THE LONDON CIGARETTE CARD COMPANY'S

CIGARETTE & TRADE CARD CATALOGUE

(INCLUDING LIEBIG & REPRINT SERIES)

2016 e

FIRST CATALOUGE I

ISBN 978-1-‹

GW00632226

Compiled by

IAN A. LAKER & Y. BERKTAY

Published by

THE LONDON CIGARETTE CARD CO. LTD
Sutton Road, Somerton, Somerset, England TA11 6QP

Telephone: 01458-273452 · Fax: 01458-273515
International Calls: Telephone: ++44 1458-273452 · Fax: ++44 1458-273515
e-mail: cards@londoncigcard.co.uk

www.londoncigcard.co.uk

CONTENTS

CARD COLLECTING

Wills
Garden Flowers
(1939)

When you mention cigarette cards, most people think of cricketers, footballers and film stars of the 1930s. This was the heyday of cigarette card issues when virtually every packet contained a little picture and the major companies like Wills and Players had their own studios and artists devoted entirely to the production of cigarette cards. It was big business, and massive print-runs often ran into hundreds of millions for each series. That's why there are still lots of them around today — sets can still be bought for around £20 upwards in very good condition, which is a major reason for their popularity for those of us wishing to indulge in nostalgia for Hollywood legends, sporting heroes, military hardware, famous trains and graceful ocean liners from a golden age.

Players
Uniforms of the
Territorial Army
(1939)

In The Beginning

In fact the hobby goes back to the 1890s, to a time when cigarettes were wrapped in paper packets. Manufacturers began inserting pieces of card to protect the contents, quickly realising that these would be useful for advertising their products. Soon these were followed by pictorial sequences, which would build up into sets. The object was to encourage repeat purchases and establish brand loyalty, and the subjects chosen were those most likely to appeal to the predominantly male customer base. Beautiful young women, sportsmen and soldiers dominated the earliest series, followed by ever more diverse topics in the early 20th century as companies competed for trade by offering something new.

Remember this was before the days of cinema, Radio or TV, let alone the modern technological wonders we now take for granted. Newspapers carried few illustrations, and living standards were much lower. For most smokers, therefore, the cards they collected from their packets were their window on the world, serving to educate, excite or amuse — they were colourful, informative and free!

Wills
Ships (1902)

Many of these early cards were from firms whose names would mean nothing to a non-collector, little companies which went out of business or were swallowed up by the big boys before World War I. And it is these cards, few of which have survived, which are often the most valuable.

The 1920s and 1930s

The 1920s and 1930s are generally regarded as the golden age of cards. Competition was fierce and rival firms were constantly looking for something different to stand out from the crowd. Players and Wills went in for adhesive-backed cards and offered special albums to stick them in. So many were produced that there are still loads around today, and they fetch only a few pounds. Another idea was cards that made up

Wills
Railway Engines (1936)

into a sectional picture of a work of art, a map or an historic event like the 1937 Coronation Procession. Some makers developed cards with push-out sections which could be made into models, whilst others came out with sequences of silk embroidered flowers, cards in miniature frames, bronze plaques, metal charms to hang on a bracelet — even little gramophone records which could actually be played!

A New Dawn

Paper shortages halted card production in 1940. Cigarette cards would never be issued on the same scale as before the war, but even so there have been quite a few over the years, starting with the blue and white pictures of film stars and footballers printed in the sliding trays in Turf Cigarettes, and progressing to many series of popular cards in packets of Tom Thumb, Doncella and Grandee Cigars. Recent anti-smoking legislation has ended any hope of new cards with tobacco products, but we will continue to welcome new trade card issues.

Brooke Bond Tea
Famous People (1969)

Trade cards, or 'trading cards' as they are often called, are picture cards issued with non-tobacco products and they have a distinguished history which pre-dates even the earliest cigarette cards. On the continent of Europe, one of the first to recognise the sales potential of cards was the Liebig Meat Extract Company, which over a period of 120 years from 1872 onwards issued no fewer than 1,800 different series. In the 1920s and '30s firms like chocolate makers Frys and Cadburys, tea companies such as Typhoo, periodical publishers etc. mimicked their tobacco counterparts by producing a regular flow of picture cards. But it was in the post-war environment that trade cards really came into their own, filling the gap left by the demise of cigarette cards.

From the 1950s onwards came a flood of 'trade' cards issued with tea, confectionery, biscuits, cereals, ice cream and so on. Among them were companies such as A & B C Gum, Bassetts and Brooke Bond, who regularly released one set after another year after year. I expect many of you will remember collecting them — and there has been a notable trend for this age group to begin collecting again, which can be satisfyingly inexpensive with some Brooke Bond cards from the 1960s and '70s priced at around £4 or £5 for a mint set.

Cards at War

Wills
Military Motors (1916)

During World War I many patriotic collections were issued — 'Recruiting Posters', 'Infantry Training', 'Modern War Weapons', 'Military Motors', 'Allied Army Leaders', 'Britain's Part in The War' and so on. All were subject to Government scrutiny to ensure no secrets reached the enemy, and 'passed for publication by the Press Bureau' is printed on many of these cards. In the run-up to World War II, out came cards demonstrating the nation's apparent military strength and preparedness for action — 'Britain's Defences', the 'R.A.F. at Work' and 'Life in the Royal Navy' to name a few. 'Aircraft of the R.A.F.' cards showed our latest fighters, the Spitfire and Hurricane ('the performance of this machine is an official secret' we are warned). It is rumoured that German agents were buying up Player's 1939 'British Naval Craft' in London to send back to U-Boat crews. Meanwhile the authorities sponsored a series of 'Air Raid Precautions', 'cigarette cards of national importance', endorsed by Home Secretary Samuel Hoare, with useful hints on how to put on a gas-mask or extinguish an incendiary bomb. How effective or otherwise these proved in the blitz we shall never know, but they raised public awareness.

The Cards That Never Were

Wills
Waterloo (c1916)

The Wagner cards were not the only ones never to see the light of day. Britain's biggest maker, W. D. & H. O. Wills of Bristol prepared a series of 50 cards to celebrate Wellington's victory over Napoleon at the Battle of Waterloo, but when the date for issue came up in 1915 their release was cancelled so as not to offend the French who were our allies fighting the Germans. And in a series of 'Musical Celebrities' all the German subjects were withdrawn and substituted by lesser-known individuals from other nationalities. Another Wills casualty was a series of 50 cards prepared to mark the coronation of King Edward VIII. Edward's abdication in 1936 put paid to this and the cards were destroyed — all except, that is, for a handful of sets presented to the firm's directors and top management.

A World Record

Early in 2007, a world record price was paid in America for a single card — $2,350,000, roughly equivalent to £1,200,000. This card was sold later on in the year for another world record price, $2,800,000 (approximately £1,500,000). The card in question featured Honus Wagner, one of the great names in U.S. baseball at the turn of the 20th century. Wagner was a dedicated non-smoker and objected when America's biggest tobacco corporation planned to picture him on a cigarette card without his permission. Threats of legal action prevented its release, but a few slipped out, and it was one of these that stunned the collecting world when it was auctioned.

Today's Hobby

Remember *The Saint, The Avengers, The Prisoner, Thunderbirds, Captain Scarlet* and *Doctor Who*? They all have huge followings and collectors are snapping up new sets as they come onto the market. The same goes for *Star Trek*, Buffy, Disney, Harry Potter and

Strictly Ink
Doctor Who 3rd Series (2002)

The Lord of the Rings. Cult TV series and blockbuster movies are sure to be pictured on cards. That goes for football too. There are hundreds of different sets to chose from, some going back to the days of Matthews, Finney and Lofthouse, others bringing us right up to date with the latest Premiership players and stars like Lampard and Rooney.

The thing is, card collecting is a living hobby with many new series being produced each year

Topps UK
Star Wars (1978)

attracting a new generation of collectors. Whatever your age or interests, you're going to be pleasantly surprised by what cards can offer. Collecting cards has come a long way since its pre-war image and people from all walks of life are now keen collectors.

The London Cigarette Card Company

In 2016 the London Cigarette Card Company will be celebrating its 89th anniversary. The firm's remarkable history as the world's first company devoted solely to the needs of card collectors began in 1927 when Colonel C.L. Bagnall D.S.O, M.C., set up business at 47 Lionel Road, Brentford with a capital of just £500. The enterprise proved popular with collectors, and card stocks quickly grew to the point where an extension had to be built to house them, and the first catalogue was published in 1929. Four years later came another momentous event — the launch of the monthly magazine *Cigarette Card News* now renamed **Card Collectors News** and still being published today. By 1933, the business had expanded to such a degree that larger premises were essential and, in October of that year, the L.C.C.C. moved to Wellesley Road, Chiswick, their address until 1977 when they moved again, this time to Somerset. Today, the company's headquarters in Sutton Road, Somerton houses one of the world's largest stocks of cigarette cards and trade cards — **MORE THAN 50 MILLION** — and serves collectors around the world. In September 1999 they set up their website (**www.londoncigcard.co.uk**) which now offers over 7,500 different series, all with sample colour illustrations.

For many years we have published the hobby's essential reference catalogues as three independent catalogues for Cigarette, Trade and Liebig issues. After extensive market research and speaking with many collectors it was decided to amalgamate all three catalogues mentioned above into one volume with prices for over 16,000 different series on every subject imaginable, thus making it the most definitive guide to collecting available today. We also publish a monthly magazine called **Card Collectors News** (available by post at £2.25 each or £27 for a year's subscription), which keeps everyone up-to-date with news about the latest card issues, stories and features. Cards can be ordered by post, telephone, fax or e-mail, and through our website.

For further information contact The London Cigarette Card Company Ltd, Sutton Road, Somerton, Somerset TA11 6QP, telephone 01458-273452, e-mail cards@londoncigcard.co.uk.

HOW TO USE THE CATALOGUE

This catalogue is published in five sections. Section 1 covers the cigarette card issues of British tobacco manufacturers for the home market with overseas series. Section 2 deals with cards issued by foreign tobacco manufacturers. Section 3 covers reprinted series of cigarette and trade cards. Section 4 covers trade card manufacturers excluding Liebig card issues, which are covered in Section 5.

In Sections 1 to 4 manufacturers are featured in alphabetical order and the issues of each firm are also catalogued alphabetically. Section 1 is also divided into appropriate sub-divisions i.e. 'British Issues', 'Overseas Issues', 'Silks' etc. Section 2 also has sub-divisions such as 'With Brand Name', 'Without Brand Name', 'Silks' etc. In Section 4 all British and overseas issues are listed in one alphabetical listing except Brooke Bond overseas issues, where these are listed under the company's code to show chronological sequence of issue. In Section 5 the issues of Liebig are listed in the same order as shown in the Italian-language *Fada Liebig Catalogue* officially recognised by the Liebig Company. However, for ease of use for collectors using Sanguinetti references, these are also listed. Where a brand name but no maker's name is shown on the card, reference should be made to the Index of Brands. Anonymous British tobacco issues are listed at the end of Section 1 and Anonymous trade card issues are listed at the end of Section 4.

Information is given in the columns from left to right as follows:

Size
(a) Sections 1 and 3 (British manufacturers and reprint series): the code letter refers to the size of the card as indicated in the chart on page xxvi. A number 1 or 2 after the letter means that the card is slightly larger or smaller than shown.
(b) Sections 2 and 4 (Foreign Tobacco manufacturers and Trade Card issuers): the absence of a code letter indicates that the series is of standard size. A code letter 'L' defines the card as being large (about 80 × 62 mm). Other codes are 'K' = smaller than standard, 'M' = between standard and large, and 'EL' = larger than large, and in the Trade Card section 'LT' = large trade (size 89 x 64mm).

Printing
(a) Sections 1 and 3 (British manufacturers and reprint series): the code indicates the printing on the front of the card. 'BW' = black-and-white; 'C' = coloured; 'CP' = colour photograph; 'P' = photograph; 'U' = uncoloured (monochrome).
(b) Sections 2 and 4 (Foreign Tobacco manufacturers and Trade Card issuers): the letter 'P' is used to show that a series consists of photographs.

Number in Set
This figure gives the number of cards in the series. A question mark alongside shows the exact number is unknown.

Title and Date
Where a series title is printed on the cards, this is used in the catalogue. For cards which do not exhibit a series title, an 'adopted' title is shown (indicated by an asterisk in the British section). Where a firm issued more than one series with the same title, these are distinguished by the addition of 'Set 1', 'Set 2', etc, or a code letter. The date of issue, where known, is shown in brackets, otherwise an approximate date is shown prefixed by 'C'.

Reference Code
(a) British issues: un-numbered series, series issued by more than one manufacturer, and different series of the same title issued by a single firm, have been given an 'H', 'OG', 'GP' or 'W' number cross-referencing them to provide further information.
   'H' refers to *The British Tobacco Issues Handbook* 2003 Edition.
   'OG' refers to *The Ogdens Reference Book* 2005 Edition.
   'GP' refers to *The Godfrey Phillips & Associated Companies Reference Book* 2008 Edition.
   'W' refers to *The W.D. & H.O. Wills Reference Book* 2011 Edition.
(b) Foreign issues: 'RB.118' or 'RB.21' followed by a number refers to the Tobacco War reference book or the British American Tobacco reference book respectively. 'WI' or 'RB.23'and 'WII' refer to World Tobacco Index Part I and Part II respectively. (Details of these publications will be found on page xiii.)
(c) Trade Card issues: reference codes in this section all relate to Cartophilic Reference Book No. 126 – The British Trade Card Handbook.

Code Letters Used After the Set Title

In Some Early series a code word has been created. This is to help identify the various manufactures that printed the same set, i.e. Actresses, Beauties, Boer War Celebrities etc. For example: Beauties 'PAC' was issued by **P**ritchard & Burton, **A**dkin and **C**ope. Some series may not include all manufactures within the coded word, therefore for full listing please use the appropriate reference number in the catalogue with their respective reference books. For Example: Beauties 'PAC' – see H.2 in the *British Tobacco Issues Handbook*.

The Definition of Multi-Backed & Vari-Backed

Where each number in the set can be collected in each advertisement back these are listed in the catalogue.

Multi-Backed: If only certain cards can be collected within a set with the same advertisement these are referred to as multi-backed. For instance in Wills Sports of All Nations numbers 1 to 9 can be collected with a Three Castles or Traveller back but not a complete set in these advertisement backs.

Vari-Backed: The term vari-backed means you can only collect one advertisement back of each card for instance numbers 1 to 9 of a set would only be available in one advertisement back and number 10 to 19 in another back and so on.

Prices and Condition of Cards

Sections 1 and 2: the last two columns show the London Cigarette Card Company's selling prices for odd cards, complete sets or albums in very good condition.

Section 3: gives a price for complete sets in mint condition.

Section 4: gives prices for odd cards, complete sets and albums the majority of which are in finest collectable to mint condition except for pre-1950 cards which are very good condition.

Section 5: the prices quoted are for cards in good average condition (the more recent series will be of a higher quality).

Please note : For sections 1 and 2, when ordering 'end' numbers, for example Nos. 1 and 50 of a set of fifty, the following applies. For series catalogued up to £1 per card, end cards are charged at treble price. For series catalogued from £1 to £3 per card, end cards are charged at £3 per card. For series catalogued at more than £3 per card there is no additional charge for end numbers.

Album prices quoted in this catalogue are for empty albums without corner mounts or cards stuck in. When albums have corner mounts or cards stuck in they would in most cases be at a much reduced price.

HOW TO ORDER

Availability

We have one of the world's largest stocks of cards and the chances are that we will be able to supply your requirements for most series at the prices shown in the catalogue. However, certain odd cards, particularly from rarer series, may not be available in top condition and in such cases it is helpful if you indicate whether cards of a lower standard are acceptable at reduced prices. If a complete set is not in stock, we may be able to offer a part set, with one or two cards missing, at the appropriate fraction of full catalogue price. In some instances we can supply sets on request in fair to good condition at half catalogue price. If in doubt, please e-mail or write for a quotation, enclosing a stamped, self-addressed envelope.

End Numbers (Sections 1 and 2)

When ordering 'end' numbers, for example Nos. 1 and 50 of a set of fifty, please note that the following applies. For series catalogued up to £1 per card, end cards are charged at treble price. For series catalogued from £1 to £3 per card, end cards are charged at £3 per card. And for series catalogued at more than £3 per card there is no additional charge for end numbers.

Postage and Handling Fee

Orders are sent post free to UK addresses, but **please note** orders under £20.00 will incur a handling fee of £2.00. Overseas postage is charged at cost and there is no handling fee.

Ordering and Payment

Please ensure that your name and full address are clearly shown. State the maker's name and the set title required (with 'first series', 'second series', date of issue, etc. as appropriate). For odds, please list each individual number wanted. Make your crossed cheque or postal order payable to The London Cigarette Card Company Limited and enclose with order. Notes and coins should be registered. Overseas payments can only be accepted by Sterling cheque drawn on a British bank or by credit/debit card. We accept Mastercard, Visa, Visa Delta, Electron, JCB, American Express and Maestro credit/debit cards. Quote your card number and the card security code (which is the last three numbers in the signature strip), expiry date (and, for Maestro cards, the issue number if one is shown, or start date); also now accepting Paypal. Please allow 14 days for delivery. Send your order to:

The London Cigarette Card Co. Ltd, Sutton Road, Somerton, Somerset TA11 6QP, England

Please note: Orders sent to addresses outside the European Community will have 15% (UK tax) deducted off card and album prices.

24-Hour Telephone Order Line (01458-273452)

For the convenience of customers, an answering machine is in operation to receive orders when the office is closed. Just leave your order, name and address with credit or debit card number, expiry date, and the card security code, which is the last three numbers on the signature strip (and, for Maestro cards, the issue number, if one is shown, or start date). Your order will be dealt with as soon as possible. Please note that we can only deal with general enquiries in office hours. Telephone number: **01458-273452** (international ++44 1458-273452).

Fax Machine (01458-273515)

Our fax machine is on 24 hours a day to receive orders. Just place your order stating your name, address, credit or debit card number, expiry date and the card security code, which is the last three numbers on the signature strip (and, for Maestro cards, the issue number, if one is shown, or start date). The fax number is **01458-273515** (international ++44 1458-273515).

Website – www.londoncigcard.co.uk

Over 7,500 series are listed on our website, each one with a sample illustration. Orders can be placed direct via our website.

E-Mail – cards@londoncigcard.co.uk

Remember that your cards will look their best when displayed in one of our albums: please see pages xviii to xix. Value Added Tax where applicable is included in all prices shown, at the current rate of 20%.

Guarantee

In the unlikely event that you, the collector, are not satisfied with the cards supplied, we guarantee to replace them or refund your money, provided the goods are returned within 14 days of receipt. This guarantee does not affect your statutory rights.

OPENING TIMES AT SUTTON ROAD

Collectors are welcome to call at our offices in Sutton Road, Somerton, where you will be able to purchase your requirements direct from the massive stocks held at the premises – sets, albums, books and accessories plus odd cards. We do not have items on display, but we are more than happy to get things out for you to view.

**Our offices are open to customers Monday to Friday
9.30am-12.30pm and 2.30pm-4.30pm**

SALE OF COLLECTIONS

Our buying department welcomes offers of collections (whether large or small), particularly early and rare cards, but please note that we are mainly interested in cards in very good condition. If in doubt please get in touch before sending anything.

NEW ISSUES

We usually have between 5 and 20 new issues (mostly trade card issues) added to stock each month, and if you wish to keep up-to-date why not subscribe to *Card Collectors News* magazine (see page xii), in which the magazine editior, gives a description of all new additions and includes sample illustrations of most of them. A sample of the back and front of each new issues can also be found on our website each month (www.londoncigcard.co.uk).

The FIRST EVER card collecting magazine!
First published in 1933
You get so much with a 12 month subscription

- 12 copies of the *Card Collectors News* magazine
- FREE sample card with every issue
- FREE monthly Auction List which has at least 400 lots
- Special offers (only for subscribers) which could save you up to 25% on over 150 sets every month
- Discount on a Set of the Month (only to subscribers)
- Details of any new issues that arrive into stock every month
- Informative articles from readers and collectors all around the world
- Competitions and prizes! (You could get a 12 month subscription for free)

Collect back issues of the magazine starting from £1
(see our website for issues available)

Subscription is £27 for the UK
£52 for European countries and
£64 for countries outside of Europe
Digital worldwide magazine subscription for only £26
(See website for details)

Keep your magazines safe in a purpose designed luxury binder to
hold 12 copies in a choice of attractive blue or maroon covers
with gold lettering — £10.00 each

CARTOPHILIC REFERENCE BOOKS

British Tobacco Issues Handbook (updated 2003 edition). Updates the original Handbooks Parts I & II, but excludes Ogden, Wills and The Godfrey Phillips Group of Companies. 369 pages **£24.00**

Handbook Part II (1920 to 1940) British Tobacco Issues. Updated by the above book, but includes Godfrey Phillips Silks listings. 164 pages, illustrated. Published at £12.00
. . . . **Special Offer Price £6.00**

The Card Issues of Abdulla/Adkin/Anstie (reprint, originally published 1943). 20 pages **£4.50**

The Card Issues of Ardath Tobacco (reprint, originally published 1943). 28 pages **£4.50**

The Card Issues of W.A. & A.C. Churchman (reprint, originally published 1948). 36 pages **£4.50**

The Card Issues of W. & F. Faulkner (reprint, originally published 1942). 12 pages **£4.50**

The Card Issues of Gallaher (reprint, originally published 1944). 40 pages **£4.50**

The Card Issues of R. & J. Hill (reprint, originally published 1942). 28 pages **£4.50**

The Card Issues of Lambert & Butler (reprint, originally published 1948). 32 pages **£4.50**

The Card Issues of Ogdens (reprint 2015 paperback edition includes 2 pages of additions and corrections from the updated 2005 edition). 333 pages **£24.00**

The Card Issues of Godfrey Phillips (reprint, originally published 1949). 40 pages . . . . **Out of Print**

The Card Issues of Godfrey Phillips & Associated Companies (updated 2008 edition). Includes Cavanders, Drapkin, Millhoff and Muratti. 256 pages **£28.00**

The Card Issues of John Player & Sons (reprint, originally published 1948). 44 pages **£4.50**

Guide Book No. 2, F. & J. Smith Cards (published 1980). 36 pages **£4.50**

The Card Issues of Taddy (reprint, originally published 1948). 32 pages **£4.50**

The Card Issues of W.D. & H.O. Wills (updated 2011 Edition). 214 pages **£25.00**

The Card Issues of Wills and B.A.T. combined (published 1942-1952, reprinted as one volume in 1998). 402 pages **£20.50**

Directory of British Tobacco Issuers (reprint, originally published 1946). 36 pages **£4.50**

World Tobacco Card Index & Handbook Part I & Part II . . . . **Out of Print**

World Tobacco Card Index & Handbook Part III. Supplement to Index I & II. 504 pages **£25.50**

World Tobacco Card Index & Handbook Part IV. Supplement to Index I, II & III. 688 pages **£19.00**

World Tobacco Card Index & Handbook Part V. Supplement to Index I, II, III & IV (published 1990). 552 pages **£19.00**

World Tobacco Issues Part 1. Issuers A to K. 344 pages **£23.00**

World Tobacco Issues Part 2. Issuers L to Z, plus Anonymous. 344 pages **£23.00**

The above two books, updated to August 2000, are a revision of the World Tobacco Indexes Parts I to V combined (but not the Handbooks) with many additions & amendments. They do not contain the Handbook and therefore do not have subject listings.

Handbook of Worldwide Tobacco and Trade Silk Issues. 342 pages, some colour illustrations . . **£50.50**

Australian and New Zealand Card Issues Part 1 . . . . **Out of Print**

Australian and New Zealand Card Issues Part 2 (published 1993). 257 pages **£16.00**

The New 'Tobacco War' Reference Book (updated 1999 edition). 236 pages **£20.50**

Glossary of Cartophilic Terms (reprint, originally published 1948). 40 pages **£4.50**

British Trade Card Index Part I, Part II & Part III . . . . **Out of Print**

British Trade Card Index Part IV (1986-1994 issues). 412 pages **£20.50**

British Trade Card Index Issues up to 1970 (2006 edition). 516 pages **£25.50**

British Trade Card Handbook Issues up to 1970 (2006 edition). 542 pages **£25.50**

Guide Book No. 1, Typhoo Tea Cards (published 1976). 36 pages **£4.50**

Guide Book No. 3, A. & B.C. Gum Cards (updated 2004 edition). 52 pages **£4.50**

BOOKS FOR THE COLLECTOR

Brooke Bond Tea Cards Reference Book

The definitive reference book with 319 colour illustrations of cards and albums including overseas issues and the story of the company's first hundred years from one shop to market leader. Published 2007. . . . . £12.50

Brooke Bond Picture Cards
'The First Forty Years'

This invaluable 72-page reference book detailing all the issues of Brooke Bond Tea from 1954 to 1994. It includes British issues as well as overseas issues with illustrations. £7.00

Classic Brooke Bond
Picture Card Collections

Mark Knowler's 320-page hardback book should appeal to all collectors, not just those specialising in Brooke Bond, because it is a wonderful advert for the hobby. Impeccably presented and with superb colour illustrations throughout, it is the kind of book you can dip into for a few minutes or browse through for hours.

As described by the publisher, 'this beautifully produced nostalgic book comprises the best 12 original albums, presented slightly larger than they were 40 to 50 years ago, to bring out the best in the wonderfully detailed illustrations. Every card is printed in its correct position, making every page an enormously colourful feast for the eyes.'

The albums that have been included are Out Into Space, British Wild Life, Wild Flowers Series 2, Freshwater Fish, African Wild Life, Asian Wild Life, British Butterflies, Wild Birds in Britain, Transport Through The Ages, Trees in Britain, Flags and Emblems of the World and History of The Motor Car, although other UK issues from Frances Pitt British Birds through to the 1999 Thank You Card are covered in the introduction. £25.00

Collecting Cigarette & Trade Cards

by Gordon Howsden. Traces the history and development of cards from their beginning to the present day and includes the background of the issuing firms, thematic collecting, printing and production, grading, pricing and so on. Authoritatively written in an easy-to-read style and beautifully illustrated in colour, the book approaches the subject from a fresh angle which will appeal to seasoned collectors and newcomers alike. Cigarette & Trade Cards is not only an indispensable reference work but also a joy to read or just browse through. 152 large-format pages with 220 colour illustrations featuring 750 cards and related ephemera. £17.50

BOOKS FOR THE COLLECTOR

Prophets of Zoom

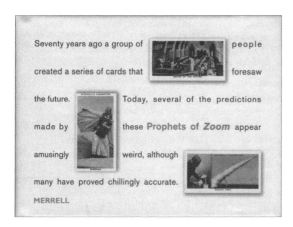

Seventy years ago a group of people created a series of cards that foresaw the future. Today, several of the predictions made by these **Prophets of Zoom** appear amusingly weird, although many have proved chillingly accurate.

MERRELL

An unusual but fascinating book, *Prophets of Zoom*, with 112 pages, reproduces the front and back of each card in Mitchell's 1936 series of 50 The World of Tomorrow, opposite which is pictured a modern equivalent – and it's surprising how many of the predictions have become true!

From author Alfredo Marcantonio's introduction, we learn that the card set was inspired by a book called *The World of Tomorrow* and drew upon images from contemporary films, in particular Alexanda Korda's *Things to Come*, as well as inventions then at the cutting edge of technology. The individual predictions range from the amazing to the amusing, and together they paint a unique picture of the world we live in now, as pre-war Britain imagined it would be.

To take just one example. The very first card informs us that 'coal-mines and oil-wells will not last forever. We shall have to gain the energy we need, not from fuel, but from the inexhaustible forces of nature', and the set forecasts wind turbines, atomic energy and solar motors as being the power sources of the future.

From space travel and giant television screens, robots and bullet trains, to London's skyscraper sky-line, this is highly entertaining stuff, and excellent value. **£7.95**

☆ BARGAIN 25 OFFER ☆

25 sets for £30, that's our terrific special bargain offer

We have selected twenty-five sets of cards issued between the 1950s and the 1990s, chosen for their wide range of interesting subjects and all in top condition. Each of the sets is individually catalogued at £2.50 or more, so this collection represents a huge saving on normal prices.

Ask for 'Bargain 25' when ordering

☆ SAMPLER COLLECTIONS ☆

We have taken one card from each of 450 post-war card series and assembled them into nine different groups of fifty. These are particularly useful for the collector who wishes to see sample cards before buying complete sets, and are also a great foundation for a 'type' collection. Each group of 50 costs only £6.

Order one collection from groups A, B, C, D, E, F, G, H or I for £6
or all nine groups for £45

REGIMENTAL BOOKS

The following series of books featuring the different Regiments and Corps of the British Army illustrated on Cigarette and Trade cards, contain History, Uniforms, Badges, Regimental Colours, Victoria Cross Winners and Personalities. Approximately 200 illustrations in each book, 56 pages with 16 in full colour, all produced by David J. Hunter.

The Coldstream Guards £8.50
The Gordon Highlanders £8.50
Queen's Own Highlanders (Seaforth & Camerons) £8.50
The Queen's Royal Lancers £8.50
The Regiments of Wales (The Welsh Guards, The Royal
Welsh Fusiliers & The Royal Regiment of Wales) £8.50
The Royal Army Medical Corps £8.50
The Royal Marines £8.50
The Royal Regiment of Fusiliers — Part 1 (The Royal
Northumberland Fusiliers & The Royal Warwickshire
Regiment) £8.50
The Royal Regiment of Fusiliers — Part 2 (The Royal
Fusiliers (City of London Regiment) & The Lancashire
Fusiliers) £8.50
The Scotts Guards £8.50
The Worcestershire & Sherwood Foresters Regiment £8.50

THE FIRST WORLD WAR ON CIGARETTE AND TRADE CARDS

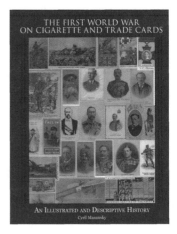

By Dr Cyril Mazansky

Published in 2015

What a wonderful advertisement for our hobby! *The First World War on Cigarette and Trade Cards* is a book illustrated with 941 cards, mostly issued at the time and including many rarities. This is no mere picture book. It is an authoritative history of the war written by an expert on the subject, employing cards from a collection built up over a period of more than thirty years. The result is a richly illustrated descriptive tapestry of this great conflict, using cards and silks to great effect both as a source of information and also as a means of showing how events, personalities and various aspects of the war were presented to the public at the time. The book is split into chapters dealing with particular topics such as Military Leaders, Armaments, War Scenes, Army Life, VC Heroes and The Home Front, plus a special section on the History of Card Collecting. The author, Dr Cyril Mazansky, will be familiar to readers of *Card Collectors News* magazine as he has contributed many articles. We cannot recommend this book too highly. It is a marvellous production, well researched, well written in a style which involves the reader in 'The War to End All Wars', and impeccably illustrated with a magnificent array of cards.

Price £37.50

LUXURY ALBUMS

LUXURY BINDER WITH 30 LEAVES £13.50
MATCHING SLIP-CASE £6.00 (only supplied with binder) • EXTRA LEAVES 17p EACH
☆ **GREY CARD INTERLEAVES — 30 FOR £4.00** ☆
Orders are sent post free to UK addresses, but PLEASE NOTE **orders under £20.00 will incur a
handling fee of £2.00. Overseas postage is charged at cost and there is no handling fee.**

Full display, front and back, is given to your cards in top quality transparent leaves held in a luxurious binder.
The leaves are made from a tough, clear optical film. Binders are available in a choice of blue or maroon
covers (with matching slip-cases as an optional extra) and each is supplied complete with 30 leaves,
of which various sizes are available as listed below.

Page Ref.	Suitable for	Pockets Per Page	Pocket size (mm) wide x deep
A	Standard size cards	10	43 x 83
M	Medium size cards	8	55 x 83
D	Doncella/Grandee/Typhoo size cards	6	111 x 55
L	Large size cards	6	73 x 83
X	Extra large cards	4	111 x 83
P	Postcards	2	111 x 170
C	Cabinet size cards, booklets etc.	1	224 x 170
K	Miniature size cards	15	43 x 55

Remember to state which colour (blue or maroon) and which page reference/s you require.

**Order by telephone (01458-273452), fax (01458-273515), e-mail (cards@londoncigcard.co.uk)
or through our website (www.londoncigcard.co.uk) 24 hours a day, 7 days a week
using your credit or debit cards, or you can order by post.**

xvii

ALBUMS FOR LARGE TRADE CARDS

☆ An album designed specifically for modern trade cards like Skybox, Comic Images, Rittenhouse, Inkworks, Topps etc

☆ The ideal way to display your large modern trade cards to their best advantage

☆ 3-ring luxury padded binders in a choice of maroon or blue

☆ There are two types of leaves:

9 pockets per sheet size 91 x 68mm, reference LT
6 pockets per sheet size 138 x 66mm, reference WV

Orders are sent post free to UK addresses, but PLEASE NOTE orders under £20.00 will incur a handling fee of £2.00. Overseas postage is charged at cost and there is no handling fee.

**COMPLETE ALBUM WITH 30 LEAVES
IN A CHOICE OF 'LT' OR 'WV' LEAVES £17.00 · EXTRA LEAVES 22p EACH**

☆ COLLECTORS' ACCESSORIES ☆

A neat and tidy way for you to deal with incomplete sets is to use our
numbered, printed 'wants' lists

30 adhesive lists numbered 1 to 50 . . . . **75p**

The professional way to wrap sets with our translucent
glascine wrapping strips

200 strips size 123 x 68 mm for standard size cards **£5.00**
200 strips size 175 x 83mm for large cards **£5.50**
200 strips size 228 x 83mm for extra-large cards **£6.00**

EXTRA LARGE ALBUMS FOR CARDS

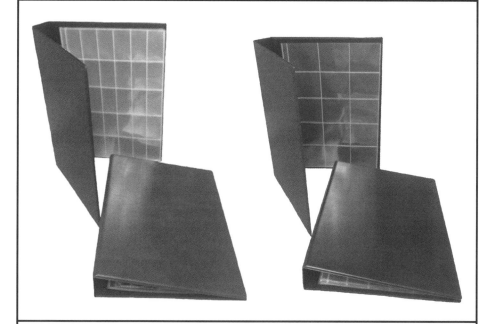

☆ Luxury 4-ring padded binder, size 415 x 333mm

☆ Albums include 20 leaves of your choice, 'XLA' or 'XLLT'

☆ Ideal for storing large volumes of cards, both cigarette and trade

☆ A choice of maroon or blue

☆ Two types of leaves available:

> 30 pocket page, pocket size 72 x 40mm, ref XLA
> 15 pocket page, pocket size 70 x 89mm, ref XLLT

Album with 20 leaves (XLA or XLLT)   £30.00
Extra packs of 20 leaves (XLA or XLLT)   £12.00

Orders are sent post free to UK addresses, but please note
orders under £20 will incur a handling fee of £2.00.
Overseas postage is charged at cost and there is no handling fee.

2016 AUCTIONS

We have been auctioning for over 75 years cards to suit every collector

Monthly 400-lot postal auctions of cigarette and trade cards and associated items with estimated values from as little as £1 up to many hundreds. Lots to interest every collector and suit their pocket.

Postal Auctions for 2016 are as follows:

Saturday,	2nd January	Saturday, 25th June
Saturday,	30th January	Saturday, 30th July
Saturday,	27th February	Saturday, 27th August
Saturday,	26th March	Saturday, 24th September
Saturday,	30th April	Saturday, 29th October
Saturday,	28th May	Saturday, 26th November

Each postal auction finishes at midnight on the above dates.

A guide to how we assess condition and how to bid can be found on our bidding sheet which comes with the free auction catalogue, so it couldn't be easier if you are an 'auction beginner'.

There are no additional charges to bidders for buyer's premium, so bidding is straightforward, with no 'hidden extras'.

Each lot is described with an estimate of its value reflecting the condition of the cards, ranging from poor right through to mint condition, and for over 75 years collectors have bid with complete confidence, knowing that every effort is made to describe the lots accurately.

Each auction contains a selection of rare sets, rare and scarce individual cards, pre-1918 issues, 1920-40 series, old and modern trade issues including Brooke Bond, errors and varieties, silks, albums, books, Liebigs, cigarette packets etc – in fact plenty to interest everyone.

Auction catalogues are available *FREE OF CHARGE*, 4 weeks before the date of sale from The London Cigarette Card Company Limited, Sutton Road, Somerton, Somerset TA11 6QP
Telephone: 01458-273452   Fax: 01458-273515
E-mail: auctions@londoncigcard.co.uk

The Auction Catalogue can also be found on our website, which contains a preview of each auction as well as facilities for on-line bidding – visit www.londoncigcard.co.uk for further details.

Also a copy of the auction catalogue is automatically sent each month to subscribers to our magazine *Card Collectors News*
(subscription details on page xii)

INDEX OF BRANDS

The following is a list of the cases so far known where cards appear without the name of issuer, but inscribed with a brand name or other indication which is the collector's only clue to the identity of the issuer. (1), (2) or (4) indicates in which section of the catalogue the manufacturer appears

GENERAL NOTE: Where no brand name appears on the cards in a lot of cases they were issued by British American Tobacco Co., Imperial Tobacco Company of Canada Ltd or United Tobacco Companies (South) Ltd which all appear in Section 2. As regards to plain back cards, in a lot of cases they will be listed under Anonymous Series (in Section 1) or British American Tobacco Co. section 'F' Plain Backs (in Section 2).

Fez Cigarettes — see American Tobacco Co. (2)
The Flor de Dindigul Cigar — see Bewlay (1)
Forecasta — see B. Morris (1)
Four Square — see Dobie (1)
Fresher Cigarettes — see Challis (1)
Fume Emblem — see Westminster Tobacco Co. (2)
Futera – see Futura or Trade Cards (Europe) Ltd (4)

GP — see Godfrey Phillips (1)
Gainsborough Cigarettes — see Cohen Weenen (1)
General Favourite Onyx — see E. Robinson (1)
Gibson Girl Virginia, Madrali Turkish and Hungarian — see Golds (1)
Gold Coin Tobacco — see Buchner (2)
Gold Flake Cigarettes — see Hill (1)
Gold Flake, Honeydew and Navy Cut Medium Cigarettes — see Hill (1)
The Greys Cigarettes — see United Kingdom Tobacco Co. (1)
Guards Cigarettes — see Carreras (1)

Hard-a-Port – see Moore & Calvi (2)
Hassan Cigarettes — see American Tobacco Co. (2)
Havelock Cigarettes — see Wills (Overseas) (2)
Hawser, Epaulet and Honey Flake Cigarettes — see Wholesale Tobacco Supply Syndicate (1)
Heart's Delight Cigarettes — see Pritchard & Burton (1)
Helmar Cigarettes — see American Tobacco Co. (2)
Herbert Tareyton Cigarettes — see American Tobacco Co. (2)
Hindu Cigarettes — see American Tobacco Co. (2)
Hoffman House Magnums — see American Tobacco Co. (2)
Honest Long Cut — see Duke or American Tobacco Co. (2)
Hornet – see D.C. Thomson (4)
Hotspur – see D.C. Thomson (4)
Hustler – see J. Knight (4)
Hustler Little Cigars — see American Tobacco Co. (2)

Imperial Tobacco Limited (Castella) — see W.D. & H.O. Wills (1)
Islander, Fags, Specials, Cubs — see Bucktrout (2)

Jack Rose Little Cigars — see American Tobacco Co. (2)
Jag – see Fleetway Publications (4)

Jersey Lily Cigarettes — see Wm. Bradford (1)
Jibco – see J.I. Batten (4)
Cigarette Job — see Societe Job (1)
Jolly Sailor – see Cunning Articifer (4)
Jubbly – see Freshmaid Ltd (4)
Junior Member Cigarettes — see Pattreiouex (1)
Just Suits Cut Plug — see American Tobacco Co. (2)

K The B – see Local Authorities Caterers' Association (4)
Kensitas Cigarettes — see J. Wix (1)
King Edward VII Cigarettes — see Cabana (1)
King Features – see Authentix (4)
Kopec Cigarettes — see American Tobacco Co. (2)

L. & Y. Tobacco Co. -— see Lancs. and Yorks. Tobacco Manufacturing Co. (1)
V.G. Langford – see Vincent Graphics (4)
Laughing Cow – see Bel UK (4)
Lennox Cigarettes — see American Tobacco Co. (2)
Leon de Cuba Cigars — see Eldons (1)
Le Roy Cigars — see Miller (2)
Levant Favourites — see B. Morris (1)
Life Ray Cigarettes — see Ray & Co. (1)
Lifeboat Cigarettes — see United Tobacco Co. (2)
Lion – see Fleetway Publications & IPC Magazines (4)
Lion and Thunder – see IPC Magazines (4)
Lord Nielson – see Mister Softee Ltd (4)
Lotus Cigarettes — see United Tobacco Co. (2)
Lucana Cigarettes — see Sandorides (1)
Lucky Strike Cigarettes — see American Tobacco Co. (2)
Luxury Cigarettes — see American Tobacco Co. (2)

Magpie Cigarettes — see Schuh (2)
Manikin Cigars — see Freeman (1)
Mascot Cigarettes — see British American Tobacco Co. (2)
Matossian's Cigarettes — see Henley & Watkins (2)
Max Cigarettes — see A. & M. Wix (1)
Mayblossom Cigarettes — see Lambert & Butler (1)
Mecca Cigarettes — see American Tobacco Co. (2)
Mickey Mouse Weekly – see Caley (4)
Mills — see Amalgamated (1)
Milo Cigarettes — see Sniders & Abrahams (2)
Miners Extra Smoking Tobacco — see American Tobacco Co. (2)

Mogul Cigarettes — see American Tobacco Co. (2)
Murad Cigarettes — see American Tobacco Co. (2)

Natural American Spirit — see Santa Fe Natural Tob. Co. (2)
Nebo Cigarettes — see American Tobacco Co. (2)
New Hotspur – see D.C. Thomson (4)
New Orleans Tobacco — see J. & T. Hodge (1)

OK Cigarettes — see African Tobacco Mfrs. (2)
Obak Cigarettes — see American Tobacco Co. (2)
Officers Mess Cigarettes — see African Tobacco Mfrs. (2)
Old Gold Cigarettes — see American Tobacco Co. (2)
Old Judge Cigarettes — see Goodwin (2)
Old Mills Cigarettes — see American Tobacco Co. (2)
1a, 27 & 33 Leigh Road, Eastleigh — see Ingram's (1)
One of the Finest — see Buchner (2)
Oracle Cigarettes — see Tetley (1)
Orient Line Steamships — see Singleton & Cole (1)
Our Little Beauties — see Allen & Ginter (2)
Oxford Cigarettes — see American Tobacco Co. (2)

Pan Handle — see American Tobacco Co. (2)
Park Drive — see Gallaher (1)
Perfection Cigarettes — see American Tobacco Co. (2)
Peter Pan Cigarettes — see Sniders & Abrahams (2)
Pibroch Virginia — see Fryer (1)
Piccadilly — see Carreras (1)
Picadilly Little Cigars — see American Tobacco Co. (2)
Pick-Me-Up Cigarettes — see Drapkin & Millhoff (1)
Piedmont Cigarettes — see American Tobacco Co. (2)
Pinhead Cigarettes — see British American Tobacco Co. (2)
Pinnace — see Godfrey Phillips (1)
Pioneer Cigarettes — see Richmond Cavendish (1)
Pirate Cigarettes — see Wills (Overseas) (2)
PO Box 5764, Johannesburg — see A. & M. Wix (1)
Polo Bear Cigarettes — see American Tobacco Co. (2)
Polo Mild Cigarettes — see Murray (1)

Private Seal Tobacco — see Godfrey Phillips (1)
Pure Virginia Cigarettes — see Thomson & Porteous (1)
Puritan Little Cigars — see American Tobacco Co. (2)
Purple Mountain Cigarettes — see Wills (Overseas) (2)

QV Cigars — see Webster (1)

RS — see Robert Sinclair (1)
Recruit Little Cigars — see American Tobacco Co. (2)
Red Cross — see Lorillard or American Tobacco Co. (2)
Reina Regenta Cigars — see B. Morris (1)
De Reszke Cigarettes — see Millhoff and Godfrey Phillips (1)
Richmond Gem Cigarettes — see Allen & Ginter (2)
Richmond Straight Cut Cigarettes — see American Tobacco Co. (2)
Ringers Cigarettes — see Edwards, Ringer & Bigg (1)
Rock City Tobacco — see Carreras (1)
Roseland Cigarettes — see Glass (1)
Rover – see D.C. Thomson (4)
Roxy – see Fleetway Publications (4)
Royal Bengal Little Cigars — see American Tobacco Co. (2)

St Dunstan's — see Carreras (1)
St Leger Little Cigars — see American Tobacco Co. (2)
Scorcher – see IPC Magazines (4)
Scorcher and Score – see IPC Magazines (4)
Scoreboard – see Merlin (4)
Scots Cigarettes — see African Tobacco Mfrs (2)
Scrap Iron Scrap — see American Tobacco Co. (2)
Senator Cigarettes — see Scerri (2)
Senior Service Cigarettes — see Pattreiouex (1)
Sensation Cut Plug — see Lorillard (2)
Shredded Wheat/Shreddies – see Nabisco Foods (4)
Sifta Sam – see Palmer Mann & Co. (4)
Silko Cigarettes — see American Tobacco Co. (2)
Skipper – see D.C. Thomson (4)
Smash – see IPC Magazines (4)
Sovereign Cigarettes — see American Tobacco Co. (2)
Spinet Cigarettes or The Spinet House — see Hill (1)

Sportsman — see Carreras (Overseas) (2)
The Spotlight Tobaccos — see Hill (1)
Springbok Cigarettes — see United Tobacco Co. (2)
Standard Cigarettes — see Carreras or Sniders & Abrahams (2)
Star of the World Cigarettes — see JLS (1)
State Express Cigarettes — see Ardath (1)
Stimorol Gum — see Scanlen (4)
Strato Gum — see Myers & Metreveli (4)
Sub Rosa Cigarros — see American Tobacco Co. (2)
Subbuteo – see P.A. Adolf (4)
Sultan Cigarettes — see American Tobacco Co. (2)
Summit — see International Tobacco Co. (1)
Sunlight Soap – see Lever Brothers (4)
Sunripe Cigarettes — see Hill (1)
Sunspot Cigarettes — see Theman (1)
Superkings – see J. Player & Sons (1)
Sweet Alva Cigarettes — see Drapkin (1)
Sweet Caporal — see Kinney or American Tobacco Co. or ITC Canada (2)
Sweet Lavender — see Kimball (2)

TSS — see Tobacco Supply Syndicate (1)
Tatley's Cigarettes — see Walker's Tobacco Co. (1)
Teal Cigarettes — see British American Tobacco Co. (2)
Three Bells Cigarettes — see J. & F. Bell (1)
Tiger – see Fleetway Publications & IPC Magazines (4)
Tiger Cigarettes — see British American Tobacco Co. (2)
Tipsy Loo Cigarettes — see H.C. Lloyd (1)
Tokio Cigarettes — see American Tobacco Co. (2)
Tolstoy Cigarettes — see American Tobacco Co. (2)
Tom Thumb — see Players (1)
Top Flight – see T.P.K. Hannah (4)

Topsy Cigarettes — see Richards & Ward (1)
Trawler, Critic and King Lud Cigarettes — see Pattreiouex (1)
Trebor Bassett – see Bassett (4)
Trebor/Topps – see Topps (UK) (4)
Triumph – see Amalgamated Press (4)
Trumps Long Cut — see Moore & Calvi (2)
Turf Cigarettes — see Carreras (1)
Turkey Red Cigarettes — see American Tobacco Co. (2)
Turkish Trophy Cigarettes — see American Tobacco Co. (2)
Twelfth Night Cigarettes — see American Tobacco Co. (2)

U.S. Marine — see American Tobacco Co. (2)
Uzit Cigarettes — see American Tobacco Co. (2)

Val Footer Gum – see Klene (4)
Valiant – see IPC Magazines (4)
Vanguard – see D.C. Thomson (4)
Vanity Fair Cigarettes — see Kimball (2)
Vice Regal Cigarettes — see Wills (Overseas) (2)
Victor – see D.C. Thomson (4)
Victory Bubble Gum – see Trebor Ltd (4)
Virginia Brights Cigarettes — see Allen & Ginter (2)

WTC — see Walker's Tobacco Co. (1)
Wings Cigarettes — see Brown & Williamson (2)
Wizard – see D.C. Thomson (4)
Woman's Realm – see Brooke Bond Tea (4)
Wow Gum – see Myers & Metreveli (4)

Yankee Doodle and Pilot – see British Australasian Tobacco Co (2)
Yankee Doodle and Champion – see British Australasian Tobacco Co (2)

Zip Bubble Gum – see Trebor Ltd (4)

INDEX OF INSCRIPTIONS found on British issues of cards

'The Cigarettes with which these Picture Cards are issued are manufactured in England and are Guaranteed Pure' — see Hill
'England expects that Every Man will do his duty — By Purchasing these Cigarettes you are supporting British labour' — issuers unknown, see Anonymous
'Issued with these Famous Cigarettes' — see Teofani
'Issued with these Fine Cigarettes' — see Teofani
'Issued with these High Grade Cigarettes' — see Teofani
'Issued with these Well-known Cigarettes' — see Teofani
'Issued with these World Famous Cigarettes' — see Teofani
'Presented with these well-known choice cigarettes' — see Teofani
'Smoke these cigarettes always' — see Teofani
'These Cigarettes are Guaranteed Best British Manufacture' — see Hill.

CARD SIZES (only applies to Section 1). Please note: (card size) *album leaf size*

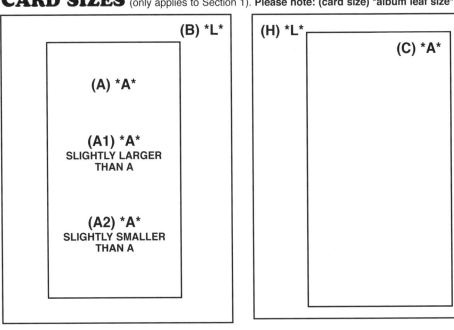

(B) *L*

(H) *L*

(C) *A*

(A) *A*

(A1) *A*
SLIGHTLY LARGER
THAN A

(A2) *A*
SLIGHTLY SMALLER
THAN A

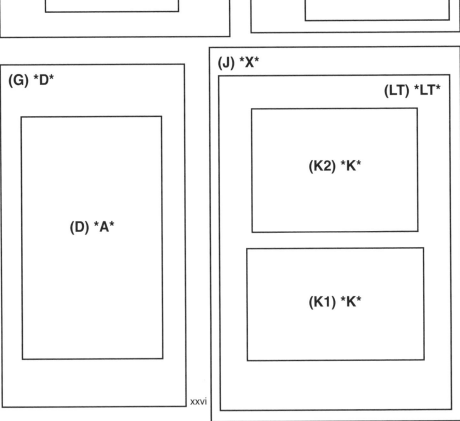

(G) *D*

(D) *A*

(J) *X*

(LT) *LT*

(K2) *K*

(K1) *K*

SECTION 1
BRITISH TOBACCO ISSUERS

Size	Print-ing	Number in set	BRITISH TOBACCO ISSUERS	Handbook reference	Price per card	Complete set
			ABDULLA & CO. LTD, London			
			20 page reference book (combined with Adkin & Anstie) — £4.50			
A	BW	50	Beauties of To-Day (1938)	GP.20	£3.60	—
	?	4	Bridge Rule Cards (various sizes) (c1935)	GP.311	£16.00	—
A	C	25	British Butterflies (1935)	GP.42	£1.20	£30.00
A	P	52	Cinema Stars Set 1 (c1933)	GP.306	£4.00	—
A2	U	30	Cinema Stars Set 2 (c1933)	GP.51	£5.00	—
A2	U	30	Cinema Stars Set 3 (c1933)	GP.52	£4.00	—
A2	U	32	Cinema Stars Set 4 (c1933)	GP.53	£2.75	£90.00
A2	C	32	Cinema Stars Set 5 (c1933)	GP.54	£2.75	£90.00
A2	C	30	Cinema Stars Set 6 (c1933)	GP.55	£3.60	—
—	C	2	Commanders of the Allies (127 x 67mm) (c1915) ...	GP.313	£85.00	—
D	C	25	Feathered Friends (1935)	GP.70	£1.40	£35.00
A2	C	50	Film Favourites (1934)	GP.71	£4.00	—
A	C	50	Film Stars (1934)	GP.73	£8.00	—
—	C	24	*Film Stars (128 x 89mm) (c1934)	GP.76	£8.00	—
—	BW	3	Great War Gift Packings Cards (78 x 48mm) (1916)	GP.314	£85.00	—
A	U	18	Message Cards (letters of the alphabet) (c1936):	GP.315		
			A Back in blue		£14.00	
			B Back in green		£14.00	
			C Back in orange		£14.00	—
K2	U	18	Message Cards (letters of the alphabet) (c1936):	GP.315		
			A Last line 'may be used'		£15.00	—
			B Last line 'of Jokers may be...'		£15.00	—
A	C	25	Old Favourites (1936) (Flowers)	GP.106	80p	£20.00
—	C	1	Princess Mary Gift Card (67 x 49mm) (1914)	GP.317	—	£30.00
A	C	40	Screen Stars (1939):	GP.307		
			A Without 'Issued by the Successors to...' back		£1.25	£50.00
			B With 'Issued by the Successors to ...' back ...		£2.50	—
A2	C	50	Stage and Cinema Beauties (1935)	GP.135	£4.00	—
A	—	30	Stars of the Stage and Screen (c1934):	GP.308		
			A Black and White		£4.00	—
			B Coloured		£6.00	—
			ADCOCK & SON, Norwich			
A1	U	12	Ancient Norwich (1928)		—	£140.00
			11/12 Ancient Norwich (No. 6 missing)		£3.00	£33.00
			ADKIN & SONS, London			
			20 page reference book (combined with Abdulla & Anstie) — £4.50			
D	BW	25	*Actresses — French. Nd. 126-150 (c1898)	H.1	£220.00	—
A	C	15	*Beauties 'PAC', multi-backed (c1898)	H.2	£340.00	—
A	C	50	Butterflies and Moths (1924)	H.80	£2.00	£100.00

1

ADKIN & SONS, London (continued)

Size	Printing	Number in set	British Tobacco Issuers	Handbook reference	Price per card	Complete set
		12	Character Sketches:	H.3		
A2	C		A Black printing on back (1901)		£8.00	£100.00
A2	C		B Green printing on back (1902)		£8.00	£100.00
—	C		C Premium issue (145 x 103mm) (1901)		£110.00	—
—	C	4	*Games — by Tom Browne, postcard back (135 x 85mm) (c1900)	H.4	£300.00	—
		12	A Living Picture (c1901):	H.5		
A2	C		A 'Adkin & Sons' at top back			
			(i) crimson		£8.00	£100.00
			(ii) scarlet		£8.00	£100.00
A2	C		B 'These cards are ...' at top back		£8.00	£100.00
—	C		C Premium issue (145 x 103mm)		£110.00	—
A	BW	25	Notabilities (1915)		£5.00	£125.00
A1	C	12	Pretty Girl Series (Actresses) (c1897)	H.7	£60.00	—
A2	C	12	*Pretty Girl Series 'RASH' (1897):	H.8		
			A Calendar back		£65.00	—
			B Advertisements back		£40.00	—
			C Figure and verse back		£40.00	—
D	C	12	A Royal Favourite (1900)	H.9	£12.50	£150.00
A	BW		Soldiers of the Queen (1899-1900):	H.10		
			A Series of 50:			
		24	(a) Nos. 1-24 '... and exclusively with'		£30.00	—
		50	(b) Nos. 1-50 and variety '... and issued with ...'		£5.50	£275.00
		59	B Series of 60, plus No. 61 (Nos 28, 33 not issued)		£5.00	—
A	BW	31	*Soldiers of the Queen and Portraits (1901)	H.11	£6.50	—
A	C	30	Sporting Cups and Trophies (1914)		£17.00	—
A	BW	25	War Trophies (1917)		£5.00	£125.00
A	C	50	Wild Animals of the World (1922)	H.77	£1.80	£90.00

AIKMAN'S, Montrose

Size	Printing	Number in set	British Tobacco Issuers	Handbook reference	Price per card	Complete set
D	C	30	*Army Pictures, Cartoons, etc. (c1916)	H.12	£130.00	—

H.J. AINSWORTH, Harrogate

Size	Printing	Number in set	British Tobacco Issuers	Handbook reference	Price per card	Complete set
D	C	30	*Army Pictures, Cartoons, etc (1916)	H.12	£130.00	—

ALBERGE & BROMET, London

Size	Printing	Number in set	British Tobacco Issuers	Handbook reference	Price per card	Complete set
A	C		*Boer War and General Interest (c1900):	H.13		
		? 11	A 'Bridal Bouquet' and 'El Benecio' wording on green leaf design back		£120.00	—
		? 2	B 'La Optima' and 'Federation' wording on green leaf design back		£180.00	—
		? 8	C 'Bridal Bouquet' and 'El Benecio' wording on brown leaf design back		£120.00	—
		? 1	D 'La Optima' and 'Federation' wording on brown leaf design back		£200.00	—
DI	C	40	*Naval and Military Phrases (c1904):	H.14		
			A 'Bridal Bouquet' and 'El Benecio'		£100.00	—
			B 'La Optima' and 'Federation'		£100.00	—
DI	C	30	*Proverbs (c1903)	H.15	£100.00	—

PHILLIP ALLMAN & CO. LTD, London

Size	Printing	Number in set	British Tobacco Issuers	Handbook reference	Price per card	Complete set
A	C	50	Coronation Series (1953)		£1.00	£50.00

PHILLIP ALLMAN & CO. LTD, London (continued)

Size	Printing	Number				Handbook ref.	Price per card	Complete set
			Pin-up Girls (1953):			H.851		
A1	C		A	First 12 subjects:				
		12	Ai	Unnumbered, 'For men only' … … … … … …			£5.00	£60.00
		12	Aii	Numbered, 'Ask for Allman always' … … … …			£4.00	£50.00
		12	Aiii	Unnumbered, 'Ask for Allman always' … … …			£4.50	£55.00
A1	C	12	B	Second 12 subjects … … … … … … … …			£5.00	—
A1	C	24	C	Inscribed '1st series of 24' … … … … … … …			£8.00	—
—	C	24	D	Large size (75 x 68mm) … … … … … … … …			£4.00	—

AMALGAMATED TOBACCO CORPORATION LTD ('Mills' Cigarettes)

Size	Printing	Number		Handbook ref.	Price per card	Complete set
—	C	25	Famous British Ships 'Series No. 1' (75 x 48mm) (1952) … … … … … … … … … …		20p	£3.50
—	C	25	Famous British Ships 'Series No. 2' (75 x 48mm) (1952) … … … … … … … … …		20p	£4.00
—	C	50	History of Aviation (75 x 48mm) (1952):			
			A Nos. 1 to 16, 18 to 25 and 27 … … … …		£2.00	—
			B Nos. 17, 26 and 28 to 50 … … … … …		24p	£6.00
A	C	25	Kings of England (1954) … … … … … …		£1.80	£45.00
A	C	25	Propelled Weapons (1953) … … … … … …		20p	£4.00

OVERSEAS ISSUES

Size	Printing	Number		Handbook ref.	Price per card	Complete set
A	C	25	Aircraft of the World (1958) … … … … … … …	H.852	80p	£20.00
A	C	25	Animals of the Countryside (1957) … … … …	H.853	30p	£7.50
A	C	25	Aquarium Fish (1960) … … … … … … … … …	H.854	24p	£6.00
A	C	25	Army Badges — Past and Present (1960) … … …		£1.00	£25.00
A	C	25	British Coins and Costumes (1958) … … … …	H.855	50p	£12.50
A	C	25	British Locomotives (1961) … … … … … …	H.856	70p	£17.50
A	C	25	British Uniforms of the 19th Century (1957) … …	H.857	£1.00	£25.00
A	C	25	Butterflies and Moths (1957) … … … … …	H.858	36p	£9.00
A	C	25	Cacti (1960) … … … … … … … … … …	H.859	50p	£12.50
A	C	25	Castles of Britain (1961) … … … … … …	H.860	£1.20	£30.00
A	C	25	Coins of the World (1960) … … … … … …	H.861	20p	£5.00
A	C	25	Communications (1961) … … … … … …	H.862	£1.00	£25.00
A	C	25	Dogs (1958) … … … … … … … … … …	H.863	70p	£17.50
A	C	25	Evolution of the Royal Navy (1957) … … … …	H.864	60p	£15.00
A	C	25	Football Clubs and Badges (1961) … … … …	H.865	£1.60	—
A	C	25	Freshwater Fish (1958) … … … … … … …	H.866	24p	£6.00
A	C	25	Guerriers à Travers les Ages (French text) (1961) …	H.882	80p	£20.00
A	C	25	Historical Buildings (1959) … … … … … …	H.867	80p	£20.00
A	C	25	Histoire de l'Aviation, 1st series (French text) (1961)	H.868	30p	£7.50
A	C	25	Histoire de l'Aviation, 2nd series (French text) (1962)	H.868	£1.00	£25.00
A	C	25	Holiday Resorts (1957) … … … … … …	H.869	20p	£3.00
A	C	25	Interesting Hobbies (1959) … … … … … …	H.870	60p	£15.00
A	C	25	Into Space (1958) … … … … … … … …	H.871	28p	£7.00
A	C	25	Les Autos Modernes (French text) (1961) … … …	H.875	50p	£12.50
A	C	25	Medals of the World (1959) … … … … … …	H.872	24p	£6.00
A	C	25	Merchant Ships of the World (1961) … … … …	H.873	80p	£20.00
A	C	25	Merveilles Modernes (French text) (1961) … … …	H.876	40p	£10.00
A	C	25	Miniature Cars and Scooters (1959) … … … …	H.874	£1.20	£30.00
A	C	25	Nature (1958) … … … … … … … … …	H.877	20p	£3.00
A	C	25	Naval Battles (1959) … … … … … … …	H.878	50p	£12.50
A	C	25	Ports of the World (1957) … … … … … …	H.869	20p	£3.50
A	C	25	Ships of the Royal Navy (1961) … … … … …	H.879	50p	£12.50
A	C	25	Sports and Games (1958) … … … … … …	H.880	£1.20	£30.00
A	C	25	Tropical Birds (1959) … … … … … … …	H.881	£1.20	—
A	C	25	Weapons of Defence (1961) … … … … … …	H.883	£1.00	£25.00
A	C	25	Wild Animals (1958) … … … … … … …	H.884	20p	£5.00

AMALGAMATED TOBACCO CORPORATION LTD (Overseas Issues continued)

A	C	25	The Wild West (1960)	H.885	£1.00	£25.00
A	C	25	World Locomotives (1959)	H.886	£1.20	£30.00

THE ANGLO AMERICAN CIGARETTE MAKING CO. LTD, London

A	C	20	Russo-Japanese War Series (1906)	H.100	£400.00	—

THE ANGLO CIGARETTE MANUFACTURING CO., London

A	C	36	Tariff Reform Series (1909)	H.16	£35.00	—

E. & W. ANSTIE, Devizes

20 page reference book (combined with Abdulla & Adkin) — £4.50

A2	C	25	Aesop's Fables (1934)	H.518	£3.20	£80.00
A	C	16	*British Empire Series (1904)	H.17	£13.00	£210.00
A	BW	40	Nature Notes (1939)		£10.00	—
A	U	50	People of Africa (1926)		£3.80	£190.00
A	U	50	People of Asia (1926)		£3.80	£190.00
A	U	50	People of Europe (1925)		£3.80	£190.00
A2	BW	40	Places of Interest (1939):			
			A Varnished front		90p	£36.00
			B Unvarnished front		£3.00	—
—	C	8	Puzzles (26 x 70mm) (1902)	H.18	£230.00	—
A	C	50	*Racing Series (1922):			
			1-25 — Racing Colours		£5.00	—
			26-50 — Horses, Jockeys, Race-courses, etc ...		£7.00	—
—	C	5	Royal Mail (70 x 50mm) (1899)	H.19	£330.00	—
A	C	50	Scout Series (1923)		£3.80	£190.00
A2	C		Sectional Series:			
		10	Clifton Suspension Bridge (1938)	H.519-1	£2.50	£25.00
		10	Stonehenge (1936)	H.519-2	£2.50	£25.00
		10	The Victory (1936)	H.519-3	£4.00	—
		20	Wells Cathedral (1935)	H.519-4	£2.50	£50.00
		20	Wiltshire Downs (1935)	H.519-6	£2.50	£50.00
		10	Windsor Castle (1937)	H.519-5	£2.50	£25.00
A2	BW	40	Wessex (1938)		£1.75	£70.00
A	U	50	The World's Wonders (1924)		£1.80	£90.00

SILKS. Anonymous unbacked woven silks. Width sizes only are quoted as the silks were prepared in ribbon form and length sizes are thus arbitrary.

—	C	10	*Flags, large (width 95mm) (c1915)	H.495-1	£11.00	—
—	C	36	*Flags, small (width 42mm) (c1915)	H.495-1	£2.50	—
—	C	85	*Regimental Badges (width 32mm) (c1915)	H.495-3	From £2.00	—
—	C		*Royal Standard and Portraits (c1915):	H.495-2		
		1	Royal Standard (width 95mm)		—	£15.00
		1	King George V:			
			(a) Large (width 71 mm), black frame		—	£70.00
			(b) Large (width 71mm), gold frame		—	£60.00
			(c) Small (width 32mm)		—	£70.00
		1	Queen Mary:			
			(a) Large (width 71 mm)		—	£60.00
			(b) Small (width 32mm)		—	£75.00
		1	Lord French (width 71mm)		—	£85.00
		1	Lord Kitchener (width 71mm)		—	£20.00

H. ARCHER & CO., London

Size	Print-ing	Number in set		Handbook reference	Price per card	Complete set
C	C		*Actresses — Selection from 'FROGA A and B' (c1900):	H.20		
		? 20	A 'Golden Returns' back		£70.00	—
		? 13	B 'M.F.H.' back		£70.00	—
C			*Beauties — 'CHOAB' (c1900):	H.21		
	U	50	A 'Bound to Win' front		£30.00	—
	C	? 4	B 'Golden Returns' back		£75.00	—
	C	? 5	C 'M.F.H.' back		£75.00	—
C	C	20	*Prince of Wales Series (c1912)	H.22	£30.00	—

ARDATH TOBACCO CO. LTD, London
28 page reference book — £4.50

Size	Print-ing	Number in set		Handbook reference	Price per card	Complete set
A1	C	50	*Animals at the Zoo (export) (c1924):	H.520		
			A Back with descriptive text		£2.50	—
			B Back without description, 'Double Ace' issue ...		£25.00	—
A	C	96	Ardath Modern School Atlas (export) (c1935)		£1.60	—
A2	P	54	Beautiful English Women (1928) (export)		£3.50	—
A	C	25	Big Game Hunting (export) (c1930):			
			A Back in blue		£4.00	—
			B Back in black		£15.00	—
—	U	30	Boucher Series (77 x 62mm) (c1915)		£3.00	—
A	U	50	Britain's Defenders (1936)		90p	£45.00
	U	50	British Born Film Stars (export) (1934):			
A2			A Small size, back white semi-glossy		£1.70	—
A2			B Small size, back cream matt		£1.70	—
—			C Medium size (67 x 53mm)		£3.00	—
	U		Camera Studies (c1939):	H.644		
—		36	A Small size (70 x 44mm)		£1.50	£55.00
—		45	B Large size (79 x 57mm)		£1.40	£65.00
—	C	25	Champion Dogs (95 x 67mm) (1934)		£1.80	£45.00
A	C	50	Cricket, Tennis and Golf Celebrities (1935):			
			A Home issue, grey back		£1.40	£70.00
			B Export issue, brownish-grey back, text revised		£2.50	£125.00
—	U	25	Dog Studies (95 x 68mm) (1938)		£5.00	£125.00
A	C	25	Eastern Proverbs (export) (c1930)	H.521	£2.00	£50.00
A	C	48	Empire Flying-Boat (sectional) (1938)		£1.80	£90.00
			Album		—	£35.00
A	C	50	Empire Personalities (1937)		80p	£40.00
A	C	50	Famous Film Stars (1934)		£1.20	£60.00
A	C	50	Famous Footballers (1934)		£1.60	£80.00
A	C	25	Famous Scots (1935)		£1.60	£40.00
—	C	25	Fighting and Civil Aircraft (96 x 68mm) (1936)		£2.60	£65.00
A	C	50	Figures of Speech (1936)		£1.50	£75.00
A	C	50	Film, Stage and Radio Stars (1935)		£1.10	£55.00
—	C	25	Film, Stage and Radio Stars (96 x 68mm) (1935)		£1.20	£30.00
—	BW	? 22	Film Stars (postcard size) (c1935)	H.645	£30.00	—
—	U	40	Franz Hals Series, Dutch back (70 x 60mm) (c1916):			
			A Without overprint		£15.00	—
			B With overprint		£25.00	—
—	C	50	From Screen and Stage (96 x 65mm) (1936)		£1.20	£60.00
—	U	30	Gainsborough Series (77 x 62mm) (c1915)	H.714	£3.00	—
—	C	30	Girls of All Nations (78 x 66mm) (c1916)		£18.00	—
A1	U	50	Great War Series (c1916)		£6.00	—
A1	U	50	Great War Series 'B' (c1916)		£6.00	—
A1	U	50	Great War Series 'C' (c1916)		£6.00	—

ARDATH TOBACCO CO. LTD, London (continued)

Size	Printing	Number in set	Description	Handbook reference	Price per card	Complete set
A2	P	35	Hand Shadows (c1930) (export)		£35.00	—
—	BW	25	Historic Grand Slams (folders) (101 x 70mm) (c1935)		£35.00	—
			Hollandsche Oude Meesters, Dutch back (70 x 60mm) (c1916):			
—	U	25	A First 25 subjects		£15.00	—
—	U	25	B Second 25 subjects		£15.00	—
J2	U	48	How to Recognise the Service Ranks (holed for binding) (c1939)	H.642	£5.00	—
			Industrial Propaganda Cards (c1942):	H.914		
H1	C	2	A Black background		£7.50	£15.00
H1	C	4	B Coloured fronts		£7.50	£30.00
LT?	BW	11	C White fronts		£4.00	£45.00
J2	U	? 171	Information Slips (holed for binding) (1938)	H.643	£3.50	—
A	U	50	Life in the Services (1938):			
			A Home issue, adhesive		70p	£35.00
			B Export issue, non-adhesive		£1.30	£65.00
			Ministry of Information Cards (1941-3):			
J2	U	5	A Calendar — 'It all depends on me'		£4.00	£20.00
J2	U	1	B Greeting Card — 'It all depends on me'		—	£10.00
—	C	24	C 'It all depends on me' (80 x 63mm)	H.913	£1.25	£30.00
—	C	1	D Union Jack Folder (60 x 46mm)		—	£10.00
—	C	1	E 'On the Cotton Front' (80 x 63mm)	H.913	—	£2.50
—	BW	1	F 'On the Kitchen Front' (70 x 55mm)	H.913	—	£2.50
A	C	50	National Fitness (1938):			
			A Home issue, adhesive		60p	£30.00
			B Export issue, non-adhesive		£1.00	£50.00
A2	CP	50	New Zealand Views (1928) (export)		£2.80	—
A	U	50	Our Empire (export) (c1937)	H.522	£1.50	£75.00
A	C		Proverbs (c1936):			
		25	A Home issue Nos 1-25		£1.40	£35.00
		25	B Export issue Nos 26-50		£3.40	—
—	U	30	Raphael Series (77 x 62mm) (c1915)		£3.00	—
—	U		Rembrandt Series (1914):			
		30	A Large size (77 x 62 mm), English back		£4.00	—
		40	B Large size (77 x 62mm), Dutch back		£16.00	—
		30	C Extra-large size (101 x 62mm)		£6.00	—
—	U	30	Rubens Series (77 x 61 mm) (c1915):			
			A English 'State Express' back		£3.00	—
			B English 'Winfred' back		£17.00	—
			C Dutch back		£17.00	—
			D New Zealand 'State Express' back		£17.00	—
	U	100	Scenes from Big Films (export) (1935):			
A			A Small size, white back		£2.00	—
A			B Small size, cream back		£4.00	—
—			C Medium Size (67 x 52mm)		£4.50	—
—	BW	20	Ships of The Royal Navy (Double Ace Cigarettes Slides) (c1955)	H.887	£20.00	—
A	C	50	Silver Jubilee (1935)		70p	£35.00
			Album		—	£35.00
A	C	50	Speed — Land, Sea and Air (1935):			
			A Home issue, 'Issued with State Express'		£1.50	£75.00
			B Export issue, Ardath name at base		£2.20	—
—	C	25	Speed — Land, Sea and Air (95 x 68mm) (1938) ...		£1.80	£45.00
A	C	50	Sports Champions (1935):			
			A Home issue, 'State Express' at base		£1.10	£55.00
			B Export issue, 'Ardath' at base		£2.20	£110.00

ARDATH TOBACCO CO. LTD, London (continued)

Size	Print-ing	Number in set		Handbook reference	Price per card	Complete set
A	C	50	Stamps — Rare and Interesting (1939)		£1.60	£80.00
A	C	50	Swimming, Diving and Life-Saving (1937) (export) ...	H.523	£2.20	—
A	C	50	Tennis (1937) (export)	H.524	£2.20	—
A	C	48	Trooping the Colour (sectional) (1939)		£2.00	£100.00
			Album		—	£30.00
—	C	12	Types of Smokers (c1910):	H.716		
			A Size 77 x 64mm		£80.00	—
			B Size 102 x 64mm		£80.00	—
—	U	30	Valasquez Series (c1915):			
			A Large size (77 x 62mm)		£3.50	—
			B Extra-large size (101 x 62mm)		£6.00	—
A	C	50	Who is This? (1936) (Film Stars)		£1.80	£90.00
J2	U	? 5	Wonderful Handicraft (c1935)	H.717	£45.00	—
—	BW	24	World Views (No. 13 not issued) (95 x 68mm) (1937)		50p	£12.00
A	C	50	Your Birthday Tells Your Fortune (1937)		80p	£40.00

PHOTOGRAPHIC ISSUES

H	P		Photocards — Numbered Series (1936)*:			
		110	'A' — Football Clubs of North West Counties		£2.00	£220.00
		110	'B' — Football Clubs of North East Counties		£2.30	—
		110	'C' — Football Clubs of Yorkshire		£1.80	£200.00
		165	'D' — Football Clubs of Scotland		£1.50	£250.00
		110	'E' — Football Clubs of Midlands		£2.00	£220.00
		110	'F' — Football Clubs of London and Southern Counties		£1.80	£200.00
		99	'Z' — General Interest (Sports):			
			Nos. 111-165		70p	£38.00
			Nos. 166-209 (Cricket etc)		70p	£32.00
		11	'A.s' (1), 'C.s' (2-3), 'E.s' (4-10), 'F.s' (11) — Football Clubs (supplementary)		£5.50	£60.00
		?	Selected cards from the above 8 series:			
			A With red overprint		£7.00	—
			B Thin paper attached to back covering front of card advertising Ardath 'Kings'		£7.00	—
	P		Photocards — 'A Continuous Series of Topical Interest' (1937):	H.525		
		22	Group A — Racehorses and Sports		£1.35	£30.00
		22	Group B — Coronation and Sports		—	£38.00
			21 Different (minus Walter Neusel)		90p	£18.00
		22	Group C — Lancashire Personalities		—	£45.00
			21 Different (minus Gracie Fields)		£1.25	£25.00
		22	Group D — Sports and Miscellaneous		£1.50	£33.00
		22	Group E — Film Stars and Sports		£1.25	£27.00
		22	Group F — Film Stars and Sportsmen		£1.50	£33.00
		66	'G.S.' — Miscellaneous subjects (export)		£2.50	—
H	P		Photocards — 'A Continuous Series of General interest', with Album offer (1938):	H.526		
		11	Group G — Australian Cricketers		£20.00	—
		22	Group H — Film, Radio and Sporting Stars		£1.25	£27.00
		22	Group I — Film Stars and Miscellaneous		£1.25	£27.00
	P		Photocards — 'A Continuous Series of General Interest', without Album offer — uncoloured (1938):	H.527		
H		22	Group J — Film Stars and General Interest		£1.10	£24.00
H		22	Group K — Film, Radio and Sporting Stars:			
			1 With 'Kings' Clause		£1.25	£27.00
			2 Without 'Kings' Clause (export)		£1.60	—
H		44	Group L — Film Stars and Miscellaneous		70p	£30.00

ARDATH TOBACCO CO. LTD, London (Photographic Issues continued)

Size	Print	Number	Description	Handbook ref	Price per card	Complete set
		45	Group M — Film Stars and Miscellaneous:			
C		1	Small size		90p	£40.00
—		2	Large size (80 x 69 mm), with 'Kings' Clause ...		90p	£40.00
—		3	Large size (80 x 69mm), without 'Kings' Clause		90p	£40.00
	P	45	Group N — Film, Stage and Radio Stars:			
C		1	Small size		90p	£40.00
—		2	Large size (80 x 69mm)		90p	£40.00
H	CP		Photocards — 'A Continuous Series of General Interest', without Album offer — Hand coloured (export) (1938):	H.528		
		22	Group 1 — Views of the World		£1.00	£22.00
		22	Group 2 — Views of the World		£1.00	£22.00
		22	Group 3 — Views of the World		80p	£17.50
			Real Photographs:			
	P	45	Group O — 'A Continuous Series of General Interest' — Films, Stage and Radio Stars (1939) ...	H.529	80p	£36.00
C	P	45	'1st Series of 45' — Film and Stage Stars (1939) ...		£1.10	—
C	P	54	'2nd Series of 54' — Film and Stage Stars (1939) ...		£1.10	—
J2	P	18	'First Series' — Views (1937)		£2.50	—
J2	P	18	'Second Series' — Film and Stage Stars (1937)		£2.50	—
J2	P	18	'Third Series' — Views (1937)		£2.50	—
J2	P	18	'Fourth Series' — Film and Stage Stars (1937)		£2.50	—
J2	P	18	'Fifth Series' — Views (1938)		£2.50	—
J2	P	18	'Sixth Series' — Film and Stage Stars (1938)		£2.50	—
H	P	44	'Series One' 'G.P.1' — Film Stars (export) (1939) ...		90p	£40.00
H	P	44	'Series Two' 'G.P.2' — Film Stars (export) (1939) ...		45p	£20.00
H	P	44	'Series Three' 'G.P.3' — Film Stars (export) (1939) ...		£3.00	—
H	CP	44	'Series Three' 'C.V.3' — Views (export) (1939)		90p	£40.00
H	CP	44	'Series Four' 'C.V.4' — Views (export) (1939)		35p	£15.00
J2	P	36	'Series Seven' — Film and Stage Stars (1938)		£1.00	—
J2	P	54	'Series Eight' — Film and Stage Stars (1938)		80p	£45.00
	P	54	'Series Nine' — Film and Stage Stars (1938):			
H			A Medium size		80p	£45.00
J2			B Extra-large size		80p	£45.00
	P	54	'Series Ten' — Film and Stage Stars (1939):			
—			A Large size (80 x 69mm)		80p	£45.00
J2			B Extra-large size		£1.00	£55.00
	P	54	'Series Eleven' — Film and Stage Stars (1939):			
—			A Large size (80 x 69mm)		80p	£45.00
J2			B Extra-large size		£1.20	—
—	P	54	'Series Twelve' — Film and Stage Stars (80 x 69mm) (1939)		80p	£45.00
—	P	54	'Series Thirteen' — Film and Stage Stars (80 x 69mm) (1939)		80p	£45.00
	P	36	'Of Famous Landmarks' (1939):			
—			A Large size (80 x 69 mm), titled 'Real Photographs'		£3.50	—
	J2		B Extra-large size, titled 'Real Photographs of Famous Landmarks'		£1.70	£60.00
	P	36	'Of Modern Aircraft' (1939):			
—			A Large size (80 x 69mm)		£4.50	—
J2			B Extra-large size		£3.50	—

SILKS

Size	Print	Number	Description	Handbook ref	Price per card	Complete set
—	C	1	Calendar for 1937 (silk) (138 x 102mm)	H.508	—	£140.00
—	C	1	Calender for 1938 (silk) (160 x 102mm)	H.508	—	£140.00

THE ASSOCIATED TOBACCO MANUFACTURERS LTD

C2	C	25	Cinema Stars (export) (c1926):	H.530		
			A 'Issued with Bond Street Turkish Cigarettes' ...		£35.00	—
			B 'Issued with John Bull Virginia Cigarettes' ...		£35.00	—
			C 'Issued with Club Virginia Cigarettes'		£35.00	—
			D 'Issued with Heliopolis Turkish Cigarettes' ...		£35.00	—
			E 'Issued with Sports Turkish Cigarettes'		£35.00	—

A. ATKINSON, London

D	C	30	*Army Pictures, Cartoons, etc (c1916)	H.12	£130.00	—

AVISS BROTHERS LTD, London

D1	C	40	*Naval and Military Phrases (c1904)	H.14	£220.00	—

J.A. BAILEY, Swansea

D1	C	40	*Naval and Military Phrases (c1904)	H.14	£270.00	—

A. BAKER & CO. LTD, London

A	BW	20	*Actresses — 'BLARM'(c1900):	H.23		
			A Long design back (64mm)		£30.00	—
			B Design altered and shortened (58mm)		£30.00	—
A	BW	10	*Actresses — 'HAGGA' (c1900)	H.24	£30.00	£300.00
	BW		*Actresses 'Baker's 3-sizes' (c1900):	H.25		
A		25	A Small cards		£32.00	—
—		25	B Extra large cards (67 x 127mm)		£250.00	—
—	BW	25	Actresses 'Baker's 3 sizes' (56 x 75mm) (c1900) ...	H.25	£50.00	—
C	BW	? 41	*Baker's Tobacconists' Shops (c1901):	H.26		
			A 'Try our 3½d Tobaccos' back		£250.00	—
			B 'Cigar, Cigarette, etc. Manufacturers' back ...		£150.00	—
C	C	25	Beauties of All Nations (c1900):	H.27		
			A 'Albert Baker & Co. (1898) ...' back		£22.00	£550.00
			B 'A. Baker & Co. ...' back		£16.00	£400.00
C	BW	16	*British Royal Family (c1902)	H.28	£50.00	—
A1	BW	20	Cricketers Series (1901)	H.29	£325.00	—
A1	C	25	*Star Girls (c1898)	H.30	£225.00	—

BAYLEY & HOLDSWORTH

A	C	26	*International Signalling Code (c1910)		£200.00	—

E.C. BEESTON, Wales

D	C	30	*Army Pictures, Cartoons etc (c1916)	H.12	£130.00	—

BELFAST SHIPS STORES CO. LTD, Belfast

C	1		*Dickens' Characters (79 x 40mm) (c1895)	H.31	£1000.00	—

J. & F. BELL LTD, Glasgow

A	BW	10	*Actresses — 'HAGGA' ('Three Bells Cigarettes') (c1900)	H.24	£80.00	—
C	C	25	*Beauties — Tobacco Leaf Back (c1898):	H.32		
			A 'Bell's Scotia Cigarettes' back		£120.00	—
			B 'Three Bells Cigarettes' back		£120.00	—
A	C	25	Colonial Series (c1901)		£45.00	—
A	BW	30	*Footballers (c1902)		£75.00	—
A	C	25	Scottish Clan Series No. 1 (c1903)	H.33	£16.00	£400.00

J. & F. BELL LTD, Glasgow (continued)

OVERSEAS ISSUES

Size	Print	Number	Description	Handbook ref	Price	Set
A	C	60	Rigsvaabner (Arms of Countries) (c1925)		£30.00	—
A	C	60	Women of Nations (1924)		£30.00	—

B. BELLWOOD, BRADFORD

| C | C | 18 | Motor Cycle Series (c1912) ... ... | H.469 | £130.00 | — |

RICHARD BENSON LTD, Bristol

	U	24	Old Bristol Series:			
—			A Original issue (80 x 70mm) (c1925):			
			i 23 different, minus No. 8		£3.00	£70.00
			ii Number 8		—	£30.00
—			B Re-issue (88 x 78-83mm) (1946)		£2.00	£50.00

BENSON & HEDGES, London

A2	C	1	Advertisement Card, The Original Shop (1973)		—	£2.00
B	C	10	B.E.A. Aircraft (1958)	H.888	£11.00	—
—	C	50	Friendly Games (75 x 45mm) (c1970)		£1.50	—

OVERSEAS ISSUES (CANADA)

| A2 | C | 48 | Ancient and Modern Fire Fighting Equipment (1947) | | £6.00 | — |
| — | BW | 12 | Oxford University Series (90 x 50mm) (c1912) ... ... | | £40.00 | — |

FELIX BERLYN, Manchester

	C	25	Golfing Series (Humorous) (c1910):			
A1			A Small size		£400.00	—
—			B Post card size (139 x 87mm)		£600.00	—

BERRY, London

| D | U | 20 | London Views (c1905) ... ... | H.34 | £275.00 | — |

BEWLAY & CO. LTD, London

D1	U		Bewlay's War Series (Generals, etc) (c1915):	H.477		
		12	A 'Caps the Lot' Smoking Mixture		£12.50	—
		6	B Try Bewlay's 'Caps the Lot' Mixture		£12.50	—
		6	C Try Bewlay's 'Modern Man' Mixture		£12.50	—
D1	U	25	Bewlay's War Series (Photogravure War Pictures) (c1915):	H.35		
			A 'Modern Man' Mixtures etc		£12.50	—
			B 'Modern Man' Cigarettes		£12.50	—
			C 'Two Great Favourites'		£12.50	—
A	C	6	*Comic Advertisement Cards (1909)	H.36	£200.00	—
—	C	6	*Comic Advertisement Cards (140 x 88mm) (c1909)	H.36	£100.00	—

W.O. BIGG & CO., Bristol

A	C	37	*Flags of All Nations (c1904):	H.37		
			A 'Statue of Liberty' back, 4d oz		£9.00	—
			B As A:— (a) altered to 4½d by hand		£9.00	—
			(b) 4 ½d red seal over 4d		£9.00	—
			C Panel design 'New York' Mixture		£9.00	—
A	C	50	Life on Board a Man of War (c1905)	H.38	£11.00	£550.00

JAS. BIGGS & SONS, London

| C | C | 26 | *Actresses — 'FROGA A' 'Two Roses' in white (c1900) ... ... | H.20 | £40.00 | — |

JAS. BIGGS & SONS, London (continued)

Size	Print-ing	Number in set		Handbook reference	Price per card	Complete set
C	C	52	*Actresses — 'FROGA A & B' 'Two Roses' in black (c1900)	H.20	£55.00	—
A	C		*Beauties, with frameline — 'CHOAB' (c1900):	H.21		
		25	A Blue typeset back		£75.00	—
		50	B Overprinted in black on Bradford cards		£70.00	—
C	C		*Beauties, no framelines — selection 'BOCCA' (c1900):	H.39		
		25	A Blue back		£75.00	—
		25	B Black back		£75.00	—
C	C	30	*Colonial Troops (c1901)	H.40	£35.00	—
C	C	30	*Flags and Flags with Soldiers (c1903)	H.41	£32.00	—
A1	C	25	*Star Girls (c1900)	H.30	£275.00	—

J.S. BILLINGHAM, Northampton

Size	Print-ing	Number in set		Handbook reference	Price per card	Complete set
D	C	30	*Army Pictures, Cartoons etc (c1916)	H.12	£130.00	—

R. BINNS, Halifax

Size	Print-ing	Number in set		Handbook reference	Price per card	Complete set
A	U	? 17	*Halifax Footballers (c1924)	H.531	£200.00	—

BLANKS CIGARETTES

Size	Print-ing	Number in set		Handbook reference	Price per card	Complete set
A	C	50	Keystrokes in Break-Building (c1935)	H.647	£500.00	—

THE BOCNAL TOBACCO CO., London

Size	Print-ing	Number in set		Price per card	Complete set
A2	U	25	Luminous Silhouettes of Beauty and Charm (1938)	£3.00	£75.00
A2	C	25	Proverbs Up-to-Date (1938)	£2.40	£60.00

ALEXANDER BOGUSLAVSKY LTD, London

Size	Print-ing	Number in set		Price per card	Complete set
—	C	12	Big Events on the Turf (133 x 70mm) (1924)	£45.00	—
A2	C	25	Conan Doyle Characters (1923):		
			A Back in black, white board	£7.00	—
			B Back in grey, cream board	£7.00	—
			C Back in green	£7.00	—
A2	C	25	Mythological Gods and Goddesses (1924)	£3.00	£75.00
A	C	25	*Sports Records, Nd. 1-25 (1925)	£2.20	£55.00
A	C	25	Sports Records, Nd. 26-50 (1925)	£2.20	£55.00
	C	25	Winners on the Turf (1925):		
A			A Small size, captions 'sans serif'	£3.60	£90.00
A			B Small size, captions with 'serif'	£5.00	—
B			C Large size	£5.50	—

R. & E. BOYD LTD, London

Size	Print-ing	Number in set		Handbook reference	Price per card	Complete set
—	U	25	Places of Interest (c1938):			
			A Size 67 x 35mm		£70.00	—
			B Size 71 x 55mm		£70.00	—
—	U	25	Wild Birds at Home (75 x 57mm) (c1938)	H.626	£70.00	—

WM. BRADFORD, Liverpool

Size	Print-ing	Number in set		Handbook reference	Price per card	Complete set
C	C	50	*Beauties 'CHOAB' (c1900)	H.21	£38.00	—
D	U	? 7	Beauties — 'Jersey Lily Cigarettes' (c1900)	H.488	£600.00	—
D2	BW	20	Boer War Cartoons (c1901)	H.42	£120.00	—

T. BRANKSTON & CO., London

Size	Print-ing	Number in set		Handbook reference	Price per card	Complete set
C	C	30	*Colonial Troops (c1901):	H.40		
			A Golf Club Mixture		£35.00	—
			B Red Virginia		£35.00	—
			C Sweet as the Rose		£35.00	—

T. BRANKSTON & CO., London (continued)

Size	Print-ing	Number in set		Handbook reference	Price per card	Complete set
A2	C	12	*Pretty Girl Series 'RASH' (c1900)	H.8	£350.00	—

BRIGHAM & CO., Reading

B	U	16	Down the Thames from Henley to Windsor (c1912)		£160.00	—
A	U	16	Reading Football Players (c1912)		£450.00	—
—	BW	3	Tobacco Growing in Hampshire (89 x 79mm) (1915)	H.470	£16.00	£50.00

BRITANNIA ANONYMOUS SOCIETY

| — | C | ? 31 | *Beauties and Scenes (60 x 40mm) (c1914) ... ... | H.532 | £80.00 | — |

BRITISH & COLONIAL TOBACCO CO., London

| A1 | C | 25 | *Armies of the World (c1900) ... ... | H.43 | £220.00 | — |

J.M. BROWN, Derby

| D | C | 30 | *Army Pictures, Cartoons etc (c1916) ... ... | H.12 | £130.00 | — |

ROBERT BRUCE LTD, Birmingham & Wolverhampton

| A | C | 18 | Motor Cycle Series (c1912) ... ... | H.469 | £200.00 | — |

JOHN BRUMFIT, London

| A | C | 50 | The Public Schools' Ties Series (Old Boys) (1925) ... | | £4.00 | £200.00 |

G.A. BULLOUGH, Castleford

| D | C | 30 | *Army Pictures, Cartoons etc (c1916) ... ... | H.12 | £130.00 | — |

BURSTEIN, ISAACS & CO., London
(The BI-CO Company, B.I. & Co. Ltd)

D	BW	25	Famous Prize-Fighters, Nd. 1-25 (1923):			
			A Front caption upper and lower case lettering		£7.00	—
			B Front caption small capital letters		£7.00	—
D	BW	25	Famous Prize-Fighters, Nd. 26-50 (1924):			
			A Front caption upper and lower case lettering		£7.00	—
			B Front caption small capital letters		£7.00	—
D	P	28	London View Series (1922)		£4.00	—

BYRTWOOD & CO., Bristol

| A2 | U | ? 37 | *Pretty Girl Series — 'BAGG' (c1900) ... ... | H.45 | £150.00 | — |

CABANA CIGAR CO., London

—	BW	2	Advertisement Card — 'Little Manturios'			
			(63 x 49mm) (1905)	H.719	£350.00	—
A2	C	40	*Home and Colonial Regiments (c1900)	H.69	£350.00	—

PERCY E. CADLE & CO. LTD, Cardiff

A1	BW	20	*Actresses 'BLARM' (c1900)	H.23	£40.00	—
C	U	26	*Actresses — 'FROGA A' (c1900):	H.20		—
			A Printed Back		£38.00	—
			B Rubber — Stamped Back		£200.00	—
C	C	26	*Actresses — 'FROGA B' (c1900)	H.20	£50.00	—
C	BW	12	*Boer War and Boxer Rebellion Sketches (c1901) ...	H.46	£60.00	—
C	BW	10	*Boer War Generals — 'FLAC' (c1901)	H.47	£70.00	—
A	BW	20	*Footballers (c1904)	H.4	£70.00	—

CARRERAS LTD, London

Size	Print-ing	Number in set			Handbook reference	Price per card	Complete set
A	CP	24	Actresses and Their Pets (1926) (export)		H.648	£5.00	—
	C	48	Alice in Wonderland (1930):				
A				A Small size, rounded corners		£1.50	£75.00
A				B Small size, square corners		£3.00	—
B2				C Large size		£1.80	£90.00
		1		D Instruction Booklet		—	£18.00
A	C	50	Amusing Tricks and How to Do Them (1937)			£1.60	£80.00
	C		Battle of Waterloo (1934):			H.533		
C		1		1 Paper insert, with instructions		—	£12.00
—		15		*2 Soldiers and Guns, large size (67 x 70mm) ...		£4.00	—
A				*3 Soldiers and Guns, small size:			
		10		Soldiers — Officers' Uniforms		£2.00	—
		12		Soldiers and Guns		£2.00	—
C1	C	50	Believe it or Not (1934)			80p	£40.00
A	C	50	Birds of the Countryside (1939)			£1.10	£55.00
D1	BW	200	The Black Cat Library (Booklets) (c1910)			£12.00	—
A	C	50	Britain's Defences (1938)			70p	£35.00
A	C	50	British Birds (1976)			20p	£4.00
			Album			—	£10.00
	C	25	British Costumes (1927):				
C2				A Small size		£1.40	£35.00
B2				B Large size		£1.40	£35.00
A	P	27	British Prime Ministers (1928) (export)			£2.00	£55.00
A1	C	1	Calendar for 1934			—	£30.00
A	C	50	Celebrities of British History (1935):				
				A Brown on cream back (two shades of ink) ...		90p	£45.00
				B Pale brown on bluish back		90p	£45.00
				Album		—	£30.00
A	C	25	Christie Comedy Girls (1928) (export)			£2.20	£55.00
A	U		Cricketers (1934):				
		30		A 'A Series of Cricketers'		£3.50	£105.00
		50		B 'A Series of 50 Cricketers':			
				1 Front in brown and white		£3.50	£175.00
				2 Front in black and white		£35.00	—
A	BW	50	Dogs and Friend (1936)			50p	£25.00
A	C	50	Do You Know? (1939)			35p	£17.50
A	C	50	Famous Airmen and Airwomen (1936)			£1.70	£85.00
	C		Famous Escapes (1926):				
A		25		A Small size		£1.60	£40.00
B2		25		B Large size		£1.40	£35.00
—		10		C Extra-large size (133 x 70mm)		£3.00	£30.00
A2	C	96	Famous Film Stars (1935)		H.534	£1.30	£125.00
A	C		Famous Footballers (1935):				
		48		A Set of 48		£1.40	£70.00
		24		B Nos. 25-48 redrawn		£1.80	£45.00
A	C	25	Famous Men (1927) (export)			£1.60	£40.00
B2	P	24	Famous Naval Men (1929) (export)			£2.00	£50.00
—	C	6	Famous Posters (folders) (65 x 41mm) (1923)		H.606	£25.00	—
B2	P	12	Famous Soldiers (1928) (export)			£6.00	£75.00
A	P	27	Famous Women (1929) (export)			£1.50	£40.00
A	C	25	Figures of Fiction (1924)			£2.20	£55.00
	P	54	Film and Stage Beauties (1939):				
A2				A Small size		50p	£27.00
—				B Medium size (70 x 60mm):			
				(a) Without full stop after 'Carreras Ltd'		65p	£35.00
				(b) With full stop after 'Carreras Ltd.'		80p	£42.00

CARRERAS LTD, London (continued)

Size	Print-ing	Number in set		Handbook reference	Price per card	Complete set
	P	36	Film and Stage Beauties:			
B1			A Large size (1939)		£1.00	£36.00
J2			B Extra-large size (1938)		£1.50	£55.00
A	C	50	Film Favourites (1938)		£1.50	£75.00
A	P	54	Film Stars — 'A Series of 54' (1937)		85p	£45.00
	P	54	Film Stars (1938):			
A			A Small size, 'Second Series of 54'		50p	£27.00
—			B Medium size (68 x 60mm), 'A Series of 54' ...		£1.00	£55.00
J2	P		Film Stars (export):			
		36	'A Series of 36' (c1935)		£3.00	—
		36	'Second Series of 36' (c1936)		£3.00	—
		36	'Third Series of 36' (c1937)		£3.00	—
		36	'Fourth Series of 36' (c1938)		£3.00	—
A2	C	50	Film Stars, by Florence Desmond (1936)		£1.00	£50.00
—		72	Film Stars, oval (70 x 30mm) (1934):			
	P		A Inscribed 'Real Photos'		£2.50	—
	U		B Without 'Real Photos'		£1.50	£110.00
			Album		—	£30.00
A	C	60	Flags of All Nations (unissued) (c1960)		50p	£30.00
—	C		*Flags of the Allies (shaped) (c1915):	H.49		
		1	Grouped Flags:'Black Cat' Cigarettes		£50.00	—
		5	Allies Flags: 'Black Cat' Cigarettes		£50.00	—
A	C	50	Flowers (1936)		50p	£25.00
A	C	50	Flowers All the Year Round (1977)		20p	£10.00
			Album		—	£10.00
A2	C	75	*Footballers (1934):			
			A 'Carreras Cigarettes' on front 27mm long		£2.00	£150.00
			B 'Carreras Cigarettes' on front 26mm long		£2.00	£150.00
	C	36	'Fortune Telling' (1926):			
A			A Small size:			
			1 Card inset		70p	£25.00
			2a Head inset, black framelines		70p	£25.00
			2b Head inset, brown framelines		£1.25	£45.00
B2			B Large size:			
			1 Card inset		70p	£25.00
			2 Head inset		70p	£25.00
		1	C Instruction Booklet:			
			1 Address 23 New North Street		—	£20.00
			2 Address 12 Bath Street		—	£11.00
	P		Glamour Girls of Stage and Films (1939):			
A2		54	A Small size		55p	£30.00
—		54	B Medium size (70 x 60mm)		65p	£35.00
—		36	C Large size (76 x 70mm)		£1.00	£36.00
J2		36	D Extra-large size		£1.25	£45.00
	C	50	'Gran-Pop' by Lawson Wood (1934):			
C1			A Small size		50p	£25.00
B			B Large size		40p	£20.00
	C	52	Greyhound Racing Game (1926):			
A			A Small size		30p	£15.00
B2			B Large size		30p	£15.00
		1	C Instruction Leaflet		—	£11.00
—	C		Guards Series (68 x 50mm):			
		4	A Military Mug Series (1971)		£1.00	—
		8	B Order Up the Guards (1970)		£1.00	—
		16	C Send for the Guards (1969)		£1.00	—
D1	BW	5	The Handy Black Cat English-French Dictionary (Booklets) (1915)		£25.00	—

CARRERAS LTD, London (continued)

Size	Printing	Number in set		Handbook reference	Price per card	Complete set
	C	48	Happy Family (1925):			
A1			A Small size		40p	£20.00
B2			B Large size		40p	£20.00
A	C	25	Highwaymen (1924)		£2.60	£65.00
A	C	50	History of Army Uniforms (1937)		£1.50	£75.00
A	C	50	History of Naval Uniforms (1937)		90p	£45.00
	C		Horses and Hounds (1926)			
A		25	A Small size		£2.20	£55.00
B2		20	B Large size		£2.25	£45.00
—		10	C Extra-large size (133 x 70mm)		£4.50	£45.00
	C	50	Kings and Queens of England (1935):			
A			A Small size		£1.60	£80.00
B2			B Large size		£2.50	£125.00
			Album (To suit either size of cards)		—	£30.00
A	C	50	Kings and Queens of England (1977)		35p	£17.50
			Album		—	£15.00
A	U	50	A 'Kodak' at the Zoo 'Series of Fifty' (1924)		80p	£40.00
A	U	50	A 'Kodak' at the Zoo '2nd Series' (1925)		80p	£40.00
A	P	27	Malayan Industries (1929) (export)		80p	£20.00
	P	24	Malayan Scenes (1928):			
A			A Small size		£3.00	—
—			B Medium size (70 x 60mm)		75p	£18.00
A	C	50	Military Uniforms (1976)		20p	£4.00
			Album		—	£10.00
—	C	7	Millionaire Competition Folders (68 x 30mm) (1971)		£2.00	—
—	C	53	*Miniature Playing Cards (44 x 32mm) (c1935)	H.535-1A	20p	£9.00
	C	50	The 'Nose' Game (1927):			
A			A Small size		50p	£25.00
B2			B Large size		50p	£25.00
		1	C Instruction Leaflet		—	£11.00
	C	50	Notable MPs (1929):			
A			A Small size		£1.20	£60.00
—			B Medium size (69 x 60mm)		60p	£30.00
A	P	25	Notable Ships — Past and Present (1929) (export)		£1.60	£40.00
	C		Old Staffordshire Figures (1926):			
A		24	A Small size		£1.25	£30.00
—		12	B Extra-large size (134 x 71mm)		£3.00	£36.00
B	C	24	Old Staffordshire Figures (different subjects) (1926)		£1.50	£36.00
	C	24	Orchids (1925):			
A			A Small size		£1.00	£25.00
B			B Large size		£1.00	£25.00
—			C Extra-large size (133 x 70mm)		£3.40	—
A	C		Our Navy (1937):			
		20	A Thick card, selected numbers		£1.20	£24.00
		50	B Thin card		£1.20	£60.00
C1	C	50	Palmistry (1933)		60p	£30.00
A	C	50	Palmistry (1980)		£1.00	—
			Album		—	£15.00
A	P	27	Paramount Stars (1929) (export)		£1.70	£45.00
A	C	25	Picture Puzzle Series (1923)	H.649	£1.60	£40.00
—	C	53	Playing Cards (68 x 42mm) (c1925)	H.535-1B	£1.20	—
	C		*Playing Cards and Dominoes (1929):	H.535-IC		
C		52	A Small size:			
			(a) Numbered		60p	—
			(b) Unnumbered		60p	—
—		26	B Large size (77 x 69mm):			
			(a) Numbered		£1.00	£26.00
			(b) Unnumbered		£1.00	£26.00

CARRERAS LTD, London (continued)

Size	Printing	Number in set		Handbook reference	Price per card	Complete set
A	C	48	Popular Footballers (1936):			
			A White back		£1.10	£55.00
			B Cream back		£1.10	£55.00
—	C		Popular Personalities, oval (70 x 30mm) (1935):	H.629		
		72	1 Normal issue		85p	£60.00
			Album		—	£30.00
		10	2 Replaced subjects (Nos. 1-10) for issue in Eire		£20.00	—
	C		Races — Historic and Modern (1927):			
A		25	A Small size		£2.40	£60.00
B		25	B Large size		£2.40	£60.00
—		12	C Extra-large size (133 x 69mm)		£5.00	£60.00
A	U	50	Radio & Television Favourites (unissued) (c1955) ...		£8.00	—
A	C	140	Raemaekers War Cartoons (1916):			
			A 'Black Cat' Cigarettes		£1.30	£185.00
			B Carreras Cigarettes		£4.00	—
	C		Regalia Series (1925):			
A		25	A Small size		50p	£12.50
B		20	B Large size		60p	£12.00
—		10	C Extra-large size (135 x 71mm)		£2.00	£20.00
—	C	50	'Round the World' Scenic Models (folders) (83 x 73mm) (c1930)		80p	£40.00
	C		School Emblems (1929):			
A		50	A Small size		90p	£45.00
B		40	B Large size		75p	£30.00
—		20	C Extra-large size (134 x 76mm)		£2.25	£45.00
A	C	50	The Science of Boxing (c1916):			
			A 'Black Cat' back		£3.00	£150.00
			B 'Carreras Ltd' back		£5.00	—
A	C	50	Sport Fish (1978)		20p	£4.00
			Album		—	£10.00
C1	C	48	Tapestry Reproductions of Famous Paintings (sectional) (1938)		80p	£40.00
A	C	50	Tools — And How to Use Them (1935)		£2.00	£100.00
A	C	80	Types of London (1919)		£1.70	£135.00
A	P	27	Views of London (1929) (export)		40p	£11.00
A	P	27	Views of the World (1927) (export)		75p	£20.00
A	C	50	Vintage Cars (1976):			
			A With word 'Filter' in white oval:			
			i Thin card, bright red oblong at top		20p	£9.00
			ii Thick card, bright red oblong at top		20p	£7.50
			iii Thin card, dull red oblong at top		40p	—
			B Without word 'Filter' in white oval		20p	£5.00
			Album		—	£10.00
A	C	25	Wild Flower Art Series (1923)		£1.40	£35.00
A	C	50	Women on War Work (c1916)		£7.50	£375.00

TURF SLIDE ISSUES

Size	Printing	Number in set		Handbook reference	Price per card	Complete set
A	U	50	British Aircraft (1953)		£180	£90.00
A	U	50	British Fish (1954)		70p	£35.00
A	U	50	British Railway Locomotives (1952)		£1.80	£90.00
A	U	50	Celebrities of British History (1951)		£1.50	£75.00
A	U	50	Famous British Fliers (1956)		£6.50	—
A	U	50	Famous Cricketers (1950)		£6.50	—
A	U	50	Famous Dog Breeds (1952)	H.889	£2.00	£100.00
A	U	50	Famous Film Stars (1949)		£3.20	—
A	U	50	Famous Footballers (1951)		£5.00	—
A	U	50	Film Favourites (1948)		£4.00	—

CARRERAS LTD, London (Turf Slide Issues continued)

A	U	50	Film Stars (1947)		£3.20	—
A	U	50	Footballers (1948)		£5.00	—
A	U	50	Olympics (1948)		£6.50	—
A	U	50	Radio Celebrities (1950)		£1.40	£70.00
A	U	50	Sports Series (1949)		£4.00	—
A	U	50	Zoo Animals (1955)		50p	£25.00

(N.B. These prices are for the full slides. If only the cut slides are required these will be half Catalogue price.)

SILKS

			Lace Motifs (c1915):	H.506		
—	—	79	A Size 63 x 63mm		£8.00	—
—	—	15	B Size 125 x 63mm		£40.00	—
—	—	7	C Size 125 x 125mm		£80.00	—
—	C	12	Miscellaneous Series Cabinet size (1915)	H.505-18	£180.00	—

OVERSEAS ISSUES (AUSTRALIA & CANADA)

—	C	20	Canadian Fish (69 x 50mm) (1985)		£2.00	—
—	C	20	Canadian Wild Animals (69 x 50mm) (1984):			
			A Complete set		£2.00	—
			B 15 Different		30p	£4.50
C2	U	72	Film Star Series (1933):			
			A Smile Away back		£3.00	—
			B Standard back		£1.50	—
C2	C	72	Football Series (1933)		£3.00	—
C2	C	24	Personality Series (1933)		£2.50	—
C2	U	72	Personality Series Film Stars (1933)		£1.50	—
C2	C	72	Personality Series Footballers (1933)		£3.00	—
—	C	216	Sportsman's Guide — Fly Fishing (Package Issue) (c1955):			
			A 25 Package (103 x 75mm)		£2.00	—
			B 20 Package (82 x 75mm)		£2.00	—

CARRICK & CO., Hull

D	C	12	*Military Terms (1901)	H.50	£80.00	—
—	U	1	Queen Victoria Jubilee 1887 (105 x 67mm)	H.720	—	£300.00

P.J. CARROLL & CO. LTD, Dundalk, Glasgow and Liverpool

D	C	25	Birds (prepared but not issued) (c1940)	H.537	70p	£17.50
D	C	25	British Naval Series (c1915)	H.51	£45.00	—
A	P	20	County Louth G.R.A. Team and Officials (1913)		£32.00	—
D	BW	25	*Derby Winners (1914-15):	H.52		
			A Back in black		£120.00	—
			B Back in green		£120.00	—
K2	BW	26	Grand Slam Spelling Bee Cards (c1935)		£16.00	—
D	C	25	Ship Series (1937)		£10.00	£250.00
D	U	24	Sweet Afton Jig-Saw Puzzles (1935)	H.650	£20.00	—

THE CASKET TOBACCO & CIGARETTE CO. LTD, Manchester

A2	U	? 1	Bowling Fixture Cards, Coupon Back (1907)	H.53	£500.00	—
A2	U	? 5	Cricket Fixture Cards, Coupon back (1905-10)	H.53	£500.00	—
A2	U	? 2	Cyclists Lighting-up Table (1909-10)		£500.00	—
A2	U	? 18	*Football Fixture Cards, Coupon back (1905-11)	H.53	£500.00	—
A2	BW	? 7	Road Maps (c1910)	H.54	£500.00	—

S. CAVANDER & CO., London and Portsea

D	BW	50	*Beauties — selection from 'Plums' (1898)	H.186	£550.00	—

CAVANDERS LTD, London and Glasgow

Size	Printing	Number in set	Description	Handbook reference	Price per card	Complete set
A	C	25	Ancient Chinese (1926)		£1.80	£45.00
A	C	25	Ancient Egypt (1928)		£1.60	£40.00
B	C	25	Ancient Egypt (different subjects) (1928)		£1.40	£35.00
A	P	36	Animal Studies (1936)		40p	£14.00
	CP	50	Beauty Spots of Great Britain (1927):			
A			A Small size		50p	£25.00
—			B Medium size (76 x 52mm)		50p	£25.00
	CP		Camera Studies (1926):			
A		54	A Small size		25p	£12.50
—		56	B Medium size (77 x 51mm)		28p	£15.00
A	C	30	Cinema Stars — Set 6 (1934)	GP.55	£1.20	£36.00
—	CP	30	The Colonial Series (77 x 51mm) (1925):	GP.330		
			A Small caption, under lmm high		50p	£15.00
			B Larger caption, over lmm high		50p	£15.00
—	C	25§	Coloured Stereoscopic (77 x 51mm) (1931)		70p	£35.00
D	C	25	Feathered Friends or Foreign Birds (1926):	GP.70		
			A Titled 'Feathered Friends'		£2.40	—
			B Titled 'Foreign Birds'		£1.60	£40.00
—	C	25§	Glorious Britain (76 x 51mm) (1930)		60p	£30.00
			The Homeland Series (1924-26):	GP.333		
A			Small size:			
	CP	50	A Back in blue		£1.00	£50.00
	CP	50	B Back in black, glossy front		£1.00	£50.00
	CP	54	C Back in black, matt front		40p	£20.00
			Medium size (77 x 51mm):			
	CP	50	D Back inscribed 'Hand Coloured Real Photos'		35p	£17.50
	CP	56	E As D, with 'Reprinted ...' at base		50p	£28.00
	CP	56	F Back inscribed 'Real Photos'		50p	£28.00
	P	56	G Back inscribed 'Real Photos'		50p	£28.00
A	C	25	Little Friends (1924)	GP.89	£1.20	£30.00
—	C	25	The Nation's Treasures (77 x 51mm) (1925)		60p	£15.00
	P		Peeps into Many Lands — 'A Series of ...' (1927):			
D		36§	A Small size		50p	£36.00
—		36§	B Medium size (75 x 50mm)		80p	£55.00
—		36	C Extra-large size (113 x 68mm)		£2.00	—
	P	36§	Peeps into Many Lands — 'Second Series ...' (1928):			
D			A Small size		£1.00	£75.00
—			B Medium size (75 x 50mm)		£1.00	£75.00
	P	24§	Peeps into Many Lands — 'Third Series ...' (1929):			
D			A Small size		40p	£20.00
			B Medium size (75 x 50mm)		90p	£45.00
—			C As B, but inscribed 'Reprinted by Special Request'		£1.50	£75.00
	P	24§	Peeps into Prehistoric Times — 'Fourth Series ...' (1930):			
D			A Small size		90p	£45.00
—			B Medium size (75 x 50mm)		£1.40	£65.00
—	P		*Photographs (54 x 38mm) (1924):	GP.337		
		30	1 Animal Studies		£1.50	—
		3	2 Royal Family		£3.30	—
—	C	48	Regimental Standards (76 x 70mm) (c1924)		£12.00	—
C	C	25	Reproductions of Celebrated Oil Paintings (1925)	GP.245	£1.40	£35.00
	CP	108	River Valleys (1926):			
A			A Small size		40p	£45.00
—			B Medium size (75 x 50mm)		40p	£45.00

CAVANDERS LTD, London and Glasgow (continued)

Size	Print-ing	Number		Handbook reference	Price per card	Complete set
A	C	25	School Badges (1928):	GP.121		
			A Back in dark blue		£1.00	£25.00
			B Back in light blue		£1.00	£25.00
—	CP	30	Wordsworth's Country (76 x 51mm) (1926)		£1.00	£30.00
			§ Stereoscopic series, consisting of a Right and a Left card for each number, a complete series is thus **double** the number shown.			

R.S. CHALLIS & CO. LTD, London

D1	C	50	Comic Animals (1936)		70p	£35.00
A	BW	44	Flickits (Greyhound Racing Flickers) (1936)	Ha.589-1	£40.00	—
D1	U	36	Wild Birds at Home (1935):	H.626		
			A Inscribed 'Issued with Baldric Cigarettes'		60p	£22.00
			B Above wording blocked out in black		£1.25	£45.00

H. CHAPMAN & Co.

D	C	30	*Army Pictures, Cartoons, etc (c1916)	H.12	£220.00	—

CHARLESWORTH & AUSTIN LTD, London

C	U	50	*Beauties — 'BOCCA' (c1900)	H.39	£35.00	—
C	BW	16	*British Royal Family (1902)	H.28	£50.00	—
C	C		Colonial Troops (c1900):	H.40		
		50	A Black back		£38.00	—
		30	B Brown back		£38.00	—
A1	BW	20	Cricketers Series (1901)	H.29	£320.00	—
C	C	30	*Flags and Flags with Soldiers (c1903)	H.41	£35.00	—

CHESTERFIELD CIGARETTES

—	C	6	Chesterfield Collection (76 x 45mm) (1979)		£3.00	—
—	C	6	Cocktails (76 x 45mm) 1980		50p	£3.00

CHEW & CO., Bradford

D	C	30	*Army, Pictures, Cartoons etc (c1916)	H.12	£130.00	—

W.A. & A.C. CHURCHMAN, Ipswich
36 page reference book — £4.50

C	C	26	*Actresses — 'FROGA A' (c1900)	H.20	£35.00	—
C	C	26	*Actresses — 'FROGA B' (c1900)	H.20	£45.00	—
C	U	24	*Actresses, 'For the Pipe' back (c1900)	H.55	£85.00	—
—	C	48	Air-Raid Precautions (68 x 53mm) (1938)	H.544	50p	£25.00
A	C	25	Army Badges of Rank (1916)	H.56	£5.00	£125.00
A	U	50	Association Footballers (1938)		70p	£35.00
A	U	50	Association Footballers, 2nd series (1939)		£1.20	£60.00
A	C	12	*Beauties — 'CERF' (1904)	H.57	£65.00	—
			*Beauties — 'CHOAB' (c1900):	H.21		
—	C	3	I Circular cards, 55mm diameter		£1500.00	—
C	C	25	II Five different backs		£120.00	—
C	U	25	*Beauties — 'FECKSA'(c1902)	H.58	£90.00	—
C	C	25	*Beauties — 'GRACC' (c1900)	H.59	£100.00	—
A	C	50	Birds and Eggs (1906)	H.60	£7.00	£350.00
D	BW	20	*Boer War Cartoons (c1901)	H.42	£110.00	—
		20	*Boer War Generals' — 'CLAM' (c1901):	H.61		
A2	BW		A Black front		£35.00	—
A	U		B Brown front		£35.00	—
A	C	25	Boxing (1922)	H.311	£6.00	—
A	U	50	Boxing Personalities (1938)		£1.80	£90.00

W.A. & A.C. CHURCHMAN, Ipswich (continued)

Size	Printing	Number in set	Description	Handbook reference	Price per card	Complete set
A	C	50	Boy Scouts (1916)	H.62	£7.00	£350.00
A	C	50	Boy Scouts, 2nd series (1916)	H.62	£7.00	£350.00
A	C	50	Boy Scouts, 3rd series (1916):	H.62		
			A Brown back		£7.00	£350.00
			B Blue back		£10.00	–
A	U	25	British Film Stars (1934)		£2.40	£60.00
A	C	55	Can You Beat Bogey at St Andrews? (1933):			
			A Without overprint		£3.00	–
			B Overprinted in red 'Exchangeable'		£3.00	–
	U		Cathedrals and Churches (1924):	H.545		
A		25	A Small size		£2.00	£50.00
J		12	B Extra-large size		£12.50	–
A	C	50	Celebrated Gateways (1925)	H.347	£2.00	£100.00
D	P	41	*Celebrities – Boer War Period (c1901)	H.63	£20.00	–
–	BW	1	Christmas Greetings Card (68 x 53mm) (1938)		–	£2.00
A	C	25	Civic Insignia and Plate (1926)		£2.00	£50.00
A	C	50	Contract Bridge (1935)		80p	£40.00
A	C	50	Cricketers (1936)		£3.40	–
	C		Curious Dwellings:			
A		25	A Small size (1926)		£2.20	£55.00
B		12	B Large size (1925)		£6.00	–
A	C	25	Curious Signs (1925)		£2.20	£55.00
A	C	38	Dogs and Fowls (1908)	H.64	£7.50	–
	C		Eastern Proverbs:	H.521		
			A Small size:			
A		25	1 'A Series of 25' (1931)		80p	£20.00
A		25	2 '2nd Series of 25' (1932)		£1.20	£30.00
			B Large size:			
B		12	1 'A Series of 12' (1931)		£4.00	–
B		12	2 '2nd Series of 12' (1933)		£3.00	£36.00
B		12	3 '3rd Series of 12' (1933)		£3.00	£36.00
B		12	4 '4th Series of 12' (1934)		£1.50	£18.00
A		50	East Suffolk Churches:			
	BW		A Black front, cream back (1912)		£2.20	£110.00
	BW		B Black front, white back (1912)		£2.20	£110.00
	U		C Sepia front (1917)		£2.20	£110.00
A	C	50	Empire Railways (1931)		£2.50	£125.00
A	C	25	Famous Cricket Colours (1928)		£4.00	£100.00
	U		Famous Golfers:			
A		50	A Small size (1927)		£10.00	–
			B Large size:			
B		12	1 'A Series of 12' (1927)		£30.00	–
B		12	2 '2nd Series of 12' (1928)		£30.00	–
	C		Famous Railway Trains:			
A		25	A Small size (1929)		£2.60	£65.00
			B Large size:			
B		12	1 'Series of 12' (1928)		£7.00	–
B		12	2 '2nd Series of 12' (1929)		£7.00	–
A	C	50	Fish and Bait (1914)	H.65	£7.00	£350.00
A	C	50	Fishes of the World (1911):	H.66	–	£250.00
			30 cards as re-issued 1924		£1.65	£50.00
			20 cards not re-issued		£11.00	–
A	C	50	Flags and Funnels of Leading Steamship Lines			
			(1912)	H.67	£7.00	–
A	C	50	Football Club Colours (1909)	H.68	£12.00	£600.00
A	U	50	*Footballers – Photogravure Portraits (c1910)		£35.00	–

W.A. & A.C. CHURCHMAN, Ipswich (continued)

Size	Printing	Number in set	Title	Handbook reference	Price per card	Complete set
A	C	50	Footballers — Action Pictures & Inset (1914)		£18.00	£900.00
A	C	52	'Frisky' (1935)		£3.50	—
A	C	50	History and Development of the British Empire			
			(1934)		£2.00	£100.00
			Album		—	£40.00
—	U	48	Holidays in Britain (Views and Maps) (68 x 53 mm)			
			(1937)		50p	£25.00
—	C	48	Holidays in Britain (views only) (68 x 53mm) (1938)		50p	£25.00
C	C	40	*Home and Colonial Regiments (1902)	H.69	£55.00	—
A	C	25	The Houses of Parliament and Their Story (1931) ...		£2.00	£50.00
	C		Howlers:			
A		40	A Small size (1937)		40p	£16.00
B		16	B Large size (1936)		50p	£8.00
A	C	25	The Inns of Court (1932)		£3.00	£75.00
A	C	50	Interesting Buildings (1905)	H.70	£8.00	£400.00
A	C	25	Interesting Door-Knockers (1928)		£2.40	£60.00
A	C	25	Interesting Experiments (1929)		£1.60	£40.00
A	C	50	'In Town To-night' (1938)		40p	£20.00
B	C	12	Italian Art Exhibition, 1930 (1931)		£2.50	£30.00
B	C	12	Italian Art Exhibition, 1930 — '2nd Series' (1931) ...		£2.50	£30.00
	C		The King's Coronation (1937):			
A		50	A Small size		30p	£12.50
B		15	B Large size		80p	£12.00
A	U	50	Kings of Speed (1939)		60p	£30.00
	C		Landmarks in Railway Progress:			
A		50	A Small size (1931)		£2.80	£140.00
			B Large size:			
B		12	1 '1st Series of 12' (1932)		£5.50	£65.00
B		12	2 '2nd Series of 12' (1932)		£5.50	£65.00
	U		Lawn Tennis (1928):	H.546		
A		50	A Small size		£4.00	£200.00
B		12	B Large size		£12.00	—
	C		Legends of Britain (1936):			
A		50	A Small size		90p	£45.00
B		12	B Large size		£1.50	£18.00
	C		Life in a Liner (1930):			
A		25	A Small size		£1.60	£40.00
B		12	B Large size		£6.00	—
A	C	50	*Medals (1910)	H.71	£7.00	£350.00
	C		Men of the Moment in Sport:			
A		50	A Small size (1928):			
			1 40 Different		£4.00	—
			2 10 Different Golfers (Nos. 24 to 33)		£10.00	—
			B Large size:			
B		12	1 '1st Series of 12' (1929):			
			A 10 Different		£9.00	—
			B Nos. 7 and 8 (Golfers)		£100.00	—
B		12	2 '2nd Series of 12' (1929):			
			A 10 Different		£9.00	—
			B Nos. 7 and 8 (Golfers)		£100.00	—
—	C	48	Modern Wonders (68 x 53mm) (1938)		40p	£20.00
A	C	25	Musical Instruments (1924)	H.547	£3.60	£90.00
	C		Nature's Architects (1930):			
A		25	A Small size		£1.40	£35.00
B		12	B Large size		£2.50	£30.00
—	U	48	The Navy at Work (68 x 53mm) (1937)		50p	£24.00

W.A. & A.C. CHURCHMAN, Ipswich (continued)

Size	Printing	Number in set	Description	Handbook reference	Price per card	Complete set
—	U	55	Olympic Winners Through The Years (Package Designs, 30 small, 25 large) (1960)	H.891	£2.00	—
A	C	50	*Phil May Sketches (1912):	H.72		
			A 'Churchman's Gold Flake Cigarettes'		£7.00	£350.00
			B 'Churchman's Cigarettes'		£8.00	—
A	C	25	Pipes of the World (1927)		£3.00	£75.00
	C		Prominent Golfers (1931):			
A		50	A Small size:			
			1 49 Different		£8.50	—
			2 No. 25 Bobby Jones		£100.00	—
B		12	B Large size:			
			1 11 Different		£20.00	—
			2 No. 5 Bobby Jones		£200.00	—
	C		The 'Queen Mary' (1936):			
A		50	A Small size		£1.60	£80.00
B		16	B Large size		£3.50	£55.00
A	C	50	Racing Greyhounds (1934)		£2.60	£130.00
—	C	48	The RAF at Work (68 x 53mm) (1938)		90p	£45.00
	C		Railway Working:	H.548		
			A Small size:			
A		25	1 'Series of 25' (1926)		£3.60	£90.00
A		25	2 '2nd Series of 25' (1927)		£2.40	£60.00
			B Large size:			
B		12	1 'Series of 12' (1926)		£10.00	—
B		13	2 '2nd Series, 13' (1927)		£10.00	—
B		12	3 '3rd Series, 12' (1927)		£10.00	—
A	C	50	*Regimental Colours and Cap Badges (1911)	H.73	£7.00	£350.00
A	BW	50	Rivers and Broads (1922):			
			A Titled 'Rivers & Broads'		£6.50	—
			B Titled 'Rivers & Broads of Norfolk & Suffolk' ...		£5.50	—
A	C	50	Rugby Internationals (1935)		£1.80	£90.00
A	C	50	Sectional Cycling Map (1913)	H.74	£6.00	£300.00
A	C	50	Silhouettes of Warships (1915)		£9.00	—
A	C	50	Sporting Celebrities (1931):			
			A 43 Different		£3.00	—
			B 7 Different Golfers (Nos. 30 to 36)		£10.00	—
	C		Sporting Trophies (1927):			
A		25	A Small size		£2.40	£60.00
B		12	B Large size		£6.00	—
A	C	25	Sports and Games in Many Lands (1929):			
			A 24 Different minus No. 25		£4.00	£100.00
			B Number 25 (Babe Ruth)		—	£50.00
	C		The Story of London (1934):			
A		50	A Small size		£1.80	£90.00
B		12	B Large size		£3.00	£36.00
	C		The Story of Navigation:			
A		50	A Small size (1936)		40p	£20.00
B		12	B Large size (1935)		£1.25	£15.00
A	C		3 Jovial Golfers in search of the perfect course (1934):			
		36	A Home issue		£3.50	—
		72	B Irish issue, with green over-printing		£9.00	—
A	C	50	A Tour Round the World (1911)	H.75	£7.00	£350.00
	C		Treasure Trove:			
A		50	A Small size (1937)		40p	£20.00
B		12	B Large size (1935)		£1.50	£18.00
A1	C	25	*Types of British and Colonial Troops (c1900)	H.76	£45.00	—

W.A. & A.C. CHURCHMAN, Ipswich (continued)

					Price per card	Complete set
	C		Warriors of All Nations:			
A		25	A Small size (1929)		£3.00	£75.00
			B Large size:			
B		12	1 'A Series of 12' (1929)		£4.00	£50.00
B		12	2 '2nd Series of 12' (1931)		£4.00	£50.00
	C		Well-known Ties (1934):			
A		50	A Small size		90p	£45.00
			B Large size			
B		12	1 'A Series of 12'		£1.75	£21.00
B		12	2 '2nd Series of 12'		£1.75	£21.00
A	C	50	Well-known Ties, '2nd Series' (1935)		70p	£35.00
A	U	25	Wembley Exhibition (1924)		£3.00	£75.00
A	U	50	West Suffolk Churches (1919)		£2.00	£100.00
A	C	50	Wild Animals of the World (1907)	H.77	£8.00	£400.00
—	C	48	Wings Over the Empire (68 x 53mm) (1939)		40p	£20.00
	C		Wonderful Railway Travel (1937):			
A		50	A Small size		60p	£30.00
B		12	B Large size		£1.50	£18.00
—	U	40	The World of Sport (Package Designs, 30 small, 10 large) (1961)	H.892	£2.00	—
A	C	50	World Wonders Old and New (prepared but not issued) (c1955)		40p	£20.00

OVERSEAS ISSUES (CHANNEL ISLANDS)

(All cards without I.T.C. clause)

—	C	48	Air Raid Precautions (68 x 53) (1938)	H.544	£1.80	—
—	U	48	Holidays in Britain (68 x 53) (1937)		£1.80	—
—	C	48	Holidays in Britain (68 x 53) (1938)		£1.80	—
—	C	48	Modern Wonders (68 x 53) (1938):			
			A I.T.C. clause blocked out in silver		£5.00	—
			B Reprinted without I.T.C. clause		£1.80	—
—	U	48	The Navy at Work (68 x 53) (1937)		£1.80	—
—	C	48	The RAF at Work (68 x 53) (1939)		£1.80	—
—	C	48	Wings Over the Empire (68 x 53) (1939)		£1.80	—

WM. CLARKE & SON, Dublin

A	C	25	Army Life (1915)	H.78	£13.00	£325.00
A1	BW	16	*Boer War Celebrities — 'CAG' (c1901)	H.79	£25.00	—
A	C	50	Butterflies and Moths (1912)	H.80	£8.00	£400.00
A	BW	30	Cricketer Series (1901)		£170.00	—
A1	BW	66	Football Series (1902)	H.81	£32.00	—
A	C	25	Marine Series (1907)		£14.00	£350.00
A	C	50	Royal Mail (1914)	H.82	£12.00	£600.00
	C	50	Sporting Terms (38 x 58mm) multi-backed (c1900):	H.83		
			14 Cricket Terms		£50.00	—
			12 Cycling Terms		£50.00	—
			12 Football Terms		£50.00	—
			12 Golf Terms		£50.00	—
—	C	20	*Tobacco Leaf Girls (shaped) (c1898)	H.84	£450.00	—
—	C	25	Well-known Sayings (71 x 32mm) (c1900)	H.85	£24.00	£600.00

J. CLAYTON, Wakefield

—	C	? 6	*Play Up Sporting Shields (c1895)	H.718	£175.00	—

Size	Printing	Number in set	BRITISH TOBACCO ISSUERS	Handbook reference	Price per card	Complete set

J.H. CLURE, Keighley

Size	Printing	Number in set		Handbook reference	Price per card	Complete set
D	C	30	*Army Pictures, Cartoons, etc (c1900):	H.12		
			A 'These Cigarettes' back		£130.00	—
			B 'Try Clure's Havana Mixture' back		£130.00	—
A	U	50	War Portraits (1916)	H.86	£100.00	—

J. LOMAX COCKAYNE, Sheffield

Size	Printing	Number in set		Handbook reference	Price per card	Complete set
A	U	50	War Portraits (1916)	H.86	£100.00	—

COHEN WEENEN & CO. LTD, London

Size	Printing	Number in set		Handbook reference	Price per card	Complete set
—	P	40	*Actresses, Footballers and Jockeys (26 x 61mm) (c1901)	GP.350	£50.00	—
A1	U	26	*Actresses — 'FROGA A' (c1900)	H.20/GP.351	£65.00	—
A	C	25	*Beauties — selection from 'BOCCA' (c1900)	H.39/GP.353	£75.00	—
A1	C	25	*Beauties — 'GRACC' (c1900)	H.59/GP.354	£110.00	—
D2	BW	25	*Boxers (c1912):	H.721/GP.362		
			A Black back		£18.00	—
			B Green back		£12.00	£300.00
			C Without Maker's Name		£18.00	—
A	BW		*Celebrities — Black and white (1901):	GP.356		
		65	A 'Sweet Crop, over 250 ...' back		£6.00	—
		? 20	B 'Sweet Crop, over 500 ...' back		£11.00	—
A	C		*Celebrities — Coloured (1901):			
		45	I 1-45 Boer War Generals etc. 'Sweet Crop, over 100 ...' back:	GP.355	—	£270.00
			A Toned back		£6.00	—
			B White back		£6.00	—
			C Plain Back		£9.00	—
		121	II 1-121 Including Royalty, etc. 'Sweet Crop, over 250 ...' back:			
			I-45 as in I	GP.355	£9.00	—
			46-121 additional subjects	GP.357	£6.00	—
—	C		*Celebrities — 'GAINSBOROUGH I' (1901):	GP.358		
—		? 21	A In metal frames (46 x 67mm)		£100.00	—
D2		39	B 'Sweet Crop, over 250 ...' back		£50.00	—
D		30	C 'Sweet Crop, over 400 ...' back		£14.00	£420.00
D1		2	D 1902 Calendar Back gilt border to front		£130.00	—
D1		39	E Plain Back, white border		£12.00	£475.00
D1		? 40	F Plain back, gilt border to front		£100.00	—
	P	? 177	*Celebrities — 'GAINSBOROUGH II' (c1901):	GP.359		
			A In metal frames (46 x 67mm)		£18.00	—
D2			B Without frames showing Frame Marks		£5.00	—
D2			C Without Frames no Frame Marks (as issued)		£10.00	—
D2	U	25	*Cricketers (1926)		£16.00	—
A2	C	20	*Cricketers, Footballers, Jockeys (c1900):	GP.361		
			A Caption in brown		£22.00	£440.00
			B Caption in grey-black		£22.00	£440.00
D	C	40	Fiscal Phrases (c1905):	GP.363		
			A 'Copyright Regd.' on front		£12.50	£500.00
			B Without 'Copyright Regd.'		£12.50	£500.00
A2	C	60	Football Captains, 1907-8 — Series No. 5	GP.364	£15.00	—
A2	BW	100	*Heroes of Sport (c1898)	GP.365	£90.00	—
A	C	40	*Home and Colonial Regiments (c1901):	H.69/GP.366		
			A 'Sweet Crop, over 100 ...' back		£9.00	£360.00
			B 'Sweet Crop, over 250 ...' back		£13.00	—
			C 1902 Calendar Back Gilt Border		£130.00	—

COHEN WEENEN & CO. LTD, London (continued)

Size	Printing	Number			Handbook ref.	Price	Complete set
A2	C	20		*Interesting Buildings and Views (1902):	GP.367		
			A	No Framelines		£12.00	£240.00
			B	*Gilt Framelines 1902 Calendar back*		£130.00	—
K2	C	52		*Miniature Playing Cards — Bandmaster Cigarettes			
				(c1910)		£4.00	—
D2	C			*Nations:	GP.369		
		20	A	Blue 'Sweet Crop, over 250 ...' back (c1902)		£12.00	£240.00
		20	B	*Plain back — gilt border* (c1902)		£100.00	—
		? 1	C	*1902 Calender back* (c1902)		£130.00	—
		20	D	Text back (1923)		£4.50	£90.00
D	C	40		Naval and Military Phrases (c1904):	H.14/GP.370		
			A	Red back, 'Series No. 1'		£16.00	£640.00
			B	'Sweet Crop, over 250 ...' back:			
				i White Border		£28.00	—
				ii Gilt Border		£130.00	—
D2	C	50		Owners, Jockeys, Footballers, Cricketers — Series			
				No. 2 (c1906)	GP.371	£15.00	£750.00
D2	C	20		Owners, Jockeys, Footballers, Cricketers — Series			
				No. 3 (c1907)	GP.372	£16.00	£320.00
D	C	30		*Proverbs, 'Sweet Crop, over 400 ...' back (c1905)	H.15/GP.373	£16.00	—
A	C	20		Russo-Japanese War Series (1904)	H.100/GP.120	£20.00	—
A	BW	25		*Silhouettes of Celebrities (c1905)	GP.374	£12.00	£300.00
D1	C	50		Star Artistes — Series No. 4 (c1905):	GP.375		
				20 With stage background		£12.00	£240.00
				30 No stage, plain background		£12.00	£360.00
D	C	50		V.C. Heroes (of World War I), Nd. 51-100 (1915):			
				51-75 — dull greyish card		£11.00	£275.00
				Without Maker's Name on back		£14.00	—
				76-100 — glossy white card		£11.00	£275.00
D	U	50		*War Series (World War I) (1915):	H.103/GP.376		
				1-25 Admirals and Warships:			
				A Thick card		£11.00	£275.00
				B Thin card		£11.00	£275.00
				26-50 Leaders of the War:			
				A Maker's Name on back		£11.00	£275.00
				B *Without Maker's Name on back*		£14.00	—
D1	C	30		Wonders of the World:	GP.378		
				A Inscribed 'Series 6', white borders (c1908) ...		£7.00	£210.00
				B Without 'Series 6', gilt borders (1923)		£3.00	£90.00
SILKS							
—	C	16		*Victoria Cross Heroes II (72 x 70mm)			
				(paper-backed) (c1915)	GP.251	£40.00	—

T.H. COLLINS, Mansfield

Size	Printing	Number			Handbook ref.	Price	Complete set
Al	U	25		Homes of England (1924):			
			A	Dark mauve front		£6.00	£150.00
			B	Grey front		£20.00	—
A	C	25		Sports and Pastimes — Series I (1923)	H.225	£7.00	£175.00

F. COLTON Jun., Retford

Size	Printing	Number			Handbook ref.	Price	Complete set
D	C	30		*Army Pictures, Cartoons, etc (c1916):	H.12		
			A	'Best House' back		£130.00	—
			B	'Our Hand-filled Cigarettes' back		£130.00	—
A	U	50		War Portraits (1916)	H.86	£100.00	—

T.W. CONQUEST, London

Size	Print-ing	Number in set		Handbook reference	Price per card	Complete set
D	C	*30	Army Pictures, Cartoons etc (c1916)	H12	£130.00	—

THE CONTINENTAL CIGARETTE FACTORY, London

Size	Print-ing	Number in set		Handbook reference	Price per card	Complete set
A	C		Charming Portraits (c1925):	H.549		
		25	A Back in blue, with firm's name		£5.00	—
		25	B Back in blue, inscribed 'Club Mixture Tobacco'		£7.00	—
		4	C Back in brown, inscribed 'Club Mixture Tobacco'		£12.00	—
		25	*D Plain back		£5.00	—

COOPER & CO'S STORES LTD, London

Size	Print-ing	Number in set		Handbook reference	Price per card	Complete set
A	BW	25	*Boer War Celebrities — 'STEW' (c1901):	H.105		
			A 'Alpha Mixture' back		£160.00	—
			B 'Gladys Cigars' back		£160.00	—

COOPERATIVE WHOLESALE SOCIETY LTD, Manchester

Size	Print-ing	Number in set		Handbook reference	Price per card	Complete set
A2	C	? 6	*Advertisement Cards (c1915)	H.106	£400.00	—
A	C	24	African Types (1936)		50p	£12.00
—	C	? 2	*Beauties (102 x 68mm) (c1915)	H.722	£100.00	—
—	U	50	Beauty Spots of Britain (76 x 51mm) (1936)		50p	£25.00
A2	C	50	Boy Scout Badges (1939)		£1.50	£75.00
A	C	25	Boy Scout Series (c1915)		£36.00	—
A	C	48	British and Foreign Birds (1938)		80p	£40.00
A	C	50	British Sport Series§ (c1914)		£32.00	—
D	C	25	*Cooking Recipes (1923)		£2.40	£60.00
A	C	28	*Co-operative Buildings and Works (c1914)	H.107	£15.00	£420.00
A	C	24	English Roses (1924)		£4.00	£100.00
A	C	50	Famous Bridges (48 + 2 added) (1937)		90p	£45.00
A	C	48	Famous Buildings (1935)		80p	£40.00
A2	C	25	How to Do It (1924):			
			A 'Anglian Mixture' back		£3.00	—
			B 'Equity Tobacco' back		£3.00	—
			C 'Jaycee Brown Flake' back		£3.00	—
			D 'Raydex Gold Leaf' back		£3.00	—
A	C	48	Musical Instruments (1934)		£4.00	£200.00
A	C	25	Parrot Series (1910)		£40.00	—
A	C	48	Poultry (1927)		£8.00	£400.00
A	C	48	Railway Engines (1936)		£3.50	£175.00
A	C	24	Sailing Craft (1935)		£1.60	£40.00
A	C	18	War Series (c1915)		£28.00	—
A2	C	48	Wayside Flowers, brown back (1923)		£2.00	£100.00
A2	C	48	Wayside Flowers, grey back (1928)		80p	£40.00
A2	C	48	Wayside Woodland Trees (1924)		£2.50	£125.00
A	C	24	Western Stars (1957)		65p	£16.00

§Note: Cards advertise non-tobacco products, but are believed to have been packed with cigarettes and/or tobacco.

COPE BROS. & CO. LTD, Liverpool

Size	Print-ing	Number in set		Handbook reference	Price per card	Complete set
	BW	20	*Actresses — 'BLARM' (c1900):	H.23		
A1			A Plain backs. Name panel ¼" from border		£35.00	—
A1			B Black design back. Name ¼" from border		£35.00	—
D			C Black design back. Name panel ¹⁄₁₆" from border		£35.00	—
A	U	? 6	*Actresses — 'COPEIS' (c1900)	H.108	£300.00	—
A	U	26	*Actresses 'FROGA A' (c1900)	H.20	£90.00	—
D1	P	50	*Actresses and Beauties (c1900)	H.109	£15.00	—

COPE BROS. & CO. LTD, Liverpool (continued)

Size	Printing	Number in set	Description	Handbook reference	Price per card	Complete set
KI	P	? 46	*Beauties, Actors and Actresses (c1900)	H.110	£30.00	—
A	C	52	*Beauties — P.C. inset (c1898)	H.111	£45.00	—
A	C	15	*Beauties 'PAC' (c1898)	H.2	£75.00	—
A1	C	50	Boats of the World (c1910)		£15.00	£750.00
D2	BW	126	Boxers (c1915):			
			1-25 Boxers		£20.00	£500.00
			26-50 Boxers		£16.00	£400.00
			51-75 Boxers		£16.00	£400.00
			76-100 Boxers		£22.00	£550.00
			101-125 Army Boxers		£16.00	£400.00
			126 'New World Champion'		—	£50.00
D	BW	25	Boxing Lessons (1935)		£4.00	£100.00
A1	C	35	*Boy Scouts and Girl Guides (c1910)	H.132	£13.00	£450.00
—	C	25	Bridge Problems (folders) (85 x 50mm) (1924)		£30.00	—
D	BW	25	British Admirals (c1915)	H.103	£14.00	£350.00
A2	C	50	British Warriors (c1912):			
			A Black on white backs		£8.00	£400.00
			B Grey on toned backs		£10.00	£500.00
A1	U	25	Castles§ (1939)		£1.20	£30.00
A1	U	25	Cathedrals§ (May, 1939)		£1.60	£40.00
A	C	50	Characters from Scott (c1900):			
			A Wide card		£12.00	£600.00
			B Narrow card — officially cut		£12.00	—
	U	115	Chinese Series (c1903):			
A1			Nos 1-20		£12.00	—
A1			Nos-2I-40:			
			A 'Bond of Union Tobacco' back		£12.00	—
			B 'Cope's Courts' back		£12.00	—
			C 'Golden Cloud' back		£12.00	—
			D 'Golden Magnet' back		£12.00	—
			E 'Solace' back		£12.00	—
			Nos 41-65:			
D			A Picture 56mm long		£12.00	—
AI			B Picture 58mm long		£12.00	—
A2			Nos 66-115:			
			A 'Bond of Union'/'Bond of Union' back		£12.00	—
			B 'Bond of Union'/'Golden Magnet' back		£12.00	—
			C 'Golden Magnet'/'Golden Magnet' back		£12.00	—
			D 'Golden Magnet'/'Bond of Union' back		£12.00	—
—	C	6	*Comic Hunting Scenes (c1890)	H.723	£300.00	—
A	C	50	Cope's Golfers (1900):			
			A Wide card		£80.00	—
			B Narrow card — officially cut		£80.00	—
—	C	25	Dickens' Character Series (75 x 58mm) (1939)		£1.20	£30.00
—	C	50	Dickens' Gallery (1900):			
A			A Back listed		£11.00	£550.00
—			B Size 70 x 43mm, 'Solace' back		£120.00	—
A	C	50	Dogs of the World (by Cecil Aldin) (c1910)		£13.00	£650.00
A	C	25	Eminent British Regiments Officers' Uniforms (c1908):		—	£325.00
			A Yellow-brown back		£13.00	—
			B Claret back		£13.00	—
A2	C	30	*Flags of Nations (c1903):	H.114		
			A 'Bond of Union' back		£12.00	£360.00
			B *Plain back*		£9.00	—
D	C	24	*Flags, Arms and Types of Nations (c1904):	H.115		
			A Numbered		£8.00	£200.00
			B Unnumbered		£100.00	—

COPE BROS. & CO. LTD, Liverpool (continued)

Size	Printing	Number in set	Title	Handbook reference	Price per card	Complete set
—	C	25	The Game of Poker§ (75 x 58mm) (1936)		50p	£12.50
—	C	50	General Knowledge§ (70 x 42mm) (1925)		£4.00	—
—	BW	32	Golf Strokes (70 x 45mm) (1923)		£15.00	—
A1	C	60	'Happy Families' (1937)		£1.65	£100.00
—	C	50	Household Hints§ (advertisement fronts) (70 x 45mm) (1925)		£1.80	£90.00
—	U	20	*Kenilworth Phrases (80 x 70mm) (c1910)	H.116	£450.00	—
C	BW	30	Lawn Tennis Strokes (1924):			
			A Numbers 1 to 25		£6.00	—
			B Numbers 26 to 30		£25.00	—
—	U	50	Modern Dancing (folders) (74 x 43mm) (1926)		£15.00	—
A2	C	50	Music Hall Artistes (c1910):			
			A Inscribed 'Series of 50'		£35.00	—
			B Without the above		£12.00	£600.00
A	U	472	Noted Footballers — 'Clips Cigarettes' (c1910):	H.474		
			1 Unnumbered — Wee Jock Simpson		—	£65.00
			120 Series of 120:			
			A Greenish-blue frame		£22.00	—
			B Bright blue frame		£22.00	—
			162 Series of 282:			
			A Greenish-blue frame		£22.00	—
			B Bright blue frame		£22.00	—
			471 Series of 500. Bright blue frame		£22.00	—
D	P	195	Noted Footballers — 'Solace Cigarettes' (c1910)	H.474	£22.00	—
A	C	24	*Occupations for Women (1897)	H.117	£100.00	—
—	C	6	*Phases of the Moon (111 x 74mm) (c1890)	H.725	£300.00	—
—	C	24	Photo Albums for the Million (c1898):	H.119		
			12 Buff cover (25 x 39mm)		£16.00	—
			12 Green cover (25 x 39mm)		£16.00	—
A2	C	25	Pigeons (c1926)		£9.00	£225.00
A	C	52	*Playing Cards. Blue backs (c1902):			
			A Rounded Corners		£16.00	—
			B Square Corners		£12.00	—
—	C	7	The Seven Ages of Man (114 x 78mm) (c1885)	H.726	£300.00	—
A	C	50	Shakespeare Gallery (c1900):			
			A Wide card		£12.00	£600.00
			B Narrow card — officially cut		£12.00	—
A2	C	25	Song Birds (c1926)		£7.00	£175.00
A1	C	25	Sports and Pastimes (1925)	H.55l	£4.00	£100.00
—	C	25	Toy Models (The Country Fair) (73 x 66mm) (c1930)	H.552	40p	£10.00
A1	C	25	*Uniforms of Soldiers and Sailors (c1900):	H.120		
			A Circular Medallion back, wide card		£30.00	—
			B Square Medallion back, wide card		£60.00	—
			C Square Medallion back, narrow card, officially cut		£25.00	—
D	BW		VC and DSO Naval and Flying Heroes:			
		50	Unnumbered (1916)	H.121	£9.00	£450.00
		25	Numbered 51-75 (1917)		£10.00	£250.00
D	BW	20	*War Pictures (1915)	H.122	£12.50	£250.00
D	BW	25	*War Series (War Leaders and Warships) (c1915)	H.103	£13.00	—
A1	C	25	Wild Animals and Birds (c1908)		£17.00	—
A	C	25	The World's Police (c1935)		£5.00	£125.00

§Joint Cope and Richard Lloyd issues.

OVERSEAS ISSUES

Size	Printing	Number in set	Title	Handbook reference	Price per card	Complete set
A2	C	30	Flags of Nations (c1903)		£80.00	—
A	C	50	Jordklodens Hunde (1912)		£35.00	—

COPE BROS. & CO. LTD, Liverpool (Overseas Issues continued)

D	C	30	Scandinavian Actors and Actresses (1910) … … …		£40.00	—
A	C	35	Speider Billeder I Hver Pakke (1910) … … … … …		£35.00	—
A	C	25	Uniformer A F Fremragende Britiske Regimenter (1908) … … … … … … … … … … … … …		£30.00	—
A	C	25	Vilde Dyr Og Fugle (1907) … … … … … … … … …		£35.00	—

E. CORONEL, London

A	C	25	*Types of British and Colonial Troops (1900) … … …	H.76	£65.00	—

DAVID CORRE & CO., London

—	C	1	Advertisement Card — The New Alliance (70 x 42mm) (c1915) … … … … … … … … … … … … …		—	£400.00
D	C	40	*Naval and Military Phrases (1900):	H.14		
			A With border … … … … … … … … … … … …		£90.00	—
			B Without border … … … … … … … … … … …		£90.00	—

JOHN COTTON LTD, Edinburgh

—	C	50	*Bridge Hands (folders) (82 x 66mm) (1934) … … …		£12.00	—
A1	U	50	*Golf Strokes — A/B (1936) … … … … … … … …		£9.00	—
A1	U	50	*Golf Strokes— C/D (1937) … … … … … … … … …		£10.00	—
A1	U	50	*Golf Strokes— E/F (1938) … … … … … … … … …		£14.00	—
A1	U	50	*Golf Strokes — G/H (1939) … … … … … … … …		£500.00	—
A1	U	50	*Golf Strokes — I/J (1939) … … … … … … … …		£500.00	—

A. & J. COUDENS LTD, London

A1	P	60	British Beauty Spots (1923):	H.553		
			A Printed back, numbered … … … … … … … …		£1.70	£100.00
			B Printed back, unnumbered … … … … … … …		£2.50	—
			*C Back rubber stamped 'Cymax Cigarettes …' …		£4.00	—
			*D Plain back		£4.00	—
A	P	60	Holiday Resorts in East Anglia (1924) … … … …		£1.25	£75.00
A2	BW	25	Sports Alphabet (1924) … … … … … … … … … …	H.551	£10.00	£250.00

THE CRAIGMILLAR CREAMERY CO. LTD, Midlothian

H	C	1	*Views of Craigmillar (c1901) … … … … … … …	H.727	—	£1200.00

W.F. DANIELL, Bristol

—	BW	? 1	*Puzzle Cards (108 x 73mm) (c1900) … … … … …	H.729	£650.00	—

W.R. DANIEL & CO., London

—	C	1	Advertisement Card (85 x 55mm) (c1901) … … … …	H.728	—	£600.00
A2	C	30	*Colonial Troops (c1902):	H.40		
			A Black back … … … … … … … … … … … …		£90.00	—
			B Brown back … … … … … … … … … … …		£90.00	—
A2	C	25	*National Flags and Flowers — Girls (c1901) … … …	H.123	£160.00	—

W.T. DAVIES & SONS, Chester

A	C	50	*Actresses — 'DAVAN' (c1902) … … … … … …	H.124	£90.00	—
A2	U	42	Aristocrats of the Turf (1924):	H.554		
			1 Nos 1-30 — 'A Series of 30' … … … … … …		£6.00	—
			2 Nos 31-42 — 'A Series of 42' … … … … … …		£20.00	—

W.T. DAVIES & SONS, Chester (continued)

Size	Printing	Number in set		Handbook reference	Price per card	Complete set
A2	U	36	Aristocrats of the Turf, Second Series (1924)	H.554	£5.50	—
A	C	25	Army Life (1915)	H.78	£12.00	—
A	BW	12	*Beauties (1903)	H.125	£60.00	—
A	C	25	Boxing (1924)	H.311	£4.40	£110.00
A	C	50	Flags and Funnels of Leading Steamship Lines (1913)	H.67	£12.00	—
A	BW	? 13	Newport Football Club (c1904)	H.126	£450.00	—
A	BW	5	Royal Welsh Fusiliers (c1904)	H.127	£450.00	—

S.H. DAWES, Luton

D	C	30	*Army Pictures, Cartoons, etc (c1916)	H.12	£130.00	—

J.W. DEWHURST, Morecambe

D	C	30	*Army Pictures, Cartoons, etc (c1916)	H.12	£130.00	—

R.I. DEXTER & CO., Hucknall

D2	U	30	*Borough Arms (1900)	H.128	£1.30	£40.00

A. DIMITRIOU, London

—	C	? 3	Advertisement Cards (100 x 65mm) (c1930)		£125.00	

GEORGE DOBIE & SON LTD, Paisley

—	C	? 22	Bridge Problems (folders) (circular 64mm diameter) (c1933)		£50.00	—
—	C	32	Four-Square Book (Nd 1-32) (75 x 50mm) (1959) ...		£2.00	—
—	C	32	Four-Square Book (Nd 33-64) (75 x 50mm) (1959) ...		£2.00	—
—	C	32	Four-Square Book (Nd 65-96) (75 x 50mm) (1960) ...		£1.50	£50.00
A	C	25	Weapons of All Ages (1924)		£8.00	£200.00

DOBSON & CO. LTD

A	C	8	The European War Series (c1917)	H.129	£45.00	—

THE DOMINION TOBACCO CO. (1929) LTD, London

A	U	25	Old Ships (1934)		£2.60	£65.00
A	U	25	Old Ships (Second Series) (1935)		80p	£20.00
A	U	25	Old Ships (Third Series) (1936)		£1.00	£25.00
A	U	25	Old Ships (Fourth Series) (1936)		£2.20	£55.00

JOSEPH W. DOYLE LTD, Manchester

—	P	18	*Beauties, Nd X.1-X.18 (89 x 70mm) (c1925)	H.653	£14.00	—
D	P	12	Dirt Track Riders Nd. CC.A.1-CC.A.12 (c1925)	H.635	£50.00	—
D	P	12	Views Nd. CC.B.1-CC.B.12 (c1925)	H.635	£30.00	—
D	P	12	Views Nd CC.C.1-CC.C.12 (c1925)	H.635	£30.00	—
D	P	12	*Beauties Nd. CC.D.1-CC.D.12 (c1925)	H.635	£30.00	—
D	P	12	*Beauties Nd CC.E.1-CC.E.12 (c1925)	H.635	£30.00	—

MAJOR DRAPKIN & CO., London

D	BW	12	*Actresses 'FRAN' (c1910)	H.175/GP.400	£8.00	—
C	C	8	*Advertisement Cards (c1925):	GP.401		
			1 Packings (4)		£7.50	£30.00
			2 Smokers (4)		£6.50	£26.00
—	BW	? 1	*Army Insignia (83 x 46mm) (c1915)	GP.402	£900.00	—

MAJOR DRAPKIN & CO., London (continued)

Size	Printing	Number	Description	Handbook ref	Price per card	Complete set
	BW	50	Around Britain (1929) (export):			
C			A Small size … … … … … … … … … …		£1.40	£70.00
B1			B Large size … … … … … … … … … …		£2.80	—
C		50	Around the Mediterranean (1926) (export):	GP.404		
C			A Small size … … … … … … … … … …		£1.50	£75.00
B1			B Large size … … … … … … … … … …		£2.80	—
A2	P	40	Australian and English Test Cricketers (1928) … … …		£2.00	£80.00
—	—	? 111	'Bandmaster' Conundrums (58 x 29mm) (c1910) …	GP.352	£10.00	—
A2	BW	? 32	Boer War Celebrities 'JASAS' — 'Sweet Alva Cigarettes' (c1901) … … … … … … … … … … …	H.133	£180.00	—
A1	U	25	British Beauties (1930) (export) … … … … … … …		£3.00	£75.00
A1	P		*Celebrities of the Great War (1916):	GP.409		
		36	A Printed back … … … … … … … … … …		80p	£30.00
		34	B Plain back … … … … … … … … … …		£1.00	£34.00
—	BW	96	Cinematograph Actors (42 x 70mm) (1913) … … …	GP.410	£13.00	—
	C	15	Dogs and Their Treatment (1924):			
A			A Small size … … … … … … … … … …		£5.50	£85.00
B2			B Large size … … … … … … … … … …		£6.50	£100.00
A	C	40	The Game of Sporting Snap (1928) … … … … …		£4.25	—
			Instruction Leaflet … … … … … … … … … …		—	£11.00
	C	50	Girls of Many Lands (1929):			
D			A Small size … … … … … … … … … …		£4.00	—
—			B Medium size (76 x 52mm) … … … … … … …		50p	£25.00
A	C	1	'Grey's' Smoking Mixture Advertisement Card (plain back) (c1935) … … … … … … … … … …		—	£7.00
A	C	25	How to Keep Fit — Sandow Exercises (c1912):	H.136		
			A 'Drapkin's Cigarettes' … … … … … … … …		£16.00	£400.00
			A1 'Drapkin's Cigarettes' short cards, cut officially		£16.00	—
			B 'Crayol Cigarettes' … … … … … … … …		£16.00	£400.00
A2	BW	54	Life at Whipsnade Zoo (1934) … … … … … … … …	GP.415	50p	£27.00
D2	C	50	'Limericks' (1929):	GP.416		
			A White card … … … … … … … … … …		£1.60	£80.00
			B Cream card … … … … … … … … … …		£1.60	£80.00
A2	P	36	National Types of Beauty (1928) … … … … … … …	GP.417	£1.00	£36.00
	C	25	Optical Illusions (1926):			
A			A Small size. Home issue, name panel (23 x 7mm) … … … … … … … … … …		£3.40	£85.00
A			B Small size. Export issue, name panel (26 x l0mm) … … … … … … … … … …		£3.00	£75.00
B2			C Large 'size. Home issue … … … … … …		£3.60	£90.00
	C	25	Palmistry:			
A			A Small size (1927) … … … … … … … … …		£3.00	£75.00
B			B Large size (1926) … … … … … … … … …		£3.00	£75.00
D	U	48	Photogravure Masterpieces (1915) … … … … … …	GP.420	£10.00	—
	C	25	Puzzle Pictures (1926):			
A			A Small size … … … … … … … … … …		£4.00	£100.00
B			B Large size … … … … … … … … … …		£4.40	£110.00
—	C	25	*Soldiers and Their Uniforms, die cut (1914):	H.138/GP.423		
			A 'Drapkin's Cigarettes':			
			i 23 Different … … … … … … …		£1.00	—
			ii 1st Life Guards … … … … … … …		£30.00	—
			iii South Wales Borderers … … … … …		£30.00	—
			B 'Crayol Cigarettes':			
			i 22 Different … … … … … … …		£1.00	£22.00
			ii Durham Light Infantry … … … … …		£20.00	—
			iii 1st Life Guards … … … … … …		£30.00	—
			iv South Wales Borderers … … … … …		£30.00	—

MAJOR DRAPKIN & CO., London (continued)

Size	Print-ing	Number in set		Handbook reference	Price per card	Complete set
A2	P	36	Sporting Celebrities in Action (1930) (export):			
			A 32 Different		£5.00	—
			B Nos. 4,5 and 6 (Golfers)		£20.00	—
			C No. 18 withdrawn		£125.00	—
D	BW		*Views of the World (c1912):	H.176/GP.425		
		12	A Caption in two lines		£5.00	£60.00
		8	B Caption in one line		£30.00	—
D	BW	8	*Warships (c1912)	GP.426	£12.00	—
SILKS						
—	C	40	Regimental Colours and Badges of the Indian Army (70 x 50mm) (paper-backed) (c1915):	H.502-5/GP.422		
			A The Buffs' back		£5.00	—
			B No brand back		£35.00	—

DRAPKIN & MILLHOFF, London

Size	Print-ing	Number in set		Handbook reference	Price per card	Complete set
A	U		*Beauties 'KEWAI' (c1898):	H.139-1		
		? 2	A 'Eldona Cigars' back		£350.00	—
		? 1	B 'Explorer Cigars' back		£350.00	—
A	BW	25	*Boer War Celebrities — 'PAM' (c1901):	H.140		
			A With PTO on front 'Pick-Me-Up Cigarettes', multi-backed		£30.00	—
			B Without PTO on front 'Pick-Me-Up Cigarettes', multi-backed		£30.00	—
			C Plain back		£55.00	—
C	C	30	*Colonial Troops, multi-backed (c1902)	H.40	£55.00	—
—	BW	? 7	*'Pick-me-up' Paper Inserts (112 x 44mm) (c1900) ...		£300.00	—
—	U	? 2	*Portraits (48 x 36mm) (c1900)	H.461	£300.00	—
A2	U	? 3	*Pretty Girl Series — 'BAGG' (c1900)	H.45	£350.00	—

J. DUNCAN & CO. LTD, Glasgow

Size	Print-ing	Number in set		Handbook reference	Price per card	Complete set
D1	C	50	'Evolution of the Steamship' (c1925)	H.559	—	£85.00
			47 different		85p	£40.00
			'Olympia II'		£25.00	—
			'Castalia' and 'Athenia'		£10.00	—
D1	C	48	*Flags, Arms and Types of Nations (c1910):	H.115		
			A Back in Blue		£30.00	—
			B Back in Green		£50.00	—
A	C	20	Inventors and Their Inventions (c1915)	H.213	£60.00	—
A	C	30	Scottish Clans, Arms of Chiefs and Tartans (c1910):	H.142		
			A Back in black		£250.00	—
			B Back in green		£20.00	—
—	C		Scottish Gems: (58 x 84mm):	H.143		
—	C	72	1st series (c1912)		£13.00	—
—	C	50	2nd series (c1913)		£13.00	—
—	C	50	3rd series (c1914)		£13.00	—
H1	BW	50	Scottish Gems (known as '4th Series') (c1925)	H.143	60p	£30.00
D	C	25	*Types of British Soldiers (c1910)	H.144	£50.00	—

G. DUNCOMBE, Buxton

Size	Print-ing	Number in set		Handbook reference	Price per card	Complete set
D	C	30	*Army Pictures, Cartoons, Etc (c1916)	H.12	£130.00	—

ALFRED DUNHILL LTD, London

Size	Print-ing	Number in set		Handbook reference	Price per card	Complete set
—	U	25	Dunhill Kingsize Ransom (75 x 45mm) (1985)		£1.80	—

EDWARDS, RINGER & CO., Bristol

Size	Print-ing	Number in set		Handbook reference	Price per card	Complete set
—	BW	50	How to Count Cribbage Hands (79 x 62mm) (c1908)		£350.00	—

EDWARDS, RINGER & BIGG, Bristol

Size	Printing	Number in set	Title	Handbook reference	Price per card	Complete set
A	U	25	Abbeys and Castles — Photogravure series (c1912):			
			A Type-set back		£9.00	£225.00
			B 'Statue of Liberty' back		£9.00	£225.00
			C 'Stag Design' back		£9.00	£225.00
A	U	25	Alpine Views — Photogravure series (c1912):			
			A 'Statue of Liberty' back		£9.00	£225.00
			B 'Stag Design' back		£9.00	£225.00
A	C	12	*Beauties — 'CERF' (1905)	H.57	£70.00	—
A	U	25	*Beauties — 'FECKSA', 1900 Calendar back	H.58	£40.00	—
A	C	50	*Birds and Eggs (1906)	H.60	£12.00	£600.00
A	BW	? 2	Boer War and Boxer Rebellion Sketches (c1901)	H.46	£180.00	—
A	BW	25	*Boer War Celebrities — 'STEW' 1901 Calendar back	H.105	£45.00	—
A	C	25	British Trees and Their Uses (1933)	H.654	£2.60	£65.00
A	C	1	Calendar for 1899	H.730	—	£600.00
A	C	1	Calendar (1905), Exmore Hunt Stag design back	H.730	—	£450.00
A	C	2	Calendar (1910)	H.730	£450.00	—
A	C	50	Celebrated Bridges (1924)	H.346	£2.50	£125.00
	U		Cinema Stars (1923):			
A2		50	A Small size		£1.80	£90.00
—		25	B Medium size (67 x 57mm)		£1.80	£45.00
A	U	25	Coast and Country — Photogravure series (1911):			
			A 'Statue of Liberty' back		£9.00	£225.00
			B 'Stag Design' back		£9.00	£225.00
A	C	23	*Dogs series (1908):	H.64		
			A 'Exmoor Hunt' back		£9.00	
			B 'Klondyke' back		£5.00	£115.00
A	C	3	Easter Manoeuvres of Our Volunteers (1897)	H.146	£325.00	—
A	C	25	Flags of All Nations, 1st series (1906)	H.37	£8.00	£200.00
A	C	12	Flags of All Nations, 2nd series (1907)	H.37	£11.00	£135.00
A	C	37	*Flags of All Nations (1907):	H.37		
			A Globe and Grouped Flags back		£8.00	
			B 'Exmoor Hunt' back:			
			i 4 ½d per oz		£8.00	—
			ii Altered to 5d by hand		£8.00	—
			iii 5d label added		£9.00	—
			C 'Stag' design back		£8.00	£300.00
			D Upright titled back		£8.00	—
A	C	25	Garden Life (1934)	H.449	£3.20	£80.00
A	C	25	How to Tell Fortunes (1929)		£4.00	£100.00
A	C	50	Life on Board a Man of War (1905)	H.38	£11.00	
—	C	1	'Miners Bound for Klondyke' (41 x 81mm) (1897)		—	£500.00
A	C	50	Mining (1925)	H.450	£2.50	£125.00
A	C	25	Musical Instruments (1924)	H.547	£4.00	£100.00
A	C	25	Optical Illusions (1936)	H.560	£3.20	£80.00
A	C	25	Our Pets (1926)	H.561	£2.40	£60.00
A	C	25	Our Pets, 2nd series (1926)	H.561	£2.40	£60.00
A	C	25	Past and Present (1928)		£3.60	£90.00
A	C	10	Portraits of His Majesty the King in Uniforms of the British and Foreign Nations (1902)	H.147	£40.00	£400.00
A	C	25	Prehistoric Animals (1924)	H.561	£5.00	£125.00
A	C	25	Sports and Games in Many Lands (1935):			
			A 24 Different minus No. 25		£5.00	£120.00
			B Number 25 (Babe Ruth)		—	£50.00
A	C	50	A Tour Round the World (Mar. 1909)	H.75	£12.00	£600.00
A	C	56	War Map of the Western Front (1916)		£12.00	—
A	U	54	War Map of the Western Front, etc Series No. 2 (1917):			
			A 'Exmoor Hunt' back		£12.00	—
			B 'New York Mixture' back		£12.00	—

Size	Print-ing	Number in set	BRITISH TOBACCO ISSUERS	Handbook reference	Price per card	Complete set

S. EISISKI, Rhyl

Size	Print-ing	Number in set		Handbook reference	Price per card	Complete set
D	U	? 25	*Actresses 'ANGOOD' (c1900)	H.187	£400.00	—
A	U	? 6	*Actresses — 'COPEIS' (c1900)	H.108	£400.00	—
A	U	? 23	*Beauties — 'FENA' (c1900)	H.148	£400.00	—
A	U	? 2	*Beauties — 'KEWA I', back inscribed 'Eisiski's New Gold Virginia Cigarettes' (c1900)	H.139	£400.00	—
A	U	? 2	*Beauties — 'KEWA I', back inscribed 'Eisiski's Rhyl Best Bird's Eye Cigarettes' (c1900)	H.139	£400.00	—
A	U	? 2	*Beauties — 'KEWA I' Rubber-stamped back (c1900)	H.139	£400.00	—

ELDONS LTD

Size	Print-ing	Number in set		Handbook reference	Price per card	Complete set
A1	C	30	*Colonial Troops — 'Leon de Cuba' Cigars (c1900)	H.40	£160.00	—

R.J. ELLIOTT & CO. LTD, Huddersfield

Size	Print-ing	Number in set		Handbook reference	Price per card	Complete set
A2	C	? 2	Advertisement Card — Bulldog (c1910)		£300.00	—

EMPIRE TOBACCO CO., London

Size	Print-ing	Number in set		Handbook reference	Price per card	Complete set
D	C	? 6	Franco-British Exhibition (c1907)	H.471	£350.00	—

THE EXPRESS TOBACCO CO. LTD, London

Size	Print-ing	Number in set		Handbook reference	Price per card	Complete set
—	U	50	'How It is Made'(Motor Cars) (76 x 51mm) (1931)		£3.50	—

L. & J. FABIAN, London

Size	Print-ing	Number in set		Handbook reference	Price per card	Complete set
—	P		The Elite Series (Beauties) (c1935):			
D1		24	A Numbered LLF 1 to 24		£40.00	—
A1		? 47	B Plain Numerals		£40.00	—

FAIRWEATHER & SONS, Dundee

Size	Print-ing	Number in set		Handbook reference	Price per card	Complete set
A	C	50	Historic Buildings of Scotland (c1914)		£50.00	—

W. & F. FAULKNER, London
12 page reference book — £4.50

Size	Print-ing	Number in set		Handbook reference	Price per card	Complete set
C	C	26	*Actresses — 'FROGA A' (c1900)	H.20	£50.00	—
A	C	25	Angling (1929)	H.655	£9.00	—
D2	C	12	*'Ation Series (1901)		£25.00	—
C	C	25	*Beauties (c1898)	H.150	£75.00	—
A	U	49	*Beauties — 'FECKSA' (1901)	H.58	£25.00	—
A	BW	16	*British Royal Family (1901)	H.28	£40.00	—
A	C	50	Celebrated Bridges (1925)	H.346	£2.50	£125.00
D2	C	12	*Coster Series (1900)	H.151	£32.00	—
A	BW	20	Cricketers Series (1901)	H.29	£300.00	—
D2	C	12	Cricket Terms (1899)	H.152	£85.00	—
D2	C	12	Football Terms, 1st Series (1900)	H.153	£35.00	—
D2	C	12	Football Terms, 2nd Series (1900)	H.153	£35.00	—
D2	C	12	*Golf Terms (1901)	H.155	£100.00	—
D2	C	12	Grenadier Guards (1899)	H.156	£30.00	—
A2	C	40	*Kings and Queens (1902)	H.157	£25.00	—
D2	C	12	Kipling Series (1900)	H.158	£27.00	—
D2	C	12	The Language of Flowers (1900):	H.159		
			A 'Grenadier' Cigarettes		£32.00	—
			B 'Nosegay' Cigarettes		£32.00	—
D2	C	12	*Military Terms, 1st series (1899)	H.50	£25.00	—
D2	C	12	*Military Terms, 2nd series (1899)	H.160	£25.00	—
D2	C	12	*Nautical Terms, 1st series (1900)	H.161	£25.00	—
D2	C	12	*Nautical Terms, 2nd series (1900):	H.162		
			A 'Grenadier' Cigarettes		£25.00	—
			B 'Union Jack Cigarettes'		£25.00	—

W. & F. FAULKNER, London (continued)

Size	Printing	Number in set			Handbook reference	Price per card	Complete set
A	C	25	Old Sporting Prints (1930)		H.563	£3.60	£90.00
A	C	25	Optical Illusions (1935)		H.560	£3.20	£80.00
D2	C		'Our Colonial Troops' (1900):				
			A	Grenadier Cigarettes:			
		30		i With copyright Nos 1-30		£30.00	—
		90		ii Without copyright Nos 1-90		£16.00	—
		60	B	Union Jack Cigarettes Nos 31-90		£18.00	—
A	C	20	Our Gallant Grenadiers, 1-20:		H.163		
			A	Without I.T.C. clause (1901):			
				i Thick card		£16.00	£320.00
				ii Thin card		£16.00	£320.00
			B	With I.T.C. clause, thin card (1902)		£27.00	£540.00
A	C	20	Our Gallant Grenadiers, 21-40 (1903)			£25.00	£500.00
A	C	25	Our Pets (1926)		H.561	£3.20	£80.00
A	C	25	Our Pets, 2nd series (1926)		H.561	£3.00	£75.00
D2	C	12	*Policemen of the World (1899):		H.164		
			A	'Grenadier' Cigarettes		£220.00	—
			B	'Nosegay' Cigarettes		£35.00	—
D2	C	12	*Police Terms (1899)		H.165	£30.00	—
A	C	25	Prominent Racehorses of the Present Day (1923) ...			£3.20	£80.00
A	C	25	Prominent Racehorses of the Present Day, 2nd series				
			(1924)			£5.00	£125.00
D2	C	12	*Puzzle series (1897):		H.166		
			A	'Grenadier Cigarettes		£225.00	—
			B	'Nosegay Cigarettes		£65.00	—
A	BW	25	*South African War Scenes (1901)		H.167	£16.00	£400.00
D2	C	12	Sporting Terms (1900)		H.168	£35.00	—
D2	C	12	Street Cries (1902)		H.169	£25.00	—

FIELD FAVOURITES CIGARETTES

D	P	? 1	*Footballers (c1895)	H.731	£2000.00	—

THE FIGARO CIGARETTE

—	C	12	Caricatures of Celebrities (101 x 57mm) (c1880) ...	H.732	£800.00	—

FINLAY & CO. LTD, Newcastle-on-Tyne and London

D1	BW	? 28	Our Girls (c1910)	H.170	£150.00	—
A	U	30	World's Aircraft (c1912)		£70.00	—

FLYNN, Dublin

A	C	26	*Beauties — 'HOL' (c1900)	H.192	£600.00	—

C.D. FOTHERGILL, St Helens

—	C	? 1	*'Play Up' Sporting Shields (c1895)	H.718	£175.00	—

FRAENKEL BROS., London

A2	C	? 2	*Beauties — 'Don Jorg (c1898)	H.733	£750.00	—
A	U	? 23	*Beauties — 'FENA' (c1898)	H.148	£130.00	—
A	C	25	*Beauties — 'GRACC' (c1898)	H.59	£160.00	—
A	U	24	*Beauties — 'HUMPS' (c1900)	H.222	£140.00	—
A	U	26	*Music Hall Artistes (c1900):	H.171		
			A Pink card		£110.00	—
			B White card		£110.00	—
A2	C	25	*Types of British and Colonial Troops (c1900)	H.76	£70.00	—

FRANKLYN, DAVEY & CO., Bristol

Size	Printing	Number in set		Handbook reference	Price per card	Complete set
A	C	12	*Beauties — 'CERF' (1905)	H.57	£70.00	—
D2	C	50	*Birds (c1895)		£70.00	—
A2	BW	10	*Boer War Generals — 'FLAC' (1901)	H.47	£90.00	—
A	C	25	Boxing (1924)	H.311	£3.20	£80.00
A	C	25	Ceremonial and Court Dress (Oct. 1915)	H.145	£12.00	—
A	C	50	Children of All Nations (1934)	H.656	90p	£45.00
—	C	? 1	Comic Dog Folder (opens to 183 x 65mm) (1898)	H.490	—	£650.00
A	C	50	*Football Club Colours (1909)	H.68	£17.00	£850.00
A	C	50	Historic Events (1924)	H.464	£2.50	£125.00
A	U	25	Hunting (1925)		£1.00	£25.00
A	U	50	Modern Dance Steps (1929)		£5.00	£250.00
A	U	50	Modern Dance Steps, 2nd series (1931)		80p	£40.00
A	C	50	Naval Dress and Badges (1916)	H.172	£12.00	—
A	C	50	Overseas Dominions (Australia) (1923)	H.451	£5.00	£250.00
A	C	25	*Star Girls (c1898)	H.30	£250.00	—
A	C	10	Types of Smokers (c1898)		£55.00	£550.00
A	C	50	Wild Animals of the World (c1902)	H.77	£12.00	£600.00

A.H. FRANKS & SONS, London

Size	Print	Number		Ref	Price	Set
D1	BW	56	*Beauties — 'Beauties Cigarettes' (c1900)	H.173	£75.00	—
D	C	24	*Nautical Expressions (c1900)	H.174	£80.00	—
A1	C	25	*Types of British and Colonial Troops (c1900)	H.76	£65.00	—

J.J. FREEMAN, London

Size	Print	Number		Ref	Price	Set
D	BW	12	*Actresses — 'FRAN' (c1912)	H.175	£45.00	—
D	BW	12	*Views of the World (c1910)	H.176	£45.00	—

J.R. FREEMAN, London

Size	Print	Number		Ref	Price	Set
C1	U	33	Football Challenge (1969)		£6.00	—
—	U	12	*'Manikin' Cards (77 x 49mm) (c1920)	H.481	£75.00	—

C. FRYER & SONS LTD, London

Size	Print	Number		Ref	Price	Set
A2	C		*Boer War and General Interest: (c1900):	H.13		
		? 10	A Brown leaf design back		£170.00	—
		? 5	B Green leaf design back		£170.00	—
		? 2	C Green daisy design back		£170.00	—
—	—	50	Clan Sketches (101 x 74mm) (paper folders with wording only) — 'Pibroch Virginia' (c1936)		£14.00	—
D	C	40	*Naval and Military Phrases (c1905)	H.14	£65.00	—
A2	BW	? 14	*'Vita Berlin' series (c1902)	H.177	£450.00	—

FRYER & COULTMAN, London

Size	Print	Number		Ref	Price	Set
D	BW	50	*Beauties — PLUMS (c1900)	H.186	£800.00	—
—	C	12	*French Phrases, 1893 Calendar back (96 x 64 mm)	H.178	£800.00	—

J. GABRIEL, London

Size	Print	Number		Ref	Price	Set
A	BW	10	*Actresses — 'HAGG A' (1900)	H.24	£80.00	—
A2	C	25	*Beauties — 'GRACC' (c1898)	H.59	£200.00	—
A	BW	20	Cricketers series (1901)	H.29	£400.00	—
A	C	40	*Home and Colonial Regiments (c1902)	H.69	£85.00	—
A	U	? 56	*Pretty Girl series — 'BAGG' (c1898)	H.45	£75.00	—
A2	C	25	*Types of British and Colonial Troops (c1900)	H.76	£75.00	—

Size	Print-ing	Number in set		Handbook reference	Price per card	Complete set

GALA CIGARETTES

Size	Print-ing	Number in set		Handbook reference	Price per card	Complete set
D1	U	? 1	Stamp Card c1910	H.589	—	£170.00

GALLAHER LTD, Belfast and London
40 page reference book — £4.50

Size	Print-ing	Number in set		Handbook reference	Price per card	Complete set
D	P	110	*Actors and Actresses (c1900)	H.179	£5.50	—
D	C	48	Aeroplanes (1939)		90p	£45.00
A2	C	25	Aesop's Fables (1931):	H.518		
			A Inscribed 'Series of 25'		£1.40	£35.00
			B Inscribed 'Series of 50'		£1.20	£30.00
D	C	25	The Allies Flags: (1914):			
			A Toned card		£6.00	—
			B White card		£6.00	—
D	C	100	Animals and Birds of Commercial Value (1921)		90p	£90.00
D	C	48	Army Badges (1939)		80p	£40.00
—	U	24	Art Treasures of the World (76 x 56mm) (1930)		80p	£20.00
D	C	100	Association Football Club Colours (1910):			
			A Grey border		£10.00	—
			B Brown border		£10.00	—
A	C	52	*Beauties (c1900):	H.180		
			A Without inset		£12.00	—
			B With Playing Card inset		£12.00	—
—	P	48	Beautiful Scotland (77 x 52mm) (1939)	H.564-I	90p	£45.00
D	C	50	*Birds and Eggs (c1905):	H.60		
			A 'Gallaher Ltd' Label		£50.00	—
			B 'Manufactured by Gallaher' Label		£9.00	—
D	C	100	Birds' Nests and Eggs series (1919):			
			A White card		£1.75	£175.00
			B Toned card		£1.75	—
D	C		Boy Scout Series grey-green back (1911):	H.630		
		100	A 'Belfast and London'		£2.75	£275.00
		86	B 'London and Belfast'		£3.00	—
D	C	100	Boy Scout Series brown back (1922)	H.630	£2.50	£250.00
D	C	48	British Birds (1937)		50p	£25.00
D	C	100	British Birds by Rankin (1923):	H.537		
			A 'By Rankin'		£20.00	—
			B 'By George Rankin'		£1.75	£175.00
D	C	75	British Champions of 1923 (1924)		£2.20	£165.00
D	U	50	British Naval series (1914)		£6.00	£300.00
D	C	48	Butterflies and Moths (1938)		40p	£20.00
D	C	25	Champion Animals & Birds of 1923 (1924)		£2.20	£55.00
D	C	48	Champions (1934):			
			A Front without letterpress		90p	£45.00
			B Front with captions, subjects re-drawn		80p	£40.00
D	C	48	Champions, 2nd Series (1935)		60p	£30.00
D	C	48	Champions of Screen & Stage (1934):			
			A Red back		70p	£35.00
			B Blue back, 'Gallaher's Cigarettes' at base ...		£1.20	£60.00
			C Blue back, 'Gallaher Ltd' at base		£2.00	£100.00
D	U	100	Cinema Stars (1926)	H.658	£1.75	£175.00
—	P	48	Coastwise (77 x 52mm) (1938)	H.564-2	£1.00	£50.00
	C	24	Dogs (1934):			
			A Captions in script letters on front:			
D			1 Small size		£2.00	£50.00
B			2 Large size		£2.00	£50.00
			B Captions in block letters on front:			
D			1 Small size		£1.00	£24.00
B			2 Large size		£1.25	£30.00

37

GALLAHER LTD, Belfast and London (continued)

Size	Print-ing	Number in set		Handbook reference	Price per card	Complete set
D	C	48	Dogs (1936)		60p	£30.00
D	C	48	Dogs Second Series (1938)		50p	£24.00
D	P	100	English and Scotch Views (c1910)		£4.00	£400.00
D	C	100	Fables and Their Morals:			
			A Numbered Outside Set Title Panel (1912) ...		£1.75	£175.00
			B & C numbered in set title panel			
			B Thin numerals 'The Moral' 16mm long (1922)			
			1 White card		£1.25	£125.00
			2 Yellow card		£1.25	£125.00
			C Thick numerals 'The Moral' 12mm long (1922)		£1.25	£125.00
D	U	100	Famous Cricketers (1926)		£3.00	£300.00
D	C	48	Famous Film Scenes (1935)		70p	£35.00
D	U	100	Famous Footballers, green back (1925)		£2.50	£250.00
D	C	50	Famous Footballers, brown back (1926)		£2.80	£140.00
D	C	48	Famous Jockeys (1936):			
			A Blue text		£1.30	£65.00
			B Mauve text:			
			1 Nos 1 to 24		£3.00	—
			2 Nos 25 to 48		£5.00	—
D	C	48	Film Episodes (1936)		70p	£35.00
D	C	48	Film Partners (1935)		80p	£40.00
—	P	48	Flying (77 x 52mm) (1938)	H.564-3	£1.70	—
D	C	100	Footballers, red back (1928):	H.659		
			1 Nos. 1-50 — Action pictures		£3.50	£175.00
			2 Nos. 51-100 — Portraits		£3.50	£175.00
D	C	50	Footballers in Action (1928)		£3.20	£160.00
D	C	48	Garden Flowers (1938)		20p	£10.00
D	C	100	The Great War series (1915)		£3.00	£300.00
D	C	100	The Great War series — Second Series (1916)		£3.00	£300.00
D	C		The Great War, Victoria Cross Heroes (1915-16):	H.735		
		25	1st series 1-25		£5.00	£125.00
		25	2nd series 26-50		£5.00	£125.00
		25	3rd series 51-75		£5.00	£125.00
		25	4th series 76-100		£5.00	£125.00
		25	5th series 101-125		£5.00	£125.00
		25	6th series 126-150		£5.00	£125.00
		25	7th series 151-175		£5.00	£125.00
		25	8th series 176-200		£5.00	£125.00
—	C	20	£½ Million Berkeley Star Competition (90 x 33mm) (1995)		£1.50	—
D	C	100	How to do it (1916)		£4.00	£400.00
D		100	Interesting Views:			
	P		A Uncoloured, glossy (1923)		£2.00	£200.00
	CP		B Hand-coloured, matt (1925)		£3.00	£300.00
D			Irish View Scenery (c1910):	H.181		
	BW	400	1-400, matt:			
			A Numbered on back		£2.00	—
			B Unnumbered, plain back		£3.00	—
	P	400	1-400, glossy — see H.181-A			
			A Black photo		90p	£360.00
			B Brown photo		£4.00	—
			C As A, but series title and No. omitted		£2.00	—
			D Numbered 1-200 plain back		£3.00	—
	P	600	1-600, glossy — see H.181-B			
			A Nos 1 to 500		90p	£450.00
			B Nos 50l to 600		£6.00	—

GALLAHER LTD, Belfast and London (continued)

Size	Print-ing	Number in set		Handbook reference	Price per card	Complete set
B2	P	48	Island Sporting Celebrities (Channel Islands) (1938)		£3.00	—
D	C	100	'Kute Kiddies' series (1916) … … … … … … … … …		£4.00	£400.00
D	P	50	Latest Actresses (1910):			
			A Black photo … … … … … … … … … … … …		£13.00	—
			B Chocolate photo … … … … … … … … …		£20.00	—
D	C	50	Lawn Tennis Celebrities (1928) … … … … … … …		£5.00	—
A	C	24	Motor Cars (1934) … … … … … … … … … … … …		£4.50	£110.00
D	C	48	My Favourite Part (1939) … … … … … … … …		60p	£30.00
D	C	48	The Navy (1937):			
			A 'Park Drive …' at base of back … … … … …		60p	£30.00
			B 'Issued by …' at base of back … … … … …		£1.20	£60.00
—	P	48	Our Countryside (72 x 52mm) (1938) … … … … …	H.564-4	£1.25	—
D	C	100	Plants of Commercial Value (1923) … … … … …		£1.00	£100.00
D	C	48	Portraits of Famous Stars (1935) … … … … …		£1.00	£50.00
D	C	48	Racing Scenes (1938) … … … … … … … … …		60p	£30.00
D	C	100	The Reason Why (1924) … … … … … … … … …		£1.00	£100.00
A	C	50	*Regimental Colours and Standards (Nd 151-200)			
			(1899) … … … … … … … … … … … … …		£7.00	£350.00
D	C	100	Robinson Crusoe (1928) … … … … … … … … …		£2.00	£200.00
A	C	50	Royalty series (1902) … … … … … … … … …		£7.00	£350.00
B2	P	48	Scenes from the Empire (1939) (export) … … … …	H.565	30p	£15.00
—	P	24	Shots from the Films (77 x 52mm) (1936) … … … …	H.566	£3.50	—
D	C	48	Shots from Famous Films (1935) … … … … … …		60p	£30.00
D	C	48	Signed Portraits of Famous Stars (1935) … … … …		£2.50	—
C1	C	20	Silk Cut Advertisements (1993) … … … … … …		£1.50	—
A	C	111	The South African series (Nd 101-211) (1901):			
			A White back … … … … … … … … … … …		£6.00	—
			B Cream back … … … … … … … … … …		£6.00	—
D	C	48	Sporting Personalities (1936) … … … … … … …		40p	£20.00
D	C	100	'Sports' series (1912) … … … … … … … … …		£7.00	£700.00
D	U	? 98	*Stage and Variety Celebrities (collotype) (c1898):	H.182		
			A 'Gallager' back … … … … … … … … …		£90.00	—
			B 'Gallaher' back … … … … … … … … …		£90.00	—
			C As B but larger lettering, etc … … … … … …		£90.00	—
D	C	48	Stars of Screen & Stage (1935):			
			A Back in green … … … … … … … … …		60p	£30.00
			B Back in brown … … … … … … … … …		£1.60	£80.00
G2	C	5	Telemania (1989) … … … … … … … … … … …		£2.00	£10.00
D	C	48	Trains of the World (1937) … … … … … … …		£1.00	£50.00
D	C	100	Tricks and Puzzles Series, green back (1913) … …		£5.50	£550.00
D	C	100	Tricks & Puzzles Series, black back (1933):			
			Nos. 1-50 … … … … … … … … … … …		£1.00	£50.00
			Nos. 51-100 … … … … … … … … … …		£1.00	£50.00
A	C	50	*Types of the British Army — unnumbered (1897):	H.183		
			A 'Battle Honours' back … … … … … … …		£12.00	—
			B 'The Three Pipe …' — green back … … … …		£12.00	—
A	C	50	*Types of the British Army — Nd 1-50 (1898):	H.183		
			A 'The Three Pipe …' — brown back … … …		£11.00	—
			B 'Now in Three …' — brown back … … … …		£11.00	—
A	C	50	*Types of British and Colonial Regiments — Nd			
			51-100 (1900):			
			A 'The Three Pipe …' — brown back … … …		£11.00	—
			B 'Now in Three …' — brown back … … … …		£11.00	—
D	C	100	Useful Hints series (1915) … … … … … … … …		£3.50	£350.00

GALLAHER LTD, Belfast and London (continued)

Size	Printing	Number in set		Handbook reference	Price per card	Complete set
	C	20	Views – Berkeley Superkings Panoramic (1994):			
G2			A Blue border (90 x 45mm)		£1.50	–
–			B Blue border (90 x 33mm)		£1.50	–
G2			C Green border (90 x 45mm)		£1.50	–
–			D Green border (90 x 33mm)		£1.50	–
G2			E Red border (90 x 45mm)		£1.50	–
–			F Red border (90 x 33mm)		£1.50	–
D	U	25	Views in North of Ireland (1912)		£60.00	–
D	C	50	Votaries of the Weed (1916)		£7.00	£350.00
D	C	100	'Why is it?' series (1915):			
			A Green back		£3.20	£320.00
			B Brown back		£3.20	£320.00
D	C	48	Wild Animals (1937)		40p	£20.00
D	C	48	Wild Flowers (1939)		70p	£35.00
D	C	100	Woodland Trees series (1912)		£5.00	£500.00
D	C	100	The 'Zoo' Aquarium (1924)		£1.30	£130.00
D	C	50	'Zoo' Tropical Birds, 1st Series (1928)		£1.60	£80.00
D	C	50	'Zoo' Tropical Birds, 2nd Series (1929)		£1.60	£80.00
SILKS						
–	C	25	Flags – Set 1 (68 x 48mm) (paper-backed) (1916)	H.501-1	£8.00	–

SAMUEL GAWITH, Kendal

–	BW	25	The English Lakeland (90 x 70mm) (1926)		£25.00	–

F. GENNARI LTD, London

A	U	50	War Portraits (1916)	H.86	£100.00	–

LOUIS GERARD LTD, London

D1	U	50	Modern Armaments (1936):	H.567		
			A Numbered		£1.00	£50.00
			B Unnumbered		£1.20	£60.00
D1	U	24	Screen Favourites (1937):	H.568		
			A Inscribed 'Louis Gerard & Company'		£4.00	–
			B Inscribed 'Louis Gerard Limited'		£4.00	–
D1	C	48	Screen Favourites and Dancers (1937):	H.569		
			A Matt front		£2.50	£125.00
			B Varnished front		£4.00	–

W.G. GLASS & CO. LTD, Bristol

A	BW	20	*Actresses – 'BLARM' (c1900)	H.23	£75.00	–
A2	BW	10	*Actresses – 'HAGG A' (c1900)	H.24	£75.00	–
A	U	25	*Beauties – 'FECKSA (c1901)'	H.58	£120.00	–
D1	BW	20	*Boer War Cartoons ('Roseland Cigarettes') (c1901)	H.42	£120.00	–
A	BW	25	*Boer War Celebrities – 'STEW' (c1901)	H.105	£90.00	–
A	BW	16	*British Royal Family (1901)	H.28	£70.00	–
A2	BW	20	Cricketers Series (1901)	H.29	£375.00	–
D	C	40	*Naval and Military Phrases (c1902)	H.14	£110.00	–
A	BW	19	*Russo-Japanese Series (1904)	H.184	£70.00	–

R.P. GLOAG & CO, London

(Cards bear advertisements for 'Citamora' and/or 'The Challenge Flat Brilliantes' without maker's name)

A2	U	? 9	*Actresses – 'ANGLO' (c1896):	H.185		
			A 'Citamora' on front		£450.00	
			B 'The Challenge Flat' on front		£450.00	

R.P. GLOAG & CO., London (continued)

Size	Printing	Number in set		Handbook reference	Price per card	Complete set
D			*Beauties — Selection from 'Plums' (c1898):	H.186		
	BW	60	A 'The Challenge Flat' front in black and white ...		£100.00	—
			B 'Citamora' front:			
	BW	? 10	(a) front in black and white		£130.00	—
	U	? 11	(b) front in brown printed back		£250.00	—
	U	? 10	(c) front in brown, plain back		£250.00	—
A	C	40	*Home and Colonial Regiments (c1900)	H.69	£45.00	—
D	C	30	*Proverbs (c1901)	H.15	£100.00	—
A2	C	25	*Types of British and Colonial Troops (c1900)	H.76	£60.00	—

GLOBE CIGARETTE CO.

Size	Printing	Number in set		Handbook reference	Price per card	Complete set
D	BW	25	*Actresses — French (c1900)	H.1	£350.00	—

GOLDS LTD, Birmingham

Size	Printing	Number in set		Handbook reference	Price per card	Complete set
A2	BW	1	Advertisement Card (Chantecler) (c1905)	H.737	—	£750.00
C	C	18	Motor Cycle Series (c1914):	H.469		
			A Back in blue, numbered		£50.00	—
			B Back in grey, numbered		£60.00	—
			C Back in grey, unnumbered		£60.00	—
—	BW	? 21	*Prints from Noted Pictures (68 x 81mm) (c1908):	H.216		
			A With firm's name, 5 brands listed back		£140.00	—
			B With firm's name, 3 brands listed back		£140.00	—
			C Without firm's name, 'Gibson Girl' back		£140.00	—

T.P. & R. GOODBODY, Dublin and London

Size	Printing	Number in set		Handbook reference	Price per card	Complete set
—	U	? 4	*Actresses — 'ANGOOD' (36 x 60mm) (c1898)	H.187	£350.00	—
A2	U	? 10	*Beauties — 'KEWA' (c1898):	H.139		
			A Back rubber stamped in mauve		£300.00	—
			B Back rubber stamped in red		£300.00	—
D	BW		*Boer War Celebrities — 'CAG' (1901):	H.79		
		25	See H.79 — Fig. 79-B		£35.00	—
		16	See H.79 — Fig. 79-C		£35.00	—
		16	See H.79 — Fig. 79-D		£35.00	—
		16	See H.79 — Fig. 79-E		£35.00	—
	C	50	Colonial Forces (c1900):	H.188		
A2			A Brown back		£75.00	—
A2			B Black back		£75.00	—
—			C Size 80 x 50mm		£500.00	—
—	U	? 67	*Dogs (1910) (36 x 60mm):	H.189		
			A 'Brown Flake' back		£100.00	—
			B 'Celebrated Greenville Plug' back		£100.00	—
			C 'Eblana Flake' back		£100.00	—
			D 'Furze Blossom Cigarettes' back		£100.00	—
			E 'Furze Blossom Navy Cut' back		£100.00	—
			F 'Golden Flake' back:			
			i Text 44mm deep		£100.00	—
			ii Text 50mm deep		£100.00	—
			G 'Silk Cut Cigarettes' back		£100.00	—
			H 'Specialities in Tins & Packets' back		£100.00	—
			I 'Two Flakes' back:			
			i Text 44mm deep		£100.00	—
			ii Text 50mm deep		£100.00	—
C	C	26	Eminent Actresses — 'FROGA A' (c1900):	H.20		
			A Front 'Goodbody' at base		£50.00	—
			B Front 'Goodbody' at top		£250.00	—

T.P. & R. GOODBODY, Dublin and London (continued)

Size	Print- ing	Number in set		Handbook reference	Price per card	Complete set
C	C	20	Irish Scenery (Five Printings) (c1905)	H.190	£40.00	—
A2	U	? 14	*Pretty Girl Series — 'BAGG' (c1898):	H.45		
			A 10 'Gold and Silver Medals' back		£300.00	—
			B 'Furze Blossom':			
			i Mauve back		£300.00	—
			ii Red back		£300.00	—
			iii Grey back		£300.00	—
D	C	50	Questions & Answers in Natural History (1924)		£2.60	£130.00
A	C	25	Sports & Pastimes — Series 1 (1925)	H.225	£7.00	£175.00
A	C	25	Types of Soldiers (c1914)	H.144	£60.00	—
D	U	20	*War Pictures (c1915)	H.122	£35.00	—
C	C	12	'With the Flag to Pretoria' (c1901)	H.191	£110.00	—

GORDON'S, Glasgow

| A2 | BW | ? 4 | Billiards — By George D. Gordon (c1910) ... ... | | £1000.00 | — |

F. GOUGH, Blackley

| — | C | ? 1 | *Play Up Sporting Shields (c1895) ... ... | H.718 | £125.00 | — |

GRAVESON, Mexboro'

A2	C	30	*Army Pictures, Cartoons, Etc (c1916):	H.12		
			A 'Wholesale Tobacconist' back		£130.00	—
			B 'Wholesale and Retail Tobacconist' back		£130.00	—
			C 'Wholesale and Retail Tobacconist Flash Cards			
			etc.' back		£130.00	—
A	U	50	War Portraits (1916)	H.86	£100.00	—

FRED GRAY, Birmingham

| A | C | 25 | *Types of British Soldiers (c1914) ... ... | H.144 | £150.00 | — |

GRIFFITHS BROS., Manchester

| — | P | 18 | *Beauties (89 x 70mm) (c1925) ... ... | H.653 | £150.00 | — |

W.J. HARRIS, London

A2	C	26	*Beauties 'HOL' (c1900)	H.192	£40.00	—
C	C	30	*Colonial Troops (c1900)	H.40	£100.00	—
A1	C	25	*Star Girls (c1899)	H.30	£300.00	—

JAS. H. HARRISON, Birmingham

| C | C | 18 | Motor Cycle Series (c1914) ... ... | H.469 | £90.00 | — |

HARVEY & DAVEY, Newcastle-on-Tyne

D1	C	50	*Birds and Eggs (c1905)	H.60	£5.00	£250.00
A1	C	35	*Chinese and South African Series (c1901)	H.193	£140.00	—
C	C	30	*Colonial Troops (c1900)	H.40	£80.00	—
A1	C	25	*Types of British and Colonial Troops (c1901)	H.76	£90.00	—

HARVEY'S NAVY CUT

| — | C | ? 3 | *Play Up Sporting Shields (c1895) ... ... | H.718 | £125.00 | — |

W. & H. HEATON, Birkby

| — | BW | ? 6 | Birkby Views (70 x 39mm) (c1912) ... ... | H.226 | £400.00 | — |

HENLY & WATKINS LTD, London

A1	C	25	Ancient Egyptian Gods — 'Matossian's Cigarettes' (1924)	H.570		
			*A Plain back		£7.00	£175.00
			B Back in blue		£7.00	£175.00

HIGNETT BROS. & CO., Liverpool

A	C	50	Actors — Natural and Character Studies (1938)	H.571-1	£1.60	£80.00
C	C	26	*Actresses — 'FROGA A' (c1900)	H.20	£60.00	—
A2	U	25	*Actresses — Photogravure (c1900)	H.194	£35.00	—
D1	BW	28	*Actresses — 'PILPI I' (c1901)	H.195	£20.00	—
D1	P	50	*Actresses — 'PILPI II' (c1901)	H.196	£12.00	—
—	C	? 3	Advertisement Cards. (c1885)		£600.00	—
A	C	50	A.F.C. Nicknames (1933)	H.571-2	£6.50	—
A	C	50	Air-Raid Precautions (1939)	H.544	£1.20	£60.00
—	C	60	Animal Pictures ... (38 x 70mm) (c1900)	H.197	£35.00	—
A	C	50	Arms and Armour (1924)	H.273	£3.00	£150.00
C	C	? 25	*Beauties — 'CHOAB' (c1900)	H.21	£220.00	—
D	U	50	*Beauties — gravure (c1898):	H.198		
			A 'Cavalier' back		£80.00	—
			B 'Golden Butterfly' back		£80.00	—
—	C	? 8	*Beauties, multi-backed (168 x 109mm) (c1900) ...	H.708	£400.00	—
A	C	50	British Birds and Their Eggs (1938)	H.571-3	£2.80	—
A	U	50	Broadcasting (1935)	H.571-4	£2.80	—
A1	C	19	Cabinet, 1900	H.199	£90.00	—
A	C	25	Cathedrals and Churches (1909)	H.545	£4.40	£110.00
A	U	50	Celebrated Old Inns (1925)		£3.00	£150.00
A	C	50	Champions of 1936 (1937)	H.571-5	£3.40	£170.00
A	C	25	Common Objects of the Sea-Shore (1924)		£2.40	£60.00
A	C	25	Company Drill (1915)		£4.40	£110.00
A	C	50	Coronation Procession (sectional) (1937)	H.571-6	£3.00	—
—	BW	6	Diamond Jubilee 1897 (156 x 156mm)	H.740	£600.00	—
A	C	50	Dogs (1936)	H.571-7	£2.20	£110.00
A	C	50	Football Caricatures (1935)	H.571-8	£3.50	£175.00
A	C	50	Football Club Captains (1935)	H.571-9	£3.50	£175.00
A	C	25	Greetings of the World (1907 — re-issued 1922) ...		£3.20	£80.00
A	U	25	Historical London (1926)		£2.80	£70.00
A	C	50	How to Swim (1935)	H.571-l0	£1.20	£60.00
A	C	50	Interesting Buildings (1905)	H.70	£6.50	£325.00
A	C	25	International Caps and Badges (1924)		£4.40	£110.00
A	C	25	Life in Pond & Stream (1925)		£3.00	£75.00
—	C	40	*Medals (34 x 72mm) (1901):	H.200		
			A 'Butterfly Cigarettes'		£25.00	—
			B Officially cut for use in other brands		£25.00	—
A	BW	25	Military Portraits (1914)	H.201	£5.00	£125.00
A	C	50	Modern Railways (1936)	H.571-11	£2.50	£125.00
A	C	25	Modern Statesmen (1906):			
			A 'Butterfly' back		£5.00	£125.00
			B 'Pioneer' back		£5.00	£125.00
A	C	20	*Music Hall Artistes (c1900)	H.202	£70.00	—
A	C	50	Ocean Greyhounds (1938)	H.571-12	£1.60	£80.00
	U	1	Oracle Butterfly (shaped) (c1898):			
			A Orange gold cellophane:			
			i Size 65 x 57mm		£125.00	—
			ii Size 51 x 40mm		£125.00	—
			iii Size 49 x 43mm		£125.00	—
			B Yellow and gold cellophane, size 51 x 38mm		£125.00	—
			C Purple and gold cellophane, size 48 x 38mm		£125.00	—

HIGNETT BROS. & CO., Liverpool (continued)

Size	Print-ing	Number in set	Title	Handbook reference	Price per card	Complete set
A	C	25	Panama Canal (1914)		£6.00	£150.00
A2	C	12	*Pretty Girl Series — 'RASH' (c1900)	H.8	£60.00	—
A	U	25	*The Prince of Wales' Empire Tour (1924)		£2.60	£65.00
A	U	50	Prominent Cricketers of 1938 (1938)	H.571-13	£3.60	£180.00
A	C	50	Prominent Racehorses of 1933 (1934)	H.571-14	£2.60	£130.00
A	C	50	Sea Adventure (1939)	H.571-15	50p	£25.00
A	C	25	Ships Flags & Cap Badges (1926)		£5.00	£125.00
A	C	25	Ships Flags & Cap Badges, 2nd Series (1927)		£5.00	£125.00
A	C	50	Shots from the Films (1936)	H.571-16	£3.50	—
—	C	6	*Story of a Boy Who Robs a Stork's Nest (118 x 88mm) (c1890)	H.742	£600.00	—
A	C	50	Trick Billiards (1934)	H.571-17	£6.00	—
A	U	25	Turnpikes (1927)		£2.60	£65.00
—	BW	25	*V.C. Heroes (35 x 72mm) (1901)	H.203	£60.00	—
A	C	20	*Yachts (c1902):	H.204		
			A Gold on black back		£75.00	—
			B Black on white back		£75.00	—
A	C	50	Zoo Studies (1937)	H.571-18	£1.00	£50.00

OVERSEAS ISSUES (NEW ZEALAND)

Size	Print-ing	Number in set	Title	Handbook reference	Price per card	Complete set
D1	P	50	Beauties, Set 1 (1926):			
			A Back without framelines, no brand mentioned		£2.00	—
			B Back with framelines, 'Chess Cigarettes'		£1.50	£75.00
D1	P	50	Beauties, Set 2 (1927)		£1.80	£90.00

R. & J. HILL LTD, London
28 page reference book — £4.50

Size	Print-ing	Number in set	Title	Handbook reference	Price per card	Complete set
A	C	26	*Actresses — 'FROGA A' (c1900)	H.20	£60.00	—
D	BW	30	*Actresses, Continental (c1905):	H.205		
			A 'The Seven Wonders' back		£18.00	—
			B 'Black and White Whisky' back		£25.00	—
			C Plain back		£18.00	—
D	BW	16	*Actresses — 'HAGG B' (c1900):	H.24		
			A 'Smoke Hill's Stockrider ...'		£35.00	—
			B 'Issued with Hill's High Class'		£35.00	—
—	BW	25	*Actresses (Belle of New York Series) (1899):	H206		
			A White back (41 x 75mm)		£25.00	—
			B Toned back, thick card (39 x 74mm)		£25.00	—
D1	U	20	*Actresses, chocolate tinted (1917):	H.207		
			A 'Hill's Tobaccos' etc back		£18.00	—
			B 'Issued with Hill's ...' back		£20.00	—
			C Plain back		£18.00	—
C	U	30	The All Blacks (1924)		£7.00	—
C	C	20	*Animal Series (1909):	H.743		
			A 'R. & J. Hill Ltd.' back		£27.00	—
			B 'Crowfoot Cigarettes' back		£27.00	—
			C 'The Cigarettes with which ...' back		£32.00	—
			D Space at back		£27.00	—
			E Plain Back		£27.00	—
A	BW	25	Aviation Series (1934):			
			A 'Issued by R. & J. Hill ...'		£3.40	£85.00
			B 'Issued with "Gold Flake Honeydew" ...'		£3.60	£90.00
A	BW	? 17	*Battleships (c1908):	H.208		
			A 'For the Pipe Smoke Oceanic ...' back		£350.00	—
			B Plain back		£50.00	—
A	C	25	*Battleships and Crests (1901)		£20.00	£500.00
D2	C	12	*Boer War Generals ('Campaigners') (c1901)	H.209	£35.00	£420.00

R. & J. HILL LTD, London (continued)

Size	Printing	Number in set	Description	Handbook reference	Price per card	Complete set
A1	C	20	Breeds of Dogs (1914):	H.211		
			A 'Archer's M.F.H.' back		£24.00	—
			B 'Hill's Badminton' back		£24.00	—
			C 'Hill's Verbena Mixture' back		£24.00	—
			D 'Spinet Tobacco' back		£24.00	—
D1	BW	? 48	*British Navy Series (c1902)	H.210	£28.00	—
	U	50	Caricatures of Famous Cricketers (1926):			
C			A Small size		£3.20	£160.00
B1			B Large size		£2.50	£125.00
A	BW	? 1	*Celebrated Pictures (c1905)	H.744	£700.00	—
D1	C	50	Celebrities of Sport (1939):			
			A 'Issued by R. & J. Hill ...'		£2.20	£110.00
			B 'Issued with "Gold Flake Honeydew" ...'		£4.00	—
A2	C	35	Cinema Celebrities (1936):	H.572		
			A Inscribed 'These Cigarettes are guaranteed' ...		£1.15	£40.00
			B Inscribed 'The Spinet House'		£1.30	£45.00
C	C		*Colonial Troops (c1900):	H.40		
		30	A i 'Hill's Leading Lines ...' back		£24.00	—
		30	A ii 'Perfection vide Dress ...' back		£24.00	—
		50	B 1-50. 'Sweet American' back		£24.00	—
D1	BW	40	Crystal Palace Souvenir:			
			A Front matt (1936)		£2.50	£100.00
			B Front varnished (1937)		£2.00	£80.00
D1	C	48	Decorations and Medals (1940):			
			A 'Issued by R. & J. Hill ...'		£1.60	£80.00
			B 'Issued with Gold Flake Cigarettes'		£3.00	—
	P		Famous Cinema Celebrities (1931):			
		? 48	Set 1:			
—			A Medium size (74 x 56mm) inscribed 'Series A':			
			1 'Kadi Cigarettes' at base of back		£5.00	—
			2 Space at base of back blank		£4.00	—
A			B1 Small size, inscribed 'Spinet Cigarettes'		£4.50	—
A			B2 Small size, without 'Spinet Cigarettes'		£4.50	—
		50	Set 2:			
—			C Small size (66 x 41mm) inscribed 'Series C':			
			1 'Devon Cigarettes' at base of back		£7.00	—
			2 'Toucan Cigarettes' at base of back		£7.00	—
			3 Space at base of back blank		£4.00	—
			D Medium size (74 x 56mm) inscribed 'Series D':			
			1 'Kadi Cigarettes' at base of back		£4.00	—
			2 Space at base of back blank		£4.00	—
D1	U	28	Famous Cricketers Series (1912):			
			A Red back, blue picture		£70.00	—
			B Deep blue back, brown picture		£70.00	—
			C Blue back, black picture		£70.00	—
C	U	40	Famous Cricketers (1923)	H.633	£5.00	£200.00
	U	50	Famous Cricketers, including the S. Africa Test Team — 'Sunripe Cigarettes' (1924):			
C			A Small size		£5.50	£275.00
B1			B Large size		£6.00	£300.00
A	U	50	Famous Dog Breeds 1954 (Airmail Cigarettes Slides)	H.889	£8.00	—
—	C	30	Famous Engravings — Series XI (80 x 61mm) (c1920)		£4.50	—
A2	BW	40	Famous Film Stars (1938):	H.634-1		
			A Text in English		£1.25	£50.00
			B *Text in Arabic, caption in English on back (see also Modern Beauties)*		£1.00	£40.00

45

R. & J. HILL LTD, London (continued)

Size	Print-ing	Number in set		Handbook reference	Price per card	Complete set
D1	BW	20	Famous Footballers Series (1912)		£27.00	£540.00
C	U	50	Famous Footballers (1923)		£4.00	£200.00
D	C	50	Famous Footballers (1939):	H.574		
			A Shoreditch address		£2.50	£125.00
			B 'Proprietors of Hy. Archer ...'		£2.60	£130.00
D	C	25	Famous Footballers, Nd. 51-75 (1939)		£3.00	£75.00
—	U	25	Famous Pictures: (41 x 70mm) (c1912):			
			A 'Prize Coupon' back		£4.00	£100.00
			B Without 'Prize Coupon' back		£4.00	£100.00
D	C	50	Famous Ships:			
			A Front matt (1939)		£1.10	£55.00
			B Front varnished (1940)		90p	£45.00
D	C	48	Film Stars and Celebrity Dancers (1935)		£1.50	£75.00
C	C	30	*Flags and Flags with Soldiers (c1902)	H.41	£25.00	—
—	C	24	*Flags, Arms and Types of Nations, 'Black & White' Whisky advert back (41 x 68mm) (c1910)	H.115	£12.50	£300.00
D	BW	20	Football Captain Series. Nd. 41-60 (1906):			
			A Small title		£50.00	—
			B Larger title, back re-drawn		£65.00	—
—		10	Fragments from France (38 x 67mm) (1916):	H.212		
	C		A Coloured, caption in script		£25.00	£250.00
	U		B Sepia-brown on buff, caption in block		£30.00	£300.00
	U		C As B, but black and white		£90.00	—
—	C	10	Fragments from France, different subjects, caption in block (38 x 67mm) (1916)	H.212	£25.00	£250.00
A1	U	25	Hill's War Series (c1916)	H.35	£13.00	£325.00
	C		Historic Places from Dickens' Classics (1926):			
D		50	A Small size		80p	£40.00
B1			B Large size:			
		25	1 Nos. 2-26, small numerals under 2mm high		70p	£17.50
		50	2 Nos. 1-50, large numerals over 2mm high		60p	£30.00
	U	50	Holiday Resorts (1925):			
C			A Small size:			
			1 Back in grey		90p	£45.00
			2 Back in brown		£1.50	—
B1			B Large size:			
			1 Back in grey		90p	£45.00
			2 Back in brown		£1.60	—
C2	C	20	Inventors and Their Inventions Series, Nd. 1-20, (1907):	H.213		
			A Black back, white card		£5.00	£100.00
			B Black back, toned card (shorter)		£6.00	—
C2	C	20	Inventors and Their Inventions Series, Nd. 21-40, (1907)		£8.00	£160.00
A	BW	20	*Inventors and Their Inventions (plain back) (1934)	H.213	£1.50	£30.00
—			*Japanese Series (40 x 66mm) (1904):	H.214		
	C	15	A 'Hills' on red tablet		£65.00	—
	C	1	B 'Hills' on blue tablet		£300.00	—
	BW	15	C 'Hills' on black tablet:			
			i With 'E F Lind Sydney'		£300.00	—
			ii Without 'E F Lind Sydney'		£50.00	—
—	C	20	Lighthouse Series — without frame lines to picture (42 x 68mm) (c1903)		£35.00	—
—	C	30	Lighthouse Series — with frame line. Nos. 1-20 re-touched and 10 cards added (c1903)		£35.00	—
			Magical Puzzles — see 'Puzzle Series'			

R. & J. HILL LTD, London (continued)

Size	Print-ing	Number in set		Handbook reference	Price per card	Complete set
A2	BW		Modern Beauties (1939):	H.634-2		
		50	A Titled 'Modern Beauties'. Text in English		£1.00	£50.00
		40	B Titled 'Famous Film Stars' (selection):			
			i Text in Arabic, No Captions, Numbered		£2.00	—
			ii Text in Arabic, No Captions, Unnumbered		£12.00	—
	C	30	Music Hall Celebrities — Past and Present (1930):			
D1			A Small size		£2.50	£75.00
B1			B Large size		£2.80	£85.00
D	C	20	National Flag Series (1914):	H.473		
			A Printed back		£8.00	£160.00
			B Plain back		£7.00	—
D	C	30	Nature Pictures — 'The Spotlight Tobaccos' (c1930)		£1.40	£42.00
C2	C	30	Nautical Songs (1937)		£1.50	£45.00
—	BW	25	*Naval Series unnumbered (42 x 64mm) (1901)	H.215	£45.00	—
D1	BW	30	Naval Series Nd. 21-50 (1902):	H.215		
			A Numbered 21-40		£13.00	—
			B Numbered 41-50		£60.00	—
	U	30	'Our Empire' (1929):			
D1			A Small size		40p	£12.00
B1			B Large size		80p	£24.00
—	BW		Popular Footballers — Season 1934-5 (68 x 49mm):			
		30	'Series A' — Nd. 1-30		£3.20	£95.00
		20	'Series B' — Nd. 31-50		£3.50	£70.00
C	C	20	Prince of Wales Series (1911)	H.22	£12.00	£240.00
	U		Public Schools and Colleges (1923):	H.575		
		50	A 'A Series of 50':			
C			1 Small size		90p	£45.00
B1			2 Large size		90p	£45.00
		75	B 'A Series of 75':			
C			1 Small size		£1.20	£90.00
B1			2 Large size		£1.20	£90.00
A1	C	50	Puzzle Series:	H.660		
			A Titled 'Puzzle Series' (1937)		£1.20	£60.00
			B Titled 'Magical Puzzles' (1938)		£2.00	£100.00
	U	50	The Railway Centenary — 'A Series of 50' (1925):			
C			A Small size		£1.50	£75.00
B1			B Large size:			
			1 Back in brown		£1.50	£75.00
			2 Back in grey		£4.00	—
	U	25	The Railway Centenary — '2nd Series — 51 to 75' (1925):			
C			A Small size		£2.00	£50.00
B1			B Large size		£2.00	£50.00
C2	P	42	Real Photographs — Set 1 (Bathing Beauties) (c1930):	H.576-1		
			A 'London Idol Cigarettes' at base of back:			
			1 Front black and white, glossy		£2.50	—
			2 Front brown, matt		£2.50	—
			B Space at base of back blank:			
			1 Front black and white, glossy		£2.50	—
			2 Front brown, matt		£2.50	—
C2	P	42	Real Photographs — Set 2 (Beauties) (c1930)	H.576-2	£3.00	—
—	BW	20	Rhymes — black and white sketches (c1905)	H.217	£30.00	—
			The River Thames — see 'Views of the River Thames'			
D1	P	50	Scenes from the Films (1932):			
			A Front black and white		£3.50	—
			B Front sepia		£3.50	—
A2	BW	40	Scenes from the Films (1938)		90p	£36.00

R. & J. HILL LTD, London (continued)

Size	Print-ing	Number in set	BRITISH TOBACCO ISSUERS	Handbook reference	Price per card	Complete set
D1		35	Scientific Inventions and Discoveries (1929):	H.213		
	C		A Small size, 'The Spinet House ...' back		£1.30	£45.00
	BW		B Small size, 'The Spotlight Tobaccos ...' back		£1.30	£45.00
B1	C		C Large size		£1.30	£45.00
DI	P	50	Sports (1934):			
			A Titled 'Sports', numbered front and back		£5.00	—
			B Titled 'Sports Series', numbered front only ...		£12.00	—
			*C Untitled, numbered front only		£15.00	—
A1	BW	30	*Statuary — Set 1 (c1900):	H.218-1		
			A Black and white front, matt		£50.00	—
	BW		B Black and white front, varnished		£12.00	—
A	BW	30	*Statuary — Set 2 (c1900)	H.218-2	£8.00	£240.00
C1	BW		*Statuary — Set 3 (c1900):	H.218-3		
		? 26	A Name panel white lettering on black background		£25.00	—
		? 4	B Name panel black lettering on grey background		£50.00	—
		? 26	C Name panel black lettering on white back-ground		£50.00	—
D1	C	100	*Transfers (c1935)		£6.50	—
D	C	20	*Types of the British Army (1914):			
			A 'Badminton' back		£30.00	—
			B 'Verbena' back		£30.00	—
B2	CP		Views of Interest:			
		48	'A First Series ...' Nd. 1-48 (1938):			
			A 'The Spinet House ...' back		30p	£15.00
			B 'Sunripe & Spinet Ovals ...' back		25p	£12.50
		48	'Second Series ...' Nd. 49-96 (1938)		25p	£12.50
		48	'Third Series ...' Nd. 97-144 (1939)		25p	£12.50
		48	'Fourth Series ...' Nd. 145-192 (1939)		50p	£25.00
		48	'Fifth Series ...' Nd. 193-240 (1939)		60p	£30.00
			Album (1st to 5th Series Combined)		—	£25.00
B2	CP		Views of Interest — British Empire Series:			
		48	'1st Issue — Canada — Nos. 1-48' (1940)		50p	£25.00
		48	'2nd Issue — India — Nos. 49-96' (1940)		£3.00	£150.00
	U	50	Views of London (1925):	H.577		
C			A Small size		£1.00	£50.00
B1			B Large size		£1.00	£50.00
	C	50	Views of the River Thames (1924):			
D			A Small size:			
			Nos. 1-25		£2.00	£50.00
			Nos. 26-50		£1.40	£35.00
B1			B Large size:			
			1 Back in green (thin card)		£1.60	£80.00
			2 Back in green and black (thick card)		£1.60	£80.00
	U	50	Who's Who in British Films (Nov. 1927):			
A2			A Small size		£1.80	£90.00
B2			B Large size		£1.80	£90.00
C	C	84	Wireless Telephony (1923)		£1.60	£135.00
B1	U	20	Wireless Telephony — Broadcasting Series (1923) ...		£2.50	£50.00
A	U	25	World's Masterpieces — 'Second Series' (c1915) ...		£2.00	£50.00
	U	50	Zoological Series (1924):	H.578		
C			A Small size:			
			1 Back in light brown		90p	£45.00
			2 Back in grey		£1.00	£50.00
B1			B Large size:			
			1 Back in light brown		£1.00	£50.00
			2 Back in dark brown		£1.00	£50.00

48

R. & J. HILL LTD, London (continued)

CANVASES. Unbacked canvases. The material is a linen fabric, glazed to give the appearance of canvas. Specimens are found rubber stamped in red on back 'The Pipe Tobacco de Luxe Spinet Mixture'.

Size	Print	Number		Ref	Price	Set
—	C	30	'Britain's Stately Homes' (78 x 61mm) (c1915) … …		£4.00	—
—	C		*Canvas Masterpieces — Series 1 (73 x 61mm) (c1915):			
			A 'Badminton Tobacco Factories …' back:			
		40	1 'H.T. & Co., Ltd., Leeds' at right base … …		£1.50	—
		20	2 Cardigan Press, Leeds' at right base			
			(Nos. 21-40) … … … … … … … …		£1.50	—
		10	3 Without printers' credit (Nos. 21-30) … …		£1.50	—
		3	4 As 3, but size 73 x 53mm (Nos. 23-25) …		£1.50	—
		40	B 'The Spinet House …' back … … … … …		£2.00	£80.00
—	C	40	*Canvas Masterpieces — Series 2, Nd. 41-80			
			(73 x 61mm) (c1915) … … … … … … … …	H.509	£2.50	£100.00
—	C	10	*Canvas Masterpieces — Series 2, Nd. 1-10 (c1915):			
			Nos. 1 to 5 … … … … … … … … … … …		£2.00	£10.00
			Nos. 6 to 10 … … … … … … … … … …		£3.00	£15.00
—	C	5	Chinese Pottery and Porcelain — Series 1			
			(132 x 108mm) (c1915) … … … … … …		—	£45.00
			4 Different (minus No. 5) … … … … … … …		75p	£3.00
—	C	11	Chinese Pottery and Porcelain — Series 2			
			(107 x 62mm) (c1915) … … … … … … … …		£6.00	—
—	C	23	*Great War Leaders — Series 10 (73 x 60mm) (1919)		£6.00	—

OVERSEAS ISSUE

A2	C	10	Chinese Series (c1912) … … … … … … … …		£80.00	—

L. HIRST & SON, Leeds

—	C	? 5	*Soldiers and their Uniforms (cutouts) (c1915) … …	H.138	£260.00	—

J.W. HOBSON, Huddersfield

C2	C	18	Motor Cycle Series (c1914) … … … … … … … …	H.469	£100.00	—

J. & T. HODGE, Glasgow

—	C	? 5	*British Naval Crests (70 x 38mm) (c1896) … … …	H.219	£750.00	—
A	BW	16	British Royal Family (c1901) … … … … … …	H.28	£300.00	—
—	U		*Scottish Views (c1898):	H.220		
		? 11	A Thick card (74 x 39mm) … … … … … … …		£220.00	—
		? 14	B Thin card (80 x 45mm) … … … … … …		£220.00	—

HOOK OF HOLLAND CIGARETTES

A	U	? 5	*Footballers (c1905) … … … … … … … … …	H.745	£700.00	—

HUDDEN & CO. LTD, Bristol

C	C	26	*Actresses — 'FROGA A' (c1900) … … … … … … …	H.20	£65.00	—
C	C	25	*Beauties — 'CHOAB' (c1900) … … … … … … … …	H.21	£60.00	—
A2	U	20	*Beauties — 'Crown Seal Cigarettes' (c1898) … …	H.221	£150.00	—
A	U	24	*Beauties — 'HUMPS' (c1898):	H.222		
			A Blue scroll back … … … … … … … …		£75.00	—
			B Orange scroll back … … … … … … …		£60.00	—
			C Typeset back in brown … … … … … …		£400.00	—
D1	C	? 12	Comic Phrases (c1900) … … … … … … … …	H.223	£110.00	—
D	U	25	Famous Boxers (1927) … … … … … … … …	H.721	£35.00	—
A	C	25	*Flags of All Nations (c1905) … … … … … …	H.37	£26.00	£650.00
—	C	48	*Flowers and Designs (55 x 34mm) (c1900):	H.224		
			A 'Hudden Cigarettes' back … … … … …		£90.00	—
			B 'Hudden's — Dandy Dot' back … … … …		£200.00	—

HUDDEN & CO. LTD, Bristol (continued)

Size	Printing	Number in set	Title	Handbook reference	Price per card	Complete set
A	C	18	*Pretty Girl Series — 'RASH' (c1900)	H.8	£90.00	—
C	U	50	Public Schools and Colleges (c1925)	H.575	£2.20	£110.00
A	C	25	Soldiers of the Century, Nd. 26-50 (1901)		£55.00	—
A	C	25	Sports and Pastimes Series 1 (c1925)	H.225	£60.00	—
A	C	25	*Star Girls (c1900)	H.30	£110.00	—
A	C	25	Types of Smokers (c1903)		£55.00	—

HUDSON

Size	Printing	Number in set	Title	Handbook reference	Price per card	Complete set
D	U	? 1	*Actresses — 'ANGOOD' (c1900)	H.187	£600.00	—
C	C	25	*Beauties — selections from 'BOCCA' (c1900)	H.39	£500.00	—

HUNTER, Airdrie

Size	Printing	Number in set	Title	Handbook reference	Price per card	Complete set
A	BW	? 11	*Footballers (c1910)	H.227	£2000.00	—

J.T. ILLINGWORTH & SONS, Kendal

Size	Printing	Number in set	Title	Handbook reference	Price per card	Complete set
—	P	48	Beautiful Scotland (77 x 52mm) (1939)	H.564-1	£2.00	—
C1	C	25	*Cavalry (1924)		£6.00	£150.00
—	P	48	Coastwise (77 x 52mm) (1938)	H.564-2	£1.00	£50.00
A	C	25	'Comicartoons'of sport (1927)		£7.00	£175.00
—	P	48	Flying (77 x 52mm) (1938)	H.564-3	£1.80	£90.00
A	C	25	*Motor Car Bonnets (1925)		£8.00	£200.00
A	C	25	*Old Hostels (1926)		£6.00	£150.00
—	P	48	Our Countryside (77 x 52mm) (1938)	H.564-4	£2.00	£100.00
—	P	24	Shots from the Films (1937)	H.566	£5.00	—
A	BW	25	Views from the English Lakes (c1895)	H.228	£250.00	—

THE IMPERIAL TOBACCO CO. (of Great Britain & Ireland) Ltd, Bristol

Size	Printing	Number in set	Title	Handbook reference	Price per card	Complete set
A	C	50	British Birds (c1910)	H.229	£6.00	—
C	C	1	Folder — Coronation of His Majesty King Edward VII (1902)		—	£100.00
—	C	10	Out of the Blue — Richmond Adverts (2002):			
			A Size 75 x 32mm		£2.00	—
			B Size 80 x 47mm		£2.00	—
			C Size 90 x 47mm		£1.50	—
G2	C	12	Supertrivia — Superkings Adverts (c2000)		£2.00	—

INGRAM'S, 1A, 27 & 33 Leigh Road, Eastleigh

Size	Printing	Number in set	Title	Handbook reference	Price per card	Complete set
D	C	30	*Army Pictures, Cartoons, etc (1916)	H.12	£130.00	—

INTERNATIONAL TOBACCO CO. LTD, London

Size	Printing	Number in set	Title	Handbook reference	Price per card	Complete set
—	C	28	Domino cards (69 x 35mm) (1938)		40p	£10.00
	U		*Famous Buildings and Monuments of Britain (1934) (bronze metal plaques without envelopes):	H.580		
		50	'Series A':			
A1			1 Nos. 1-30, small size		£1.20	£36.00
H2			2 Nos. 31-50, large size		£1.20	£24.00
		50	'Series B':			
A1			1 Nos. 51-80, small size		£2.00	£60.00
H2			2 Nos. 81-100, large size		£2.00	£40.00
—	—	100	Empty envelopes with text for numbers 1 to 100		£1.00	—
			*The same plaques were also used for an export issue, with envelopes inscribed 'International Tobacco (Overseas), Ltd.'			
A2	C	100	Film Favourites (c1937):	H.581		
			A Back in grey		£2.40	
			B Back in black		£2.40	

INTERNATIONAL TOBACCO CO. LTD, London (continued)

	C	100	'Gentlemen! The King!' — (60 small, 40 large) (1937):	H.582		
—			A Back in blue … … … … … … … … … …		50p	£50.00
			B Back in black … … … … … … … … … …		20p	£20.00
A	C	50	International Code of Signals (1934) … … … … … …		80p	£40.00
D	C	48	Screen Lovers — 'Summit' (unissued) (c1940) … …		£3.50	—

J.L.S. TOBACCO CO., London
('Star of the World' Cigarettes)

D	BW	20	*Boer War Cartoons (1901) … … … … … … … … …	H.42	£150.00	—
B2	BW	? 32	*Boer War Celebrities — 'JASAS' (c1901) … … … …	H.133	£225.00	—
A2	C	30	*Colonial Troops (c1901) … … … … … … … …	H.40	£100.00	—

PETER JACKSON, London

	P		Beautiful Scotland (1939):	H.564-1		
D		28	A Small size … … … … … … … … … … …		£1.35	£40.00
—		48	B Medium size, 77 x 52mm … … … … … …		£1.00	£50.00
	P		Coastwise (1938):	H.564-2		
D		28	A Small size … … … … … … … … … … …		£1.35	£40.00
—		48	B Medium size, 77 x 52mm … … … … … …		£1.25	£60.00
D	P	28	Famous Film Stars (1935) … … … … … … … …		£3.50	£100.00
D	P	27	Famous Films (1934) … … … … … … … … … …		£3.50	£100.00
D	P	28	Film Scenes (1936) … … … … … … … … … …		£3.50	£100.00
B	P	28	Film Scenes (1936) … … … … … … … … … …		£4.50	£125.00
	P		Flying (1938):	H.564-3		
D		28	A Small size … … … … … … … … … … …		£3.00	—
—		48	B Medium size (77 x 52mm) … … … … … …		£3.50	—
—	C	100	'Gentlemen! The King!' (60 small, 40 large) (1937):	H.582		
			A Overprinted on International black back … …		£1.00	£100.00
			B Overprinted on International blue back … … …		£1.00	—
			C Reprinted with Jackson's name at base:			
			i Back in black … … … … … … … … …		£1.00	—
			ii Back in blue … … … … … … … … …		£2.00	—
			Album … … … … … … … … … … … …		—	£30.00
D	P	28	Life in the Navy (1937) … … … … … … … …		£2.00	£55.00
B	P	28	Life in the Navy (1937) … … … … … … … …		£2.50	£70.00
	P		Our Countryside (1938):	H.564-4		
D		28	A Small size … … … … … … … … … … …		£1.00	£28.00
—		48	B Medium size (77 x 52mm) … … … … … …		£1.25	£60.00
—	C	150	The Pageant of Kingship — 90 small, 60 large (1937):			
			A Inscribed 'Issued by Peter Jackson' … … … …		50p	£75.00
			B Inscribed 'Issued by Peter Jackson (Overseas), Ltd.':			
			1 Printed on cream matt board … … … …		50p	£75.00
			2 Printed on white glossy board … … … …		50p	£75.00
			3 Printed on white glossy paper … … … …		33p	£50.00
			Album … … … … … … … … … … … …		—	£30.00
	P		Shots from the Films (1937):	H.566		
D		28	A Small size … … … … … … … … … … …		£3.00	£85.00
—		24	B Medium size (77 x 52mm) … … … … … …		£3.25	£80.00
—	C	250	Speed — Through the Ages (170 small, 80 large) (1937) … … … … … … … … … … … …	H.583	30p	£75.00
D	P	28	Stars in Famous Films (1935) … … … … … … …		£3.50	£100.00

JACOBI BROS. & CO. LTD, London

A	BW	? 32	*Boer War Celebrities — 'JASAS' (c1901):	H.133		
			A Black and white front … … … … … … … …		£220.00	—
			B As A, but mauve tinted … … … … … … …		£220.00	—

JAMES & CO. (Birmingham) LTD

—	C	20	Arms of Countries (c1915):			
			A Size 70 x 40mm		£160.00	—
			B Size 70 x 49mm		£160.00	—

JAMES'S (GOLD LEAF NAVY CUT)

A	U	? 11	Pretty Girl Series — 'BAGG' (c1898)	H.45	£400.00	—

J.B. JOHNSON & CO., London

A	C	25	*National Flags and Flowers — Girls (c1900)	H.123	£350.00	—

JOHNSTON'S CIGARETTES

A	U	? 3	*British Views (c1910)	H.746	£650.00	—

JONES BROS., Tottenham

A	BW	20	*Spurs Footballers:	H.230		
			A 12 Small titles (1911):			
			i 10 Different		£15.00	—
			ii F Bentley		£100.00	—
			iii H Middlemiss		£150.00	—
			B 6 Large titles (1912):			
			i 4 Different		£15.00	—
			ii E J Lightfoot		£200.00	—
			iii R McTavish		£150.00	—
			C 1 Team Group of 36 (1910-11)		£1000.00	—
			D 1 Team Group of 34 (1911-12)		£1000.00	—

A.I. JONES & CO. Ltd, London

—	C	1	*Advertisement Card — Alexia Mixture (80 x 46mm)			
			(c1900)	H.748	—	£750.00
D	C	12	Nautical Terms (c1905)	H.231	£50.00	—

A.S. JONES, Grantham

D	C	30	Army Pictures, Cartoons, etc (c1916)	H.12	£130.00	—

ALEX. JONES & CO., London

D2	U		*Actresses — 'ANGOOD' (c1898):	H.187		
		? 15	A Front in brown		£250.00	—
		? 1	B Front in green		£500.00	—
A	BW	1	Portrait of Queen Victoria 1897		—	£150.00

T.E. JONES & CO., Aberavon

D	C	? 2	*Conundrums (c1900)	H.232	£225.00	—
A2	C	50	*Flags of All Nations (c1899)	H.233	£85.00	—
D	C	12	Well-known Proverbs (c1900)	H.235	£225.00	—
—	BW	52	Welsh Rugby Players (64 x 34mm) (1899)	H.234	£250.00	—

C.H. JORDEN LTD, London

—	P	? 12	*Celebrities of the Great War (c1915) (35 x 64mm) ...	H.236	£90.00	—

J. & E. KENNEDY, Dublin

A	U	25	*Beauties — 'FECKSA' (c1900)	H.58	£50.00	—

RICHARD KENNEDY, Dundee

—	C	? 25	*Naval & Military Cartoons (130 x 90mm) (c1905) ...	H.701	£650.00	—
A	U	50	War Portraits (1916)	H.86	£100.00	—

Size	Print-ing	Number in set		Handbook reference	Price per card	Complete set
			KINNEAR LTD, Liverpool			
A	C	? 13	*Actresses (c1898) ...	H.237	£120.00	—
D1	BW	? 15	*Australian Cricketers (1897) ...	H.238	£250.00	—
—	BW	? 1	Cricket Fixture Folder (89 x 69mm) (1903) ...	H.750	£1500.00	—
A	C	? 18	*Cricketers (c1895) ...	H.269	£500.00	—
A2	C	25	*Footballers and Club Colours (c1898) ...	H.239	£220.00	—
—	U	1	The Four Generations (Royal Family) (65 x 70mm) (1897) ...	H.749	—	£500.00
—	BW	1	'A Gentleman in Kharki' (44 x 64mm) (1900) ...		—	£85.00
A	C		*Jockeys (1896):	H.240		
		12	— see H.240—I-1 ...		£65.00	—
		1	— see H.240—I-2 ...		£110.00	—
		25	— see H.240—II-A ...		£110.00	—
		4	— see H.240—II-B ...		£110.00	—
A	C	? 2	*Prominent Personages (c1902) ...	H.479	£800.00	—
D1	U	13	*Royalty (1897) ...	H.241	£45.00	—
—	U	? 32	Views (49 x 35mm) (c1899) ...	H.751	£400.00	—
			B. KRIEGSFELD & CO., Manchester			
—	C	1	*Advertisement Card— Apple Blossom (c1900) ...	H.752	—	£1500.00
A2	U		*Beauties — 'KEWA' (c1900):	H.139		
		? 63	A Matt surface ...		£90.00	—
		? 6	B Glossy surface ...		£160.00	—
A	C	? 10	Celebrities (c1900):	H.242		
			A Backs Horizontal Format ...		£200.00	—
			B Backs Vertical Format ...		£200.00	—
A	C	50	*Flags of All Nations (c1900) ...	H.233	£65.00	—
A	C	50	*Phrases and Advertisements (c1900) ...	H.243	£90.00	—
			A. KUIT LTD, Manchester			
—	C	? 12	*Arms of Cambridge Colleges (17 x 25mm) (c1914)*	H.458	£120.00	—
—	C	? 12	*Arms of Companies (30 x 33mm) (c1914)* ...	H.459	£120.00	—
—	C	30	British Beauties — oval card (36 x 60mm) (c1914) ...	H.244	£50.00	—
—	P	? 44	*'Crosmedo'Bijoucards (55 x 37mm) (c1915) ...	H.245	£130.00	—
A	U	25	Principal Streets of British Cities and Towns (1916)		£100.00	—
A	CP	50	Types of Beauty (c1914) ...	H.246	£100.00	—
			LAMBERT & BUTLER, London			
			32 page reference book — £4.50			
Al	BW	20	*Actresses — 'BLARM' (c1900) ...	H.23	£35.00	£700.00
—	C	10	*Actresses and Their Autographs (c1898):	H.247		
			A Wide card (70 x 38mm): 'Tobacco' back ...		£150.00	—
			B Narrow card (70 x 34mm): 'Cigarettes' back ...		£125.00	—
A2	BW	50	*Admirals (1900):	H.248		
			A 'Flaked Gold Leaf Honeydew' back ...		£18.00	—
			B 'May Blossom' back ...		£18.00	—
			C 'Prize Medal Bird's Eye' back ...		£18.00	—
			D 'Viking' back ...		£24.00	—
—	C	12	Advertisement Cards — Facts about Lambert & Butler (2002):			
			A Size 75 x 32mm ...		£2.00	—
			B Size 80 x 47mm ...		£1.50	£18.00
C	C	1	*Advertisement Card — Spanish Dancer (1898) ...	H.249	—	£500.00

LAMBERT & BUTLER, London (continued)

Size	Print-ing	Number in set	Description	Handbook reference	Price per card	Complete set
A	C	50	Aeroplane Markings (1937)		£1.80	£90.00
A	C	40	Arms of Kings and Queens of England (1906)		£5.00	£200.00
A	C	25	Aviation(1915)		£4.40	£110.00
A2	C	26	*Beauties — 'HOL' (c1900):	H.192		
			A 'Flaked Gold Leaf Honey Dew' back		£32.00	—
			B 'Log Cabin' back		£32.00	—
			C 'May Blossom' back		£32.00	—
			D 'Viking Navy Cut' back		£32.00	—
A	C	50	Birds and Eggs (1906)	H.60	£3.50	£175.00
C	BW	25	*Boer War and Boxer Rebellion — Sketches (1904)	H.46	£32.00	—
C	U	20	*Boer War Generals — 'CLAM' (1900):	H.61		
			I 10. No frame lines to back:			
			A Brown back		£35.00	—
			B Black back		£35.00	—
			II 10. With frame lines to back:			
			A Brown back		£35.00	—
			B Black back		£35.00	—
C	B	10	*Boer War Generals — 'FLAC' (1901)	H.47	£40.00	—
C	U	1	*Boer War Series — 'The King of Scouts' (Col. R.S.S. Baden-Powell) (1901)	H.753	—	£500.00
A	C	25	British Trees and Their Uses (1927)	H.654	£2.20	£55.00
A	C	25	Common Fallacies (1928)		£2.00	£50.00
—	C	50	*Conundrums (38 x 57mm) (1901):	H.250		
			A Blue back — thick card		£22.00	—
			B Green back		£16.00	—
A2	C	12	Coronation Robes (1902)	H.251	£18.00	£220.00
A	C	25	Dance Band Leaders (1936)		£4.00	£100.00
A	C	50	Empire Air Routes (1936)		£2.00	£100.00
A	BW	25	Famous British Airmen and Airwomen (1935)		£2.00	£50.00
A	U	25	Fauna of Rhodesia (1929)		£1.40	£35.00
A	C	50	Find Your Way:			
			A Address 'Box No. 152, London' (1932)		£1.50	£75.00
			B Address 'Box No. 152, Drury Lane, London' (1932)		£1.50	£75.00
			C Overprinted in red (1933)		£1.50	£75.00
A	BW	1	D Joker Card:			
			i Without overprint (1932)		—	£12.00
			ii With overprint (1933)		—	£12.00
A	C	50	Footballers 1930-1 (1931)		£4.50	—
A	C	25	Garden Life (1930)	H.449	£1.00	£25.00
A	C	25	Hints and Tips for Motorists (1929)		£4.00	£100.00
A	U	25	A History of Aviation:			
			A Front in green (1932)		£2.00	£50.00
			B Front in brown (1933)		£2.80	£70.00
A	C	50	Horsemanship (1938)		£2.50	£125.00
A	C	25	How Motor Cars Work (1931)		£2.20	£55.00
A	C	50	Interesting Customs and Traditions of the Navy, Army and Air Force (1939)		£1.00	£50.00
A	C	25	Interesting Musical Instruments (1929)		£2.80	£70.00
A	C	50	Interesting Sidelights on the Work of the GPO (1939)		£1.20	£60.00
A	C	20	International Yachts (1902)		£65.00	—
A	C	25	Japanese Series (1904):			
			A Thick toned card		£8.00	£200.00
			B Thin white card		£8.00	£200.00
—	C	4	*Jockeys, no frame lines (35 x 70mm) (c1903)	H.252	£55.00	£220.00
—	C	10	*Jockeys with frame lines (35 x 70mm) (c1903)	H.252	£55.00	£550.00
A	C	50	Keep Fit (1937)		80p	£40.00

LAMBERT & BUTLER, London (continued)

Size	Printing	Number in set	Description	Handbook reference	Price per card	Complete set
A	C	25	London Characters (1934):			
			A With Album Clause		£2.40	£60.00
			B Without Album Clause		£20.00	—
			Album		—	£40.00
A	C	1	*Mayblossom Calendar, 1900		—	£750.00
A	C	25	Motor Car Radiators (1928)		£6.00	£150.00
A	C	25	Motor Cars — 'A Series of 25', green back (1922)		£2.60	£65.00
A	C	25	Motor Cars — '2nd Series of 25' (1923)		£2.60	£65.00
A	C	50	Motor Cars — '3rd Series of 50' (1926)		£4.00	£200.00
A	C	25	Motor Cars — 'A Series of 25', grey back (1934)		£3.60	£90.00
A	C	50	Motor Cycles (1923)		£3.50	£175.00
A	C	50	Motor Index Marks (1926)		£2.80	£140.00
A	C	25	Motors (1908):	H.703		
			A Green back		£28.00	—
			B Plain back		£28.00	—
A	BW	25	Naval Portraits (1914)		£4.00	£100.00
A	BW	50	Naval Portraits, incl. above 25 (1915)		£4.00	£200.00
—	C	3	Packet Redesign of The Pack (1998):			
			A Size 75 x 32mm		£2.00	—
			B Size 80 x 47mm		£2.00	—
A	C	25	Pirates and Highwaymen (1926)		£1.60	£40.00
A	U	25	Rhodesian Series (1928)		£1.40	£35.00
A	C	50	The Thames from Lechlade to London:	H.754		
			A Small numerals about 1mm high (1907)		£7.00	£350.00
			B Large numerals about 2mm high (1908)		£7.00	£350.00
			C Plain back (unnumbered)		£7.00	—
A	U	25	Third Rhodesian Series (1930)		60p	£15.00
—	C	12	Total Experience Total Trivia — Size 80 x 47mm (1999)		£2.00	—
—	C	4	*Types of the British Army & Navy (35 x 70mm) (c1897):	H.254		
			A 'Specialities' back in brown		£70.00	—
			B 'Specialities' back in black		£70.00	—
			C 'Viking' back in black		£70.00	—
A	C	25	*Waverley series (1904)	H.255	£13.00	£325.00
A	C	25	Winter Sports (1914)		£5.00	£125.00
A	C	25	Wireless Telegraphy (1909)		£5.00	£125.00
A	C	25	Wonders of Nature (1924)		80p	£20.00
A	C	25	World's Locomotives, Nd. 1-25 (1912)		£4.40	£110.00
A	C	50	World's Locomotives Nd. 1-50 (1912)		£5.50	£275.00
A	C	25	World's Locomotives, Nd. 1A-25A (c1913)		£5.00	£125.00

OVERSEAS ISSUES

Size	Printing	Number in set	Description	Handbook reference	Price per card	Complete set
D2	U	50	Actors and Actresses — 'WALP' (1905)	W.32	£3.50	—
		250	Actresses — 'ALWICS' (1905):	W.33		
D2	U		A Portraits in black, border in red:			
			i Scout back		£5.00	—
			ii With firm's name		£3.50	—
D2	BW		B Portraits and border in black		£7.00	—
D2	U	50	Beauties red tinted (1908):	W.146		
			A Scout back		£4.00	—
			B With firm's name		£4.00	—
A	C	83	Danske Byvaabner (c1915)		£15.00	—
	BW	26	Etchings of Dogs (1926):			
A			A Small size		£30.00	—
—			B Medium size (80 x 54mm)		£30.00	—
D2	C	25	Flag Girls of All Nations (1908)	W.64	£13.00	—
A2	P	50	Homeland Events (1928)		£2.50	£125.00
A	P	50	London Zoo (1927)		£1.50	—

LAMBERT & BUTLER, London (Overseas Issues continued)

Size	Printing	Number in set		Handbook reference	Price per card	Complete set
A	C	50	Merchant Ships of the World (1924)		£2.50	—
D2	BW	30	Music Hall Celebrities (1916)	W.269	£6.50	—
A	P	50	Popular Film Stars (1926):			
			A Series title in one line, no brand quoted		£1.50	£75.00
			B Series title in two lines, inscribed 'Varsity			
			Cigarettes'		£2.50	—
			C Series title in two lines, no brand quoted		£1.50	£75.00
A	P	50	The Royal Family at Home and Abroad (1927)		£1.50	£75.00
A	BW	100	Royalty, Notabilities and Events 1900-1902 (1902) ...	W.28	£14.00	—
D2	BW	100	Russo Japanese series (1905)		£7.00	—
D	P	50	Types of Modern Beauty (1927)		£1.50	£75.00
A	P	50	Who's Who in Sport (1926)		£3.00	£150.00
A	P	50	The World of Sport (1927)		£2.00	£100.00
A	U	50	Zoological Studies (c1928)		£10.00	—

LAMBKIN BROS., Cork

Size	Printing	Number in set		Handbook reference	Price per card	Complete set
A	C	36	*Country Scenes — Small size (1924) (6 sets of 6):			
			Series 1 — Yachting		£7.00	—
			Series 2 — Country		£7.00	—
			Series 3 — Far East		£7.00	—
			Series 4 — Sailing		£7.00	—
			Series 5 — Country		£7.00	—
			Series 6 — Country		£7.00	—
C	C	36	*Country Scenes — Large size (1924) (6 sets of 6):			
			Series 7 — Yachting		£7.00	—
			Series 8 — Country		£7.00	—
			Series 9 — Far East		£7.00	—
			Series 10 — Sailing		£7.00	—
			Series 11 — Country		£7.00	—
			Series 12 — Windmill Scenes		£7.00	—
—	C	? 9	*Irish Views, anonymous. inscribed 'Eagle, Cork' (68			
			x 67mm) (c1925)	H.585	£40.00	—
—	C	? 5	*'Lily of Killarney' Views (73 x 68mm) (c1925)	H.586	£200.00	—

LANCS & YORKS TOBACCO MANUFACTURING CO. LTD, Burnley
(L. & Y. Tob. Mfg. Co.)

Size	Printing	Number in set		Handbook reference	Price per card	Complete set
C	C	26	*Actresses — 'FROGA A' (c1900)	H.20	£500.00	—

C. & J. LAW, Hertford

Size	Printing	Number in set		Handbook reference	Price per card	Complete set
A	C	25	*Types of British Soldiers (c1914)	H.144	£30.00	—
A	U	50	War Portraits (1916)	H.86	£100.00	—

R.J. LEA LTD, Manchester

Size	Printing	Number in set		Handbook reference	Price per card	Complete set
A	C	1	*Advertisement Card — Swashbuckler (c1913)		—	£1000.00
A1	C	50	Chairman Miniatures 1-50 (1912):			
			A No border		£3.00	£150.00
			B Gilt border		£3.00	£150.00
			Album		—	£40.00
A1	C	50	Chairman and Vice Chair Miniatures, 51-100 (1912)		£3.00	£150.00
—	C	1	Chairman Puzzles Picture No 1 (diamond shaped			
			54 x 31mm) (c1910)	H.755	£300.00	—
—	C	12	Chairman Puzzles Picture No 2 (60 x 21mm)			
			(c1910)	H.755	£300.00	—
A1	BW	25	Chairman War Portraits (marked 'War Series' on front)			
			(1915)		£5.00	£125.00

R.J. LEA LTD, Manchester (continued)

Size	Printing	Number in set	Description	Handbook reference	Price per card	Complete set
A	C	70	Cigarette Transfers (Locomotives) (1916)		£9.00	—
A	BW	25	Civilians of Countries Fighting with the Allies (1914)		£13.00	£325.00
		48	Coronation Souvenir (1937):			
A2	P		A Small size, glossy:			
			1 Lea's name		60p	£30.00
			2 'Successors to ...'		40p	£20.00
A2	BW		B Small size, matt:			
			1 Lea's name		£1.00	£50.00
			2 Successors to		50p	£25.00
—	P		C Medium size (77 x 51mm)		60p	£30.00
A2	C	50	Dogs (1923):			
			1 Nos. 1-25 — A White card		£4.40	—
			B Cream card		£4.40	—
			2 Nos. 26-50		£6.40	—
A2	C	25	English Birds (1922):			
			A Glossy front		£3.20	£80.00
			B Matt front		£6.00	—
A2	C	25	The Evolution of the Royal Navy (1925)		£2.40	£60.00
A2	P	54	Famous Film Stars (1939)		£1.30	£70.00
	CP	48	Famous Racehorses of 1926 (1927):			
A2			A Small size ...		£3.00	£150.00
			B Medium size (75 x 50mm)		£8.00	—
		48	Famous Views (1936):			
A2	P		A Small size — 1 Glossy		30p	£15.00
	BW		2 Matt		£1.00	£50.00
—	P		B Medium size (76 x 51mm)		50p	£25.00
A2	P	36	Film Stars — 'A First Series ...' (1934)		£3.40	£120.00
A2	P	36	Film Stars — 'A Second Series ...' (1934)		£3.00	£110.00
A2	C	25	Fish (1926)		£2.40	£60.00
A1	C	50	Flowers to Grow (The Best Perennials) (1913)		£4.00	£200.00
A2		48	Girls from the Shows (1935):			
	P		A Glossy front		£2.20	£110.00
	BW		B Matt front		£2.50	£125.00
			Album		—	£40.00
A1	C	50	Modern Miniatures (1913)	H.756	—	£390.00
			46 different, less 1, 8, 12, 32		£1.90	£90.00
A1	C	12	More Lea's Smokers (1906):	H.256		
			A Green borders		£80.00	—
			B Red borders		£120.00	—
			Album		—	£50.00
A1	C	50	Old English Pottery and Porcelain, 1-50 (1912)		£2.00	£100.00
			Album		—	£35.00
A1	C	50	Old Pottery and Porcelain, 51-100 (1912):			
			A 'Chairman Cigarettes'		£1.60	£80.00
			B 'Recorder Cigarettes'		£6.00	—
			Album		—	£35.00
A1	C	50	Old Pottery and Porcelain, 101-150 (1912):			
			A 'Chairman Cigarettes'		£1.60	£80.00
			B 'Recorder Cigarettes'		£6.00	—
			Album		—	£35.00
A1	C	50	Old Pottery and Porcelain, 151-200 (1913)		£1.60	£80.00
			Album		—	£35.00
A1	C	50	Old Pottery and Porcelain, 201-250 (1913)		£1.60	£80.00
			Album		—	£35.00
—	C	24	Old English Pottery and Porcelain (138 x 89mm) ...	H.257	£6.00	—
			(Inscribed Chairman Cigarette Series or other firms' names, postcard format back) (c1910)			

R. J. LEA LTD, Manchester (continued)

A2		54	Radio Stars (1935):			
	P		A Glossy front		£2.20	£120.00
	BW		B Matt front		£3.00	£160.00
A2	C	50	Roses (1924)		£1.80	£90.00
A2	C	50	Ships of the World (1925)		£1.90	£95.00
A	BW	25	War Pictures (1915)		£4.40	£110.00
		48	Wonders of the World (1938):			
A2	P		A Small size — 1 Glossy		60p	£30.00
	BW		2 Matt		£1.40	£65.00
	P		B Medium size (76 x 50mm)		60p	£30.00

SILKS. All paper-backed.

—	C		*Butterflies and Moths III (c1925):	H.505-7		
		12	1 Small size (70 x 44mm)		£4.50	£55.00
		12	2 Large size (70 x 88mm)		£4.00	£50.00
		6	3 Extra-large size (143 x 70mm)		£4.50	£27.00
—	C	54	*Old Pottery — Set 1 (68 x 38mm) (c1915)	H.505-14	£1.00	£55.00
—	C	72	*Old Pottery — Set 2 (61 x 37mm) (c1915)	H.505-14	£1.00	£75.00
—	C	50	Regimental Crests and Badges — Series I (48mm sq.) (c1920)	H.502-4	£1.80	—
—	C	50	Regimental Crests and Badges — Series II (48 mm sq.) (c1920)	H.502-4	£2.00	—

ALFRED L. LEAVER, London

—	U	12	Manikin Cards (79 x 51mm) (c1925)	H.481	£150.00	—

J. LEES, Northampton

A	C	? 21	Northampton Town Football Club (No. 301-321) (c1912)		£120.00	—

A. LEWIS & CO. (WESTMINSTER) LTD, London

A2	C	52	Horoscopes (1938)	H.587	80p	£42.00

H.C. LLOYD & SON, Exeter

A	U	28	Academy Gems (c1900):	H.258		
			A Red-brown tint		£50.00	—
			B Purple tint		£50.00	—
			C Green tint		£50.00	—
D	BW	? 26	*Actresses and Boer War Celebrities (c1900)	H.260	£45.00	—
—	BW		*Devon Footballers and Boer War Celebrities (c1901):	H.259		
		? 42	Set 1 — Without framelines (70 x 41mm)		£50.00	—
		? 6	Set 2 — With framelines (70 x 45mm)		£225.00	—
A1	C	25	*Star Girls — 'Tipsy Loo Cigarettes' (c1898):	H.30		
			A Brand name in capitals:			
			i Black		£400.00	—
			ii Blue		£400.00	—
			iii Red		£400.00	—
			B Brand name in upper and lower case		£400.00	—
—	BW	36	War Pictures (73 x 69mm) (c1914)		£325.00	—

RICHARD LLOYD & SONS, London

Most cards inscribed 'Branch of Cope Bros. & Co., Ltd.' See also under 'Cope Bros'.

A	C	25	Atlantic Records (1936)		£3.00	£75.00
—	BW	25	*Boer War Celebrities (35 x 61mm) (1899)	H.261	£40.00	—

RICHARD LLOYD & SONS, London (continued)

Size	Printing	Number in set		Handbook reference	Price per card	Complete set
A2	P	27	Cinema Stars, glossy — 'A Series of 27', Nd. 1-27 (c1934)		£7.00	—
A2	P	27	Cinema Stars, glossy — 'A Series of 27', Nd. 28-54 (c1934)		£2.50	£70.00
A2	P	27	Cinema Stars, glossy — 'Third Series of 27', Nd. 55-81 (1935)		£7.00	—
A2	U	25	Cinema Stars, matt — 'A Series of 25' (c1937)		£2.40	£60.00
A	BW	25	*Famous Cricketers (Puzzle Series) (1930)	H.661	£7.00	—
—	U	? 23	*General Interest — Actresses, Celebrities and Yachts (62 x 39mm) (c1900)	H.262	£100.00	—
Al	C	96	*National Types, Costumes and Flags (c1900)	H.263	£35.00	—
D	C		Old Inns:			
		25	A1 Titled 'Old English Inns' (1923)		£1.60	£40.00
		25	A2 Titled 'Old Inns — Series 2' (1924)		£3.00	£75.00
		50	B Titled 'Old Inns' (1925)		£1.60	£80.00
A	C	10	*Scenes from San Toy* (c1905)	H.462	£11.00	£110.00
A	BW	25	Tricks and Puzzles (1935)		£1.00	£25.00
A2	U	25	Types of Horses (1926):			
			A Back in light brown		£4.00	£100.00
			B Back in dark brown		£4.00	£100.00
A2	U	25	'Zoo' Series (1926)	H.588	£1.00	£25.00

A. LOWNIE, Abroath

A	C	30	*Army Pictures, Cartoons, etc. (c1916)	H.12	£130.00	—

LUSBY LTD, London

D	C	25	Scenes from Circus Life (c1900)	H.264	£130.00	—

HUGH McCALL, Edinburgh, Glasgow and Aberdeen

C	C	? 1	*RAF Advertisement Card (c1924)	H.594	£400.00	—

D. & J. MACDONALD, Glasgow

A	C	? 10	*Actresses — 'MUTA' (c1891)	H.265	£120.00	—
A	BW	25	*Cricketers (c1902)	H.266	£500.00	—
—	BW	? 24	*Cricket and Football Teams (71 x 69mm) (c1902):	H.267		
			A 'Winning Team' Cigarettes		£500.00	—
			B 'Tontine' Cigarettes		£500.00	—
—	C	? 1	County Cricket Team (71 x 69mm) (1900)	H.267	£2500.00	—

MACKENZIE & CO., Glasgow

—	P	50	*Actors and Actresses (32 x 58mm) (c1902)	H.268	£22.00	—
—	U	50	Victorian Art Pictures — Photogravure (32 x 58mm) (c1908)		£24.00	—
A	BW	50	The Zoo (c1910)		£28.00	—

WM. M'KINNELL, Edinburgh

A	C	12	European War Series (1915)	H.129	£75.00	—
A	U	50	War Portraits (1916)	H.86	£100.00	—

MACNAUGHTON, JENKINS & CO. LTD, Dublin

—	C	50	Castles of Ireland (1924):	H.662		
			A Size 76 x 45mm		£4.00	£200.00
			B Size 74 x 44mm		£4.50	—
D	C	50	Various Uses of Rubber (1924)		£3.00	£150.00

A. McTAVISH, Elgin

Size	Print-ing	Number in set		Handbook reference	Price per card	Complete set
D	C	30	*Army Pictures, Cartoons etc (c1916)	H12	£130.00	—

McWATTIE & SONS, Arbroath

D	C	30	*Army Pictures, Cartoons etc (c1916)	H.12	£130.00	—

THE MANXLAND TOBACCO CO., Isle of Man

D	BW	? 6	*Views in the Isle of Man (c1900):	H.491		
			A Varnished front		£500.00	—
			B Matt front		£500.00	—

MARCOVITCH & CO., London

A2	P	18	*Beauties (anonymous with plain backs, numbered left base of front) (1932)	GP.490	£1.00	£18.00
			The Story in Red and White (1955):	GP.494		
A	U	6	A Standard size		£4.00	—
—	U	7	B Size 75 x 66mm		£2.00	£14.00

MARCUS & CO., Manchester

A	C	? 18	*Cricketers, 'Marcus Handicap Cigarettes' (1895) ...	H.269	£550.00	—
A	C	25	*Footballers and Club Colours (1896)	H.239	£225.00	—
—	BW	1	The Four Generations (Royal Family) (65 x 70mm)			
			(1897)	H.749	—	£350.00

T.W. MARKHAM, Bridgwater

—	BW	? 28	Views of Bridgwater (68 x 42mm) (c1906)	H.709	£120.00	—

MARSUMA LTD, Congleton

A	BW	50	*Famous Golfers and Their Strokes (c1914)		£50.00	—

C. MARTIN, Moseley

D	C	30	*Army Pictures, Cartoons etc. (c1916)	H12	£130.00	—

MARTINS LTD, London

A	C	1	''Arf a Mo', Kaiser!' (c1915)		—	£75.00
—	U		Carlyle Series — folding card (c1918):	H.270		
			A Second page 'Martin Bros.'			
		? 3	i Size 83 x 38mm		£125.00	—
		? 14	ii Size 83 x 78mm		£125.00	—
		? 4	B Third page 'Martin Bros.'		£125.00	—
		? 3	C Second Page 'Martin's Ltd'		£125.00	—
—	U	? 781	The Performer Tobacco Fund Photographs –			
			Celebrities (140 x 88mm) (c1916)		£7.00	—
D	U	25	*VC Heroes (c1916)		£28.00	£700.00

R. MASON & CO., London

C	C	30	*Colonial Troops (c1902)	H.40	£55.00	—
D2	C	40	*Naval and Military Phrases (c1904):	H.14		
			A White Border		£50.00	—
			B No Border		£50.00	—

JUSTUS VAN MAURIK

—	C	12	*Dutch Scenes (108 x 70mm) (c1920)	H.622	£160.00	—

MAY QUEEN CIGARETTES

| | C | 12 | Interesting Pictures (68 x 48mm) (c1960) ... ... | | £1.00 | — |

MENTORS LTD, London

| | C | 32 | Views of Ireland (42 x 67mm) (c1912) ... ... | H.271 | £12.00 | — |

J. MILLHOFF & CO. LTD, London

Size	Print-ing	Number in set	Description	Handbook reference	Price per card	Complete set
	CP		Antique Pottery (1927):			
A2		54	A Small size		90p	£50.00
—		56	B Medium size (74 x 50mm)		80p	£45.00
	C		Art Treasures:			
D		30	A Small size (1927)		£1.00	£30.00
B		50	B Large size (1926)		70p	£35.00
B	C	25	Art Treasures — '2nd Series of 50', Nd. 51-75 (1928)		£1.00	£25.00
B	C	25	England, Historic and Picturesque — 'Series of 25' (1928)		£1.20	£30.00
B	C	25	England, Historic and Picturesque — 'Second Series ...'(1928)		£1.00	£25.00
A2	P	27	Famous Golfers (1928)		£14.00	—
	P	27	Famous 'Test' Cricketers (1928):			
A2			A Small size		£6.00	—
			B Medium size (76 x 51mm)		£6.00	—
—	C	25	Gallery Pictures (76 x 51mm) (1928)		£1.40	£35.00
A2	C	50	'Geographia' Map Series (sectional) (1931)	GP.506	£1.80	£90.00
	CP		The Homeland Series (1933):	GP.333		
A2		54	A Small size		40p	£20.00
—		56	B Medium size (76 x 51mm)		50p	£28.00
A2	P	36	In the Public Eye (1930)		£1.70	£60.00
D	C	25	Men of Genius (1924)		£5.00	£125.00
B	C	25	Picturesque Old England (1931)		£1.40	£35.00
A2	P		Real Photographs:	GP.7		
		27	'A Series of 27' —			
			A Matt front (c1931)		£1.00	£27.00
			B Glossy front (c1931)		40p	£11.00
		27	'2nd Series of 27' (c1931)		80p	£22.00
		27	'3rd Series of 27' (c1932)		40p	£11.00
		27	'4th Series of 27' (c1932)		80p	£22.00
		27	'5th Series of 27' (c1933)		£1.10	£30.00
		27	'6th Series of 27' (c1933)		£1.10	£30.00
C	C	25	Reproductions of Celebrated Oil Paintings (1928) ...	GP.338	£1.60	£40.00
—	U		'RILETTE' Miniature Pictures (60 x 45mm) (c1925):	GP.512		
		20	A Inscribed Series of 20		£3.50	—
		25	B Inscribed Series of 25		£3.50	—
		30	C Inscribed Series of 30		£3.50	—
		42	D Inscribed Series of 42		£3.50	—
		43	E Inscribed Series of 43		£3.50	—
		56	F Inscribed Series of 56		£3.50	—
		74	G Inscribed Series of 74		£3.50	—
B	C	25	Roses (1927)		£3.00	£75.00
			Theatre Advertisement Cards, multi-backed (c1905):			
—	BW	? 9	A Medium size (83 x 56mm)		£180.00	—
—	BW	? 2	B Large size (108 x 83mm)		£250.00	—
A2	C	50	Things to Make — 'De Reszke Cigarettes' (1935) ...		60p	£30.00
A2	C	50	What the Stars Say — 'De Reszke Cigarettes' (1934)		90p	£45.00
A2	P	36	Zoological Studies (1929)		40p	£14.00

MIRANDA LTD, London

Size	Printing	Number in set	Title	Handbook ref	Price per card	Complete set
A	C	20	Dogs (c1925)	H.211	£8.00	—
A	C	25	Sports and Pastimes — Series I (c1925)	H.225	£7.00	£175.00

STEPHEN MITCHELL & SON, Glasgow

Size	Printing	Number in set	Title	Handbook ref	Price per card	Complete set
C	C	51	*Actors and Actresses — Selection from 'FROGA B and C' (c1900)	H.20	£24.00	—
C	U	25	*Actors and Actresses — 'FROGA C' (c1900)	H.20	£24.00	—
C	U	50	*Actors and Actresses — 'FROGA D' (c1900)	H.20	£24.00	—
C	U	26	*Actresses — 'FROGA B' (c1900)	H.20	£24.00	—
A	U	1	Advertisement Card 'Maid of Honour' (c1900)		—	£750.00
A	C	50	Air Raid Precautions (1938)	H.544	£1.00	£50.00
A	C	25	Angling (1928)	H.655	£7.00	£175.00
A	C	50	Arms and Armour (1916)	H.273	£4,00	£200.00
A	C	25	Army Ribbons and Buttons (1916)		£4.00	£100.00
C	BW	25	*Boxer Rebellion — Sketches (c1904)	H.46	£30.00	—
D1	BW	25	British Warships, 1-25 (1915)		£7.00	£175.00
D1	BW	25	British Warships, Second series 26-50 (1915)		£7.00	£175.00
A	C	50	Clan Tartans — 'A Series of 50' (1927)	H.663	£2.00	£100.00
A	C	25	Clan Tartans — '2nd Series, 25' (1927)		£1.20	£30.00
A	C	25	Empire Exhibition, Scotland, 1938 (1938)		£1.00	£25.00
			Album		—	£35.00
A2	C	25	Famous Crosses (1923)		70p	£17.50
A	C	50	Famous Scots (1933)		£2.00	£100.00
A	U	50	First Aid (1938)		£1.40	£70.00
A	U	50	A Gallery of 1934 (1935)		£3.00	£150.00
			Album		—	£40.00
A	U	50	A Gallery of 1935 (1936)		£1.90	£95.00
A	C	50	Humorous Drawings (1924)	H.590	£2.50	£125.00
A	C	50	Interesting Buildings (1905)	H.70	£8.00	£400.00
A	C	40	London Ceremonials (1928)		£1.50	£60.00
A	C	25	Medals (1916)	H.71	£5.00	£125.00
A	C	30	A Model Army (cut-outs) (1932)		£1.20	£36.00
A	C	25	Money (1913)		£5.00	£125.00
A	C	25	Old Sporting Prints (1930)	H.563	£1.60	£40.00
A	U	50	Our Empire (1937)	H.522	50p	£25.00
A	C	25	*Regimental Crests, Nicknames and Collar Badges (1900)	H.274	£14.00	£350.00
A	C	70	River and Coastal Steamers (1925)		£4.00	—
A	C		A Road Map of Scotland (1933):			
		50	A Small numerals		£3.50	£175.00
		50	B Large numerals in circles		£3.50	£175.00
		50	C Overprinted in red		£4.50	£225.00
		1	D Substitute card (Blue)		—	£16.00
A	C	50	Scotland's Story (1929)		£3.00	£150.00
A	C	25	Scottish Clan Series No. 1 (1903)	H.33	£14.00	£350.00
A	U	50	Scottish Football Snaps (1935)		£3.00	£150.00
			Album		—	£40.00
A	U	50	Scottish Footballers (1934)		£3.00	£150.00
			Album		—	£40.00
A	C	25	Seals (1911)		£5.00	£125.00
A	C	25	Sports (1907)	H.275	£15.00	£375.00
A	C	25	Stars of Screen and History (1939)		£2.80	£70.00
A	C	25	Statues and Monuments (l914)		£4.80	£120.00
—	C	25	Village Models Series (1925):	H.664		
A			A Small size		£2.40	£60.00
			B Medium size (68 x 62mm)		£5.00	£125.00

STEPHEN MITCHELL & SON, Glasgow (continued)

Size	Printing	Number in set	Description	Handbook reference	Price per card	Complete set
—	C	25	Village Models Series — 'Second' (1925):	H.664		
A			A Small size:			
			1 Inscribed 'Second Series'		£2.40	£60.00
			2 Not inscribed 'Second Series'		£5.00	—
			B Medium size (68 x 62mm)		£5.00	£125.00
A	U	50	Wonderful Century (1937)		70p	£35.00
A	U	50	The World of Tomorrow (1936)		£1.80	£90.00

MOORGATE TOBACCO CO., London

Size	Printing	Number in set	Description	Handbook reference	Price per card	Complete set
—	BW	30	The New Elizabethan Age (20 small, 10 large) (1953):			
			A Matt front		£3.50	—
			B Varnished front		£2.00	£60.00

B. MORRIS & SONS LTD, London

Size	Printing	Number in set	Description	Handbook reference	Price per card	Complete set
—	BW	30	*Actresses (41 x 68mm) (1898)	H.276	£2.00	£60.00
C	U	26	*Actresses — 'FROGA A (c1900):	H.20		
			A 'Borneo Queen' back		£32.00	—
			B 'Gold Seals' back		£32.00	—
			C 'Morris's Cigarettes' back		£32.00	—
			D 'Tommy Atkins' back		£80.00	—
—	C	? 4	*Actresses — selection from 'FROGA B' — 'Morris's High Class Cigarettes' on front (76 x 66mm) (c1900)	H.20	£1500.00	—
A1	P	1	*Advertisement Card (Soldier and Girl) (c1900)	H.758	—	£2000.00
A1	C	50	Animals at the Zoo (1924):	H.520		
			A Back in blue		80p	£40.00
			B Back in grey		90p	£45.00
A1	C	35	At the London Zoo Aquarium (1928)		50p	£17.50
A1	BW	25	Australian Cricketers (1925)		£4.00	£100.00
A	C	50	*Beauties — 'CHOAB' (c1900):	H.21		
			A 'Gold Flake Honeydew' back		£50.00	—
			B 'Golden Virginia' back		£50.00	—
			C 'Levant Favourites' back		£50.00	—
			D 'Reina Regenta' back		£50.00	—
A	U	? 53	*Beauties — Collotype, multi-backed (c1897)	H.278	£190.00	—
A	U	21	*Beauties — 'MOM' (c1900):	H.277		
			A 'Borneo Queen' back		£32.00	—
			B 'Gold Seals' back		£32.00	—
			C 'Morris's Cigarettes' back		£32.00	—
			D 'Tommy Atkins' back		£80.00	—
A	C	20	Boer War, 1900 (VC Heroes)	H.279	£35.00	—
A	BW	25	*Boer War Celebrities — 'PAM' (c1901)	H.140	£30.00	—
A2	C	25	Captain Blood (1937)		£1.20	£30.00
D	U	50	Film Star Series (1923)		£3.50	—
A	C	30	*General Interest — six cards each entitled (c1910):	H.280		
			i Agriculture in the Orient		£7.00	£42.00
			ii Architectural Monuments		£7.00	£42.00
			iii The Ice Breaker		£7.00	£42.00
			iv Schools in Foreign Countries		£7.00	£42.00
			v Strange Vessels		£7.00	£42.00
D	U	25	Golf Strokes Series (1923)		£6.00	£150.00
A1	—	12	Horoscopes (wording only) (1936):			
			A White card		£1.00	—
			B Cream card		70p	£8.50
A2	C	25	How Films are Made (1934):			
			A White card		£1.20	£30.00
			B Cream Card		£1.40	£35.00

B. MORRIS & SONS LTD, London (continued)

Size	Printing	Number in set		Handbook reference	Price per card	Complete set
A1	BW	50	How to Sketch (1929)		£1.20	£60.00
D	BW	20	London Views (c1905):	H.34		
			A 'American Gold' back		£32.00	−
			B 'Morris's Gold Flake' back		£32.00	−
			C 'Smoke Borneo Queen' back		£32.00	−
			D 'Smoke Reina Regenta' back		£32.00	−
A	C	25	Marvels of the Universe Series (c1912)	H.281	£4.00	£100.00
A1	C	25	Measurement of Time (1924)		£1.40	£35.00
D	U	25	Motor Series (Motor parts) (1922)		£4.40	£110.00
D	C	50	National and Colonial Arms (1917)	H.704	£6.00	£300.00
A1	C	25	The Queen's Dolls' House (1925)		£3.20	£80.00
D	U	25	Racing Greyhounds − 'Issued by Forecasta' (1939)		£1.60	£40.00
A1	BW	24	Shadowgraphs (1925)		£2.60	£65.00
A1	C	13	Treasure Island (1924)		£2.00	£26.00
A1	C	50	Victory Signs (1928)		70p	£35.00
C	U	25	War Celebrities (1915)		£6.00	£150.00
D	C	25	War Pictures (1916)	H.51	£8.00	£200.00
A	C	25	Wax Art Series (1931)		50p	£12.50
A	C	25	Whipsnade Zoo (1932)		60p	£15.00
D	C	25	Wireless Series (1923)		£4.80	£120.00

SILKS

Size		Number		Handbook	Price	Complete
−	C	24	Battleship Crests (70 x 50mm) (paper backed) (c1915)	H.504-3	£35.00	−
−	C		English Flowers (78 x 56mm) (paper backed) (c1915):	H.505-4		
		25	A Series of 25:			
			i Back text 5th line with 'Crewel'		£4.00	−
			ii Back text 5th line overprinted with 'Cruel'		£9.00	−
			iii Back Without 'Crewel' or 'Cruel'		£7.00	−
		50	B Series of 50		£4.50	−
−	C	25	English and Foreign Birds (78 x 56mm) (paper backed) (c1915)	H.505-1	£5.00	£125.00
−	C	25	*Regimental Colours IV (75 x 55m) (unbacked and anonymous (c1915))	H.502-9	£4.00	−
−	C	4	*Regimental Colours (210 x 190mm) (c1915)	H.502-13	£70.00	−

PHILIP MORRIS & CO. LTD, London

Size		Number		Handbook	Price	Complete
	U	50	British Views (1924):			
C			A Small size		£3.00	−
−			B Large size (79 x 67mm)		£3.00	−
C	−	108	Classic Collection (90 x 47mm) (1985)	H.894	£1.25	−
C	−	72	Motormania (75 x 45mm) (1986)		£1.50	−

P. MOUAT & CO., Newcastle-on-Tyne

Size		Number		Handbook	Price	Complete
C	C	30	*Colonial Troops (c1902)	H.40	£300.00	−

MOUSTAFA LTD, London

Size		Number		Handbook	Price	Complete
D2	CP	50	Camera Studies (1923):	GP.541		
			A Front with number and caption, back in black		£3.20	−
			*B Front without letterpress, plain back		£3.20	−
D2	C	25	Cinema Stars − Set 8 (1924)	GP.542	£5.00	−
A2	C	40	Leo Chambers Dogs Heads (1924)		£3.50	£140.00
D2	C	25	Pictures of World Interest (1923)		£3.60	−
A2	P	25	Real Photos (Views) (1925)		44p	£11.00

MUNRO, Glasgow

Size		Number		Handbook	Price	Complete
C	C	30	Colonial Troops (c1900)		£500.00	−

Size	Printing	Number in set	BRITISH TOBACCO ISSUERS	Handbook reference	Price per card	Complete set

B. MURATTI, SONS & CO. LTD, Manchester and London

Size	Print-ing	Number in set		Handbook reference	Price per card	Complete set
—	U	? 24	*Actresses, cabinet size, collotype (106 x 69mm) (c1898)	GP.551	£125.00	—
C	C	26	*Actresses — 'FROGA A' (c1900):	H.20		
			A 'To the Cigarette Connoisseur' back		£27.00	—
			B 'Muratti's Zinnia Cigarettes' back		£35.00	—
—	C		*Actresses and Beauties — Green Corinthian column framework — 'Neb-Ka' vertical backs (117 x 67mm) (c1900):			
		? 18	Actresses — selection from 'FROGA C'	H.20	£160.00	—
		? 3	Beauties — selection from 'MOM'	H.277/GP.555	£300.00	—
—	C		*Actresses and Beauties — brown and yellow ornamental framework (117 x 67mm) (c1900):			
			I 'Neb-Ka' horizontal backs:			
		26	i Actresses — selection from 'FROGA A'	H.20	£140.00	—
		50	ii Beauties — selection from 'CHOAB' ...	H.21	£140.00	—
		25	II Rubber stamped back. Beauties — selection from 'CHOAB'	H.21	£140.00	—
		25	III Plain back — Beauties — selection from 'CHOAB'	H.21	£140.00	—
—	C		*Advertisement Cards, Globe design back (88 x 66mm) (c1900):	GP.552		
		? 10	i Brown borders to front		£400.00	—
		? 19	ii White borders to front		£400.00	—
A2	P	24	Australian Race Horses (export) (c1930)		£1.00	£25.00
C	C	50	*Beauties — 'CHOAB' (Zinnia back) (c1900):	H.21/GP.554		
			A Black printing on back		£45.00	—
			B Olive green printing on back		£60.00	—
—	C	? 66	*Beautiful Women, Globe design back (54 x 75mm) (c1900)	H.284/GP.32	£90.00	—
—	BW	20	*Boer War Generals — 'CLAM' (35 x 61mm) (c1901)	H.61/GP.556	£38.00	—
—	C	15	*Caricatures (42 x 62mm) (c1903):	GP.558		
			A 'Sole Manufacturers of ...' brown back		£30.00	—
			B 'Muratti's Zinnia Cigarettes' brown back		£32.00	—
			C 'Muratti's Zinnia Cigarettes' black back		£30.00	—
			D 'Muratti's Vassos Cigarettes' (not seen)		—	—
			E As D, but 'Vassos' blocked out, brown back ...		£50.00	—
—	C	35	Crowned Heads (53 x 83mm) (c1913)		£14.00	—
C	C	52	*Japanese Series, Playing Card inset (c1904)	GP.560	£17.00	—
			Plain back		£15.00	—
—	P		Midget Post Card Series (1902):	GP.561		
		? 124	A Matt Front (90 x 70mm)		£11.00	—
		? 18	B Matt Front (80 x 65mm)		£11.00	—
			C Glossy front (85 x 65mm few 75-80 x 65mm):			
		? 96	i With serial numbers		£11.00	—
		? 136	ii Without serial numbers		£11.00	—
—	P	? 127	'Queens' Post Card Series (90 x 70mm) (c1902):	GP.562		
			A Front in black/sepia		£15.00	—
			B Front in reddish brown		£15.00	—
A1	BW	19	*Russo-Japanese Series (1904)	H.184/GP.563	£15.00	£285.00
A1	C	25	*Star Girls (c1898)	H.30	£250.00	—
A	U	? 51	*Views of Jersey (c1912):	GP.564		
			A Plain back		£18.00	—
			B 'Opera House, Jersey' back		£19.00	—
A	U	25	*War Series — 'MURATTI I', white card (1916)	GP.565	£22.00	—
A	U	50	*War Series — 'MURATTI II', toned card (1917)			
			Nos. 1-25 (and alternative cards)	H.290/GP.566	£14.00	—

B. MURATTI, SONS & CO. LTD, Manchester and London (continued)

SILKS

—	C		*Flags — Set 3 (70 x 52mm) (paper backed) (c1915):		
		25	1st Series — Series C, Nd. 20-44	GP.579	£3.75	—
		24	2nd Series:		
			Series A, Nd. 26-49	GP.578	£3.75	—
			Series E, Nd. 48-72, paper backing in grey (No.		
			52 unissued)	GP.582	£3.75	—
			Series E, Nd. 48-72, paper backing in green (No.		
			52 unissued)	GP.582	£3.75	—
—	C		*Flags — Set 8 (paper backed) (c1915):		
		3	Series A, Nd. 1-3 (89 x 115mm)	GP.577	£10.00	—
		1	Series B, Nd. 19 (70 x 76mm)	GP.586	—	£12.00
		18	Series C, Nd. 1-18 (89 x 115mm)	GP.580	£10.00	—
		3	Series D, Nd. 45-47 (89 x 115mm)	GP.581	£10.00	—
		6	Series F, Nd. 73-78 (89 x 115mm)	GP.583	£10.00	—
—	C	18	*Great War Leaders — Series P (89 x 115mm) (paper		
			backed) (c1916)	GP.584	£15.00	—
—	C		*Regimental Badges I (paper backed) (c1915):	H.502-1	
		25	Series A, Nd. 1-25 (70 x 52mm)	GP.585	£4.50	—
		48	Series B, Nd. I-48 (76 x 70mm)	GP.587	£6.00	—
		15	Series B, Nd. 4-18 (76 x 70mm)	GP.586	£6.00	—
		16	Series G, Nd. 79-94 (76 x 70mm)	GP.588	£8.00	—
—	C	25	*Regimental Colours I — Series CB (76 x 70mm)		
			(paper backed) (c1915)	GP.589	£10.00	—
—	C	72	*Regimental Colours V — Series RB (70 x 52 mm)		
			(paper backed) (c1915)	GP.590	£6.00	—

CANVASES. Unbacked canvases. The material is not strictly canvas, but a linen fabric glazed to give the
tappearance of canvas.

—	C	40	Canvas Masterpieces — Series M (71 x 60mm)		
			(c1915):	H.509/GP.575	
			A Shaded back design, globe 12mm diam		£5.50	—
			B Unshaded back design, globe 6mm diam		£2.50	£100.00
—	C	16	Canvas Masterpieces — Series P (114 x 90mm)		
			(c1915)		£12.00	—

MURRAY, SONS & CO. LTD, Belfast

A	BW	20	*Actresses — 'BLARM' (c1900):	H.23		
			A 'Pineapple Cigarettes' back		£90.00	—
			B 'Special Crown Cigarettes' back		£100.00	—
D1	P	22	Bathing Beauties (1929)		£6.00	—
A1	BW	40	Bathing Belles (1939)	H.592	40p	£16.00
C	C	15	Chess and Draughts Problems — Series F (1912) ...	H.291	£90.00	—
D1	P	22	Cinema Scenes (1929)		£6.00	—
A	BW	54	*Cricketers and Footballers — Series H (c1912):	H.292		
			20 Cricketers. A Thick card		£75.00	—
			B Thin card		£75.00	—
			C Brown Printing		£175.00	—
			34 Footballers. A Thick card		£50.00	—
			B Thin card		£50.00	—
A1	BW	25	Crossword Puzzles (c1925)		£300.00	—
D1	P	26	Dancers (1929)		£5.00	—
D	P		Dancing Girls (1929):		
		25	A 'Belfast-Ireland' at base		£3.40	£85.00
		25	B 'London & Belfast' at base		£3.40	£85.00
		26	C Inscribed 'Series of 26'		£3.40	

MURRAY, SONS & CO. LTD, Belfast (continued)

Size	Printing	Number in set		Handbook reference	Price per card	Complete set
—	C	? 29	Football Flags (shaped) (60 x 32mm) (c1905):	H.759		
			A Maple Cigarettes		£70.00	—
			B Murray's Cigarettes		£70.00	—
C	C	25	*Football Rules (c1911)		£30.00	—
A	BW	104	*Footballers — Series J (c1910)	H.293	£50.00	—
A	C	20	Holidays by the LMS (1927)	H.593	£10.00	—
A1	C	20	Inventors Series (1924)	H.213	£5.00	£100.00
C	U	25	*Irish Scenery Nd. 101-125 (1905):			
			A 'Hall Mark Cigarettes'		£22.00	—
			B 'Pine Apple Cigarettes'		£22.00	—
			C 'Special Crown Cigarettes'		£22.00	—
			D 'Straight Cut Cigarettes'		£22.00	—
			E 'Yachtsman Cigarettes'		£22.00	—
C	BW	25	Polo Pictures — E Series (1911)	H.294	£28.00	—
—	U	50	Prominent Politicians — B Series (41 x 70mm) (1909):	H.295		
			A Without '... in two strengths' in centre of back		£18.00	—
			B With '... in two strengths' in centre of back ...		£3.00	£150.00
—	C	50	Puzzle Series (1925):	H.660		
A1			A With coupon attached at top		£20.00	—
			B Without coupon		£8.00	—
C	U	25	Reproduction of Famous Works of Art — D Series			
			(1910)	H.296	£25.00	£625.00
C	U	24	Reproductions of High Class Works of Art — C Series			
			(1910)	H.297	£25.00	£600.00
D2	C	50	Stage and Film Stars — 'Erinmore Cigarettes'			
			(c1926)		£4.00	£200.00
A1	BW	25	Steam Ships (1939)		£1.60	£40.00
A1	C	50	The Story of Ships (1940)		40p	£20.00
A2	C	25	Types of Aeroplanes (1929)		£1.40	£35.00
C	C	20	Types of Dogs (1924):	H.211		
			A Normal back		£7.00	—
			B Normal back, with firm's name rubber-stamped			
			in red		£7.00	—
A1	C	35	*War Series — Series K (1915)	H.298	£27.00	—
C2	U	25	*War Series — Series L, Nd. 100-124 (c1916):			
			A Sepia		£4.00	£100.00
			B Grey-brown		£4.00	—
			C Purple-brown		£4.00	—

SILKS

Size	Printing	Number in set		Handbook reference	Price per card	Complete set
—	C	? 16	*Flags, small (70 x 42mm) — 'Polo Mild Cigarettes'			
			(plain paper backing) (c1915)	H.498-1	£20.00	—
—	C	? 3	*Flags and Arms, large (102 x 71mm) — 'Polo Mild			
			Cigarettes' (plain paper backing) (c1915)	H.498-2	£65.00	—
—	C	? 31	*Orders of Chivalry II, 'Series M' (70 x 42mm) (paper			
			backed, Nd. 35-65) (c1915)	H.504-15	£18.00	—
—	C	? 25	*Regimental Badges (70 x 42mm) — 'Polo Mild			
			Cigarettes' (plain paper backing) (c1915)	H.498-3	£18.00	—

H.J. NATHAN, London

Size	Printing	Number in set		Handbook reference	Price per card	Complete set
D	C	40	Comical Military and Naval Pictures (c1905):	H.14		
			A White Border		£60.00	—
			B No Border		£60.00	—

JAMES NELSON, London

Size	Printing	Number in set		Handbook reference	Price per card	Complete set
A	P	? 23	*Beauties — 'FENA' (c1899)	H.148	£1000.00	—

NETTLETON AND MITCHELL, Ossett

Size	Print-ing	Number in set		Handbook reference	Price per card	Complete set
A	C	30	*Army Pictures, Cartoons, etc. (c1916)	H.12	£150.00	—

THE NEW MOSLEM CIGARETTE CO., London

D	C	30	*Proverbs (c1902)	H.15	£110.00	—

E.J. NEWBEGIN, Sunderland

—	P	50	*Actors and Actresses (39 x 60mm) (c1902)	H.299	£55.00	—
A	BW	10	*Actresses — 'HAGG A' (c1900)	H.24	£180.00	—
D	C	? 4	Advertisement Cards (c1900)	H.761	£1000.00	—
A	BW	20	Cricketers Series (1901)	H.29	£500.00	—
A	BW	19	*Russo-Japanese Series (1904)	H.184	£150.00	—
D	C	12	Well-Known Proverbs (c1905)	H.235	£150.00	—
D	C	25	Well-Known Songs (c1905)	H.300	£150.00	—

W.H. NEWMAN, Birmingham

C	C	18	Motor Cycle Series (c1914)	H.469	£110.00	—

THOS. NICHOLLS & CO., Chester

A	C	50	Orders of Chivalry (1916)	H.301	£8.00	£400.00

THE NILMA TOBACCO COY., London

A	C	40	*Home and Colonial Regiments (c1903)	H.69	£120.00	—
D	C	30	*Proverbs (c1903)	H.15	£100.00	—

M.E. NOTARAS LTD, London

A2	P	36	National Types of Beauty (c1925)	GP.625	£1.00	£36.00
—	U	24	*Views of China (68 x 43mm) (1925)		80p	£20.00

A. NOTON, Sheffield

—	U	12	'Manikin' Cards (79 x 51mm) (c1920)	H.481	£120.00	—

OGDENS LTD, Liverpool

333 page reference book (updated paperback 2015 Edition) – £24.00

Home Issues (*excluding 'Guinea Gold' and 'Tabs', but including some early issued abroad*).

A	C	25	ABC of Sport (1927)		£3.20	£80.00
A	C	50	Actors — Natural and Character Studies (1938)	H.571-1	£1.00	£50.00
C	C	25	*Actresses — coloured, 'Ogden's Cigarettes contain no glycerine' back (c1895):	OG.3		
			A Titled in black		£90.00	—
			B Titled in brown		£90.00	—
D2	U	? 1	*Actresses — green, green borders (c1900)	OG.4	£1000.00	—
D1	U	50	*Actresses — green photogravure (c1900)	OG.5	£12.00	—
D	P	? 589	*Actresses — 'Ogden's Cigarettes' at foot (c1900) ...	OG.6	£3.50	—
D	P		*Actresses and Beauties — collotype (c1895):	OG.12		
		? 83	i named:			
			A *Plain back*		£85.00	—
			B 'Midnight Flake' back		£65.00	—
		? 21	ii unnamed:			
			A *Plain back*		£85.00	—
			B 'Midnight Flake' back:			
			i blue back		£65.00	—
			ii red back		£130.00	—

Size	Printing	Number in set		Handbook reference	Price per card	Complete set

OGDENS LTD, Liverpool (continued)

Size	Print-ing	Number in set		Handbook reference	Price per card	Complete set
D	P		*Actresses and Beauties — collotype, 'Ogden's Cigarettes' back (1895):	OG.12		
		? 54	i named		£65.00	—
		? 45	ii unnamed		£65.00	—
A	P	? 205	*Actresses and Beauties — woodbury-type (c1894)	OG.13	£40.00	—
A	C	50	AFC Nicknames (1933)	H.571-2	£4.50	£225.00
A	C	50	Air-Raid Precautions (1938)	H.544	90p	£45.00
A	C	50	Applied Electricity (1928)		£1.30	£65.00
—	C	192	Army Crests and Mottoes (39 x 59mm) (c1902)	OG.20	£6.00	—
			Album		—	£50.00
A	U	36	Australian Test Cricketers, 1928-29	OG.21	£3.60	£130.00
A	C	28	*Beauties — 'BOCCA' (c1900)	H.39/OG.23	£28.00	—
—	C	50	*Beauties — 'CHOAB' (c1900):	H.21/OG.24		
			Nos 1-25 (size 65 x 36mm)		£30.00	—
			Nos 26-50 (size 67 x 37mm)		£30.00	—
A	C	26	*Beauties — 'HOL' (c1900):	H.192/OG.25		
			A 'Guinea Gold' red rubber stamp back		£250.00	—
			B Blue Castle Design back		£22.00	£570.00
A2	C	52	*Beauties — 'Playing Card' series (c1900):	OG.26		
			A 52 with playing card inset		£32.00	—
			B 26 without playing card inset		£37.00	—
A2	C	52	*Beauties and Military — PC inset (c1898)	OG.29	£32.00	—
—	P	50	Beauty Series, numbered, 'St. Julien Tobacco' (36 x 54mm) (c1900)	OG.30	£3.00	£150.00
D	P	? 83	Beauty Series, unnumbered, issued Australia (c1900)	OG.31	£70.00	—
A	C	50	Billiards, by Tom Newman (1928)	OG.33	£2.50	£125.00
A	C	50	Birds' Eggs (1904):			
			A White back		£2.00	£100.00
			B Toned back		£1.80	£90.00
A	C	50	Bird's Eggs (cut-outs) (1923)		£1.20	£60.00
A	C	50	The Blue Riband of the Atlantic (1929)		£2.50	£125.00
D	P	? 142	*Boer War and General Interest — 'Ogden's Cigar-ettes' at foot (c1900)	OG.38	£3.50	
H2	P	? 68	*Boer War and General Interest — 'Ogden's Cigarettes' at foot (c1900)	OG.38	£45.00	
—	P	? 3	*Boer War & General Interest (Liners) 'Ogdens Cigarettes' at foot (72 x 55mm) (c1900)	OG.38	£175.00	
A	C	50	Boxers (1915)		£7.00	£350.00
A	C	25	Boxing (1914)	H.311/OG.40	£6.00	£150.00
—	C	? 6	*Boxing Girls (165 x 94mm) (c1895)	OG.69	£600.00	—
A	C	50	Boy Scouts (1911):	H.62/OG.41		
			A Blue back		£3.50	£175.00
			B Green back		£5.00	£250.00
A	C	50	Boy Scouts, 2nd series (1912):	H.62/OG.42		
			A Blue back		£3.50	£175.00
			B Green back		£5.00	£250.00
A	C	50	Boy Scouts, 3rd series (1912):	H.62/OG.43		
			A Blue back		£3.50	£175.00
			B Green back		£5.00	£250.00
A	C	50	Boy Scouts, 4th series, green back (1913)		£3.50	£175.00
A	C	25	Boy Scouts, 5th series, green back (1914)		£3.60	£90.00
A	C	50	Boy Scouts (1929)	OG.46	£2.80	£140.00
A	C	50	British Birds:	H.229/OG.47		
			A White back (1905)		£2.00	£100.00
			B Toned back (1906)		£1.80	£90.00
A	C	50	British Birds, Second Series (1908)		£2.20	£110.00
A	C	50	British Birds (Cut-Outs) (1923)	OG.49	£1.00	£50.00

OGDENS LTD, Liverpool (continued)

Size	Print-ing	Number in set		Handbook reference	Price per card	Complete set
A	C	50	British Birds and Their Eggs (1939)	H.571-3	£2.60	£130.00
A	C	50	British Costumes from 100 BC to 1904 (1905)	OG.51	£6.00	£300.00
A	U	50	Broadcasting (1935)	H.571-4	£1.80	£90.00
A	C	50	By the Roadside (1932)		£1.10	£55.00
A	C	44	Captains of Association Football Clubs and Colours (1926)		£3.00	£130.00
A	U	50	Cathedrals and Abbeys (1936):			
			A Cream card		£1.20	£60.00
			B White card		£1.20	£60.00
A	C	50	Champions of 1936 (1937)	H.571-5	£1.80	£90.00
A	C	50	Children of All Nations (cut-outs) (1923)	H.656/OG.58	£1.00	£50.00
A	C	50	Club Badges (1914)		£5.00	£250.00
A	C	50	Colour in Nature (1932)		£1.00	£50.00
—	C	? 27	*Comic Pictures (1890-95) (size varies)	OG.62	£350.00	—
A	C	50	Construction of Railway Trains (1930)		£2.50	£125.00
A	C	50	Coronation Procession (sectional) (1937)	H.571-6	£1.80	£90.00
			Album		—	£40.00
A	U	50	Cricket, 1926		£2.80	£140.00
A2	C	12	*Cricket and Football Terms — Women (c1896)	OG.69	£400.00	—
D2	U	50	*Cricketers and Sportsmen (c1898)	OG.70	£90.00	—
A	C	25	Derby Entrants, 1926		£2.60	£65.00
A	C	50	Derby Entrants, 1928		£2.20	£110.00
A	U	50	Derby Entrants, 1929		£2.40	£120.00
A	C	50	Dogs (1936)	H.571-7	£2.40	£120.00
A	U	28	*Dominoes — Actresses — 'FROGA A' back (c1900):	H.20/OG.75		
			A Mitred corners (7 backs)		£25.00	—
			B Unmitred corners (7 backs)		£25.00	—
A	U	56	*Dominoes — Beauties — 'MOM' back (c1900)	H.277/OG.77	£25.00	—
A2	BW	55	*Dominoes — black back (1909)		£1.80	£100.00
A	C	25	Famous Dirt-Track Riders (1929)		£5.40	£135.00
A	C	50	Famous Footballers (1908)		£4.50	£225.00
A	U	50	Famous Rugby Players (1926-27)		£2.50	£125.00
A	C	50	Flags and Funnels of Leading Steamship Lines (1906)	H.67/OG.81	£4.00	£200.00
A	C	50	Football Caricatures (1935)	H.571-8	£2.60	£130.00
—	C	43	*Football Club Badges (shaped for buttonhole) (c1910)	OG.85	£8.00	—
A	C	50	Football Club Captains (1935)	H.571-9	£2.80	£140.00
			Album		—	£35.00
A	C	51	Football Club Colours (1906):	H.68/OG.86		
			Nos. 1-50		£4.00	£200.00
			No. 51		—	£5.00
A	C	50	Foreign Birds (1924)		90p	£45.00
A	C	50	Fowls, Pigeons and Dogs (1904)	H.64/OG.88	£3.20	£160.00
A	U	25	Greyhound Racing — '1st Series ...' (1927)		£4.40	£110.00
A	U	25	Greyhound Racing — '2nd Series ...' (1928)		£4.40	£110.00
—	C	1	*History of the Union Jack (threefold card) (51 x 37mm closed) (1901)	OG.102	—	£225.00
A	C	50	How to Swim (1935)	H.571-10	£1.00	£50.00
A	BW	50	Infantry Training (1915)	OG.105	£3.00	£150.00
A	C	50	Jockeys, and Owners' Colours (1927)		£2.50	£125.00
A	C	50	Jockeys 1930 (1930)		£2.50	£125.00
A	C	50	Leaders of Men (1924)		£1.80	£90.00
A	C	25	Marvels of Motion (1928)		£2.40	£60.00
K2	C	52	*Miniature Playing Cards — Actresses and Beauties back (c1900):	OG.115		
			I Unnamed, no numeral (76 backs known)		£5.00	—
			II Unnamed, 'numeral 40' (26 backs known) ...		£5.00	—
			III Named, 'numeral 46' (26 backs known)		£5.00	—
			IV Named, no numeral (26 backs known)		£5.00	—

OGDENS LTD, Liverpool (continued)

Size	Printing	Number in set	Description	Handbook reference	Price per card	Complete set
K2	C	52	*Miniature Playing Cards, blue Tabs 'Shield and Flower' design back (1909)	OG.118	£3.00	—
K2	C	52	*Miniature Playing Cards, yellow 'Coolie Cut Plug' design back:	OG.116		
			A Yellow back (1904)		£3.00	—
			B Yellow back with white border (1904)		£4.00	—
A	C	50	Modern British Pottery (1925)		£1.10	£55.00
A	C	50	Modern Railways (1936)	H.571-11	£2.20	£110.00
A	BW	50	Modern War Weapons (1915):	OG.122		
			A Original numbering		£3.50	£175.00
			B Numbering re-arranged		£11.00	—
A	C	25	Modes of Conveyance (1927)		£2.40	£60.00
A	C	50	Motor Races 1931 (1931)		£2.80	£140.00
A	C	50	Ocean Greyhounds (1938)	H.571-12	£1.20	£60.00
A	C	25	Optical Illusions (1923)	H.560/OG.127	£3.40	£85.00
A	C	50	Orders of Chivalry (1907)		£3.50	£175.00
A	C	25	Owners, Racing Colours and Jockeys (1914)		£4.00	£100.00
A	C	50	Owners, Racing Colours and Jockeys (1906)		£3.20	£160.00
A	C	25	Picturesque People of the Empire (1927)		£1.40	£35.00
A	U	50	Picturesque Villages (1936)		£1.40	£70.00
A	C	25	Poultry (1915):			
			A 'Ogden's Cigarettes' on front		£5.40	£135.00
			B Without 'Ogden's Cigarettes' on front		£5.40	£135.00
A	C	25	Poultry, 2nd series, as 'B' above (1916)		£5.40	£135.00
A	C	25	Poultry Alphabet (1924)		£4.40	£110.00
A	C	25	Poultry Rearing and Management — '1st Series ...' (1922)		£3.00	£75.00
A	C	25	Poultry Rearing and Management — '2nd Series ...' (1923)		£3.00	£75.00
A	U	50	Prominent Cricketers of 1938 (1938)	H.571-13	£2.50	£125.00
A	C	50	Prominent Racehorses of 1933 (1934)	H.571-l4	£2.00	£100.00
A	C	25	Pugilists and Wrestlers, Nd. 1-25 (1908)		£5.60	£140.00
A	C	25	Pugilists and Wrestlers, Nd.26-50:			
			A White back (1909)		£5.60	£140.00
			B Toned back (1908)		£5.60	£140.00
A	C	25	Pugilists and Wrestlers, 2nd series, Nd. 51-75 (1909)		£6.00	£150.00
A	U	50	Pugilists in Action (1928)		£3.60	£180.00
A	C	50	Racehorses (1907)		£3.80	£190.00
A	C	50	Racing Pigeons (1931)		£4.00	£200.00
A	C	25	Records of the World (1908)		£3.20	£80.00
A	C	50	Royal Mail (1909)	H.82/OG.147	£4.20	£210.00
A	C	50	Sea Adventure (1939)	H.571-15	50p	£25.00
A	C	50	Sectional Cycling Map (1910)	H.74/OG.150	£3.20	£160.00
A	C	50	*Shakespeare Series (c1903):	OG.151		
			A Unnumbered		£13.00	£650.00
			B Numbered		£13.00	£650.00
A	C	50	Shots from the Films (1936)	H.571-16	£2.00	£100.00
A	U	25	Sights of London (1923)		£2.00	£50.00
A	C	50	Smugglers and Smuggling (1932)		£2.20	£110.00
A	C		Soldiers of the King (1909):	OG.156		
		50	A Grey printing on front		£5.00	£250.00
		25	B Brown printing on front		£6.00	—
A	U	50	Steeplechase Celebrities (1931)		£2.00	£100.00
A	C	50	Steeplechase Trainers, and Owners' Colours (1927)		£2.00	£100.00
A	C	50	The Story of Sand (1934)		£1.00	£50.00
A	C	50	Swimming, Diving and Life-Saving (1931)	H.523/OG.161	£1.50	£75.00

OGDENS LTD, Liverpool (continued)

Size	Printing	Number in set	Description	Handbook reference	Price per card	Complete set
D	C	25	*Swiss Views, Nd. 1-25 (c1905)		£4.00	£100.00
D	C	25	*Swiss Views, Nd. 26-50 (c1905)		£5.00	£125.00
A	C	25	Trainers, and Owners' Colours — '1st Series ...' (1925)		£2.60	£65.00
A	C	25	Trainers, and Owners' Colours — '2nd Series ...' (1926)		£3.20	£80.00
A	C	50	Trick Billiards (1934)	H.571-17	£1.60	£80.00
A	C	50	Turf Personalities (1929)		£2.40	£120.00
D	C	48	Victoria Cross Heroes (1901)	OG.168	£16.00	£800.00
A	C	25	Whaling (1927)		£3.00	£75.00
A	C	50	Yachts and Motor Boats (1930)		£2.50	£125.00
A	C	50	Zoo Studies (1937)	H.571-18	60p	£30.00

'GUINEA GOLD' SERIES

(The Set ...S and X numbers represent the reference numbers quoted in the original Ogden's Reference Book).

Size	Printing	Number in set	Description	Handbook reference	Price per card	Complete set
D	P	1148	1-1148 Series (c1901):	OG.330S		
			Nos. 1-200		80p	£160.00
			Nos. 201-500		£1.70	—
			Nos. 501-900, excl. 523 and 765		£1.40	—
			Nos. 901-1000, excl. 940, 943, 947 and 1000		£2.00	—
			Nos. 1001-1148, excl. 1003, 1006-8, 1024, 1030, 1033, 1034, 1037, 1040, 1042, 1048, 1066, 1081, 1082, 1088		£2.00	—
			Scarce Nos: 523, 940, 943, 947, 1000, 1003, 1007, 1008, 1024, 1030, 1033, 1034, 1037, 1040, 1042, 1048, 1066, 1088		£65.00	—
			Very scarce Nos. 765, 1006, 1081, 1082		—	—
D	CP	?	Selected numbers from 1-1148 Series (c1900)		£5.00	—
D	P		400 New Series I (c1902)		£1.25	£500.00
D	P		400 New Series B (c1902)		£1.50	£600.00
D	P		300 New Series C (c1902)		£1.20	£360.00
D	P	? 323	Set 73S Base B Actresses (c1900)	OG.340S	£3.00	—
			Set 75S Base D (c1900):	OG.350S		
D	P	? 318	List DA — White Panel Group		£1.20	—
D	P	? 58	List DB — The Denumbered Group		£2.75	—
D	P	? 62	List DC — The Political Group		£1.30	—
D	P	? 193	List DD — Boer War etc		£1.20	—
D	P	? 46	List DE — Pantomime and Theatre Group		£4.00	—
D	P	? 376	List DF — Actors and Actresses		£1.50	—
D	P	? 40	Set 76S Base E Actors and Actresses (c1900)	OG.355S	£3.75	—
D	P	? 59	Set 77S Base F Boer War etc (c1901)	OG.360S	£1.20	—
			Set 78S Base I (c1900):	OG.365S		
			List IA — The small Machette Group:			
D	P	83	I Actors and Actresses		£1.30	—
D	P	14	II London Street Scenes		£3.50	—
D	P	32	III Turner Pictures		£2.00	—
D	P	11	IV Cricketers		£14.00	—
D	P	18	V Golf		£25.00	—
D	P	10	VI Views and Scenes Abroad		£1.75	—
D	P	30	VII Miscellaneous		£1.30	—
D	P	639	List IB — The Large Machette Group		£1.30	—
D	P	5	List IC — The White Panel Group		£5.00	—
D	P	30	Set 79S Base J Actresses (c1900)	OG.370S	£4.00	—
D	P	238	Set 80S Base K Actors and Actresses (c1900)	OG.375S	£3.00	—
D	P	216	Set 81S Base L Actors and Actresses (c1900)	OG.380S	£2.50	—

OGDENS LTD, Liverpool ('Guinea Gold' Series continued)

Size	Print-ing	Number in set		Handbook reference	Price per card	Complete set
			Set 82S Base M (c1901):	OG.385S		
D	P	3	List Ma Royalty		£3.00	£9.00
D	P	77	List Mb Cricketers		£28.00	—
D	P	50	List Mc Cyclists		£6.00	—
D	P	150	List Md Footballers		£23.00	—
D	P	50	List Me Pantomime and Theatre Group		£6.50	—
D	P	33	List Mf Footballers and Cyclists		£15.00	—
D	P	27	List Mg Boer War and Miscellaneous		£1.20	—
D	P ?	2951	List Mh Actors and Actresses		£1.30	—

Guinea Gold Series, Large and Medium

Size	Print-ing	Number in set		Handbook reference	Price per card	Complete set
H	P	77	Set 73X Actresses Base B (c1900)	OG.340X	£18.00	—
H2	P	1	Set 74X Actress Base C (c1900)	OG.345X	—	£50.00
—	P	55	Set 75X Base D List DX1 medium size (73 x 55mm) (c1901)	OG.350X	£15.00	—
			Set 75X Base D large size (c1901):	OG.350X		
H	P	50	List DB – The Denumbered Group		£3.00	—
H	P	158	List DD – Boer War etc.		£2.00	—
H	P	45	List DE – Pantomime and Theatre Group		£6.00	—
H	P	270	List DX2 – Actors and Actresses		£2.00	—
H	P	24	Set 78X Actresses Base I (c1900)	OG.365X	£40.00	—
H	P	406	Set 82X Actors, Actresses, Boer War Etc Base M (c1901)	OG.385X	£2.00	—

'TABS' SERIES

(The listing includes both home and overseas 'Tabs' issues.)

Size	Print-ing	Number in set		Handbook reference	Price per card	Complete set
D	BW	200	*Actresses (c1900)	OG.7	£2.75	—
D	BW	200	*Actresses and Foreign Views (c1900)	OG.14	£2.30	—
D	BW ?	331	*Composite Tabs Series, with 'Labour Clause' (1901)	OG.63		
		1	General de Wet		—	£5.00
		1	General Interest		—	£6.00
		17	Heroes of the Ring		£7.50	—
		1	HM the Queen		—	£5.00
		2	HRH the Prince of Wales		£4.00	£8.00
		14	Imperial Interest		£1.20	£17.00
		106	Imperial or International Interest		£1.20	—
		3	International Interest		£2.00	£6.00
		14	International Interest or a Prominent British Officer		£1.20	£17.00
		22	Leading Athletes		£3.00	—
		15	Leading Favourites of the Turf		£4.50	—
		54	Leading Generals at the War		£1.20	£65.00
		2	Members of Parliament		£3.50	£7.00
		11	Notable Coursing Dogs		£7.50	—
		12	Our Leading Cricketers		£15.00	—
		17	Our Leading Footballers		£10.00	—
		37	Prominent British Officers		£1.20	£42.00
		1	The Yacht 'Columbia'		—	£7.00
		1	The Yacht 'Shamrock'		—	£7.00
D	BW ?	71	*Composite Tabs Series, without 'Labour Clause' (c1900):	OG.64		
		40	General Interest		£26.00	—
		31	Leading Artists of the Day		£22.00	—
D	BW ?	114	*Composite Tabs Series, Sydney issue (c1900):	OG.65		
		1	Christian de Wet		£10.00	—
		1	Corporal G. E. Nurse, VC		£10.00	—
		15	English Cricketer Series		£60.00	—
		1	Imperial Interest		£10.00	—

OGDENS LTD, Liverpool ('Tabs' Series continued)

Size	Printing	Number in set		Handbook reference	Price per card	Complete set
			*Composite Tabs Series, Sydney issue (continued):			
		29	Imperial or International Interest		£8.00	—
		6	International Interest		£8.00	—
		1	Lady Sarah Wilson		£10.00	—
		41	Leading Generals at the War		£8.00	—
		13	Prominent British Officers		£8.00	—
D	BW	150	General Interest, Series 'A' (1901)	OG.89	£1.10	—
D	BW	200	General Interest, Series 'B' (1902)	OG.90	£1.00	£200.00
D	BW	470	General Interest, Series 'C' (1902):			
			C.1-200	OG.91	£1.00	£200.00
			C.201-300		£2.20	
			C.301-350		£1.20	£60.00
			No Letter, Nd 1-120		£1.20	
D	BW	200	General Interest, Series 'D' (1902)	OG.92	£1.00	£200.00
D	BW	120	General Interest, Series 'E' (1902)	OG.93	£1.20	—
D	BW	420	General Interest, Series 'F' (1902):	OG.94		
			F.1-200		£1.40	
			F.201-320		£1.40	
			F.321-420		£3.00	—
D	BW ?	400	General Interest, Sydney issue (c1902):	OG.99		
			Nd 1-100 on front		£3.00	—
			Nd 101-400 on back		£3.00	—
	?	106	Unnumbered, mostly similar numbered cards			
			101-200		£6.00	—
D	BW	196	*General Interest, unnumbered, similar style			
			C.201-300 (1902):	OG.95		
			76 Stage Artistes		£1.20	—
			41 Celebrities		£1.20	—
			56 Footballers		£2.50	—
			23 Miscellaneous		£1.20	—
D	BW	100	*General Interest, unnumbered, similar style			
			C.301-350 (1902):	OG.96		
			28 Actresses		£1.20	—
			40 Castles		£1.20	—
			12 Dogs		£1.25	—
			20 Miscellaneous		£2.00	—
D	BW	300	*General Interest, unnumbered, similar style			
			F.321-420 (1903):	OG.97		
			A 100 with full stop after caption		£1.40	£140.00
			B Without full stop after caption:			
			79 I Stage Artistes		£1.20	—
			21 II Cricketers		£10.00	—
			25 III Football		£6.00	—
			15 IV Golf		£22.00	—
			10 V Cyclists		£5.00	—
			9 VI Fire Brigades		£5.00	—
			5 VII Aldershot Gymnasium		£3.00	£15.00
			36 VIII Miscellaneous		£1.20	—
D	BW ?	111	*General Interest, 'oblong' back (c1900)	OG.98	£15.00	
D	BW	? 75	*Leading Artistes of the Day, numbered 126-200, plain			
			backs (c1900)	H.1/OG.109	£14.00	—
D	BW	? 71	Leading Artistes of the Day with 'Labour Clause'			
			(c1900):	OG.110		
			A Type-set back		£1.40	
			B Plain back		£20.00	—

OGDENS LTD, Liverpool ('Tabs' Series continued)

Size	Print-ing	Number in set		Handbook reference	Price per card	Complete set
D	BW	? 25	Leading Artistes of the Day, without 'Labour Clause' (c1900):	OG.111-1		
			A With caption, type-set back … … … … … …		£15.00	—
			B With caption, plain back … … … … … … … …		£15.00	—
			C Without caption, type-set back … … … … …		£15.00	—
D	BW	? 91	Leading Artistes of the Day, without 'Labour Clause' (c1900):	OG.111-2		
			A Type-set back … … … … … … … … … … …		£12.00	—
			B Plain back … … … … … … … … … … … …		£12.00	—
D	BW	25	Leading Generals at the War, with descriptive text (c1900):	OG.112		
			A 'Ogden's Cigarettes' back … … … … … …		£2.00	—
			B 'Ogden's Tab Cigarettes' back … … … … …		£1.40	£35.00
D	BW		Leading Generals at the War, without descriptive text (c1900):	OG.113		
		? 47	A 'Ogden's Tab Cigarettes' back (47 known) …		£1.00	—
		? 25	B 'Ogden's Lucky Star' back (25 known) … … …		£6.00	—
D	BW	50	*Stage Artistes and Celebrities (c1900) … … … … …	OG.157	£3.00	£150.00

OVERSEAS ISSUES

Size	Print-ing	Number in set		Handbook reference	Price per card	Complete set
D2	BW	51	Actresses, black and white Polo issue (1906) … …	OG.10	£3.20	—
D	U	30	Actresses, unicoloured Polo issue (1908):	OG.11		
			A Tin foil at back white … … … … … … … …		£3.00	£90.00
			B Tin foil at back shaded … … … … … … …		£3.40	£100.00
D2	C	17	Animals Polo issue (1916) … … … … … … … …	OG.18	£12.00	—
A1	C	60	Animals — cut-outs:	OG.17		
			A Ruler issue (1912) … … … … … … … …		£3.20	—
			B Tabs issue (1913):			
			i With captions … … … … … … … …		£3.20	—
			ii Without captions … … … … … … …		£4.50	—
D2	C	50	Aviation series Tabs issue (1912):	OG.22		
			A Ogdens at base … … … … … … … …		£7.00	—
			B Ogdens England at base … … … … … …		£8.00	—
			Beauties green net design back 1901:	OG.27		
D	BW	? 66	A Front black & white … … … … … … …		£15.00	—
D	C	? 98	B Front coloured … … … … … … … … …		£28.00	—
D2	C	45	Beauties Picture Hats Polo issue (1911) … … …	OG.28	£6.50	—
D	C	50	Best Dogs of Their Breed Polo issue (1916):	OG.32		
			A Back in red … … … … … … … … … …		£8.00	—
			B Back in blue with Eastern characters … … …		£8.00	—
			C Back in blue without Eastern characters … …		£8.00	—
D	C	52	Birds of Brilliant Plumage Ruler issue (1914):	OG.36		
			A Fronts with framelines … … … … … … …		£3.40	—
			B Fronts without framelines … … … … … …		£3.40	—
A	C	25	British Trees and Their Uses, Guinea Gold issue (1927) … … … … … … … … … … … … …	OG.52	£2.00	£50.00
D	C	25	China's Famous Warriors, Ruler issue (1913) … …	OG.59	£6.00	—
A	C	25	Famous Railway Trains, Guinea Gold issue (1928) …	OG.79	£3.00	£75.00
D2	C	20	Flowers, Polo issue (1915):	OG.82		
			A Without Eastern inscription … … … … … …		£6.00	—
			B With Eastern inscription … … … … … … …		£6.00	—
D2	U	25	Indian Women, Polo issue (1919):	OG.104		
			A Framework in light apple green … … … … …		£6.00	—
			B Framework in dark emerald green … … … …		£6.00	—
—	C	52	Miniature Playing Cards, Polo issue (56 x 38mm) (c1910) … … … … … … … … … … … … …	OG.117	£13.00	—

OGDENS LTD, Liverpool (Overseas Issues continued)

D2	BW		Music Hall Celebrities (1911):	OG.125		
		30	A Polo issue		£6.00	—
		50	B Tabs issue		£6.00	—
A	C	50	Riders of the World, Polo issue (1911)	OG.146	£4.00	—
D2	U	50	Russo-Japanese series (1905)	OG.148	£22.00	—
D2	C	36	Ships and Their Pennants, Polo issue (1911)	OG.153	£6.50	—
D2	C	32	Transport of the World, Polo issue (1917)	OG.165	£6.00	—

THE ORLANDO CIGARETTE & CIGAR CO., London

A	C	40	*Home & Colonial Regiments (c1901)	H.69	£600.00	—

OSBORNE TOBACCO CO. LTD, Portsmouth & London

A	U	50	Modern Aircraft (1953):	H.895		
			A Dark Blue back:			
			i Firm's name in one line		50p	£25.00
			ii Firm's name in two lines		£2.00	—
			B Light Blue back		£1.00	£50.00
			C Brown back		50p	£25.00

W.T. OSBORNE & CO., London

D	C	40	*Naval and Military Phrases (c1904):	H.14		
			A White Border		£45.00	—
			B No Border		£45.00	—

PALMER & CO., Bedford

—	U	12	'Manikin' Cards (79 x 51mm) (c1920)	H.481	£120.00	—

J.A. PATTREIOUEX, Manchester

	P		Beautiful Scotland (1939):	H.564-1		
D		28	A Small size		£1.10	£30.00
—		48	B Medium size (77 x 52mm)		35p	£17.50
—	P	48	The Bridges of Britain (77 x 52mm) (1938)		35p	£17.50
—	P	48	Britain from the Air (77 x 52mm) (1939)		30p	£15.00
A	C	50	British Empire Exhibition Series (c1928)		£2.80	£140.00
—	P	48	British Railways (77 x 52mm) (1938)		70p	£35.00
A	C	50	Builders of the British Empire (c1929)		£3.40	£170.00
—	C	24	Cadet's Jackpot Jigsaws (90 x 65mm) (1969)		£1.50	—
A	C	50	Celebrities in Sport (c1930):			
			A 46 Different		£4.00	—
			B Nos. 39,40 and 41 (Golfers)		£20.00	—
			C No. 38 Bobby Jones		£50.00	—
	P		Coastwise (1939):	H.564-2		
D		28	A Small size		£1.25	£35.00
—		48	B Medium size (77 x 52mm)		30p	£15.00
A	C	75	Cricketers Series (1926)	H.665	£11.00	—
A	C	50	Dirt Track Riders (1929)		£11.00	—
D	P	54	Dirt Track Riders (1930):			
			A Descriptive back		£12.00	—
			* B Non-descriptive back		£25.00	—
—	P	48	Dogs (76 x 51mm) (1939)		50p	£25.00
A	C	30	Drawing Made Easy (c1930)		£2.50	£75.00
A	C	52	The English and Welsh Counties (c1928)		£2.20	£115.00
	P		Flying (1938):	H.564-3		
D		28	A Small size		£2.00	—
—		48	B Medium size (77 x 52mm)		60p	£30.00

J.A. PATTREIOUEX, Manchester (continued)

Size	Printing	Number in set	Description	Handbook reference	Price per card	Complete set
A2	P	78	Footballers in Action (1934)		£4.00	—
A	C		Footballers Series (1927):			
		50	A Captions in blue		£9.00	—
		100	B Captions in brown		£9.00	—
—	P	48	Holiday Haunts by the Sea (77 x 52mm) (1937)		35p	£17.50
A	C	25	'King Lud' Problems (c1935)	H.638	£18.00	—
A	C	26	Maritime Flags (c1932)		£10.00	—
—	P	48	The Navy (1937):			
			A Large captions on back, text width 35mm		70p	£35.00
			B Smaller captions on back, text width 30mm ...		80p	£40.00
	P		Our Countryside (1938):	H.564-4		
D		28	A Small size		£1.50	£42.00
—		48	B Medium size (77 x 52mm)		30p	£15.00
A	U	25	Photos of Football Stars (c1930)	H.666	£32.00	—
D	C	50	Railway Posters by Famous Artists (c1930)		£8.00	—
A2	P	54	Real Photographs of London (1936)		£2.50	—
D	P	28	Shots from the Films (1938)	H.566	£2.75	—
—	P	48	Sights of Britain — 'Series of 48' (76 x 51 mm) (1936)		50p	£25.00
—	P	48	Sights of Britain — 'Second Series ...' (76 x 51mm) (1936):			
			A Large captions on back 2mm high		30p	£15.00
			B Smaller captions on back 1mm high		35p	£17.50
—	P	48	Sights of Britain — 'Third Series ...' (76 x 51mm) (1937)		50p	£25.00
—	P	48	Sights of London — 'First Series ...' (76 x 51mm) (1935)		£1.25	£60.00
—	P	12	Sights of London — 'Supplementary Series of 12 Jubilee Pictures' (76 x 51mm) (1935)		£1.00	£12.00
A2	P	54	Sporting Celebrities (1935)		£4.50	—
—	P	96	Sporting Events and Stars (76 x 50mm) (1935):			
			A 92 Different		£2.00	—
			B Nos. 18, 20 and 21 (Golfers)		£10.00	—
			C No. 19 Bobby Jones		£40.00	—
A	C	50	Sports Trophies (c1931)		£3.00	£150.00
—	C	24	Treasure Island (65 x 45mm) (1968)		£1.50	—
A2	CP	51	*Views (c1930)	H.597	£1.30	£65.00
A2	P	54	Views of Britain (1937)		£1.70	—
—	P	48	Winter Scenes (76 x 52mm) (1937)		30p	£15.00

1920s PHOTOGRAPHIC SERIES   Listed in order of letters and/or numbers quoted on cards.

Size	Printing	Number in set	Description	Handbook reference	Price per card	Complete set
H2	P	50	*Animals and Scenes — unnumbered 'Junior Member' back (c1925)	H.595-1	£1.50	—
H2	P	50	Animals and Scenes, Nd 1-50 (c1925)		£1.50	—
H2	P	50	*Scenes, Nd 201-250 'Junior Member' back (c1925)		£1.30	—
C	P	96	Animals and Scenes, Nd 250-345 (c1925):	H.595-2B		
			A 'Casket/Critic' back (i) grey		£1.20	—
			(ii) brown		£1.20	—
			* B 'Junior Member' back		£1.20	—
C	P	96	Animals and Scenes, Nd 346-441 (c1925):			
			A 'Casket/Critic' back		£1.20	—
			B 'Club Member' back		£1.20	—
			* C 'Junior Member' back		£1.20	—
H	P	50	*Animal Studies, Nd A42-A91 'Junior Member' back (c1925)		£1.20	—
H	P	50	*Animal Studies, Nd A92-A141 'Junior Member' back (c1925)		£1.20	—

J.A. PATTREIOUEX, Manchester (1920s Photographic Series continued)

Size	Printing	Number in set	Description	Handbook reference	Price per card	Complete set
H	P	50	*Animal Studies, Nd A151-A200 'Junior Member' back (c1925) … … … … … … … … …		£1.20	—
C	P		*Natives and Scenes (c1925):	H.595-2G		
		36	A 'Series 1/36 B' on front, Nd 1-36 'Junior Member' back … … … … … … … … …		£1.50	—
		96	B 'Series 1/96 B' on front, Nd 1-96 'Junior/Club Member' back … … … … … … … …		£1.50	—
C	P	96	*Foreign Scenes, Nd 1/96C-96/96C (c1925) … … …		£1.20	—
C	P	96	Cricketers, Nd C1-C96, 'Casket Cigarettes' on front (c1925):	H.595-2C		
			A Printed back … … … … … … … … …		£50.00	—
		*	B Plain back … … … … … … … … …		£50.00	—
C	P	96	*Animals — 'Series Nos CA1 to 96'. Back 7 (c1925)	H.595-2A	£1.50	—
C	P	96	*Natives and Scenes (c1925):			
			A 'C.B.1 to 96' on front. 'Club/Critic Member' back:			
			1 Nd 1-96 … … … … … … … … …		£1.20	—
			2 Nd C.B.1-C.B.96 … … … … … …		£1.20	—
			B 'J.S. 1 to 96' on front. 'Junior Member' back …		£1.20	—
C	P	96	*Animals and Scenes — 'CC1 to 96' on front (c1925)		£1.40	—
H2	P	50	*British Scenes — 'Series C.M.1-50.A' on front (c1925)		£1.20	—
H2	P	50	*Foreign Scenes (c1925):			
			A 'Series CM. 1/50 B' on front … … … … …		£1.20	—
			B 'J.M. Series 1/50' on front … … … … …		£1.20	—
H2	P	50	*Foreign Scenes (c1925):	H.595-2H		
			A 'Series C.M. 101-150.S' on front … … … …		£1.20	—
			B Nd S.101-S.150 on front … … … … …		£1.20	—
C	P	96	*Foreign Scenes, Nd 1/96D-96/96D (c1925) … … …		£1.80	—
H2	P	50	*Foreign Scenes, Nd 1/50E-50/50E (c1925) … … …		£1.30	—
H2	P	50	*Foreign Scenes, Nd 1/50F-50/50F (c1925) … … …		£1.30	—
C	P	96	Footballers, Nd F.1-F.96. 'Casket' and 'Critic' back (c1925) … … … … … … … … … …		£12.00	—
C	P	95	Footballers, Nd F.97-F.191. 'Casket' and 'Critic' back styles (c1925) … … … … … … … … …		£11.00	—
H	P	50	Football Teams, Nd F.192-F.241. ('Casket' and 'Critic') (1922) … … … … … … … … …	H.595-2F	£50.00	—
C	P	96	*Footballers — 'Series F.A. 1/96' on front (c1922) …		£10.00	—
C	P	96	*Footballers — 'Series F.B. 1/96' on front (1922) …	H.595-2D	£10.00	—
C	P	96	*Footballers — 'Series F.C. 1/96' on front (c1922) …	H.595-2E	£10.00	—
H2	P	50	*Scenes — 'G. 1/50' on front (c1925) … … … … …		£1.50	—
H2	P	50	*Scenes — '1/50. H' on front (c1925) … … … … …	H.595-2J	£1.50	—
H2	P	50	*Animals and Scenes, Nd I.1-I.50 (c1925) … … … …		£1.50	—
H2	P	50	Famous Statues — 'J.C.M. 1 to 50 C' on front (c1925) … … … … … … … … … … … … …		£2.00	—
H2	P	50	*Scenes, Nd JCM 1/50D-JCM 50/50D (c1925):			
			A 'Junior/Club Member' back … … … … … …		£1.30	—
			B 'Junior Member' back … … … … … … …		£1.30	—
B1	P	30	Child Studies, Nd J.M. No. 1-J.M. No. 30 (c1925) …		£4.00	—
B1	P	30	*Beauties, Nd J.M.1-J.M.30 (c1925) … … … … … …		£3.50	—
H2	P	50	*Foreign Scenes — 'J.M. 1 to 50 A' on front (c1925)	H.595-2I	£1.20	—
H2	P	50	British Empire Exhibition 'J.M. 1 to 50 B' on front (c1925) … … … … … … … … … … … …		£2.00	—
C	P	96	*Animals and Scenes — 'J.S. 1/96A'on front (c1925)		£1.20	—
H2	P	50	*Scenes, Nd S.1-S.50.' Junior Member' back (c1925)		£1.20	—
H2	P	50	*Scenes, Nd S.5l-S.100.' Junior Member' back (c1925)		£1.20	—
B1	P	50	*Cathedrals and Abbeys, Nd S.J. 1-S.J. 50. Plain back (c1925) … … … … … … … … … … … … …		£3.00	—

J.A. PATTREIOUEX, Manchester (1920s Photographic Series continued)

B1	P	50	*British Castles. Nd S.J. 51-S.J. 100. Plain back*			
			(c1925)		£3.00	—
H2	P	4	*Scenes, Nd V.1-V.4. 'Junior Member' back (c1925)	H.595-1	£5.00	—

W. PEPPERDY

A	C	30	*Army Pictures, Cartoons, etc (c1916)	H.12	£130.00	—

M. PEZARO & SON, London

D	C	25	*Armies of the World (c1900):	H.43		
			A Cake Walk Cigarettes		£140.00	—
			B Nestor Virginia Cigarettes		£140.00	—
D	C	? 19	Song Titles Illustrated (c1900)	H.323	£320.00	—

GODFREY PHILLIPS LTD, London

The Card Issues of Godfrey Phillips & Associated Companies (2009 Edition) reference book,
256 pages — £28.00

D1	C	25	*Actresses 'C' Series, Nd 101-125 (c1900): GP.1			
			A Blue Horseshoe design back		£35.00	—
			B Green back, 'Carriage' Cigarettes		£30.00	—
			C Blue back, 'Teapot' Cigarettes		£85.00	—
			D Blue back, 'Volunteer' Cigarettes		£85.00	—
			E Blue back, 'Derby' Cigarettes		£85.00	—
			F Blue back 'Ball of Beauty' Cigarettes		£85.00	—
—	C	50	*Actresses — oval card (38 x 62mm) (1916): GP.2			
			A With name		£7.00	—
			B Without Maker's and Actress's Name		£6.00	£300.00
A2	C	1	*Advertisement Card — 'Grand Cut' (1934) GP.2		—	£15.00
A2	C	1	*Advertisement Card — 'La Galbana Fours' (1934) ... GP.2		—	£15.00
A	C	50	Aircraft (1938) GP.5		£2.20	£110.00
A2	C	54	Aircraft — Series No. 1 (1938): GP.4			
			A Millhoff and Philips names at base		£4.00	—
			B Phillips and Associated Companies at base:			
			1 Front varnished		£3.00	£160.00
			2 Front matt		50p	£27.00
D	C	40	Animal Series (c1905)		£6.50	£260.00
—	C	30	Animal Studies (61 x 53mm) (1936)		30p	£9.00
A2	C	50	Annuals (1939): GP.9			
			A Home issue		25p	£12.50
			B New Zealand issue (dates for planting 4-6			
			months later). See Overseas Issues			
B	C	25	Arms of the English Sees (1924)		£4.80	£120.00
A	BW		B.D.V. Package Issues (1932-34):			
		17	Boxers	GP.161	£7.00	—
		55	Cricketers	GP.162	£8.00	—
		68	Film Stars	GP.168	£2.50	—
		136	Footballers	GP.163	£6.00	—
		19	Jockeys	GP.164	£4.50	—
		21	Speedway Riders	GP.165	£9.00	—
		28	Sportsmen	GP.166	£4.50	—
D1	C	25	*Beauties, Nd B.801-825 (c1902)	GP.12	£12.00	£300.00
A1	U	24	*Beauties, collotype — 'HUMPS' (c1895):	H.222/GP.24		
			A 'Awarded 7 Gold Medals 1895' on front		£85.00	
			B 'PLUMS' on front		£600.00	—

GODFREY PHILLIPS LTD, London (continued)

Size	Printing	Number in set	Description	Handbook reference	Price per card	Complete set
A	C	30	*Beauties, 'Nymphs' (c1896)	GP.14	£90.00	—
D			*Beauties — 'PLUMS' (1897):	H.186/GP.16		
	BW	? 60	A Front in black and white		£175.00	—
	C	50	B Plum-coloured background		£70.00	—
	C	50	C Green background		£70.00	—
DA	C	44	Beauties of Today, small — 'A Series of 44 ...' (1937)		£1.60	—
A	C	50	Beauties of Today, small — 'A Series of 50 ...' (1938)	GP.20	£1.20	£60.00
A2	P	54	Beauties of Today, small — 'A Series of Real Photographs ...' (1939)		£1.40	£75.00
A	C	36	Beauties of Today, small — 'A Series of 36 ... Second Series' (1940)		£1.10	£40.00
—	P		Beauties of Today, large (83 x 66mm) (c1938):	GP.24		
		36	First arrangement, known as 'Series A'		£3.50	—
		36	Second arrangement, known as 'Series B'		£6.00	—
J2	P	36	Beauties of Today, extra-large, unnumbered (1937)	GP.25	£1.50	£55.00
J2	P	36	Beauties of Today, extra-large — 'Second Series' (1938)		£1.25	£45.00
J2	P	36	Beauties of Today, extra-large — 'Third Series' (1938)		£1.10	£40.00
J2	P	36	Beauties of Today, extra-large — 'Fourth Series' (1938)		£1.10	£40.00
J2	P	36	Beauties of Today, extra-large — 'Fifth Series' (1938)		£1.00	£36.00
J2	P	36	Beauties of Today, extra-large — 'Sixth Series' (1939)		£1.00	£36.00
J2	P	36	Beauties of Today, extra-large — Unmarked (1939):	GP.31		
			A Back 'Godfrey Phillips Ltd'		£1.00	£36.00
			B Back 'Issued with B.D.V. Medium Cigarettes ...'		50p	£18.00
A2	BW	36	Beauties of the World — Stage, Cinema, Dancing Cele-brities (1931)		£1.50	£55.00
A2	C	36	Beauties of the World — Series No. 2 — Stars of Stage and Screen (1933)		£1.65	£60.00
A1	C	50	Beautiful Women (c1905):	H.284/GP.32		
			A Inscribed 'W.I. Series'		£12.00	—
			B Inscribed 'I.F. Series'		£12.00	—
—	C	50	Beautiful Women, Nd W.501-550 (55 x 75mm) (c1905)	H.284/GP.32	£24.00	—
—	C	30	Beauty Spots of the Homeland (126 x 89mm) (1938)		50p	£15.00
A	C	50	Bird Painting (1938)		90p	£45.00
D1	C	25	*Boxer Rebellion — Sketches (1904)	H.46/GP.35	£32.00	—
—	C	30	*British Beauties — Oval Card (36 x 60mm) Plain back (c1910)	H.244/GP.15	£3.00	£90.00
D	U	50	'British Beauties' photogravure (c1916)	GP.38	£8.00	£400.00
—	PC	76	British Beauties (37 x 51mm) (c1916)		£3.50	£265.00
A	C	54	British Beauties Nd 1-54 (1914):	GP.36		
			(a) Blue back, grey-black, glossy front		£2.75	£150.00
			(b) Plain back, grey-black, glossy front		£3.50	—
			(c) Plain back, sepia, matt front		£3.50	—
A	C	54	British Beauties Nd 55-108 (1914):	GP.37		
			A Blue back, grey-black, semi-glossy front		£2.75	£150.00
			B Blue back, grey-black matt front		£2.75	£150.00
			C Plain back, grey-black matt front		£3.50	—
A	C	50	British Birds and Their Eggs (1936)		£1.20	£60.00
D1	C	30	British Butterflies, No. 1 issue (1911)		£5.00	£150.00
A	C	25	British Butterflies:	GP.42		
			A Back in pale blue (1923)		£1.60	£40.00
			B Back in dark blue (1927)		£1.20	£30.00
			C 'Permacal' transfers (1936)		80p	£20.00

GODFREY PHILLIPS LTD, London (continued)

Size	Print-ing	Number in set	Description	Handbook reference	Price per card	Complete set
A2	C	25	British Orders of Chivalry and Valour (1939):	GP.43		
			A Back 'Godfrey Phillips Ltd'		£3.00	£75.00
			B Back 'De Reszke Cigarettes' (no maker's name)		£3.00	£75.00
D1	U	25	British Warships, green photo style (1915)		£9.00	£225.00
L	U	25	British Warships, green photo style (1915)		£40.00	—
A1	P	80	British Warships, 'real photographic' (c1916)	GP.45	£17.00	—
D1	C	50	*Busts of Famous People (1906):			
			A Pale green back, caption in black		£30.00	—
			B Brown back, caption in black		£50.00	—
			C Green back, caption in white		£8.00	£400.00
—	C	36	Characters Come to Life (61 x 53mm) (1938)		£1.00	£36.00
D1	C	25	*Chinese Series (c1910):	GP.48		
			A Back in English		£8.00	£200.00
			B 'Volunteer' Cigarettes back		£10.00	£250.00
—	P	25	*Cinema Stars — Circular (57mm diam.) (1924)	GP.49	£3.40	—
A	P	52	Cinema Stars — Set 1 (1929)	GP.50	£3.00	—
A2	U	30	Cinema Stars — Set 2 (1924)	GP.51	£3.00	—
A2	BW	30	Cinema Stars — Set 3 (1931)	GP.52	£1.70	£50.00
A2	C	32	Cinema Stars — Set 4 (1934)	GP.53	£1.70	£55.00
A2	BW	32	Cinema Stars — Set 5 (1934)	GP.54	£1.75	£55.00
A	C	50	*Colonial Troops (1904)	H.40/GP.56	£27.00	—
			Come to Life Series — see 'Zoo Studies'			
	C		Coronation of Their Majesties (1937):	GP.57		
A2		50	A Small size		30p	£15.00
—		36	B Medium size (61 x 53mm)		27p	£10.00
—		24	C Postcard size (127 x 89mm):			
			i Back with postcard format		£1.40	£35.00
			ii Back without postcard format		£4.00	—
	P		Cricketers (1924):	GP.58		
K2		198	*A Miniature size, 'Pinnace' photos (Nd 16c-225c)		£9.00	—
D		192	B Small size, brown back (selected Nos)		£9.00	—
B1		? 157	*C Large size, 'Pinnace' photos		£40.00	—
B1		25	D Large size, brown back (selected Nos)		£24.00	—
—		? 180	*E Cabinet size		£40.00	—
D	BW	1	Cricket Fixture Card (Radio Luxembourg) (1936) ...		—	£7.00
D	C	25	Derby Winners and Jockeys (1923)		£4.00	£100.00
D1	C	30	Eggs, Nests and Birds, No. 1 issue (1912):			
			A Unnumbered	GP.60	£6.00	£180.00
			B Numbered		£6.00	£180.00
D1	C	25	Empire Industries (1927)	GP.61	£1.40	£35.00
A2	C	50	Evolution of the British Navy (1930)		—	£95.00
			49 different (minus No 40)		£1.10	£55.00
D	C	25	Famous Boys (1924)		£2.80	£70.00
D	C	32	Famous Cricketers (1926)		£5.50	—
A	C	25	Famous Crowns (1938)		44p	£11.00
A2	C	50	Famous Footballers (1936)	GP.66	£2.20	£110.00
—	C	36	Famous Love Scenes (60 x 53mm) (1939)		70p	£25.00
A2	C	50	Famous Minors (1936)		30p	£15.00
—	C	26	Famous Paintings (128 x 89mm) (1938)	GP.69	£1.30	£35.00
D	C	25	Feathered Friends (1928)	GP.70	£1.80	£45.00
A2	C	50	Film Favourites (1934)	GP.71	70p	£35.00
A2	C	50	Film Stars (1934)	GP.73	80p	£40.00
—	C	24	*Film Stars — '... No. ... of a series of 24 cards ...' (128 x 89mm) (1934):	GP.74		
			A Postcard format back		£3.00	£75.00
			B Back without postcard format		£4.00	£100.00

GODFREY PHILLIPS LTD, London (continued)

Size	Print.	No.	Description	Handbook ref.	Price per card	Complete set
—	C	24	*Film Stars — '... No. ... of a series of cards', Nd 25-48 (128 x 89mm) (1935):	GP.75		
			A Postcard format back		£3.00	—
			B Back without postcard format		£6.00	—
—	C	24	*Film Stars '... No. ... of a series of cards', vivid backgrounds (128 x 89mm) (1936):	GP.76		
			A Postcard format back		£2.00	—
			B Back without postcard format		£3.00	—
D	C	25	First Aid Series, green back (1914)	GP.78	£7.00	£175.00
D	C	50	First Aid, black back (1923)	GP.77	£1.60	£80.00
D	C	25	*Fish (1924)		£3.00	£75.00
	C	30	Flower Studies (1937):			
—			A Medium size (61 x 53mm)		25p	£7.50
—			*B Postcard size (128 x 89mm)		70p	£21.00
	P	2462	Footballers — 'Pinnace' photos (1922-24):			
K2			A Miniature size (prices shown apply to numbers 1 to 940, for numbers above 940 prices are doubled):	GP.155		
		112	1a 'Oval' design back, in brown		£4.00	—
		400	1b 'Oval' design back, in black		£2.00	—
		? 388	2 Double-lined oblong back		£2.20	—
		? 890	3 Single-lined oblong back, address 'Photo'		£1.40	—
		? 2350	4 Single-lined oblong back, address 'Pinnace' photos		£1.40	—
			B Large size (83 x 59mm):	GP.156		
—		? 400	1 'Oval' design back		£3.50	—
			2 Double-lined oblong back:			
		? 63	a Address 'Photo'		£10.00	—
		? 2462	b Address 'Pinnace' photos		£3.50	—
—		? 2462	C Cabinet size (153 x 111mm)	GP.157	£10.00	—
—		? 24	D Football Teams (153 x 111mm)	GP.157	£500.00	—
—	C	30	Garden Studies (128 x 89mm) (1938)		50p	£15.00
A	C	13	*General Interest (c1895)	GP.83	£45.00	£600.00
—	BW	100	*Guinea Gold Series, unnumbered (64 x 38mm) Inscribed 'Phillips' Guinea Gold', matt (1899)	GP.87	£6.50	—
—	BW	90	*Guinea Gold Series, numbered 101-190 (68 x 41mm). Inscribed 'Smoke Phillips ...' (1902):	GP.88		
			A Glossy		£5.00	—
			B Matt		£5.00	—
			*Guinea Gold Series, unnumbered (63 x 41mm) (c1900):	GP.89		
			Actresses:			
	BW	135	A Black front		£5.00	—
	U	100	B Brown front		£10.00	—
	BW	26	Celebrities, Boer War		£5.00	—
A2	C	25	Home Pets (1924)	GP.90	£2.20	£55.00
A2	U	25	How to Build a Two Valve Set (1929)		£2.60	£65.00
D1	C	25	How to Do It Series (1913)		£8.00	£200.00
D	C	25	How to Make a Valve Amplifier ..., Nd 26-50 (1924)		£3.20	£80.00
A	C	25	How to Make Your Own Wireless Set (1923)		£2.80	£70.00
D	C	25	Indian Series (1908)		£14.00	£350.00
A2	C	54	In the Public Eye (1935)		60p	£32.00
A2	C	50	International Caps (1936)	GP.66	£2.00	£100.00
A2	C	37	Kings and Queens of England (1925):			
			Nos 1 and 4		£30.00	—
			Other numbers		£2.00	£70.00

GODFREY PHILLIPS LTD, London (continued)

Size	Printing	Number in set	Description	Handbook reference	Price per card	Complete set
A2	U	25	Lawn Tennis (1930)		£3.00	£75.00
K1	C	52	*Miniature Playing Cards (c1905)	GP.99	£120.00	—
K2	C	53	*Miniature Playing Cards (1932-34):	GP.100		
			A Back with exchange scheme:			
			1 Buff. Offer for 'pack of playing cards'		60p	—
			2 Buff. Offer for 'playing cards, dominoes or chess'		60p	£30.00
			3 Buff. Offer for 'playing cards, dominoes or draughts'		60p	£30.00
			4 Lemon		60p	—
			5 White, with red over-printing		60p	—
			B *Blue scroll back*		60p	£30.00
A2	C	25	Model Railways (1927)	GP.101	£3.20	£80.00
D1	C	30	Morse and Semaphore Signalling (1916):	GP.102		
			'Morse Signalling' back		£11.00	£330.00
			'Semaphore Signalling' back		£11.00	£330.00
D	C	50	Motor Cars at a Glance (1924)		£4.00	£200.00
D	C	20	Novelty Series (1924)		£13.00	—
A2	C	48	The 'Old Country' (1935)		80p	£40.00
A	C	25	Old Favourites (1924)	GP.107	£1.80	£45.00
—	C	36	Old Masters (60 x 53mm) (1939)		50p	£18.00
A	U	36	Olympic Champions Amsterdam, 1928		£2.75	£100.00
A	C	25	Optical Illusions (1927)		£2.60	£65.00
	C		'Our Dogs' (1939):	GP.110		
A2		36	A Small size (export)		£1.60	£60.00
—		30	B Medium size (60 x 53mm)		60p	£18.00
—		30	*C Postcard size (128 x 89mm)		£3.40	—
—	BW	48	'Our Favourites' (60 x 53mm) (1935)		25p	£12.50
—	C	30	Our Glorious Empire (128 x 89mm) (1939)		70p	£21.00
	C	30	'Our Puppies' (1936):	GP.113		
—			A Medium size (60 x 53mm)		£1.65	£50.00
—			*B Postcard size (128 x 89mm)		£1.80	£55.00
A2	C	25	Personalities of Today (Caricatures) (1932)		£2.20	£55.00
A2	C	25	Popular Superstitions (1930)		£1.60	£40.00
J2		20	'Private Seal' Wrestling Holds (export) (c1920)		£35.00	—
A	C	25	Prizes for Needlework (1925)	GP.116	£2.20	£55.00
D	C	25	Railway Engines (1924)		£3.60	£90.00
—	P	27	Real Photo Series — Admirals and Generals of the Great War. Cut-outs for buttonhole (28 x 40mm) (c1915)	GP.118	£8.00	—
D	C	25	Red Indians (1927)	GP.119	£3.60	£90.00
A	C	20	Russo-Japanese War Series (1904)	H.100/GP.120	£325.00	—
A	C	25	School Badges (1927)	GP.121	£1.20	£30.00
A	C		Screen Stars (1936):			
		48	First arrangement, known as 'Series A':	GP.122		
			i Frame embossed		£1.20	£60.00
			ii Frame not embossed		£1.60	£80.00
		48	Second arrangement, known as 'Series B'	GP.123	£1.00	£50.00
A2	C		A Selection of B.D.V. Wonderful Gifts:			
		48	'… based on 1930 Budget' (1930)	GP.84	£1.20	—
		48	'… based on 1931 Budget' (1931)	GP.85	£1.20	—
		48	'… based on 1932 Budget' (1932)	GP.86	£1.00	£50.00
		30	Semaphore Signalling — see 'Morse and Semaphore Signalling'			
D	C	25	Ships and Their Flags (1924)	GP.124	£3.00	£75.00
—	C	36	Ships that have Made History (60 x 53mm) (1938)		60p	£22.00
—	C	48	Shots from the Films (60 x 53mm) (1934)	GP.126	80p	£40.00

GODFREY PHILLIPS LTD, London (continued)

Size	Printing	Number in set	Description	Handbook reference	Price per card	Complete set
A2	C	50	Soccer Stars (1936)	GP.66	£1.80	£90.00
A2	C	36	Soldiers of the King (1939):	GP.127		
			A Inscribed 'This surface is adhesive'		£1.60	—
			B Without the above:			
			1 Thin card		70p	£25.00
			2 Thick card		70p	£25.00
	C		Special Jubilee Year Series (1935):	GP.128		
—		20	A Medium size (60 x 53mm)		40p	£8.00
—		12	B Postcard size (128 x 89mm)		£2.00	£24.00
A2	U	30	Speed Champions (1930)		£2.00	£60.00
A2	U	36	Sporting Champions (1929)		£2.75	£100.00
D1	C	25	Sporting Series (c1910)	GP.131	£20.00	—
D	C	25	Sports (1923):	GP.131		
			A White card		£4.00	—
			B Grey card		£4.00	—
A2	C	50	*Sportsmen — 'Spot the Winner' (1937):			
			A Inverted back		£1.10	£55.00
			B Normal back		£1.50	£75.00
A	BW		Sports Package Issues:			
		25	Cricketers (1948)	GP.171	£9.00	—
		25	Cricketers (1951)	GP.177	£9.00	—
		25	Footballers (1948)	GP.172	£8.00	—
		50	Footballers (1950)	GP.176	£8.00	—
		25	Footballers (1951)	GP.178	£8.00	—
		25	Football & Rugby Players (1952)	GP.180	£7.00	—
		25	Jockeys (1952)	GP.179	£5.00	—
		25	Radio Stars (1949)	GP.175	£3.50	—
		50	Sportsmen (1948)	GP.173	£5.00	—
		25	Sportsmen (1949)	GP.174	£5.00	—
		25	Sportsmen (1953)	GP.181	£5.00	—
		25	Sportsmen (1954)	GP.182	£5.00	—
A2	C		Stage and Cinema Beauties (1933):			
		35	First arrangement — known as 'Series A'	GP.133	£1.15	£40.00
		35	Second arrangement — known as 'Series B'	GP.134	£1.15	£40.00
A2	C	50	Stage and Cinema Beauties (1935)	GP.135	£1.20	£60.00
A	U	?	Stamp Cards (four colours, several wordings) (c1930)	GP.287	£2.50	—
A2	CP	54	Stars of the Screen — 'A Series of 54' (1934)		£1.20	£65.00
A2	C	48	Stars of the Screen — 'A Series of 48' (1936):			
			A Frame not embossed		90p	£45.00
			B Frame embossed		90p	£45.00
			C In strips of three, per strip		£2.50	£40.00
D1	C	25	*Statues and Monuments (cut-outs) (1907):	GP.139		
			A Provisional Patent No. 20736		£9.00	£225.00
			B Patent No. 20736		£9.00	£225.00
D	C	25	*Territorial Series (Nd 51-75) (1908)		£25.00	—
A	U	25	The 1924 Cabinet (1924)		£2.00	£50.00
A	C	50	This Mechanized Age — First Series (1936):			
			A Inscribed 'This surface is adhesive'		30p	£15.00
			B Without the above		36p	£18.00
A	C	50	This Mechanized Age — Second Series (1937)		50p	£25.00
A1	C	25	*Types of British and Colonial Troops (1899)	H.76/GP.145	£45.00	—
D1	C	25	*Types of British Soldiers (Nd M.651-75) (1900)	H.144/GP.146	£25.00	£625.00
A	C	63	*War Photos (1916)	GP.149	£9.00	—
—	C	30	Zoo Studies — Come to Life Series (101 x 76mm) (1939)		£1.50	£45.00
			Spectacles for use with the above		—	£8.00

GODFREY PHILLIPS LTD, London (continued)

SILKS Known as 'the B.D.V. Silks'. All unbacked. Inscribed 'B.D.V. Cigarettes' or 'G.P.' (Godfrey Phillips), or anonymous. Issued about 1910-25. 'Ha' prefix refers to original Handbook Part II. Nos 201 to 253 refer to new Godfrey Phillips Reference Book.

Size	Print-ing	Number in set		Handbook reference	Price per card	Complete set
—	C	62	*Arms of Countries and Territories (73 x 50mm) —			
			Anonymous … … … … … … … … … … … …	Ha.504-12/201	£4.00	—
—	C	32	*Beauties — Modern Paintings (B.D.V.):	Ha.505-13/202		
			A Small size (70 x 46mm) … … … … … … …		£12.00	
			B Extra-large size (143 x 100mm) … … … … …		£40.00	—
—	C	100	*Birds II (68 x 42mm) — B.D.V … … … … … … …	Ha.505-2/203	£3.00	—
—	C	12	*Birds of the Tropics III — B.D.V.:	Ha.505-3/204		
			A Small size (71 x 47mm) … … … … … … …		£11.00	—
			B Medium size (71 x 63mm) … … … … … …		£13.00	—
			C Extra-large size (150 x 100mm) … … …		£17.00	—
—	U	24	*British Admirals (83 x 76mm) — Anonymous … …	Ha.504-5/205	£6.50	—
—	C		*British Butterflies and Moths II — Anonymous:	Ha.505-6/206		
		40	Nos 1-40. Large size, 76 x 61mm … … … … …		£6.00	—
		10	Nos 41-50. Medium size. 70 x 51mm … … … …		£6.00	—
—	C	108	*British Naval Crests II:	Ha.504-4/207		
			A B.D.V., size 70 x 47mm … … … … … …		£2.00	—
			B Anonymous, size 70 x 51mm … … … … …		£2.00	—
—	C	25	*Butterflies I (70 x 48mm) — Anonymous … … … …	Ha.505-5/208	£10.00	—
—	C	47	Ceramic Art — B.D.V.:	Ha.505-16/209		
			A Small size (70 x 43mm) … … … … … … … …		£1.00	£47.00
			B Small size (70 x 48mm) … … … … … … … …		£1.00	—
			C Medium size (70 x 61mm) … … … … … … …		£1.75	—
—	C		*Clan Tartans:	Ha.505-15/210		
			A Small size (71 x 48mm):			
		49	1 Anonymous … … … … … … … … … …		£1.10	£55.00
		65	2 B.D.V … … … … … … … … … … … …		£1.10	£70.00
		56	B Medium size (70 x 60mm) — B.D.V … … …		£3.00	—
		12	C Extra-large size (150 x 100mm) B.D.V.			
			(selected Nos.) … … … … … … … … …		£5.50	—
—	C	108	*Colonial Army Badges (71 x 50mm) — Anonymous	Ha.502-3/211	£2.80	—
—	C	17	County Cricket Badges (69 x 48mm):	Ha.505-8/212		
			A Anonymous … … … … … … … … … … …		£18.00	—
			B B.D.V … … … … … … … … … … … …		£18.00	—
—	C	108	*Crests and Badges of the British Army II:	H.502-2/213		
			A1 Small size (70 x 48mm) Anonymous:			
			(a) Numbered … … … … … … … … …		£1.30	£140.00
			(b) Unnumbered … … … … … … … … …		£1.30	£140.00
			A2 Small size (70 x 48mm) — B.D.V … … … …		£1.30	£140.00
			A3 Medium size (70 x 60mm):			
			(a) Anonymous … … … … … … … … …		£1.50	—
			(b) B.D.V … … … … … … … … … … …		£1.50	—
—	C		*Flags — Set 4 — Anonymous:	Ha.501-4/214		
		? 143	A 'Long' size (82 x 53mm) … … … … … … …		£1.70	—
			B 'Short' size (70 x 48mm):			
		? 143	1 First numbering arrangement (as A) …		£1.40	—
		? 108	2 Second numbering arrangement … … …		£1.00	—
		? 113	3 Third numbering arrangement … … …		£1.00	—
—	C		*Flags — Set 5 — Anonymous:	Ha.501-5/215		
			A Small size (70 x 50mm):			
		20	1 With caption … … … … … … … …		£1.00	—
		6	2 Without caption, flag 40 x 29mm … …		£1.20	—
		? 6	3 Without caption, flag 60 x 41mm … …		£1.20	—
		? 8	B Extra-large size (155 x 108mm) … … … … …		£14.00	—

GODFREY PHILLIPS LTD, London (Silks continued)

Size/Print	Number in set	Description	Handbook reference	Price per card	Complete set
— C	18	*Flags — Set 6 — Anonymous:	Ha.501-6/216		
		A　Size 69 x 47mm		£1.00	£18.00
		B　Size 71 x 51mm		£1.00	£18.00
— C	20	*Flags — Set 7 (70 x 50mm) — Anonymous	Ha.501-7/217	£1.00	—
— C	50	*Flags — Set 9 — ('5th Series') (70 x 48mm) —			
		Anonymous	Ha.501-9/218	£1.80	£90.00
— C		*Flags — Set 10:	Ha.501-10/219		
	120	'7th Series' (70 x 48mm) — Anonymous		90p	—
	120	'10th Series' (70 x 62mm) — Anonymous		£1.00	—
	120	'12th Series' (70 x 48mm) — Anonymous		90p	—
	65	'15th Series' (70 x 62mm) (selected Nos.) — B.D.V.		£1.20	—
	65	'16th Series' (70 x 62mm) (selected Nos.) — B.D.V.		£1.20	—
		'20th Series' (70 x 48 mm) — B.D.V.:			
	132	A　B.D.V. in brown		£1.00	—
	48	B　B.D.V. in orange		£2.50	—
	126	'25th Series' (70 x 48mm) — B.D.V.		90p	—
	62	'25th Series' '(70 x 62mm) (selected Nos.) — B.D.V.		£3.00	—
		'26th Series' (70 x 48mm) — B.D.V.:			
	112	A　26th Series in brown		£1.00	—
	55	B　26th Series in blue		£4.00	—
	70	'28th Series' (70 x 48mm) (selected Nos.) — B.D.V.		£1.00	—
— C		*Flags — Set 12:	Ha.501-12/220		
	1	A　'Let 'em all come' (70 x 46mm) — Anonymous		—	£11.00
		B　Allied Flags (grouped):			
	1	Four Flags — Anonymous:			
		1　Small size (70 x 46mm)		—	£9.00
		2　Extra-large size (163 x 120mm)		—	£40.00
	1	Seven Flags (165 x 116mm):			
		1　Anonymous		—	£9.00
		2　B.D.V. in brown or orange		—	£9.00
	1	Eight Flags (165 x 116mm) — B.D.V.		—	£40.00
— C		*Flags — Set 13:	Ha.501-13/221		
	? 23	A　Size 163 x 114mm — Anonymous		£2.25	—
	? 27	B　Size 163 x 114mm — B.D.V. in brown, orange,			
		blue, green or black		£2.25	—
	? 23	C　Size 150 x 100mm — B.D.V.		£2.25	—
— C	26	*Flags — Set 14 ('House Flags') (68 x 47mm) —			
		Anonymous	Ha.501-14/229	£8.50	—
— C	25	*Flags — Set 15 (Pilot and Signal Flags) (70 x 50mm):	Ha.501-15/244		
		A　Numbered 601-625 — Anonymous		£3.60	£85.00
		B　Inscribed 'Series II' — B.D.V.		£2.40	£60.00
— C		*Football Colours:	Ha.505-9/222		
	? 21	A　Anonymous. size 68 x 49mm		£8.00	—
	? 86	B　B.D.V., size 68 x 49mm		£6.00	—
	? 78	C　B.D.V., size 150 x 100mm		£6.00	—
— C	126	G.P. Territorial Badges (70 x 48mm)	Ha.502-12/223	£2.20	—
— U	25	*Great War Leaders II (81 x 68mm) — Anonymous	Ha.504-7/224	£6.40	—
— U	50	*Great War Leaders III and Warships, sepia, black or			
		blue on white or pink material (70 x 50mm) —			
		Anonymous	Ha.504-10/225	£6.40	—
— C		*Great War Leaders IV and Celebrities:	Ha.504-11/226		
	3	A　Small size (70 x 48mm) — Anonymous		£6.00	—
	4	B　Small size (70 x 48mm) — B.D.V.		£6.50	—
	3	C　Medium size (70 x 63mm) — Anonymous ...		£6.00	—
	2	D　Medium size (70 x 63mm) — B. D.V.		£6.00	—
	? 18	E　Extra-large size (150 x 100mm) — B.D.V. ...		£6.00	—
	? 4	F　Extra-large size (150 x 110mm) — Anonymous		£6.00	£24.00
	? 1	G　Extra-large size (150 x 110mm) — B.D.V. ...		—	£15.00

GODFREY PHILLIPS LTD, London (Silks continued)

*Great War Leaders IV and Celebrities (continued):

Size	Print- ing	Number in set		Handbook reference	Price per card	Complete set
		? 25	H Extra-large size (163 x 117mm) — Anonymous		£6.00	—
		? 44	I Extra-large size (163 x 117mm) — B.D.V. ...		£6.00	—
—	C		Heraldic Series — B.D.V.:	Ha.504-17/228		
		25	A Small size (68 x 47mm)		£1.20	£30.00
		25	B Small size (68 x 43mm)		£1.20	£30.00
		25	C Medium size (68 x 60mm)		£3.00	—
		12	D Extra-large size (150 x 100mm) (selected Nos)		£5.50	£65.00
—	C	10	*Irish Patriots — Anonymous:	Ha.505-11/230		
			A Small size (67 x 50mm)		£12.00	—
			B Large size (83 x 76mm)		£12.00	—
			C Extra-large size (152 x 110mm)		£17.00	—
—	C	1	*Irish Republican Stamp (70 x 50mm)	Ha.505-12/231	—	£2.00
—	C	10	Miniature Rugs (89 x 55mm) (c1920)	GP.232	£9.00	—
—	C	54	*Naval Badges of Rank and Military Headdress (70 x 47mm) — Anonymous	Ha.504-9/233	£6.00	—
—	C	40	*Old Masters — Set 1 (155 x 115mm) — B.D.V.	Ha.503-1/235	£32.00	—
—	C	20	*Old Masters — Set 2 (150 x 105mm):	Ha.503-2/236		
			A Anonymous		£4.00	—
			B B.D.V. wording above picture		£4.00	—
			C B.D.V. wording below picture		£6.00	—
—	C		*Old Masters — Set 3A (70 x 50mm):	Ha.503-3A/237		
		40	A B.D.V.		£3.00	—
		55	B Anonymous		£2.50	—
—	C	30	*Old Masters — Set 3B (70 x 50mm) — Anonymous	Ha.503-3B/237	£2.50	—
—	C	120	*Old Masters — Set 4 (70 x 50mm) — Anonymous	Ha.503-4/238	£2.00	—
—	C		*Old Masters — Set 5 (70 x 50mm):	Ha.503-5/239		
		20	A Unnumbered — Anonymous		£3.00	—
		60	B Nd. 1-60 — B.D.V		£1.20	£72.00
		20	C Nd. 101-120 — Anonymous:			
			1 Numerals normal size		£2.00	—
			2 Numerals very small size		£2.00	£40.00
		20	D Nd. 101-120 — B.D.V.		£1.80	£36.00
—	C	50	*Old Masters — Set 6 (67 x 42mm) — B.D.V.	Ha.503-6/240	£1.20	£60.00
—	C	50	*Old Masters — Set 7, Nd. 301-350 (67 x 47mm) — Anonymous	Ha.503-7/241	£2.50	—
—	C	50	*Orders of Chivalry I (70 x 48mm) — Anonymous ...	Ha.504-14/242	£2.20	—
—	C	24	*Orders of Chivalry — Series 10 (70 x 50mm):	Ha.504-16/243		
			A Nd. 1-24 — B.D.V.		£1.80	£45.00
			B Nd. 401-424 — G.P		£2.00	£50.00
—	C	72	*Regimental Colours II (76 x 70mm) — Anonymous	Ha.502-7/245	£4.50	—
—	C		*Regimental Colours and Crests III:	Ha.502-8/246		
			A Small size (70 x 51mm):			
		40	1 Colours with faint backgrounds — Anonymous		£1.60	—
		120	2 Colours without backgrounds — Anonymous		£1.75	—
		120	3 Colours without backgrounds — B.D.V.		£1.75	—
		120	B Extra-large size (165 x 120mm):			
			1 Anonymous — unnumbered		£6.50	—
			2 B.D.V. — numbered		£6.00	—
—	C	50	*Regimental Colours — Series 12 (70 x 50mm) — B.D.V.	Ha.502-11/247	£2.00	£100.00
—	C	10	*Religious Pictures — Anonymous:	Ha.505-10/248		
			A Small size (67 x 50mm)		£18.00	—
			B Large size (83 x 76 mm)		£20.00	—
			C Extra-large size (155 x 110mm)		£27.00	—

GODFREY PHILLIPS LTD, London (Silks continued)

—	C	75	*Town and City Arms — Series 30 (48 unnumbered, 27 numbered 49-75) — B.D.V.:	Ha.504-13/250		
			A Small size (70 x 50mm)		£2.00	—
			B Medium size (70 x 65mm)		£3.00	—
—	C	25	*Victoria Cross Heroes I (70 x 50mm) — Anonymous	Ha.504-1/251	£12.00	—
—	C	? 25	*Victoria Cross Heroes II (70 x 50mm) — Anonymous	Ha.504-2/252	£12.00	—
—	C	90	*War Pictures (70 x 48mm) — Anonymous	Ha.504-8/253	£6.00	—

OVERSEAS ISSUES (AUSTRALIA AND NEW ZEALAND)

A2	U	50	*Animal Studies (c1930)	GP.7	£2.00	—
A2	C	50	Annuals (1939) (New Zealand issue)	GP.9	£1.50	£75.00
D	BW	50	Australian Sporting Celebrities (1932)		£3.20	—
D	BW	50	Film Stars (1934)		£2.00	—
D	C	50	Stars of British Films (1934):			
			A Back 'B.D.V. Cigarettes'		£2.00	—
			B Back 'Grey's Cigarettes ...'		£2.00	—
			C Back 'De Reszke Cigarettes'		£2.00	—
			D Back 'Godfrey Phillips (Aust)'		£2.00	—
D	BW	38	Test Cricketers, 1932-1933:			
			A 'Issued with Grey's Cigarettes'		£3.50	—
			B 'Issued with B.D.V. Cigarettes'		£3.50	—
			C Back 'Godfrey Phillips (Aust.)'		£3.50	—
D2	C		Victorian Footballers (1933):			
		50	1 'Series of 50':			
			A 'Godfrey Phillips (Aust.)'		£4.50	—
			B 'B.D.V. Cigarettes ...'		£4.50	—
			C 'Grey's Cigarettes'		£4.50	—
		75	2 'Series of 75':			
			D 'B.D.V. Cigarettes ...'		£6.00	—
D	BW	50	Victorian League and Association Footballers (1934)		£6.00	—
A2	C	100	*Who's Who in Australian Sport (1933)	GP.150	£4.00	—

JOHN PLAYER & SONS, Nottingham
44 page reference book — £4.50

NOTE: The Imperial Tobacco Co. clause (I.T.C. clause) appears on Home issues dated between 1902 and 1940, excluding those issued in the Channel Islands. For series without I.T.C. clause, see the Overseas section.

A	C	25	*Actors and Actresses (1898)	H.337	£25.00	£625.00
A1	BW	50	*Actresses (1897)	H.339	£25.00	—
A	C	8	*Advertisement Cards (1893-94) multi-backed	H.338	From £300.00	—
	C	1	*Advertisement Card (Sailor) (c1930):			
A			A Small size		—	£5.00
B			B Large size		—	£20.00
B	BW	1	Advertisement Card — Wants List (1936)		—	£1.00
A	C	50	Aeroplanes (1935):			
			A Home issue — titled 'Aeroplanes (Civil)'		£1.10	£55.00
			Album (with price)		—	£22.00
			B Irish issue — titled 'Aeroplanes'		£1.50	£75.00
A	C	50	Aircraft of the Royal Air Force (1938):			
			A Home issue — with I.T.C. clause		£1.00	£50.00
			Album		—	£22.00
			B Channel Islands issue — without I.T.C. clause		£1.50	£75.00
J	C	10	Allied Cavalry or Regimental Uniforms:	H.340		
			Allied Cavalry (1914)		£10.00	£100.00
			Regimental Uniforms (1914)		£9.00	£90.00

JOHN PLAYER & SONS, Nottingham (continued)

Size	Print-ing	Number in set		Handbook reference	Price per card	Complete set
A	C	50	Animals of the Countryside (1939):			
			A Home issue — adhesive, with I.T.C. clause ...		25p	£12.50
			Album		—	£22.00
			B Irish issue — non-adhesive, green numerals overprinted		£1.00	—
			C Channel Islands issue — adhesive, without I.T.C. clause		80p	£40.00
B	C	25	Aquarium Studies (1932)		£1.80	£45.00
B	C	25	Architectural Beauties (1927)		£2.20	£55.00
A	C	50	Arms and Armour (1909):	H.273		
			A Home issue — with I.T.C. clause		£2.50	£125.00
			B Overseas issue — without I.T.C. clause — see Overseas section			
A	C	50	Army Corps and Divisional Signs, 1914-1918 (1924)		60p	£30.00
A	C	100	Army Corps and Divisional Signs, 1914-1918, '2nd Series' (1925):			
			Nos. 51-100		80p	£40.00
			Nos. 101-150		80p	£40.00
A	C	25	Army Life (1910)	H.78	£2.00	£50.00
J	C	12	Artillery in Action (1917)		£5.00	£60.00
A	U	50	Association Cup Winners (1930)	H.667	£1.80	£90.00
A	C	50	Aviary and Cage Birds:			
			A Small size (1933):			
			1 Cards		£1.00	£50.00
			2 Transfers		50p	£25.00
			Album		—	£30.00
B		25	B Large size (1935)		£3.60	£90.00
A	C	50	Badges and Flags of British Regiments (1904):	H.341		
			A Brown back, unnumbered		£2.50	£125.00
			B Brown back, numbered		£2.50	£125.00
A	C	50	Badges and Flags of British Regiments (1903):			
			A Green back, thick card		£2.50	£125.00
			B Green back, thin card		£2.50	£125.00
A	C	50	Birds and Their Young (1937):			
			A Home issue — adhesive, with I.T.C. clause ...		25p	£12.50
			Album			
			A Cream Cover		—	£22.00
			B Grey Cover		—	£22.00
			B Irish issue:			
			1 Adhesive, with large green numerals ...		£1.00	—
			2 Non-adhesive, with large green numerals		£1.00	—
			C Channel Islands issue — adhesive, without I.T.C. clause		70p	£35.00
A	C	25	Birds and Their Young, 1st series (unissued) (1955)		24p	£6.00
A	C	25	Birds and Their Young, 2nd series (unissued) (1955)		20p	£4.00
—	P	10	*Bookmarks — Authors (139 x 51mm) (1905)		£65.00	—
A	C	25	Boxing (1934)		£6.00	—
			Album		—	£40.00
A	C	50	Boy Scout and Girl Guide Patrol Signs and Emblems (1933):			
			A Cards		50p	£25.00
			B Transfers		50p	£25.00
			Album		—	£30.00
B	C	25	British Butterflies (1934)		£4.40	£110.00
A	C	50	British Empire Series (1904):	H.343		
			A Grey-white card, matt		£1.40	£70.00
			B White card, semi-glossy		£1.60	£80.00

JOHN PLAYER & SONS, Nottingham (continued)

Size	Printing	Number in set	Description	Handbook reference	Price per card	Complete set
	C	25	British Livestock:			
A			A Small card (1915)		£3.00	£75.00
			B Medium card — see Overseas section			
J			C Extra-large card, brown back (1916)		£4.00	£100.00
J			D Extra-large card, blue back (1923)		£3.60	£90.00
B	C	25	British Naval Craft (1939)		£1.00	£25.00
J	C	20	British Pedigree Stock (1925)		£4.50	£90.00
B	C	25	British Regalia (1937)		£1.20	£30.00
A	C	50	Butterflies (1932):			
			A Cards		£1.30	£65.00
			B Transfers		50p	£25.00
			Album		—	£30.00
A	C	50	Butterflies and Moths (1904)	H.80	£1.90	£95.00
	C		Bygone Beauties:			
A		25	A Small card (1914)		£1.60	£40.00
J		10	B Extra-large card (1916)		£4.50	£45.00
—	U	? 32	*Cabinet Size Pictures, 1898-1900 (220 x 140mm):	H.476		
			A Plain back		£90.00	—
			B Printed back		£90.00	—
A	C	20	Castles, Abbeys etc (c1894):	H.345		
			A Without border		£28.00	£560.00
			B White border		£28.00	£560.00
B	C	24	Cats (1936)		£7.00	—
A	C	50	Celebrated Bridges (1903)	H.346	£3.00	£150.00
A	C		Celebrated Gateways (1909):	H.347		
		50	A Thick card		£1.50	£75.00
		25	B Thinner card (26-50 only)		£1.80	—
A	C	25	Ceremonial and Court Dress (1911)	H.145	£1.80	£45.00
B	C	25	Championship Golf Courses (1936)		£8.00	£200.00
	C		Characters from Dickens:	H.348		
A		25	Small card, lst series (1912)		£2.40	£60.00
J		10	Extra-large card (1912)..		£6.00	£60.00
A	C	25	Characters from Dickens, 2nd series (1914)	H.348	£2.40	£60.00
A	C	50	Characters from Dickens (1st & 2nd series combined) (1923)	H.348	£1.40	£70.00
B	C	25	Characters from Fiction (1933)		£4.00	£100.00
A	C	25	Characters from Thackeray (1913)		£1.60	£40.00
A	C	50	Cities of the World (1900):			
			A Grey-mauve on white back		£4.50	—
			B Grey-mauve on toned back		£4.50	—
			C Bright mauve on white back		£4.50	—
B	C	20	Clocks — Old and New (1928)		£5.00	£100.00
A	C	25	Colonial and Indian Army Badges (1916)		£1.40	£35.00
A	C	50	Coronation Series Ceremonial Dress (1937):			
			A Home issue — with I.T.C. clause		35p	£17.50
			Album		—	£22.00
			B Channel Islands issue — without I.T.C. clause		£1.00	£50.00
A	C	25	*Counties and Their Industries:	H.349		
			A Unnumbered (c1910)		£2.60	£65.00
			B Numbered (1914)		£2.60	£65.00
A	C	50	*Countries — Arms and Flags:			
			A Thick card (1905)		90p	£45.00
			B Thin Card (1912)		£1.10	£55.00
A	C	50	*Country Seats and Arms (1906)		£1.00	£50.00
A	C		*Country Seats and Arms, 2nd series (1907):			
		25	A Nd. 51-75 First printing		£1.60	£40.00
		50	B Nd. 51-100 Second printing		£1.00	£50.00
A	C	50	*Country Seats and Arms, 3rd series (1907)		£1.00	£50.00

JOHN PLAYER & SONS, Nottingham (continued)

Size	Print-ing	Number in set	Description	Handbook reference	Price per card	Complete set
B	C	25	Country Sports (1930) ……………………………		£6.00	£150.00
A	C	50	Cricketers, 1930 (1930) ……………………………		£1.50	£75.00
A	C	50	Cricketers, 1934 (1934) ……………………………		£1.20	£60.00
A	C	50	Cricketers, 1938 (1938):			
			A Home issue — with I.T.C. clause …………		£1.00	£50.00
			Album …………………………………		—	£22.00
			B Channel Islands issue — without I.T.C. clause …………………………		£2.00	£100.00
A	C	50	Cricketers, Caricatures by 'Rip' (1926) …………		£2.00	£100.00
	C		Cries of London:	H.350		
A		25	Small cards, 1st series (1913) …………………		£2.00	£50.00
J		10	Extra-large cards, 1st series (1912) …………		£4.50	£45.00
J		10	Extra-large cards, 2nd series (1914) …………		£4.00	£40.00
A	C	25	Cries of London, 2nd series (1916):			
			A Blue back		£1.00	£25.00
			B Black back (unissued)		£7.00	—
A	C	50	Curious Beaks (1929) …………………………		80p	£40.00
A	C	50	Cycling (1939):			
			A Home issue — adhesive, with I.T.C. clause …		90p	£45.00
			Album …………………………………		—	£22.00
			B Irish issue:			
			1 Adhesive, with large green numerals …		£1.60	—
			2 Non-adhesive, with large green numerals …………………………		£1.60	—
			C Channel Islands issue — adhesive, without I.T.C. clause …………………………		£1.50	£75.00
	C		Dandies (1932):			
A		50	A Small size ………………………………		40p	£20.00
B		25	B Large size ………………………………		£1.80	£45.00
A	C	50	Decorations and Medals (unissued) (c1940) ……		£2.00	£100.00
A	C	50	Derby and Grand National Winners (1933):			
			A Cards ………………………………		£1.70	£85.00
			B Transfers ……………………………		50p	£25.00
			Album …………………………………		—	£30.00
	C		Dogs (1924) — Scenic backgrounds:			
A		50	A Small size ………………………………		£1.00	£50.00
J		12	B Extra-large size ………………………		£3.25	£40.00
	C		Dogs — Full length:	H.668		
A		50	A Small size (1931):			
			1 Cards ……………………………		90p	£45.00
			2 Transfers ………………………		50p	£25.00
			Album ……………………………		—	£30.00
B		25	B Large size (1933) ………………………		£2.60	£65.00
	C		Dogs — Heads:			
A		50	A Small size — Home issue (1929) ………		£1.00	£50.00
A		25	B Small size — Irish issue, 'A Series of 25', with I.T.C. clause (1927) …………………		£2.00	£50.00
A		25	C Small size — Irish issue, '2nd Series of 25', with I.T.C. clause (1929) …………………		£2.00	£50.00
			D Small size — Overseas issue, without I.T.C. clause (1927) — see Overseas section			
B		20	E Large size — Home issue, 'A Series of 20' (1926) ………………………………		£2.75	£55.00
B		20	F Large size — Home issue, '2nd Series of 20' (1928) ………………………………		£2.75	£55.00
A	C	50	Dogs' Heads (silver-grey backgrounds) (1940) ……		£3.00	—
A	C	50	Dogs' Heads by Biegel (unissued) (c1955) ………		90p	£45.00
B	C	25	Dogs — Pairs and Groups (unissued) (c1955) ……		£1.40	£35.00

JOHN PLAYER & SONS, Nottingham (continued)

Size	Print-ing	Number in set		Handbook reference	Price per card	Complete set
A	C	50	Drum Banners and Cap Badges (1924):			
			A Base panel joining vertical framelines		90p	£45.00
			B Fractional space between the above		80p	£40.00
A	C	25	Egyptian Kings and Queens, and Classical Deities			
			(1911)		£2.00	£50.00
J	C	10	Egyptian Sketches (1915)	H.351	£4.00	£40.00
	C	25	*England's Military Heroes (1898):	H.352		
A1			A Wide card		£40.00	—
A1			*A1 Wide card plain back*		£40.00	—
—			B Narrow card (68 x 28mm)		£32.00	—
—			*B2 Narrow card, plain back (68 x 28mm)*		£30.00	—
	C	25	England's Naval Heroes (1897):	H.353		
A1			A Wide card		£40.00	—
—			B Narrow card (68 x 28mm)		£26.00	£650.00
	C	25	England's Naval Heroes (1898), descriptions on back:	H.353		
A1			A Wide card		£40.00	—
A1			*A2 Wide card, plain back*		£40.00	—
—			B Narrow card (68 x 29mm)		£28.00	£700.00
—			*B2 Narrow card, plain back (68 x 29mm)*		£28.00	—
A	C	25	Everyday Phrases by Tom Browne (1901):	H.354		
			A Thickcard		£18.00	£450.00
			B Thin card		£18.00	£450.00
B	BW	25	Fables of Aesop (1927)		£2.40	£60.00
	C	20	Famous Authors and Poets (1902):			
A			A Wide card		£30.00	£600.00
—			B Narrow card (67 x 30mm)		£20.00	£400.00
B	C	25	Famous Beauties (1937):			
			A Home issue — with I.T.C. clause		£1.80	£45.00
			B Channel Islands issue — without I.T.C.			
			clause		£2.40	£60.00
A	C	50	Famous Irish-Bred Horses (1936)		£3.60	£180.00
			Album		—	£40.00
A	C	50	Famous Irish Greyhounds (1935)		£5.50	—
			Album		—	£40.00
J	C	10	Famous Paintings (1913)	H.355	£3.50	£35.00
A	C	50	Film Stars — 'Series of 50' (1934)		£1.30	£65.00
			Album		—	£22.00
A	C	50	Film Stars — 'Second Series ...':			
			A Home issue — Album 'price one penny'			
			(1934)		£1.00	£50.00
			Album (with price)		—	£22.00
			B Irish issue — Album offer without price (1935)		£1.60	£80.00
			Album (without price)		—	£40.00
A	C	50	Film Stars — Third Series:			
			A Home issue — titled 'Film Stars — with I.T.C.			
			clause (1938)		90p	£45.00
			Album		—	£22.00
			B Irish issue — titled 'Screen Celebrities' (1939)		£2.20	—
			C Channel Islands issue — titled 'Film Stars',			
			without I.T.C. clause (1938)		£1.50	£75.00
B	BW	25	Film Stars — Large size (1934):			
			A Home issue — with Album offer		£3.20	£80.00
			Album		—	£30.00
			B Irish issue — without Album offer		£7.00	—
A	C	50	Fire-Fighting Appliances (1930)		£1.60	£80.00
A	C	50	Fishes of the World (1903)	H.66	£2.40	£120.00
A	C	50	Flags of the League of Nations (1928)		50p	£25.00

JOHN PLAYER & SONS, Nottingham (continued)

Size	Print-ing	Number in set		Handbook reference	Price per card	Complete set
A	C	50	Football Caricatures by 'Mac' (1927) … … … … …		£1.40	£70.00
A	C	50	Footballers Caricatures by 'Rip' (1926) … … … … …		£1.40	£70.00
A	C	50	Footballers, 1928 (1928) … … … … … … … … …		£1.80	£90.00
A	C	25	Footballers, 1928-9 — '2nd Series' (1929) … … … …		£1.80	£45.00
—	C	?	Football Fixture Folders (1935-61) … … … … … …		£15.00	—
	C		Fresh-Water Fishes:			
A		50	A Small size, Home issue:			
			1 Pink card (1933) … … … … … … … …		£1.50	£75.00
			2 White card (1934) … … … … … … … …		£1.70	£85.00
			Album (titled British Fresh-Water Fishes)		—	£22.00
B		25	B Large size, Home issue — adhesive (1935) …		£2.80	£70.00
B		25	C Large size, Irish issue — non-adhesive (1935)		£5.00	£125.00
A	C	25	From Plantation to Smoker (1926) … … … … … …		40p	£10.00
	C	50	Gallery of Beauty (1896):	H.356		
			A Wide Card:			
A			I Set of 50 … … … … … … … … … … … …		£23.00	—
A			II 5 Alternative Pictures (Nos 20, 24, 25, 48, 49) … … … … … … … … … … … …		£65.00	—
			B Narrow Card official cut:			
—			I Set of 50 … … … … … … … … … … …		£20.00	—
—			II 5 Alternative Pictures (Nos 20, 24, 25, 48, 49) … … … … … … … … … … …		£60.00	—
	C		Game Birds and Wild Fowl:			
A		50	A Small size (1927) … … … … … … … … … …		£1.50	£75.00
B		25	B Large size (1928) … … … … … … … … … …		£5.00	£125.00
A	C	25	Gems of British Scenery (1914) … … … … … …		£1.20	£30.00
	C		Gilbert and Sullivan — 'A Series of …':			
A		50	A Small size (1925) … … … … … … … … …		£1.20	£60.00
J		25	B Extra-large size (1926) … … … … … … … …		£3.40	£85.00
	C		Gilbert and Sullivan — '2nd Series of …':			
A		50	A Small size (1927) … … … … … … … … …		£1.20	£60.00
B		25	B Large size (1928) … … … … … … … … …		£4.00	£100.00
B	C	25	Golf (1939):			
			A Home issue — with I.T.C. clause … … … …		£7.50	£190.00
			B Channel Islands issue — without I.T.C. clause … … … … … … … … … … …		£7.00	£175.00
A	C	25	Hidden Beauties (1929) … … … … … … … … …		30p	£7.50
A	C	25	Highland Clans (1908) … … … … … … … … …		£5.00	£125.00
A	C	50	Hints on Association Football (1934) … … … … … …	H.669	£1.00	£50.00
			Album … … … … … … … … … … … … …		—	£22.00
J	C	10	Historic Ships (1910):			
			A Thick card … … … … … … … … … … …		£5.50	£55.00
			B Thin card … … … … … … … … … … …		£5.50	£55.00
	C		History of Naval Dress:			
A		50	A Small size (1930) … … … … … … … … …		£1.20	£60.00
B		25	B Large size (1929) … … … … … … … … …		£2.00	£50.00
A	C	50	International Air Liners:			
			A Home issue — Album 'price one penny', with I.T.C. clause (1936) … … … … … … … …		50p	£25.00
			Album (with price) … … … … … … … … …		—	£22.00
			B Irish issue — Album offer without price, with I.T.C. clause (1937) … … … … … … … …		£1.00	£50.00
			Album (without price) … … … … … … … …		—	£40.00
			C Channel Islands issue — without Album offer or I.T.C. clause (1936) … … … … … …		£1.20	£60.00
A	C	25	Irish Place Names — 'A Series of 25' (1927) … … …		£3.20	£80.00
A	C	25	Irish Place Names — '2nd Series of 25' (1929) … …		£3.20	£80.00

JOHN PLAYER & SONS, Nottingham (continued)

Size	Print-ing	Number in set		Handbook reference	Price per card	Complete set
A	C	1	Joker Card – Card Scheme (1937)		—	£5.00
	C	50	Kings and Queens of England (1935):	H.670		
A			A Small size		£1.60	£80.00
			Album		—	£22.00
B			B Large size		£2.80	£140.00
			Album		—	£30.00
A	C	50	Life on Board a Man of War in 1805 and 1905 (1905)	H.38	£2.50	£125.00
A	C	25	Live Stock (1925)		£4.00	£100.00
A	C	50	Military Head-Dress (1931)		£1.20	£60.00
A	C	50	Military Series (1900)		£22.00	—
A	C	50	Military Uniforms of the British Empire Overseas (1938):			
			A Home issue — adhesive, with I.T.C. clause ...		80p	£40.00
			Album		—	£22.00
			B Channel Islands issue:			
			1 Adhesive, without I.T.C. clause		£1.50	£75.00
			2 Non-adhesive, without I.T.C. clause		£1.50	£75.00
A	C	25	Miniatures (1916)		50p	£12.50
A	C	50	Modern Naval Craft (1939):			
			A Home issue — adhesive, with I.T.C. clause ...		50p	£25.00
			Album		—	£22.00
			B Irish issue — non-adhesive		£1.00	—
			C Channel Islands issue — adhesive, without I.T.C. clause		£1.00	£50.00
A	C	50	Motor Cars — 'A Series of 50' (1936):			
			A Home issue — Album 'price one penny'		£1.50	£75.00
			Album (with price)		—	£22.00
			B Irish issue — Album offer without price		£2.20	—
			Album (without price)		—	£40.00
			C Channel Islands issue — without Album offer		£2.00	£100.00
A	C	50	Motor Cars — 'Second Series ...' (1937):			
			A Home issue — with I.T.C. clause		£1.00	£50.00
			Album		—	£22.00
			B Channel Islands issue — without I.T.C. clause		£1.80	£90.00
B	U	20	Mount Everest (1925)		£5.00	£100.00
A	C	25	Napoleon (1915)	H.364	£2.20	£55.00
A	C	50	National Flags and Arms:			
			A Home issue — Album 'price one penny' (1936)		45p	£22.50
			Album (with price)		—	£22.00
			B Irish issue — Album offer without price (1937)		£1.00	£50.00
			Album (without price)		—	£40.00
			C Channel Islands issue — without Album offer (1936)		80p	£40.00
B	C	25	The Nation's Shrines (1929)		£2.20	£55.00
	C		Natural History:			
A		50	A Small size (1924)		40p	£20.00
J		12	B Extra-large size — 'A Series of 12' (1923) ...		£1.25	£15.00
J		12	C Extra-large size — '2nd Series of 12' (1924) ...		£1.25	£15.00
B	C	24	A Nature Calendar (1930)		£5.00	£125.00
	C		Nature Series:			
A		50	Small card (1908)		£1.50	£75.00
J		10	Extra-large card (Birds) (1908)		£12.00	—
J		10	Extra-large card (Animals) (1913)		£6.00	£60.00
A	C	50	Old England's Defenders (1898)		£22.00	—
B	C	25	'Old Hunting Prints' (1938):			
			A Home issue — with I.T.C. clause		£3.00	£75.00
			B Channel Islands issue — without I.T.C. clause		£4.40	—

Size	Print-ing	Number in set		Handbook reference	Price per card	Complete set

JOHN PLAYER & SONS, Nottingham (continued)

Size	Print-ing	Number in set	Description	Handbook reference	Price per card	Complete set
B	C	25	Old Naval Prints (1936):			
			A Home issue — with I.T.C. clause … … … …		£2.60	£65.00
			B Channel Islands issue — without I.T.C. clause		£4.00	—
J	BW	25	Old Sporting Prints (1924) … … … … … … … …		£4.40	£110.00
B	C	25	Picturesque Bridges (1929) … … … … … … … …		£3.00	£75.00
B	C	25	Picturesque Cottages (1929) … … … … … …		£3.60	£90.00
B	C	25	Picturesque London (1931) … … … … … … …		£5.00	£125.00
A	C	25	Players — Past and Present (1916) … … … … …		£1.00	£25.00
A	C	25	Polar Exploration (1915) … … … … … … … …		£2.80	£70.00
A	C	25	Polar Exploration, 2nd series (1916) … … … … …		£2.20	£55.00
B	C	25	Portals of the Past (1930) … … … … … … …		£2.20	£55.00
A	C	50	Poultry (1931):	H.671		
			A Cards … … … … … … … … … … … …		£1.80	£90.00
			B Transfers … … … … … … … … … … …		50p	£25.00
			Album … … … … … … … … … … … … …		—	£30.00
A	C	25	Products of the World:			
			A Thick card (1909) … … … … … … … …		80p	£20.00
			B Thin card (1908) … … … … … … … …		£1.20	£30.00
A	C	50	Products of the World — Scenes only (1928) … … …		30p	£15.00
A	C	25	Racehorses (1926) … … … … … … … … … …		£5.40	£135.00
A	U	40	Racing Caricatures (1925) … … … … … … … …		90p	£36.00
B	C	25	Racing Yachts (1938):			
			A Home issue — with I.T.C. clause … … …		£3.80	£95.00
			B Channel Islands issue — without I.T.C. clause		£5.00	—
A	C	50	RAF Badges (1937):			
			A Home issue — with I.T.C. clause:			
			1 Without motto … … … … … … … …		60p	£30.00
			2 With motto … … … … … … … … …		60p	£30.00
			Album … … … … … … … … … … …		—	£22.00
			B Channel Islands issue — without I.T.C. clause		£1.00	£50.00
A	C	50	*Regimental Colours and Cap Badges (1907) — title box with side indent … … … … … … … … …	H.73	£1.30	£65.00
A	C	50	*Regimental Colours and Cap Badges — Territorial Regiments (1910) — title box without side indent:			
			A Blue back … … … … … … … … … …		£1.30	£65.00
			B Brown back … … … … … … … … … …		£1.30	£65.00
A	C	50	Regimental Standards and Cap Badges (1930) … …		80p	£40.00
J	C	10	Regimental Uniforms — see 'Allied Cavalry'			
A	C	50	Regimental Uniforms (1-50):			
			A Blue back (Jul. 1912) … … … … …		£2.20	£110.00
			B Brown back (Jul. 1914) … … … … … …		£2.40	£120.00
A	C	50	Regimental Uniforms (51-100) (1914) … … … …		£1.40	£70.00
A	C	50	Riders of the World:	H.358		
			A Thick grey card (1905) … … … … … …		£1.70	£85.00
			B Thinner white card (1914) … … … … …		£1.70	£85.00
—	P	6	The Royal Family (101 x 154mm) (1902) … … …	H.359	—	£270.00
—	C	1	The Royal Family (55 x 66mm) (1937) … … … …		—	£2.50
—	P	? 30	Rulers and Views (101 x 154mm) (1902) … … … …	H.363	£100.00	—
			Screen Celebrities — see Film Stars			
A	C	50	Sea Fishes:			
			A Home issue — Album 'price one penny', with I.T.C. clause (1935) … … … … … … … …		40p	£20.00
			Album (with price) … … … … … … … … …		—	£22.00
			B Irish issue — Album offer without price, with I.T.C. clause (1937) … … … … … … … …		£1.00	—
			Album (without price) … … … … … … … …		—	£40.00
			C Channel Islands issue — without Album or I.T.C. clause (1935) … … … … … … … …		80p	£40.00

JOHN PLAYER & SONS, Nottingham (continued)

Size	Print-ing	Number in set	Title	Handbook reference	Price per card	Complete set
A	C	50	A Sectional Map of Ireland (1937)		£2.50	—
A	U	1	A Sectional Map of Ireland Joker (1937)		—	£15.00
A	C	25	Shakespearean Series (1914)		£1.80	£45.00
B	C	20	Ship-Models (1926)		£3.00	£60.00
A	C	50	Shipping (unissued) (1960)		£1.50	£75.00
A	C	25	Ships' Figureheads (1912):			
			A Numerals 'sans serif'		£2.80	£70.00
			B Numerals with serif		£2.60	£65.00
B	C	25	Ships' Figure-Heads (1931)		£2.00	£50.00
—	C	8	Snap Cards (93 x 65mm) (c1930)	H.672	£7.00	—
A	C	50	Speedway Riders (1937)		£1.80	£90.00
			Album:			
			A Cream Cover		—	£30.00
			B Grey Cover		—	£30.00
A	BW ?	148	Stereoscopic Series (c1900)	H.357	£125.00	—
A	C	50	Straight Line Caricatures (1926)		60p	£30.00
A	C	25	Struggle for Existence (1923)		32p	£8.00
A	C	50	Tennis (1936)	H.524	90p	£45.00
			Album		—	£22.00
A	C	25	Those Pearls of Heaven (1914)		£1.40	£35.00
A	BW	66	Transvaal Series (1902):	H.360		
			A Black front		£5.00	—
			B Violet-black front		£5.00	—
B	C	25	Treasures of Britain (1931)		£1.80	£45.00
A	C	25	Treasures of Ireland (1930)		£2.00	£50.00
B	C	25	Types of Horses (1939):			
			A Home issue — with I.T.C. clause		£4.00	£100.00
			B Channel Islands issue — without I.T.C. clause		£4.60	—
A	C	50	Uniforms of the Territorial Army (Oct. 1939)		90p	£45.00
			Album		—	£22.00
A	C	50	Useful Plants and Fruits (1904)	H.361	£2.50	£125.00
A	C	25	Victoria Cross (1914)		£2.80	£70.00
A	C	90	War Decorations and Medals (1927)		90p	£80.00
	C		Wild Animals:	H.673		
A		50	A Small size — 'Wild Animals' Heads' (1931)		70p	£35.00
A		25	B Small transfers, number in series not stated (1931)		£1.50	—
A		50	C Small transfers — 'A Series of 50' (1931)		50p	£25.00
			Album		—	£30.00
B		25	D Large size — 'Wild Animals — A Series of ...' (1927)		£1.80	£45.00
B		25	E Large size — 'Wild Animals — 2nd Series ...' (1932)		£1.80	£45.00
A	C	50	Wild Animals of the World (1902):	H.77		
			A 'John Player & Sons Ltd.'		£3.00	£150.00
			B 'John Player & Sons, Branch, Nottingham'		£4.50	—
			C1 As B, 'Branch' omitted but showing traces of some or all of the letters		£4.50	—
			C2 As B. New printing with 'Branch' omitted		£3.00	£150.00
A2	C	45	Wild Animals of the World, narrow card (1902):	H.77		
			A 'John Player & Sons Ltd.'		£5.00	£225.00
			B 'John Player & Sons, Branch, Nottingham'		£7.00	—
			C1 As B, 'Branch' omitted but showing traces of some or all of the letters		£5.00	—
			C2 As B. New printing with 'Branch' omitted		£5.00	£225.00

JOHN PLAYER & SONS, Nottingham (continued)

Size	Printing	Number in set			Handbook reference	Price per card	Complete set
	C		Wild Birds:				
A		50	A	Small size (1932):			
				1 Cards … … … … … … … … …		50p	£25.00
				2 Transfers … … … … … … …		50p	£25.00
				Album … … … … … … … …		—	£30.00
B		25	B	Large size (1934) … … … … …		£2.80	£70.00
B	C	25	Wild Fowl (1937) … … … … … …			£3.20	£80.00
A	C	50	Wonders of the Deep (1904) … …	H.365	£2.00	£100.00
A	C	25	Wonders of the World:		H.362		
				A Blue back (1913) … … … … …		80p	£20.00
				B Grey back (1926) … … … … …		£1.40	£35.00
J	C	10	Wooden Walls (1909):				
				A Thick card … … … … … …		£6.00	£60.00
				B Thin card … … … … … … …		£6.00	£60.00
A	C	25	Wrestling and Ju-Jitsu:				
				A Blue back (1911) … … … … …		£2.40	£60.00
				B Grey back (1925) … … … …		£1.60	£40.00
A	C	26	Your Initials (transfers) (1932) … … …		70p	£18.00
B	C	25	Zoo Babies (1938):				
				A Home issue — with I.T.C. clause … … … …		80p	£20.00
				B Channel Islands issue — without I.T.C. clause		£2.00	—

POST-1960 ISSUES

Size	Printing	Number in set			Handbook reference	Price per card	Complete set
G	C	30	African Wildlife (1990) … … … … … …		50p	£15.00
			Album … … … … … … … … …		—	£15.00
—	BW	9	Basket Ball Fixtures (114 x 71mm) (1972) … … … …		£6.00	—
	C	44	Black Jack (1984):		H.896		
—			A Size 75 x 35mm … … … …		£1.00	—
—			B Size 80 x 47mm … … … …		60p	—
G2			C Size 90 x 47mm … … … …		60p	—
G	C	32	Britain's Endangered Wildlife:				
				A Grandee Issue (1984) … … … … …		25p	£8.00
				Album … … … … … … … …		—	£15.00
				B Doncella Issue (1984) … … … … …		30p	£9.00
				Album … … … … … … … …		—	£15.00
H2	C	30	Britain's Maritime History (1989) … … … …		40p	£12.00
			Album … … … … … … … … …		—	£10.00
G	C	30	Britain's Nocturnal Wildlife:				
				A Grandee Issue (1987) … … … … …		27p	£8.00
				Album … … … … … … … …		—	£15.00
				B Doncella Issue (1987) … … … … …		£1.00	£30.00
				Album … … … … … … … …		—	£15.00
G	C	30	Britain's Wayside Wildlife (1988) … … … … …		30p	£9.00
			Album … … … … … … … …		—	£15.00
G	C	30	Britain's Wild Flowers:				
				A Grandee Issue (1986) … … … … …		25p	£7.50
				Album … … … … … … … …		—	£15.00
				B Doncella Issue (1986) … … … … …		60p	£18.00
				Album … … … … … … … …		—	£15.00
G	C	32	British Birds (1980) … … … … … …		60p	£18.00
			Album/Folder … … … … … … …		—	£15.00
G	C	32	British Butterflies:				
				A Grandee Issue (1983) … … … … …		40p	£13.00
				Album … … … … … … … …		—	£15.00
				B Doncella Issue (1984) … … … … …		60p	£19.00
				Album … … … … … … … …		—	£15.00

JOHN PLAYER & SONS, Nottingham (Post-1960 Issues continued)

Size	Printing	Number in set	Description	Handbook reference	Price per card	Complete set
G	C	30	British Mammals:			
			A Grandee Issue (1982):			
			1 Imperial Tobacco Ltd		27p	£8.00
			2 Imperial Group PLC		40p	£12.00
			Album		—	£15.00
			B Doncella Issue (1983)		50p	£15.00
			Album		—	£15.00
G	C	32	Country Houses and Castles (1981)		33p	£10.00
			Album/Folder		—	£15.00
—	U	116	Corsair Game (63 x 38mm) (1965)	H.897	£1.00	—
H2	C	32	Exploration of Space (1983)		22p	£7.00
			Album		—	£8.00
G	C	28	Famous MG Marques (1981)		90p	£25.00
			Album/Folder		—	£15.00
G	C	24	The Golden Age of Flying (1977)	H.898	25p	£6.00
			Album/Folder		—	£15.00
G	C	1	The Golden Age of Flying Completion Offer (1977) ...	H.898	—	£3.50
G	C	24	The Golden Age of Motoring (1975):	H.899		
			A With set completion offer		£4.00	—
			B Without set completion offer		27p	£6.50
			Album/Folder		—	£15.00
G	C	24	The Golden Age of Sail (1978)		25p	£6.00
			Album/Folder		—	£10.00
G	C	1	The Golden Age of Sail Completion Offer (1978) ...		—	£3.50
G	C	24	The Golden Age of Steam (1976)	H.900	27p	£6.50
			Album/Folder		—	£15.00
G	C	1	The Golden Age of Steam Completion Offer (1976)	H.900	—	£3.50
G	U	7	Grandee Limericks (1977)		£10.00	—
H2	C	30	History of Britain's Railways (1987)		80p	£24.00
			Album		—	£15.00
H2	C	30	History of British Aviation (1988)		80p	£24.00
			Album		—	£15.00
H2	C	30	History of Motor Racing (1986):			
			A Imperial Tobacco Ltd		90p	£27.00
			B Imperial Group PLC		£1.20	£36.00
			Album		—	£15.00
G	C	24	History of the VC (1980)		£1.00	£24.00
			Album/Folder		—	£15.00
G	C	1	History of the VC completion offer (1980)		—	£5.00
—	BW	5	Jubilee Issue (70 x 55mm) (1960)	H.901	£1.50	£7.50
G	C	30	The Living Ocean:			
			A Grandee Issue (1985)		25p	£7.50
			Album		—	£15.00
			B Doncella Issue (1985)		40p	£12.00
			Album		—	£15.00
H2	C	32	Myths and Legends (1982)		£1.00	£32.00
			Album/Folder		—	£15.00
G	C	24	Napoleonic Uniforms (1979)		25p	£6.00
			Album/Folder		—	£15.00
G	C	1	Napoleonic Uniforms Completion Offer (1979)		—	£4.00
G	C	7	Panama Puzzles (1975)		£7.00	—
G	BW	6	Play Ladbroke Spot-Ball (1975)		£7.00	—
G	C	6	Play Panama Spot Six (1977)		£7.00	—
G1	C		Player Clues:	H.902		
		?	A Closing Date 30-1-87, red headings		50p	—
		?	B Closing Date 31-7-87, blue headings		50p	—

JOHN PLAYER & SONS, Nottingham (Post-1960 Issues continued)

Size	Print-ing	Number in set	Description	Handbook reference	Price per card	Complete set
G1	C		Player Games:	H.903		
		?	A Closing Date 28-1-83 ……………………		60p	—
		?	B Closing Date 29-7-83 ……………………		60p	—
		?	C Closing Date 30-12-83 ……………………		60p	—
		?	D Closing Date 30-4-84 ……………………		60p	—
		?	E Closing Date 31-8-84 ……………………		60p	—
		?	F Closing Date 31-1-85 ……………………		60p	—
G1	C	?	Player Prize Closing Date 29-1-88 …………	H.904	50p	—
G1	C		Player Quiz:	H.905		
		?	A Closing Date 31-7-85, green headings ………		50p	—
		?	B Closing Date 28-2-86, red headings ………		50p	—
		?	C Closing Date 31-7-86 blue headings ………		50p	—
	C	50	Supercars (1987):	H.906		
—			A Size 90 x 35mm ………………………		60p	—
G2			B Size 90 x 47mm ………………………		60p	—
	C	60	Superdeal (1985):	H.907		
—			A Size 75 x 35mm ………………………		60p	—
—			B Size 80 x 47mm ………………………		60p	—
—			C Size 90 x 35mm ………………………		60p	—
G2			D Size 90 x 47mm ………………………		60p	—
	C	108	Superyear 88 (1988):	H.908		
—			A Size 90 x 35mm ………………………		60p	—
G2			B Size 90 x 47mm ………………………		60p	—
—	U	4	Tom Thumb Record Breakers (82 x 65mm) (1976) …	H.909	£7.00	—
G	C	25	Top Dogs (1979) ……………………………		£1.20	£30.00
			Album/Folder ………………………………		—	£15.00
—	C	4	Vanguard Limericks (80 x 45mm) (1981) ………	H.910	£2.50	—
H2	C	32	Wonders of the Ancient World (1984) …………		40p	£12.50
			Album ………………………………………		—	£15.00
H2	C	30	Wonders of the Modern World (1985) …………		30p	£9.00
			Album ………………………………………		—	£15.00
G	C	6	World of Gardening (1976) ………………………		£10.00	—
	C	156	World Tour (1986):	H.911		
—			A Size 80 x 35mm ………………………		60p	—
—			B Size 80 x 47mm ………………………		60p	—
—			C Size 90 x 35mm ………………………		60p	—
G2			D Size 90 x 47mm ………………………		60p	—

OVERSEAS ISSUES

Size	Print-ing	Number in set	Description	Handbook reference	Price per card	Complete set
A	C	50	Aeroplane Series (1926) …………………………		£2.40	—
A	C	50	Arms and Armour (1926) …………………………		£3.00	£150.00
		50	Beauties 1st series (1925):			
—	P		A Black and white fronts (63 x 41mm) ……		£1.60	£80.00
—	PC		B Coloured fronts (63 x 44mm) ……………		£1.80	£90.00
—	PC	50	Beauties 2nd series (63 x 41mm) (1925) ………		£1.60	£80.00
D2	C	52	Birds of Brilliant Plumage (1927) ……………		£3.50	—
A	C	25	Bonzo Dogs (1923) ……………………………		£5.00	—
A	C	50	Boy Scouts (1924) ……………………………		£3.50	—
—	C	25	British Live Stock (80 x 54mm) (1924) ………		£7.50	—
A	C	50	Butterflies (Girls) (1928) ………………………		£6.00	—
A	C	25	Dogs (Heads) (1927) …………………………		£1.60	£40.00
D	C	32	Drum Horses (1911) ……………………………		£9.00	—
D2	C	25	Flag Girls of All Nations (1908) ………………		£9.00	—
A	C	50	Household Hints (1928-29) ……………………		£1.10	£55.00
A	C	50	Lawn Tennis (1928) ……………………………		£4.50	—
A	C	50	Leaders of Men (1925) ………………………		£2.50	£125.00
A	U	48	Pictures of the East (1931) ……………………		£2.50	£125.00
A	C	25	Picturesque People of the Empire (1928) ………		£2.40	£60.00

JOHN PLAYER & SONS, Nottingham (Overseas Issues continued)

Size	Print-ing	Number in set		Handbook reference	Price per card	Complete set
—	C	53	Playing Cards (68 x 45mm) (1929)		£1.40	—
A	U	50	Pugilists in Action (1928)		£4.50	—
A	C	50	Railway Working (1926)		£2.20	£110.00
A	P	50	The Royal Family at Home and Abroad (1927)		£2.80	—
A	C	50	Ships Flags and Cap Badges (1930)		£2.20	£110.00
A	C	50	Signalling series (1926)		£2.00	—
A	C	25	Whaling (1930)		£3.00	£75.00

JAS. PLAYFAIR & CO., London

Size	Print-ing	Number in set		Handbook reference	Price per card	Complete set
A	C	25	How to Keep Fit — Sandow Exercises (c1912)	H.136	£35.00	—

THE PREMIER TOBACCO MANUFACTURERS LTD, London

Size	Print-ing	Number in set		Handbook reference	Price per card	Complete set
D	U	48	Eminent Stage and Screen Personalities (1936) ...	H.569	£2.00	—
K2	C	52	*Miniature Playing Cards (c1935)		£7.50	—
—	BW		Stage and Screen Personalities (57 x 35mm) (1937):	H.674		
		100	A Back in grey		£1.50	—
		50	B Back in brown (Nos. 51-100)		£2.20	—

PRITCHARD & BURTON LTD, London

Size	Print-ing	Number in set		Handbook reference	Price per card	Complete set
A2	C	51	*Actors and Actresses — 'FROGA B and C' (c1900):	H.20		
			A Blue back		£22.00	—
			B Grey-black back		£75.00	—
A	C	15	*Beauties 'PAC' (c1900)	H.2	£60.00	—
D	BW	20	*Boer War Cartoons (1900)	H.42	£120.00	—
A1	C		*Flags and Flags with Soldiers (c1902):	H.41		
			A Flagstaff Draped:			
		30	1st printing		£18.00	£540.00
		15	2nd printing		£20.00	—
		15	B Flagstaff not Draped (Flags only)		£20.00	—
D	U	25	*Holiday Resorts and Views (c1902)	H.366	£20.00	—
A	C	40	*Home Colonial Regiments (c1901)	H.69	£55.00	—
D	U	25	*Royalty Series (1902)	H.367	£24.00	—
D	U	25	*South African Series (1901)	H.368	£24.00	—
A2	C	25	*Star Girls (c1900)	H.30	£220.00	—

G. PRUDHOE, Darlington

Size	Print-ing	Number in set		Handbook reference	Price per card	Complete set
C	C	30	*Army Pictures, Cartoons, etc (c1916)	H.12	£130.00	—

JAMES QUINTON LTD, London

Size	Print-ing	Number in set		Handbook reference	Price per card	Complete set
A	C	26	*Actresses — 'FROGA A' (c1900)	H.20	£200.00	—

RAY & CO. LTD, London

Size	Print-ing	Number in set		Handbook reference	Price per card	Complete set
—	C		*Flags of The Allies (Shaped) (c1915):	H.49		
		1	A Grouped Flag 'All Arms' Cigarettes		£80.00	—
		5	B Allies Flags 'Life Ray' Cigarettes		£80.00	—
A	BW	25	War Series — 1-25 — Battleships (c1915)	H.472	£15.00	—
A	C	75	War Series — 26-100 — British and Foreign Uniforms (c1915)	H.472	£12.00	—
A	C	24	War Series — 101-124 — British and Dominion Uniforms (c1915)	H.472	£25.00	—

RAYMOND REVUEBAR, London

Size	Print-ing	Number in set		Handbook reference	Price per card	Complete set
—	P	25	Revuebar Striptease Artists (72 x 46mm) (1960) ...		£18.00	—

RECORD CIGARETTE & TOBACCO CO., London

Size	Printing	Number in set	Title	Handbook reference	Price per card	Complete set
—	U	? 2	Gramophone Records (100mm Diameter) (c1935) ...	H.675	£100.00	—
—	U	? 34	The 'Talkie' Cigarette Card — (gramophone record on reverse) (70mm square) (c1935):			
			A Back 'Record Tobacco Company'		£50.00	—
			B Back 'Record Cigarette Company'		£50.00	—

J. REDFORD & CO., London

Size	Printing	Number in set	Title	Handbook reference	Price per card	Complete set
A	BW	20	*Actresses — 'BLARM' (c1900)	H.23	£75.00	—
A2	C	25	*Armies of the World (c1901)	H.43	£60.00	—
A2	C	25	*Beauties — 'GRACC' (c1899)	H.59	£130.00	—
A2	C	30	*Colonial Troops (c1902)	H.40	£55.00	—
D	C	24	*Nautical Expressions (c1900)	H.174	£80.00	—
D2	C	40	*Naval and Military Phrases (c1904)	H.14	£65.00	—
A	C	25	Picture Series (c1905)	H.369	£65.00	—
A	C	25	Sports and Pastimes Series 1 (c1905)	H.225	£80.00	—
D1	BW	50	Stage Artistes of the Day (c1908)	H.370	£20.00	—

RELIANCE TOBACCO MFG. CO. LTD

Size	Printing	Number in set	Title	Handbook reference	Price per card	Complete set
A2	C	24	British Birds (c1935)	H.604	£5.00	—
A2	C	35	*Famous Stars* (c1935)	H.572	£5.00	—

RICHARDS & WARD

Size	Printing	Number in set	Title	Handbook reference	Price per card	Complete set
A1	P	? 13	*Beauties — 'Topsy Cigarettes' (c1900)	H.371	£750.00	—

A.S. RICHARDSON, Luton

Size	Printing	Number in set	Title	Handbook reference	Price per card	Complete set
—	U	12	*Manikin Cards (82 x 51mm) (c1920)	H.481	£120.00	—

THE RICHMOND CAVENDISH CO. LTD, London

Size	Printing	Number in set	Title	Handbook reference	Price per card	Complete set
A2	C	26	*Actresses — 'FROGA A' (c1900)	H.20	£32.00	—
D2	BW	28	*Actresses — 'PILPI I' (c1902)	H.195	£15.00	—
D	P	50	*Actresses 'PILPI II' (c1902)	H.196	£11.00	—
A	U		*Actresses Photogravure, 'Smoke Pioneer Cigarettes' back (c1905):	H.372		
		50	I Reading bottom to top		£8.00	£400.00
		? 179	IIA Reading top to bottom. Different subjects		£7.00	—
		? 13	B Plain back		£11.00	—
A	C	14	*Beauties 'AMBS' (1899):	H.373		
			A 'The Absent Minded Beggar' back:			
			i '1st Verse' back		£50.00	—
			ii '2nd Verse' back		£50.00	—
			iii '3rd Verse' back		£50.00	—
			iv '4th Verse' back		£50.00	—
			v 'Chorus (1st verse)' back		£50.00	—
			vi 'Chorus (2nd verse)' back		£50.00	—
			vii 'Chorus (3rd verse)' back		£50.00	—
			viii 'Chorus (4th verse)' back		£50.00	—
			B 'The Soldiers of The Queen' back:			
			i '1 Britons once did' back		£50.00	—
			ii '2 War clouds gather' back		£50.00	—
			iii '3 Now we're roused' back		£50.00	—
			iv 'Chorus' back		£50.00	—
A	C	52	*Beauties — 'ROBRI' playing card inset (c1898)	H.374	£50.00	—
—	C	40	*Medals (34 x 72mm) (c1900)	H.200	£22.50	£900.00
A2	C	20	Music Hall Artistes (c1902)	H.202	£50.00	—
A	C	12	*Pretty Girl Series — 'RASH' (c1900)	H.8	£50.00	—

THE RICHMOND CAVENDISH CO. LTD, London (continued)

Size	Print	Number		Handbook	Price	Complete
A	C	20	*Yachts (c1900):	H.204		
			A Gold on black back		£65.00	—
			B Black on white back		£65.00	—

OVERSEAS ISSUES

D	C	28	Chinese Actors and Actresses (1922)	W.361	£4.00	—
A	P	50	Cinema Stars (1926)		£3.50	—

RIDGWAYS, Manchester

—	C	? 2	*'Play Up' Sporting Shields (c1895)	H.718	£150.00	—

R. ROBERTS & SONS, London

A2	C	26	*Actresses — 'FROGA A' (c1900)	H.20	£75.00	—
A	C	25	*Armies of the World (c1900):	H.43		
			A 'Fine Old Virginia' back		£50.00	—
			B Plain back		£50.00	—
A2	C	50	*Beauties — 'CHOAB' (c1900):	H.21		
			1-25 without borders to back		£70.00	—
			26-50 with borders to back		£85.00	—
—	C	50	*Beautiful Women (60 x 43mm) (c1900)	H.284	£275.00	—
A2	C	50	*Colonial Troops (c1902)	H.40	£40.00	—
A	BW	28	*Dominoes (c1905)		£80.00	—
K1	C	52	*Miniature Playing Cards (c1905):			
			A Blue background		£65.00	—
			B Pink background		£65.00	—
			C Yellow background		£65.00	—
D2	C	24	*Nautical Expressions (c1900):	H.174		
			A 'Navy Cut Cigarettes' on front		£65.00	—
			B Firm's name only on front		£65.00	—
A2	C	70	Stories without words (c1905)		£60.00	—
A2	C	25	*Types of British and Colonial Troops (c1900)	H.76	£50.00	—

ROBINSON & BARNSDALE LTD, London

—	C	1	*Advertisement Card — Soldier, 'Colin Campbell Cigars' (29 x 75mm) (c1897):	H.764		
			A With equal 'E' back		—	£200.00
			B With unequal 'E' back		—	£150.00
—	BW	? 24	*Actresses, 'Colin Campbell Cigars' (c1898):	H.375		
			A Size 43 x 70mm		£140.00	—
			B Officially cut narrow — 32 x 70mm		£140.00	—
A	P	? 33	*Actresses, 'Cupola' Cigarettes (c1898)	H.376	£250.00	—
A1	P		*Beauties — collotype (c1895):	H.377		
		? 9	A 'Our Golden Beauties' back in black		£250.00	—
		? 18	B 'Nana' back in red on white		£250.00	—
		? 1	C 'Nana' back in vermillion on cream		£250.00	—
A	C	? 1	*Beauties — 'Blush of Day' (c1898)		£350.00	—
—	C	? 16	*Beauties — 'Highest Honors' (44 x 73mm) (c1895)	H.379	£350.00	—
A2	U	? 3	Beauties 'KEWA II' (c1895)	H.139	£350.00	—

E. ROBINSON & SONS LTD, Stockport

A1	C	10	*Beauties 'ROBRI' (c1900):	H.374		
			A 'Forget-Me-Not Mixture' back		£60.00	—
			B 'Gold Flake Honeydew' back		£60.00	—
			C 'Gold Leaf Navy Cut' back		£60.00	—
			D 'Jack's Best Tobacco' back		£60.00	—
			E 'Jack Tar Navy Cut' back		£60.00	—
			F 'Man Friday Mixture' back		£60.00	—

E. ROBINSON & SONS LTD, Stockport (continued)

*Beauties 'ROBRI' (continued):

Size	Printing	Number in set		Handbook reference	Price per card	Complete set
			G 'Reliable Tobaccos' back		£60.00	—
			H 'Stockport Snuff' back		£60.00	—
			I 'Thin Twist & Thick Twist' back		£60.00	—
			J 'Three Decker Cigarettes' back		£60.00	—
A	BW	? 49	Derbyshire and the Peak (c1905)	H.380	£225.00	—
A2	C	25	Egyptian Studies (c1914)		£25.00	—
A	C	25	King Lud Problems (c1934)	H.638	£22.00	—
A	C	6	Medals and Decorations of Great Britain (c1905):	H.484		
			A Vertical back with firm's name		£250.00	—
			B Horizontal back with 'General Favourite Onyx'		£500.00	—
A2	C	40	Nature Studies (c1912)		£24.00	—
A2	C	25	Regimental Mascots (1916)		£70.00	—
A	C	25	Types of British Soldiers (1900)	H.144	£400.00	—
A2	C	25	Wild Flowers (c1915)		£20.00	£500.00

ROMAN STAR CIGARS

Size	Printing	Number in set		Handbook reference	Price per card	Complete set
C	C	26	*Actresses 'FROGA A' (c1900)	H.20	£175.00	—
A	C	25	*Beauties 'BOCCA' (c1900)	H.39	£175.00	—

ROTHMAN'S LTD, London

Size	Printing	Number in set		Handbook reference	Price per card	Complete set
	C		Beauties of the Cinema (1936):	H.605		
D1		40	A Small size		£1.75	£70.00
—		24	B Circular cards, 64mm diam:			
			1 Varnished		£4.00	£100.00
			2 Unvarnished		£4.00	£100.00
A2	P	24	Cinema Stars — Small size (c1925)		£1.60	£40.00
B	P	25	Cinema Stars — Large size (c1925)		£1.00	£25.00
—	C	30	Country Living (Consulate) (112 x 102mm) (1973) ...		—	£18.00
—	C	6	Diamond Jubilee Folders (127 x 95mm) (1950)		£12.00	—
C2	C	50	Football International Stars (unissued) (1984) ...	H.912	50p	£25.00
C	U	36	Landmarks in Empire History (c1936)		£1.25	£45.00
			Album		—	£50.00
		?	Metal Charms (c1930)		£4.00	—
D1	U	50	Modern Inventions (1935)		£1.20	£60.00
B2	P	54	New Zealand (c1930)		£1.00	£55.00
D1	U	24	Prominent Screen Favourites (1934)	H.568	£1.20	£30.00
A2	BW	50	'Punch Jokes' (c1935)		60p	£30.00
A1	C	5	Rare Banknotes (1970)		£4.00	—
			Album		—	£10.00

WM. RUDDELL LTD, Dublin and Liverpool

Size	Printing	Number in set		Handbook reference	Price per card	Complete set
K	U	? 3	*Couplet Cards (c1925)	H.676	£30.00	—
D	C	25	Grand Opera Series (1924)		£7.40	£185.00
A2	C	25	Rod and Gun (1924)		£7.00	£175.00
D	C	50	Songs that will Live for Ever (c1925)		£4.00	£200.00

RUTHERFORD

Size	Printing	Number in set		Handbook reference	Price per card	Complete set
A	BW	? 6	Footballers (c1900)	H.765	£2000.00	—

I. RUTTER & CO., Mitcham

Size	Printing	Number in set		Handbook reference	Price per card	Complete set
D	BW	15	*Actresses — 'RUTAN' (c1900):	H.381		
			A Rubber-stamped on plain back		£90.00	—
			B Red printed back		£60.00	—
			C Plain back		£35.00	—

I. RUTTER & CO., Mitcham (continued)

Size	Printing	Number in set		Handbook reference	Price per card	Complete set
A	BW	1	Advertisement Card 'Tobacco Bloom' (1899)	H.485	—	£1200.00
A	BW	7	*Boer War Celebrities (c1901)	H.382	£60.00	—
D1	C	54	*Comic Phrases (c1905)	H.223	£20.00	—
A	BW	20	Cricketers Series (1901)	H.29	£325.00	—
C	C		*Flags and Flags with Soldiers (c1902):	H.41		
		15	A Flagstaff Draped, 2nd printing		£26.00	—
		15	B Flagstaff not Draped (Flags only)			
			(a) white back		£26.00	—
			(b) cream back		£26.00	—
C	C	24	*Girls, Flags and Arms of Countries (c1900):	H.383		
			A Blue back		£35.00	—
			B Plain back		£25.00	—
A	C	25	Proverbs (c1905):	H.384		
			A Green Seal on front		£45.00	—
			B Red Seal on front		£45.00	—
A	C	25	*Shadowgraphs (c1905)	H.44	£45.00	—

S.D.V. TOBACCO CO. LTD, Liverpool

Size	Printing	Number in set		Handbook reference	Price per card	Complete set
A	BW	16	British Royal Family (c1901)	H.28	£600.00	—

ST. PETERSBURG CIGARETTE CO. LTD, Portsmouth

Size	Printing	Number in set		Handbook reference	Price per card	Complete set
A	BW	? 17	Footballers (c1900)	H.410	£1800.00	—

SALMON & GLUCKSTEIN LTD, London

Size	Printing	Number in set		Handbook reference	Price per card	Complete set
—	C	1	*Advertisement Card ('Snake Charmer' Cigarettes) (73 x 107mm) (c1897)	H.767	—	£500.00
C	C	15	*Billiard Terms (c1905):			
			A Small numerals about 2mm high		£80.00	—
			B Larger numerals about 3mm high		£80.00	—
A	C	12	British Queens (c1897)	H.480	£45.00	—
—	C	30	*Castles, Abbeys and Houses (76 x 73mm) (c1906):			
			A Brown back		£18.00	—
			B Red back		£25.00	—
C	C	32	*Characters from Dickens (c1903)	H.385	£30.00	—
A	C	25	Coronation Series (1911)		£12.00	£300.00
—	U	25	*Famous Pictures — Brown photogravure (57 x 76mm) (c1910)	H.386	£10.00	£250.00
—	U	25	*Famous Pictures — Green photogravure (58 x 76mm) (c1910)	H.387	£9.00	£225.00
A2	C	6	Her Most Gracious Majesty Queen Victoria (1897):	H.388		
			A Thin card		£50.00	£300.00
			B Thick card		£50.00	£300.00
A	C	50	The Great White City (c1908)		£14.00	£700.00
C	C	40	Heroes of the Transvaal War (1901)	H.389	£15.00	£600.00
D2	C	25	Magical Series (1923)		£7.00	£175.00
C	C	30	*Music Hall Celebrities (c1902)		£55.00	—
—	C	25	*Occupations (64 x 18mm) (c1898)	H.390	£550.00	—
C	C	20	'Owners and Jockeys' Series (c1900)	H.392	£85.00	—
—	C	48	*The Post in Various Countries (41 x 66mm) (c1900)	H.391	£28.00	—
A2	C	6	*Pretty Girl Series — 'RASH' (c1900)	H.8	£65.00	—
—	C	22	Shakespearian Series (c1902):	H.393		
			A Large format, frame line back (38 x 69mm) ...		£35.00	—
			B Re-drawn, small format, no frame line back (37 x 66mm)		£35.00	—

SALMON & GLUCKSTEIN LTD, London (continued)

Size	Print-ing	Number in set		Handbook reference	Price per card	Complete set
A	C	25	*Star Girls (c1900):	H.30		
			A Red back … … … … … … … … … … … …		£120.00	—
			B Brown back, different setting … … … … … …		£120.00	—
A	C	25	Traditions of the Army and Navy (c1917):			
			A Large numerals, dome above number 2mm wide		£16.00	£400.00
			B Smaller numerals, back redrawn, dome above number 1mm wide … … … … … … … …		£16.00	£400.00
A2	C	25	Wireless Explained (1923) … … … … … … … … …		£6.00	£150.00

SILKS

Size	Print-ing	Number in set		Handbook reference	Price per card	Complete set
—	C	50	*Pottery Types (paper-backed) (83 x 55mm) (c1915):	H.505-17		
			A Numbered on front and back … … … …		£4.50	—
			B Numbered on back only … … … … … … …		£4.50	—

W. SANDORIDES & CO. LTD, London

Size	Print-ing	Number in set		Handbook reference	Price per card	Complete set
	U	25	Aquarium Studies from the London Zoo (1925):	H.607		
C2			A Small size:			
			1 Small lettering on back … … … … … …		£3.60	£90.00
			2 Larger lettering on back … … … … …		£3.60	£90.00
B1			B Large size … … … … … … … … … … … …		£3.60	£90.00
	C	25	Cinema Celebrities (1924):	H.530		
C2			A Small size … … … … … … … … … … … …		£2.60	£65.00
—			B Extra-large size (109 x 67mm) … … … …		£4.00	£100.00
	C	25	Cinema Stars (export) (c1924):	H.530		
C2			A Small size, with firm's name at base of back …		£6.00	—
C2			B Small size, 'Issued with Lucana Cigarettes …		£6.00	—
C2			C Small size, 'Issued with Big Gun Cigarettes …'		£8.00	—
—			D Extra-large size (109 x 67mm) 'Issued with Big Gun Cigarettes … … … … … … … …		£2.60	£65.00
—			E Extra-large size (109 x 67mm) issued with Lucana 66 … … … … … … … … … …		£8.00	—
	U	50	Famous Racecourses (1926) — 'Lucana':	H.608		
C2			A Small size … … … … … … … … … …		£4.00	£200.00
B1			B Large size … … … … … … … … … …		£5.00	£250.00
C2	U	50	Famous Racehorses (1923):	H.609		
			1A Back in light brown … … … … … … … …		£3.20	£160.00
			1B Back in dark brown … … … … … … … …		£3.20	£160.00
			2 As 1A, with blue label added, inscribed 'Issued with Sandorides Big Gun Cigarettes …' …		£12.00	—
—	BW	12	London Views (57 x 31mm) (c1936) — see Teofani			
A	C	25	Sports & Pastimes — Series 1 — 'Big Gun Cigarettes (c1924) … … … … … … … … … … … …	H.225	£12.00	—

SANSOM'S CIGAR STORES, London

Size	Print-ing	Number in set		Handbook reference	Price per card	Complete set
—	P	? 2	*London Views (52 x 37mm) (c1915) … … … … …	H.768	£650.00	—

NICHOLAS SARONY & CO., London

Size	Print-ing	Number in set		Handbook reference	Price per card	Complete set
	C	50	Around the Mediterranean (1926):	GP.404		
C2			A Small size … … … … … … … … … …		£1.20	£60.00
			Album … … … … … … … … … … … … …		—	£30.00
B1			B Large size … … … … … … … … … …		£1.20	£60.00
—	U	? 7	Boer War Scenes (67 x 45mm) (c1901) … … … …	GP.701	£800.00	—
	U	25	Celebrities and Their Autographs, Nd 1-25 (1923):			
C1			A Small size … … … … … … … … … …		£1.00	£25.00
B1			B Large size … … … … … … … … … …		£1.00	£25.00

NICHOLAS SARONY & CO., London (continued)

Size	Print-ing	Number in set		Handbook reference	Price per card	Complete set
	U	25	Celebrities and Their Autographs, Nd 26-50 (1924):			
C1			A Small size:			
			1 Small numerals		£1.00	£25.00
			2 Large numerals		£1.00	£25.00
B1			B Large size:			
			1 Small numerals		£1.00	£25.00
			2 Large numerals		£1.00	£25.00
	U	25	Celebrities and Their Autographs. Nd 51-75 (1924):			
C1			A Small size		£1.00	£25.00
B1			B Large size		£1.00	£25.00
	U	25	Celebrities and Their Autographs, Nd 76-100 (1925):			
C1			A Small size		£1.00	£25.00
B1			B Large size		£1.00	£25.00
A2	U	50	Cinema Stars — Set 7 (1933)	GP.703	£1.50	£75.00
—	U		Cinema Stars — Postcard size (137 x 85mm):			
		38	'of a Series of 38 Cinema Stars' (1929)		£9.00	—
		42	'of a second Series of 42 Cinema Stars' (c1930) ...		£5.00	£210.00
		50	'of a third Series of 50 Cinema Stars' (c1930) ...		£5.00	£250.00
		42	'of a fourth Series of 42 Cinema Stars' (c1931) ...		£5.00	£210.00
		25	'of a fifth Series of 25 Cinema Stars' (c1931)		£5.00	£125.00
D	U	25	Cinema Studies (1929)		£1.20	£30.00
	C	25	A Day on the Airway (1928):			
C2			A Small size		£1.40	£35.00
B2			B Large size		£1.40	£35.00
A2	P	54	Life at Whipsnade Zoo (1934)	GP.415	60p	£32.50
	BW	25	Links with the Past — First 25 subjects, Nd 1-25 (1925):	GP.711		
C1			A Small size		50p	£12.50
B			B Large size		60p	
	BW	25	Links with the Past — Second 25 subjects (1926):	GP.711		
C			A Home issue, Nd 26-50:			
			1 Small size		50p	£12.50
B			2 Large size, descriptive back		40p	£10.00
B			3 Large size, advertisement back		£1.80	—
			B Sydney issue, Nd 1-25:			
C			1 Small size		£1.00	£25.00
B			2 Large size		£1.00	£25.00
			C Christchurch issue, Nd 1-25:			
C			1 Small size		£1.00	£25.00
B			2 Large size		40p	£10.00
	BW	25	Museum Series (1927):	GP.712		
			A Home issue:			
C2			1 Small size		30p	£7.50
B			2 Large size, descriptive back		30p	£7.50
B			3 Large size, advertisement back		£1.00	£25.00
			Booklet Cover for large size		—	£4.00
B			B Sydney issue, large size		70p	£17.50
			C Christchurch issue:			
C2			1 Small size		60p	£15.00
B			2 Large size		70p	£17.50
	P	36	National Types of Beauty (1928):	GP.417		
A2			A Small size		50p	£18.00
—			B Medium size (76 x 51mm)		40p	£14.00
	C	15	Origin of Games (1923):			
A			A Small size		£5.00	£75.00
B2			B Large size		£6.00	£90.00

NICHOLAS SARONY & CO., London (continued)

	C	50	'Saronicks' (1929):	GP.414		
D2			A Small size		40p	£20.00
—			B Medium size (76 x 51 mm)		40p	£20.00
	C	50	Ships of All Ages (1929):			
D			A Small size		80p	£40.00
—			B Medium size (76 x 52mm)		£1.20	£60.00
D	C	25	Tennis Strokes (1923)		£3.60	£90.00

T.S. SAUNT, Leicester

D	C	30	*Army Pictures, Cartoons etc (c1916)	H.12	£130.00	—

SCOTTISH COOPERATIVE WHOLESALE SOCIETY LTD, Glasgow ('S.C.W.S.')

A2	C	25	Burns (1924):	H.611		
			A Printed back:			
			1 White card		£2.80	—
			2 Cream card		£1.60	£40.00
			*B Plain back		£7.50	—
C	C	20	Dogs (1925)	H.211	£12.00	—
A2	C	25	Dwellings of All Nations (1924):	H.612		
			A Printed back:			
			1 White card		£3.50	—
			2 Cream card		£2.20	£55.00
			*B Plain back		£7.50	—
B	C	25	Famous Pictures (1924)		£8.00	—
H2	C	25	Famous Pictures — Glasgow Gallery (1927):			
			A Non-adhesive back		£2.40	£60.00
			B Adhesive back		£1.40	£35.00
H2	C	25	Famous Pictures — London Galleries (1927):			
			A Non-adhesive back		£2.40	£60.00
			B Adhesive back		£1.40	£35.00
A2	C	50	Feathered Favourites (1926):			
			A Grey borders		£2.50	£125.00
			B White borders:			
			1 Non-adhesive back		£2.50	£125.00
			2 Adhesive back		£1.80	£90.00
A	C	25	Racial Types (1925)		£8.00	£200.00
A2	C	50	Triumphs of Engineering (1926):			
			A Brown border		£2.50	£125.00
			B White border		£2.60	—
A2	C	50	Wireless (1924)		£4.50	£225.00

SELBY'S TOBACCO STORES, Cirencester

—	U	12	'Manikin' Cards (79 x 51mm) (c1920)	H.481	£120.00	—

SHARPE & SNOWDEN, London

A	U	? 1	*Views of England (c1905)	H.769	£750.00	—
A	U	? 23	*Views of London (c1905)	H.395	£350.00	—

W.J. SHEPHERD, London

A	U	25	*Beauties — 'FECKSA' (c1900)	H.58	£100.00	—

SHORT'S, London

—	BW		*Short's House Views (c1925):	H.562		
		? 13	1 Numbered (75 x 60mm)		£60.00	—
		? 6	2 Unnumbered (77 x 69mm)		£40.00	—

JOHN SINCLAIR LTD, Newcastle-on-Tyne

Size	Print-ing	Number in set		Handbook reference	Price per card	Complete set
D2	U	? 92	*Actresses (42 x 63 mm) (c1900)	H.396	£85.00	—
—	P		*Birds (1924):	H.613		
C		? 41	A Small size, back 'Specimen Cigarette Card' ...		£8.00	—
C		48	B Small size, descriptive back:			
			1 White front		£3.00	—
			2 Pinkish front		£3.00	—
—		50	C Large size (78 x 58mm)		£6.50	—
A	C	50	British Sea Dogs (1926)		£6.00	£300.00
	P		Champion Dogs — 'A Series of ...' (1938):			
A2		54	A Small size		75p	£40.00
B2		52	B Large size		75p	£40.00
	P		Champion Dogs — '2nd Series ...' (1939):			
A2		54	A Small size		£3.25	£175.00
B2		52	B Large size		£3.50	—
A2	P	50	English and Scottish Football Stars (1935)		£1.50	£75.00
A	P	54	Film Stars — 'A Series of 54 Real Photos' (1934) ...		£2.20	£120.00
A	P	54	Film Stars — 'A Series of Real Photos', Nd 1-54 (1937)		£1.70	£90.00
A	P	54	Film Stars — 'A Series of Real Photos', Nd 55-108 (1937)		£1.30	£70.00
	P		*Flowers and Plants (1924):	H.614		
C		? 37	A Small size, back 'Specimen Cigarette Card' ...		£7.50	—
C		96	B Small size, descriptive back:			
			1 White front		£2.50	—
			2 Pinkish front		£2.50	—
D	P	? 52	Football Favourites (c1910)		£170.00	—
A	BW	4	*North Country Celebrities (c1905)	H.397	£75.00	£300.00
D	P	? 55	Northern Gems (c1902)		£75.00	—
A	C	50	Picture Puzzles and Riddles (c1910)		£27.00	—
A	P	54	Radio Favourites (1935)		£1.50	£80.00
K2	C	53	Rubicon Cards (miniature playing cards) (1933):			
			A Without overprint		£6.00	—
			B With red overprint		£8.00	—
A	C	50	Trick Series (c1910)		£30.00	—
A	BW	50	Well-Known Footballers — North Eastern Counties (1938)		£1.20	£60.00
A	BW	50	Well-Known Footballers — Scottish (1938)		£1.20	£60.00
D2	C	50	World's Coinage (c1915)	H.398	£20.00	£1000.00

SILKS

Size	Print-ing	Number in set		Handbook reference	Price per card	Complete set
—	C	? 1	The Allies (140 x 100mm) (numbered 37) (c1915) ...	H.501-2	—	£35.00
—	C		*Flags — Set 2 (70 x 52mm) (unbacked and anonymous) (c1915):	H.501-2		
		? 12	A Numbered Nos 25-36		£14.00	—
			B Unnumbered:			
		? 24	1 Caption in red		£8.00	—
		? 24	2 Caption in myrtle-green		£7.00	—
		? 24	3 Caption in bright green		£7.00	—
		? 24	4 Caption in blue		£8.00	—
		? 25	5 Caption in black		£12.00	—
—	C		*Flags — Set 11 (unbacked and anonymous) (c1915):	H.501-11		
		50	'Fourth Series' (49 x 70mm)		£6.00	—
		50	'Fifth Series' (49 x 70mm)		£6.00	—
		50	'Sixth Series':			
			1 Nos 1-25 (49 x 70mm)		£7.00	—
			2 Nos 26-50 (68 x 80mm)		£7.00	—
		? 10	'Seventh Series' (115 x 145mm)		£60.00	—

JOHN SINCLAIR LTD, Newcastle-on-Tyne (Silks continued)

	C	50	*Regimental Badges I (paper backed) (70 x 52mm) (c1915)	H.502-1	£6.00	—
—	C	? 24	*Regimental Colours II (unbacked and anonymous) (c1915):	H.502-7		
			1 Nos 38-49 (No. 49 not seen) (76 x 70mm)		£13.00	—
			2 Nos 50-61 (65 x 51mm)		£13.00	

ROBERT SINCLAIR TOBACCO CO. LTD, Newcastle-on-Tyne

C2	C		Billiards by Willie Smith (1928):			
		10	1 First set of 10		£9.00	£90.00
		15	2 Second Set of 15		£11.00	£165.00
		3	3 Third Set of 25 (Nos 26-28 only issued)		£16.00	£48.00
A2	U	28	Dominoes (c1900)		£60.00	
			*Footballers (c1900):	H.399		
A2	U	? 4	A Mauve Collotype		£1500.00	—
D2	BW	? 16	B Black & White Collotype		£1000.00	—
D	C	12	*Policemen of the World (c1899)	H.164	£220.00	—
	C	12	The 'Smiler' Series (1924):			
A			A Small size (inscribed '... 24 cards'), ...		£7.50	—
H			B Large size		£13.00	—

SILKS. *Unbacked silks, inscribed with initials 'R.S.' in circle.*

—	C	4	*Battleships and Crests (73 x 102mm) (c1915)	H.499-1	£60.00	—
—	C	10	*Flags (70 x 51 mm) (c1915)	H.499-2	£26.00	—
—	C	6	*Great War Area — Cathedrals and Churches (140 x 102mm) (c1915)	H.499-3	£50.00	—
—	C	10	*Great War Heroes (70 x 51 mm) (c1915)	H.499-4	£40.00	—
—	C	1	*Red Cross Nurse (73 x 102mm) (c1915)	H.499-5	—	£50.00
—	C	5	*Regimental Badges (70 x 51 mm) (c1915)	H.499-6	£32.00	—

J. SINFIELD, Scarborough

A	U	24	*Beauties — 'HUMPS' (c1900)	H.222	£1400.00	—

SINGLETON & COLE LTD, Shrewsbury

A	C	50	*Atlantic Liners (1910)		£24.00	—
A	C	25	Bonzo Series (1928)	H.678	£8.00	£200.00
D1	BW	50	*Celebrities — Boer War Period (c1901):	H.400		
			25 Actresses		£22.00	£550.00
			25 Boer War Celebrities		£22.00	£550.00
A2	BW	35	Famous Boxers (1930):			
			A Numbered		£16.00	—
			B Unnumbered		£45.00	—
A2	BW	25	Famous Film Stars (1930)		£11.00	—
A	BW	35	Famous Officers — Hero Series (1915):			
			A1 'Famous Officers' on back toned card		£15.00	£525.00
			A2 'Famous Officers' thin white card		£35.00	—
			B 'Hero Series' on back		£400.00	—
D1	BW	50	*Footballers (c1905)		£150.00	—
C	C	40	*Kings and Queens (1902)	H.157	£25.00	—
—	U	12	'Manikin' Cards (77 x 49mm) (c1920)	H.481	£110.00	—
A	C	25	Maxims of Success (c1905):	H.401		
			A Orange border		£30.00	—
			B Lemon yellow border		£250.00	—
A	BW		Orient Royal Mail Line (c1905):	H.402		
		8	A 'Orient-Pacific Line' front, Manager's back ...		£65.00	—
		8	B 'Orient Royal Mail Line' front, Singleton and Cole back		£45.00	—

SINGLETON & COLE LTD, Shrewsbury (continued)

Orient Royal Mail Line (continued):

Size	Print	Number	Description	Handbook ref	Price	Complete
		10	C 'Orient Line' front, Manager's back (5 ports) ...		£45.00	—
		10	D 'Orient Line' front, Manager's back (11 ports)		£45.00	—
A	C	25	Wallace Jones — Keep Fit System (c1910)		£26.00	—

SILKS

—	C	110	Crests and Badges of the British Army (paper-backed) (66 x 40mm) (c1915)	H.502-2	£4.00	—

F. & J. SMITH, Glasgow
36 page reference book — £4.50

Size	Print	Number	Description	Handbook ref	Price	Complete
A	C	25	*Advertisement Cards (1899)	H.403	£250.00	—
A	C	50	Battlefields of Great Britain (1913):			
			A 'Albion Gold Flake Cigarettes' back		£16.00	—
			B 'Auld Brig Flake' back		£16.00	—
			C 'Cut Golden Bar Twilight Brand' back		£16.00	—
			D 'Glasgow Mixture Cigarettes' back		£16.00	—
			E 'Glasgow Mixture Tobacco' back		£16.00	—
			F 'Goodwill Virginia' back		£16.00	—
			G 'Kashan Cigarettes' back		£16.00	—
			H 'No. 1 Mixture' back		£16.00	—
			I 'Orchestra Cigarettes' back		£16.00	—
			J 'Pinewood Cigarettes' back		£16.00	—
			K 'Pinewood Mixture' back		£16.00	—
			L 'Squaw Thick Black Tobacco' back		£16.00	—
			M 'Studio Cigarettes' back		£16.00	—
			N 'Sun Cured Mixture' back		£16.00	—
			O 'Wild Geranium Cigarettes' back		£16.00	—
A1	BW	25	*Boer War Series 'Studio' Cigarettes back (1900) ...		£75.00	—
A	C	50	*Boer War Series (1900)		£30.00	—
D	BW		*Champions of Sport (1902):	H.404		
		50	A Red back. Numbered, multi-backed		£90.00	—
		50	B Blue back. Unnumbered		£90.00	—
A	C	25	'Cinema Stars' (1920):	H.615		
			A 'Compeer Cigarettes' back		£12.00	—
			B 'Glasgow Mixture Mild, Medium & Full' back ...		£12.00	—
			C 'Kashan Cigarettes' back		£12.00	—
			D 'Luxury Mixture' back		£12.00	—
			E 'Orchestra Cigarettes, Mild & Medium' back ...		£12.00	—
			F 'Pinewood Cigarettes' back		£12.00	—
			G 'Studio Cigarettes' back		£12.00	—
			H 'Sun Cured Mixture' back		£12.00	—
A	U	50	Cricketers (1912)		£16.00	£800.00
A	U	20	Cricketers, 2nd Series, Nd 51-70 (1912)		£30.00	£600.00
A	U	50	Derby Winners (1913)		£15.00	£750.00
A	C	50	Famous Explorers (1911)		£16.00	£800.00
A	C	50	Football Club Records, 1913 to 1917 (1918)		£18.00	£900.00
A	C	50	Football Club Records, 1921-22 (1922)		£18.00	£900.00
D	U	120	*Footballers, brown back (1902)		£45.00	—
A	U	50	*Footballers, blue back Nd 1-52 (Nos 1 and 13 not issued) (1910):			
			A Black portrait		£14.00	
			B Brown portrait		£14.00	
A	U	50	*Footballers, blue back. Nd 55-104 (Nos 53 and 54 not issued) (1910):			
			A Black portrait		£14.00	
			B Brown portrait		£14.00	

F. & J. SMITH, Glasgow (continued)

Size	Printing	Number in set		Handbook reference	Price per card	Complete set
A	U	150	*Footballers, yellow frame line (1914):			
			A Pale blue back … … … … … … … … …		£14.00	—
			B Deep blue back … … … … … … … … …		£14.00	—
A	C	50	Fowls, Pigeons and Dogs (1908) … … … … … … …	H.64	£10.00	£500.00
A	C	25	Holiday Resorts (1925) … … … … … … … … …		£8.00	£200.00
A	C		*Medals:	H.71		
		20	A Unnumbered — thick card (1902) … … … …		£15.00	£300.00
		50	B Numbered. 'F. & J. Smith' thick card, multi-backed (1902) … … … … … … … … …		£11.00	£550.00
		50	C Numbered. 'The Imperial Tobacco Co.' very thin card (1903) … … … … … … … …		£35.00	—
		50	D Numbered. 'The Imperial Tobacco Company' thin card, multi-backed (1906) … … … … …		£11.00	£550.00
A	C	50	Nations of the World (1923) … … … … … … … …	H.454	£7.00	£350.00
A	C	50	Naval Dress and Badges:	H.172		
			A Descriptive back, multi-backed (1911) … … …		£10.00	£500.00
			B Non-descriptive back, multi-backed (1914) …		£10.00	£500.00
A	C	50	Phil May Sketches:	H.72		
			A Blue-grey back, multi-backed (1908) … … …		£10.00	
			B Brown back (1924):			
			1 'Albion (Empire Grown) Smoking Mixture' back … … … … … … … … … …		£7.00	—
			2 'Glasgow Smoking Mixture' back … …		£7.00	—
			3 'High Class Virginia Cigarettes' back …		£7.00	—
			4 'Seal Virginia Cigarettes' back … … …		£7.00	—
A	C	25	Prominent Rugby Players (1924) … … … … … … …		£12.00	£300.00
A	C	40	Races of Mankind (1900):	H.483		
			A Series title on front, multi-backed … … … …		£45.00	—
			*B Without series title, multi-backed … … … … …		£65.00	—
A	C	25	Shadowgraphs (1915):			
			A Glasgow Mixture, Mild, Medium & Full … … …		£8.00	—
			B Orchestra Cigarettes … … … … … … … …		£8.00	—
			C Pinewood Cigarettes … … … … … … … …		£8.00	—
			D Pinewood Mixture … … … … … … … … …		£8.00	—
			E Squaw Thick Black Tobacco … … … … …		£8.00	—
			F Studio Cigarettes … … … … … … … … …		£8.00	—
			G Sun Cured Mixture … … … … … … … …		£8.00	—
A	C	50	*A Tour Round the World:			
			A Script Advertisement back (1904) … … … …		£22.00	—
			B Post-card format back (1905) … … … … …		£40.00	—
A	C	50	A Tour Round the World (titled series, multi-backed) (1906) … … … … … … … … … … … … …	H.75	£11.00	£550.00
A	BW	25	War Incidents (1914):			
			A White back … … … … … … … … … … …		£8.00	£200.00
			B Toned back … … … … … … … … … … …		£8.00	£200.00
A	BW	25	War Incidents, 2nd series (1915):			
			A White back … … … … … … … … … … …		£8.00	£200.00
			B Toned back … … … … … … … … … … …		£8.00	£200.00

SNELL & CO., Plymouth and Devonport

Size	Printing	Number in set		Handbook reference	Price per card	Complete set
A	BW	25	*Boer War Celebrities — 'STEW' (c1901) … … … …	H.105	£250.00	—

SOCIETE JOB, London (and Paris)

Size	Printing	Number in set		Handbook reference	Price per card	Complete set
A	C	25	British Lighthouses (c1925) … … … … … … … …		£8.00	£200.00

SOCIETE JOB, London (and Paris) (continued)

—	U		*Cinema Stars (c1926):	H.616		
		48	A Unnumbered size (58 x 45mm):			
			1 Complete Set		—	£75.00
			2 46 different (minus Love, Milovanoff) ...		£1.00	£46.00
		43	B Unnumbered size (58 x 36mm)		£3.00	—
		?	C Numbered 100-192 (56 x 45mm) (sepia)		£4.00	—
		? 1	D Numbered 39 (57 x 45mm) (reddish brown) ...		£10.00	—
D	BW	25	*Dogs (1911)	H.406	£28.00	£700.00
D	BW	25	*Liners (1912)	H.407	£34.00	—
D1	C	52	*Miniature Playing Cards (c1925)		£7.00	—
A2	C	25	Orders of Chivalry (1924)		£4.00	£100.00
A2	C	25	Orders of Chivalry (Second series) (1927)		£4.00	£100.00
A2	C	3	Orders of Chivalry (unnumbered) (1927)		£8.00	£24.00
D	BW	25	*Racehorses — 1908-09 Winners (1909)	H.408	£26.00	£650.00

LEON SOROKO, London

—	U	6	Jubilee series (1935):			
			A Small size (75 x 41mm)		£200.00	—
			B Large size (83 x 73mm)		£200.00	—

SOUTH WALES TOB. MFG CO. LTD, Newport and London

A	BW	? 91	Game of Numbers (c1910)		£80.00	—
A	U	25	*Views of London (c1910)	H.409	£26.00	£650.00

SOUTH WALES TOBACCO CO. (1913) LTD, Newport

D	C	30	*Army Pictures, Cartoons, etc. (c1916)	H.12	£130.00	—

S.E. SOUTHGATE & SON, London

A1	C	25	*Types of British and Colonial Troops (c1900)	H.76	£130.00	—

T. SPALTON, Macclesfield

D	C	30	*Army Pictures, cartoons etc (c1916)	H.12	£130.00	—

SPIRO VALLERI & CO.

A	BW	? 10	Noted Footballers (c1905)	H.772	£2000.00	—

G. STANDLEY, Newbury

—	U	12	'Manikin' Cards (77 x 49mm) (c1920)	H.481	£120.00	—

A. & A.E. STAPLETON, Hastings

—	U	12	*'Manikin' Cards (79 x 51mm) (c1920)	H.481	£120.00	—

H. STEVENS & CO., Salisbury

A1	C	20	*Dogs (1923)	H.211	£11.00	—
A1	U	25	*Zoo series (1926)	H.588	£7.00	—

A. STEVENSON, Middleton

A	U	50	War Portraits (1916)	H.86	£100.00	—

ALBERT STOCKWELL, Porthcawl

D	C	30	*Army Pictures, Cartoons, etc (c1916).	H.12	£130.00	—

STRATHMORE TOBACCO CO. LTD, London

—	U	25	British Aircraft (76 x 50mm) (1938)		£3.00	£75.00

TADDY & CO., London

32 page reference book — £4.50

Size	Printing	Number in set	Description	Handbook reference	Price per card	Complete set
—	U	? 72	*Actresses — collotype (40 x 70mm) (c1897)	H.411	£120.00	—
A	C	25	*Actresses — with Flowers (c1900)		£90.00	—
A	BW	37	Admirals and Generals — The War (c1915):			
			A 25 Commoner Cards	H.412	£18.00	
			B 12 Scarce Cards (Nos 8, 9, 10, 13, 14, 17, 18, 21, 22, 23, 24, 25)		£40.00	
A	BW	25	Admirals and Generals — The War (South African printing) (c1915)	H.412	£35.00	—
A	C	25	Autographs (c1910)	H.413	£22.00	£550.00
A	C	20	Boer Leaders: (c1901)			
			A White back		£28.00	£560.00
			B Cream back		£28.00	—
A	C	50	British Medals and Decorations — Series 2 (c1905)		£13.00	£650.00
A	C	50	British Medals and Ribbons (c1903)		£13.00	£650.00
A	C	20	*Clowns and Circus Artistes (c1915)	H.414	£900.00	—
C2	C	30	Coronation series (1902):			
			A Grained card		£25.00	—
			B Smooth card		£25.00	—
A	BW	238	County Cricketers (c1907)	H.415	£40.00	—
A	C	50	Dogs (c1900)	H.487	£32.00	—
C	U	5	*English Royalty — collotype (c1898)	H.416	£900.00	—
A	C	25	Famous Actors — Famous Actresses (c1903)		£24.00	£600.00
A	BW	50	Famous Horses and Cattle (c1912)		£120.00	—
A2	C	25	Famous Jockeys (c1905):	H.417		
			A Without frame line — blue title		£36.00	—
			B With frame line — brown title		£32.00	—
A	BW	50	Footballers (export issue) (c1906)	H.418	£100.00	—
A	C	25	'Heraldry' series (c1910)		£22.00	£550.00
A	C	25	Honours and Ribbons (c1910)		£26.00	£650.00
C	C	10	Klondyke series (c1900)		£70.00	£700.00
C	BW	60	Leading Members of the Legislative Assembly (export issue) (c1900)		£900.00	—
A	C	25	*Natives of the World (c1900)	H.419	£70.00	—
A	C	25	Orders of Chivalry (c1911)	H.301	£22.00	£550.00
A	C	25	Orders of Chivalry, second series (c1912)	H.301	£26.00	£650.00
A	BW		Prominent Footballers — Grapnel and/or Imperial back:	H.420		
		? 596	A Without 'Myrtle Grove' footnote (1907)		£25.00	—
		? 403	B With 'Myrtle Grove' footnote (1908-9)		£25.00	—
A	BW	? 409	Prominent Footballers — London Mixture back (1913-14)	H.420	£45.00	—
—	C	20	*Royalty, Actresses, Soldiers (39 x 72mm) (c1898) ...	H.421	£225.00	—
A	C	25	'Royalty' series (c1908)		£20.00	£500.00
A	C	25	*Russo-Japanese War (1-25) (1904)		£22.00	£550.00
A	C	25	*Russo-Japanese War (26-50) (1904)		£26.00	£650.00
A	BW	16	South African Cricket Team 1907	H.422	£60.00	—
A	BW	26	South African Football Team 1906-07	H.423	£28.00	—
A	C	25	Sports and Pastimes — Series 1 (c1912)	H.225	£24.00	£600.00
A	C	25	Territorial Regiments — Series 1 (1908)		£24.00	£600.00
A	C	25	Thames series (c1903)		£36.00	£900.00
C	C	20	Victoria Cross Heroes (1-20) (c1900)		£75.00	—
C	C	20	Victoria Cross Heroes (21-40) (c1900)		£75.00	—
A	C	20	VC Heroes — Boer War (41-60) (1901):			
			A White back		£23.00	—
			B Toned back		£23.00	£460.00

TADDY & CO., London (continued)

Size	Print-ing	Number in set		Handbook reference	Price per card	Complete set
A	C	20	VC Heroes — Boer War (61-80) (1901):			
			A White back		£23.00	—
			B Toned back		£23.00	£460.00
A	C	20	VC Heroes — Boer War (81-100) (1902):			
			A White back		£25.00	—
			B Toned back		£25.00	£500.00
A	C	25	Victoria Cross Heroes (101-125) (1905)		£65.00	—
A2	BW	2	*Wrestlers (c1910)	H.424	£300.00	—

TADDY & CO., London and Grimsby

Size	Print-ing	Number in set		Handbook reference	Price per card	Complete set
—	C	8	Advertisement Cards, three sizes (1980)		60p	£5.00
A	C	26	Motor Cars, including checklist (1980):			
			A 'Clown Cigarettes' back		40p	£10.00
			B 'Myrtle Grove Cigarettes' back		40p	£10.00
A	C	26	Railway Locomotives including checklist (1980):			
			A 'Clown Cigarettes' back		60p	£15.00
			B 'Myrtle Grove Cigarettes' back		40p	£10.00

W. & M. TAYLOR, Dublin

Size	Print-ing	Number in set		Handbook reference	Price per card	Complete set
A	C	8	European War series (c1915):	H.129		
			A 'Bendigo Cigarettes' back		£45.00	—
			B 'Tipperary Cigarettes' back		£45.00	—
A	U	25	*War series — 'Muratti II' (c1915):	H.290		
			A 'Bendigo Cigarettes' back		£60.00	—
			B 'Tipperary Cigarettes' back		£20.00	£500.00

TAYLOR WOOD, Newcastle

Size	Print-ing	Number in set		Handbook reference	Price per card	Complete set
C	C	18	Motor Cycle series (c1914)	H.469	£120.00	—

TEOFANI & CO. LTD, London

(Cards mostly without Teofani's name.)

Size	Print-ing	Number in set		Handbook reference	Price per card	Complete set
C2	U	25	Aquarium Studies from the London Zoo ('Lucana' cards with green label added, inscribed 'Issued with Teofani Windsor Cigarettes') (c1925)	H.607	£12.00	—
D1	U	50	Cinema Celebrities (c1928):			
			A 'Presented with Broadway Novelties'		£5.00	—
			B 'Presented with these well-known ...'		£3.50	—
	C	25	Cinema Stars (c1928):	H.530		
			1 Anonymous printings:			
C2			A Small size		£7.00	—
			B Extra-large size (109 x 67mm)		£7.00	—
			2 Teofani printings:			
C2			A Small size — 'Issued with Blue Band Cigarettes		£7.00	—
C2			B Small size — 'Three Star Cigarettes'		£7.00	—
C2			C Small size — 'Three Star Magnums'		£7.00	—
C2			D Small Size — 'The Favourite Cigarettes'		£7.00	—
—			E Extra-large size (109 x 67mm) — 'Three Star Magnums'		£7.00	—
D	U	25	*Famous Boxers — 'Issued with The 'Favourite Magnums ...' (c1925)	H.721	£12.00	—
C2	P	32	Famous British Ships and Officers — 'Issued with these High Grade Cigarettes' (1934)		£4.00	£130.00
B1	U	50	Famous Racecourses ('Lucana' cards with mauve label added, inscribed 'Issued with The Favourite Cigarettes' (c1926)	H.608	£20.00	—

TEOFANI & CO. LTD, London (continued)

Size	Print-ing	Number in set		Handbook reference	Price per card	Complete set
A	U	? 24	Famous Racehorses (c1925)	H.609	£12.00	—
—	BW	12	*Film Actors and Actresses (56 x 31mm) (plain back)			
			(1936)	H.618	£1.50	£18.00
C2	C	20	Great Inventors (c1924)	H.213	£5.00	—
A	C	20	*Head Dresses of Various Nations (plain back) (c1925)		£16.00	—
—	BW	12	*London Views (57 x 31mm) (c1936):	H.620		
			A Plain back		50p	£6.00
			B Back 'Our Agent Raoul Savon' with brand name:			
			i 'Big Gun' back		£5.00	—
			ii 'Fine' back		£5.00	—
			iii 'Hudavend' back		£5.00	—
			iv 'K.O.G.' back		£5.00	—
			v 'Lucana 66' back		£5.00	—
			vi 'Lucana C.T.' back		£5.00	—
			vii 'Palace' back		£5.00	—
			viii 'Pharoah's' back		£5.00	—
			ix 'Teofani No. 1' back		£5.00	—
			x 'Three Dogs' back		£5.00	—
			xi 'Three Star' back		£5.00	—
			xii 'West End' back		£5.00	—
D2	U	48	Modern Movie Stars and Cinema Celebrities (1934)	H.569	£1.00	£50.00
A	C	50	*Natives in Costume (plain back) (c1925)		£18.00	—
A2	C	24	Past and Present — Series A — The Army (1938):			
			A With framelines		£2.00	£50.00
			B Without framelines		£1.70	£40.00
A2	C	24	Past and Present — Series B — Weapons of War			
			(1938)		£1.00	£25.00
A2	C	4	Past and Present — Series C — Transport (1940) ...	H.679	£5.00	—
C	U	50	Public Schools and Colleges — 'Issued with these			
			Fine Cigarettes' (c1924)	H.575	£3.60	—
D	C	50	Ships and Their Flags — 'Issued with these well-			
			known cigarettes' (c1925)	GP.124	£4.00	£200.00
A	C	25	Sports and Pastimes Series I — 'Smoke these			
			cigarettes always' (c1925)	H.225	£14.00	—
—	P	22	*Teofani Gems I — Series of 22 (53 x 35mm) (plain			
			back) (c1925)		£3.00	
—	P	28	*Teofani Gems II — Series of 28 (53 x 35mm) (plain			
			back) (c1925)		£1.00	
—	P	36	*Teofani Gems III — Series of 36 (53 x 35mm) (plain			
			back) (c1925)		£3.00	
—	P	2	Teofani Gems — unnumbered (53 x 35mm) (plain			
			back) (c1925)		£3.00	£6.00
A2	P	36	Views of the British Empire — 'Issued with these			
			Famous Cigarettes' (c1928):			
			A Front in black and white		£1.25	£45.00
			B Front in light brown		£1.25	£45.00
C	U	50	Views of London — 'Issued with these World Famous			
			Cigarettes' (c1925)	H.577	£4.00	—
C2	U	24	Well-Known Racehorses (c1924)	H.609	£10.00	—
A	C	50	*World's Smokers (plain back) (c1925)		£18.00	—
	U	50	Zoological Studies (c1924):	H.578		
C			A Standard Size		£4.00	—
B1			B Large Size		£7.00	—

OVERSEAS ISSUE

Size	Print-ing	Number in set			Price per card	Complete set
H1	BW	50	Teofani's Icelandic Employees (1930)		£7.00	—
H	P	50	Theatre Artistes and Scenes (c1930)		£25.00	—

TETLEY & SONS LTD, Leeds

A2	C	1	*'The Allies' (grouped flags) (c1915)	H.425	—	£1200.00
A	U	50	War Portraits (c1916)	H.86	£100.00	—
D	C	25	World's Coinage (1914)	H.398	£70.00	—

THEMANS & CO., Manchester

A	—	55	Dominoes (Sunspot brand issue) (c1914)		£80.00	—
C	C	18	Motor Cycle series (c1914)	H.469	£85.00	—
A	C	? 2	Riddles and Anecdotes (c1913)	H.426	£1000.00	—
A	U	50	*War Portraits (1916)	H.86	£70.00	—
—	C	14	War Posters (63 x 41 mm) (c1916)	H.486	£400.00	—

SILKS

Anonymous silks with blue border, plain board backing. Reported also to have been issued with firm's name rubber stamped on backing.

—	C		*Miscellaneous Subjects (c1915):	H.500		
		? 8	Series B1 — Flags (50 x 66mm)		£10.00	—
		? 3	Series B2 — Flags (50 x 66mm)		£10.00	—
		? 12	Series B3 — Regimental Badges (50 x 66mm) ...		£7.00	—
		? 12	Series B4 — Ship's Badges (50 x 66mm)		£20.00	—
		? 7	Series B5 — British Views and Scenes (50 x 66mm)		£20.00	—
		? 48	Series B6 — Film Stars (50 x 66mm)		£10.00	—
		? 2	Series C1 — Flags (65 x 55mm)		£12.00	—
		? 3	Series C2 — Flags (70 x 65mm)		£12.00	—
		? 4	Series C3 — Regimental Badges (64 x 77mm) ...		£10.00	—
		? 2	Series C4 — Crests of Warships (64 x 77mm) ...		£10.00	—
		? 1	Series D1 — Royal Standard (138 x 89mm)		£15.00	—
		? 1	Series D2 — Shield of Flags (138 x 89mm)		£15.00	—
		? 1	Series D3 — Regimental Badge (138 x 89mm) ...		£15.00	—
		? 1	Series D5 — British Views and Scenes (138 x 89mm)		£20.00	—
		? 14	Series D6 — Film Stars (138 x 89mm)		£10.00	—

THOMSON & PORTEOUS, Edinburgh

D2	C	50	Arms of British Towns (c1905)		£17.00	£850.00
A	BW	25	*Boer War Celebrities — 'STEW' (c1901)	H.105	£60.00	—
A	C	20	European War series (c1915)	H.129	£15.00	£300.00
A	C	25	*Shadowgraphs (c1905)	H.44	£45.00	—
A	C	41	VC Heroes (c1915):	H.427		
			A Front with firm's name at base:			
			i 40 Different (minus No. 6)		£14.00	£560.00
			ii Number 6		—	£60.00
			B Front with firm's name at top		£60.00	—
			C Without firm's name, with 'Pure Virginia Cigarettes'		£14.00	£575.00

TOBACCO SUPPLY SYNDICATE, London (T.S.S.)

D	C	24	*Nautical Expressions (c1900)	H.174	£120.00	—

TOM NODDY

—	C	12	Children of the Year Series (140 x 90mm) (1904) ...		£100.00	—

TURKISH MONOPOLY CIGARETTE CO. LTD

—	C	? 16	*Scenes from the Boer War (113 x 68mm, folded in three) (c1901)	H.478	£600.00	—

UNITED KINGDOM TOBACCO CO., London

Size	Print-ing	Number in set		Handbook reference	Price per card	Complete set
A	C	50	Aircraft — 'The Greys Cigarettes' (1938)	GP.5	£1.80	£90.00
—	U	48	Beautiful Britain — 'The Greys Cigarettes' (140 x 90mm) (1929)	GP.406	£1.70	£85.00
—	U	48	Beautiful Britain — Second series 'The Greys Cigarettes' (140 x 90mm) (1929)	GP.407	£1.50	£75.00
A2	C	25	British Orders of Chivalry and Valour — 'The Greys Cigarettes' (1936)	GP.43	£1.40	£35.00
A	U	24	Chinese Scenes (1933)		75p	£18.00
A2	U	32	Cinema Stars — Set 4 (1933)	GP.53	£1.70	£55.00
A2	U	50	Cinema Stars — Set 7 (1934):	GP.703		
			A Anonymous back		£2.50	£125.00
			B Back with firm's name		£1.70	£85.00
A2	C	36	Officers Full Dress (1936)		£2.00	£70.00
A2	C	36	Soldiers of the King — 'The Greys Cigarettes' (1937)	GP.127	£2.20	£80.00

UNITED SERVICES MANUFACTURING CO. LTD, London

A1	C	50	Ancient Warriors (1938)		£2.40	£120.00
A	C	25	Ancient Warriors (1954)		£4.40	—
A1	BW	50	Bathing Belles (1939)	H.592	£1.00	£50.00
D	U	100	Interesting Personalities (1935)		£3.50	—
D	U	50	Popular Footballers (1936)		£6.00	—
D	U	50	Popular Screen Stars (1937)		£4.00	—

UNITED TOBACCONISTS' ASSOCIATION LTD

A	C	10	*Actresses — 'MUTA' (c1900)	H.265	£250.00	—
A2	C	12	*Pretty Girl Series 'RASH' (c1900)	H.8	£550.00	—

WALKER'S TOBACCO CO. LTD, Liverpool

C	P	60	*British Beauty Spots (c1925)	H.553	£20.00	—
A	BW	28	*Dominoes 'Old Monk' issue (1908)		£65.00	—
D2	U	28	*Dominoes 'W.T.C.' Monogram back (c1925)	H.535-2	£6.00	—
A2	P	32	Film Stars — 'Tatley's Cigarettes' (1936)	H.623	—	£80.00
			31 Different (minus Lombard)		£1.50	£46.00
A2	P	48	*Film Stars — Walker's name at base (1937)	H.623	£4.50	—

WALTERS TOBACCO CO. LTD, London

B	U	6	Angling Information (wording only) (1939)	H.624	£1.50	£9.00

E.T. WATERMAN, Coventry

D	C	30	*Army Pictures, Cartoons, etc. (1916)	H.12	£130.00	—

WEBB & RASSELL, Reigate

A	U	50	War Portraits (1916)	H.86	£100.00	—

H.C. WEBSTER (Q.V. Cigars)

—	BW	? 7	*Barnum and Bailey's Circus (60 x 42mm) (c1900) ...	H.428	£400.00	—

HENRY WELFARE & CO., London

D	P	? 22	Prominent Politicians (c1911)	H.429	£80.00	—

WESTMINSTER TOBACCO CO. LTD, London

Inscribed 'Issued by the Successors in the United Kingdom to the Westminster Tobacco Co., Ltd.' For other issues without the above see Overseas Issues.

A2	P	36	Australia — 'First Series' (1932)		25p	£9.00

WESTMINSTER TOBACCO CO. LTD, London (continued)

Size	Printing	Number in set	Description	Handbook reference	Price per card	Complete set
A2	P	36	Australia, Second Series, plain back, unissued. (1933)	H.680	25p	£9.00
A2	P	48	British Royal and Ancient Buildings (1925):			
			A Unnumbered, without descriptive text		90p	£45.00
			B Numbered, with descriptive text		£1.20	£60.00
A2	P	48	British Royal and Ancient Buildings — 'A Second Series ...' (1926)		50p	£25.00
A2	P	36	Canada — 'First Series' (1927)		70p	£25.00
A2	P	36	Canada — 'Second Series' (1928)		70p	£25.00
A2	P	48	Indian Empire — 'First Series' (1926)		50p	£25.00
A2	P	48	Indian Empire — 'Second Series' (1927)		50p	£25.00
A2	P	36	New Zealand — 'First Series' (1929)		50p	£18.00
A2	P	36	New Zealand — 'Second Series' (1930)		25p	£9.00
A2	P	36	South Africa — 'First Series' (1930)		75p	£27.00
A2	P	36	South Africa — 'Second Series' (1931)		75p	£27.00

OVERSEAS ISSUES

Size	Printing	Number in set	Description	Price per card	Complete set
—	BW	332	Adamsons Oplevelser (68 x 50mm) (1930)	£20.00	—
—	P	50	Beauties (63 x 48mm) (1924)	£3.20	—
—	P	100	Beautiful Women (65 x 49mm) (1915)	£3.20	—
—	C	50	Birds, Beasts and Fishes (63 x 48mm) (1923)	£3.00	—
			British Beauties (1915):		
—	CP	102	A Coloured (60 x 41mm)	£4.00	—
—	P	86	B Uncoloured (57 x 41mm)	£4.00	—
A2	P	48	British Royal and Ancient Buildings (1925)	£1.20	£60.00
—	C	50	Butterflies and Moths (70 x 42mm) (1920)	£3.00	—
A2	P	36	Canada 1st series (1926)	£1.10	£40.00
A2	P	36	Canada 2nd series (1928)	£1.10	£40.00
D2	U	30	Celebrated Actresses (1921)	£6.00	—
—	C	25	Champion Dogs (anonymous back) (95 x 67mm) (1934)	£5.00	—
A	BW	100	Cinema Artistes green back (1929-33)	£3.50	—
A	BW	50	Cinema Artistes grey back (1929-33)	£3.50	—
A	C	48	Cinema Celebrities (1935)	£3.50	—
A	P	50	Cinema Stars (1926)	£3.50	—
—	P	50	Cinema Stars (63 x 48mm) (1930)	£3.50	—
—	CP	50	Cinema Stars (63 x 48mm) (1930)	£3.50	—
—	C	27	Dancing Girls (63 x 44mm) (1917)	£6.00	—
A	C	50	Do You Know (1922)	£2.50	—
D2	C	24	Fairy Tale (booklets) (1926)	£7.50	—
—	C	100	Famous Beauties (64 x 48mm) (1916):		
			A Captions in brown	£2.50	—
			B Captions in blue	£2.80	—
—	U	35	Famous Fighting Ships of Various Nations (138 x 92mm) (c1910)	£50.00	—
		52	Film Favourites (64 x 48mm) (1927):		
—	P		A Uncoloured	£4.00	—
—	CP		B Coloured	£4.00	—
—	U	50	Film Personalities (64 x 48mm) (1931)	£4.50	—
—	C	50	Garden Flowers of the World (70 x 50mm) (1917)	£3.20	—
A1	U	40	The Great War Celebrities (1914)	£9.00	—
A2	P	48	Indian Empire 1st series (1925)	£1.10	£55.00
A2	P	48	Indian Empire 2nd series (1926)	£1.10	£55.00
—	P	50	Islenzkar Eimskipamyndir (Trawlers) (77 x 52mm) (1931)	£3.20	£160.00
—	P	50	Islenzkar Landslagmyndir (Views) (77 x 52mm) (1928)	£2.40	£120.00
—	P	50	Islenzkar Landslagmyndir 2nd series (Views) (77 x 52mm) (1929)	£2.40	£120.00

WESTMINSTER TOBACCO CO. LTD, London (Overseas Issues continued)

Size	Printing	Number in set	Title	Handbook reference	Price per card	Complete set
A1	C	40	Merrie England Studies (1914)		£8.00	—
A	BW	36	Modern Beauties (1938)		£3.50	—
—	CP	52	Movie Stars (63 x 48mm) (1925)		£3.80	—
A2	P	36	New Zealand 1st series (1928)		£1.25	£42.00
A2	P	36	New Zealand 2nd series (1929)		£1.25	£42.00
—	C	53	Playing Cards (63 x 41mm) (1934):			
			A With Exchange Scheme		£3.00	—
			B Without Exchange Scheme		£3.00	—
—	C	55	Playing Cards (72 x 49mm) (1934):			
			A Blue back		£2.00	—
			B Red back		£2.00	—
A	P	50	Popular Film Stars (1926)		£3.50	—
A2	P	36	South Africa 1st series (1928)		£1.10	£40.00
A2	P	36	South Africa 2nd series (1928)		£1.10	£40.00
—	C	49	South African Succulents (72 x 50mm) (1936)		35p	£17.50
—	C	100	Stage and Cinema Stars, captions in grey (63 x 47mm) (1921)		£2.50	—
—	C	100	Stage and Cinema Stars, captions in black (63 x 47mm) (1921)		£3.25	—
—	CP	50	Stars of Filmland (63 x 48mm) (1927):			
			A 'Westminster' lettering brown on white		£3.50	—
			B 'Westminster' lettering white on brown		£3.50	—
C2	C	50	Steamships of the World (1920)		£10.00	—
—	C	50	Uniforms of All Ages (69 x 47mm) (1917)		£12.00	—
A	P	50	Views of Malaya (1930)		£7.00	—
D	C	25	Wireless (1923)		£5.00	—
—	C	50	Women of Nations (70 x 49mm) (1922)		£5.00	—
A	BW	50	The World of Tomorrow (1938)		£1.50	£75.00

SILK ISSUES

Size	Printing	Number in set	Title	Handbook reference	Price per card	Complete set
—	C	50	Garden Flowers of the World (82 x 51mm) (c1914)		£6.00	—
—	C	24	Miniature Rugs (93 x 52mm) (1924)		£20.00	—

WHALE & CO.

Size	Printing	Number in set	Title	Handbook reference	Price per card	Complete set
A	C	? 11	Conundrums (c1900)	H.232	£450.00	—

M. WHITE & CO., London

Size	Printing	Number in set	Title	Handbook reference	Price per card	Complete set
—	BW	20	*Actresses — 'BLARM' (c1900)	H.23	£220.00	—

WHITFIELD'S, Walsall

Size	Printing	Number in set	Title	Handbook reference	Price per card	Complete set
D	C	30	*Army Pictures, Cartoons etc. (c1916)	H.12	£130.00	—

WHITFORD & SONS, Evesham

Size	Printing	Number in set	Title	Handbook reference	Price per card	Complete set
C2	C	20	*Inventors series (c1924)	H.213	£45.00	—

WHOLESALE TOBACCO SUPPLY CO., London ('Hawser' Cigarettes)

Size	Printing	Number in set	Title	Handbook reference	Price per card	Complete set
A	C	25	Armies of the World (c1902)	H.43	£70.00	—
A	C	40	Army Pictures (c1902)	H.69	£100.00	—

P. WHYTE, England

Size	Printing	Number in set	Title	Handbook reference	Price per card	Complete set
D	C	30	*Army Pictures, Cartoons, etc. (1916)	H.12	£130.00	—

W. WILLIAMS & CO., Chester

Size	Printing	Number in set	Title	Handbook reference	Price per card	Complete set
A	U	30	Aristocrats of the Turf (c1925)	H.554	£8.00	£240.00
A	U	36	Aristocrats of the Turf 2nd series (c1925)	H.554	£14.00	—
A	BW	25	*Boer War Celebrities 'STEW' (c1901)	H.105	£75.00	—

W. WILLIAMS & CO., Chester (continued)

Size	Print	Number	Description	Handbook ref	Price	Complete set
A	C	25	Boxing (c1924)	H.311	£10.00	£250.00
A	C	50	Interesting Buildings (c1910)	H.70	£14.00	£700.00
A	BW	12	Views of Chester (c1910)	H.430	£35.00	£420.00
A	BW	12	Views of Chester — As It Was (c1910):	H.430		
			A Toned card		£35.00	£420.00
			B Bleuté card		£35.00	—

W.D. & H.O. WILLS, Bristol

212 page reference book The Card Issues of W.D. & H.O. Wills (2011 Edition)— £25.00

NOTE: The Imperial Tobacco Co. clause (I.T.C. clause) appears on Home issues
dated between 1902 and 1940, excluding those issued in the Channel Islands.
For series without I.T.C. clause, see the Overseas section.

Size	Print	Number	Description	Handbook ref	Price	Complete set
A	U		*Actresses — collotype (c1894):			
		25	A 'Wills' Cigarettes'	W.2-1	£100.00	—
		43	B 'Wills's Cigarettes'	W.2-2	£100.00	—
A	C	20	*Actresses, brown type-set back (c1895)	W.3-A	£1000.00	—
A	C	52	*Actresses, brown scroll back, with PC inset (c1898)	W.3-C	£18.50	£950.00
A	C	52	*Actresses, grey scroll back (c1897):	W.3-D		
			A Without PC inset		£18.50	£950.00
			B With PC inset		£18.50	£950.00
A	U		*Actresses and Beauties — collotype, 'Three Castles' and 'Firefly' front (c1895):	W.2-4		
	?	125	Actresses		£100.00	—
	?	33	Beauties		£100.00	—
A	C		*Advertisement Cards:	W.1		
	?	4	1888 issue (cigarette packets)		£2000.00	—
	?	1	1889-90 issue (serving maid)		£800.00	—
	?	11	1890-93 issues (tobacco packings)		£1000.00	—
	?	3	1893 issue (showcards):			
			A 'Autumn Gold Cigarettes' back		£350.00	—
			B 'Best Bird's Eye Cigarettes' back		£350.00	—
			C 'Eothen Cigarettes' back		£350.00	—
			D 'Passing Clouds' back		£350.00	—
			E 'Pole Star Cigarettes' back		£350.00	—
			F 'Sahara Cigarettes' back		£350.00	—
			G 'The Three Castles Cigarettes' back		£350.00	—
	?	6	1893-94 issue (posters)		£350.00	—
B	BW	1	Advertisement Card — Wants List (1935)		—	75p
—	C	4	*Advertisement Postcards of Wills Packings (139 x 88mm) (1902)	W.398	£150.00	—
A	C		Air Raid Precautions (1938):	W.123		
		50	A Home issue — adhesive back, with I.T.C. clause		90p	£45.00
			Album (with price)		—	£22.00
		40	B Irish issue — non-adhesive back		£1.75	—
		50	C Channel Islands issue – adhesive back, without I.T.C. clause		£1.20	£60.00
A	C	50	Allied Army Leaders (1917)	W.35	£1.70	£85.00
A	C	50	Alpine Flowers (1913)		90p	£45.00
A	C	48	Animalloys (sectional) (1934)	W.124	40p	£20.00
A	C	50	*Animals and Birds in Fancy Costumes (c1896)	W.4	£45.00	—
B	C	25	Animals and Their Furs (1929)		£2.00	£50.00
A	C	50	Arms of the Bishopric (1907)		£1.00	£50.00
A	C	50	Arms of the British Empire (1910)	W.40	80p	£40.00
B	C	25	Arms of the British Empire — 'First Series' (1931) ...		£1.80	£45.00

W.D. & H.O. WILLS, Bristol (continued)

Size	Printing	Number in set	Title	Handbook reference	Price per card	Complete set
B	C	25	Arms of the British Empire — 'Second Series' (1932)		£1.80	£45.00
A	C	50	Arms of Companies (1913) … … … … … … … … …		90p	£45.00
A	C	50	Arms of Foreign Cities (1912):	W.42		
			A White card … … … … … … … … … … … … …		80p	£40.00
			B Cream card … … … … … … … … … … … …		90p	—
			C As A, with 'Mark' … … … … … … … … … …		£1.00	—
B	C	42	Arms of Oxford and Cambridge Colleges (1922) …		£1.40	£60.00
B	C	25	Arms of Public Schools — '1st Series' (1933) … …		£2.20	£55.00
B	C	25	Arms of Public Schools — '2nd Series' (1934) … …		£2.20	£55.00
B	C	25	Arms of Universities (1923) … … … … … … … …		£1.60	£40.00
A	C	50	Association Footballers 'Frameline' back (1935):	W.134		
			A Home issue – with I.T.C. clause … … … … …		£1.30	£65.00
			Album … … … … … … … … … … … … … …		—	£22.00
			B Channel Islands issue – without I.T.C. clause		£2.50	£125.00
A	C	50	Association Footballers – 'No frameline' back (1939):	W.135		
			A Home issue — adhesive back … … … … …		£1.30	£65.00
			B Irish issue — non-adhesive back … … … …		£2.40	£120.00
B	C	25	Auction Bridge (1926) … … … … … … … … …		£2.40	£60.00
A	C	50	Aviation (1910) … … … … … … … … … … …	W.46	£2.60	£130.00
A	U	? 20	*Beauties — collotype (c1894):	W.2-3		
			A 'W.D. & H.O. Wills' Cigarettes' … … … … …		£175.00	—
			B 'Firefly' Cigarettes … … … … … … … …		£175.00	—
A1	C	? 10	*Beauties ('Girl Studies'), type-set back (c1895) … …	W.3-B	£1200.00	—
A	C		*Beauties, brown backs (c1897):	W.3-E		
		52	A With PC inset — scroll back … … … … …		£22.00	£1100.00
		10	B As A, 10 additional pictures … … … … … …		£70.00	—
		? 53	C 'Wills' Cigarettes' front, scroll back … … … …		£175.00	—
		? 29	D 'Wills' Cigarettes' front, type-set back … … …		£250.00	—
K	C	52	*Beauties, miniature cards, PC inset, grey scroll back			
			(c1896) … … … … … … … … … … … … …	W.3-F	£26.00	—
B	C	25	Beautiful Homes (1930) … … … … … … … … …		£2.60	£65.00
A	C	50	Billiards (1909) … … … … … … … … … … …		£2.20	£110.00
—	—	10	Boer War Medallions (c1901) … … … … … … …	W.18	£90.00	—
A	C	50	*Borough Arms (1-50):			
			A Scroll back, unnumbered (1904) … … … … …	W.19	£1.10	£55.00
			B Scroll back, numbered on front (1904) … … …		£10.00	—
			C Descriptive back, numbered on back (1905) …		£1.10	£55.00
			D 2nd Edition — 1-50 (1906) … … … … … …		£1.10	£55.00
A	C	50	*Borough Arms (51-100):	W.19		
			A 2nd Series (1905) … … … … … … … … …		80p	£40.00
			B 2nd Edition, 51-100 (1906) … … … … … …		80p	£40.00
A	C	50	*Borough Arms (101-150):	W.19		
			A 3rd Series, Album clause in grey (1905) … …		£1.00	£50.00
			B 3rd Series, Album clause in red (1905) … …		80p	£40.00
			C 2nd Edition, 101-150 (1906) … … … … … …		80p	£40.00
A	C	50	*Borough Arms (151-200), 4th series (1905) … … …	W.19	80p	£40.00
A	C	24	*Britain's Part in the War (1917) … … … … … …		£1.00	£25.00
A	C	50	British Birds (1917) … … … … … … … … … …		£1.50	£75.00
A	C	50	British Butterflies (1927) … … … … … … … … …	W.156	£1.10	£55.00
B	C	25	British Castles (1925) … … … … … … … … … …		£3.00	£75.00
—	BW	1	British Commanders in the Transvaal War 1899-1900			
			(booklet) (206 x 114mm) (1900):	W.511		
			A With 'Bristol & London' on front … … … … …		—	£100.00
			B Without 'Bristol & London' on front … … … …		—	£100.00
—	C	12	The British Empire (133 x 101mm) (c1930) … … …		£9.00	—
B	C	25	British School of Painting (1927) … … … … … …		£1.40	£35.00
—	BW	48	British Sporting Personalities (76 x 52mm) (1937) …		£1.00	£50.00

W.D. & H.O. WILLS, Bristol (continued)

Size	Print-ing	Number in set	Description	Handbook reference	Price per card	Complete set
A	C	50	Builders of the Empire (1898):	W.20		
			A White card		£8.00	£400.00
			B Cream card		£8.00	£400.00
B	C	40	Butterflies and Moths (1938)		90p	£36.00
A	C	1	*Calendar for 1911 (1910)		—	£15.00
A	C	1	*Calendar for 1912 (1911)		—	£10.00
B	C	25	Cathedrals (1933)		£5.00	£125.00
B	U	25	Celebrated Pictures (1916):	W.165		
			A Deep brown back		£2.00	£50.00
			B Yellow-brown back		£1.80	£45.00
B	U	25	Celebrated Pictures, 2nd Series (1916)	W.166	£2.20	£55.00
A	C	50	Celebrated Ships (1911)		£1.30	£65.00
A	C	25	Cinema Stars — 'First Series' (1928)		£1.60	£40.00
A	C	25	Cinema Stars — 'Second Series' (1928)		£1.60	£40.00
A	U	50	Cinema Stars — 'Third Series' (1931)		£2.20	£110.00
—	C	12	Cities of Britain (133 x 101mm) (c1930)		£9.00	—
A	C	60	Coronation Series (1902):	W.6		
			A 2mm wide arrow at side of text, back		£6.00	£360.00
			B 1mm narrow arrow at side of text, back		£6.00	£360.00
A	C	50	The Coronation Series (1911)		£1.10	£55.00
A	C	50	*Cricketers (1896)	W.7	£90.00	—
A	C		Cricketers Series, 1901:	W.8		
		50	A With Vignette		£25.00	—
		25	B Without Vignette		£25.00	—
A	C		Cricketers (1908):	W.58		
		25	A 1-25 'Wills' S' at top front		£9.00	£225.00
		50	B 1-50 'Wills's' at top front		£7.50	£375.00
A	C	50	Cricketers, 1928 (1928)	W.178	£1.80	£90.00
A	C	50	Cricketers — '2nd Series' (1929)		£1.80	£90.00
B	C	25	Dogs (1914)		£3.60	£90.00
B	C	25	Dogs, 2nd Series (1915)		£3.60	£90.00
A	C	50	Dogs — Light backgrounds (1937):	W.187		
			A Home issue — adhesive back, with I.T.C. clause		60p	£30.00
			Album		—	£22.00
			B Irish issue — non-adhesive back		£1.50	£75.00
			C Channel Islands issue – adhesive back, without I.T.C. clause		£1.30	£65.00
A	C		*Double Meaning (1898):	W.5		
		50	A Without PC inset		£10.00	£500.00
		52	B With PC inset		£10.00	£520.00
A	C		Do You Know:			
		50	'A Series of 50' (1922)	W.188	50p	£25.00
		50	'2nd Series of 50' (1924)	W.189	50p	£25.00
		50	'3rd Series of 50' (1926)	W.190	50p	£25.00
		50	'4th Series of 50' (1933)	W.191	60p	£30.00
A	C	50	Engineering Wonders (1927)	W.193	£1.00	£50.00
A	C	50	English Period Costumes (1929)		£1.00	£50.00
B	C	25	English Period Costumes (1927)	W.195	£2.60	£65.00
B	C	40	Famous British Authors (1937)		£1.75	£70.00
B	C	30	Famous British Liners — 'First Series' (1934)		£5.50	—
B	C	30	Famous British Liners — 'Second Series' (1935)		£4.00	£120.00
B	C	25	Famous Golfers (1930)		£16.00	—
A	C	50	Famous Inventions (1915)	W.60	£1.00	£50.00
A	C		A Famous Picture — (sectional):			
		48	Series No. 1 — 'Between Two Fires' (1930)	W.207	40p	£20.00
		48	Series No. 2 — 'The Boyhood of Raleigh' (1930)	W.208	40p	£20.00

W.D. & H.O. WILLS, Bristol (continued)

Size	Printing	Number in set		Handbook reference	Price per card	Complete set
			A Famous Picture (continued):			
		48	Series No. 3 — 'Mother and Son' (1931)	W.209	40p	£20.00
		48	'The Toast' (1931):	W.210		
			A Home issue — Series No. 4		50p	£24.00
			B Irish issue — Series No. 1		£2.00	—
		48	'The Laughing Cavalier' (1931):	W.211		
			A Home issue — Series No. 5:			
			1 No stop after numeral		40p	£20.00
			2 Full stop after numeral		40p	£20.00
			B Irish issue — Series No. 2		£2.00	—
		49	Series No. 6 — 'And When did you Last See Your Father?' (1932)	W.212	£1.00	£50.00
A	C	50	First Aid:			
			A Without Album Clause (1913)		£1.50	£75.00
			B With Album Clause (1915)		£1.50	£75.00
A	C	50	Fish & Bait (1910)	W.62	£3.00	£150.00
—	C	6	Flags of the Allies (shaped) (1915)	W.67	£13.00	—
A	C	25	Flags of the Empire (1926)	W.215	£1.60	£40.00
A	C	25	Flags of the Empire — '2nd Series' (1929)		£1.20	£30.00
A	C	50	Flower Culture in Pots (1925)	W.217	45p	£22.50
B	C	30	Flowering Shrubs (1935)		£1.10	£33.00
A	C	50	Flowering Trees and Shrubs (1924)		80p	£40.00
A	U	66	*Football Series (1902)	W.22	£10.00	—
A	C	50	Garden Flowers (1933)	W.225	70p	£35.00
A	C	50	Garden Flowers by Richard Sudell (1939):	W.222		
			A Home issue – Album offer with price		25p	£12.50
			B Irish issue – Album offer without price		50p	£25.00
			C Channel Islands issue – no Album offer		50p	£25.00
B	C	40	Garden Flowers — New Varieties — 'A Series' (1938)		60p	£24.00
B	C	40	Garden Flowers — New Varieties — '2nd Series' (1939)		50p	£20.00
A	C	50	Garden Hints (1938):	W.226		
			A Home issue — Album offer with price		25p	£12.50
			B Irish issue — Album offer without price		50p	£25.00
			C Channel Islands issue – no Album offer		50p	£25.00
A	C	50	Garden Life (1914)	W.69	70p	£35.00
A	C	50	Gardening Hints (1923)	W.227	40p	£20.00
A	C	50	Gems of Belgian Architecture (1915)		70p	£35.00
A	C	50	Gems of French Architecture (1917):			
			A White card		£1.40	£70.00
			B Bleuté card		£1.60	—
			C Rough brown card		£1.60	—
A	P	50	Gems of Italian Architecture (1960) (reprint)	W.388	70p	£35.00
A	C	50	Gems of Russian Architecture (1916)		70p	£35.00
B	C	25	Golfing (1924)		£9.00	—
—	C	32	Happy Families (non-insert) (91 x 63mm) (c1935) ...		£5.00	—
B	C	25	Heraldic Signs and Their Origin (1925)	W.230	£2.00	£50.00
A	C	50	Historic Events (1912)	W.74	£1.20	£60.00
A2	P	54	Homeland Events (1932)	W.232	60p	£32.00
A	C	50	Household Hints (1927)	W.234	60p	£30.00
A	C	50	Household Hints — '2nd Series' (1930)		60p	£30.00
A	C	50	Household Hints (1936):	W.236		
			A Home issue — Album offer with price		25p	£12.50
			B Irish issue — Album offer without price		50p	£25.00
			C Channel Islands issue – no Album offer		50p	£25.00
A	BW	50	Hurlers (1927)		£1.80	£90.00

W.D. & H.O. WILLS, Bristol (continued)

Size	Print-ing	Number in set	Description	Handbook reference	Price per card	Complete set
—	C	12	Industries of Britain (133 x 101mm) (c1930)		£9.00	—
A	C	25	Irish Beauty Spots (1929)		£5.00	—
A	C	25	Irish Holiday Resorts (1930)		£5.00	—
A	C	50	Irish Industries (1937):			
			A Back 'This surface is adhesive ...'		£3.00	—
			B Back 'Ask your retailer ...'		£1.20	£60.00
A	U	25	Irish Rugby Internationals (1928)		£12.00	—
A	C	50	Irish Sportsmen (1935)		£4.50	—
			Album		—	£40.00
A	C	50	Japanese Series (c1900)	W.23	£38.00	—
B	C	40	The King's Art Treasures (1938)		30p	£12.00
	C		*Kings and Queens:	W.9		
A1		50	A Short card (1897):			
			a Grey back, thin card		£6.50	£325.00
			b Grey back, thick card		£6.50	£325.00
			c Brown back		£10.00	—
A			B Standard size card (1902):			
		51	a Blue-grey back with 5 substitute titles:			
			i 50 different		£6.50	£325.00
			ii Edward The Martyr		—	£50.00
		50	b Grey back, different design, thinner card		£13.00	—
B	C	25	Lawn Tennis, 1931 (1931)		£10.00	—
A	C	50	Life in the Hedgerow (c1950) (unissued)		50p	£25.00
A	C	50	Life in the Royal Navy (1939):	W.253		
			A Home issue – with Album offer		40p	£20.00
			Album		—	£22.00
			B Channel Islands issue – without Album offer ...		50p	£25.00
A	C	50	Life in the Tree Tops (1925)	W.254	40p	£20.00
A	C	50	Life of King Edward VIII (1936) (unissued)		—	£1000.00
A	C		*Locomotive Engines and Rolling Stock:	W.24		
		50	A Without I.T.C. clause (1901)		£9.00	£450.00
		7	B As A, 7 additional cards (1901)		£30.00	—
		50	C With I.T.C. clause (1902)		£9.00	£450.00
A	C	50	Lucky Charms (1923)	W.256	60p	£30.00
A	C	50	*Medals (1902):	W.25		
			A White card		£3.00	£150.00
			B Toned card		£3.00	£150.00
A	C	50	Merchant Ships of the World (1924)	W.257	£1.40	£70.00
A	C	50	Military Motors (1916):			
			A Without 'Passed for ... Press Bureau'		£1.80	£90.00
			B With 'Passed for ... Press Bureau'		£1.80	£90.00
K2	C	53	*Miniature Playing Cards (1932-34):	W.260		
			A Home issue, blue back — 'narrow 52'			
			(2 printings)		50p	£25.00
			B Home issue, blue back — 'wide 52' (4 printings)		50p	£25.00
			C Home issue, pink back (3 printings)		60p	—
			D Irish issue, blue back (7 printings)		£1.00	—
A	C	50	Mining (1916)	W.81	£1.50	£75.00
B	C	25	Modern Architecture (1931)		£1.60	£40.00
B	U	30	Modern British Sculpture (1928)		£1.30	£40.00
A	C	50	Musical Celebrities (1911)	W.83	£2.50	£125.00
A	C	50	Musical Celebrities — Second Series (1916):	W.83		
			Set of 50 with 8 substituted cards		£3.50	£175.00
			8 original cards (later substituted)		£275.00	—
A	C	25	*National Costumes (c1895)	W.26	£200.00	—
A	C	? 8	*National Types (c1893)	W.396	£1300.00	—
A	C	50	Naval Dress & Badges (1909)	W.84	£3.50	£175.00

W.D. & H.O. WILLS, Bristol (continued)

Size	Print-ing	Number in set		Handbook reference	Price per card	Complete set
A	C	50	Nelson Series (1905) … … … … … … … … … …	W.85	£5.50	£275.00
A	C	50	Old English Garden Flowers (1911) … … … … …		£1.50	£75.00
A	C	50	Old English Garden Flowers, 2nd Series (1913) … …		£1.00	£50.00
B	C	25	Old Furniture — '1st Series' (1923) … … … … …		£2.80	£70.00
B	C	25	Old Furniture — '2nd Series' (1924) … … … … …		£2.80	£70.00
B	C	40	Old Inns — 'A Series of 40' (1936) … … … … …		£3.00	£120.00
B	C	40	Old Inns — 'Second Series of 40' (1939) … … … …		£1.75	£70.00
B	C	25	Old London (1929) … … … … … … … … … … …		£3.60	£90.00
B	C	30	Old Pottery and Porcelain (1934) … … … … … …		£1.20	£36.00
B	C	25	Old Silver (1924) … … … … … … … … … …		£2.40	£60.00
B	C	25	Old Sundials (1928) … … … … … … … … …		£2.80	£70.00
A	C	20	Our Gallant Grenadiers (c1901):	W.27		
			A Deep grey on toned card … … … … …		£32.00	—
			B Blue-grey on bluish card … … … … … …		£32.00	—
A	BW	50	Our King and Queen (1937):	W.286		
			A Home issue – with Album offer … … … … …		30p	£15.00
			Album … … … … … … … … … … … …		—	£22.00
			B Channel Islands issue – without Album offer …		50p	£25.00
A	C	50	Overseas Dominions (Australia) (1915) … … … … …	W.87	80p	£40.00
A	C	50	Overseas Dominions (Canada) (1914) … … … … …		60p	£30.00
A	C	50	Physical Culture (1914) … … … … … … … …		£1.00	£50.00
—	—	1	Pinchbeck Medallion (1897) … … … … … … …		£100.00	—
A	C	25	Pond and Aquarium 1st Series (c1950) (unissued) …		32p	£8.00
A	C	25	Pond and Aquarium 2nd Series (c1950) (unissued) …		32p	£8.00
A	U	100	*Portraits of European Royalty (1908):			
			Nos. 1-50 … … … … … … … … … … … …		£1.50	£75.00
			Nos. 51-100 … … … … … … … … … … …		£1.50	£75.00
B	C	25	Public Schools (1927) … … … … … … … … …		£2.40	£60.00
B	U	25	Punch Cartoons (1916):			
			A Toned card … … … … … … … … … …		£4.00	£100.00
			B Glossy white card … … … … … … … … …		£6.00	—
B	U	25	Punch Cartoons — Second Series (1917) … … … …		£18.00	—
B	C	40	Puppies (c1950) (unissued) … … … … … … …		—	—
B	C	40	Racehorses and Jockeys, 1938 (1939) … … … … …		£2.25	£90.00
A	C	50	Radio Celebrities — 'A Series …' (1934):	W.301		
			A Home issue — back 'This surface …' … … …		90p	£45.00
			Album … … … … … … … … … … … …		—	£22.00
			B Irish issue — back 'Note. This surface …' … .		£1.50	—
A	C	50	Radio Celebrities — 'Second Series — (1935):	W.302		
			A Home issue — back 'This surface …' … … …		50p	£25.00
			Album … … … … … … … … … … … …		—	£22.00
			B Irish issue — back 'Note. This surface …' …		£1.30	—
A	C	50	Railway Engines (1924) … … … … … … … … …	W.303	£1.20	£60.00
A	C	50	Railway Engines (1936):	W.304		
			A Home issue — back 'This surface …' … … …		£1.00	£50.00
			Album (with price) :			
			A Cream Cover … … … … … … … … …		—	£22.00
			B Grey Cover … … … … … … … … … …		—	£22.00
			B Irish issue — back 'Note. This surface …' …		£1.60	£80.00
			Album (without price) … … … … … … …		—	£40.00
A	C	50	Railway Equipment (1939):	W.305		
			A Home issue – with Album offer … … … … …		40p	£20.00
			B Channel Islands issue – without Album offer …		70p	£35.00
A	C	50	Railway Locomotives (1930) … … … … … … …		£1.80	£90.00
A	C	12	Recruiting Posters (1915) … … … … … … … …	W.92	£7.50	£90.00
A	C	50	The Reign of H.M. King George V (1935) … … … …		80p	£40.00
			Album … … … … … … … … … … … …		—	£22.00

W.D. & H.O. WILLS, Bristol (continued)

Size	Print-ing	Number in set			Handbook reference	Price per card	Complete set
B	C	25	Rigs of Ships (1929)			£3.80	£95.00
A	C	50	Romance of the Heavens (1928):		W.313		
			A	Thin card		£1.20	£60.00
			B	Thick card		£1.20	£60.00
A	C	50	Roses (1912)		W.94	£1.60	£80.00
A	C	50	Roses, 2nd Series (1914)		W.94	£1.60	£80.00
A	C	50	Roses (1926)		W.94	£1.10	£55.00
B	C	40	Roses (1936)			£1.60	£65.00
—	BW	48	Round Europe (66 x 52mm) (1937)			40p	£20.00
A	C	50	Rugby Internationals (1929)			£2.00	£100.00
A	C	50	Safety First (1934):		W.321		
			A	Home issue — 'This surface ...'		£1.20	£60.00
				Album (with price)		—	£22.00
			B	Irish issue — 'Note. This surface ...'		£2.00	—
A	C	50	School Arms (1906)		W.96	80p	£40.00
A	C	50	The Sea-Shore (1938):		W.322		
			A	Home issue — adhesive with Album offer		30p	£15.00
				Album		—	£22.00
			B	Irish issue — non-adhesive		70p	£35.00
			C	Channel Islands issue – adhesive without Album offer		60p	£30.00
A	C	50	Seaside Resorts (1899):		W.10		
			A	'Best Bird's Eye' back		£12.00	—
			B	'Capstan Navy Cut' back		£12.00	—
			C	'Gold Flake' back		£12.00	—
			D	'The Three Castles' back		£12.00	—
			E	'Traveller' back		£12.00	—
			F	'Westward Ho!' back		£12.00	—
A	U	40	Shannon Electric Power Scheme (1931)			£1.75	£70.00
A	C		*Ships:		W.11		
		25	A	Without 'Wills' on front (1895):			
				a	'Three Castles' back	£30.00	£750.00
				b	Grey scroll back	£30.00	£750.00
		50	B	With 'Wills' on front, dark grey back (1896)		£20.00	—
		100	C	Green scroll back on brown card (1898-1902):			
				i	1898-25, Group 1	£20.00	—
				ii	1898-50, Group 2	£20.00	—
				iii	1902-25 additional subjects, Group 3	£20.00	—
A	U	50	Ships' Badges (1925)		W.328	80p	£40.00
A	C	50	Signalling Series (1911)		W.97	£1.80	£90.00
A	C	50	*Soldiers and Sailors (c1894):		W.13		
			A	Grey back		£45.00	—
			B	Blue back		£45.00	—
A	C		*Soldiers of the World (1895-7):		W.12		
			A	Without PC inset:			
		100		a	With 'Ld.' back, thick card	£9.00	£900.00
		100		b	With 'Ld.' back, thin card	£9.00	—
		100		c	Without 'Ld.' back, thin card	£9.00	£900.00
		1			Additional card (as c) 'England, Drummer'	—	£150.00
		52	B	With PC inset		£24.00	£1250.00
A	C	50	Speed (1930)			£1.60	£80.00
A	C	50	Speed (1938):		W.330		
			A	Home issue — Album offer with price		40p	£20.00
			B	Irish issue — Album offer without price		80p	£40.00
			C	Channel Islands issue – no Album offer		60p	£30.00
A	C	50	Sports of All Nations, multi-backed (1900)		W.14	£11.00	£550.00
A	C	50	Strange Craft (1931)			£1.00	£50.00

W.D. & H.O. WILLS, Bristol (continued)

Size	Printing	Number in set		Handbook reference	Price per card	Complete set
A	C	50	Time and Money in Different Countries (1906)	W.104	£1.80	£90.00
A	BW		Transvaal Series:	W.30		
		50	A With black border (1899)		£9.00	—
		66	Bi Without black border (1900-01)		£1.75	£115.00
		258	Bii Intermediate cards — additions and alternatives (1900-01)		£1.75	
		66	C Final 66 subjects, as issued with 'Capstan' back (1902)		£6.00	—
B	C	40	Trees (1937)		£1.60	£65.00
B	C	25	University Hoods and Gowns (1926)		£3.20	£80.00
A	C		'Vanity Fair' Series (1902):	W.31		
		50	1st series		£7.00	£350.00
		50	2nd series		£7.00	£350.00
		50	Unnumbered — 43 subjects as in 1st and 2nd, 7 new subjects		£7.00	£350.00
A	C	50	Waterloo (c1916) (unissued)		£120.00	—
A	C		Wild Animals of the World (c1900):	W.15		
		50	A Green scroll back		£7.00	£350.00
		52	B Grey back, PC inset		£12.00	£600.00
		? 16	C Text back		£35.00	—
A	C	50	Wild Flowers (1923):	W.345		
			A With dots in side panels		70p	£35.00
			B Without dots in side panels		70p	£35.00
A	C	50	Wild Flowers — 'Series of 50' (1936):	W.346		
			A Home issue — back 'This surface ...'		50p	£25.00
			Album (with price)		—	£22.00
			B Irish issue — back 'Note. This surface ...' ...		80p	—
			C Channel Islands issue – without Album offer or I.T.C. clause		60p	£30.00
A	C	50	Wild Flowers — '2nd Series.' (1937):	W.37		
			A Home issue — adhesive back, with Album offer		20p	£10.00
			Album (with price)		—	£22.00
			B Irish issue — non-adhesive back		70p	£35.00
			C Channel Islands issue – adhesive back without Album offer		60p	£30.00
A	C	50	Wonders of the Past (1926)	W.348	70p	£35.00
A	C	50	Wonders of the Sea (1928)	W.349	50p	£25.00
A	C	25	The World's Dreadnoughts (1910)	W.115	£3.00	£75.00

POST-1965 ISSUES

Size	Printing	Number in set		Handbook reference	Price per card	Complete set
H2	C	30	Britain's Motoring History (1991)	W.416	£1.40	£42.00
			Album		—	£15.00
—	C	6	Britain's Motoring History (149 x 104mm) (1991) ...	W.416	£1.25	£7.50
H2	C	30	Britain's Steam Railways (1998)	W.416	£1.20	£36.00
			Album		—	£15.00
G2	C	30	British Aviation (1994)	W.418	£1.20	£36.00
			Album		—	£15.00
	C	6	British Aviation (1994) Beer Mats	W418	50p	£3.00
	C	56	Caribbean Treasure Cruise (1985):	W.419		
—			A Size 75 x 35mm		60p	—
—			B Size 80 x 47mm		60p	—
G2	C	30	Classic Sports Cars (1996)		£1.20	£36.00
			Album		—	£8.00
G2	C	30	Donington Collection (1993)	W.422	£1.20	£36.00
			Album		—	£15.00
—	C	6	Donington Collection (1993) Beer Mats	W.422	£1.25	
—	C	12	Embassy World Snooker Championship 17 April-3 May (80 x 47mm) (2004)	W.443	£3.00	—

W.D. & H.O. WILLS, Bristol (Post-1965 Issues continued)

Size	Printing	Number in set		Handbook reference	Price per card	Complete set
	C	12	Embassy World Snooker Championship 16 April-2 May (2005):	W.444		
—			A Size 75 x 32mm		£3.00	—
—			B Size 80 x 47mm		£3.00	—
G2	BW	48	Familiar Phrases (1986)		£1.20	£60.00
	C	26	Focus on What's What (1989):	W.425		
—			A Size 75 x 32mm		60p	—
—			B Size 80 x 47mm		60p	—
G2	C	10	Golden Era (1999)	W.426	£2.00	£20.00
			Album		—	£15.00
H2	C	30	History of Britain's Railways (1987)	W.428	£1.20	£36.00
			Album		—	£15.00
H2	C	30	History of Motor Racing (1987)	W.429	£1.50	—
			Album		—	£15.00
G2	C	30	In Search of Steam (1992)	W.430	£1.20	£36.00
			Album		—	£15.00
—	C	6	In Search of Steam (1992) Beer Mats	W.430	£1.25	—
G2	BW	5	Pica Punchline (1984)		£1.20	£6.00
H2	U	144	Punch Lines (1983)	W.433	80p	—
G2	U	288	Punch Lines (1983)	W.433	80p	—
G2	U	48	Ring the Changes (1985):	W.434		
			A With 'Wills' name		£1.20	£60.00
			B Without 'Wills' Name		£1.60	—
—	C	12	Russ Abbot Advertising Cards (80 x 47mm) (1993)		£1.50	£18.00
	C	56	Showhouse (1988):	W.435		
—			A Size 60 x 43mm		60p	—
—			B Size 80 x 35mm		60p	—
—			C Size 68 x 47mm		60p	—
—			D Size 80 x 47mm		60p	—
G2			E Size 90 x 47mm		60p	—
G2	C	30	Soldiers of Waterloo (1995)		£1.20	£36.00
			Album		—	£15.00
G2	BW	10	Spot the Shot (1986)		£2.50	£25.00
G2	C	30	The Tank Story (1997)		£1.20	£36.00
			Album		—	£15.00
			Three Castles Sailing Ship Model advertisement cards (1965):			
A	C	1	A View from Stern:			
			Three Castles Filter:			
			I. Three Castles Cigarettes		—	£4.00
			II. In the eighteenth century		—	£1.50
A	C	1	B Views from Bows:			
			I. Three Castles Filter		—	£1.50
			II. Three Castles Filter magnum		—	£1.50
A	BW	1	C Sailing Ship Black Line Drawing		—	£5.00
A	BW	1	D Three Castles Shield Black Line Drawing		—	£5.00
—	C		200th Anniversary Presentation Packs (2 sets of Playing Cards) (1986)	W.661	—	£90.00
	C	?	Wheel of Fortune (1985):	W.439		
—			A Size 75 x 35mm		60p	—
—			B Size 80 x 47mm		60p	—
—	C	56	Wonders of the World (1986):	W.440		
			A Size 90 x 47mm		50p	£28.00
			B Size 80 x 47mm		70p	£40.00
			C Size 80 x 35mm		90p	—
C1	C	36	World of Firearms (1982)		25p	£9.00
			Album		—	£10.00

Size	Print-ing	Number in set		Handbook reference	Price per card	Complete set

W.D. & H.O. WILLS, Bristol (Post-1965 Issues continued)

Size	Print.	No.	Description	Ref	Price	Set
C1	C	36	World of Speed (1981) …… …… …… …… …… ……		25p	£9.00
			Album …… …… …… …… …… …… …… …… ……		—	£20.00

OVERSEAS ISSUES

D2	U	50	Actors and Actresses, scroll backs in green (1905):	W.32		
			A Portraits in black and white …… …… …… ……		£3.50	—
			B Portraits flesh tinted …… …… …… …… ……		£2.75	—
D	U	30	Actresses — brown and green (1905) Scissors issue	W.116	£3.30	£100.00
D2	U	50	Actresses — four colours surround (c1904):	W.117		
			A Scissors issue …… …… …… …… …… …… ……		£7.00	—
			B Green scroll back issue …… …… …… …… ……		£3.00	—
D	U	30	Actresses — orange/mauve surround (c1916) Scissors issue:	W.118		
			A Surround in Orange …… …… …… …… ……		£2.50	£75.00
			B Surround in mauve …… …… …… …… ……		£1.70	£50.00
D2	U	100	Actresses (c1903):	W.34		
			A Capstan issue …… …… …… …… …… ……		£3.25	—
			B Vice Regal issue …… …… …… …… …… ……		£3.25	—
D	U		Actresses (c1903):	W.33		
		250	A Front portrait in black, border in red …… …… ……		£3.00	—
		50	B Front portrait in red, border in red …… …… ……		£3.00	—
D	BW	25	Actresses — Tabs type numbered (1902) …… ……	W.16	£20.00	
D2	BW	50	Actresses — Tabs type unnumbered, Scissors issue (c1905) …… …… …… …… …… …… …… ……	W.119	£12.00	—
D	U	30	Actresses unicoloured I (1908):	W.120		
			A Scissors issue, back in red …… …… …… ……		£2.00	£60.00
			B Scissors issue, back in purple brown …… ……		£2.50	£75.00
A	U	30	Actresses — unicoloured II (c1908) Scissors issue …	W.121	£2.00	£60.00
A	C	1	*Advertisement Card 'Capstan' (1902) …… …… ……	W.402	—	£300.00
A	C	50	Aeroplanes (1926) …… …… …… …… …… …… ……		£3.50	—
A	C	60	Animals (cut-outs) (1913):	W.37		
			A Havelock issue …… …… …… …… …… ……		£2.00	
			B Wills' Specialities issue …… …… …… ……		£1.00	£60.00
	C	50	Animals and Birds:	W.17		
A			A With text, without title (c1902) …… …… ……		£15.00	—
D2			B Without text, with title (1912) …… …… ……		£5.00	—
D2			C Without text or title (1909) …… …… …… ……		£6.00	—
A	C	50	Arms and Armour (1910):	W.38		
			A Capstan issue …… …… …… …… …… ……		£2.00	—
			B Havelock issue …… …… …… …… …… ……		£3.00	—
			C Vice Regal issue …… …… …… …… ……		£2.00	—
			D United Service issue …… …… …… …… …		£3.20	£160.00
A	C	50	Arms of the British Empire (1910):	W.40		
			A Backs in black …… …… …… …… …… ……		£1.20	£60.00
			B Wills' Specialities issue …… …… …… ……		£1.20	—
			C Havelock issue …… …… …… …… …… ……		£7.00	—
A	C	25	Army Life (1914) Scissors issue …… …… …… ……	W.133	£2.80	£70.00
—	U	50	Art Photogravures 1st series (1912):	W.43		
			A Size 67 x 33mm …… …… …… …… …… ……		£1.00	—
			B Size 67 x 44mm …… …… …… …… ……		£1.00	—
A	U	50	Art Photogravures 2nd series (1914) …… …… ……	W.44	£1.00	—
A	C		Australian Club Cricketers (1905):	W.59-1		
		40	A Dark blue back, front blue frameline with state		£18.00	—
		40	B Dark blue back, front blue frameline without state …… …… …… …… …… …… …… ……		£18.00	—
		40	C Green back …… …… …… …… …… ……		£18.00	—
		46	D Pale blue back, front brown frameline:			
			i Numbers 1-40 (minus Nos 28 & 33) …… ……		£25.00	—
			ii Numbers 41-48 …… …… …… …… …… ……		£50.00	—

W.D. & H.O. WILLS, Bristol (Overseas Issues continued)

Size	Printing	Number in set	Description	Handbook reference	Price per card	Complete set
A	C	25	Australian and English Cricketers (1903)	W.59-2	£17.00	—
D2	U	25	Australian and English Cricketers (1909):	W.59-3		
			A Capstan issue:			
			i Framework in scarlet		£17.00	—
			ii Framework in blue		£17.00	—
			B Vice Regal issue:			
			i Framework in scarlet		£17.00	—
			ii Framework in blue		£17.00	—
D2	U	60	Australian and South African Cricketers (1910):	W.59-4		
			A Capstan issue:			
			i Framework in scarlet		£17.00	—
			ii Framework in blue		£17.00	—
			B Havelock issue:			
			i Framework in scarlet		£40.00	—
			ii Framework in blue		£40.00	—
			C Vice Regal issue:			
			i Framework in scarlet		£17.00	—
			ii Framework in blue		£17.00	—
—	P	100	Australian Scenic Series (69 x 52mm) (1928)	W.138	£1.10	—
A	C	50	Australian Wild Flowers (1913):			
			A Wills' Specialities issue, grey-brown back		£1.10	£55.00
			B Wills' Specialities issue, green back		£2.00	—
			C Havelock issue		£3.50	—
A	C		Aviation (1910):	W.46		
		85	A Black backs 'Series of 85':			
			i Capstan issue		£3.00	—
			ii Vice Regal issue		£3.00	—
		75	B Black backs 'Series of 75':			
			i Capstan issue		£2.30	—
			ii Havelock issue		£3.00	—
			iii Vice Regal issue		£2.30	—
		75	C Green back 'Series of 75':			
			i Capstan issue		£2.50	—
			ii Havelock issue		£3.50	—
			iii Vice Regal issue		£2.50	—
D2	C	50	Aviation Series (1911):	W.47		
			A W.D. and H.O. Wills back		£3.50	—
			B Anonymous backs with album clause		£3.50	—
			C Anonymous backs without album clause		£3.50	—
A	C	? 95	Baseball Series (1912) Pirate issue	W.353	£500.00	—
A	U	40	Beauties — brown tinted (1913):	W.139		
			A Scissors issue		£1.70	£70.00
			B Star circle and leaves issue		£3.00	—
D2	U	30	Beauties — 'Celebrated Actresses' Scissors issue (c1912)	W.140	£5.00	—
A2	C	52	Beauties — Heads and shoulders set in background (1911) PC inset:	W.141		
			A Scissors issue:			
			i Background to packets plain		£6.50	—
			ii Background to packets latticework design		£3.20	£170.00
			iii No packet back		£40.00	—
			B Star circle and leaves issue		£6.00	—
—	CP	50	Beauties 1st series (63 x 45mm) (1925)	W.142	£4.00	—
—	P	25	Beauties 1st Series (64 x 40mm) (1925)	W.142	£3.50	—
—	P	50	Beauties 2nd series (64 x 40mm) (1925)	W.143	£3.50	—
A2	C	32	Beauties — Picture Hats (1914):	W.144		
			A Scissors issue		£3.75	—
			B Star circle and leaves issue		£5.50	—

Size	Printing	Number in set		Handbook reference	Price per card	Complete set
			W.D. & H.O. WILLS, Bristol (Overseas Issues continued)			
—	CP	72	Beauties — red star and circle back (70 x 47mm) (1923) ...	W.145	£12.00	—
D2	U	50	Beauties — red tinted (1905) ...	W.146	£2.50	£125.00
D	C	30	Beauties and Children (c1910) Scissors issue ...	W.147	£2.50	£75.00
A	P	50	Beautiful New Zealand (1928) ...		40p	£20.00
D2	C	50	Best Dogs of Their Breed (1914):	W.48		
			A Havelock issue ...		£7.50	—
			B Wills' Specialities issue ...		£5.00	—
			C Anonymous back, Wills' on front ...		£9.00	—
D2	C	30	Birds and Animals (1911) Ruby Queen issue ...	W.354	£3.00	—
D1	C	50	Birds, Beasts and Fishes (1924) ...	W.151	50p	£25.00
A	C	100	Birds of Australasia:			
			A Green backs (1912):			
			i Capstan issue ...		£1.50	£150.00
			ii Havelock issue ...		£2.50	—
			iii Vice Regal issue ...		£1.50	£150.00
			B Yellow backs (1915):			
			i Havelock issue ...		£2.50	—
			ii Wills' Specialities issue ...		£1.50	—
D	C	52	Birds of Brilliant Plumage:	W.152		
			A Four Aces issue (1924) ...		£3.25	—
			B Pirate Issue:			
			i With border on front (1916) ...		£4.00	—
			ii Without border on front (1916) ...		£4.00	—
			C Red star, circle and leaves issue (1914) ...		£4.50	—
D2	C	25	Birds of the East 1st series Ruby Queen issue (1912)	W.355	£1.60	£40.00
D2	C	25	Birds of the East 2nd series Ruby Queen issue (1927) ...	W.356	£1.60	£40.00
D2	C	36	Boxers (1911):	W.153		
			A Scissors issue ...		£10.00	—
			B Green star and circle issue ...		£10.00	—
D2	U		Britain's Defenders (1915):	W.51		
			A Wills' Specialities issue:			
		50	i Inscribed 'A Series of 50' ...		£1.50	£75.00
		8	ii Without inscription 'A Series of 50' ...		£10.00	—
		50	B Havelock issue ...		£3.00	—
		50	C Scissors issue:			
			i Red upright 'Scissors' packet ...		£1.80	£90.00
			ii Green upright 'Scissors' packet ...		£2.00	£100.00
			iii Red slanting 'Scissors' packet ...		£1.80	£90.00
		50	D Green star and circle issue ...		£2.20	—
D2	C	43	British Army Boxers (1913) Scissors issue ...		£6.00	—
D2	C	50	British Army Uniforms (c1910):	W.106		
			A Wild Woodbine issue ...		£6.00	£300.00
			B Flag issue ...		£5.50	—
			C Scissors issue ...		£5.50	£275.00
—	C	101	British Beauties (59 x 41mm) (c1915) ...	W.155	£2.50	—
A	C	50	British Empire Series (1912):			
			A Capstan issue ...		£1.20	£60.00
			B Havelock issue ...		£2.00	—
			C Vice Regal issue ...		£1.20	£60.00
A	P	48	British Royal and Ancient Buildings (1925) ...		50p	£25.00
A	BW	45	British Rugby Players (1930) ...		£2.70	—
A	U	50	Chateaux (1925) ...	W.167	£6.00	—
A	C	50	Children of All Nations (1925) ...		90p	£45.00

W.D. & H.O. WILLS, Bristol (Overseas Issues continued)

Size	Print-ing	Number in set		Handbook reference	Price per card	Complete set
D2	C	100	China's Famous Warriors (1911) Pirate issue:			
			A First 25 subjects	W.357	£3.00	£75.00
			B Second 25 subjects	W.358	£3.00	£75.00
			C Third 25 subjects	W.359	£3.00	£75.00
			D Fourth 25 subjects	W.360	£3.00	£75.00
D2	C	28	Chinese Actors and Actresses (1907) Pirate issue	W.361	£3.00	—
D2	C	25	Chinese Beauties 1st Series (1907) Pirate issue:	W.362		
			A Vertical back		£2.00	£50.00
			B Horizontal back		£2.20	£55.00
D2	C	25	Chinese Beauties 2nd series (1909) Pirate issue:	W.363		
			A With framelines on front		£2.00	£50.00
			B Without framelines on front		£2.00	£50.00
D2	C	30	Chinese Children's Games (1911) Ruby Queen issue	W.364	£3.00	—
D2	C	50	Chinese Costumes Pirate issue (1928)	W.365	£5.00	—
—	C	25	Chinese Pagodas (1911) Pirate issue (138 x 88mm)	W.366	£50.00	—
D2	U	50	Chinese Proverbs brown (138 x 88mm) (1928):	W.367		
			A Pirate issue		£1.80	—
			B Ruby Queen issue		£5.00	—
D2	C	50	Chinese Proverbs coloured (1914-16) Pirate issue:	W.368		
			A Back in blue:			
			i Without overprint		£1.80	—
			ii With overprint		£1.80	—
			B Back in olive green		£1.80	—
D2	C	40	Chinese Trades (c1905) Autocar issue	W.369	£7.00	—
D2	C	50	Chinese Transport (1914) Ruby Queen issue	W.370	£3.50	—
D2	U	50	Cinema Stars Four Aces issue (1926):	W.172		
			A Numbered		£1.80	£90.00
			B Unnumbered		£2.00	£100.00
D2	U	25	Cinema Stars (1916) Scissors issue	W.173	£2.60	£65.00
A1	P	50	Cinema Stars (1926)	W.382	£5.00	—
A	C	50	Coaches and Coaching Days (1925)		£2.20	£110.00
A	C		Conundrums (c1900):	W.21		
		25	A With album clause		£13.00	—
		25	B Without album clause		£13.00	—
		25	C Without album clause redrawn		£13.00	—
		50	D Without album clause inscribed '50 Different'		£13.00	—
—	C	68	Crests and Colours of Australian Universities, Colleges and Schools (70 x 48mm) (1929)	W.176	80p	£55.00
A	P	63	Cricketers (c1925)	W.59-5	£8.00	—
A	U	25	Cricketer Series (1902)	W.59-6	£140.00	—
A	U	50	Cricketer Series (1901)	W.59-7	£140.00	—
A	P	48	Cricket Season 1928-29	W.177	£3.50	—
D2	C	27	Dancing Girls (1915) Scissors issue:	W.180		
			A Inscribed '28 Subjects' (No. 3 not issued)		£3.00	—
			B Inscribed '27 Subjects'		£3.00	—
D2	C	25	Derby Day Series (1914):	W.181		
			A Scissors issue:			
			i With title		£8.00	—
			ii Without title		£10.00	—
			B Star and circle issue		£9.00	—
A	C	50	Dogs — Scenic backgrounds (1925)		£1.00	£50.00
—	C	20	Dogs — Heads 1st series (70 x 63mm) (1927):			
			A Wills' World Renown Cigarettes issue:			
			i With album clause		£3.50	—
			ii Without album clause		£3.50	—
			B Three Castles and Vice Regal Cigarettes issue		£3.50	—
—	C	20	Dogs — Heads 2nd series (70 x 63mm) (1927)		£3.50	—

W.D. & H.O. WILLS, Bristol (Overseas Issues continued)

Size	Print-ing	Number in set		Handbook reference	Price per card	Complete set
D2	C	32	Drum Horses (1909):	W.192		
			A Scissors issue:			
			i Vertical format, open Scissors packet ...		£9.00	—
			ii Horizontal format, closed Scissors packet		£7.00	—
			B United Service issue		£6.50	—
			C Green star, circle and leaves issue		£7.50	—
A	P	25	English Cricketers (1926)		£3.20	£80.00
—	C	25	English Period Costumes (70 x 55mm) (1928):	W.195		
			A White card		£2.00	—
			B Cream card		£2.00	£50.00
—	P	10	English Views & Buildings (145 x 108mm) (c1928)	W.407	£13.00	—
	BW		Etchings (of Dogs) (1925):			
A		26	A Small size English language issues:			
			i With 'Gold Flake Cigarettes'		£7.00	—
			ii Without 'Gold Flake Cigarettes'		£2.50	—
A		26	B Small size Dutch language issues:			
			i With framelines to back		£8.00	—
			ii Without framelines to back		£8.00	—
—		26	C Medium size (78 x 54mm)		£5.00	—
D	C	25	The Evolution of the British Navy (1915)		£3.00	£75.00
		10	Famous Castles (c1928):	W.408		
—	P		A Size 145 x 108mm		£12.00	—
—	U		B Size 140 x 75mm		£12.00	—
	U		Famous Film Stars (1934):			
A		100	A Small size		£1.50	—
—		100	B Medium size (67 x 53mm):			
			i White card		£2.50	—
			ii Cream card		£2.50	—
—	P	100	Famous Film Stars (68 x 51mm) (c1936)		£3.40	—
A2	U	50	Famous Footballers (1914):			
			A Scissors issue		£10.00	—
			B Star and circle issue		£10.00	—
A	C	50	Famous Inventions (without ITC clause) (1926)	W.60	£1.00	£50.00
D2	U	75	Film Favourites Four Aces issue (1928)		£1.80	—
A	C	50	Fish of Australasia (1912):			
			A Capstan issue		£1.50	£75.00
			B Havelock issue		£2.50	—
			C Vice Regal issue		£1.50	£75.00
D2	C		Flag Girls of All Nations (1908):	W.64		
		50	A Capstan issue		£2.00	—
		50	B Vice Regal issue		£2.00	—
		25	C United Service issue		£3.00	£75.00
		25	D Scissors issue:			
			i Numbered		£10.00	—
			ii Unnumbered		£10.00	—
		25	E Green star, circle and leaves issue		£3.00	£75.00
—	C	8	Flags, shaped metal (1915)	W.65	£10.00	—
D2	C	126	Flags and Ensigns (1903)	W.66	£1.60	—
A	C	25	Flags of the Empire (no ITC clause) (1926)	W.215	£7.00	—
D2	C		Flowers Purple Mountain issue (1914):			
		20	A Numbered	W.371	£12.00	—
		100	B Unnumbered	W.372	£12.00	—
D2	C	50	Football Club Colours Scissors/Special Army Quality issue (1907)	W.220	£9.00	—
A	C	28	Football Club Colours and Flags (1913):	W.68		
			A Capstan issue		£5.00	—
			B Havelock issue		£7.00	—

W.D. & H.O. WILLS, Bristol (Overseas Issues continued)

Size	Printing	Number in set		Handbook reference	Price per card	Complete set
	U	200	Footballers (1933):			
A			A Small size … … … … … … … … … …		£1.70	—
—			B Medium size (67 x 52mm) … … … … … … …		£3.50	—
—	C	? 5	Footballers Shaped Die Cut (59 x 30mm) (1910) …	W.404	£150.00	—
D2	C	50	Girls of All Nations (1908):	W.73		
			A Capstan issue … … … … … … … … … …		£3.00	—
			B Vice Regal issue … … … … … … … …		£3.00	—
			C Green star, circle and leaves issue … … … …		£3.00	—
D2	C	25	Governor-General of India Scissors issue (1912) …	W.229	£7.40	—
—	C	25	Heraldic Signs and Their Origins (77 x 59mm) (1925) … … … … … … … … … … … …	W.230	£1.60	£40.00
D2	C	30	Heroic Deeds (1913) Scissors issue … … … … … …		£5.00	—
A	C	50	Historic Events (1913):	W.74		
			A Wills' Specialities issue … … … … … … …		£1.40	£70.00
			B Havelock issue … … … … … … … … …		£2.50	—
—	C	25	History of Naval Dress (75 x 55mm) (1930) … … …		£35.00	—
A2	P	50	Homeland Events (1927) … … … … … … …	W.233	80p	£40.00
A2	C	50	Horses of Today (1906):	W.75		
			A Capstan issue … … … … … … … … …		£3.20	—
			B Havelock issue … … … … … … … … …		£5.00	—
			C Vice Regal issue … … … … … … … …		£3.20	—
A	C	50	Household Hints (1927):	W.236		
			A With 'Wills' Cigarettes' at top back … … … …		60p	—
			B Without 'Wills' Cigarettes' at top back … … …		£1.50	—
D2	C		Houses of Parliament (c1912):	W.237		
		33	A Pirate issue … … … … … … … … … …		£1.40	£45.00
		32	B Star and circle issue … … … … … … … …		£2.25	£72.00
D2	C	50	Indian Regiments (1912):	W.239		
			A Scissors issue … … … … … … … … …		£9.00	—
			B Star and circle issue … … … … … … … …		£9.00	—
A	C	2	Indian Series – see Bukhsh Ellallie & Co.			
A	C	50	Interesting Buildings (1905) … … … … … … … …	W.76	£2.80	£140.00
D2	BW	67	International Footballers Season 1909-1910:	W.242		
			A Scissors issue (1910) … … … … … … … …		£12.00	—
			B United Services issue (1910) … … … … …		£12.00	—
			C Flag issue (1911) … … … … … … … …		£12.00	—
A	U	5	Islands of the Pacific (c1916) … … … … … …	W.375	£250.00	—
D2	C	50	Jiu-Jitsu (c1910):			
			A Scissors issue … … … … … … … … …		£6.50	—
			B Flag issue … … … … … … … … … …		£6.00	—
D1	C	53	Jockeys and Owners Colours with PC inset Scissors issue (1914) … … … … … … … … … … …		£8.00	—
A	C	50	Lighthouses (1926) … … … … … … … … …		£1.80	£90.00
A	U		Maori Series (c1900):	W.77		
		100	A White border … … … … … … … … … …		£90.00	—
		? 44	B Green border. Numbered bottom left … … …		£90.00	—
		? 3	C Green border. Numbered top left … … … …		£200.00	—
		? 4	D Green border. Unnumbered … … … … …		£200.00	—
		? 100	E White border. Plain back (anonymous) … … …		£75.00	—
A	C	45	Melbourne Cup Winners (1906) … … … … … …	W.78	£9.00	—
A	C	50	Merchant Ships of the World (1925) (without I.T.C. clause) … … … … … … … … … … … …	W.257	£1.40	£70.00
A1	C	40	Merrie England Studies (Male) (1916) … … … …	W.79	£7.00	—
A	U	24	Merveilles du Monde (1927) … … … … … … …	W.258	£7.00	—
A	BW	25	Military Portraits (1917) Scissors issue … … … … …		£4.00	—
—	C	25	Miniatures — oval medallions (62 x 45mm) (1914)	W.261	£55.00	—

W.D. & H.O. WILLS, Bristol (Overseas Issues continued)

Size	Print-ing	Number in set	Description	Handbook reference	Price per card	Complete set
K2	C	52	Miniature Playing Cards Scissors issue (1906) … …		£11.00	—
A	U	50	Modern War Weapons (1915):	W.82		
			A Wills' Specialities issue … … … … … … …		£2.00	—
			B Havelock issue … … … … … … … … …		£3.00	—
A	C	25	Modes of Conveyance (1928) Four Aces issue … …		£2.00	£50.00
A	C	48	Motor Cars (1923) … … … … … … … … … …		£2.20	£110.00
A	P	50	Motor Cars (1927) … … … … … … … … …		£1.80	£90.00
A	C	50	Motor Cycles (1926) … … … … … … … …		£3.20	£160.00
A1	P	48	Movie Stars (1927) … … … … … … … …		£3.50	—
D2	BW	50	Music Hall Celebrities (1911) Scissors issue … … …	W.269	£6.50	—
A	C	50	National Flags and Arms (1938) … … … … …		£1.50	—
—	C	25	The Nation's Shrines (71 x 55mm) (1928) … … … …		£1.40	£35.00
A	P	50	Nature Studies (1928) … … … … … … …		£1.50	—
A	C	50	New Zealand Birds (1925) … … … … … …		£1.20	£60.00
A	P	50	New Zealand — Early Scenes and Maori Life			
			(1926) … … … … … … … … … … …		50p	£25.00
A	P	50	New Zealand Footballers (1927) … … … … …		£1.60	£80.00
A	U	50	New Zealand Race Horses (1928):			
			A Cream card … … … … … … … … …		£1.00	£50.00
			B White card … … … … … … … … …		£1.00	—
A	C	50	N.Z. Butterflies, Moths and Beetles (1925) … … …		£1.00	£50.00
A	C	25	Past and Present (1929) … … … … … … …		£1.40	£35.00
A1	C	50	Past and Present Champions (1908):	W.89		
			A Capstan Cigarette issue … … … … …		£12.00	—
			B Capstan Tobacco issue … … … … … …		£12.00	—
A	C	25	Picturesque People of the Empire (1928) … … … …		£1.40	£35.00
A	C	25	Pirates and Highwaymen (1925) … … … … …		£1.60	£40.00
A	C	25	Police of the World (1910) … … … … … …	W.290	£10.00	—
—	C	70	Practical Wireless (69 x 62mm) (1923) … … … …		£8.00	—
D2	C		Products of the World — Maps and Scenes (1913):	W.293		
		50	A Pirate issue … … … … … … … … …		£1.40	—
		25	B Green star, circle and leaves issue … … … …		£1.80	—
A	C	50	Products of the World — Scenes only (1929) … … …		50p	£25.00
A	C	50	Prominent Australian and English Cricketers (1907)	W.59-8	£14.00	—
D2	C	23	Prominent Australian and English Cricketers (1907)	W.59-9	£18.00	—
D2	BW	59	Prominent Australian and English Cricketers (1911):	W.59-10		
			A Capstan issue:			
			i 'A Series of 50' … … … … … … … …		£14.00	—
			ii 'A Series of …/A Series of 59' … … … …		£17.00	—
			B Vice Regal issue:			
			i 'A Series of 50' … … … … … … …		£14.00	—
			ii 'A Series of …/A Series of 59' … … … …		£17.00	—
			C Havelock issue … … … … … … … …		£40.00	—
D2	C	25	Puzzle Series (1910) Scissors/United Service issue:	W.298		
			A Background blue-green … … … … … … …		£7.00	—
			B Background light yellow … … … … … …		£7.00	—
D	C	50	Races of Mankind (1911) … … … … … …		£13.00	—
A	C	50	Railway Engines (1924) … … … … … … … …	W.303	£1.30	£65.00
A	C	50	Railway Working (1927) … … … … … … …		£2.20	—
A	C	50	Regimental Colours and Cap Badges (1907):			
			A Scissors issue … … … … … … … …		£1.60	£80.00
			B United Service issue:			
			i Red back … … … … … … … … …		£1.60	£80.00
			ii Blue back … … … … … … … …		£1.60	£80.00
D2	C	33	Regimental Pets (1911) Scissors issue … … … … …	W.309	£6.50	—
A	C	50	Regimental Standards and Cap Badges (1928) … …		80p	£40.00

W.D. & H.O. WILLS, Bristol (Overseas Issues continued)

Size	Print-ing	Number in set		Handbook reference	Price per card	Complete set
A	C	50	Riders of the World:	W.93		
			A Capstan/Vice Regal/Pennant/Wills' Specialities issue (1913)		£1.70	—
			B Havelock issue (1913)		£3.50	—
			C Back in red-brown (1931)		£1.20	£60.00
A	C	50	Romance of the Heavens (1928) (No ITC clause) ...		£1.50	—
D2	C	25	Roses (1912):	W.373		
			A Purple Mountain issues:			
			i With Wills' Cigarettes on front		£6.40	—
			ii Without Wills' Cigarettes on front		£6.40	—
			B Plain backs with Wills' Cigarettes on front ...		£6.40	—
A	P	50	The Royal Family at Home and Abroad (1927) ...		£1.60	—
A	C	50	Royal Mail (with Wills' Cigarettes on fronts) (1913):	W.95		
			A Capstan issue		£4.00	£200.00
			B Havelock issue (without Wills' Cigarettes on fronts)		£5.00	—
			C Vice Regal issue		£4.00	£200.00
			D With anonymous backs		£6.50	—
			E With plain back		£6.50	—
A	P	50	The Royal Navy (1929)		£1.80	£90.00
A	BW	100	Royalty, Notabilities and Events 1900-1902 (1902) ...	W.28	£3.00	—
D1	U	27	Rulers of the World (1911)	W.320	£8.00	—
D2			Russo-Japanese Series (1905):	W.29		
	BW	100	A Fronts in black		£2.00	£200.00
	U	50	B Fronts in red		£8.00	—
A	C	50	Safety First (1937)	W.321	90p	£45.00
B	CP	48	Scenes from the Empire (1939)		£2.00	£100.00
D2	C	30	Semaphore Signalling (1910)		£3.50	£105.00
A	P	50	Ships and Shipping (1928)		90p	£45.00
D2	C	36	Ships and Their Pennants (1913)		£6.00	—
A	C	50	Ships' Badges (1925)	W.328	90p	£45.00
A	C	50	Signalling Series (1912):	W.97		
			A Capstan issue		£1.40	£70.00
			B Havelock issue		£2.50	—
			C Vice Regal issue		£1.40	£70.00
D2	BW	40	Sketches in black and white (1905)	W.98	£2.50	—
	C		Soldiers of the World (1903):	W.12		
A		50	A Numbered		£9.00	—
D2		75	B Unnumbered		£10.00	—
A	BW	100	South African Personalities (1894)	W.99	£140.00	—
—	P	10	Splendours of New Zealand (140 x 75mm) (c1928)		£12.00	—
D2	C	30	Sporting Girls (1913) Scissors issue	W.331	£9.00	—
	P	50	A Sporting Holiday in New Zealand (1928):	W.332		
A			A Small size		80p	£40.00
—			B Medium size (70 x 57mm)		£1.00	£50.00
D2	C	25	Sporting Terms (1905):	W.100		
			A Capstan issue		£15.00	—
			B Vice Regal issue		£15.00	—
D	C	50	Sports of the World (1917)		£5.00	—
D2		50	Stage and Music Hall Celebrities (1904) (Portrait in oval frame):	W.102		
	BW		A Capstan issue		£3.50	—
	BW		B Vice Regal issue		£3.50	—
	U		C Havelock issue		£4.50	—
D2	BW	50	Stage and Music Hall Celebrities (1908) (Portrait in oblong frame)	W.103	£3.50	

W.D. & H.O. WILLS, Bristol (Overseas Issues continued)

Size	Print-ing	Number in set		Handbook reference	Price per card	Complete set
D1	P	52	Stars of the Cinema (1926):			
			A Text back		£6.00	—
			B Four Aces issue		£6.00	—
A	C	50	Time and Money in Different Countries (1908):	W.104		
			A Capstan issue		£1.60	—
			B Havelock issue		£2.80	—
			C Vice Regal issue:			
			i With album clause		£1.60	£80.00
			ii Without album clause		£1.60	£80.00
A	C	50	A Tour Round the World (1907)	W.105	£3.00	—
D2	C	50	Types of the British Army (1912):	W.106		
			A Capstan issue		£2.40	—
			B Vice Regal issue		£2.40	—
A	C	50	Types of the Commonwealth Forces (1910):	W.107		
			A Capstan issue		£2.60	—
			B Vice Regal issue		£2.60	—
			C Havelock issue		£5.00	—
A	C	25	United States Warships (1911):	W.108		
			A Capstan issue		£3.40	—
			B Havelock issue		£5.40	—
			C Vice Regal issue		£3.40	—
A	P	50	Units of the British Army and RAF (1928)		60p	£30.00
A	C	50	USS Co's Steamers (1930)		£2.60	—
A	C	50	VCs (1926)		£2.00	£100.00
D2	C	25	Victoria Cross Heroes (1915):			
			A Havelock issue		£4.00	—
			B Wills' Specialities issue		£2.60	£65.00
			C Scissors issue		£3.60	£90.00
A	C	10	Victorian Football Association (1908):	W.110		
			A Capstan on front		£5.00	—
			B Havelock on front		£7.00	—
A	C	19	Victorian Football League (1908):	W.111		
			A Capstan on front		£5.00	—
			B Havelock on front		£7.00	—
—	P	215	Views of the World (66 x 28mm) (1908):	W.112		
			A Numbers 1-50 plain backs (anonymous)		£1.00	—
			B Numbers 51-215 blue back Capstan issue ...		£1.00	—
			C Numbers 51-215 green back Vice Regal issue		£1.00	—
A	C	25	Village Models Series (1925):			
			A Small size		£1.40	£35.00
			B Medium size		£6.00	—
D2	C	50	War Incidents 1st series (1915):	W.113		
			A Wills' Specialities issue		£2.40	—
			B Havelock issue		£3.50	—
			C Scissors issue		£2.50	£125.00
D2	C	50	War Incidents 2nd series (1915):	W.113		
			A Wills' Specialities issue		£3.20	£160.00
			B Havelock issue		£5.00	—
A	BW	50	War Pictures (1915):	W.114		
			A Wills' Specialities issue		£1.40	£70.00
			B Havelock issue		£2.50	—
A	C	50	Warships (1926)		£1.80	£90.00
D2	C	30	What It Means (1916) Scissors issue		£1.50	£45.00
	C		Wild Animals (1934):			
A		50	A Small size titled 'Wild Animals' Heads		70p	£35.00
—		25	B Medium size titled 'Wild Animals' (69 x 55mm)		£1.40	£35.00

W.D. & H.O. WILLS, Bristol (Overseas Issues continued)

Size	Printing	Number in set	Description	Handbook reference	Price per card	Complete set
A	C	50	Wild Animals of the World (1906):	W.15		
			A Bristol and London issue		£12.00	—
			B Celebrated Cigarettes issue		£6.00	£300.00
			C Star, circle and leaves issue		£8.50	—
A	C	25	Wonders of the World (1926)		£1.20	£30.00
A	C	25	The World's Dreadnoughts (1910):	W.115		
			A Capstan issue		£2.60	—
			B Vice Regal issue		£2.60	—
			C No ITC clause		£2.80	£70.00
A	P	50	Zoo (1927):			
			A Scissors issue without descriptive back		£5.00	—
			B Wills' issue with descriptive back		30p	£15.00
—	P	50	Zoological Series (70 x 60mm) (1922)		£1.80	—

SILK ISSUES 1911-17

Size	Printing	Number in set	Description	Handbook reference	Price per card	Complete set
—	C	50	Arms of the British Empire (70 x 48mm)	W.126	£3.00	—
—	C	50	Australian Butterflies (70 x 51mm)		£3.00	—
—	C	50	Birds and Animals of Australia (70 x 48mm)		£3.20	—
			Crests and Colours of Australian Universities, Colleges and Schools (70 x 48mm):			
—	C	50	A Numbered		£3.00	—
—	C	1	B Unnumbered		£25.00	—
—	C	1	Flag (Union Jack) (162 x 112mm)		£30.00	—
—	C	28	Flags of 1914-18 Allies (64 x 42mm):	W.214		
			A Backs with letterpress in capitals		£2.25	—
			B Backs with letterpress in small lettering		£2.25	—
—	C	13	*Flags on Lace* (71 x 50mm)	W.405	£6.00	—
A	C	38	Kings and Queens of England	W.251	£5.00	—
—	C	50	Popular Flowers (72 x 51mm):			
			A Backs inscribed 'Now being inserted in the large packets'		£4.50	—
			B Backs inscribed 'Now being inserted in the 1/- packets'		£4.50	—
—	C	67	War Medals (82 x 53mm)	W.341	£3.50	—

WILSON & CO., Ely

Size	Printing	Number in set	Description	Handbook reference	Price per card	Complete set
A	U	50	War Portraits (1916)	H.86	£100.00	—

W. WILSON, Birmingham

Size	Printing	Number in set	Description	Handbook reference	Price per card	Complete set
D	C	30	*Army Pictures. Cartoons, etc (1916)	H.12	£130.00	—
A	U	50	War Portraits (1916)	H.86	£100.00	—

HENRI WINTERMANS (UK) LTD

Size	Printing	Number in set	Description	Handbook reference	Price per card	Complete set
G	C	30	Disappearing Rain Forest (1991)		40p	£12.00
			Album		—	£15.00
G	C	30	Wonders of Nature (1992)		50p	£15.00
			Album		—	£15.00

A. & M. WIX, London and Johannesburg

Size	Printing	Number in set	Description	Handbook reference	Price per card	Complete set
—	—		Cinema Cavalcade (50 coloured, 200 black and white; sizes — 70 small, 110 large, 70 extra-large):			
		250	'A Series of 250 ...' ('Max Cigarettes') (1939) ...		£1.30	—
		250	'2nd Series of 250 ...' ('Max Cigarettes') (1940)		£1.50	—
A2	C	100	Film Favourites — 'Series of 100 ...' (c1937)	H.581-1	£2.75	—
A2	C	100	Film Favourites — '2nd Series of 100 ...' (1939) ...	H.581-2	£2.75	—

A. & M. WIX, London and Johannesburg (continued)

Size	Print-ing	Number in set		Handbook reference	Price per card	Complete set
A2	C	100	Film Favourites — '3rd Series of 100 ...' (c1939) ...	H.581-3	£1.50	£150.00
J1	C	100	*Men of Destiny (folders) (P.O. Box 5764, Johannesburg) (c1935)		£2.25	—
—	C	250	Speed Through the Ages (171 small, 79 large) (1938):	H.583		
			A Back in English and Afrikaans		32p	£80.00
			B Back in English		40p	£100.00
—	C	250	This Age of Power and Wonder (170 small, 80 large) ('Max Cigarettes') (c1935)		30p	£75.00

J. WIX & SONS LTD, London

Size	Print-ing	Number in set		Handbook reference	Price per card	Complete set
—	C	80	Bridge Favours and Place Cards (diecut) (1937) ...	H.681	£18.00	—
—	C	50	Bridge Hands (140 x 105mm) (1930)	H.682	£30.00	—
C	C	50	Builders of Empire — 'Kensitas' (1937)		60p	£30.00
—	U	42	Card Tricks by Jasper Maskelyne (c1935):	H.535-3		
			A Size 70 x 34mm		£6.00	—
			B Size 70 x 47mm		£6.00	—
A2	C	50	Coronation (1937):			
			A J. Wix and 'Kensitas' back:			
			1 Linen finish		25p	£12.50
			2 Varnished		60p	£30.00
			B 'Kensitas' back		25p	£12.50
	C		Henry:	H.625		
			'A Series of ...' (1935):			
B1		50	A Large size		90p	£45.00
			Album		—	£30.00
—		25	B Extra-large size		£3.20	£80.00
			'2nd Series ...' (1935):			
B1		50	A Large size:			
			i With album price		£1.20	£60.00
			ii Without album price		£3.50	—
			Album		—	£35.00
—		25	B Extra-large size:			
			i Last line of text 'Throat'		£3.00	£75.00
			ii Last line of text 'Your Throat'		£6.00	—
B1		50	3rd Series, nothing after 'copyright reserved' (1936)		80p	£40.00
B1		50	4th Series, with full stop after 'copyright reserved' (1936)		70p	£35.00
B1		50	5th Series, with dash after 'copyright reserved' (1936)		60p	£30.00
	U		Jenkynisms:			
			A 'The K4's' Series (c1932):			
B2		102	I Known as 1st Series	H.636-1	80p	—
B2		50	II Known as 2nd Series	H.636-2	80p	£40.00
B2		30	III Known as 3rd Series	H.636-3	80p	—
B2		1	IV Known as 4th Series	H.636-4	—	£2.50
			B The Red Bordered series (c1932):			
	U	50	I Series of Quotations:	H.637-1		
A2			A Size 65 x 38mm		£4.50	—
—			B Size 69 x 54mm		£4.50	—
	U		II 'Today's Jenkynisms':	H.637-2		
A2			A Size 65 x 38mm:			
		? 44	i Without letter		£4.50	—
		? 30	ii Series B		£4.50	—
		? 19	iii Series C		£4.50	—
		? 34	iv Series D		£4.50	—

J. WIX & SONS LTD, London (continued)

Jenkynisms: B The Red Bordered series (c1932):

    II 'Today's Jenkynisms' (continued):

Size	Printing	Number in set		Handbook ref	Price per card	Complete set
—			B Size 69 x 54mm:			
		? 44	i Without letter		£4.50	—
		? 30	ii Series B		£4.50	—
		? 19	iii Series C		£4.50	—
		? 34	iv Series D		£4.50	—
—	C		Ken-cards (102 x 118mm):			
		12	Series 1 Starters/Snacks (1969)		—	£5.00
		12	Series 2 Main Courses (1969)		—	£5.00
		12	Series 3 Desserts (1969)		—	£5.00
		12	Series 4 Motoring (1969)		—	£5.00
		12	Series 5 Gardening (1969)		—	£5.00
		12	Series 6 Do It Yourself (1969)		—	£5.00
		12	Series 7 Home Hints (1969)		—	£5.00
		12	Series 8 Fishing (1969)		—	£5.00
	U	25	Love Scenes from Famous Films — 'First Series' (1932):			
C2			A Small size		£3.00	£75.00
B1			B Large size		£3.00	£75.00
—			C Extra-large size (127 x 88mm)		£6.50	—
	U	19	Love Scenes from Famous Films — 'Second Series' (1932) (Nos. 5, 9, 13, 20, 23, 24 withdrawn):			
C2			A Small size		£2.80	£55.00
B1			B Large size		£3.25	£65.00
			C Extra-large size (127 x 88mm)		£8.00	—
K2	C	53	*Miniature Playing Cards (anonymous) (c1935):	H.535-3		
			A Scroll design:			
			1 Red back		20p	£9.00
			2 Blue back		25p	£12.50
			B Ship design:			
			1 Red border — Nelson's 'Victory'		35p	£17.50
			2 Black border — Drake's 'Revenge'		35p	£17.50
U		25	Scenes from Famous Films — 'Third Series' (1933):			
C2			A Small size		£3.00	£75.00
—			B Extra-large size (127 x 88mm)		£8.00	—

SILKS

Size	Printing	Number in set		Handbook ref	Price per card	Complete set
—	C	48	British Empire Flags — 'Kensitas' (78 x 54mm) (1933)	H.496-4		
			A Inscribed 'Printed in U.S.A.'		£1.00	£50.00
			B Without 'Printed in U.S.A.'		£1.00	£50.00
			Album		—	£30.00
—	C	60	Kensitas Flowers — 'First Series', small (68 x 40mm) (1934):	H.496-1		
			A Back of folder plain		£3.00	—
			B Back of folder printed in green:			
			i Centre oval 19mm deep		£3.00	—
			ii Centre oval 22mm deep		£3.00	—
			iii As ii, inscribed 'washable ...'		£3.00	—
			Album		—	£35.00
—	C	60	Kensitas Flowers — 'First Series', medium (76 x55mm) (1934):	H.496-1		
			A Back of folder plain		£4.50	—
			B Back of folder printed in green:			
			i Line commencing 'Kensitas' 46mm long		£4.50	—
			ii Line commencing 'Kensitas' 50mm long		£4.50	—
			iii As ii, inscribed 'Washable'		£4.50	—
			Album		—	£35.00

J. WIX & SONS LTD, London (Silks continued)

	C	30	Kensitas Flowers — 'First Series' Extra-large			
			(138 x96mm) (1934):	H.496-1		
			A Back of folder plain … … … … … … …		£40.00	—
			B Back of folder printed in green:			
			i Word 'More' half in oval … … … … …		£40.00	—
			ii Word 'More' outside oval … … … … …		£40.00	—
			iii As ii, inscribed 'Washable' … … … … …		£40.00	—
—	C	40	Kensitas Flowers — 'Second Series' (1935):	H.496-2		
			A Small size, 68 x 40mm			
			1 Nos 1-30 … … … … … … … … …		£6.00	—
			2 Nos. 31 to 40 … … … … … …		£25.00	—
			Album … … … … … … … … … … …		—	£35.00
			B Medium size, 76 x 55mm			
			1 Nos 1-30 … … … … … … … … …		£6.00	—
			2 Nos. 31 to 40 … … … … …		£26.00	—
			Album … … … … … … … … … …		—	£35.00
	C	60	National Flags — 'Kensitas' (78 x 54mm) (1934) …	H.496-3	£1.25	£75.00
			Album … … … … … … … … …		—	£30.00

OVERSEAS ISSUE

A2	P	24	Royal Tour in New Zealand (1928) … … … … …		£13.00	—

WOOD BROS., England

—	BW	28	Dominoes (63 x 29mm) (c1910) … … … … …		£70.00	—

T. WOOD, Cleckheaton

D	C	30	*Army Pictures, Cartoons, etc (1916) … … … … …	H.12	£130.00	—

JOHN J. WOODS, London

A	BW	? 23	*Views of London (c1905) … … … … … … … … …	H.395	£270.00	—

W.H. & J. WOODS LTD, Preston

—	C	1	Advertisement Card 'Perfection Flake' (86 x 35mm)			
			(c1900) … … … … … … … … … … … … … …	H.773	—	£1000.00
A2	U	25	Aesop's Fables (c1932) … … … … … … … … … …	H.518	£1.80	£45.00
A2	P	50	Modern Motor Cars (c1936) … … … … … … … …		£6.00	£300.00
D	C	25	Romance of the Royal Mail (c1933) … … … … …		£1.20	£30.00
A	C	25	*Types of Volunteers and Yeomanry (c1902) … … …	H.455	£36.00	£900.00

J. & E. WOOLF

A	U	? 5	*Beauties 'KEWA' (c1900) … … … … … … … …	H.139	£1200.00	—

M.H. WOOLLER, London

A	—	25	Beauties 'BOCCA' (c1900) … … … … … … … …		£1500.00	—

T.E. YEOMANS & SONS LTD, Derby

—	C	72	Beautiful Women (75 x 55mm) (c1900) … … … … …	H.284	£250.00	—
A	U	50	War Portraits (1916) … … … … … … … … … … …	H.86	£100.00	—

JOHN YOUNG & SONS LTD, Bolton

A2	C	12	Naval Skits (c1904) … … … … … … … … … …	H.457	£150.00	—
A2	C	12	*Russo-Japanese Series (1904) … … … … … … …	H.456	£90.00	—

A. ZICALIOTTI

A	C	1	Advertisement Card 'Milly Totty' (c1900) … … … …	H.774	—	£1800.00

ANONYMOUS SERIES

A WITH LETTERPRESS ON BACK OF CARD

Size	Print-ing	Number in set	Description	Handbook reference	Price per card	Complete set
A2	C	20	Animal Series — see Hill:			
			A 'The cigarettes with which …' back			
			B Space at back			
A	U	? 35	*Beauties — 'KEW A' 'England Expects…' back c1900	H.139	£125.00	—
D	BW	25	*Boxers, green back — see Cohen Weenen			
A1	C	? 2	*Celebrities — Coloured. 1902 Calendar back — see			
			Cohen Weenen			
D	C	? 2	*Celebrities — 'GAINSBOROUGH I', 1902			
			Calendar back, gilt border to front — see Cohen			
			Weenen	H.90		
	C	25	Cinema Stars — see Teofani:	H.530		
C2			A Small size			
—			B Extra-large size (109 x 67mm)			
A2	U	50	Cinema Stars — Set 7 — see United Kingdom			
			Tobacco Co.	GP.703		
D2	C	25	Cinema Stars — Set 8 — see Moustafa	GP.542		
A2	C	50	Evolution of the British Navy — see Godfrey Phillips			
A2	BW	40	Famous Film Stars, text in Arabic (two series) — see			
			Hill			
A2	C	50	Famous Footballers — see Godfrey Phillips			
A2	C	35	Famous Stars — see Reliance Tobacco Mfg. Co. ...	H.572		
C2	C	20	Great Inventors — see Teofani	H.213		
A2	C	20	*Interesting Buildings and Views, 1902, Calendar			
			back — see Cohen Weenen	H.96		
D2	U	48	Modern Movie Stars and Cinema Celebrities — see			
			Teofani	H.569		
D2	C	? 1	*Nations, 1902 Calendar back — see Cohen Weenen	H.97		
D2	C	25	Pictures of World Interest — see Moustafa			
A	C	25	*Types of British Soldiers, 'General Favourite Onyx'			
			back — see E. Robinson	H.144		
D	C	25	V.C. Heroes (Nos. 51-75 — see Cohen Weenen) ...			
A	C	41	V.C. Heroes — 'Pure Virginia Cigarettes' — Dobson			
			Molle & Co. Ltd — Printers — see Thomson and			
			Porteous	H.427		
D	U	50	*War Series (Cohen Weenen — Nos. 1-50)	H.103		
C2	U	24	Well-Known Racehorses — see Teofani	H.609		

B WITH PLAIN BACK

Size	Print-ing	Number in set	Description	Handbook reference	Price per card	Complete set
A	U	25	*Actors and Actresses — 'FROGA C' (c1900)	H.20	£12.00	—
D2	U	? 9	*Actresses — 'ANGLO' (c1896)	H.185	£90.00	—
	U		*Actresses — 'ANGOOD' (c1898):	H.187		
			A Brown tinted:			
		? 22	i Thick board		£40.00	—
		? 14	ii Thin board		£40.00	—
		? 10	B Green tinted		£60.00	—
		? 30	C Black tinted		£40.00	—
A1	BW	20	*Actresses — 'BLARM' (c1900)	H.23	£14.00	—
D	U	20	*Actresses — Chocolate tinted — see Hill	H.207		
A	C	? 50	*Actresses — 'DAVAN' (c1902):	H.124		
			A Portrait in red only		£50.00	—
			B Portrait in colour		£50.00	—
D	BW	12	*Actresses — 'FRAN' — see Drapkin	H.175		
A		26	*Actresses — 'FROGA A' (c1900):	H.20		
	C		i Coloured		£12.00	—
	U		ii Unicoloured		£12.00	—
A1	BW	10	*Actresses — 'HAGG A' (c1900)	H.24	£12.00	—

Size	Printing	Number in set		Handbook reference	Price per card	Complete set
			ANONYMOUS SERIES (With Plain Back continued)			
A1	BW	? 13	*Actresses — 'HAGG B' (c1900)	H.24	£12.00	—
A	BW	15	*Actresses — 'RUTAN' — see Rutter	H.381		
—	C	50	*Actresses Oval Card — see Phillips	H.324		
A1	U		*Actresses and Beauties — Collotype — see Ogden	H.306		
C	C	20	*Animal Series — see Hill			
	C	? 12	*Arms of Cambridge Colleges (17 x 25mm) — see Kuit	H.458		
—	C	? 12	*Arms of Companies (30 x 33mm) — see Kuit	H.459		
A2	P	36	Australia. Second Series — see Westminster			
A2	BW	? 13	*Battleships — see Hill	H.208		
A	C	25	*Beauties — 'BOCCA' (c1900)	H.39	£16.00	—
A		50	*Beauties — 'CHOAB' (c1900):	H.21		
	U		A Unicoloured		£12.00	—
	C		B Coloured		£12.00	—
A			*Beauties — 'FECKSA' (c1901):	H.58		
	U	50	A Plum-coloured front		£12.00	—
	C	? 6	B Coloured front		£50.00	—
D2	U	? 23	*Beauties — 'FENA' (c1900)	H.148	£50.00	—
A2	C	25	*Beauties — 'GRACC' (c1900)	H.59	£20.00	—
A	C	26	*Beauties — 'HOL' (c1900)	H.192	£12.00	—
A	U	? 14	*Beauties 'KEWA' (c1900)	H.139	£50.00	—
A	U	? 7	Beauties — 'NANA' (c1895)	H.377	£150.00	—
D	BW	50	*Beauties — 'PLUMS' (c1900)	H.186	£45.00	—
—	C	30	*Beauties — Oval card (36 x 60mm) — see Phillips	H.244		
A2	P	18	*Beauties — see Marcovitch	GP.490		
D1	U		*Bewlay's War Series (c1915):	H.477		
		12	1 Front without captions		£20.00	—
		? 1	2 Front with captions		£30.00	—
A2	BW	20	*Boer War Cartoons (c1901)	H.42	£20.00	—
A	C		*Boer War and General Interest (c1901):	H.13		
		? 20	A Plain cream back		£40.00	—
		? 22	B Brown Leaf Design back		£40.00	—
		? 12	C Green Leaf Design back		£40.00	—
		? 6	D Green Daisy Design back		£60.00	—
A2	BW	? 16	*Boer War Celebrities — 'CAG' (1901)	H.79	£25.00	—
A		? 7	Boer War Celebrities 'RUTTER' (1901):	H.382		
	BW		A Front in black and white		£35.00	—
	U		B Front in light orange brown		£35.00	—
D2	BW	20	*Boer War Generals — 'CLAM' (1901)	H.61	£16.00	—
A1	BW	? 10	*Boer War Generals — 'FLAC' (1901)	H.47	£16.00	—
D	C	25	*Boxer Rebellion — Sketches (1904)	H.46	£12.00	—
A	C	54	*British Beauties (Phillips) (1-54)	H.328		
A	C	54	*British Beauties (Phillips) (55-108) Matt	H.328		
A1	P	60	*British Beauty Spots — see Coudens	H.553		
B1	P	50	*British Castles, Nd. S.J.51-S.J.100 — see Pattreiouex			
—	C	108	*British Naval Crests (74 x 52mm) (c1915)	H.504-4/GP.207	£3.50	—
A	C	12	British Queens (c1897)	H.480	£30.00	—
A	BW	16	*British Royal Family (1902)	H.28	£12.00	—
D2	CP	50	*Camera Studies — see Moustafa			
B1	P	50	*Cathedrals and Abbeys. Nd. S.J.1-S.J.50 — see Pattreiouex			
A	C	45	*Celebrities — Coloured — see Cohen Weenen ...	GP.357		
D2	C	39	*Celebrities — 'GAINSBOROUGH I' — see Cohen Weenen	GP.358		
D2	BW ?	147	*Celebrities — 'GAINSBOROUGH II' — see Cohen Weenen	GP.359		

ANONYMOUS SERIES (With Plain Back continued)

Size	Print-ing	Number in set	Title	Handbook reference	Price per card	Complete set
A1	P	36	*Celebrities of the Great War (1916) — see Major Drapkin & Co … … … … … … … … …			
A	BW	? 12	Celebrities of the Great War (c1916) … … … … …	H.236	£90.00	—
A	C	25	*Charming Portraits — see Continental Cigarette Factory … … … … … … … … … … …	H.549		
A2	U	30	*Cinema Stars — Set 3 (1931) … … … … … …	GP.52	£2.00	—
A2	U	30	*Cinema Stars — Set 6 (1935) … … … … … …	GP.55	£1.00	£30.00
A	C		*Colonial Troops (c1901):	H.40		
		30	A Cream card … … … … … … … … … … …		£15.00	—
		50	B White card … … … … … … … … … … …		£15.00	—
—	C	110	*Crests and Badges of the British Army (74 x 52mm):	GP.245		
			A Numbered (c1915) … … … … … … …		£4.00	—
			B Unnumbered (c1915) … … … … … … …		£3.00	—
A	BW	20	Cricketers Series (1901) … … … … … … … …	H.29	£250.00	—
A	C	50	Dogs (as Taddy) (c1900):	H.487		
			A Borders in green … … … … … … … …		£30.00	—
			B Borders in white … … … … … … … …		£30.00	—
A	C	25	*England's Military Heroes — see Player:	H.352		
			A Wide card … … … … … … … … … …			
			B Narrow card … … … … … … … … …			
A	C	25	*England's Naval Heroes — see Player:	H.353		
			A Wide card … … … … … … … … … …			
			B Narrow card … … … … … … … … …			
A	C	20	*The European War Series (c1915) … … … … …	H.129	£12.00	—
—	BW	12	*Film Actors and Actresses (56 x 31mm) — see Teofani … … … … … … … … … … …	H.618		
A	C		*Flags, Arms and Types of Nations (c1910):	H.115		
		24	A Numbered … … … … … … … … … …		£12.00	—
		? 2	B Unnumbered … … … … … … … … …		£50.00	—
A	C		*Flags and Flags with Soldiers (c.1902):	H.41		
		30	A Flagstaff draped … … … … … … … …		£12.00	—
		15	B Flagstaff not draped (flags only) … … … …		£12.00	—
A1	C	30	*Flags of Nations — see Cope … … … … … …	H.114		
A1	C	24	*Girls, Flags and Arms of Countries — see Rutter …	H.383		
A	C	20	*Head Dresses of Various Nations — see Teofani …			
A	C	40	*Home and Colonial Regiments (c1901) … … … …	H.69	£12.00	—
A	—	20	*Inventors and Their Inventions — see Hill … … …	H.213		
—	C	? 9	*Irish Views (68 x 67mm) — see Lambkin … … … …	H.585		
A	C	52	*Japanese Series, P.C. Inset — see Muratti … … …			
A1	P	? 2	*King Edward and Queen Alexandra (c1902) … … …	H.460	£20.00	—
—	BW	12	*London Views (57 x 31mm) — see Teofani … … …	H.620		
C	C	20	*National Flag Series — see Hill … … … … …			
D	C	20	*Nations, gilt border — see Cohen Weenen … … …	GP.369		
A	C	50	*Natives in Costume — see Teofani … … … … …			
D	C	40	*Naval and Military Phrases (c1904):	H.14		
			A Plain front (no border) … … … … … … …		£12.00	—
			B Front with gilt border … … … … … … …		£60.00	—
—	P	30	*Photographs (Animal Studies) (64 x 41mm) (c1925)	GP.337	£2.00	—
—	U	? 2	*Portraits — see Drapkin & Millhoff (48 x 36mm) …	H.461		
A	U	? 42	*Pretty Girl Series — 'BAGG' (c1900) … … … …	H.45	£20.00	—
A2	C	12	*Pretty Girl Series 'RASH' (c1897) … … … … …	H.8	£18.00	—
A1	C	20	*Prince of Wales Series (c1911) … … … … … …	H.22	£12.00	—
D	C	30	*Proverbs (c1903) … … … … … … … … … …	H.15	£12.00	—
—	C	? 48	*Regimental Colours II (76 x 70mm) (c1915) … … …	H.502-7	£12.00	—
A	BW	19	Russo-Japanese Series (1904) … … … … … …	H.184	£20.00	—
A	C	20	Russo-Japanese War Series (1904) … … … … …	H.100	£20.00	—
A	C	10	Scenes from San Toy — see Richard Lloyd … … …	H.462		

ANONYMOUS SERIES (continued)

Size	Print-ing	Number in set		Handbook reference	Price per card	Complete set
A	C	25	Sports and Pastimes Series No. 1 (c1912) … … …	H.225	£12.00	—
A	C	25	*Star Girls (c1900) … … … … … … … … … … … …	H.30	£15.00	—
A1	BW	? 28	*Statuary A-D — see Hill … … … … … … … … … …	H.218		
—	P	22	*Teofani Gems I — Series of 22 (53 x 35mm) — see Teofani … … … … … … … … … … … … … … …			
—	P	28	*Teofani Gems II — Series of 28 (53 x 35mm) see Teofani … … … … … … … … … … … … … … …			
—	P	36	*Teofani Gems III — Series of 36 (53 x 35mm) — see Teofani … … … … … … … … … … … … … …			
A	C	25	*Types of British and Colonial Troops (c1900) … …	H.76	£20.00	—
A2	C	25	*Types of British Soldiers (c1914) … … … … … …	H.144	£12.00	—
—	U	? 24	Views and Yachts (narrow, about 63 x 30mm) (c1900)	H.262-2	£50.00	—
D	BW	12	*Views of the World — see Drapkin … … … … … …	H.176		
D	BW	8	*Warships — see Drapkin … … … … … … … … …	GP.426		
D			*War Series (c1915):	H.103		
	U	? 2	A Front in brown … … … … … … … … … … … …		£30.00	—
	BW	? 4	B Front in black and white … … … … … … … …		£30.00	—
A	C	50	*World's Smokers — see Teofani … … … … … … …			

C WITH DESIGNS ON BACK

Size	Print-ing	Number in set		Handbook reference	Price per card	Complete set
A	BW	25	Careless Moments (1922) … … … … … … … … …		80p	£20.00
D2	U	28	*Dominoes ('W.T.C.' monogram back) — see Walker's Tobacco Co. … … … … … … … … …	H.535-2		
—	C	53	*Miniature Playing Cards (68 x 42mm) (red back, black cat trade mark in centre) — see Carreras …	H.535-1		
K2	C	53	*Miniature Playing Cards (blue scroll back) — see Godfrey Phillips … … … … … … … … … … …			
K2	C	53	*Miniature Playing Cards — see J. Wix:	H.535-3		
			A Scroll design:			
			1 Red back … … … … … … … … … … … …			
			2 Blue back … … … … … … … … … … …			
			B Ship design:			
			2 Black border — Drake's 'Revenge' … … …			
C			*Playing Cards and Dominoes — see Carreras:	H.535-1		
C		52	A Small size:			
			1 Numbered … … … … … … … … … … …			
			2 Unnumbered … … … … … … … … … …			
—		26	B Large size (77 x 69mm):			
			1 Numbered … … … … … … … … … … …			
			2 Unnumbered … … … … … … … … … …			

D ANONYMOUS SERIES SILKS AND OTHER NOVELTY ISSUES

For Anonymous Metal Plaques — see International Tobacco Co.
For Anonymous Metal Charms — see Rothman's.
For Anonymous Miniature Rugs — see Godfrey Phillips.
For Anonymous Lace Motifs — see Carreras.
For Anonymous Woven Silks — see Anstie and J. Wix.
For Anonymous Printed Silks with Blue Borders — see Themans.

SECTION 2
FOREIGN TOBACCO ISSUERS

AFRICAN CIGARETTE CO. LTD, Egypt

	50	Actresses ALWICS (c1905)	£9.00	—
L	25	Auction Bridge (c1925)	£7.00	—

AFRICAN TOBACCO MANUFACTURERS, South Africa

A CARD ISSUES

L	29	All Blacks South African Tour (1928)	£20.00	—
	60	Animals (c1920):		
		A Cut Outs	£3.50	—
		B Not Cut Out	£3.50	—
	25	The Arcadia Fair (1924)	£10.00	—
MP	48	British Aircraft (1932)	£5.00	—
	50	Chinese Transport (1930)	£5.00	—
MP	48	Cinema Artistes (1930)	£4.00	—
	50	Cinema Stars 'OMBI' Officers Mess Issue 1st Series (1921)	£2.00	£100.00
	50	Cinema Stars 'OMBI' Officers Mess Issue 2nd Series (1921)	£2.20	£110.00
M	50	Famous and Beautiful Women (1938)	£2.50	—
L	50	Famous and Beautiful Women (1938)	£3.00	—
	33	Houses of Parliament (c1920)	£6.00	—
	58	Miniatures (c1925)	£6.50	—
MP	48	National Costume (1930)	£3.50	—
K	53	Playing Cards MP-SA Virginia Cigarettes (c1930)	£3.00	—
K	53	Playing Cards, OK Cigarettes (c1930)	£1.80	—
K	53	Playing Cards, Scotts Cigarettes (c1930)	£1.80	—
MP	48	Popular Dogs (1930)	£5.00	—
M	100	Postage Stamps, Rarest Varieties (1929)	£1.70	£170.00
M	80	Prominent NZ and Australian Rugby Players and Springbok 1937 Touring Team (1937)	£5.50	—
L	80	Prominent NZ and Australian Rugby Players and Springbok 1937 Touring Team (1937)	£3.50	—
	25	The Racecourse (1924) W.181	£10.00	—
M	132	S. African Members of the Legislative Assembly (1921)	£40.00	—
M	100	The World of Sport (1938)	£4.00	—
L	100	The World of Sport (1938)	£3.50	—

B SILK ISSUES

M	30	Some Beautiful Roses (c1925)	£9.00	—
M	25	Types of British Birds (c1925)	£9.00	—
M	20	Types of British Butterflies (c1925)	£11.00	—
M	25	Types of Railway Engines (c1925)	£26.00	—
M	25	Types of Sea Shells (c1925)	£13.00	—

ALLEN & GINTER, USA

ALL SERIES ISSUED 1885-95

	?	Actors and Actresses (sepia photographic)	£7.00	—

ALLEN & GINTER, USA (continued)

	?	Actresses and Beauties (coloured)	£11.00	—
	50	American Editors	£35.00	—
L	50	American Editors	£40.00	—
L	50	The American Indian	£60.00	—
	50	Arms of All Nations	£26.00	—
	50	Birds of America	£16.00	£800.00
L	50	Birds of America	£32.00	—
	50	Birds of the Tropics	£18.00	£900.00
L	50	Birds of the Tropics	£30.00	—
	50	Celebrated American Indian Chiefs	£40.00	—
	50	City Flags	£16.00	—
	50	Fans of the Period	£28.00	—
	50	Fish from American Waters	£17.00	—
L	50	Fish from American Waters	£30.00	—
	50	Flags of All Nations (series title curved)	£11.00	£550.00
	48	Flags of All Nations (series title in straight line)	£11.00	£550.00
	50	Flags of All Nations, 2nd series	£13.00	£650.00
	47	Flags of the States and Territories	£14.00	—
	50	Fruits	£25.00	—
	50	Game Birds	£16.00	£800.00
L	50	Game Birds	£32.00	—
	50	General Government and State Capitol Buildings	£16.00	—
	50	Great Generals	£45.00	—
	50	Natives in Costume	£35.00	—
	50	Naval Flags	£16.00	£800.00
	50	Parasol Drill	£25.00	—
	50	Pirates of the Spanish Main	£40.00	—
	50	Prize and Game Chickens	£26.00	—
	50	Quadrupeds	£17.00	—
L	50	Quadrupeds	£30.00	—
	50	Racing Colors of the World:		
		A Front with white frame	£27.00	—
		B Front without white frame	£27.00	—
	50	Song Birds of the World	£16.00	£800.00
L	50	Song Birds of the World	£32.00	—
	50	Types of All Nations	£26.00	—
	50	Wild Animals of the World	£18.00	—
	50	The World's Beauties, 1st series	£25.00	—
	50	The World's Beauties, 2nd series	£25.00	—
	50	The World's Champions, 1st series	£50.00	—
	50	The World's Champions, 2nd series	£60.00	—
L	50	The World's Champions, 2nd series	£100.00	—
	50	The World's Decorations	£16.00	£800.00
L	50	The World's Decorations	£28.00	—
	50	World's Dudes	£25.00	—
	50	The World's Racers	£30.00	—
	50	World's Smokers	£22.00	—
	50	World's Sovereigns	£32.00	—

ALLEN TOBACCO CO., USA

L	?	Views and Art Studies (c1910)	£5.00	—

THE AMERICAN CIGARETTE CO. LTD, China

	10	Admirals and Generals Ref RB.118/155 (c1900)	£60.00	—
	25	Beauties Group 1 Ref RB.118/8 (c1900)	£18.00	—
?	15	Beauties Group 2 Ref RB.118/21-2 (c1900)	£30.00	—

THE AMERICAN CIGARETTE CO. LTD, China (continued)

53	Beauties with Playing Card inset Ref RB.118/23 (c1900) … … … … …	£50.00	—
50	Flowers Ref RB.118/161 (c1900) … … … … … … … … … … … … …	£15.00	—

AMERICAN EAGLE TOBACCO CO., USA

20	Actresses blue border (c1890):		
	A With firm's name … … … … … … … … … … … … … … …	£80.00	—
	B 'Double 5' back … … … … … … … … … … … … … … … …	£70.00	—
15	Actresses sepia (c1890) … … … … … … … … … … … … … … …	£75.00	—
15	Beauties 'PAC' (c1895) … … … … … … … … … … … … … … …	£100.00	—
36	Flags of Nations (c1890):		
	A Size 70 x 39mm … … … … … … … … … … … … … … …	£35.00	—
	B Size 64 x 39mm … … … … … … … … … … … … … … …	£35.00	—
36	Flags of States (c1890):		
	A Size 70 x 39mm … … … … … … … … … … … … … … …	£35.00	—
	B Size 64 x 39mm … … … … … … … … … … … … … … …	£35.00	—
50	Occupations for Women (c1895) … … … … … … … … … … … …	£70.00	—
	Photographic Cards Actresses (c1890):		
? 33	A Size 69 x 37mm … … … … … … … … … … … … … … …	£20.00	—
L 6	B Size 102 x 52mm … … … … … … … … … … … … … … …	£30.00	—
23	Presidents of the U.S. (c1890) … … … … … … … … … … … … …	£60.00	—

THE AMERICAN TOBACCO COMPANY, USA

ALL SERIES ISSUED 1890-1902

A   TYPESET BACK IN BLACK (see RB.118 index Fig C-1 for design on back)

28	Beauties Domino Girls RB.118/66 … … … … … … … … … … …	£20.00	—
25	Beauties Group 1 RB.118/4 … … … … … … … … … … … … …	£4.00	—
? 1	Beauties Group 2 RB.118/20	—	—
25	Beauties Group 3 RB.118/25 … … … … … … … … … … … … …	£4.00	—
25	Beauties Group 3 RB.118/26 … … … … … … … … … … … … …	£4.00	£110.00
25	Beauties Group 3 RB.118/27 … … … … … … … … … … … … …	£4.00	—
25	Beauties Group 3 RB.118/29 … … … … … … … … … … … … …	£4.00	—
	Beauties Group 4 RB.118/36:		
50	a Coloured … … … … … … … … … … … … … … … … …	£4.00	£200.00
? 50	b Sepia … … … … … … … … … … … … … … … … … …	£15.00	—
52	Beauties PC Inset … … … … … … … … … … … … … … … …	£10.00	£520.00
25	Beauties — Star Girls RB.118/76 … … … … … … … … … … …	£17.00	—
25	Dancers RB.118/52 … … … … … … … … … … … … … … … …	£14.00	—
50	Dancing Women RB.118/135 … … … … … … … … … … … … …	£22.00	—
50	Fancy Bathers RB.118/136 … … … … … … … … … … … … …	£22.00	—
36	Japanese Girls RB.118/139 … … … … … … … … … … … … …	£70.00	—
25	Military Uniforms RB.118/101 … … … … … … … … … … … …	£16.00	—
25	Military Uniforms RB.118/102 … … … … … … … … … … … …	£14.00	—
27	Military Uniforms RB.118/103 … … … … … … … … … … … …	£10.00	—
50	Musical Instruments RB.118/140 … … … … … … … … … … …	£16.00	—
50	National Flag and Arms RB.118/141 … … … … … … … … … …	£12.00	—
25	National Flag and Flowers — Girls RB.118/142 … … … … … …	£23.00	—
50	Savage Chiefs and Rulers RB.118/144 … … … … … … … … …	£25.00	—

B   NET DESIGN BACK IN GREEN (see RB.118 index Fig C-2 for design on back)

25	Beauties Black background RB.118/62 … … … … … … … … …	£14.00	—
25	Beauties Curtain background RB.118/65 … … … … … … … … …	£13.00	£325.00
25	Beauties Flower Girls RB.118/67 … … … … … … … … … … …	£13.00	—
25	Beauties Group 1 RB.118/1 … … … … … … … … … … … … …	£4.00	—
27	Beauties Group 1 RB.118/2 … … … … … … … … … … … … …	£4.00	—
25	Beauties Group 1 RB.118/3 … … … … … … … … … … … … …	£4.00	—
24	Beauties Group 1 RB.118/4 … … … … … … … … … … … … …	£4.00	—
25	Beauties Group 1 RB.118/5 … … … … … … … … … … … … …	£4.00	—

THE AMERICAN TOBACCO COMPANY, USA (1890-1902 continued)

B   NET DESIGN BACK IN GREEN (continued)

	25	Beauties Group 1 RB.118/6	£4.00	—
	50	Beauties Group 1 RB.118/10	£4.00	—
	25	Beauties Group 2 RB.118/16	£4.00	—
	25	Beauties Group 2 RB.118/17	£4.00	—
	? 24	Beauties Group 2 RB.118/18	£4.00	—
	25	Beauties Group 2 RB.118/19	£4.00	—
	25	Beauties Group 2 RB.118/20	£4.00	—
	25	Beauties Group 2 RB.118/21	£5.00	—
	36	Beauties Group 2 RB.118/22	£6.00	—
	25	Beauties Group 3 RB.118/25	£4.00	—
	? 10	Beauties Group 3 RB.118/28	—	—
	25	Beauties Group 3 RB.118/30	£4.00	—
	25	Beauties Group 3 RB.118/31	£8.00	—
	25	Beauties Group 3 RB.118/32	£4.00	—
	50	Beauties Marine and Universe Girls RB.118/71	£30.00	—
	25	Beauties Palette Girls RB.118/74	£12.00	—
	25	Beauties Star Girls RB.118/76	£18.00	—
	25	Beauties — Stippled background RB.118/78	£13.00	—
	20	Beauties — thick border RB.118/79	£32.00	—
	52	Beauties with Playing Card inset Set 1 RB.118/85 (Head & Shoulder)	£12.00	—
	52	Beauties with Playing Card inset Set 2 RB.118/86 (Half Length)	£12.00	—
	25	Boer War Series II — Series A RB.118/100:		
		a) numbered	£6.00	£150.00
		b) unnumbered	£7.00	—
		c) unnumbered and untitled 'series A'	£8.00	—
	22	Boer War Series II — Series B RB.118/100	£8.00	—
	25	Chinese Girls RB.118/111	£13.00	—
	25	Fish from American Waters RB.118/137	£10.00	—
	25	International Code Signals RB.118/43	£13.00	—
	27	Military Uniforms numbered RB.118/103	£9.00	—
	25	Military Uniforms unnumbered RB.118/104	£15.00	—
	50	National Flags and Arms RB.118/141	£10.00	—
	25	Old and Ancient Ships 1st Series RB.118/143	£6.00	£150.00
	25	Old and Ancient Ships 2nd Series RB.118/143	£10.00	£250.00
	25	Star Series — Beauties RB.118/77	£17.00	—

C   NET DESIGN BACK IN BLUE (see RB.118 index Fig C-2 for design on back)

		Actresses RB.118-90:		
P	? 300	A Large Letter Back (word 'Brands' 29mm)	£4.00	—
P	? 300	B Small Letter Back (word 'Brands' 25mm)	£5.00	—
	25	Beauties blue frameline RB.118/64:		
		A Matt	£22.00	—
		B Varnished	£22.00	—
	28	Beauties — Domino Girls RB.118/66	£22.00	—
	25	Beauties Group 1 dull backgrounds RB.118/7.2	£14.00	—
	25	Beauties Group 1 vivid coloured backgrounds set 1 RB.118/7.3	£14.00	—
	25	Beauties Group 1 vivid coloured backgrounds set 2 RB.118/9	£14.00	—
	25	Beauties numbered RB.118/72:		
		A Front in black and white	£18.00	—
		B Front in mauve	£16.00	—
	24	Beauties — orange framelines RB.118/73	£30.00	—
		Beauties — playing cards RB.118/87:		
	52	A Inscribed 52 subjects	£12.00	—
	53	B Inscribed 53 subjects	£12.00	—
	32	Celebrities RB.118/94	£7.50	—
	25	Comic Scenes RB.118/113	£10.00	—
P	? 149	Views RB.118/96	£3.00	—

THE AMERICAN TOBACCO COMPANY, USA (1890-1902 continued)

D '*OLD GOLD' BACK* (see RB.118 index Fig C-3 for design on back)

25	Beauties Group 1 RB.118/1	£4.00	—
27	Beauties Group 1 RB.118/2	£4.00	—
25	Beauties Group 1 RB.118/3	£4.00	—
24	Beauties Group 1 RB.118/4	£4.00	—
25	Beauties Group 1 RB.118/5	£4.00	—
25	Beauties Group 1 RB.118/6	£4.00	—
? 47	Beauties Group 2 RB.118/16, 17, 18	£4.00	—
25	Beauties Group 2 RB.118/22	£4.00	—
27	Beauties Group 3 RB.118/25	£4.00	—
25	Beauties Group 3 RB.118/26	£4.00	—
25	Beauties Group 3 RB.118/27	£4.00	—
25	Beauties Group 3 RB.118/28	£4.00	—
25	Beauties Group 3 RB.118/30	£4.00	—
25	Flowers Inset on Beauties RB.118/41	£10.00	£250.00
25	International Code Signals:		
	A With series title RB.118/42	£11.00	£275.00
	B Without series title RB.118/43	£11.00	£275.00

E *LABELS BACK* (see RB.118 index Fig C-4/6 for design on back)

35	Beauties Group 1 RB.118/2-3	£5.00	—
25	Beauties Group 2 1st Set RB.118/15	£5.00	—
25	Beauties Group 2 2nd Set RB.118/16	£5.00	—
	Beauties Group 3 RB.118/25:		
27	A Old Gold Label	£5.00	—
26	B Brands Label	£5.00	—

F *OTHER BACKS WITH NAME OF FIRM*

P	100	Actresses RB.118/91	£5.00	—
	44	Australian Parliament RB.118/92	£6.00	—
	25	Battle Scenes RB.118/130	£14.00	—
	1	Columbian and Other Postage Stamps (1892)	—	£13.00
	50	Congress of Beauty — Worlds Fair RB.118/134	£22.00	—
	25	Constellation Girls	£25.00	—
	50	Fish from American Waters RB.118/137	£13.00	—
	50	Flags of All Nations RB.118/138	£10.00	—
	25	Flower Inset on Beauties RB.118/41	£12.00	£300.00
	25	International Code Signals RB.118/42	£12.00	£300.00
	25	Songs A RB.118/46 (1896):		
		A Thicker board size 70 x 39mm	£15.00	—
		B Thinner board size 67 x 39mm	£15.00	—
	25	Songs B RB.118/47 (1898):		
		A Size 70 x 39mm	£15.00	—
		B Size 67 x 39mm	£15.00	—
	25	Songs C 1st series RB.118/48 (1900)	£10.00	—
	25	Songs C 2nd series RB.118/48 (1900)	£12.00	—
	25	Songs D RB.118/49 (1899)	£10.00	£250.00
	27	Songs E RB.118/50 (1901)	£13.00	—
	25	Songs F RB.118/51 (1897):		
		A Size 70 x 36mm, with scroll at base	£13.00	—
		B Size 67 x 38mm, without scroll at base	£13.00	—
	25	Songs G RB.118/53 (1899)	£12.00	—
	25	Songs H RB.118/54 (1901)	£18.00	—
	25	Songs I RB.118/55 (1895)	£22.00	—

ISSUES 1903-1940

L	50	Actors	£7.00	—
	85	Actress Series	£7.00	—
L	50	Actresses	£10.00	—

THE AMERICAN TOBACCO COMPANY, USA (1903-1940 continued)

Size	Number in set		Price per card	Complete set
		Animals:		
L	40	A Descriptive back	£2.60	—
L	40	B Non descriptive back	£2.60	—
L	25	Arctic Scenes	£6.00	—
M	15	Art Gallery Pictures	£5.00	—
M	50	Art Reproductions	£5.00	—
	21	Art Series	£17.00	—
	18	Ask Dad	£13.00	—
L	50	Assorted Standard Bearers of Different Countries	£6.50	—
	25	Auto-drivers	£15.00	—
M	50	Automobile Series	£14.00	—
L	50	Baseball Folder series (T201) (1911)	£35.00	—
M	121	Baseball series (T204)	£50.00	—
	208	Baseball series (T205) (1911)	£25.00	—
	522	Baseball series (T206)	£25.00	—
	200	Baseball series (T207) (1910)	£35.00	—
	565	Baseball series (T210)	£35.00	—
	75	Baseball series (T211)	£35.00	—
	426	Baseball series (T212)	£35.00	—
	180	Baseball series (T213)	£35.00	—
	90	Baseball series (T214)	£110.00	—
	100	Baseball series (T215)	£35.00	—
L	76	Baseball Triple Folders (T202) (1912)	£45.00	—
		Bird series:		
	50	A With white borders	£2.60	—
	50	B With gold borders	£2.60	—
	30	Bird Series with Fancy Gold Frame	£3.20	—
M	360	Birthday Horoscopes	£2.20	—
M	24	British Buildings 'Tareyton' issue	£3.00	—
M	42	British Sovereigns 'Tareyton' issue	£3.00	—
M	50	Butterfly Series	£5.00	—
L	153	Champion Athlete & Prize Fighter series (size 73 x 64mm) (1911)	£8.00	—
L	50	Champion Athlete and Prize Fighter series (size 83 x 63 mm)	£14.00	—
L	50	Champion Pugilists	£23.00	—
EL	100	Champion Women Swimmers	£10.00	—
M	150	College series	£3.00	—
M	50	Costumes and Scenery for All Countries of the World	£3.50	—
L	49	Cowboy series	£7.50	—
M	38	Cross Stitch	£9.00	—
M	17	Embarrassing Moments or Emotional Moments	£35.00	—
M	50	Emblem Series	£3.50	—
L	100	Fable Series	£3.20	—
LP	53	Famous Baseball Players, American Athletic Champions and Photoplay Stars	£55.00	—
	50	Fish Series inscribed '1 to 50' — 1st 50 subjects	£2.80	—
	50	Fish Series inscribed '1 to 100' — 2nd 50 subjects	£2.80	—
	200	Flags of All Nations	£2.00	—
M	100	Flags of All Nations	£16.00	—
	50	Foreign Stamp Series	£6.50	—
L	505	Fortune Series	£2.20	—
M	79	Henry 'Tareyton' issue	£2.50	—
L	50	Heroes of History	£9.00	—
M	50	Historic Homes	£5.00	—
L	25	Historical Events Series	£8.00	—
M	25	Hudson — Fulton Series	£7.00	—
L	50	Indian Life in the 60s (1910)	£8.50	—
L	221	Jig Saw Puzzle Pictures	£11.00	—

THE AMERICAN TOBACCO COMPANY, USA (1903-1940 continued)

Size	Number in set		Price per card	Complete set
L	50	Light House Series	£8.00	—
L	50	Men of History	£9.00	—
M	100	Military Series white borders	£5.00	—
	50	Military Series gilt borders	£6.00	—
	50	Military Series 'Recruit' issue:		
		A Uncut cards	£6.00	—
		B Die-cut cards	£6.00	—
	50	Movie Stars	£5.00	—
L	100	Movie Stars	£5.00	—
	33	Moving Picture Stars	£22.00	—
EL	50	Murad Post Card Series	£9.00	—
	100	Mutt & Jeff Series (black and white)	£5.00	—
	100	Mutt & Jeff Series (coloured)	£5.00	—
EL	16	National League and American League Teams	£55.00	—
	50	Pugilistic Subjects	£30.00	—
EL	18	Puzzle Picture Cards	£17.00	—
M	200	Riddle Series	£3.00	—
EL	60	Royal Bengal Souvenir Cards	£9.00	—
M	150	Seals of the United States and Coats of Arms of the World	£2.00	—
L	25	Series of Champions	£30.00	—
L	50	Sights and Scenes of the World	£4.00	—
L	50	Silhouettes	£9.00	—
L	25	Song Bird Series	£40.00	—
	39	Sports Champions	£35.00	—
	45	Stage Stars	£8.00	—
	25	State Girl Series	£8.00	—
L	50	Theatres Old and New Series	£8.00	—
M	50	Toast Series	£9.00	—
M	550	Toast Series	£2.20	—
L	25	Toasts	£15.00	—
	50	Types of Nations:		
		A Without series title	£3.00	—
		B With series title	£3.00	—
		C Anonymous back	£3.00	—
L	25	Up to Date Baseball Comics	£30.00	—
L	25	Up to Date Comics	£10.00	—
P	340	World Scenes and Portraits	£4.00	—
	250	World War I Scenes	£2.50	—
L	50	World's Champion Athletes	£12.00	—
L	25	The World's Greatest Explorers	£6.00	—

THE AMERICAN TOBACCO CO. OF NEW SOUTH WALES LTD, Australia

	25	Beauties Group 1 RB.118/8 (c1900)	£14.00	—
	25	Beauties Group 2 (c1900)	£14.00	—

THE AMERICAN TOBACCO CO. OF VICTORIA LTD, Australia

?	98	Beauties Group 2 (c1900)	£14.00	—

ASHEVILLE TOBACCO WORKS AND CIGARETTE CO., USA

	39	Actresses (c1890)	£75.00	—

ATLAM CIGARETTE FACTORY, Malta

M	65	Beauties back in blue (c1925)	£2.80	—
	150	Beauties back in brown (c1925)	£6.00	—
M	519	Celebrities (c1925)	£1.20	—

ATLAM CIGARETTE FACTORY, Malta (continued)

L	50	Views of Malta (c1925)	£6.00	—
M	128	Views of the World (c1925)	£5.50	—

BANNER TOBACCO CO., USA

L	? 41	Actors and Actresses (c1890)	£75.00	—
EL	25	Girls (c1890) RB.22/X2-453	£38.00	—

THOMAS BEAR & SONS LTD

50	Aeroplanes (1926)	£4.50	—
50	Cinema Artistes Set 2 (c1935)	£3.80	—
50	Cinema Artistes Set 4 (c1935)	£3.80	—
50	Cinema Stars coloured (1930)	£3.00	£150.00
50	Do You Know (1923)	£1.80	£90.00
270	Javanese series 1 blue background (c1925)	£2.00	—
100	Javanese series 4 yellow background (c1925)	£8.00	—
50	Stage and Film Stars (1926)	£4.00	—

AUG BECK & CO. USA

? 44	Picture Cards (c1890)	£60.00	—
23	Presidents of U.S. (coloured) (c1890)	£70.00	—
23	Presidents of U.S. (sepia) (c1890)	£70.00	—
? 14	State Seals (c1890)	£75.00	—

BRITISH AMERICAN TOBACCO CO. LTD

A   WITH MAKER'S NAME NET DESIGN IN GREEN (ISSUES 1902-05)

25	Beauties Art series RB.118/61	£13.00	—
25	Beauties — Black background RB.118/62	£12.00	—
25	Beauties — Blossom Girls RB.118/63	£40.00	—
25	Beauties — Flower Girls RB.118/67	£11.00	—
25	Beauties — Fruit Girls RB.118/68	£14.00	—
25	Beauties — Girls in Costumes RB.118/69	£14.00	—
20	Beauties Group 1 RB.118/9	£11.00	—
25	Beauties — Lantern Girls RB.118/70	£11.00	£275.00
50	Beauties — Marine and Universe Girls RB.118/71	£12.00	—
25	Beauties — Palette Girls RB.118/74:		
	A Plain border to front	£11.00	—
	B Red border to front	£14.00	—
24	Beauties — Smoke Girls RB.118/75	£16.00	—
25	Beauties — Star Girls RB.118/76	£16.00	—
25	Beauties — Stippled background RB.118/78	£11.00	£275.00
25	Beauties — Water Girls RB.118/80	£11.00	£275.00
50	Buildings RB.118/131	£11.00	—
25	Chinese Girls 'A' RB.118/111	£11.00	—
25	Chinese Girls 'B' RB.118/112:		
	A Background plain	£11.00	—
	B Background with Chinese letters	£11.00	—
25	Chinese Girls 'C' RB.118/113	£11.00	—
	Chinese Girls 'D' RB.118/114:		
20	A Back design 53mm long	£11.00	—
25	B Back design 60mm long	£11.00	—
25	Chinese Girls 'E' RB.118/115	£11.00	—
25	Chinese Girls 'F' Set 1 RB.118/116:		
	A Fronts reddish background	£11.00	—
	B Fronts sepia background	£11.00	—

BRITISH AMERICAN TOBACCO CO. LTD (continued)

A WITH MAKER'S NAME NET DESIGN IN GREEN (ISSUES 1902-05) (continued)

	25	Chinese Girls 'F' Set 2 RB.118/116:		
		A Yellow border	£11.00	—
		B Gold border	£13.00	—
	50	Chinese Girls 'F' Set 3 RB.118/116:		
		A Plain background	£11.00	—
		B Chinese characters background	£12.00	—
	40	Chinese Trades RB.118/108	£8.00	—

B WITH MAKER'S NAME NET DESIGN IN BLUE (ISSUES 1902-05)

	25	Beauties — numbered RB.118/72	£18.00	—
	53	Beauties — Playing Cards RB.118/87	£11.00	—

C WITH MAKER'S NAME OTHER BACKS

MP	50	Beauties (1925)	£2.50	—
MP	40	Beauties (1926)	£2.50	—
M	50	Birds, Beasts and Fishes (1925)	£2.00	£100.00
	50	Danish Athletes (1905)	£15.00	—
	28	Dominoes (1905)	£6.00	—
	48	Fairy Tales (1926)	£4.00	—
	48	A Famous Picture — The Toast (c1930)	£3.00	—
	25	New York Views (c1908)	£12.00	—
	53	Playing Cards (1905)	£11.00	—
M	50	Wild Animals (c1930)	£2.50	—

D SERIES WITH BRAND NAMES

ALBERT CIGARETTES

M	50	Aeroplanes (Civils) (1935)	£12.00	—
	50	Artistes de Cinema Nd 1-50 (1932)	£3.00	—
	50	Artistes de Cinema Nd 51-100 (1933)	£3.00	—
	50	Artistes de Cinema Nd 101-150 (1934)	£3.00	—
MP	? 67	Beauties (c1928)	£4.50	—
M	75	Belles Vues de Belgique (c1930)	£3.00	—
M	50	Birds, Beasts & Fishes (c1930)	£4.00	—
M	50	Butterflies (Girls) (1926)	£6.00	—
M	50	Cinema Stars (brown photogravure) (c1927)	£3.00	—
M	100	Cinema Stars (numbered, coloured) (c1928)	£3.00	—
M	208	Cinema Stars (unnumbered, coloured) (c1929)	£3.00	—
M	100	Circus Scenes (c1930)	£3.50	—
M	100	Famous Beauties (1916)	£3.50	—
M	50	L'Afrique Equitoriale de l'Est a l'Ouest (c1930)	£3.00	—
M	100	La Faune Congolaise (c1930)	£1.50	—
M	50	Les Grandes Paquebots du Monde (1924)	£7.00	—
M	50	Merveilles du Monde (1927)	£3.50	—
M	50	Women of Nations (Flag Girls) (1922)	£4.00	—

ATLAS CIGARETTES

	50	Buildings (1907)	£6.00	—
	25	Chinese Beauties (1912)	£4.00	—
	50	Chinese Trades Set IV (1908)	£3.00	—
	85	Chinese Trades Set VI (1912)	£3.00	—

BATTLE AX CIGARETTES

M	100	Famous Beauties (1916)	£5.00	—
M	50	Women of Nations (Flag Girls) (1917)	£6.00	—

COPAIN CIGARETTES

	52	Birds of Brilliant Plumage (1927)	£6.00	—

DOMINO CIGARETTES

	25	Animaux et Reptiles (1961)	30p	£7.50
	25	Corsaires et Boucaniers (1960)	20p	£3.00
	25	Figures Historiques 1st series (1961)	50p	£12.50

BRITISH AMERICAN TOBACCO CO. LTD (continued)

D SERIES WITH BRAND NAMES: DOMINO CIGARETTES (continued)

Size			Price per card	Complete set
25	Figures Historiques 2nd series (1961)		80p	£20.00
25	Fleurs de Culture (1960)		20p	£3.00
25	Les Oiseaux et l'Art Japonais (1961)		£1.00	—
25	Les Produits du Monde (1960)		20p	£3.00
50	Voitures Antiques (1961)		£1.40	—

EAGLE BIRD CIGARETTES

50	Animals and Birds (1909)		£2.00	—
50	Aviation series (1912)		£4.00	—
25	Birds of the East (1912)		£2.00	£50.00
25	China's Famous Warriors (1911)		£4.00	—
25	Chinese Beauties 1st series (1908):			
	A	Vertical back	£3.00	—
	B	Horizontal back	£3.00	—
25	Chinese Beauties 2nd series (1909):			
	A	Front without framelines	£3.00	—
	B	Front with framelines	£3.00	—
50	Chinese Trades (1908)		£2.60	—
25	Cock Fighting (1911)		£16.00	—
60	Flags and Pennons (1926)		£1.40	£85.00
50	Romance of the Heavens (1929)		£2.70	—
50	Siamese Alphabet (1922)		£1.50	£75.00
50	Siamese Dreams and Their Meanings (1923)		£1.20	£60.00
50	Siamese Horoscopes (c1915)		£1.20	£60.00
50	Siamese Play-Inao (c1915)		£1.40	£70.00
50	Siamese Play-Khun Chang Khun Phaen 1st series (c1915)		£1.40	£70.00
50	Siamese Play-Khun Chang Khun Phaen 2nd series (c1915)		£1.40	£70.00
36	Siamese Play-Phra Aphaiu 1st series (c1918)		£1.50	£55.00
36	Siamese Play-Phra Aphaiu 2nd series (1919)		£1.50	£55.00
150	Siamese Play — Ramakien I (c1913)		£1.40	—
50	Siamese Play — Ramakien II (1914)		£1.40	£70.00
50	Siamese Uniforms (1915)		£2.00	£100.00
50	Views of Siam (1928)		£3.00	£150.00
50	Views of Siam (Bangkok) (1928)		£4.00	£200.00
30	War Weapons (1914)		£3.00	£90.00

KONG BENG CIGARETTES

60	Animals (cut-outs) (1912)		£7.00	—

MASCOT CIGARETTES

100	Cinema Stars (Nd 201-300) (1931)		£3.20	—
M 208	Cinema Stars unnumbered (1924)		£2.80	—

MILLBANK CIGARETTES

60	Animals (cut-outs):			
	A	'1516' at base of back (1922)	£1.40	—
	B	'3971' at base of back (1923)	£1.40	—

NASSA CIGARETTES

M 50	Birds, Beasts and Fishes (1924)		£5.00	—

PEDRO CIGARETTES (see also Imperial Tobacco Co. of India)

50	Actors and Actresses (c1905)		£3.50	—
40	Nautch Girls. Coloured (1905)		£2.50	—
37	Nautch Girls. Red border (c1905)		£2.50	—

PINHEAD CIGARETTES

50	Chinese Modern Beauties (1912)		£4.00	—
33	Chinese Heroes Set 1 (1912)		£4.00	—
50	Chinese Heroes Set 2 (1913)		£4.00	—
50	Chinese Trades Set III (1908)		£4.00	£200.00
50	Chinese Trades Set IV (1909)		£4.00	£200.00

Size Number
in set   FOREIGN TOBACCO ISSUERS   Price   Complete
                                                                        per card   set

BRITISH AMERICAN TOBACCO CO. LTD (continued)

D   SERIES WITH BRAND NAMES: PINHEAD CIGARETTES (continued)

Size	Number in set			Price per card	Complete set
	50	Chinese Trades Set V (1910)		£4.00	£200.00
	50	Types of the British Army (1909)		£5.00	—

RAILWAY CIGARETTES (see also Imperial Tobacco Co. of India)

| | 37 | Nautch Girls series (1907) | | £3.00 | — |

TEAL CIGARETTES

	30	Chinese Beauties (c1915)		£5.00	—
	50	Cinema Stars (1930):			
		A	Back in blue	£2.20	—
		B	Back in red brown	£2.20	—
	30	Fish series (1916)		£3.50	—
	50	War Incidents (1916)		£2.80	£140.00

TIGER CIGARETTES

	52	Nautch Girls series (1911):			
		A	Without frameline to front	£3.00	—
		B	With frameline to front:		
			i With crossed cigarettes on back	£3.00	—
			ii Without crossed cigarettes on back	£3.00	—

NO BRAND NAME BLUE FLAG PACKET WITH SIAMESE TEXT

	50	Puzzle Sectional Series (c1915) RB.21/492-1		£2.00	—
	50	Siamese Dancers (c1915) RB.21/492-2		£1.50	£75.00
	50	Siamese Life (c1915) RB.21/492-3		£1.50	£75.00
	50	Siamese Proverbs (c1915) RB.21/492-4		£1.60	£80.00
	50	Types of the British Army (c1916)		£4.00	—

E   PRINTED ON BACK NO MAKER'S NAME OR BRAND

(See also Imperial Tobacco Co. of Canada Ltd and United Tobacco Companies (South) Ltd)

Size	Number in set			Price per card	Complete set
		Actresses 'ALWICS' (c1905):			
	175	A	Portrait in black	£3.75	—
	50	B	Portrait in red	£4.00	—
	50	Aeroplanes (1926)		£3.20	£160.00
	50	Aeroplanes of Today (1936)		£1.20	£60.00
	25	Angling (1930)		£5.00	—
	50	Arms and Armour (1910)		£6.00	—
	25	Army Life (c1910)		£6.80	—
	50	Art Photogravures (1913)		£1.10	—
	1	Australia Day (1915)		—	£15.00
	22	Automobielen (c1925)		£8.00	—
	75	Aviation (1910)		£4.50	—
	50	Aviation series (1911):			
		A	With album clause	£4.00	—
		B	Without album clause	£4.00	—
		Beauties Set I (1925):			
P	50	A	Black and white	£2.30	£115.00
MP	50	B	Coloured	£2.00	—
P	50	Beauties 2nd series (1925):			
		A	Black and white	£2.30	£115.00
		B	Coloured	£2.00	—
P	50	Beauties 3rd series (1926)		£1.50	£75.00
	50	Beauties red tinted (c1906)		£3.20	—
		Beauties tobacco leaf back (c1908):			
	52	A	With PC inset	£3.50	£175.00
	50	B	Without PC inset	£4.50	£225.00
P	50	Beauties of Great Britain (1930):			
		A	Non-stereoscopic	70p	£35.00
		B	Stereoscopic	£2.50	—
P	50	Beautiful England (1928)		50p	£25.00

BRITISH AMERICAN TOBACCO CO. LTD (continued)

E   PRINTED ON BACK NO MAKER'S NAME OR BRAND (continued)

Size	No.	Title	Price per card	Complete set
MP	60	La Belgique Monumentale et Pittoresque (c1925)	£3.25	—
	50	Best Dogs of Their Breed (1916)	£4.50	—
	50	Billiards (1929)	£2.20	—
	50	Birds, Beasts and Fishes (1937)	70p	£35.00
M	50	Birds, Beasts and Fishes (1929)	£1.20	£60.00
	24	Birds of England (1924)	£2.60	£65.00
	50	Boy Scouts (1930) — without album clause	£2.80	£140.00
	50	Britain's Defenders (1915):		
		A Blue grey fronts	£2.20	—
		B Mauve fronts	£2.00	£100.00
	50	British Butterflies (1930)	£1.10	£55.00
	50	British Empire series (1913)	£3.00	—
	25	British Trees and Their Uses (1930)	£2.20	£55.00
	50	British Warships and Admirals (1915)	£5.00	—
	50	Butterflies and Moths (1911):		
		A With album clause	£3.00	—
		B Without album clause	£2.50	—
	50	Butterflies (Girls) (1928)	£6.00	£300.00
M	50	Butterflies (Girls) (1928)	£7.50	£375.00
M	50	Celebrities of Film and Stage (1930):		
		A Title on back in box	£2.00	£100.00
		B Title on back not in box	£2.00	£100.00
LP	48	Channel Islands Past and Present (1939):		
		A Without '3rd Series'	£1.20	—
		B With '3rd Series'	40p	£20.00
	40	Characters from the Works of Charles Dickens (1919):		
		A Complete set	—	£50.00
		B 38 different (— Nos 33, 39)	70p	£27.00
	50	Cinema Artistes, black and white set 1 (Nd 1-50) (c1928)	£1.80	£90.00
	50	Cinema Artistes black and white set 4 (Nd 101-150) (c1928)	£1.80	£90.00
		Cinema Artistes brown set 1 (c1930):		
	60	A With 'Metro Golden Mayer'	£2.50	—
	50	B Without 'Metro Golden Mayer'	£2.50	—
	50	Cinema Artistes brown set 2 (c1931):		
		A Oblong panel at top back	£2.00	£100.00
		B Oval panel at top back	£2.00	£100.00
L	48	Cinema Artistes set 3 (c1931)	£2.00	£100.00
	48	Cinema Celebrities (C) (1935)	£1.20	£60.00
L	48	Cinema Celebrities (C) (1935)	£1.50	£75.00
L	56	Cinema Celebrities (D) (1936)	£2.70	—
	50	Cinema Favourites (1929)	£2.20	£110.00
	50	Cinema Stars Set 2 (Nd 1-50) (1928)	£1.20	£60.00
	50	Cinema Stars Set 3 (Nd 51-100) (1929)	£3.00	—
	50	Cinema Stars Set 4 (Nd 101-150) (1930)	£1.20	—
	100	Cinema Stars 'BAMT' (coloured) (1931)	£2.30	—
P	50	Cinema Stars Set 1 (c1928)	£1.50	—
P	50	Cinema Stars Set 2 (c1928)	£1.20	£60.00
P	50	Cinema Stars Set 3 (c1928)	£1.50	—
MP	52	Cinema Stars Set 4 (c1928)	£1.80	—
MP	52	Cinema Stars Set 5 (c1928)	£1.80	—
MP	52	Cinema Stars Set 6 (c1928)	£2.50	—
LP	48	Cinema Stars Set 7 (c1928)	£3.00	—
P	50	Cinema Stars Set 8 (Nd 1-50) (c1928)	£1.20	£60.00
P	50	Cinema Stars Set 9 (Nd 51-100) (c1928)	£2.50	—
P	50	Cinema Stars Set 10 (Nd 101-150) (c1928)	£2.50	—
P	50	Cinema Stars Set 11 (Nd 151-200) (c1928)	£2.50	—

BRITISH AMERICAN TOBACCO CO. LTD (continued)

E   *PRINTED ON BACK NO MAKER'S NAME OR BRAND* (continued)

	25	Derby Day series (1914)	£10.00	—
	50	Do You Know? (1923)	50p	£25.00
	50	Do You Know? 2nd series (1931)	50p	£25.00
	25	Dracones Posthistorici (c1930)	£9.00	—
	25	Dutch Scenes (1928)	£3.20	£80.00
	50	Engineering Wonders (1930)	80p	£40.00
	40	English Costumes of Ten Centuries (1919)	£1.50	£60.00
P	25	English Cricketers (1926)	£3.00	£75.00
	26	Etchings (of Dogs) (1926)	£2.50	£65.00
P	50	Famous Bridges (1935)	£1.00	£50.00
	50	Famous Footballers Set 1 (1923)	£5.00	—
	50	Famous Footballers Set 2 (1924)	£5.00	—
	50	Famous Footballers Set 3 (1925)	£5.00	—
	25	Famous Racehorses (1926)	£3.00	£75.00
	25	Famous Railway Trains (1929)	£2.40	£60.00
	50	Favourite Flowers (c1925)	£1.00	£50.00
	50	Film and Stage Favourites (c1925)	£1.80	£90.00
	75	Film Favourites (1928)	£1.50	£115.00
	50	Flags of the Empire (1928)	80p	£40.00
	50	Foreign Birds (1930)	80p	£40.00
	50	Game Birds and Wild Fowl (1929)	£1.40	£70.00
LP	45	Grace and Beauty (Nos 1-45) (1938)	50p	£22.50
LP	45	Grace and Beauty (Nos 46-90) (1939)	30p	£13.50
LP	48	Guernsey, Alderney and Sark Past and Present 1st series (1937)	50p	£25.00
LP	48	Guernsey, Alderney and Sark Past and Present 2nd series (1938)	40p	£20.00
L	80	Guernsey Footballers Priaulx League (1938)	60p	£50.00
P	52	Here There and Everywhere:		
		A Non stereoscopic (1929)	40p	£20.00
		B Stereoscopic (1930)	80p	£40.00
	25	Hints and Tips for Motorists (1929)	£2.60	£65.00
P	50	Homeland Events (1928)	80p	£40.00
	50	Horses of Today (1906)	£5.00	—
	32	Houses of Parliament (red back) (1912)	£2.00	—
	32	Houses of Parliament (brown backs with verse) (1912)	£9.00	—
	50	Indian Chiefs (1930)	£10.00	—
	50	Indian Regiments series (1912)	£10.00	—
	50	International Air Liners (1937)	80p	£40.00
	25	Java Scenes (1929)	£9.00	—
LP	48	Jersey Then and Now 1st series (1935)	£1.00	£50.00
LP	48	Jersey Then and Now 2nd series (1937)	80p	£40.00
	50	Jiu Jitsu (1911)	£3.80	—
	50	Keep Fit (1939)	90p	£45.00
	50	Leaders of Men (1929)	£3.50	—
	50	Life in the Tree Tops (1931)	50p	£25.00
	50	Lighthouses (1926)	£2.00	£100.00
	40	London Ceremonials (1929)	£1.50	£60.00
P	50	London Zoo (1927)	70p	£35.00
	50	Lucky Charms (1930)	£1.50	£75.00
	25	Marvels of the Universe series (c1925)	£2.60	£65.00
	45	Melbourne Cup Winners (1906)	£7.50	—
	50	Merchant Ships of the World (1925)	£5.00	—
	25	Merchant Ships of the World (1925)	£3.50	—
	25	Military Portraits (1917)	£3.00	—
	36	Modern Beauties 1st series (1938)	£1.10	£40.00
	36	Modern Beauties 2nd series (1939)	60p	£22.00
MP	54	Modern Beauties 1st series (1937)	£1.00	£55.00

BRITISH AMERICAN TOBACCO CO. LTD (continued)

E *PRINTED ON BACK NO MAKER'S NAME OR BRAND* (continued)

Size	Number		Price per card	Complete set
MP	54	Modern Beauties 2nd series (1938)	£1.00	£55.00
MP	36	Modern Beauties 3rd series (1938)	£1.50	£55.00
MP	36	Modern Beauties 4th series (1939)	£1.00	£36.00
ELP	36	Modern Beauties 1st series (1936)	£1.10	£40.00
ELP	36	Modern Beauties 2nd series (1936)	75p	£27.00
ELP	36	Modern Beauties 3rd series (1937)	85p	£30.00
ELP	36	Modern Beauties 4th series (1937)	£1.50	£55.00
ELP	36	Modern Beauties 5th series (1938)	£1.00	£36.00
ELP	36	Modern Beauties 6th series (1938)	85p	£30.00
ELP	36	Modern Beauties 7th series (1938)	£1.25	£45.00
LP	36	Modern Beauties 8th series (1939)	£1.50	£55.00
LP	36	Modern Beauties 9th Series (1939)	£1.50	£55.00
LP	36	Modern Beauties (1939)	£1.25	£45.00
	50	Modern Warfare (1936)	£1.50	£75.00
M	48	Modern Wonders (1938)	£3.00	—
	25	Modes of Conveyance (1928)	£2.20	£55.00
	48	Motor Cars green back (1926)	£4.00	—
	36	Motor Cars brown back (1929)	£6.00	—
	50	Motorcycles (1927)	£3.70	—
P	50	Native Life in Many Lands (1932)	£1.50	£75.00
P	50	Natural and Man Made Wonders of the World (1937)	60p	£30.00
P	50	Nature Studies stereoscopic (1928)	60p	£30.00
P	48	Nature Studies stereoscopic (1930)	£1.00	£50.00
	50	Naval Portraits (1917)	£3.00	—
	25	Notabilities (1917)	£2.80	£70.00
	25	Past and Present (1929)	£1.80	£45.00
P	48	Pictures of the East (1930):		
		A 'A Series of 48' 17mm long	£1.50	£75.00
		B 'A Series of 48' 14mm long	£1.50	£75.00
M	48	Picturesque China (c1925):		
		A With 'P' at left of base	£1.60	£80.00
		B Without 'P' at left of base	£1.60	£80.00
M	53	Playing Cards Ace of Hearts Back (c1935)	40p	£20.00
K	53	Playing Cards designed back (c1935):		
		A Blue back	£1.00	—
		B Red back	£1.00	—
	36	Popular Stage, Cinema and Society Celebrities (c1928)	£3.50	—
	25	Prehistoric Animals (1931)	£3.20	£80.00
	50	Prominent Australian and English Cricketers (1911)	£40.00	—
	25	Puzzle series (1916)	£6.00	—
	50	Railway Working (1927)	£1.80	£90.00
	10	Recruiting Posters (1915)	£7.00	—
	33	Regimental Pets (1911)	£7.00	—
	50	Regimental Uniforms (1936)	£1.60	£80.00
	50	Romance of the Heavens (1929)	90p	£45.00
P	50	Round the World in Pictures stereoscopic (1931)	£1.20	£60.00
	50	Royal Mail (1912)	£4.00	—
P	50	Royal Navy (1930)	£2.00	—
	27	Rulers of the World (1911)	£8.00	—
	40	Safety First (1931)	£2.00	£80.00
	25	Ships' Flags and Cap Badges 1st series (1930)	£3.00	£75.00
	25	Ships' Flags and Cap Badges 2nd series (1930)	£3.00	£75.00
P	50	Ships and Shipping (1928)	90p	£45.00
	50	Signalling series (1913)	£3.50	—
	100	Soldiers of the World (tobacco leaf back) (c1902)	£13.00	—
	50	Speed (1938)	70p	£35.00

BRITISH AMERICAN TOBACCO CO. LTD (continued)

E PRINTED ON BACK NO MAKER'S NAME OR BRAND (continued)

Size	No.	Description	Price per card	Complete set
	25	Sports and Games in Many Lands (1930):		
		A 24 Different minus No. 25	£5.00	£120.00
		B Number 25 (Babe Ruth)	—	£50.00
	50	Stage and Film Stars (1926)	£1.60	—
M	50	Stars of Filmland (1927)	£2.50	—
	100	Transfers (Spanish wording headed 'Moje la calcomania') RB.21/587 c1930:		
		A Size 55 x 35mm	£4.00	—
		B Size 62 x 40mm wording 37mm deep	£3.00	—
		C Size 62 x 40mm wording 44mm deep	£4.00	—
	48	Transport Then and Now (1940)	50p	£25.00
	32	Transport of the World (1917)	£9.00	—
	20	Types of North American Indians (c1930)	£15.00	—
P	50	Types of the World (1936)	80p	£40.00
P	270	Views of the World stereoscopic (1908)	£3.00	—
	50	War Incidents (brown back) (1915)	£2.00	£100.00
	50	War Incidents (blue back) (1916)	£2.00	£100.00
	25	Warriors of All Nations (gold panel) (1937)	£1.80	£45.00
	50	Warships (1926)	£5.00	—
	25	Whaling (1930)	£2.40	£60.00
P	50	Who's Who in Sport (1926)	£2.50	£125.00
	50	Wild Animals of the World (tobacco leaf back) (1902)	£9.00	—
	25	Wireless (1923)	£4.40	—
	50	Wonders of the Past (1930)	80p	£40.00
	50	Wonders of the Sea (1929)	70p	£35.00
	25	Wonders of the World (c1928)	80p	£20.00
	40	World Famous Cinema Artistes (1933)	£1.65	£65.00
M	40	World Famous Cinema Artistes (1933)	£1.65	£65.00
	50	World's Products (1929)	50p	£25.00
P	50	The World of Sport (1927)	£2.00	£100.00
P	50	Zoo (1935)	60p	£30.00
	50	Zoological Studies (1928):		
		A Brown back	50p	£25.00
		B Black back	£1.50	

F PLAIN BACKS

Size	No.	Description	Price per card	Complete set
	50	Actors and Actresses 'WALP' (c1905):		
		A Portraits in black and white, glossy	£2.50	£125.00
		B Portraits flesh tinted, matt	£2.50	£125.00
	50	Actresses 'ALWICS' (c1905)	£2.50	—
	50	Actresses, four colours surround (c1905) W.117	£2.50	£125.00
	30	Actresses unicoloured (c1910):		
		A Fronts in purple brown	£1.00	£30.00
		B Fronts in light brown	£1.00	£30.00
	50	Animals and Birds (1912)	£2.00	—
	60	Animals — cut-outs (1912)	£1.10	—
	50	Art Photogravures (1912)	£2.00	—
	50	Aviation series (1911)	£4.00	—
	40	Beauties — brown tinted (1913)	£2.50	—
	50	Beauties with backgrounds (1911)	£2.50	—
	50	Beauties 'LAWHA' (c1906) W.146	£3.00	—
	32	Beauties Picture Hats I with borders (1914)	£3.00	—
	45	Beauties Picture Hats II without borders (1914)	£3.00	—
	30	Beauties and Children (c1910)	£5.00	—
	30	Beauties 'Celebrated Actresses' (c1910)	£3.00	—
	52	Birds of Brilliant Plumage — PC inset (1914)	£3.00	—

BRITISH AMERICAN TOBACCO CO. LTD (continued)

F PLAIN BACKS (continued)

	25	Bonzo series (1923):		
		A With series title ………………………………………………	£4.00	—
		B Without series title ……………………………………………	£4.00	—
	30	Boy Scouts Signalling (c1920):		
		A Captions in English …………………………………………	£4.00	£120.00
		B Captions in Siamese ……………………………………………	£4.00	£120.00
	50	British Man of War series (1910) ……………………………………	£10.00	—
	50	Butterflies and Moths (1910) ……………………………………	£1.80	—
	50	Cinema Artistes (c1928) ……………………………………………	£2.50	—
	50	Cinema Stars RB.21/259 (c1930):		
		A Front matt …………………………………………………	£1.50	£75.00
		B Front glossy …………………………………………………	£1.50	—
	50	Cinema Stars RB.21/260 (Nd 1-50) (c1930) …………………………	£1.50	—
	50	Cinema Stars RB.21/260 (Nd 51-100) (c1930) ………………………	£1.50	—
	50	Cinema Stars RB.21/260 (Nd 101-150) (c1930) ……………………	£1.50	—
	100	Cinema Stars RB.21/260 (Nd 201-300) (c1930) ……………………	£1.20	£120.00
	50	Cinema Stars 'FLAG' (c1930) ……………………………………	£1.50	—
	27	Dancing Girls (1913) ……………………………………………	£2.00	—
	32	Drum Horses (1910) ……………………………………………	£5.00	—
	50	English Period Costumes …………………………………………	90p	£45.00
	50	Flag Girls of All Nations (1911) …………………………………	£2.00	—
		Flags, Pennons and Signals (c1910):		
	70	A Numbered 1-70 ………………………………………………	£1.40	—
	70	B Unnumbered …………………………………………………	£1.40	—
	50	C Numbered 71-120 ……………………………………………	£1.40	—
	45	D Numbered 121-165 …………………………………………	£1.40	—
	20	Flowers (1915) …………………………………………………	£1.50	£30.00
	50	Girls of All Nations (1908) ………………………………………	£2.20	—
	30	Heroic Deeds (1913) ……………………………………………	£3.00	—
	25	Hindou Gods (1909) ……………………………………………	£10.00	—
	32	Houses of Parliament (1914) ……………………………………	£3.25	—
	25	Indian Mogul Paintings (1909) …………………………………	£10.00	—
LP	48	Jersey Then and Now 3rd series (c1940) ………………………	£2.00	—
	53	Jockeys and Owners Colours — PC inset (c1914) ………………	£4.00	—
	30	Merrie England Female Studies (1922) …………………………	£5.00	—
K	36	Modern Beauties 1st series (1938) ………………………………	£3.00	—
	36	Modern Beauties 2nd series (1939) ……………………………	£3.00	—
P	48	Movie Stars (c1930) ……………………………………………	£1.70	—
	50	Music Hall Celebrities (1911):		
		A Blue border …………………………………………………	£2.50	—
		B Gilt border …………………………………………………	£2.50	—
		C Red border …………………………………………………	£2.50	—
		D Yellow border ………………………………………………	£4.00	—
P	50	New Zealand, Early Scenes and Maori Life (c1928) ……………	£1.60	—
	50	Poultry and Pidgeons (c1926) …………………………………	£7.00	—
	25	Products of the World (1914) ……………………………………	£1.00	£25.00
	25	Roses (1912) W.373 ……………………………………………	£8.00	—
	50	Royal Mail (1912) ………………………………………………	£5.00	—
	36	Ships and Their Pennants (1913) ………………………………	£2.50	—
	75	Soldiers of the World (c1902) …………………………………	£9.00	—
	30	Sporting Girls (1913) W.331 ……………………………………	£6.00	—
	50	Sports of the World (1917):		
		A Brown front …………………………………………………	£4.00	—
		B Coloured front ………………………………………………	£4.00	—
M	50	Stars of Filmland (1927) ………………………………………	£2.00	—
	32	Transport of the World (1917) …………………………………	£1.50	—

BRITISH AMERICAN TOBACCO CO. LTD (continued)

F PLAIN BACKS (continued)

	50	Types of the British Army (1908):		
		A Numbered	£3.60	—
		B Unnumbered	£3.60	—
P	50	Types of the World (1936)	£2.50	—
P	50	Units of the British Army and RAF (c1930)	£2.00	—
M	50	Women of Nations (Flag Girls) (1922)	£4.00	—

G PAPER BACKED SILKS ISSUED 1910-1917

M	25	Arabic Proverbs	£14.00	—
M	50	Arms of the British Empire:		
		A Back in blue	£3.00	—
		B Back in brown	£4.00	—
M	50	Australian Wild Flowers	£3.50	—
M	50	Best Dogs of Their Breed	£6.00	—
	110	Crests and Badges of the British Army	£2.50	—
M	108	Crests and Badges of the British Army	£2.50	—
M	50	Crests and Colours of Australian Universities, Colleges and Schools	£2.50	—

BRITISH AMERICAN TOBACCO COMPANY (CHINA) LTD

	32	Sectional Picture — 'Beauties of Old China' (1934)	£5.00	—

BRITISH AMERICAN TOBACCO CO. LTD, Switzerland

	30	Series Actrices (1921) RB.21/200-140	£6.00	—

BRITISH AUSTRALASIAN TOBACCO CO., Australia

		Flags of all Nations (c1903):		
?126		A Yankee Doodle and Pilot	£10.00	—
		B Yankee Doodle and Champion:		
126		i Subjects as Wills Reference W.66	£10.00	—
?22		ii Other Flags	£12.00	—
?106		iii Steamship Company Flags	£12.00	—

BRITISH CIGARETTE CO. LTD, China

	25	British and Foreign Actresses and Beauties (c1900)	£75.00	—
	25	South African War Scenes (c1900)	£32.00	—

BROWN & WILLIAMSON TOBACCO CORP, USA (Wings Cigarettes)

M	50	Modern American Airplanes (c1938):		
		A Inscribed 'Series A'	£4.00	—
		B Without 'Series A'	£3.20	—
M	50	Modern American Airplanes 'Series B' (c1938)	£3.20	—
M	50	Modern American Airplanes 'Series C' (c1938)	£3.20	—
	50	Movie Stars (1940) (Golden Grain Tobacco)	£5.00	—

D. BUCHNER & CO., USA

	48	Actors (1887)	£32.00	—
L	50	Actresses (1891)	£30.00	—
L	? 61	American Scenes with a Policeman (c1890)	£70.00	—
	144	Baseball Players (c1890)	£160.00	—
L	28	Butterflies and Bugs (c1890)	£70.00	—
L	51	Morning Glory Maidens (c1890)	£55.00	—
L	23	Musical Instruments (c1890)	£65.00	—
L	21	Yacht Club Colours (c1890)	£65.00	—

BUCKTROUT & CO. LTD, Guernsey, Channel Islands

M	416	Around the World (1926):		
		A Inscribed 'Places of Interest' Nd. 1-104	50p	£52.00
		B Inscribed 'Around the World' Nd. 105-208	50p	£52.00
		C Inscribed 'Around the World' Nd. 209-312	50p	£52.00
		D Inscribed 'Around the World' Nd. 313-416	50p	£52.00
	24	Birds of England (1923)	£3.25	£80.00
	50	Cinema Stars, 1st series (1921)	£2.00	£100.00
	50	Cinema Stars, 2nd series (1922)	£2.20	£110.00
M	50	Football Teams (1924)	£3.40	—
M	22	Football Teams of the Bailiwick (1924)	£1.00	£22.00
	123	Guernsey Footballers (c1925)	£5.00	—
	20	Inventors Series (1924)	£1.25	£25.00
	25	Marvels of the Universe Series (1923)	£3.00	£75.00
M	54	Playing Cards (1928)	80p	£42.00
	25	Sports and Pastimes (1925)	£5.00	—

BUKHSH ELLAHIE & CO., India

	53	Indian Girl Playing Card inset (c1898):		
		A Full length girl seated	£25.00	—
		B Full length girl standing	£25.00	—
		C Bust length	£25.00	—
	2	Indian Series (c1898) W.240	£350.00	—

CALCUTTA CIGARETTE CO., India

	25	Actresses — 'ALWICS' (c1905):		
		A Fronts in blue	£25.00	—
		B Fronts in chocolate	£30.00	—

A. G. CAMERON & SIZER, USA (including Cameron & Cameron)

	25	The New Discovery (1889):		
		A Without overprint	£34.00	—
		B With overprint	£34.00	—
	24	Occupations for Women (1895)	£50.00	—
		Photographic Cards (c1895) RB.29/C7-6:		
	? 230	Actresses	£18.00	—
L	? 6	Actresses	£22.00	—
	75	Framed Paintings	£15.00	—

V. CAMILLERI, Malta

MP	104	Popes of Rome (1922):		
		A Nd. 1-52	£2.00	£100.00
		B Nd. 53-104	£2.00	£100.00

CAMLER TOBACCO COY, Malta

P	250	Footballers (c1925)	£9.00	—
M	96	Maltese Families Coats of Arms:		
		A Thick board (c1925)	£1.20	—
		B Thin board (1958)	£1.20	—

CHING & CO., Jersey, Channel Islands

L	24	Around and About in Jersey, 1st series (1963)	30p	£7.50
		Album	—	£15.00
L	24	Around and About in Jersey, 2nd series (1964)	80p	£20.00
		Album	—	£20.00
	25	Do You Know? (1962)	20p	£3.00
		Album	—	£8.00

CHING & CO., Jersey, Channel Islands (continued)

	48	Flowers (1962)	£1.00	£50.00
L	24	Jersey Past and Present, 1st series (1960)	25p	£6.00
L	24	Jersey Past and Present, 2nd series (1961)	60p	£15.00
		Album (1st & 2nd Series combined)	—	£15.00
L	24	Jersey Past and Present, 3rd series (1961)	20p	£5.00
		Album	—	£10.00
	25	Ships and Their Workings (1961)	20p	£3.00
	50	Veteran and Vintage Cars (1960)	50p	£25.00
		Album	—	£15.00

THE CIGARETTE COMPANY, Jersey, Channel Islands

	72	Jersey Footballers (c1910)	£8.00	—

LA CIGARETTE ORIENTAL DE BELGIQUE, Belgium

L	100	Famous Men Throughout the Ages (c1940)	50p	£50.00

C. COLOMBOS, Malta

MP	200	Actresses (c1900)	£3.50	—
MP	59	Actresses (c1900)	£16.00	—
	50	Actresses (coloured) (c1900)	£16.00	—
MP	57	Celebrities (c1900)	£20.00	—
P	136	Dante's Divine Comedy (c1914)	£2.50	—
		Famous Oil Paintings (c1910):		
MP	72	1 Series A	£1.00	—
MP	108	2 Series B	£1.00	—
MP	240	3 Series C	£1.00	—
MP	100	4 Series D	£1.00	—
LP	91	5 Large size	£7.00	—
MP	100	Life of Napoleon Bonaparte (c1914)	£3.00	—
MP	70	Life of Nelson (c1914)	£3.00	—
MP	70	Life of Wellington (c1914)	£3.00	—
MP	100	National Types and Costumes (c1910)	£3.00	—
MP	30	Opera Singers (c1900)	£32.00	—
	120	Paintings and Statues (c1912)	£1.00	—
M	112	Royalty and Celebrities (c1910)	£3.50	—

COLONIAL TOBACCOS (PTY) LTD, South Africa

EL	150	World's Fairy Tales (c1930)	£4.00	—

D. CONDACHI & SON, Malta

?	15	Artistes & Beauties (c1905)	£22.00	—

CONSOLIDATED CIGARETTE CO., USA

		Ladies of the White House (c1895):		
	14	A Size 73 x 43mm, white borders	£40.00	—
	25	B Size 70 x 38mm, no borders	£35.00	—

A.G. COUSIS & CO., Malta

		Actors and Actresses (c1910):		
P	100	A Back with framework	£2.50	—
KP	100	B Back without framework	£2.50	—
K	254	Actors and Actresses (c1925)	£1.50	—
KP	100	Actresses Series I (c1910)	£2.00	—
KP	80	Actresses Series II (c1910)	£2.00	—

A.G. COUSIS & CO., Malta (continued)

Size	Number in set			Price per card	Complete set
P	100	Actresses (c1910):			
		A	Series I	£2.00	—
		B	Series II	£2.00	—
		C	Series III	£2.00	—
		D	Series IV	£2.00	—
		E	Series V	£2.00	—
		F	Series VI	£2.00	—
		G	Series VII	£2.00	—
		H	Series VIII	£2.00	—
		I	Series IX	£2.00	—
		J	Series X	£2.00	—
		K	Series XI	£2.00	—
		L	Series XII	£2.00	—
		M	Series XIII	£2.00	—
		N	Series XIV	£2.00	—
		O	Series XV	£2.00	—
		P	Series XVI	£2.00	—
		Q	Series XVII	£2.00	—
		R	Series XVIII	£2.00	—
		S	Series XIX	£2.00	—
		Actresses (c1910):			
KP	2281	A	Miniature size 50 x 30mm	£1.25	—
P	1283	B	Small size 58 x 39mm	£1.25	—
MP	325	Actresses, Celebrities and Warships (c1910)		£10.00	—
		Actresses, Partners and National Costumes (c1910):			
KP	200	A	Miniature size 50 x 30mm	£2.25	—
P	100	B	Small size 60 x 39mm	£2.50	—
MP	50	Beauties, Couples and Children (c1908):			
		A	Back inscribed 'Collection No. 1'	£3.50	—
		B	Back inscribed 'Collection No. 2'	£3.50	—
		C	Back inscribed 'Collection No. 3'	£3.50	—
K	50	Beauties, Couples and Children (red back) (c1925)		£2.50	—
P	402	Celebrities numbered matt (c1910):			
		A	Front inscribed 'Cousis' Dubec Cigarettes', Nd. 1-300	£1.80	—
		B	Front inscribed 'Cousis' Cigarettes', Nd. 301-402	£1.80	—
P	2162	Celebrities unnumbered (c1910):			
		A	Miniature size 50 x 30mm	£1.25	—
		B	Small size 59 x 39mm	£1.25	—
MP	72	Grand Masters of the Order of Jerusalem (c1910)		£3.50	—
P	100	National Costumes (c1910)		£2.75	—
MP	? 57	Paris Exhibition 1900 (c1901)		£30.00	—
MP	102	Paris Series (1902)		£30.00	—
		Popes of Rome (c1910):			
MP	182	A	Back inscribed 'A.G. Cousis & Co'	£2.00	—
MP	81	B	Back inscribed 'Cousis' Dubec Cigarettes'	£3.20	—
P	100	Statues and Monuments (c1910):			
		A	Numbered	£2.00	—
		B	Unnumbered	£2.00	—
KP	127	Views of Malta (c1910)		£2.50	—
P	115	Views of Malta numbered (c1910)		£1.50	—
MP	127	Views of Malta numbered (c1910)		£1.50	—
MP	? 65	Views of Malta unnumbered (c1910)		£1.50	—
P	559	Views of the World (c1910):			
		A	Small size 59 x 39mm	£1.50	—
		B	Medium size 65 x 45mm	£1.50	—
P	99	Warships, white border (c1910)		£3.50	—

A.G. COUSIS & CO., Malta (continued)

Warships, Liners and Other Vessels (c1904):

MP	105	A 'Cousis' Dubec Cigarettes' … … … … … … … … …	£7.50	—
MP	22	B 'Cousis' Excelsior Cigarettes' … … … … … … … …	£7.50	—
MP	40	C 'Cousis' Superior Cigarettes' … … … … … … …	£7.50	—
MP	851	D 'Cousis' Cigarettes' … … … … … … … … … …	£2.00	—
KP	851	E 'Cousis' Cigarettes' … … … … … … … … … …	£2.00	—

CROWN TOBACCO CO., India

National Types, Costumes and Flags (c1900):

	? 19	A Size 70 x 40mm. Back 'These Pictures are used' … … … … … …	£40.00	—
	? 14	B Size 88 x 49mm. Back 'Smoke Crown's High-Class' … … … … …	£45.00	—

DIXSON, Australia

	50	Australian MPs and Celebrities (c1900) … … … … … … … … … …	£20.00	—

DOMINION TOBACCO CO., Canada

	50	The Smokers of the World (c1905) … … … … … … … … … … …	£65.00	—

DOMINION TOBACCO CO. LTD, New Zealand

	50	Coaches and Coaching Days (c1928) … … … … … … … … …	£2.50	—
	50	People and Places Famous in New Zealand History (c1928) … … … …	£1.80	—
	50	Products of the World (c1928) … … … … … … … … … … … …	£1.00	£50.00
	50	USS Co's Steamers (c1928) … … … … … … … … … … …	£3.00	—

DUDGEON & ARNELL, Australia

K	16	1934 Australian Test Team (1934) … … … … … … … … … … …	£9.00	—
K	55	Famous Ships (1933) … … … … … … … … … … … … … …	£4.00	—

W. DUKE, SONS & CO., USA

ALL SERIES ISSUED 1885-95

	50	Actors and Actresses Series No. 1 … … … … … … …	£18.00	—
M	50	Actors and Actresses Series No. 1 … … … … … … …	£38.00	—
	50	Actors and Actresses Series No. 2 … … … … … … …	£18.00	—
M	50	Actors and Actresses Series No. 2 … … … … … … …	£38.00	—
EL	30	Actors and Actresses (3 subjects per card) … … … … …	£36.00	—
	25	Actresses RB.118/27 … … … … … … … …	£11.00	—
EL	25	Actresses (black border) … … … … … … … … … …	£40.00	—
EL	25	Actresses (Folders) … … … … … … … … … … …	£50.00	—
EL	25	Albums of American Stars:		
		A Folder with card … … … … … … … … …	£50.00	—
		B Card only without folder … … … … … … … …	£40.00	—
EL	25	Battle Scenes … … … … … … … … … … … …	£40.00	—
EL	25	Bicycle and Trick Riders … … … … … … … … …	£40.00	—
EL	25	Breeds of Horses … … … … … … … … … …	£38.00	—
EL	25	Bridges … … … … … … … … … … … … …	£30.00	—
EL	25	Burlesque Scenes … … … … … … … … … …	£40.00	—
	50	Coins of All Nations:		
		A White background … … … … … … … … …	£18.00	—
		B Shaded background … … … … … … … … …	£18.00	—
EL	25	Comic Characters … … … … … … … … … …	£30.00	—
EL	25	Cowboys Scenes … … … … … … … … … … …	£40.00	—
EL	50	Fairest Flowers in the World … … … … … … … …	£28.00	—
	50	Fancy Dress Ball Costumes … … … … … … … …	£18.00	—
M	50	Fancy Dress Ball Costumes … … … … … … … …	£36.00	—
EL	50	Fancy Dress Ball Costumes … … … … … … … …	£30.00	—
	50	Fishers and Fish … … … … … … … … … … …	£18.00	—

W. DUKE, SONS & CO., USA (continued)

Size	Number in set		Price per card	Complete set
EL	25	Fishes and Fishing (2 subjects per card)	£36.00	—
EL	25	Flags and Costumes	£34.00	—
	50	Floral Beauties and Language of Flowers	£17.00	—
EL	25	French Novelties	£30.00	—
EL	25	Gems of Beauty:		
		A Back 'Fair Play Long Cut'	£30.00	—
		B Back 'Honest Long Cut'	£30.00	—
	50	Great Americans	£26.00	—
EL	16	Great Americans (3 subjects per card)	£40.00	—
	25	Gymnastic Exercises	£30.00	—
EL	25	Habitations of Man	£28.00	—
	50	Histories of Generals (Booklets) (1888)	£40.00	—
EL	50	Histories of Generals (Cards)	£40.00	—
	50	Histories of Poor Boys who have become rich and other famous people		
		(Booklets)	£32.00	—
	50	Holidays	£18.00	£900.00
EL	25	Illustrated Songs	£30.00	—
EL	25	Industries of the States	£38.00	—
	50	Jokes:		
		A With A.T.C. name	£18.00	—
		B Without A.T.C. name	£18.00	—
EL	25	Jokes (2 subjects per card)	£36.00	—
EL	25	Lighthouses (die cut)	£30.00	—
EL	25	Miniature Novelties	£30.00	—
	50	Musical Instruments	£24.00	—
EL	25	Musical Instruments of the World (2 subjects per card)	£36.00	—
	36	Ocean and River Steamers	£28.00	—
M	240	Photographs from Life RB.23/D76-84	£6.00	—
	53	Playing Cards	£12.00	—
	50	Popular Songs and Dancers	£24.00	—
	50	Postage Stamps	£17.00	—
EL	25	Presidential Possibilities	£36.00	—
		Rulers, Flags and Coats of Arms (1888):		
EL	50	A Thick card type	£26.00	—
EL	50	B Thin folders (titled Rulers, Coats of Arms & Flag)	£18.00	—
	50	Scenes of Perilous Occupations	£25.00	—
EL	25	Sea Captains	£36.00	—
	50	Shadows	£18.00	£900.00
EL	25	Snap Shots from Puck	£30.00	—
EL	25	Stars of the Stage, 1st series (bust poses, white edge) RB.22/X2-129:		
		A With 'Duke'	£32.00	£800.00
		B Inscribed 'Third Series'	£32.00	—
EL	25	Stars of the Stage, 2nd series (full length poses) RB.22/X2-130	£32.00	—
EL	25	Stars of the Stage, 3rd series (bust poses, black edge) RB.22/X2-131	£32.00	£800.00
EL	25	Stars of the Stage, 4th series (die cut) RB.22/X2-132	£32.00	—
EL	48	State Governors' Coats of Arms	£30.00	—
EL	48	State Governors' Coats of Arms (Folders)	£18.00	—
EL	25	Talk of the Diamond	£90.00	—
	50	The Terrors of America and Their Doings	£18.00	—
M	50	The Terrors of America and Their Doings	£36.00	—
EL	50	The Terrors of America and Their Doings	£30.00	—
	50	Tinted Photos RB.22/X2-89:		
		A Standard size	£24.00	—
		B Die cut to shape	£17.00	—
EL	24	Tricks With Cards	£55.00	—
EL	25	Types of Vessels (die cut)	£30.00	—
	50	Vehicles of the World	£25.00	—

W. DUKE, SONS & CO., USA (continued)

	50	Yacht Colors of the World	£18.00	—
M	50	Yacht Colours of the World	£36.00	—
EL	50	Yacht Colours of the World	£36.00	—

PHOTOGRAPHIC CARDS

	340	Actors and Actresses, 'Cross-Cut Cigarettes' with number and caption in design, Group 1	£5.00	—
	260	Actors and Actresses, 'Cross-Cut Cigarettes' in design, number and caption at base, Group 2	£5.00	—
	?	Actors and Actresses, 'Cross-Cut Cigarettes' and all wording at base, Group	£5.00	—
	148	Actors and Actresses, 'Dukes Cameo Cigarettes' in design, number and caption at base, Group 4	£5.00	—
	?	Actors and Actresses, 'Dukes Cameo Cigarettes', number and caption at base, Group 5	£5.00	—
	?	Actors and Actresses, 'Dukes Cigarettes' in design, number and caption at base, Group 6	£5.00	—
	?	Actors and Actresses, 'Dukes Cigarettes' and all wording at base, Group 7	£5.00	—
	?	Actors, Actresses and Celebrities, printed back:		
		1 Horizontal 'Dukes Cameo Cigarettes' back	£5.00	—
		2 Vertical 'Sales 1858' back	£5.00	—
		3 Horizontal 'Dukes Cigarettes' back	£5.00	—
EL	?	Actors, Actresses, Celebrities etc	£7.00	—

H. ELLIS & CO., USA

	25	Breeds of Dogs (c1890):		
		A 'Bengal Cheroots'	£45.00	—
		B 'Tiger Cigarettes'	£45.00	—
		C 'Triplex Cigarettes'	£45.00	—
	25	Costumes of Women (c1890)	£65.00	—
	25	Generals of the Late Civil War (c1890)	£85.00	—
	25	Photographic Cards — Actresses (c1887)	£17.00	—

JOHN FINZER & BROS., USA

L	10	Inventors and Inventions (c1891)	£50.00	—

FOH CHONG, China

M	10	Chinese Series (c1930)	—	£20.00

G.W. GAIL & AX., USA

EL	25	Battle Scenes (c1890)	£40.00	—
EL	25	Bicycle and Trick Riders (c1890)	£40.00	—
EL	25	French Novelties (c1890)	£36.00	—
EL	25	Industries of the States (c1890)	£36.00	—
EL	25	Lighthouses (die cut) (c1890)	£32.00	—
EL	25	Novelties (die cut) (c1890)	£34.00	—
EL	?	Photographic Cards (c1890)	£7.00	—
EL	25	Stars of the Stage (c1890)	£32.00	—

GENERAL CIGAR COMPANY, Montreal, Canada

		Northern Birds:		
EL	24	A With series title Nd. 1-24 (1968)	£1.20	—
EL	12	B Without series title, Nd. 25-36 (1977)	£1.40	—

G.G. GOODE LTD, Australia

	17	Prominent Cricketers Series 1924	£100.00	—

GOODWIN & CO., USA

15	Beauties — 'PAC' (c1888)	£60.00	—
50	Champions (c1888)	£55.00	—
50	Dogs of the World (c1888):		
	A Captions front and back	£25.00	—
	B Captions front only	£25.00	—
	C Captions back only	£25.00	—
50	Flowers (c1888)	£24.00	—
50	Games and Sports Series (c1888)	£35.00	—
50	Holidays (c1888)	£32.00	—
50	Occupations for Women (c1888)	£55.00	—
10	Old Judge Actresses (thick card) (c1888)	£90.00	—
	Photographic Cards (c1888):		
?	Actors and Actresses	£7.00	—
?	Baseball Players	£60.00	—
?	Celebrities and Prizefighters	£35.00	—
50	Vehicles of the World (c1888)	£30.00	—
50	Wild Animals of the World (c1888)	£30.00	—

GUERNSEY TOBACCO CO., Channel Islands

		A Famous Picture:		
	49	A And When Did You Last See Your Father? (1934)	£2.50	—
	48	B The Laughing Cavalier (1935)	£2.50	—
	48	C The Toast (1936)	£2.50	—
K	52	Miniature Playing Cards (1933)	£1.20	—

THOS. H. HALL, USA

4	Actresses RB.23/-H6-1 (1880)	£75.00	—
14	Actresses RB.23/-H6-2, multi-backed (c1885)	£18.00	—
140	Actors and Actresses RB.23/-H6-3, multi-backed (c1885)	£18.00	—
112	Actresses and Actors RB.23/-H6-4, multi-backed (c1885)	£18.00	—
? 196	Actresses and Actors RB.23/-H6-5, multi-backed (c1885)	£18.00	—
? 158	Actresses and Actors RB.23/-H6-6, multi-backed (c1885)	£18.00	—
52	Actresses RB.23/-H6-7 (c1885)	£20.00	—
12	Actresses RB.23/-H6-8 (c1885)	£38.00	—
25	Actresses RB.23/-H6-9 (c1885)	£32.00	—
11	Actresses RB.23/-H6-10 (c1885)	£80.00	—
12	Athletes RB.23/-H6-3 (1881)	£70.00	—
4	Presidential Candidates RB.23/-H6-1 (1880)	£75.00	—
22	Presidents of the United States RB.23/-H6-11 (c1888)	£37.00	—
25	Theatrical Types RB.23/-H6-12 (c1890)	£36.00	—

HARTLEY'S TOBACCO CO., South Africa

L	19	South African English Cricket Tour 1929	£80.00	—

THE HILSON CO., USA

L	25	National Types (1900)	£26.00	—

IMPERIAL CIGARETTE & TOBACCO CO., Canada

? 24	Actresses (c1900)	£60.00	—

IMPERIAL TOBACCO COMPANY OF CANADA LTD, Canada

A **WITH FIRM'S NAME**

	25	Beauties — Girls in Costume (c1903) RB.118/69	£55.00	—
	24	Beauties — Smoke Girls (c1903) RB.118/75	£55.00	—
M	50	Birds, Beasts and Fishes (1923)	£1.60	£80.00

IMPERIAL TOBACCO COMPANY OF CANADA LTD (continued)

A   WITH FIRM'S NAME (continued)

Size	No.	Title	Price	Set
L	100	Birds of Canada (1924)	£3.50	—
L	100	Birds of Canada (Western Canada) (1925)	£5.50	—
	50	British Birds (1923)	£1.00	£50.00
	48	Canadian History Series (1926)	£1.80	—
	50	Children of All Nations (1924)	£1.00	£50.00
	23	Dogs Series (1924)	£2.00	£45.00
	50	Dogs, 2nd series (1925)	£1.50	£75.00
	50	Famous English Actresses (1924)	£1.00	£50.00
	50	Film Favourites (1925):		
		A English Issue:		
		i Numbered	£3.00	—
		ii Unnumbered	£3.20	—
		B French Issue:		
		i Numbered	£6.00	—
		ii Unnumbered	£6.00	—
	50	Fish and Bait (1924)	£1.60	£80.00
	50	Fishes of the World (1924)	£2.50	£125.00
	50	Flower Culture in Pots (1925)	80p	£40.00
	30	Game Bird Series (1925)	£2.20	£65.00
	50	Gardening Hints (1923)	70p	£35.00
M	25	Heraldic Signs and Their Origins (1925)	£1.40	£35.00
	50	How to Play Golf (1925)	£9.00	—
	50	Infantry Training (1915):		
		A Glossy card	£2.50	
		B Matt card	£2.50	
L	48	Mail Carriers and Stamps (1903)	£27.00	—
	50	Merchant Ships of the World (1924)	£1.30	£65.00
	25	Military Portraits (1914)	£2.60	—
	50	Modern War Weapons, 'Sweet Caporal' issue (1914)	£3.60	—
	56	Motor Cars (1924)	£2.00	—
	50	Naval Portraits (1914)	£2.60	—
	25	Notabilities (1914)	£2.60	—
	53	Poker Hands (1924)	£1.50	—
	53	Poker Hands, New Series (1925)	£1.50	—
	25	Poultry Alphabet (1924)	£3.00	—
	50	Railway Engines (1924):		
		A With 'Wills' blanked out	£1.30	—
		B Without 'Wills'	£1.20	£60.00
	50	The Reason Why (1924)	£1.00	£50.00
	127	Smokers Golf Cards (1925)	£5.50	—

B   WITHOUT FIRM'S NAME

Size	No.	Title	Price	Set
	50	Actresses — Framed Border (Plain back) RB.21/321 (c1910)	£4.00	—
	50	Arms of the British Empire (1911)	£2.60	—
	50	Around the World (c1910):		
		A Numbered	£3.50	—
		B Unnumbered	£6.00	—
	90	Baseball Series (1912)	£40.00	—
	30	Bird Series (c1910)	£2.65	—
	50	Boy Scouts (1911) — with album clause	£6.00	—
	50	Canadian Historical Portraits (1913)	£6.00	—
	50	Canadian History Series (1914)	£2.00	—
	50	Fish Series (c1910)	£2.50	—
	50	Fowls, Pigeons and Dogs (1911)	£3.50	—
	45	Hockey Players (1912)	£25.00	—
	36	Hockey Series (coloured) (1911)	£25.00	—

IMPERIAL TOBACCO COMPANY OF CANADA LTD (continued)

B **WITHOUT FIRM'S NAME** (continued)

	50	How To Do It (c1910)	£3.00	—
	100	Lacrosse Series (coloured), Leading Players (c1910)	£8.00	—
	100	Lacrosse Series (coloured) (c1910)	£8.00	—
	50	Lacrosse Series (black and white) (c1910)	£8.00	—
	50	L'Historie du Canada (1926)	£1.50	—
	50	Movie Stars (c1930)	£2.00	—
L	50	Pictures of Canadian Life (c1910):		
		A Brown front	£7.00	—
		B Green front	£7.00	—
	50	Prominent Men of Canada (c1910)	£4.00	—
	50	Tricks and Puzzles (c1910)	£7.00	—
	50	Types of Nations (c1910)	£3.00	—
	25	Victoria Cross Heroes (blue back) (1915)	£3.20	£80.00
L	45	Views of the World (c1910)	£6.00	—
L	25	Wild Animals of Canada (c1910)	£12.00	—
M	144	World War I Scenes and Portraits (1916)	£3.00	—
	25	The World's Dreadnoughts (1910)	£4.00	—

C **SILKS ISSUED 1910-25**

M	55	Animals with Flags	£4.00	—
EL	50	Canadian History Series	£11.00	—
M	121	Canadian Miscellany	£5.00	—
M	55	Garden Flowers of the World	£2.50	—
M	55	Orders and Military Medals	£3.50	—
M	55	Regimental Uniforms of Canada	£3.50	—
L	50	Yachts, Pennants and Views	£7.00	—

THE IMPERIAL TOBACCO CO. OF INDIA LTD, India

	25	Indian Historical Views (1915):		
		A Set 1, First Arrangement	£2.60	—
		B Set 2, Second Arrangement	£2.60	—
	40	Nautch Girl Series:		
		A 'Pedro Cigarettes' (c1905)	£3.00	—
		B 'Railway Cigarettes' (c1907)	£2.75	—
	52	Nautch Girl Series, PC inset:		
		A 'Pedro Cigarettes' (c1905)	£3.00	—
		B 'Railway Cigarettes' (c1907)	£2.75	—
K	53	Playing Cards, red back (1919)	£1.50	—
K	52	Playing Cards, blue back (1933)	£1.50	—

THE JERSEY TOBACCO CO. LTD, Channel Islands

K	53	Miniature Playing Cards (1933)	£1.00	—

JUST SO, USA

EL	?	Actresses (c1890)	£11.00	—

KENTUCKY TOBACCO PTY. LTD, South Africa

L	120	The March of Mankind (1940)	£2.25	—

KHEDIVIAL CO., USA

M	10	Aeroplane Series (c1910):		
		A Back 'Duke of York Cigarettes'	£25.00	—
		B Back 'Oxford Cigarettes'	£25.00	—
M	10	Prize Dog Series (c1910):		
		A Back 'Duke of York Cigarettes'	£25.00	—
		B Back 'Oxford Cigarettes'	£25.00	—

KHEDIVIAL CO., USA (continued)

Size	Number		Price	Complete
M	25	Prize Fight Series No. 101 (c1910):		
		A Back with Fight Details ………………………………………	£30.00	—
		B Back without Fight Details ……………………………………	£30.00	—
M	25	Prize Fight Series No. 102 (c1910) …………………………………	£30.00	—

WM. S. KIMBALL & CO., USA

ALL SERIES ISSUED 1885-95

Size	Number		Price	Complete
	? 46	Actresses collotypes c1888 …………………………………………	£150.00	—
	72	Ancient Coins:		
		A Title Ancient Coins ………………………………………	£32.00	—
		B Title Facsimile of Ancient Coins ……………………………	£32.00	—
	48	Arms of Dominions …………………………………………………	£24.00	—
	50	Ballet Queens ………………………………………………………	£26.00	—
	52	Beauties with Playing Card Insets ………………………………	£26.00	—
EL	20	Beautiful Bathers …………………………………………………	£45.00	—
	50	Butterflies ……………………………………………………………	£26.00	—
		Champions of Games and Sports:		
	25	A Front with Firm's name ………………………………………	£60.00	—
	50	B Front without Firm's name …………………………………	£60.00	—
	50	Dancing Girls of the World ………………………………………	£25.00	—
	50	Dancing Women ……………………………………………………	£25.00	—
	50	Fancy Bathers ………………………………………………………	£25.00	—
EL	25	French Novelties ……………………………………………………	£45.00	—
EL	25	Gems of Beauty ……………………………………………………	£40.00	—
	50	Goddesses of the Greeks & Romans ……………………………	£32.00	—
EL	25	Household Pets ……………………………………………………	£38.00	—
	?	Photographic Actresses RB.23/K26-15-2 ………………………	£8.00	—
EL	20	Pretty Athletes ……………………………………………………	£40.00	—
	50	Savage and Semi Barbarous Chiefs and Rulers ………………	£32.00	—

KINNEY BROS., USA

ALL SERIES ISSUED 1885-95

Size	Number		Price	Complete
	25	Actresses Group 1 Set 1 RB.118/1 ……………………	£8.00	—
	25	Actresses Group 1 Set 2 RB.118/2 ……………………	£12.00	—
	25	Actresses Group 1 Set 3 RB.118/3 ……………………	£13.00	—
	25	Actresses Group 1 Set 4 RB.118/4 ……………………	£15.00	—
	25	Actresses Group 1 Set 5 RB.118/5 ……………………	£15.00	—
	25	Actresses Group 2 RB.118/15 ……………………………	£7.00	—
	25	Actresses Group 2 RB.118/16:		
		A Subjects named ……………………………………	£7.00	—
		B Subjects unnamed …………………………………	£7.00	—
	25	Actresses Group 3 RB.118/26 ……………………………	£7.00	—
	25	Actresses Group 3 RB.118/29 ……………………………	£7.00	—
	50	Actresses Group 4 RB.118/36 (black text back) ………	£7.00	—
	129	Actresses Group 4 RB.118/36-37 (plain back) ………	£6.50	—
	25	Animals ……………………………………………………	£20.00	—
	10	Butterflies of the World. Light background ……………	£22.00	—
	50	Butterflies of the World. Gold background ……………	£20.00	—
	25	Famous Gems of the World ………………………………	£24.00	—
	52	Harlequin Cards 1st series ………………………………	£25.00	—
	53	Harlequin Cards 2nd series (1889) ……………………	£25.00	—
L	50	International Cards ………………………………………	£40.00	—
K	24	Jocular Oculars …………………………………………	£40.00	—
	25	Leaders:		
		A Standard size ………………………………………	£26.00	£650.00
		B Narrow card — officially cut ………………………	£26.00	£650.00

KINNEY BROS., USA (continued)

50	Magic Changing Cards (1881)	£26.00	—
622	Military Series:		
	A Coloured background:		
50	1 Inscribed '7' on front	£7.00	—
50	2 Inscribed '8' on front	£7.00	—
30	3 Inscribed '9' on front	£7.00	—
50	4 Without numeral	£7.00	—
50	5 Foreign 1886 Types	£7.00	—
	6 Other coloured background:		
18	A U.S. Continental	£7.00	—
3	B Vatican	£60.00	—
5	C Decorations	£50.00	—
	B Plain white or lightly coloured background:		
51	1 U.S Army and Navy	£7.00	—
85	2 U.S. State Types	£7.00	—
60	3 U.S and Foreign Types	£10.00	—
50	4 England and N.G.S.N.Y.	£16.00	—
50	5 Foreign 1853 Types	£10.00	—
50	6 Foreign Types 1886	£7.00	—
15	7 French Army and Navy	£7.00	—
5	8 State Seals	£50.00	—
	National Dances:		
50	A Front with white border	£20.00	—
26	B Front without border	£24.00	—
25	Naval Vessels of the World	£24.00	—
50	New Year 1890 (1889)	£25.00	—
25	Novelties Type 1. Thick circular, no border RB.26/Fig K32-17	£26.00	—
50	Novelties Type 2. Thin circular with border RB.26/Fig K32-18	£14.00	—
	Novelties Type 3. Die cut RB.26/Fig K32-19-1 and 2:		
25	A Inscribed '25 Styles'	£10.00	—
50	B Inscribed '50 Styles'	£10.00	—
75	C Inscribed '75 Styles'	£10.00	—
50	Novelties Type 5. Standard size cards	£13.00	—
14	Novelties Type 6. Oval RB.26/XA2-120	£30.00	—
	Photographic Cards:		
?	A Actors and Actresses. Horizontal back with Kinney's name	£4.00	—
?	B Actors and Actresses. Vertical, Sweet Caporal backs	£4.00	—
45	C Famous Ships	£12.00	—
	Racehorses (1889):		
25	1 American Horses:		
	A Back with series title 'Famous Running Horses'	£26.00	—
	B Back 'Return 25 of these small cards' 11 lines of text	£24.00	—
25	2 English Horses 'Return 25 of these cards' with 6 lines of text	£24.00	—
25	3 Great American Trotters	£28.00	—
50	Surf Beauties	£25.00	—
52	Transparent Playing Cards	£16.00	—
25	Types of Nationalities (folders)	£30.00	—

KRAMERS TOBACCO CO. (PTY) LTD, South Africa

50	Badges of South African Rugby Football Clubs (1933)	£8.00	—

LEWIS & ALLEN CO. USA

L	? 120	Views and Art Studies (c1910)	£6.00	—

LONE JACK CIGARETTE CO., USA

25	Inventors and Inventions (c1888)	£70.00	—

LONE JACK CIGARETTE CO., USA (continued)

	50	Language of Flowers (1888):		
		A Front 'Lone Jack Cigarettes'	£30.00	—
		B Front 'Ruby Cigarettes'	£30.00	—
		C Front 'Unknown Cigarettes'	£30.00	—

P. LORILLARD CO., USA

For issues after 1900 see American Tobacco Co.

ALL SERIES ISSUED 1885-98

M	25	Actresses RB.23/L70-4-3	£30.00	—
M	25	Actresses RB.23/L70-5	£30.00	—
EL	25	Actresses RB.23/L70-6:		
		A 'Red Cross' long cut	£30.00	—
		B 'Sensation Cut Plug' front and back	£30.00	—
		C 'Sensation Cut Plug' front only	£30.00	—
EL	25	Actresses RB.23/L70-8	£30.00	—
EL	25	Actresses in Opera Roles RB.23/L70-9	£45.00	—
M	25	Ancient Mythology Burlesqued RB.23/L70-10	£30.00	—
M	50	Beautiful Women RB.23/L70-11:		
		A '5c Ante' front and back	£28.00	—
		B 'Lorillard's Snuff' front and back	£28.00	—
		C 'Tiger' front and back	£28.00	—
EL	25	Circus Scenes	£85.00	—
	25	National Flags	£30.00	—
EL	50	Prizefighters	£130.00	—
M	25	Types of the Stage	£30.00	—

W.C. MACDONALD INC., Canada

	?	Aeroplanes and Warships (c1940)	£1.30	—
M	53	Playing Cards (different designs) (1926-47)	70p	—

B. & J.B. MACHADO, Jamaica

	25	British Naval series (1916)	£22.00	—
	50	The Great War — Victoria Cross Heroes (1916)	£24.00	—
P	50	Popular Film Stars (1926)	£6.00	—
P	50	The Royal Family at Home and Abroad (1927)	£5.00	—
P	52	Stars of the Cinema (1926)	£6.00	—
P	50	The World of Sport (1928)	£8.00	—

MACLIN-ZIMMER-MCGILL TOB. CO., USA

EL	53	Playing Cards — Actresses (c1890)	£24.00	—

MALTA CIGARETTE CO., Malta

	135	Dante's Divine Comedy (c1905)	£15.00	—
	M40	Maltese Families Arms & Letters (c1905)	£7.00	—
	? 44	Prominent People (c1905)	£15.00	—

H. MANDELBAUM, USA

	36	Flags of Nations (c1890)	£40.00	—
	20	Types of People (c1890)	£60.00	—

MARBURG BROS., USA

	50	National Costume Cards (c1890):		
		A Front 'Greenback Smoking Mixture'	£60.00	—
		B Front 'Seal of Virginia Smoking Mixture'	£60.00	—
	50	Typical Ships (c1890)	£60.00	—

MASPERO FRERES LTD, Palestine

| | 50 | Birds, Beasts and Fishes (1925) .... | £4.00 | — |

P.H. MAYO & BROTHER, USA

	25	Actresses RB.23/M80-1 (c1890)	£32.00	—
M	25	Actresses RB.23/M80-3 (c1890)	£32.00	—
L	12	Actresses RB.23/M80-4 (c1890)	£75.00	—
?	39	Actresses RB.23/M80-5 (c1890)	£32.00	—
	40	Baseball Players (c1890)	£150.00	—
	20	Costumes and Flowers (c1890)	£32.00	—
	25	Head Dresses of Various Nations (c1890)	£34.00	—
M	25	National Flowers (Girl and Scene) (c1890)	£34.00	—
	20	Naval Uniforms (c1890)	£34.00	—
	35	Prizefighters (c1890)	£70.00	—
	20	Shakespeare Characters (c1890)	£34.00	—

M. MELACHRINO & CO., Switzerland

	52	Peuples Exotiques 1st series (c1925)	£1.00	—
	52	Peuples Exotiques 2nd series (c1925)	£1.00	—
	52	Peuples Exotiques 3rd series (c1925)	£1.00	—

MEXICAN PUFFS, USA

| | 20 | Actresses (c1890) .... | £75.00 | — |

MIFSUD & AZZOPARDI, Malta

| KP | 59 | First Maltese Parliament (1922) .... | £8.00 | — |

L. MILLER & SONS, USA

M	25	Battleships (c1900)	£32.00	—
M	25	Generals and Admirals (Spanish War) (c1900)	£32.00	—
M	24	Presidents of US (c1900)	£26.00	—
M	50	Rulers of the World (c1900)	£24.00	—

CHAS. J. MITCHELL & CO., Canada

	26	Actresses — 'FROGA A' (1900):		
		A Backs in brown	£38.00	—
		B Backs in green	£36.00	—
	26	Actresses – 'FROGA B' with Playing Card inset (1900)	£60.00	—

MITSUI & CO., Japan

| | ? | Japanese Women (c1908) .... | £10.00 | — |

MOORE & CALVI, USA

EL	53	Playing Cards — Actresses (c1890):		
		A 'Trumps Long Cut' back	£27.00	—
		B 'Hard-A-Port' with maker's name	£25.00	—
		C 'Hard-A-Port' without maker's name	£25.00	—

MURAI BROS. & CO., Japan

	150	Actresses — 'ALWICS' (c1905) W.33	£10.00	—
	100	Beauties — 'THIBS' (c1900)	£35.00	—
	50	Beauties Group 1 (c1902)	£15.00	—
	25	Chinese Beauties 1st series Peacock issue (c1910)	£4.00	£100.00
	25	Chinese Beauties 3rd series Peacock issue (c1910)	£5.00	—
	50	Chinese Beauties, back in red (c1908)	£6.50	—

MURAI BROS. & CO., Japan (continued)

	50	Chinese Children's Games without border Peacock issue (c1910)	£3.40	£170.00
	20	Chinese Children's Games with border Peacock issue (c1910)	£3.40	—
	54	Chinese Girls Set 3 (c1905)	£7.50	—
	50	Chinese Pagodas Peacock issue (c1910)	£4.00	—
	30	Chinese Series Peacock issue (c1910)	£3.50	—
	40	Chinese Trades I, back in black (c1905)	£25.00	—
	40	Chinese Trades II, back in olive, Peacock issue (c1910)	£5.00	—
	50	Dancing Girls of the World (c1900)	£40.00	—

NATIONAL CIGARETTE CO., Australia

	13	English Cricket Team 1897-8:		
		A Front black and white	£400.00	—
		B Front yellow-brown	£400.00	—

NATIONAL CIGARETTE AND TOBACCO CO., USA

		National Types (Sailor Girls) (c1890):		
	25	A Back 'Julius Bien & Co'	£30.00	—
	25	B Back 'The Girsch Lithographing Co.'	£30.00	—
	25	C Back without printer's credit	£30.00	—
	26	D Back 'Sackett Wilhelms Litho Co.'	£30.00	—

PHOTOGRAPHIC CARDS

	?	Actresses (c1888):		
		A Plain back	£8.00	—
		B Printed back	£9.00	—

NATIONAL TOBACCO WORKS, USA

EL	13	Art Miniatures (1892)	£25.00	—
EL	?	Cabinet Pictures (c1890)	£25.00	—

OLD FASHION, USA

L	? 200	Photographic Cards — Actresses (c1890)	£15.00	—

PENINSULAR TOBACCO CO. LTD, India

	50	Animals and Birds (1910)	£3.00	—
	52	Birds of Brilliant Plumage (1916):		
		A Back with single large packings	£3.20	—
		B Back with two small packings	£3.20	—
	25	Birds of the East, 1st series (1912)	£3.00	—
	25	Birds of the East, 2nd series (1912)	£3.00	£75.00
	25	China's Famous Warriors:		
		A Back 'Monchyr India'	£3.60	£90.00
		B Back 'India' only	£3.60	£90.00
	25	Chinese Heroes (1913)	£3.40	£90.00
	50	Chinese Modern Beauties (1912)	£6.50	—
	50	Chinese Trades (1908):		
		A Back with 'Monchyr'	£3.20	—
		B Back without 'Monchyr'	£3.20	—
	30	Fish series (1916)	£3.00	—
	25	Hindoo Gods (1909)	£3.20	£80.00
	37	Nautch Girl series (1910)	£7.00	—
	25	Products of the World (1915)	£2.40	60.00

PIZZUTO, Malta

	50	Milton's Paradise Lost (c1910)	£18.00	—

Size Number
in set FOREIGN TOBACCO ISSUERS Price Complete
per card set

PLANTERS' STORES & AGENCY CO. LTD, India

? 47	Actresses — 'FROGA' (1900)		£38.00	—
25	Beauties 'FECKSA' (1900)		£40.00	—

POLICANSKY BROS., South Africa

50	Beautiful Illustrations of South African Fauna (1925):			
	A	Back 'Mast Cigarettes'	£10.00	—
	B	Back 'Mignon Cigarettes'	£10.00	—

R.J. REYNOLDS (Doral), USA

	America's Backyard (plants) (2006):			
23	A	Set of 23	£1.25	—
1	B	Limited Edition Holographic Card	—	£5.00
	America On The Road (2004):			
25	A	Set of 24 plus List Card	£1.25	—
1	B	Limited Edition Card	—	—
	American Treasures (2005):			
25	A	Set of 24 plus List Card	£1.25	—
1	B	Limited Edition Card	—	—
4	Doral's Employees (2006)		£1.25	£5.00
	The 50 States (2000):			
52	A	Set of 50 plus 2 List Cards	£1.25	—
2	B	Limited Edition Cards (Washington and Lady Liberty)	£5.00	—
1	C	Limited Edition Card We The People	£10.00	—
8	Freshwater Fishing Hall of Fame (1999)		£2.00	—
	Great American Festivals (2003):			
31	A	Set of 30 plus List Card	£1.25	—
1	B	Limited Edition Card	—	—
	Smoking Moments (2007):			
24	A	Set of 24	£1.25	—
1	B	Limited Edition Card — At The Drive In	—	—
	Snapshots of The Century (2001):			
36	A	Set of 35 plus Title Card	£1.25	—
1	B	Limited Edition Card	—	£3.00
1	C	Special Edition Card	—	£6.00

D. RITCHIE & CO., Canada

52	Beauties Playing Card inset, multi-backed (c1890)		£35.00	—
52	Playing Cards, mutli-backed (c1890)		£35.00	—

RUGGIER BROS., Malta

M	50	Story of the Knights of Malta (c1925)	£6.50	—

SANTA FE NATURAL TOBACCO CO., USA

36	A Tribute To The Endangered Set 1 (2001)		£1.25	—
36	A Tribute To The Endangered Set 2 (2001)		£1.25	—
36	Century of The Great American Spirit Set 1 (2000)		£1.25	—
36	Century of The Great American Spirit Set 2 (2000)		£1.25	—
25	Music of America (2003)		£1.25	—
36	Spirit of The Old West Series 1 (1999)		£1.25	—
36	Spirit of The Old West Series 2 (1999)		£1.25	—

SCERRI, Malta

	Beauties and Children (c1930):			
150	A	Black and white, no borders	£1.20	—
? 86	B	Black and white, white border	£15.00	—
45	C	Coloured	£1.80	—

SCERRI, Malta (continued)

MP	50	Beautiful Women (c1935)	£3.20	£160.00
MP	480	Cinema Artists (c1935)	£2.50	—
MP	180	Cinema Stars (c1935)	£2.80	—
MP	50	Famous London Buildings (c1935)	£4.00	—
MP	60	Film Stars 1st series Nos 1-60 (c1935)	£3.20	—
MP	60	Film Stars 2nd series Nos 61-120 (c1935)	£3.20	—
	52	Interesting Places of the World (c1936)	50p	£26.00
P	25	International Footballers (c1935)	£30.00	—
M	401	Malta Views (c1930)	80p	—
M	51	Members of Parliament — Malta (c1930)	44p	£22.00
	146	Prominent People (c1930)	£1.50	—
MP	100	Scenes from Films (c1935)	£3.00	—
LP	100	Talkie Stars (c1930)	£3.00	—
M	100	World's Famous Buildings (c1930)	55p	£55.00

J.J. SCHUH TOBACCO CO. PTY LTD, Australia

ALL SERIES ISSUED 1920-25

	60	Australian Footballers series A (half-full length)	£13.00	—
	40	Australian Footballers series B (Rays)	£13.00	—
	59	Australian Footballers series C (oval frame)	£23.00	—
		Australian Jockeys:		
	30	A Numbered	£7.00	—
	30	B Unnumbered	£7.00	—
P	72	Cinema Stars	£2.50	—
	60	Cinema Stars	£2.75	—
L	12	Maxims of Success	£40.00	—
P	72	Official War Photographs	£4.00	—
P	96	Portraits of Our Leading Footballers	£6.00	—

G. SCLIVAGNOTI, Malta

	50	Actresses and Cinema Stars (1923)	£3.00	—
MP	71	Grand Masters of the Orders of Jerusalem (1897)	£11.00	—
P	102	Opera Singers (1897)	£15.00	—
M	100	Opera Singers (1897)	£15.00	—

SIMONETS LTD, Jersey, Channel Islands

MP	36	Beautiful Women (c1925) GP.417	£6.00	—
P	24	Cinema Scenes series (c1925)	£7.50	—
P	27	Famous Actors and Actresses (c1925)	£6.50	—
	50	Local Footballers (c1914)	£6.50	—
	25	Picture Series (c1920)	£5.00	—
P	27	Sporting Celebrities (c1930)	£10.00	—
LP	50	Views of Jersey (plain back) (c1940)	£2.50	—

THE SINSOCK & CO., Korea

	20	Korean Girls (c1905)	£20.00	—

SNIDERS & ABRAHAMS PTY LTD, Australia

		Actresses (c1905):		
	30	A Gold background	£7.00	—
	14	B White Borders	£7.00	—
	20	Admirals and Warships of USA (1908)	£9.00	—
	60	Animals (c1912)	£4.00	—
	60	Animals and Birds (c1912):		
		A 'Advertising Gifts' issue	£3.00	—
		B 'Peter Pan' issue	£3.50	—

SNIDERS & ABRAHAMS PTY LTD, Australia (continued)

15	Australian Cricket Team (1905)	£50.00	—
16	Australian Football Incidents in Play (c1906)	£16.00	—
24	Australian Footballers (full length) series AI, back with 'O & A' (1905)	£22.00	—
50	Australian Footballers (full length) series AII, back without 'O & A' (1905)	£22.00	—
76	Australian Footballers (½ length) series B (1906)	£22.00	—
76	Australian Footballers (½ length) series C (1907)	£22.00	—
140	Australian Footballers (head and shoulders) series D (1908)	£20.00	—
60	Australian Footballers (head in oval) series E (1910)	£20.00	—
60	Australian Footballers (head in rays) series F (1911)	£20.00	—
60	Australian Footballers (with pennant) series G (1912)	£20.00	—
60	Australian Footballers (head in star) series H (1913)	£20.00	—
60	Australian Footballers (head in shield) series I (1914)	£20.00	—
56	Australian Footballers (½-¾ length) series J (1910)	£20.00	—
48	Australian Jockeys, back in blue (1907)	£5.00	—
83	Australian Jockeys, back in brown (1908)	£5.50	—
56	Australian Racehorses, horizontal back (1906)	£6.00	—
56	Australian Racehorses, vertical back (1907)	£6.00	—
40	Australian Racing Scenes (1911)	£6.00	—
? 133	Australian VCs and Officers (1917)	£7.00	—
12	Billiard Tricks (c1910)	£20.00	—
60	Butterflies and Moths, captions in small letters (c1912)	£2.00	—
60	Butterflies and Moths, captions in block letters (c1912)	£2.00	—
60	Cartoons and Caricatures (c1908):		
	A Front with border	£6.50	—
	B Front without border	£6.50	—
12	Coin Tricks (c1910)	£16.00	—
64	Crests of British Warships (1915):		
	A Back in blue	£5.50	—
	B Back in green	£5.50	—
40	Cricketers in Action (1906)	£65.00	—
12	Cricket Terms (c1906)	£32.00	—
32	Dickens series (c1910)	£6.00	—
16	Dogs (c1910):		
	A 'Standard' issue	£10.00	—
	B 'Peter Pan' issue:		
	1 White panel	£10.00	—
	2 Gilt panel	£10.00	—
	C 'Coronet' issue £10.00	—	
6	Flags (shaped metal) (c1910)	£7.00	—
6	Flags (shaped card) (c1910)	£7.00	—
60	Great War Leaders and Warships (c1915):		
	A Front in green (Peter Pan issue)	£5.00	—
	B Front in sepia brown	£5.00	—
30	How to Keep Fit (c1908)	£7.00	—
60	Jokes (c1906):		
	A 'Aristocratica' back in brown	£4.50	—
	B 'Standard' back in blue	£4.50	—
	C 'Milo' back in green	£4.50	—
12	Match Puzzles (c1910)	£16.00	—
48	Medals and Decorations (c1915)	£7.00	—
M 48	Melbourne Buildings (c1915)	£8.50	—
48	Natives of the World (c1906)	£20.00	—
25	Naval Terms (c1906)	£9.00	—
12	Oscar Ashe, Lily Brayton and Lady Smokers (1911)	£7.00	—
29	Shakespeare Characters (c1908)	£6.00	—
40	Signalling — Semaphore and Morse (c1916)	£7.00	—
30	Statuary (c1906)	£10.00	—
14			

SNIDERS & ABRAHAMS PTY LTD, Australia (continued)

	60	Street Criers in London, 1707 (c1916) … … … … … … … …	£9.00	—
	32	Views of Victoria in 1857 (c1908):		
		A Green back … … … … … … … … … … … …	£10.00	—
		B Brown back … … … … … … … … … … … …	£10.00	—
P	250	Views of the World 1908 … … … … … … … … … … … … … …	£4.00	—

STAR TOBACCO CO., India

	52	Beauties (PC inset), multi-backed (c1898) … … … … … … … …	£28.00	—
	52	Indian Native Types (PC inset) (c1898) … … … … … … … … …	£28.00	—

SUM MUYE & CO., Siam

	50	Siamese Royalty (c1912) … … … … … … … … … … …	£8.00	—
	220	Movie Stars (1915) … … … … … … … … … … … … …	£3.00	—
	100	Movie Stars (sepia) (c1915) … … … … … … … … … …	£4.00	—
	120	Movie Stars (portrait in oval) (c1915) … … … … … … …	£4.00	—

TOBACCO PRODUCTS CORPORATION OF CANADA LTD

	? 45	Canadian Sports Champions (c1920) … … … … … … …	£18.00	—
	60	Do You Know (1924) … … … … … … … … … … … …	£6.00	—
	60	Hockey Players (1926) … … … … … … … … … … …	£35.00	—
	120	Movie Stars (c1920) … … … … … … … … … … … …	£3.00	—
	100	Movie Stars (sepia) (c1920) … … … … … … … … …	£4.00	—
	L20	Movie Stars Series 3 (Mack Sennett Girls) … … … … … … …	£5.00	—
	? 120	Movie Stars Set 4 (c1920) … … … … … … … … … …	£3.50	—
	? L67	Movie Stars Series 5 (c1920) … … … … … … … …	£5.00	—
	L100	Movie Stars (sepia) (c1920) … … … … … … … … …	£5.00	—

TUCKETT LIMITED, Canada

	25	Autograph Series (c1913) … … … … … … … … … …	£32.00	—
	? 210	Beauties and Scenes (c1910) … … … … … … … … …	£8.00	—
	25	Boy Scout Series (c1915) … … … … … … … … … …	£27.00	—
P	100	British Views without Tucketts on front (c1912) … … … … …	£2.50	—
P	? 224	British Views with Tucketts on front (c1912):		
		A Back 'Karnak Cigarettes' … … … … … … … …	£2.50	—
		B Back 'T & B' trade mark … … … … … … … … …	£2.50	—
		C Back 'Tuckett's Special Turkish Cigarettes' … … … … …	£2.50	—
P	80	British Warships (c1915):		
		A Back 'T & B' trade mark … … … … … … … … …	£9.00	—
		B Back 'Tuckett's Special Turkish Cigarettes' … … … …	£9.00	—
P	50	Canadian Scenes (c1912) … … … … … … … … … …	£2.50	—
	53	Playing Card Premium Certificates (c1930) … … … … … …	£7.50	—
	52	Tucketts Aeroplane Series (1930) … … … … … … … …	£4.50	—
	52	Tucketts Aviation Series (1929) … … … … … … … …	£4.50	—
	52	Tucketts Auction Bridge Series (1930) … … … … … …	£7.00	—

TURKISH-MACEDONIAN TOBACCO CO., Holland (TURMAC)

The illustration numbers are taken from Reference Book No. 138
Handbook of Worldwide Tobacco & Trade Silk issues

ANONYMOUS SILK ISSUES:

M	20	Arms of Cities and Dutch Provinces Ref 611 c1930 … … … … …	£4.00	—
EL	18	Arms of Dutch Cities and Towns Ref 617 c1930 … … … … …	£5.00	—
M	18	Arms of Dutch East and West Indies Ref 613 c1930 … … … …	£4.00	—
M	20	Decorations and Medals Ref 619 c1930 … … … … … …	£7.00	—
	100	Dutch Celebrities Ref 620 c1930 … … … … … … …	£5.00	—
	57	Flowers Ref 636 c1930 … … … … … … … … … …	£7.00	—
M	25	Flower and Leaf Design Series A Ref 626 c1930 … … … … …	£5.00	—

TURKISH-MACEDONIAN TOBACCO CO., Holland (TURMAC) (continued)

ANONYMOUS SILK ISSUES (continued)

M	16	Flower and Leaf Design Series B Ref 626 c1930	£5.00	—
M	16	Flower and Leaf Design Series C Ref 626 c1930	£5.00	—
M	16	Flower and Leaf Design Series D Ref 626 c1930	£5.00	—
M	16	Flower and Leaf Design Series E Ref 626 c1930	£5.00	—
M	20	Flowers (Europa/Afrika) Ref 627 c1930	£6.00	—
M	3	Girls of Many Lands (black silk) Ref 628 c1930	£8.00	—
M	50	Girls of Many Lands (white silk) Ref 629 c1930	£5.00	—
		Illustrated Initials c1930:		
M	26	A Single letters Ref 630	£4.00	—
M	28	B Double letters Ref 631	£4.00	—
M	33	Japanese Subjects Ref 638 c1930	£8.00	—
M	46	Javanese Figures Ref 633 c1930	£6.00	—
M	34	National and Provincial Costumes Ref 635 c1930	£4.00	—
M	66	National Flags (white silk) Ref 642 c1930	£4.00	—
		National Flags, Standards and Arms c1930:		
		A Size 75 x 50mm:		
M	83	i National Flags Ref 643	£2.00	—
M	83	ii National Standards Ref 643	£2.00	—
M	83	iii National Arms Ref 643	£2.00	—
M	76	B Size 65 x 50mm National Arms Ref 643	£3.00	—
		C Size 65 x 36mm:		
	81	i National Flags with caption Ref 643	£3.00	—
	79	ii National Flags without caption Ref 643	£3.00	—
M	145	National Flags (paper backed) Ref 644 c1930	£4.00	—
M	16	Nature Calendar Ref 645 c1930	£5.00	—
M	20	Ships of All Ages Ref 650 c1930	£10.00	—
		Sport and Nature Series c1930:		
M	55	A Sports Subjects Ref 657	£6.00	—
M	27	B Animals and Birds Ref 657	£5.00	—
M	10	C Butterflies Ref 657	£5.00	—
M	34	D Flowers Ref 657	£5.00	—
		Sporting and Other Figures (size 45 x 30mm) c1930:		
K	16	Series A Sport (No. 16 size 75 x 55mm) Ref 652	£7.00	—
K	15	Series B Music Ref 652	£7.00	—
K	17	Series C Transport Ref 652	£7.00	—
K	14	Series D Flying (No. 4 size 75 x 55mm) Ref 652	£7.00	—
K	24	Series E Miscellaneous Ref 652	£7.00	—
M	25	Sporting Figures (Numbered CA1 to CA25) Ref 653 c1930	£7.00	—
M	74	Towns and Village Arms Ref 614 c1930	£4.00	—
M	47	World Celebrities and Film Stars Ref 655 c1930	£8.00	—

UNITED TOBACCO COMPANIES (SOUTH) LTD, South Africa

A WITH FIRM'S NAME

	50	Aeroplanes of Today (1936):		
		A 'Box 78 Capetown'	£1.80	£90.00
		B 'Box 1006 Capetown'	£1.80	£90.00
	50	Animals and Birds Koodoo issue (1923)	£7.00	—
L	24	Arms and Crests of Universities and Schools of South Africa (1930)	£1.40	£35.00
L	52	Boy Scout, Girl Guide and Voortrekker Badges (1932)	£2.20	—
L	62	British Rugby Tour of South Africa (1938)	£1.80	—
	50	Children of All Nations (1928)	£1.00	—
	50	Cinema Stars 'Flag Cigarettes' (1924)	£2.20	£110.00
	60	Do You Know? (1929)	60p	£36.00
	50	Do You Know 2nd series (1930)	60p	£30.00
	50	Do You Know 3rd series (1931)	60p	£30.00
K	28	Dominoes 'Ruger Cigarettes' (1934)	£6.00	—

UNITED TOBACCO COMPANIES (SOUTH) LTD (Continued)

A WITH FIRM'S NAME (continued)

Size	Number	Title	Price	Complete set
L	50	Exercises for Men and Women (1932)	£1.20	£60.00
	48	Fairy Tales 1st series Flag issue (1928)	£2.00	—
	48	Fairy Tales 2nd series Flag issue (1928)	£2.00	—
	24	Fairy Tales (1926) (booklets)	£10.00	—
L	120	Farmyards of South Africa (1934)	£1.70	—
M	50	Household Hints (1926)	£2.00	—
	25	Interesting Experiments (1930)	£1.40	£35.00
L	100	Medals and Decorations of the British Commonwealth of Nations (1941)	90p	—
	50	Merchant Ships of the World (1925)	£1.20	£60.00
	50	Motor Cars (1923)	£4.00	—
L	100	Our Land (1938)	25p	£25.00
L	200	Our South Africa Past and Present (1938)	25p	£50.00
L	24	Pastel Plates (1938)	£1.40	£35.00
L	88	Philosophical Sayings (1938)	£1.20	—
	25	Picturesque People of the Empire (1929)	£1.80	£45.00
K	53	Playing Cards 'Flag' Cigarettes	£1.80	—
K	53	Playing Cards 'Lifeboat' Cigarettes (1934)	£2.00	—
M	53	Playing Cards 'Lotus Cigarettes' (1934)	£2.50	—
L	53	Playing Cards 'Loyalist Cigarettes' (1934)	£2.00	—
K	53	Playing Cards 'MP Cigarettes' (1934)	£2.00	—
K	53	Playing Cards 'Rugger Cigarettes' (1934)	£3.00	—
L	50	Racehorses South Africa Set 1 (1929)	£2.20	—
L	52	Racehorses South Africa Set 2 (1930):		
		A Inscribed 'a series of 50'	£2.20	—
		B Inscribed 'a series of 52'	£2.20	—
	50	Regimental Uniforms (1937)	£2.00	£100.00
	50	Riders of the World (1931)	£1.50	£75.00
L	52	S. A. Flora (1935):		
		A With 'CT Ltd'	60p	—
		B Without 'CT Ltd'	50p	£26.00
	25	South African Birds 1st series (1927)	£2.00	—
	25	South African Birds 2nd series (1927)	£2.00	—
L	52	South African Butterflies (1937)	80p	£42.00
L	52	South African Coats of Arms (1931)	50p	£26.00
L	65	South African Rugby Football Clubs (1933)	£2.00	—
L	52	Sports and Pastimes in South Africa (1936)	£3.00	—
L	47	Springbok Rugby and Cricket Teams (1931)	£3.00	—
L	28	1912-13 Springboks (1913)	£75.00	—
	25	Studdy Dogs (1925)	£5.00	—
?	98	Transfers (c1925)	£6.00	—
L	40	Views of South African Scenery 1st series (1918):		
		A Text back	£4.50	—
		B Anonymous plain back	£4.50	—
L	36	Views of South African Scenery 2nd series (1920)	£4.50	—
	25	Wild Flowers of South Africa 1st series (1925)	£1.80	—
	25	Wild Flowers of South Africa 2nd series (1926)	£1.80	—
	50	The World of Tomorrow (1938)	£1.10	£55.00

B WITHOUT FIRM'S NAME

Size	Number	Title	Price	Complete set
	50	African Fish (1937)	£1.80	£90.00
	50	British Aeroplanes (1933)	£1.80	—
EL	25	Champion Dogs (1934)	£5.00	—
	30	Do You Know (1933)	80p	£24.00
	50	Eminent Film Personalities (1930)	£2.20	—
	50	English Period Costumes (1932)	£1.00	£50.00
	25	Famous Figures from South African History (1932)	£2.60	—

UNITED TOBACCO COMPANIES (SOUTH) LTD, South Africa (continued)

B *WITHOUT FIRM'S NAME* (continued)

L	100	Famous Works of Art (1939)	30p	£30.00
	25	Flowers of South Africa (1932)	£2.00	—
M	50	Humour in Sport (1929)	£3.70	—
L	100	Our Land (1938)	30p	—
M	150	Our South African Birds (1942)	50p	£75.00
L	150	Our South African Birds (1942)	40p	£60.00
M	100	Our South African Flora (1940)	25p	£25.00
L	100	Our South African Flora (1940)	20p	£20.00
M	100	Our South African National Parks (1941)	25p	£25.00
L	100	Our South African National Parks (1941)	22p	£22.00
L	50	Pictures of South Africa's War Effort (1942)	45p	£22.50
	50	Riders of the World (1931)	£1.50	£75.00
	50	Safety First (1936)	£1.20	£60.00
	40	Ships of All Times (1931)	£2.00	—
	25	South African Birds 2nd series	£2.80	—
L	17	South African Cricket Touring Team (1929):		
		A Fronts with autographs	£22.00	—
		B Fronts without autographs	£22.00	—
M	100	South African Defence (1939)	26p	£26.00
L	50	South African Places of Interest (1934)	40p	£20.00
P	50	Stereoscopic Photographs Assorted Subjects (1928)	£1.20	—
P	50	Stereoscopic Photographs of South Africa (1929)	£1.20	—
	50	The Story of Sand (1934)	£1.00	£50.00
M	50	Tavern of the Seas (1939)	50p	£25.00
	25	Warriors of All Nations (crossed swords at base) (1937)	£2.00	£50.00
	25	What's This (1929)	£2.00	£50.00
	50	Wild Animals of the World (1932)	£1.50	£75.00
M	40	Wonders of the World (1931)	£1.25	—
M	100	World Famous Boxers (c1935)	£6.00	—

C *SILK ISSUES*

M	20	British Butterflies (c1920)	£11.00	—
M	30	British Roses (c1920)	£11.00	—
M	65	Flags of All Nations (c1920)	£3.00	—
M	25	Old Masters (c1920)	£8.00	—
M	50	Pottery Types (c1920)	£7.00	—
M	50	South African Flowers Nd 1-50 (c1920)	£4.00	—
M	50	South African Flowers Nd 51-100 (c1920)	£4.00	—

UNIVERSAL TOBACCO CO. PTY LTD, South Africa

	835	Flags of All Nations (1935)	£1.30	—

S.W. VENABLE TOBACCO CO., USA

EL	? 56	Actresses, multi-backed (c1890)	£40.00	—

GEO. F. YOUNG & BRO., USA

L	?	Actresses (c1890)	£34.00	—

ANONYMOUS SERIES — Chinese Language

M	10	Chinese Beauties (Ref ZE2-11) (c1930)	—	£20.00
M	10	Chinese Series (Ref ZE9-31) (c1930)	—	£20.00
	10	Chinese Views & Scenes (Ref ZE9-49) (c1930) (San Shing)	—	£20.00
	48	Hints on Association Football (Ref ZE3-2) (c1930)	—	£10.00
	30	Safety First (Ref ZE9-41) (c1930) (Hwa Ching)	—	£45.00

SECTION 3

REPRINT SERIES

During the past twenty years or so, around 350 classic cigarette and trade card series have been reprinted. Many of the originals are extremely rare and do not often turn up in collections, so reprints provide an opportunity to enjoy cards rarely seen. At such low prices, reprints have established a following in their own right, and have also become popular for framing to make an interesting decorative feature. The quality of reproduction is very good, and they are clearly marked as reprints to avoid confusion.

NOTE: C.C.S. = Card Collectors Society

Size	Print-ing	Number in set	REPRINT SERIES	Complete set
			ADKIN & SONS	
—	C	4	Games by Tom Browne (135 x 83mm) c1900 (reprinted 2001) … … … … …	£4.00
			A.W. ALLEN LTD (Australia)	
D2	U	18	Bradman's Records (Cricketer) 1932 (reprinted 2002) … … … … … … …	£7.00
			ALLEN & GINTER/GOODWIN/KIMBALL (USA)	
A	C	28	Baseball Greats of 1890 (reprinted 1991) … … … … … … … … … … …	£8.00
			ALLEN & GINTER (USA)	
A	C	50	Celebrated American Indian Chiefs 1888 (reprinted 1989) … … … … …	£15.00
A	C	50	Fans of The Period 1890 (reprinted 2005) … … … … … … … … … …	£8.50
A	C	50	Fruits (Children) 1891 (reprinted 1989) … … … … … … … … … … …	£8.50
A	C	50	Pirates of the Spanish Main 1888 (reprinted 1996) … … … … … … …	£15.00
A	C	50	Prize and Game Chickens c1890 (reprinted 2000) … … … … … … … …	£10.00
D2	U	9	Women Baseball Players c1888 (reprinted 2001) … … … … … … … …	£3.00
—	C	50	The World's Champions 2nd Series (82 x 73mm) c1890 (reprinted 2001) …	£17.50
			AMERICAN TOBACCO CO. (USA)	
B	C	50	Lighthouse Series 1912 (reprinted 2000) … … … … … … … … … … …	£12.00
A	C	25	Military Uniforms — numbered (green net design back) 1900 (reprinted 2003)	£6.25
			ARDATH TOBACCO CO. LTD	
A2	C	35	Hand Shadows c1930 (reprinted 2001) … … … … … … … … … … …	£7.50
			A. BAKER & CO. LTD	
A	C	25	Star Girls c1898 (reprinted 2001) … … … … … … … … … … … …	£6.00
			BARBERS TEA LTD	
A	C	24	Cinema & Television Stars 1955 (reprinted 1993) … … … … … … … …	£6.50

BENSDORP COCOA (Holland)

| — | C | 3 | Deep Sea Divers (99 x 70mm) c1900 (reprinted c1995) ... ... | £2.50 |

FELIX BERLYN

| A | C | 25 | Golfing Series Humorous 1910 (reprinted 1989) ... ... | £6.00 |

ALEXANDER BOGUSLAVSKY LTD

—	C	12	Big Events on the Turf (133 x 70mm) 1924 (reprinted 1995)	£18.00
A	C	25	Conan Doyle Characters 1923 (reprinted 1996)	£6.25
A	C	25	Winners on the Turf 1925 (reprinted 1995)	£6.25

BOWMAN GUM INC. (USA)

| — | C | 108 | Jets-Rockets-Spacemen (80 x 54mm) 1951 (reprinted 1985) ... ... | £9.00 |

WM BRADFORD

| D2 | U | 20 | Boer War Cartoons c1901 (reprinted 2001) ... ... | £5.00 |

BRIGHAM & CO

| B2 | BW | 16 | Down The Thames From Henley to Windsor c1912 (reprinted 2001) ... ... | £6.50 |

BRITISH AMERICAN TOBACCO CO. LTD

A	C	50	Aeroplanes 1926 (reprinted 2001)	£8.50
D	C	25	Beauties — Blossom Girls c1904 (reprinted 2001)	£6.00
A	C	32	Drum Horses 1910 (reprinted 2001)	£6.25
A	C	50	Indian Regiments 1912 (reprinted 2001)	£8.50
A	C	50	Lighthouses 1926 (reprinted 2000)	£8.50
A	C	45	Melbourne Cup Winners 1906 (reprinted 1992)	£8.50
A	C	50	Motorcycles 1927 (reprinted 1991)	£12.50
A	C	33	Regimental Pets 1911 (reprinted 1998)	£6.25

CADBURY BROS. LTD

| — | C | 6 | Sports Series (109 x 35mm) c1905 (reprinted 2001) ... ... | £3.00 |

CARRERAS LTD

| A | C | 50 | Famous Airmen & Airwomen 1936 (reprinted 1996) ... ... | £8.50 |
| A | C | 75 | Footballers 1934 (reprinted 1997) ... ... | £13.50 |

H. CHAPPEL & CO.

| A2 | C | 10 | British Celebrities 1905 (reprinted 2001) ... ... | £3.00 |

W.A. & A.C. CHURCHMAN

A	U	50	Boxing Personalities 1938 (reprinted 1990)	£8.50
A	C	50	Cricketers 1936 (C.C.S. reprinted 1999)	£10.00
A	C	52	Frisky 1935 (reprinted 1994)	£8.50
A	C	50	In Town To-Night 1938 (C.C.S. reprinted 1999)	£10.00
A	C	50	Landmarks in Railway Progress 1931 (reprinted 1994)	£8.50
A	C	50	Pioneers 1956 (reprinted 2000)	£9.50
A	C	25	Pipes of The World 1927 (C.C.S. reprinted 2000)	£6.50
A	C	50	Prominent Golfers 1931 (reprinted 1989)	£8.50
B	C	12	Prominent Golfers 1931 (reprinted 1989)	£6.00
A	C	50	Racing Greyhounds 1934 (reprinted 1989)	£8.50
—	C	48	The RAF at Work (68 x 53mm) 1938 (reprinted 1995)	£16.00
A	C	50	The Story of Navigation 1936 (C.C.S. reprinted 1999)	£10.00

WM. CLARKE & SON

A	BW	30	Cricketer Series 1901 (reprinted 2001) …… …… …… …… …… …… …… ……	£7.50

COHEN WEENEN & CO. LTD

A	C	60	Football Club Captains 1907-8 (reprinted 1998) …… …… …… …… ……	£10.00
A	C	40	Home & Colonial Regiments 1901 (reprinted 1998) …… …… …… ……	£8.50
A	C	50	Star Artistes 1905 (reprinted 1998) …… …… …… …… …… ……	£8.50
A	C	50	V.C. Heroes (of World War I) 1915 (reprinted 1998) …… …… …… ……	£8.50

COOPERATIVE WHOLESALE SOCIETY LTD (C.W.S.)

A	C	25	Parrot Series 1910 (reprinted 1996) …… …… …… …… …… …… ……	£6.00
A	C	48	Poultry 1927 (reprinted 1996) …… …… …… …… …… …… …… ……	£8.50

COPE BROS. & CO. LTD

A	C	50	British Warriors 1912 (reprinted 1996) …… …… …… …… ……	£8.50
A	C	50	Cope's Golfers 1900 (reprinted 1983) …… …… …… …… ……	£12.50
A	C	50	Dickens Gallery 1900 (reprinted 1989) …… …… …… …… ……	£15.00
—	C	7	The Seven Ages of Man (114 x 78mm) c1885 (reprinted 2001) …… ……	£6.00
A	C	50	Shakespeare Gallery 1900 (reprinted 1989) …… …… …… ……	£15.00
A	C	25	Uniforms of Soldiers and Sailors 1898 (reprinted 1996) …… ……	£6.25
A	C	25	The World's Police 1935 (reprinted 2005) …… …… …… …… ……	£6.00

DAH TUNG NAN (China)

—	C	18	Golf Girl Series (65 x 50mm) c1920 (reprinted 1997) …… …… …… ……	£6.00

W. DUKE, SONS & CO (USA)

A	C	25	Fishers c1890 (reprinted 2002) …… …… …… …… …… …… ……	£6.00
A	C	30	Generals of American Civil War (Histories of Generals) 1888 (reprinted 1995)	£6.25

J. DUNCAN & CO. LTD

D1	C	50	Evolution of The Steamship 1925 (reprinted 2002) …… …… …… …… ……	£8.50

H. ELLIS & CO. (USA)

A	C	25	Generals of the Late Civil War 1890 (reprinted 1991) …… …… …… ……	£6.00

EMPIRE TOBACCO CO.

D	C	6	Franco-British Exhibition 1907 (reprinted 2001) …… …… …… …… ……	£3.00

W. & F. FAULKNER

C	C	25	Beauties (coloured) c1898 (reprinted 2001) …… …… …… …… ……	£6.00
D	C	12	Cricket Terms 1899 (reprinted 1999) …… …… …… …… …… ……	£3.00
D	C	12	Football Terms 1st Series 1900 (reprinted 1999) …… …… …… ……	£3.00
D	C	12	Football Terms 2nd Series 1900 (reprinted 1999) …… …… …… ……	£3.00
D	C	12	Golf Terms (with "Faulkners" on front) 1901 (reprinted 1999) …… ……	£5.00
D2	C	12	Golf Terms (without "Faulkners" titled Golf Humour) 1901 (reprinted 1998) …	£3.00
D	C	12	Grenadier Guards 1899 (reprinted 1999) …… …… …… …… ……	£3.00
D	C	12	Military Terms 1st Series 1899 (reprinted 1999) …… …… …… ……	£3.00
D	C	12	Military Terms 2nd Series 1899 (reprinted 1999) …… …… …… ……	£3.00
D	C	12	Nautical Terms 1st Series 1900 (reprinted 1999) …… …… …… ……	£3.00
D	C	12	Nautical Terms 2nd Series 1900 (reprinted 1999) …… …… …… ……	£3.00
D	C	12	Policemen of the World 1899 (reprinted 1999) …… …… …… ……	£3.00
D	C	12	Police Terms (with "Faulkners" on front) 1899 (reprinted 1999) …… ……	£3.00
D2	C	12	Police Terms (without "Faulkners" titled Police Humour) 1899 (reprinted 1998)	£3.00
A	C	25	Prominent Racehorses of the Present day 1923 (reprinted 1993) …… ……	£6.00

W. & F. FAULKNER (continued)

D	C	12	Puzzle Series 1897 (reprinted 1999)	£3.00
D	C	12	Sporting Terms 1900 (reprinted 1999)	£3.00
D	C	12	Street Cries 1902 (reprinted 1999)	£3.00

FRANKLYN, DAVEY & CO.

A	C	25	Boxing 1924 (reprinted 2002)	£6.00

J.S. FRY & SONS LTD

A	C	25	Days of Nelson 1906 (reprinted 2003)	£6.25
A	C	25	Days of Wellington 1906 (reprinted 2003)	£6.25

J. GABRIEL

A	BW	20	Cricketers Series 1901 (reprinted 1992)	£5.00

GALLAHER LTD

A	C	48	Army Badges 1939 (reprinted 2001)	£8.50
A	C	50	The Great War Nos. 1-50 1915 (reprinted 2001)	£8.50
A	C	50	The Great War Nos. 51-100 1915 (reprinted 2003)	£8.50
A	C	25	The Great War Victoria Cross Heroes 1st Series 1915 (reprinted 2001)	£6.25
A	C	25	The Great War Victoria Cross Heroes 2nd Series 1915 (reprinted 2001)	£6.25
A	C	25	The Great War Victoria Cross Heroes 3rd Series 1915 (reprinted 2001)	£6.25
A	C	25	The Great War Victoria Cross Heroes 4th Series 1915 (reprinted 2001)	£6.25
A	C	25	The Great War Victoria Cross Heroes 5th Series 1915 (reprinted 2003)	£6.25
A	C	25	The Great War Victoria Cross Heroes 6th Series 1915 (not issued)	—
A	C	25	The Great War Victoria Cross Heroes 7th Series 1915 (reprinted 2003)	£6.25
A	C	25	The Great War Victoria Cross Heroes 8th Series 1915 (reprinted 2003)	£6.25
A	C	50	Lawn Tennis Celebrities 1928 (reprinted 1997)	£8.50
A	C	25	Motor Cars 1934 (reprinted 1995)	£6.25
A	C	50	Regimental Colours and Standards 1899 (reprinted 1995)	£8.50
A	C	48	Signed Portraits of Famous Stars 1935 (reprinted 1997)	£8.50
A	C	50	South African Series No. 101-150 (Boer War Uniforms) (reprinted 2000) ...	£8.50
A	C	50	South African Series No. 151-200 (Boer War Uniforms) (reprinted 2000) ...	£8.50
A	C	50	Types of the British Army No. 1-50 1900 (reprinted 1995)	£8.50
A	C	50	Types of the British Army No. 51-100 1900 (reprinted 1996)	£8.50

GLOBE CIGARETTE CO.

D	BW	25	Actresses — French c1900 (reprinted 2001)	£6.00

GLOBE INSURANCE

—	U	11	Famous Golfers (75 x 60mm) 1929 (reprinted 1996)	£6.00

G.G. GOODE LTD (Australia)

D2	U	17	Prominent Cricketer Series 1924 (reprinted 2001)	£5.00

THOS. H. HALL (USA)

C1	C	8	Presidential Candidates & Actresses 1880 (reprinted 2001)	£3.00

HIGNETT BROS. & CO.

A	C	25	Greetings of The World 1907 (C.C.S. reprinted 2000)	£6.50
A	C	50	Prominent Racehorses of 1933 (C.C.S. reprinted 2000)	£10.00

R. & J. HILL LTD

A	C	25	Battleships and Crests 1901 (reprinted 1995)	£6.25
A	C	20	Types of The British Army 1914 (reprinted 2001)	£6.25

HUDDEN & CO. LTD

A C 25 Famous Boxers 1927 (reprinted 1992) £6.25

HUNTLEY & PALMER (France)

— C 12 Aviation (114 x 85mm) c1908 (reprinted 2001) £7.50

IMPERIAL TOBACCO COMPANY OF CANADA LTD

A C 45 Hockey Players 1912 (reprinted 1987) £15.00
A C 36 Hockey Series 1911 (reprinted 1987) £15.00

INTERNATIONAL CHEWING GUM (USA)

— C 24 Don't Let It Happen Over Here (80 x 64mm) 1938 (reprinted 1984) £10.00

JAMES & CO.

— C 20 Arms of Countries (70 x 52mm) c1915 (reprinted 2001) £7.50

JONES BROS., Tottenham

A BW 18 Spurs Footballers 1912 (reprinted 1986) £3.00

WM. S. KIMBALL & CO. (USA)

A1 C 50 Champions of Games & Sports c1890 (reprinted 2001) £10.00

KINNEAR LTD

D1 BW 15 Australian Cricketers 1897 (reprinted 2001) £4.00

KINNEY BROS. (USA)

A C 25 Famous English Running Horses 1889 (reprinted 1996) £6.25
A C 25 Leaders 1889 (reprinted 1990) £6.00

J. KNIGHT (HUSTLER SOAP)

A C 30 Regimental Nicknames 1924 (reprinted 1996) £6.25

B. KRIEGSFELD & CO.

A C 50 Phrases and Advertisements c1900 (reprinted 2001) £10.00

A. KUIT LTD

A U 25 Principal Streets of British Cities and Towns 1916 (reprinted 2001) £6.00

LACY'S CHEWING GUM

A BW 50 Footballers c1925 (reprinted 2001) £10.00

LAMBERT & BUTLER

A C 25 Aviation 1915 (reprinted 1997) £6.00
A C 25 Dance Band Leaders 1936 (reprinted 1992) £6.00
A C 50 Empire Air Routes 1936 (C.C.S. reprinted 2000) £10.00
A C 25 Hints and Tips for Motorists 1929 (reprinted 1994) £6.00
A C 50 Horsemanship 1938 (reprinted 1994) £8.50
A C 50 Interesting Sidelights On The Work of The GPO 1939 (C.C.S. reprinted 1999) £10.00
A C 20 International Yachts 1902 (reprinted 2001) £5.00
A C 25 London Characters 1934 (reprinted 1992) £6.00
A C 25 Motor Cars 1st series 1922 (reprinted 1988) £6.25
A C 25 Motor Cars 2nd series 1923 (reprinted 1988) £6.25
A C 25 Motor Cars 1934 (reprinted 1992) £6.25

LAMBERT & BUTLER (continued)

Size	Print	Number		Complete
A	C	50	Motor Cycles 1923 (reprinted 1990)	£8.50
A	C	25	Motors 1908 (reprinted 1992)	£6.00
A	C	25	Winter Sports 1914 (reprinted 1998)	£10.00
A	C	50	World's Locomotives 1912 (reprinted 1988)	£8.50

R. J. LEA LTD

A	C	50	Flowers to Grow 1913 (reprinted 1997)	£8.50

LEAF GUM CO. (USA)

—	BW	72	Star Trek (87 x 61mm) 1967 (reprinted 1981)	£12.50

J. LEES

A	C	20	Northampton Town Football Club c1912 (reprinted 2001)	£5.00

LIEBIG (France)

J2	C	6	Famous Explorers (F1088) 1914 (reprinted 2001)	£5.00

LUSBY LTD

D	C	25	Scenes From Circus Life c1900 (reprinted 2001)	£6.00

MARBURG BROS. (USA)

A	C	15	Beauties "PAC" c1890 (reprinted 2001)	£4.00

P.H. MAYO & BROTHER (USA)

C	U	35	Prizefighters c1890 (reprinted 2001)	£7.50

STEPHEN MITCHELL & SON

A	C	25	Angling 1928 (reprinted 1993)	£6.00
A	C	50	Famous Scots 1933 (C.C.S. reprinted 1999)	£10.00
A	C	50	A Gallery of 1935 (C.C.S. reprinted 1999)	£10.00
A	C	50	Humorous Drawings 1924 (C.C.S. reprinted 1999)	£10.00
A	C	25	Money 1913 (C.C.S. reprinted 2000)	£6.50
A	C	25	Regimental Crests, Nicknames and Collar Badges 1900 (reprinted 1993) ...	£6.50
A	C	50	Scotland's Story (C.C.S. reprinted 2000)	£10.00

MURRAY, SONS & CO. LTD

A	BW	20	Cricketers 1912 (reprinted 1991)	£7.50
A	C	20	War Series K — Uniforms 1915 (reprinted 2000)	£6.25
A	C	15	War Series K — World War I Leaders & Generals 1915 (reprinted 2000) ...	£12.50

NATIONAL CIGARETTE CO. (Australia)

A	BW	13	English Cricket Team 1897-8 (reprinted 2001)	£4.00

NATIONAL EXCHANGE BANK, USA

—	C	9	Seven Ages of Golf (85 x 57mm) c1885 (reprinted 1995)	£4.50

OGDENS LTD

A	C	50	A.F.C. Nicknames 1933 (reprinted 1996)	£8.50
A	C	50	Air Raid Precautions 1938 (C.C.S. reprinted 1999)	£10.00
A	C	50	British Birds 1905 (C.C.S. reprinted 2000)	£12.50
A	C	50	By The Roadside 1932 (C.C.S. reprinted 2000)	£10.00
A	C	50	Champions of 1936 (C.C.S. reprinted 2000)	£10.00
D2	U	50	Cricketers and Sportsmen c1898 (reprinted 2001)	£10.00

OGDENS LTD (continued)

A	C	50	Flags and Funnels of Leading Steamship Lines 1906 (reprinted 1997)	£8.50
A	C	50	Jockeys 1930 (reprinted 1990)	£15.00
A	C	50	Modern Railways 1936 (reprinted 1996)	£8.50
A	C	50	Motor Races 1931 (reprinted 1993)	£12.50
A	C	25	Poultry 1st Series 1915 (reprinted 1998)	£6.00
A	C	25	Poultry 2nd Series 1916 (reprinted 2000)	£10.00
A	C	50	Shakespeare Series 1903 (C.C.S. reprinted 2000)	£10.00
A	C	50	Smugglers & Smuggling 1931 (C.C.S. reprinted 1999)	£12.50
A	C	50	Soldiers of the King 1909 (reprinted 1993)	£8.50
A	C	50	The Story of the Life Boat c1950 (reprinted 1989)	£15.00
A	C	50	The Story of The Lifeboat c1950 (without "Ogdens") (reprinted 2001)	£8.50
A	C	50	Swimming, Diving and Life-Saving 1931 (C.C.S. reprinted 2000)	£10.00

OLD CALABAR BISCUIT CO. LTD

J2	C	16	Sports and Games c1900 (reprinted 2001)	£7.50

THE ORLANDO CIGARETTE & CIGAR CO.

A	C	40	Home & Colonial Regiments c1901 (reprinted 2001)	£8.50

PALMER MANN & CO (Sifta Sam)

A	C	25	Famous Cricketers (set 24 plus 1 variety) 1950 (reprinted 2001)	£6.00

J.A. PATTREIOUEX, Manchester

A	C	75	Cricketers Series 1926 (reprinted 1997)	£13.50

GODFREY PHILLIPS LTD

A	C	30	Beauties "Nymphs" c1896 (reprinted 2001)	£7.50
A	C	25	Railway Engines 1924 (reprinted 1997)	£12.50
A	C	20	Russo-Japanese War Series 1904 (reprinted 2001)	£5.00
A	C	25	Territorial Series 1908 (reprinted 2001)	£6.25
A	C	25	Types of British Soldiers 1900 (reprinted 1997)	£6.25

JOHN PLAYER & SONS

A	C	50	Aeroplanes (Civil) 1935 (reprinted 1990)	£8.50
A	C	50	Aircraft of The Royal Air Force 1938 (reprinted 1990)	£8.50
A	C	50	Animals of The Countryside 1939 (C.C.S. reprinted 1999)	£10.00
A	C	50	Aviary & Cage Birds 1933 (reprinted 1989)	£12.50
B	C	25	Aviary and Cage Birds 1935 (reprinted 1987)	£8.50
A	C	50	British Empire Series 1904 (C.C.S. reprinted 1999)	£10.00
A	C	50	Butterflies & Moths 1904 (C.C.S. reprinted 2000)	£12.50
B	C	24	Cats 1936 (reprinted 1986)	£8.50
A	C	25	Characters from Dickens 1912 (reprinted 1990)	£6.00
A	C	25	Characters from Dickens 2nd series 1914 (reprinted 1990)	£6.00
A	C	50	Cities of The World 1900 (C.C.S. reprinted 1999)	£10.00
B	C	25	Country Sports 1930 (reprinted 2000)	£8.50
A	C	50	Cricketers 1930 (reprinted 2000)	£8.50
A	C	50	Cricketers 1934 (reprinted 1990)	£8.50
A	C	50	Cricketers 1938 (C.C.S. reprinted 2000)	£10.00
A	C	50	Cricketers Caricatures by "Rip" 1926 (reprinted 1993)	£8.50
A	C	50	Derby and Grand National Winners 1933 (reprinted 1988)	£8.50
A	C	50	Dogs' Heads (silver-grey backgrounds) 1940 (reprinted 1994)	£8.50
A2	C	25	England's Naval Heroes 1898 descriptive (reprinted 1987)	£15.00
A	C	50	Film Stars 1st Series 1934 (C.C.S. reprinted 2000)	£10.00
A	C	50	Film Stars 3rd series 1938 (reprinted 1989)	£8.50
A	C	50	Fire-Fighting Appliances 1930 (reprinted 1991)	£8.50

JOHN PLAYER & SONS (continued)

Size	Printing	Number in set		Complete set
A	C	50	Game Birds and Wild Fowl 1927 (C.C.S. reprinted 1999)	£10.00
B	C	25	Game Birds and Wild Fowl 1928 (reprinted 1987)	£8.50
A	C	50	Gilbert & Sullivan 2nd series 1927 (reprinted 1990)	£8.50
B	C	25	Golf 1939 (reprinted 1986)	£8.50
A	C	25	Highland Clans 1908 (reprinted 1997)	£8.00
A	C	50	Kings & Queens 1935 (reprinted 1990)	£10.00
A	C	50	Military Head-Dress 1931 (C.C.S. reprinted 1999)	£10.00
A	C	50	Military Series 1900 (reprinted 1983)	£8.50
A	C	50	Motor Cars 1st series 1936 (reprinted 1990)	£8.50
A	C	50	Motor Cars 2nd series 1937 (C.C.S. reprinted 2000)	£10.00
A	C	25	Napoleon 1916 (reprinted 1989)	£6.00
A	C	50	Nature Series 1908 (C.C.S. reprinted 2000)	£10.00
A	C	50	Old England's Defenders 1898 (reprinted 1987)	£15.00
B	C	25	Old Hunting Prints 1938 (reprinted 1989)	£8.50
B	C	25	Old Naval Prints 1936 (reprinted 1989)	£8.50
B	C	25	Picturesque London 1931 (reprinted 1997)	£8.50
A	C	50	Poultry 1931 (reprinted 1993)	£8.50
A	C	50	Products of The World 1928 (C.C.S. reprinted 1999)	£10.00
B	C	25	Racing Yachts 1938 (reprinted 1987)	£8.50
A	C	50	Regimental Standards & Cap Badges 1930 (reprinted 1993)	£8.50
A	C	50	Regimental Uniforms Nd. 51-100 1914 (reprinted 1995)	£8.50
A	C	50	Speedway Riders 1937 (C.C.S. reprinted 2000)	£12.50
A	C	50	Tennis 1936 (C.C.S. reprinted 1999).	£10.00
B	C	24	Treasures of Britain 1931 (reprinted 1996)	£8.50
B	C	25	Types of Horses 1939 (reprinted 1998)	£8.50
A	C	50	Uniforms of the Territorial Army 1939 (reprinted 1990)	£8.50
B	C	25	Wild Birds 1934 (reprinted 1997)	£8.50

JOHN PLAYER & SONS (OVERSEAS)

A	C	50	Ships, Flags and Cap Badges 1930 (reprinted 1997)	£15.00

REEVES LTD

D	C	25	Cricketers 1912 (reprinted 1993)	£8.00

RICHMOND CAVENDISH CO. LTD

A	C	20	Yachts c1900 (reprinted 2001)	£5.00

E. ROBINSON & SONS LTD

A	C	6	Medals & Decorations of Great Britain c1905 (reprinted 2001)	£3.00
A2	C	25	Regimental Mascots 1916 (reprinted 2001)	£6.00

S.D.V. TOBACCO CO. LTD

A1	BW	16	British Royal Family c1901 (reprinted 2001)	£4.00

SALMON & GLUCKSTEIN LTD

A	C	15	Billiard Terms 1905 (reprinted 1997)	£5.00
A	C	25	Coronation Series 1911 (C.C.S. reprinted 2000)	£6.50
C2	C	30	Music Hall Celebrities c1902 (reprinted 2001)	£7.50

JOHN SINCLAIR LTD

A	C	50	British Sea Dogs 1926 (reprinted 1997)	£8.50

SINGLETON & COLE LTD

A	BW	35	Famous Boxers 1930 (reprinted 1992)	£6.25
D	BW	50	Footballers c1905 (reprinted 2001)	£10.00

F. & J. SMITH

Size	Print.	No.		Price
A	C	25	Advertisement Cards 1899 (reprinted 2001)	£6.00
D	BW	50	Champions of Sport (unnumbered) 1902 (reprinted 2001)	£10.00
A	C	25	Cinema Stars 1920 (reprinted 1987)	£6.50
A	C	50	Fowls, Pigeons and Dogs 1908 (C.C.S. reprinted 2000)	£10.00
A	C	25	Holiday Resorts 1925 (C.C.S. reprinted 2000)	£6.50
A	C	25	Prominent Rugby Players 1924 (reprinted 1992)	£8.00

SPIRO VALLERI & CO.

A1	U	10	Noted Footballers c1905 (reprinted 2001)	£3.00

SPRATTS PATENT LTD

C2	C	12	Prize Dogs c1910 (reprinted 2001)	£3.50

TADDY & CO.

Size	Print.	No.		Price
A	C	20	Clowns & Circus Artists 1920 (reprinted 1991)	£6.00
A	BW	238	County Cricketers 1907 (reprinted 1987)	£48.00
			Individual Counties of the above set:	
		15	Derbyshire	£3.00
		15	Essex	£3.00
		16	Gloucestershire	£3.00
		15	Hampshire	£3.00
		15	Kent	£3.00
		15	Lancashire	£3.00
		14	Leicestershire	£3.00
		15	Middlesex	£3.00
		15	Northamptonshire	£3.00
		14	Nottinghamshire	£3.00
		15	Somersetshire	£3.00
		15	Surrey	£3.00
		15	Sussex	£3.00
		15	Warwickshire	£3.00
		14	Worcestershire	£3.00
		15	Yorkshire	£3.00
A	U	5	English Royalty c1898 (reprinted 2001)	£3.00
A	C	25	Famous Jockeys 1910 (reprinted 1996)	£6.25
A	C	25	Natives of the World c1900 (reprinted 1999)	£6.00
A	BW	15	Prominent Footballers Aston Villa 1907 (reprinted 1992)	£3.00
A	BW	15	Prominent Footballers Chelsea 1907 (reprinted 1998)	£3.00
A	BW	15	Prominent Footballers Everton 1907 (reprinted 1998)	£3.00
A	BW	15	Prominent Footballers Leeds 1907 (reprinted 1992)	£3.00
A	BW	15	Prominent Footballers Liverpool 1907 (reprinted 1992)	£3.00
A	BW	15	Prominent Footballers Manchester Utd 1907 (reprinted 1992)	£3.00
A	BW	15	Prominent Footballers Middlesbrough 1907 (reprinted 1998)	£3.00
A	BW	15	Prominent Footballers Newcastle Utd 1907 (reprinted 1992)	£3.00
A	BW	15	Prominent Footballers Queens Park Rangers 1907 (reprinted 1992)	£6.00
A	BW	15	Prominent Footballers Sunderland 1907 (reprinted 1998)	£3.00
A	BW	15	Prominent Footballers Tottenham Hotspur 1907 (reprinted 1998)	£3.00
A	BW	15	Prominent Footballers West Ham Utd 1907 (reprinted 1998)	£3.00
A	BW	15	Prominent Footballers Woolwich Arsenal 1907 (reprinted 1992)	£3.00
A2	C	20	Royalty, Actresses, Soldiers c1898 (reprinted 2001)	£5.00
A	C	25	Royalty Series 1908 (reprinted 1998)	£6.25
A	BW	15	South African Cricket Team 1907 (reprinted 1992)	£7.50
A	C	25	Territorial Regiments 1908 (reprinted 1996)	£6.25
A	C	25	Thames Series 1903 (reprinted 1996)	£6.25
A	C	20	Victoria Cross Heroes (Nos 1-20) 1900 (reprinted 1996)	£8.00
A	C	20	Victoria Cross Heroes (Nos 21-40) 1900 (reprinted 1996)	£6.25

TADDY & CO. (continued)

Size	Printing	Number in set		Complete set
A	C	20	VC Heroes — Boer War (Nos 41-60) 1901 (reprinted 1997)	£6.25
A	C	20	VC Heroes — Boer War (Nos 61-80) 1901 (reprinted 1997)	£6.25
A	C	20	VC Heroes — Boer War (Nos 81-100) 1902 (reprinted 1997)	£6.25
A	C	25	Victoria Cross Heroes (Nos 101-125) 1905 (reprinted 1996)	£6.25

TEOFANI & CO. LTD

A	C	24	Past and Present The Army 1938 (reprinted 2001)	£6.25
A	C	24	Past and Present Weapons of War 1938 (reprinted 2001)	£6.25

D. C. THOMSON

A	C	24	Motor Bike Cards 1929 (reprinted 1993)	£6.00
A	C	20	Motor Cycles 1923 (Wizard Series) (reprinted 1993)	£6.00

TOPPS CHEWING GUM INC. (USA)

—	C	56	Mars Attacks (90 x 64mm) 1962 (reprinted 1987)	£12.50
—	C	51	Outer Limits (90 x 64mm) 1964 (reprinted 1995)	£12.50

UNION JACK

—	C	8	Police of All Nations (70 x 45mm) 1922 (reprinted 2005)	£4.00

UNITED TOBACCONISTS' ASSOCIATION LTD

A	C	10	Actresses "MUTA" c1900 (reprinted 2001)	£3.00

HENRY WELFARE & CO.

D	BW	22	Prominent Politicians c1911 (reprinted 2001)	£6.00

W.D. & H.O. WILLS

—	C	4	Advert Postcards of Packings (140 x 90mm) 1902 (reprinted 1988)	£5.00
A	C	50	Allied Army Leaders 1917 (C.C.S reprinted 2000)	£10.00
A	C	50	Arms of Companies 1913 (C.C.S reprinted 1999).	£10.00
A	C	50	Builders of The Empire 1898 (C.C.S. reprinted 1999)	£12.50
B	C	7	Cathedrals 1933 (from set of 25) (reprinted 2000)	£2.50
A	C	50	Cricketers 1896 (reprinted 1982)	£8.50
A	C	50	Cricketers 1901 (reprinted 1983)	£15.00
B	C	25	Dogs 1914 (reprinted 1987)	£8.50
A	C	50	Double Meaning 1898 (C.C.S. reprinted 1999)	£10.00
A	C	50	Engineering Wonders 1927 (C.C.S. reprinted 1999)	£10.00
B	C	25	Famous Golfers 1930 (reprinted 1987)	£8.50
A	C	50	Fish & Bait 1910 (reprinted 1990)	£8.50
A	C	50	Flower Culture In Pots 1925 (C.C.S. reprinted 2000)	£10.00
A	C	50	Household Hints 1st Series 1927 (C.C.S. reprinted 1999)	£10.00
B	C	25	Lawn Tennis 1931 (reprinted 1988)	£8.50
A	C	50	Life in the Hedgerow 1950 (reprinted 1991, Swan Vestas)	£12.50
A	C	50	Life In The Royal Navy 1939 (C.C.S. reprinted 1999)	£10.00
A	C	50	Military Aircraft (unissued c1967) (reprinted 1991)	£8.50
A	C	50	Military Motors 1916 (reprinted 1994)	£8.50
A	C	58	Musical Celebrities 2nd series including 8 substituted cards 1914 (reprinted 1987)	£9.50
A	C	25	National Costumes c1895 (reprinted 1999)	£6.00
A	C	50	Naval Dress & Badges 1909 (reprinted 1997)	£8.50
A	C	25	Naval Dress & Badges 1909 (Nos. 1 to 25 Naval Dress only reprinted) Inscribed 'Commissioned by Sydney Cigarette Card Company, Australia' (reprinted 1993)	£6.25
A	C	50	Old English Garden Flowers 2nd Series 1913 (reprinted 1994)	£8.50
B	C	40	Puppies by Lucy Dawson (unissued) (reprinted 1990)	£12.50

W.D. & H.O. WILLS (continued)

A	C	50	Railway Engines 1924 (reprinted 1995)	£8.50
A	C	50	Railway Engines 1936 (reprinted 1992)	£8.50
A	C	50	Railway Equipment 1939 (reprinted 1993)	£8.50
A	C	50	Railway Locomotives 1930 (reprinted 1993)	£8.50
A	C	12	Recruiting Posters 1915 (reprinted 1987)	£3.00
B	C	25	Rigs of Ships 1929 (reprinted 1987)	£8.50
A	C	50	Roses 1st series 1912 (reprinted 1994)	£8.50
A	C	50	Rugby Internationals 1929 (reprinted 1996)	£8.50
A	C	50	School Arms 1906 (C.C.S. reprinted 2000)	£10.00
A	C	50	Ships Badges 1925 (C.C.S. reprinted 2000)	£10.00
A	C	50	Waterloo 1915 (reprinted 1987)	£20.00
A	C	50	Wild Flowers 1923 (C.C.S. reprinted 1999)	£10.00
A	C	50	Wild Flowers 1st series 1936 (reprinted 1993)	£15.00
A	C	50	Wonders of The Sea 1928 (C.C.S. reprinted 2000)	£10.00
A	C	25	World's Dreadnoughts 1910 (reprinted 1994)	£6.00

W.D. & H.O. WILLS (Australia)

A	C	50	Types of the British Army 1912 (reprinted 1995)	£8.50
A	C	50	War Incidents 2nd Series 1917 (reprinted 1995)	£8.50

W.H. & J. WOODS LTD

A	C	25	Types of Volunteers & Yeomanry 1902 (reprinted 1996)	£8.50

ILLUSTRATIONS OF CIGARETTE CARDS

1   Carreras Vintage Cars
2   Cope Wild Animals & Birds
3   Carreras Sport Fish
4   Wills Dogs
5   Pattreiouex British Railways
6   Dobie Four-Square Book (Nd 65- 96)
7   American Tob. Co. Cowboy Series
8   Ching Jersey Past & Present 2nd Series
9   Carreras History of Naval Uniforms
10 Players Football Caricatures by 'Mac'
11 Drapkin Australian & English Test Cricketers
12 Players Cries of London 2nd Series
13 Carreras British Birds
14 Players Butterflies & Moths
15 Rothman's Punch Jokes
16 Players Drum Banners & Cap Badges
17 Carreras Military Uniforms
18 Ogdens Fowls, Pigeons & Dogs
19 Cope V.C. & D.S.O. Naval & Flying Heroes
20 Murray Bathing Belles
21 Wills Rugby Internationals
22 Churchman In Town Tonight
23 Wills Coronation Series 1902
24 Pattreiouex Sporting Celebrities
25 National Cig. & Tob. Co. National Types
26 Gallaher The Allies Flags
27 Salmon & Gluckstein Coronation Series 1911
28 Wills Musical Celebrities 2nd Series
29 Duncan Scottish Gems 4th Series
30 Wills Merchant Ships of the World
31 Ardath Photocards Group B Coronation and Sports
32 Sniders & Abrahams Animals & Birds
33 Gallaher The Great War 1st Series
34 Abdulla Cinema Stars Set 4
35 Wills Overseas Lighthouses
36 Ogdens Club Badges
37 Sandorides Cinema Celebritioo
38 Lambert & Butler Birds & Eggs
39 Gallaher Famous Footballers (green back)
40 United Tob. Co. South Africa Boy Scout, Girl Guide & Voortrekker Badges
41 Churchman Eastern Proverbs 1st Series
42 United Tob. Co. South Africa Our South African National Parks
43 G. Phillips Beauties of Today 2nd Series

44 Players Kings & Queens of England
45 Gallaher British Birds
46 Churchman Frisky
47 Hill Famous Ships
48 Lambert & Butler Motor Cars 1934
49 Taddy Railway Locomotives
50 R.J. Lea (Silks) Butterflies & Moths
51 Wills Garden Flowers New Varieties 2nd Series
52 G. Phillips (Silks) Old Masters Set 6
53 United Tob. Co. South Africa Ships of All Times
54 Wills Football Series 1902
55 R.J. Lea Old Pottery & Porcelain 4th Series
56 British American Tobacco Modern Beauties 2nd Series
57 F. & J. Smith Footballers 1914
58 Players Uniforms of the Territorial Army
59 Lambert & Butler Winter Sports
60 Wills Pond & Aquarium 2nd Series
61 Ogdens A.F.C. Nicknames
62 Players Useful Plants & Fruits
63 Robinson Wild Flowers
64 Charlesworth & Austin British Royal Family
65 Players Film Stars 3rd Series
66 Wills Donington Collection
67 Lambert & Butler Jockeys
68 Salmon & Gluckstein The Great White City
69 Morris Measurement of Time
70 Lambert & Butler Condundrums (green back)
71 Wills Garden Hints
72 Wills Overseas Chateaux
73 Brown & Williamson Modern American Airplanes Series A
74 Wills Butterflies & Moths
75 Hill Views of Interest 1st Series
76 Taddy Motor Cars
77 Players British Naval Craft
78 Wills World of Firearms
79 Wills World of Speed
80 Wills Kings & Queens 1902
81 F. & J. Smith Champions of Sport (red back)
82 Wills Speed 1938
83 Colombos Life of Nelson
84 Players Golden Age of Steam
85 Carreras Flags of All Nations

ILLUSTRATIONS OF TRADE CARDS

1

2

3

4

5

6

7

8

9

PLAYER'S CIGARETTES

ALBERT MC INROY

10

11

PLAYER'S CIGARETTES

SMALL COALE.

12

13

PLAYER'S CIGARETTES

14

15

16

17

CARRIER.

OGDEN'S CIGARETTES

18

COPE'S

Captain E. H. Edwards, R.N., D.S.O.

CIGARETTES

19

Maxine Jennings

20

WILLS'S CIGARETTES.

TOM ARTHUR

21

CHURCHMAN'S CIGARETTES

HAROLD DAVY

22

WILLS'S Cigarettes.

PRINCE CHARLES OF DENMARK.

CORONATION SER. N° 35.

23

FOOTBALL - T. BRADSHAW, LIVERPOOL.

24

AMERICAN ADMIRAL

25

SCOTLAND.

GALLAHER'S CIGARETTES.

26

SALMON & GLUCKSTEIN'S CIGARETTES

THE SWORD OF STATE

CORONATION 1911.

27

WILLS'S CIGARETTES

L. GODOWSKI

28

SCOTTISH GEMS

SCOTT MONUMENT, EDINBURGH

29

WILLS'S CIGARETTES.

S.S. EMPRESS OF CANADA

30

EPSOM 1937
THEIR MAJESTIES THE KING AND QUEEN.

31

BLACK SWAN.

32

Gallaher's Cigarettes.

MILITARY HAND GRENADE.

33

MARLENE DIETRICH

34

LONGSHIPS LIGHTHOUSE.
LANDS END

35

OGDEN'S CIGARETTES.

LONDON ATHLETIC CLUB.

36

66 'Lucana' 66
CIGARETTES

PEGGY HYLAND.

37

Sparrow
Hawk.

38

FRED REED
WEST BROM. ALBION

39

SCOUT BADGES
FOR SCOUTS

BOY
SCOUTS

HEALTHYMAN

40

The reply to a Turkish question
should be in Turkish.

41

42

CONSTANCE BENGEN

43

PLAYER'S CIGARETTES

EDWARD VII

44

GREEN WOODPECKER

45

25   FOXY SLY

CHURCHMAN'S CIGARETTES

46

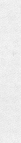

QUEEN MARY

47

LAMBERT & BUTLER'S CIGARETTES

FORD 8 H.P. SALOON

48

Taddy & C⁰ Cigarettes Railway Locomotives

TURBINE-DRIVEN LOCOMOTIVE, L.M.S.R. N° 21

49

50

WILLS'S CIGARETTES

SUNFLOWER   Variety: PRIMROSE DAME

51

Rembrandt

The Young Jewess
B.D.V. CIGARETTES

52

SLAVE DHOW

53

Football Series No. 21.

M. Sanders, Barrow-in-Furness.
Photo by Thiele, London

54

OLD POTTERY AND
PORCELAIN.
(ENGLISH.)

FELL. SEWELL & DONKIN.
Sheriff Hill Pottery,
No. 155. NEWCASTLE.

55

EDIE ADAMS

56

J. BLAIR
CLYDE F.C.

57

PLAYER'S CIGARETTES

1ST/4TH BN, THE KING'S OWN
(ROYAL LANCASTER REGT.) 1915

58

LAMBERT & BUTLER'S
CIGARETTES.

SKATE SAILING.

59

WILLS'S CIGARETTES

CARDAMINE

60

OGDEN'S CIGARETTES

LIVERPOOL

61

PLAYER'S CIGARETTES.

BRAZIL NUT

62

63

QUEEN VICTORIA
ON HER CORONATION, AGE 19.

64

PLAYER'S CIGARETTES

Errol Flynn

ERROL FLYNN

65

CASTELLA CIGARS

McLaren M23

66

F. RICKABY

67

THE BRITISH TEXTILES BUILDING

68

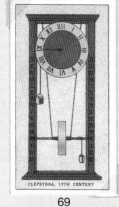

CLEPSYDRA, 17TH CENTURY

69

What is the difference between

A Honeycomb

and A Honeymoon?

70

WILLS'S CIGARETTES

DIVIDING AND REPLANTING RHUBARB

71

CHATEAU DE COMBOURG

72

AERONCA MODEL LA

73

WILLS'S CIGARETTES

CLOUDED YELLOW BUTTERFLY

74

FORD 'POPULAR' SALOON   TADDY & Cº CIGARETTES   Nº 10

76

PLAYER'S CIGARETTES

H. M. S. "REVENGE"

77

Seven-barrelled Volley Gun

78

Mallard

79

ATHELSTAN. 925-940.

80

BARRY

81

WILLS'S CIGARETTES

"PRINCESS ELIZABETH", L.M.S.R.

82

LORD HOTHAM'S ACTION, 1795

No. 13

Combos' Aristocratic Cigarettes

83

84

UNITED STATES OF AMERICA

85

86

87

88

89

90

104. 7th (Princess Royal's)
Dragoon Guards.

91

26. Fight Back

92

93

94

95

96

97

THE DALEKS

98

99

100

101

102

103

104

105

106

COLLECTORS' MINIATURES

DEUTSCHE REICHSBAHN. CLASS 05 EXPRESS LOCOMOTIVE NO. 05003 BUILT 1937

107

COUNTY OF MERIONETH No. 1019

108

109

110

POPEYE

ARF! LEGS LIKE HIS'N IS FEW AN'FAR BETWEEN!

112

113

111

114

Wall's

115

ROYAL NORFOLK REGIMENT
(9th)

116

117

118

119

ALBION REIVER

120

HOBBY

121

PAULETTE GODDARD

122

123

124

125

126

REJUVENATE
15

127

WARRIOR MONKS

128

H.M. QUEEN MARY

129

RALEIGH CANADIAN MODEL 99

130

131

Trees of the Countryside

Ty.phoo Series of 25   No. 22
SYCAMORE   ORDER
Acer Pseudo-   Aceraceae
platanus

Average height .... 60 feet.
Trunk upright. Bark ashy-grey,
smooth, scaling; fissuring later.

Leaves, green above,
grayish below, have
five pointed lobes.

Fruit.   Flowers,
                          pendent.

132

OTHELLO   Othello

Characters from Shakespeare.

Covered with honour gained in battle
against the foes of Venice, Othello the
Moor married the fair Desdemona. She
loved her husband passionately but
Iago, former Lieutenant to the Moor,
caused unfounded suspicion to fall
upon her. In a fit of jealousy Othello
smothered Desdemona, subsequently
learning her innocence, he put an end
to his own life.

Ty-phoo Series of 25   No. 24

133

134

POINTER

135

LIVERPOOL LEGENDS
FIFTEEN OF THEIR GREATEST STARS

BOB PAISLEY
MANAGER 1974-1983

136

SCORE

MARTIN DOBSON
Everton

137

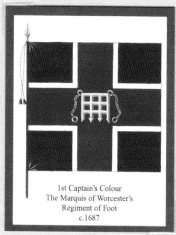

1st Captain's Colour
The Marquis of Worcester's
Regiment of Foot
c.1687

138

STAR TREK
VOYAGER
CLOSER TO HOME

LIVING WITNESS

139

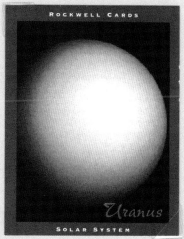

ROCKWELL CARDS

Uranus

SOLAR SYSTEM

140

141

142

143

144

145

146

147

148

SECTION 4
TRADE CARD ISSUES

Size & quantity		Date	Handbook reference	Price per card	Complete set
	TRADE CARD ISSUES				
	A-1 DAIRIES LTD				
25	Birds and Their Eggs	1964	HX-1	£1.60	£40.00
25	Butterflies and Moths	1965	HX-2	28p	£7.00
25	The Story of Milk	1967	HX-3	£1.00	—
	A-1 DOLLISDALE TEA				
25	Do You Know about Shipping and Trees?	1962	HX-4	20p	£2.50
	AAA SPORTS (USA)				
LT100	Decision 92 (United States Presidential Election)	1992		—	£8.00
	ABC (Cinema)				
10	An Adventure in Space (Set 3)	1950		£3.50	—
10	Animals (Set 5)	1952		£2.00	—
10	Birds (Set 19)	1958		£1.20	—
10	Birds and Bird Watching (Set 7)	1953		£3.00	—
10	British Athletes (Set 11)...	1955		£2.00	£20.00
20	British Soldiers:				
	A Brown Back				
	i 17 different (minus numbers 14, 15 and 18)	1950		50p	£8.50
	ii Numbers 14, 15 and 18	1950		£3.00	—
	B Black Back				
	i 19 different (minus number 5)	1950		£1.00	£19.00
	ii Number 5	1950		£6.00	—
10	Colorstars 1st Series	1961		75p	£7.50
10	Colorstars 2nd Series	1962		£4.00	—
10	Colorstars 3rd Series	1962		£2.50	—
10	Dogs (Set 17)	1957		£2.50	£25.00
10	Film Stars (Set 1)...	1950		£3.00	—
10	Horses (Set 21)	1959		£2.00	—
10	Interesting Buildings (Set 10)...	1955		80p	£8.00
10	Journey by Land (Set 8)	1954		£2.75	—
10	Journey by Water (Set 9)	1954		£2.75	—
10	Journey to the Moon (Set 12)	1956		£2.75	—
10	Parliament Buildings (Set 18)...	1958		£1.00	£10.00
10	Railway Engines (Set 4)	1951		£5.00	—
10	Scenes from the Films (Set 6)	1953		£5.00	—
10	Sea Exploration (Set 16)	1958		£1.25	£12.50
10	Sea Scenes (Set 20)	1958		80p	£8.00
10	Sports on Land (Set 15)	1956		80p	£8.00
10	Travel of the Future (Set 14)	1957		£1.00	£10.00
10	Water Sports (Set 13)	1957		£1.00	£10.00

ABC (Monogram)

L16	Film Stars		1935	HX-43	£5.00	—
12	Star Series (Film Stars)...		1936		£5.00	—

A & BC

(AMERICAN & BRITISH CHEWING GUM LTD)

(44-page Illustrated Reference Book, revised 2004 edition — £4.50)

M120	All Sports		1954		£5.00	—
EL17	Banknotes		1971	HA-1	£4.00	—
L55	Batman (pink back):					
	A With 'Batman Fan Club'		1966		£2.60	—
	B Without 'Batman Fan Club'		1966		£1.80	£100.00
L55	Batman (number on front)		1966		£2.75	—
L44	Batman (Nd 1A to 44A)...		1966		£3.50	—
L44	Batman (Nd 1B to 44B)...		1966		£5.00	—
L38	Batman (black back):					
	A English text		1966		£4.50	—
	B Dutch text		1966		£6.00	—
M1	Batman Secret Decoder (for Series of 38) (3 lines of code)		1966		—	£15.00
	Battle:					
L73	A Complete set		1966		—	£140.00
L69/73	B (Minus Nos 32, 39, 42, 44)		1966		£1.60	£110.00
LT66	Battle of Britain		1970		£1.60	—
LT60	Bazooka Joe and His Gang		1968		£4.50	—
L60	Beatles (black and white)		1964		£5.00	—
L45	Beatles (black and white) 2nd Series		1965		£8.00	—
L40	Beatles (coloured)		1965		£12.00	—
K114	Car Stamps (Set of 21 sheets each holding 5 or 6 stamps with 21 albums, price per sheet and album)		1971	HA-2	£7.00	—
L45	The Champions (TV Series)		1969		£4.00	—
M1	The Champions Secret Decoder (4 lines of code)		1969		—	£20.00
M56	Christian Name Stickers		1967	HA-7	£3.50	—
EL15	Civil War Banknotes		1965	HA-4	£3.80	—
L88	Civil War News		1965		£3.80	—
EL43	Comic Book Foldees		1968		£2.50	—
EL24	Crazy Disguises		1970		£9.00	—
L66	Creature Feature (pink backs)		1974		£1.50	£100.00
L48	Cricketers		1959		£2.50	—
L48	Cricketers 1961 Test Series:					
	A Size 90 × 64mm		1961		£3.20	—
	B Size 94 × 68mm		1961		£3.20	—
L66	Elvis Presley Series		1959		£15.00	—
L36	Exploits of William Tell		1960		£2.75	—
M22	Famous Indian Chiefs		1968		£6.00	—
EL54	Fantastic Twisters		1972		£6.50	—
M48	Film and TV Stars 1st Series		1953		£3.80	—
M48	Film and TV Stars 2nd Series		1953		£3.80	—
M48	Film and TV Stars 3rd Series...		1954		£3.80	—
L48	Film Stars:			HX-30.1		
	A Set of 48 (grey back)		1955		£3.00	—
	B Set of 48 (white back)		1955		£3.20	—
	C Set of 24 (white back with stand)		1955		£3.20	—
40	Flag Stickers		1966		£5.50	—
L73	Flags		1971	HA-8	£1.10	—

A & BC (continued)

Size & quantity		Date	Handbook reference	Price per card	Complete set
L80	Flags of the World:				
	A Size 95 × 67mm	1959		£1.50	£120.00
	B Size 82 × 57mm	1963		£1.50	£120.00
L46	Footballers 1st Series:				
	A Front without 'Planet Ltd'	1958		£3.40	—
	B Front inscribed 'Planet Ltd'	1958		£3.20	—
L46	Footballers 2nd Series:				
	A Front without 'Planet Ltd'	1958		£9.00	—
	B Front with 'Planet Ltd'	1958		£6.50	—
L49	Footballers (in Action) 1st Series (red)	1959		£4.00	—
L49	Footballers (in Action) 2nd Series (red)	1959		£7.00	—
LT42	Football 1st Series (black)	1960		£4.00	—
LT42	Football 2nd Series (black)	1960		£7.00	—
LT64	Footballers	1961		£6.00	—
LT44	Footballers — Scottish	1961		£13.00	—
L82	Footballers (Bazooka)	1962		£8.00	—
L55	Footballers 1st Series (blue)	1963		£5.00	—
L55	Footballers 2nd Series (blue)	1963		£5.00	—
L81	Footballers — Scottish (green)	1963		£13.00	—
L58	Footballers 1st Series (red)	1964		£4.00	—
L45	Footballers 2nd Series (red)	1964		£10.00	—
L46	Footballers 3rd Series (red)	1964		£12.00	—
L81	Footballers — Scottish (green)	1964		£12.00	—
M110	Footballers (black and white, issued in pairs) 1st Series	1966	HA-12.1	£5.00	—
M110	Footballers (black and white, issued in pairs) 2nd Series	1966	HA-12.2	£7.50	—
M54	Footballers — Scottish (coloured, Nos 1 to 42, issued in pairs)	1966	HA-12.3	£12.00	—
L55	Football Star Players	1967		£4.00	—
EL12	Footballers (Posters)	1967	HA-13	£8.50	—
L54	Footballers 1st Series (yellow)	1968	HA-14	£4.50	—
L47	Footballers 2nd Series (yellow)	1968		£4.00	—
L45	Footballers — Scottish (yellow)	1968		£9.00	—
EL26	Football Team Pennants — English	1968	HA-11	£8.00	—
M20	Football Team Emblems	1968	HA-10	£8.00	—
L65	Footballers 1st Series (green)	1969		£2.25	—
L54	Footballers 2nd Series (green)	1969		£2.25	£125.00
L55	Footballers 3rd Series (green)	1969		£2.25	£125.00
MP36	Footballers	1969	HA-15.1	£3.00	—
L42	Footballers — Scottish 1st Series (blue)	1969		£8.00	—
L35	Footballers — Scottish 2nd Series (blue)	1969		£9.00	—
MP15	Football Photos — Scottish	1969	HA-15.2	£6.00	—
LT84	Footballers 1st Series (orange)	1970		£1.20	£100.00
LT85	Footballers 2nd Series (orange)	1970		£1.00	£85.00
LT86	Footballers 3rd Series (orange)	1970		£4.50	—
EL14	Footballers Pin Ups	1970	HA-17.1	£7.00	—
M72	Football Colour Transparencies	1970	HA-16	£7.50	—
LT85	Footballers — Scottish 1st Series (green)	1970		£4.50	—
LT86	Footballers — Scottish 2nd Series (green)	1970		£4.50	—
EL28	Footballers Pin Ups — Scottish	1970	HA-17.2	£9.00	—
L109	Footballers 1st Series (purple)	1971	HA-18	£2.75	—
L110	Footballers 2nd Series (purple)	1971	HA-18	£2.75	—
L71	Footballers 3rd Series (purple)	1971		£5.50	—
M23	Football Club Crests	1971	HA-9A	£2.50	—
M23	Football Superstars	1971	HA-19	£8.00	—
L73	Footballers — Scottish 1st Series (purple)	1971		70p	£50.00
L71	Footballers — Scottish 2nd Series (purple)	1971		£7.00	—

Size &
quantity
TRADE CARD ISSUES
Date
Handbook
reference
Price
per card
Complete
set

A & BC (continued)

		Date	Handbook reference	Price per card	Complete set
M16	Football Club Crests — Scottish...	1971	HA-9B	£3.00	£50.00
L109	Footballers 1st Series (orange/red)...	1972	HA-20	£3.20	£350.00
L110	Footballers 2nd Series (orange/red)	1972	HA-20	£4.00	£440.00
M22	Football Card Game...	1972		£1.50	—
L89	Footballers — Scottish 1st Series (blue)	1972		£5.50	£490.00
L88	Footballers — Scottish 2nd Series (orange/red) (No. 164 not issued)	1972		£7.00	—
L131	Footballers 1st Series (blue)	1973		£4.50	—
L130	Footballers 2nd Series (blue) (Nos 235 and 262 not issued)	1973		£4.50	—
M32	Football Photos	1973		£3.50	—
EL16	Football Giant Team Posters	1973		£10.00	—
L90	Footballers — Scottish 1st Series (red)	1973		£5.50	—
L88	Footballers — Scottish 2nd Series (red)	1973		£5.50	—
L132	Footballers (red)	1974		£2.00	£265.00
L132	Footballers — Scottish (green)	1974		£4.00	—
L40	Fotostars	1961	HA-21	£4.00	—
LT66	Funny Greetings	1961		£1.50	—
LT66	Funny Valentines	1961		£4.00	—
L25	Girl from Uncle	1967	HA-22	£3.60	—
	Golden Boys:		HA-23		
L36	A Size 96 × 67mm	1960		£5.00	—
LT40	B Size 89 × 64mm	1960		£6.00	—
M27	Grand Prix (sectional)	1970	HA-24	40p	£10.00
L36	The High Chaparral	1969		£2.75	£100.00
L55	Huck Finn:				
	A Inscribed 'Hanna-Barbera Production Inc.'	1968		£3.00	£165.00
	B Inscribed ILAMI 1968'	1968		£3.00	—
L60	Kung Fu	1974		£2.20	—
L55	Land of the Giants	1969		£5.00	—
L54	The Legend of Custer	1968		£3.00	—
L55	Lotsa Laffs (various back colours, not purple)	1970	HA-25	£3.00	—
L84	Love Initials...	1970	HA-26	£2.00	—
L36	Magic	1967		£4.00	£145.00
L55	Man from UNCLE...	1965		£1.50	£90.00
	Man on the Moon:		HA-27		
LT55	Space Ship Back	1970		£3.50	—
LT19	Text Back	1970		£3.50	—
L52	Mickey Takers	1970	HA-28	£4.50	—
M24	Military Emblem Stickers	1966	HA-29	£4.50	—
L55	Monkees (black and white)	1967		£1.60	£90.00
L55	Monkees (coloured)	1967		£3.00	—
L30	Monkees Hit Songs	1967		£4.00	—
EL16	Monster Tattoos	1970		£5.00	—
EL16	Olympic Posters	1972		£4.00	—
L36	Olympics...	1972		£4.50	—
L55	Partridge Family	1972		£2.40	—
L120	Planes:				
	A Size 94 × 67mm	1958		£2.50	—
	B Size 88 × 64mm	1958		£2.50	—
L44	Planet of the Apes	1968		£5.50	—
L33	Put-on Stickers	1969	HA-32	£3.00	—
LT48	Railway Quiz	1958		£1.30	£65.00
L72	Railway Quiz	1959		£2.75	—
L40	The Rolling Stones	1965		£12.00	—
M24	Royal Portraits...	1953		£3.00	£75.00
L25	Sir Francis Drake	1961		£5.00	—

A & BC (continued)

LT88	Space Cards	1958		£5.50	—
L44	Stacks of Stickers	1971	HA-34	£4.50	—
L55	Star Trek	1969		£9.00	—
L66	Superman in the Jungle	1968		£2.50	—
L16	Superman in the Jungle (jig-saw)	1968		£4.00	—
L50	Top Stars	1964		£4.00	—
L40	Top Stars	1964		£5.50	—
EL15	TV Cartoon Tattoos	1972		£9.00	—
L44	Ugly Stickers	1967		£3.00	—
EL88	Wacky Plaks	1965		£3.00	—
EL15	Walt Disney Characters Tattoos	1973		£11.00	—
EL16	Wanted Posters	1968	HA-39	£6.00	—
L56	Western Series	1959	HA-36	£3.25	—
LT70	Who-Z-At Star?	1961		£3.25	—
L55	Winston Churchill	1965		75p	£40.00
L37	World Cup Footballers	1970	HA-41	£6.50	—
EL16	World Cup Posters	1970		£7.00	—
L48	You'll Die Laughing (purple backs)	1967	HA-25	£2.00	—

AMA GROUP (USA)

LT60	Desert Storm Operation Yellow Ribbon	1991	—	£9.50

A & P PUBLICATIONS

24	Post-war British Classic Cars	1992	20p	£4.50

A.W. SPORTS (USA)

LT100	All World Racing (Motor Racing)	1991	—	£9.50
LT100	All World Racing (Motor Racing)	1992	—	£9.50

ABBEY GRANGE HOTEL

15	Fighting Vessels	1986	—	£6.00

ACTION STARS

20	Action Stars (1950s Footballers) 1st Series	2010	—	£7.50
20	Action Stars (1950s Footballers) 2nd Series	2010	—	£7.50
20	Action Stars (1950s Footballers) 3rd Series	2011	—	£7.50

P.A. ADOLPH (Subbuteo Table Soccer)

24	Famous Footballers 1st Series of 24	1954	£1.00	£25.00
24	Famous Footballers 2nd Series of 24	1954	£1.00	£25.00
50	Famous Footballers 'A Series of 50'	1954	£16.00	—

AHC (Ace High Confectionery)

25	Wonders of the Universe	1955	HX-14	70p	£17.50

ALICE'S ATTIC

EL16	Fry's Chocolate Advertising Postcards from the Early 1900s	2012	—	£10.00

ALL INC.

L20	Actors (and Actresses) (Caricatures by Bob Hoare)	2003	50p	£10.00
L25	Films (Caricatures by Bob Hoare)	2003	50p	£12.50
L20	Musicians (Caricatures by Bob Hoare)	2003	50p	£10.00
L30	Politicians (Caricatures by Bob Hoare)	2003	50p	£15.00
L13	Sports (Caricatures by Bob Hoare)	2003	50p	£7.00

ALL SPORTS INC. (USA)

LT100	Exotic Dreams — Cars	1992		—	£9.50

A.W. ALLEN LTD (Australia)

32	Bradman's Records	1931		£40.00	—
72	Butterflies and Moths	c1920		£2.20	—
36	Cricketers (brown fronts)	1932		£15.00	—
36	Cricketers (dark brown fronts)	1933		£15.00	—
36	Cricketers (flesh tinted, frameline back)	1934		£12.00	—
36	Cricketers (flesh tinted, no frameline back)	1936		£12.00	—
36	Cricketers (coloured)	1938		£12.00	—
144	Footballers (striped background)	1933		£7.00	—
72	Footballers (Club flag)	1934		£7.00	—
48	Footballers (players in action)	1939		£11.00	—
49	Kings and Queens of England	1937/53		£1.80	—
36	Medals	1938		£3.00	—
36	Royalty Series	1937		£5.00	—
36	Soldiers of The Empire	1938		£3.00	—
36	Sports and Flags of Nations	1936		£3.50	—

J. ALLEN SPORTS

25	Sportsmen	1997		—	£9.50

ALMA CONFECTIONERY

48	James Bond 007 Moonraker	1980		£4.50	—

JAMES ALMOND

25	Sports and Pastimes	c1925	HX-225	£10.00	—

AMABILINO PHOTOGRAPHIC

M30	Display Fireworks.......................................	1988		—	£7.00

AMALGAMATED PRESS LTD

24	Aeroplanes (plain back)	c1930	HA-56	£4.00	—
M12	Catchy Tricks and Teasers	1933	HA-58	£5.00	—
M22	English League (Div. 1) Footer Captains	1926		£4.50	—
M16	Exploits of the Great War	1929		£3.00	—
16	Famous Aircraft	1927		£4.00	—
M24	Famous Footer Internationals	1926		£5.00	—
M22	Famous Shipping Lines...............................	1926		£6.00	—
M32	Famous Test Match Cricketers	1926		£6.50	—
24	Famous Trains & Engines	c1930	HA-62	£4.00	—
M16	Great War Deeds.......................................	1927		£3.50	—
M32	Great War Deeds.......................................	1928		£3.50	—
M24	The Great War — 1914-1918........................	1928		£3.50	—
M16	The Great War — 1914-1918 — New Series	1929		£3.50	—
M16	Heroic Deeds of the Great War	1927		£3.50	—
32	Makes of Motor Cars and Index Marks	1923		£3.00	—
24	Motors (plain black)	c1930	HA-65	£4.00	—
M16	RAF at War (plain black)	1940	HA-66	£5.50	—
24	Ships of the World	1924		£3.00	—
33	Ships of the World	c1935	HA-67	£3.75	—
M12	Sports 'Queeriosities'	1933		£4.50	—
MP66	Sportsmen	1922		£1.80	—
32	Sportsmen of the World	c1935	HA-68	£3.50	—
M32	Thrilling Scenes from the Great War	1927		£3.50	—
M16	Thrills of the Dirt Track	1929		£10.00	—

AMALGAMATED PRESS LTD (continued)

M16	Tip-Top Tricks and Teasers	1927		£4.00	—
M14	VCs and Their Glorious Deeds of Valour (plain back)	c1930	HA-70	£4.00	—
	AUSTRALIAN ISSUES				
M32	Australian and English Cricket Stars	1932		£12.50	—
M16	England Test Match Cricketers	1928		£12.50	—
M16	Famous Australian Cricketers	1928		£12.50	—
16	Famous Film Stars	1927		£6.00	—
32	Makes of Motor Cars and Index Marks (with date) ...	1924		£4.00	—
16	Modern Motor Cars	1926		£6.00	—
M24	Wonderful London	1926		£6.00	—

AMANDA'S FLOWERS

L12	Flower Children	1990		35p	£4.00

AMARAN TEA

25	The Circus	1968	HX-79	36p	£9.00
25	Coins of the World	1965	HX-6	60p	£15.00
25	Dogs' Heads	1965	HX-16	50p	£12.50
25	Do You Know	1969	HX-166.4	80p	£20.00
25	Flags and Emblems	1964	HX-17	40p	£10.00
25	Naval Battles	1971	HX-21	£1.00	—
25	Old England	1969		20p	£2.50
25	Science in the 20th Century	1966	HX-18	20p	£2.50
25	Veteran Racing Cars	1966	HX-19	80p	£20.00

AMBER TIPS TEA (New Zealand)

M20	The Living Seashore...	1975		20p	£3.00

AMBERVILLE CARDS

15	Jayne Mansfield	2014		—	£6.50

THE ANGLERS MAIL

EL3	Terminal Tackle Tips	1976		—	£6.00

ANGLING TIMES

M15	Series 1 Floats	1980		30p	£4.50
M15	Series 2 Species	1980		30p	£4.50
M15	Series 3 Baits	1980		30p	£4.50
M15	Series 4 Sea Fish	1980		30p	£4.50
M24	Fish	1987		30p	£7.50
M24	Fishing Floats	1986		20p	£4.50

ANGLO-AMERICAN CHEWING GUM LTD

LT66	The Horse	1966		40p	£25.00
L36	Kidnapped	c1955		£6.00	—
M12	M.G.M. Film Stars	1935	HA-74	£10.00	—
40	Underwater Adventure	1966		20p	£4.00
50	Zoo Stamps of the World	1966		80p	£40.00
	Waxed Paper Issues:				
M72	Animal World (2 pictures per card)	c1965		£2.50	—
M72	Coaching Secrets...	1964		£2.00	—
M32	Famous International Teams (inscribed 'Series of 72')	1960		£2.50	—
M128	Famous Soccer Clubs	1960		£2.50	—
M36	Flags of The Nations	c1965		£2.00	—
M36	Men of Courage	1958		£3.00	—

ANGLO-AMERICAN CHEWING GUM LTD (Waxed Paper Issues continued)

Waxed Paper Issues (continued)

M48	Men of Progress	1958	£3.00	—
M72	Noted Football Clubs	1961	£2.00	—
M48	Race Around The World	1959	£3.00	—
M72	Soccer Hints	1961	£2.00	—
M48	Sports Gallery	c1960	£4.00	—
M48	Sports Parade	1957	£4.00	—
M48	Strange But True	1957	£3.00	—
M72	Strange World	1964	£2.00	—
M72	Swimming Know-How	1962	£2.00	—
M36	Transport Through the Ages	c1960	£3.00	—
M48	World of Wonders	1957	£3.00	—
M36	World Airlines	1960	£4.00	—
	Albums or Folders with cards printed therein:			
72	Strange World	1965	—	£10.00

ANGLO CONFECTIONERY LTD

LT66	The Beatles — Yellow Submarine	1968	£12.00	—
LT66	Captain Scarlet and the Mysterons	1968	£3.00	—
L12	Football Hints (Booklet Folders)	1970	£1.65	—
L84	Football Quiz	1969	£1.60	—
LT66	The Horse	1966	£2.00	—
LT66	Joe 90	1968	£4.00	—
L56	The New James Bond 007 On Her Majesty's Secret Service	1970	£12.00	—
L84	Railway Trains and Crests	1974	£1.20	—
LT66	Space	1967	£1.35	£90.00
LT66	Tarzan	1967	£1.35	£90.00
L64	UFO	1970	£3.00	£190.00
L78	Walt Disney Characters	1971	£5.50	—
L66	Wild West	1970	£2.50	—
L48	World Cup 1970 (Football)	1970	£2.50	—

APLIN & BARRETT

L25	Whipsnade (Zoo)	1937	£1.50	£37.50

ARDMONA (Australia)

L50	International Cricket Series III	1980	—	£12.50

ARMITAGE BROS. LTD

25	Animals of the Countryside	1965	HX-9	20p	£3.00
25	Country Life	1968	HX-11	20p	£3.00

ARMY RECRUITING OFFICE

M24	British Regiments 1st Series (without text)	1992	30p	£7.50
M24	British Regiments 2nd Series (with text)	1992	30p	£7.50

THE ARROW CONFECTIONERY CO.

13	Conundrums	c1905	HX-232	£32.00	—
12	Shadowgraphs	c1905		£32.00	—

ARTBOX (USA)

LT90	Charlie and The Chocolate Factory — The Film	2005	—	£9.50
LT72	Dexter's Laboratory	2001	—	£8.00
LT72	Finding Nemo — Film Cardz (Disney Film)	2003	—	£12.00

ARTBOX (USA) (continued)

LT54	Harry Potter and the Deathly Hallows Part 2	2011		£9.50
LT90	Harry Potter & The Goblet of Fire 1st Series	2005		£12.00
LT90	Harry Potter & The Goblet of Fire 2nd Series	2006		£9.50
LT90	Harry Potter & The Half-Blood Prince 1st Series	2009		£11.00
LT90	Harry Potter & The Order of The Phoenix 1st Series ...	2008		
LT90	Harry Potter & The Order of The Phoenix 2nd Series	2008		£9.50
LT90	Harry Potter & The Prisoner of Azkaban 1st Series ...	2004		£15.00
LT90	Harry Potter & The Prisoner of Azkaban 2nd Series ...	2004		£9.50
LT72	Harry Potter & The Prisoner of Azkaban Film Cardz ...	2004		£12.00
LT90	Harry Potter & The Sorcerer's Stone	2005		£11.00
LT72	Harry Potter Memorable Moments 1st Series	2006		£12.00
LT72	Harry Potter Memorable Moments 2nd Series	2009		£9.50
M18	Pokemon Chrome Series	1999		£7.00
M80	Pokemon 3-D Action Cards	1999	25p	£16.00
M40	Pokemon Premier Edition (3-D Action Cards)	1999		£12.00
LT72	The Powerpuff Girls 1st Series	2000		£8.50
LT12	The Powerpuff Girls 1st Series Foil Series	2000		£3.50
M40	Sailor Moon — 3D	2000		£10.00
LT45	The Simpsons	2000		£16.00
LT72	Terminator 2 Judgment Day — Film Cardz	2003	20p	£9.50
LT24	Terminator 2 Judgment Day — Film Cardz Cyberetch			
	Series	2003	40p	£9.50
LT40	World Wrestling Federation Lenticular Series 2	2001		£10.00

ASKEYS

25	People and Places	1968	HX-26	20p	£3.00
25	Then and Now	1968	HX-27	20p	£4.00

THE ASSEMBLY ROOMS (Briggate)

50	War Portraits	1916	HX-86	£100.00	—

ASTON & ERDINGTON POLICE

L24	Cop Card-Toons (including album)	1989		£6.00

ASTON CARDS

LT24	Speedway Programme Covers 1st Series Inaugural			
	Season 1928	2002		£16.00
LT24	Speedway Programme Covers ,2nd Series The Early			
	Years 1920/30s	2003		£16.00
LT24	Speedway Programme Covers 3rd Series More Early			
	Years 1920/30s	2003		£16.00
LT24	Speedway Programme Covers 4th Series The			
	Fabulous '40s	2004		£16.00
LT24	Speedway Programme Covers 5th Series			
	More Early Years 1930s	2005		£16.00
LT24	Speedway Programme Covers 6th Series			
	More Early Years 1920/40s	2006		£16.00
LT24	Speedway Programme Covers 7th Series			
	More Fabulous '40s	2008		£16.00

ATLANTIC SERVICE STATIONS (Australia)

M32	Australia in the 20th Century 1st Series	1959	£1.25	—
M32	Australia in the 20th Century 2nd Series	1960	80p	£25.00
M32	English Historical Series	c1961	£1.25	—
M32	Queensland's Centenary	1959	£1.25	—

AUSTIN MOTOR CO. LTD

L13	Famous Austin Cars	1953		£12.00	—

AUSTRALIAN BUTTER

L54	Cricketers	1982		—	£15.00
L50	Cricketers	1983		25p	£12.50

AUSTRALIAN DAIRY CORPORATION

L63	Kanga Cards (Cricket)	1985		—	£15.00

AUTHENTIX (USA)

LT50	Beetle Bailey	1995		—	£9.50
LT50	Blondie (Comic Strip)	1995		—	£9.50
LT50	Hagar The Horrible	1995		—	£9.50

AUTOBRITE (Car Polish)

25	Vintage Cars	1965	HX-33	60p	£15.00

AUTOGRAPH ADICTS

L16	England Rugby World Cup Winners	2003		—	£10.00

AUTOMATIC MACHINE CO. LTD

25	Modern Aircraft	1958	HX-219	30p	£7.50

AUTOMATIC MERCHANDISING CO. LTD

L25	Adventure Twins and the Treasure Ship:				
	A Coloured	1959		£1.40	£35.00
	B Black, White and Pink only	1959		£1.40	£35.00

AVON & SOMERSET POLICE

L37	British Stamps	1985		£1.20	—

AVON RUBBER CO. LTD

30	Leading Riders of 1963 (Motor Cyclists)	1963		£2.00	£60.00
	Folder			—	£4.00

B.B.B. PIPES

25	Pipe History	c1925		£12.00	—

B.J.B. CARDS (Canada)

L25	Famous Golfers of the 40s and 50s	1992		—	£15.00

B.N.A. (Canada)

LT49	Canadian Winter Olympic Winners	1992		—	£8.00

B.P. PETROL

25	Team England (Football World Cup)	1998		30p	£7.50
	Album			—	£4.00

B.T. LTD

25	Aircraft	1964	HX-36	£1.00	—
25	British Locomotives	1961		£1.00	—
25	Do You Know?	1967	HX-166.2	40p	£10.00

B.T. LTD (continued)

25	Holiday Resorts	1963	HX-38	20p	£4.00
25	Modern Motor Cars	1962	HX-39	£1.60	—
25	Occupations	1962		40p	£10.00
25	Pirates and Buccaneers	1961	HX-40	£1.60	—
25	The West	1966	HX-42	30p	£7.50

BAD AXE STUDIOS (USA)

LT52	Dungeon Dolls — Adult Fantasy Art	2011		—	£9.50

BADSHAH TEA CO.

25	British Cavalry Uniforms of the 19th Century	1963	HX-43	60p	£15.00
25	Butterflies and Moths	1967	HX-2	20p	£3.00
25	Fish and Bait	1965	HX-44	24p	£6.00
25	Fruit of Trees and Shrubs	1965	HX-45	36p	£9.00
25	Garden Flowers	1963	HX-46	50p	£12.50
24	The Island of Ceylon	1962	HX-47	£4.00	—
25	Naval Battles	1968	HX-21	70p	£17.50
25	People and Places	1968	HX-26	20p	£2.50
25	Regimental Uniforms of the Past	1971		20p	£3.00
25	Romance of the Heavens	1968	HX-48	£1.40	—
25	Wonders of the World	1967	HX-49	36p	£9.00

J. BAINES & SON

L?	Cricket and Football Cards, etc. (Shapes)	c1905		£40.00	—

BAKE-A-CAKE LTD

56	Motor Cars	1952		£5.00	—

BAKER, WARDELL & CO. LTD

25	Animals in the Service of Man	c1964	HX-51	£2.60	—
36	Capital Tea Circus Act	c1960		£4.50	—
25	Do You Know 1st Series	c1962	HX-166.3	£3.60	—
25	Do You Know 2nd Series	c1962	HX-166.3	£3.60	—
25	History of Flight 1st Series...	c1966		£10.00	—
25	History of Flight 2nd Series	c1966		£10.00	—
25	Irish Patriots	c1960		£10.00	—
25	They Gave Their Names	c1963	HX-52	£3.00	—
25	Transport — Present and Future	c1956		£5.00	—
25	World Butterflies	c1960		£6.00	—

BARBERS TEA LTD

1	Advertisement Card — Cinema & TV Stars	1955		—	£5.00
1	Advertisement Card — Dogs	1960		—	£1.50
1	Advertisement Card — Railway Equipment	1958		—	£4.00
25	Aeroplanes	1954		£1.00	—
24	Cinema and Television Stars	1955		£3.00	—
24	Dogs	1960		20p	£4.00
25	Locomotives	1953		£1.40	£35.00
	Album			—	£30.00
24	Railway Equipment	1958		50p	£12.00

JOHN O. BARKER (Ireland) LTD (Gum)

EL24	Circus Scenes	1960		£2.00	£50.00
EL24	Famous People	1960	HX-53	£1.80	£45.00
25	The Wild West	1960	HX-55.3	£4.00	—

BARRATT & CO. LTD
(AFTER 1973 SEE GEO. BASSETT)

Size & quantity		Date	Handbook reference	Price per card	Complete set
M30	Aircraft	1941	HB-6	£6.00	—
M30	Aircraft	1943	HB-7	£6.00	—
25	Animals in the Service of Man	1964	HX-51	20p	£5.00
16	Australian Cricketers Action Series	1926		£16.00	—
15	Australian Test Players	1930	HB-10	£30.00	—
45	Beauties Picture Hats	c1910		£20.00	—
25	Birds	1960	HX-71	80p	£20.00
50	Botany Quest	1966		£1.80	—
25	British Butterflies	1965		£2.60	—
25	Butterflies and Moths	1960	HX-2	24p	£6.00
25	Cage and Aviary Birds	1960		50p	£12.50
50	Captain Scarlet and The Mysterons	1967		£3.80	—
50	Cars of the World	1965		£1.80	£90.00
	Characters From Fairy Stories and Fiction (plain back):				
M53	Characters From Fairy Stories	c1940	HB-16	£10.00	—
M12	Gulliver's Travels	c1940	HB-51	£10.00	—
M12	Pinocchio	c1940	HB-65	£10.00	—
M36	Snow White and the Seven Dwarfs	c1940	HB-75	£10.00	—
M12	The Wizard of Oz	1939	HB-82	£10.00	—
	Cricketers, Footballers and Football Teams:		HB-25		
81	Cricketers	c1925		£30.00	—
201	Footballers	c1925		£16.00	—
3	Football Teams	c1925		£50.00	—
M20	Cricket Team Folders	1933		£24.00	—
M60	Disneyland 'True Life'	1956		£1.80	—
M50	FA Cup Winners 1883-1935	1935		£25.00	—
25	Fairy Stories	c1925		£3.80	—
11	Famous British Constructions, Aircraft Series	c1930		£20.00	—
M25	Famous Cricketers — 1930	1930	HB-29	£13.00	—
M50	Famous Cricketers — 1932	1932	HB-30	£13.00	—
M9	Famous Cricketers — 1932	1932	HB-31	£24.00	—
M34	Famous Cricketers — 1934	1934	HB-32	£18.00	—
M7	Famous Cricketers — 1936	1936	HB-33	£18.00	—
M60	Famous Cricketers — 1937, unnumbered	1937	HB-34	£12.00	—
M40	Famous Cricketers — 1938, numbered	1938		£12.00	—
35	Famous Film Stars	1960		£3.00	—
M100	Famous Footballers — 1935-36, unnumbered (black back)	1935	HB-35A	£13.00	—
M98	Famous Footballers — 1936-37, unnumbered (sepia back)	1936	HB-35B	£13.00	—
M100	Famous Footballers — 1937-38, numbered	1937	HB-35C	£13.00	—
M20	Famous Footballers — 1938-39, numbered	1938	HB-35D	£13.00	—
M110	Famous Footballers — 1939-40, numbered	1939	HB-35E	£13.00	—
M50	Famous Footballers — 1947-48	1947	HB-37A	£12.00	—
M50	Famous Footballers — 1948-49	1948	HB-37B	£12.00	—
M50	Famous Footballers — 1949-50	1949	HB-37C	£12.00	—
M50	Famous Footballers New Series — 1950-51	1950	HB-38	£8.00	—
M50	Famous Footballers New Series — 1951-52	1951	HB-38	£8.00	—
M50	Famous Footballers New Series — 1952-53	1952	HB-38	£8.00	—
M50	Famous Footballers, Series A.1	1953	HX-57	£6.00	—
M50	Famous Footballers, Series A.2	1954	HX-58	£6.00	—
M50	Famous Footballers, Series A.3	1955	HX-59	£6.00	—
60	Famous Footballers, Series A.4	1956		£6.00	—
60	Famous Footballers, Series A.5	1957		£6.00	—
60	Famous Footballers, Series A.6	1958		£6.00	—
60	Famous Footballers, Series A.7	1959		£6.00	—

BARRATT & CO. LTD (continued)

Size & quantity		Date	Handbook reference	Price per card	Complete set
50	Famous Footballers, Series A.8	1960		£6.00	—
50	Famous Footballers, Series A.9:		HB-39		
	A Back Series A.8 Error printing	1961		£6.50	—
	B Back Series A.9	1961		£6.00	—
50	Famous Footballers, Series A.10	1962		£2.00	—
50	Famous Footballers, Series A.11	1963	HB-40	£5.00	—
50	Famous Footballers, Series A.12	1964		£5.00	—
50	Famous Footballers, Series A.13	1965		£5.00	—
50	Famous Footballers, Series A.14	1966		£5.00	—
50	Famous Footballers, Series A.15	1967		£1.00	£50.00
50	Famous Sportsmen:		HB-41		
	A 27 Scarce cards	1971		£4.00	—
	B 23 Common cards (Nos 2, 3, 5, 9, 10, 15, 22, 23, 26, 27, 29, 31, 32, 35, 36, 38, 42, 43, 44, 46, 47, 48, 49)	1971		£1.00	£23.00
M45	Fastest on Earth	1953	HX-60	£2.20	—
32	Felix Pictures	c1930	HX-56	£30.00	—
50	Film Stars (without name of film company)	c1940	HB-42	£8.00	—
50	Film Stars (with name of film company)	c1940	HB-43	£8.00	—
25	Fish and Bait	1962	HX-44	80p	£20.00
12	Footballers Action Caricatures	c1930	HB-49	£27.00	—
100	Football 'Stars'...	c1930	HB-47	£27.00	—
50	Football 'Stars'...	1973		£7.00	—
M66	Football Teams — 1st Division	c1930	HB-48	£16.00	—
M22	Football Team Folders, English League Division I	1932	HB-28.1	£28.00	—
M22	Football Team Folders, English League Division I	1933	HB-28.1	£28.00	—
M22	Football Team Folders, English League Division I	1934	HB-28.1	£28.00	—
M22	Football Team Folders, English League Division II ...	1932	HB-28.2	£28.00	—
M22	Football Team Folders, English League Division II ...	1933	HB-28.2	£28.00	—
M22	Football Team Folders, English League Division II ...	1934	HB-28.2	£28.00	—
M1	Football Team Folder, English League Division III	c1933	HB-28.3	£28.00	—
M20	Football Team Folders, Scottish League Divison I	1934	HB-28.4	£28.00	—
M3	Football Team Folders, Irish League	c1933	HB-28.5	£45.00	—
M1	Football Team Folder, Rugby Union	1934		£45.00	—
48	Giants in Sport...	1959		£6.50	—
EL12	Gold Rush (Package Issue)	c1960	HB-50	£8.00	—
25	Head-Dresses of the World	1962	HX-197	32p	£8.00
25	Historical Buildings	1960	HX-72	32p	£8.00
25	History of the Air	1960	HX-180	40p	£10.00
32	History of the Air	1959		£5.00	—
48	History of the Air:				
	A Cream card	1959		£1.30	—
	B White card	1959		£1.30	—
25	Interpol — back with chain frameline	1964		£3.60	—
25	Interpol — back without chain frameline (different subjects)	1964		£8.00	—
48	Leaders of Sport	c1930		£16.00	—
35	Magic Roundabout	1968		£1.60	—
25	Merchant Ships of the World:		HX-63		
	A Black back	1962		70p	£17.50
	B Blue back	1962		50p	£12.50
M40	Modern Aircraft	1955		£3.00	—
M45	Modern British Aircraft	1949	HB-56	£4.00	—
13	National Flags	c1915	HB-57	£22.00	—
64	Natural History Series	c1935	HB-62	£6.00	—
M24	Naval Ships...	c1940	HB-63	£8.00	—
M6	Our King and Queen	c1940	HB-64	£9.00	—

BARRATT & CO. LTD (continued)

Size & quantity	Title	Date	Handbook reference	Price per card	Complete set
25	People and Places	1965	HX-26	20p	£3.00
25	Pirates and Buccaneers	1960	HX-40	£1.00	£25.00
12	Prominent London Buildings	c1910	HB-67	£22.00	—
M5	Regimental Uniforms	c1930	HB-70	£12.00	—
36	Robin Hood	1957		£2.50	—
30	Robin Hood	1961		£3.00	£90.00
36	Sailing Into Space	1959	HX-123	£2.75	—
35	Sea Hunt	1961		£2.60	—
50	The Secret Service	1970		£2.20	—
50	Soccer Stars	1972		£3.80	—
50	Soldiers of the World	1966		50p	£25.00
16	South African Cricketers Series	c1930	HB-76	£22.00	—
25	Space Mysteries	1966		40p	£10.00
L20	Speed Series	c1930		£9.00	—
50	Tarzan	1967		35p	£17.50
35	Test Cricketers by E.W. Swanton, Series A	1956		£6.00	—
48	Test Cricketers, Series B	1957		£7.50	—
50	Thunderbirds 1st Series	1966		£3.80	—
50	Thunderbirds 2nd Series	1967		£1.00	£50.00
50	Tom and Jerry	1971		50p	£25.00
50	Trains	1970		32p	£16.00
50	Trains of the World	1964		30p	£15.00
35	TV's Huckleberry Hound and Friends	1961		£1.70	£60.00
35	TV's Yogi Bear	1963		£5.00	—
35	TV's Yogi Bear and Friends	1964		90p	—
70	UFO	1971	HX-179	£1.20	—
M35	Walt Disney Characters	1955	HX-65	£5.50	—
50	Walt Disney Characters 2nd Series	1957		£5.50	—
35	Walt Disney's True Life	1962		£1.50	—
25	Warriors Through the Ages	1962		£1.00	£25.00
25	What Do You Know?	1964		20p	£3.50
L72	Wild Animals	1970		90p	—
M50	Wild Animals by George Cansdale:		HX-68		
	A With 'printed in England'	1954		£1.80	—
	B Without 'printed in England'	1954		£1.80	—
36	Wild West Series No.1	1959		£2.00	—
24	The Wild West	1961		50p	£12.50
25	The Wild West	1963	HX-55.2	36p	£9.00
50	The Wild Wild West	1968		£1.80	—
25	Willum	1961		£6.50	—
50	Wisecracks 1st Series	1969		20p	£4.00
50	Wisecracks 2nd Series	1970		50p	£25.00
50	Wisecracks 3rd Series	1971		50p	£25.00
50	Wonders of the World	1962	HX-49	20p	£7.50
25	World Locomotives	1963	HX-70	80p	—
50	Wunders der Welt	1968		20p	£7.50
25	The Young Adventurer	1964		£2.60	£65.00
50	Zoo Pets	1964		£1.20	£60.00

GEO. BASSETT & CO. LTD

Size & quantity	Title	Date	Handbook reference	Price per card	Complete set
30	Adventures With Ben and Barkley	2001		20p	£6.00
50	Age of the Dinosaurs:				
	A Complete set	1979		£1.20	—
	B 35 Different	1979		—	£25.00
40	Ali-Cat Magicards	1978		£2.00	—
50	Asterix in Europe	1977		50p	£25.00
	Album			—	£25.00

GEO. BASSETT & CO. LTD (continued)

Size & quantity	Title	Date	Handbook reference	Price per card	Complete set
M20	The A Team...	1986		75p	—
50	Athletes of the World	1980		40p	—
48	Bananaman...	1985		20p	£4.00
	Album...			—	£4.00
M20	Battle (Package Issue)	1985		£2.50	
50	The Conquest of Space — 1980-81	1980		50p	£25.00
	Album ...			—	£18.00
50	Cricket	1978		£9.00	—
50	Cricket 2nd Series	1979		£3.80	—
48	Dandy Beano Collection (black back)	1989		20p	£10.00
48	Dandy/Beano 2nd Series (blue back)	1990		20p	£8.00
48	Dinosaurs and Prehistoric Creatures	1994		£2.00	—
8	Dinosaurs and Prehistoric Creatures	1997		—	—
50	Disney/Health and Safety	1977		25p	£12.50
EL6	Europe's Best (Footballers)	1992		£1.50	—
EL6	Europe's Best — Captains (Footballers)	1992		—	£6.00
EL6	Europe's Best — Defenders (Footballers)	1992		£1.50	—
EL6	Europe's Best — Goalkeepers (Footballers)...	1992		—	£6.00
EL6	Europe's Best — Midfielders (Footballers)	1992		—	£6.00
EL6	Europe's Best — Strikers Series 1 (Footballers)	1992		—	£6.00
EL6	Europe's Best — Strikers Series 2 (Footballers)	1992		—	£7.50
50	Football Action...	1976		£4.80	—
50	Football Action...	1977		£4.80	—
EL6	Football Action...	1991		£1.50	—
50	Football — 1978-79:				
	A Complete set ...	1978		—	£125.00
	B 42 Different (Minus Nos 26, 31, 33, 43, 44, 45,				
	49, 50) ...	1978		£1.00	£45.00
	Album ...			—	£25.00
50	Football — 1979-80 ...	1979		50p	£25.00
	Album ...			—	£20.00
50	Football — 1980-81 ...	1980		50p	£25.00
	Album ...			—	£20.00
50	Football — 1981-82 ...	1981		£3.50	—
	Album ...			—	£20.00
50	Football — 1982-83 ...	1982		£2.50	—
	Album ...			—	£20.00
50	Football — 1983-84 ...	1983		20p	£8.00
	Album...			—	£4.00
50	Football — 1984-85 ...	1984		£1.40	—
	Album ...			—	£20.00
48	Football — 1985-86 ...	1985		20p	£10.00
	Album ...			—	£20.00
48	Football — 1986-87 ...	1986		30p	£15.00
	Album...			—	£4.00
48	Football — 1987-88 ...	1987		£1.00	—
48	Football — 1988-89 ...	1988		20p	£10.00
48	Football 1989-90:				
	A Red back ...	1989		20p	£10.00
	B Purple-red back ...	1989		20p	£9.00
48	Football 1990-91 ...	1990		40p	£20.00
48	Football 1991-92 ...	1991		70p	£35.00
48	Football 1992-93 ...	1992		35p	£17.50
48	Football 1995-96 ...	1995		60p	£30.00
50	Football Stars ...	1974		£2.00	—
50	Football Stars — 1975-76 ...	1975		£3.50	—
EL6	Great Defenders (Footballers) ...	1992		—	£6.00

GEO. BASSETT & CO. LTD (continued)

EL6	Great Goalkeepers (Footballers)	1991		£1.50	—
EL6	Great Grounds (Football)	1991		£1.50	—
EL6	Great Managers 1st Series (Football)	1991		£1.50	—
EL6	Great Managers 2nd Series (Football)	1992		—	£6.00
M50	Guinness Book of Records	1990		—	£15.00
48	Hanna Barbera's Cartoon Capers	1983		£1.60	—
	Album			—	£5.00
24	Holograms:				
	A Red back	1986		25p	£6.00
	B Plain back	1986		50p	£12.00
	Album, Poster and Badge			—	£5.00
50	House of Horror	1982		£1.50	—
20	Jurassic Park (package issue)	1993		—	£10.00
40	Knight Rider	1987		40p	£16.00
	Album			—	£5.00
50	Living Creatures of Our World	1979		20p	£10.00
	Album			—	£20.00
45	Looney Tunes (blue border & blue back)	1995		20p	£9.00
30	Looney Tunes Cartoons (yellow border)	1997		25p	£7.50
25	Looney Tunes Cartoons (blue border, purple back)	1999		40p	£10.00
32	Lord of The Rings	2003		80p	£25.00
12	The Magic Sword Quest for Camelot	1998		25p	£3.00
EL6	Midfield Dynamos (Footballers)	1992		—	£6.00
25	Motor Cars — Vintage and Modern	1968		80p	£20.00
25	Nursery Rhymes	1967		80p	£20.00
	Album			—	£20.00
50	Play Cricket	1980		32p	£16.00
	Album			—	£12.00
25	Pop Stars	1974		50p	£12.50
EL25	Pop Stars	1984		£1.00	—
25	Popular Dogs	1966		50p	£12.50
	Album			—	£20.00
48	Premier Players (Footballers)	1994		20p	£10.00
EL6	Premier Players — Goalkeepers (Footballers)	1994		—	£6.00
EL6	Premier Players — Midfielders (Footballers)	1994		£1.50	—
35	Secret Island 1st Series	1976		£1.50	—
40	Secret Island 2nd Series	1976		20p	£3.00
20	Sky Fighters (Package Issue)	1986		£2.00	—
48	Sonic the Hedgehog	1994		20p	£7.00
50	Space 1999:				
	A Complete set	1976		—	£80.00
	B 49 different (minus No. 42)	1976		60p	£30.00
50	Super Heroes	1984		£1.00	—
	Album			—	£10.00
50	Survival on Star Colony 9	1979		40p	£20.00
40	Swim and Survive	1982		40p	£16.00
50	Tom and Jerry	1974		£2.50	—
EL6	Top Strikers 1st Series (Footballers)	1991		£1.50	—
EL6	Top Strikers 2nd Series (Footballers)	1992		£1.50	—
70	UFO	1974		25p	£17.50
25	Victoria Cross Heroes in Action:				
	A Title black print on white	1970		60p	£15.00
	B Title white print on black	1970		£3.00	—
	Album			—	£20.00
EL6	Winners in 1992 (Football Teams)	1992		—	£6.00
48	World Beaters (Footballers)	1993		35p	£17.50
EL6	World Beaters (Footballers)	1993		—	£6.00

GEO. BASSETT & CO. LTD (continued)

50	World Cup Stars/World Cup '74	1974		20p	£8.00
40	World Heroes (Footballers):				
	A 'Bassett's & Beyond' at top	1999		£1.00	£40.00
	B 'Barratt' at top...	1999		£1.25	—
40	World of The Vorgans	1978		£2.25	—
50	World Record Breakers...	1983		£1.30	—
48	World Stars (Football)	1997		£1.20	—
EL6	World's Greatest Teams (Football)	1991		£1.50	—
50	Yogi's Gang...	1976		£1.80	—

BATGER & CO.

20	Batgers Sweet Advertisement Series	c1905		£50.00	—

J.I. BATTEN & CO. LTD ('Jibco' Tea)

28	Dominoes	c1955		£3.50	—
K25	Screen Stars 1st Series	1955		£4.00	—
K25	Screen Stars 2nd Series	1956		80p	£20.00

S.P. BATTEN

50	War Portraits	1916	HX-8C	£100.00	—

BATTLE PICTURE WEEKLY

16	Weapons of World War II — Germany	c1975		£1.25	—
16	Weapons of World War II — Great Britain	c1975		£1.25	—
16	Weapons of World War II — Japan...	c1975		£1.25	—
16	Weapons of World War II — USA	c1975		£1.25	—
16	Weapons of World War II — USSR...	c1975		£1.25	—

BATTLEAXE TOFFEE

24	British and Empire Uniforms	1915		£30.00	—

J.C. BATTOCK

?M78	Cricket and Football Cards	c1920	HB-85/6	£65.00	—

BAYTCH BROS LTD

64	Fighting Favourites	1951	HX-8	£12.00	—

BEANO LTD

50	Conquest of Space	1956	HX-73	20p	£7.50
25	Fascinating Hobbies...	1950	HX-74	£4.00	—
50	Modern Aircraft	1953	HX-35	£1.20	—
50	Ships of the Royal Navy	1955	HX-76	40p	£20.00
50	This Age of Speed — No.1 Aeroplanes	1954		60p	£30.00
50	This Age of Speed — No. 2 Buses and Trams	1954		£2.00	—
50	Wonders of Modern Transport	c1955	HX-35	80p	£40.00

BEANSTALK CARDS

15	Saturday Afternoon Heroes (Footballers)...	2003		—	£5.50
15	Vintage Football Stars	2003		—	£5.50

BEATALLS

?22	Beauties	c1920	HB-88	£30.00	—

S.N. BEATTIE & CO. LTD

24	Safety Signs	1955		£6.00	—

S.N. BEATTIE & CO. LTD (continued)

12	Southgate Series (Prize scheme with letters):				
	A Titled Southgate Series in box at top	1955		£6.00	—
	B Text back without series title	1955		£7.00	—
	C Plain back	1955		£7.00	—

J.J. BEAULAH LTD

1	Boston Stump Advertisement Card				
	A 'Boston Stump' in black	1953		—	60p
	B 'Boston Stump' in blue	1954		—	60p
25	Coronation Series	1953		£1.60	£40.00
24	Marvels of the World	1954		20p	£3.00
24	Modern British Aircraft	1953		20p	£5.00

BEAUTIFUL GAME LTD

LT50	Football Greats	1999		—	£20.00
LT4	Football Greats Sir Tom Finney	1999		—	£4.00

BEAVERBROOK NEWSPAPERS (Daily Express)

L59	Car Cards '71	1971	HD-2	20p	£6.00
L53	Star Cards (pop stars)	1972		£1.00	—

T.W. BECKETT & CO. LTD (South Africa)

M50	Animals of South Africa, Series 3	1966		20p	£9.00
	Album			—	£20.00
M50	Birds of South Africa 1st Series	1965		20p	£9.00
	Album			—	£15.00
M50	Birds of South Africa 2nd Series...	1966		20p	£9.00
	Album			—	£15.00

THE BEEHIVE

25	British Uniforms of the 19th Century	1959	HX-78	80p	£20.00

BEL UK (Laughing Cow)

M12	Animal Antics	1997		£1.25	—
L8	Chicken Run	2000		£1.25	—

BELL TEA (New Zealand)

EL20	Historic New Zealand	1991		—	£12.00

BELL'S WHISKY

42	Other Famous Bells (shaped)	1975		60p	£25.00
	Album			—	£20.00

J. BELLAMY & SONS LTD

25	Vintage and Modern Trains of the World 1st Series ...	1968		32p	£8.00

BENSEL WORKFORCE LTD

20	Occupations	1991		—	£5.00

BETTER PUBS LTD

EL20	East Devon Inn Signs + 2 varieties...	1976		£1.00	£20.00

J. BIBBY & SONS LTD (Trex)

L25	Don't You Believe It	1956		£1.00	—
	Album			—	£20.00

J. BIBBY & SONS LTD (Trex) (continued)

L25	Good Dogs	1956		£2.60	—
	Album			—	£20.00
L25	How, What and Why?	1956		£1.00	—
	Album			—	£15.00
L25	Isn't It Strange?	1956		£1.00	—
	Album			—	£18.00
L25	They Gave it a Name	1956		£2.20	—
	Album			—	£20.00
L25	This Wonderful World	1956		£1.00	—
	Album			—	£15.00

BIRCHGREY LTD

L25	Panasonic European Open (Golf)	1989		—	£15.00

ALFRED BIRD & SONS

K49	Happy Families	1938		£1.50	—

BIRD'S EYE

EL12	Recipe Cards	c1965	HB-104	40p	£5.00
30	Wonders of the Seven Seas	c1975		£1.25	—

BIRKUM (Denmark)

25	Motor Cars	1956		£1.20	—

BISHOPS STORTFORD DAIRY FARMERS LTD (Tea)

25	Dogs' Heads	1965	HX-16	£1.00	£25.00
25	Freshwater Fish	1964	HX-80	£1.40	—
25	Historical Buildings	1964	HX-72	60p	£15.00
25	History of Aviation	1964	HX-36	60p	£15.00
25	Passenger Liners	1965	HX-82	20p	£3.00
25	Pond Life	1966	HX-81	20p	£3.00
25	Science in the 20th Century	1966	HX-18	20p	£3.00
25	The Story of Milk	1966	HX-3	30p	£7.50

BLACK ROOK PRESS

10	Classic Football Stars (1960s) Series 1	2010		—	£5.00
10	Classic Football Stars (1960/70s) 2nd Series	2010		—	£5.00

BLACKCAT CARDS

15	Sunderland F.C. Cup Kings of '73	2003		—	£5.50

BLACKPOOL PROGRAMME & MEMORABILIA COLLECTORS CLUB (BPMCC)

13	Blackpool FC Legends	2004		—	£13.00

BLAKEY'S BOOT PROTECTORS LTD

72	War Pictures	c1916	HX-200	£7.00	—

BLUE BAND

24	History of London's Transport:				
	A Black printing	1954		£1.00	—
	B Blue printing	1954		£1.00	—
	C Red printing	1954		£1.00	—

BLUE BAND (continued)

			Date	Handbook reference	Price per card	Complete set
24		History of London's Transport 2nd Series	1955		£2.50	—
16		See Britain by Coach:		HX-84		
	A	Black back	1954		30p	£5.00
	B	Blue back	1954		£1.00	—

THE BLUE BIRD

		Date	Handbook reference	Price per card	Complete set
M10	Famous Beauties of the Day	1922	HB-112	£9.00	—

BLUE BIRD STOCKINGS

		Date		Price per card	Complete set
EL12	Exciting Film Stars 3rd Series	1954		—	£36.00

BLUE CAP LTD

Flixies Coloured Film Transparencies:

			Date	Price per card	Complete set
K12	i	Ancient Monuments	1959	£1.00	—
K12	ii	Aviation Series	1959	£1.00	—
K12	iii	British Bird Series	1959	£1.00	£12.00
K12	iv	Butterflies	1959	£1.00	—
K12	v	Dog Series	1959	£1.00	£12.00
K12	vi	Flowers...	1959	£1.00	£12.00
K12	vii	Football Teams	1959	£1.00	—
K12	viii	Military Uniforms	1959	£1.00	—
K12	ix	Robin Hood	1959	£1.00	£12.00
K12	x	Ships	1959	£1.00	—
K12	xi	Sport Series	1959	£1.00	—
K12	xii	Tropical Fish	1959	£1.00	—
	Album for Series ii, iii, v, xi			—	£7.00
	Album for Series i, viii, ix, xii			—	£7.00
	Album for Series iv, vi, vii, x			—	£7.00

BON AIR (USA)

		Date	Price per card	Complete set
LT50	Birds and Flowers of the States	1991	—	£10.00
LT20	Civil War The Heritage Collection 1st Series	1991	—	£12.00
LT12	Civil War The Heritage Collection 2nd Series	1992	—	£8.00
LT100	18 Wheelers 1st Series (Lorries)	1994	—	£9.50
LT100	18 Wheelers 2nd Series (Lorries)	1995	—	£9.50
LT62	Federal Duck Stamps (ducks featured on stamps) ...	1992	—	£8.50
LT100	Fire Engines 1st Series...	1993	—	£15.00
LT100	Fire Engines 2nd Series	1993	—	£15.00
LT100	Fire Engines 3rd Series	1994	—	£15.00
LT100	Fire Engines 4th Series...	1994	—	£15.00
LT100	Fire Engines 5th Series...	1998	—	£12.00
LT90	Native Americans	1995	—	£9.50
LT63	On Guard The Heritage Collection	1992	—	£9.50
LT50	Wildlife America	1991	—	£10.00

E.H. BOOTH & CO. LTD (Tea)

		Date	Handbook reference	Price per card	Complete set
25	Badges and Uniforms of Famous British Regiments and Corps	1964		20p	£5.00
24	The Island of Ceylon	c1955	HX-47	£5.00	—
25	Ships and Their Workings	1963	HX-85	£1.20	—

BOW BELLS

		Date	Price per card	Complete set
MP6	Handsome Men of the British Screen	1922	£8.00	—

BOWATER-SCOTT

EL9	Scotties Famous Football Teams	1969		£3.00	—
EL3	Scotties Grand Prix Series I	1968		£3.00	—
EL4	Scotties Grand Prix Series II	1969		£3.00	—

BOWMAN GUM INC. (USA)

M108	Jets-Rockets-Spacemen	1951		—	—

BOYS' CINEMA

M24	Boys' Cinema Famous Heroes	1922		£4.50	—
MP6	Cinema Stars (plain back)	1932	HB-129	£4.50	—
MP6	Famous Film Heroes	1922		£4.50	—
EL8	Favourite Film Stars	c1930	HB-131	£4.50	—
7	Film Stars	c1930	HB-133	£3.50	—
MP8	Film Stars, brown glossy photos...	1930		£4.50	—
MP8	Film Stars, black glossy photos	1931		£4.50	—

BOYS' COMIC LIBRARY

4	Characters from Boys' Fiction	c1910	HB-137	£18.00	—
4	Heroes of the Wild West	c1910		£18.00	—
6	One and All Flowers	c1910	HB-138	£18.00	—

BOYS' FRIEND

3	Famous Boxers Series	1911		£15.00	—
3	Famous Flags Series	1911		£10.00	—
3	Famous Footballers Series	1911		£20.00	—
3	Famous Regiments Series	1911		£10.00	—
MP4	Footballers, half length studies	1923		£6.00	—
MP5	Footballers, two players on each card	1922		£6.00	—
MP15	Rising Boxing Stars	1922		£4.50	—

BOYS' MAGAZINE

M8	Coloured Studies of Famous Internationals	1922	HB-140	£6.00	—
P10	Famous Cricketers Series	1928		£6.00	—
P12	Famous Footballers Series	c1930		£6.00	—
MP10	Football Series	c1930		£4.50	—
EL9	Football Teams	c1925	HB-145	£13.00	—
	Sportsmen:				
M8	Boxers	c1926	HB-139	£9.00	—
M10	Cricketers	c1926	HB-142	£10.00	—
M30	Footballers (picture 49 × 39mm)	c1926	HB-147	£6.00	—
M64	Footballers and Miscellaneous				
	(picture 56 × 35mm)	c1926	HB-148	£6.00	—
12	'Zat' Cards, Cricketers	c1930	HB-154	£10.00	—
M11	'Zat' Cards, Cricketers	1932		£10.00	—

BOYS' REALM

MP15	Famous Cricketers	1922		£3.50	—
MP9	Famous Footballers	1922		£5.00	—

BRAINTREE TOWN F.C.

M12	Braintree Town F.C. 1st Series (Nos 1 to 12)	2012		—	£5.00
M12	Braintree Town F.C 2nd Series (Nos 13 to 24)	2014		—	£5.00

BREWER'S

24	Nursery Rhymes	c1920	HX-25A	£10.00	—

BREYGENT (USA)

LT72	American Horror Story Season 1	2014		—	£8.50
LT72	Classic Vintage Poster Collection Movie Posters (black back)	2007		—	£8.50
LT72	Classic Vintage Posters Stars – Monsters – Comedy (yellow orange back)	2009		—	£8.50
LT72	Dexter Seasons 1 and 2	2009		—	£8.00
LT72	Dexter Season 3	2011		—	£8.00
LT72	Dexter Season 4	2012		—	£8.50
LT72	Dexter Season 5 and 6	2014		—	£8.50
LT72	Ghost Whisperer Seasons 1 and 2	2009		—	£8.00
LT72	Ghost Whisperer Seasons 3 and 4	2010		—	£8.00
LT72	Grimm Season 1	2013		—	£8.50
LT72	Grimm Season 2	2015		—	£8.50
LT72	Marilyn Monroe (Photos by Shaw Family Archives)	2007		—	£8.50
LT72	The Three Stooges	2005		—	£8.50
LT72	Transformers Optimum Collection (First Three Movies)	2013		—	£8.50
LT72	The Tudors Seasons I, II & III	2011		—	£9.50
LT72	Vampirella — Adult Fantasy Art	2011		—	£8.00
LT72	Warlord of Mars	2012		—	£8.50
LT72	Witchblade	2014		—	£8.50
LT72	The Wizard of Oz	2006		—	£8.50

C. & T. BRIDGEWATER LTD

KP48	Coronation Series	1937		20p	£7.50
KP96	Film Stars (CE over No.) (No. 54 without CE)	1932		50p	£50.00
KP96	Film Stars (E below No.)	1933		£1.00	£100.00
KP96	Film Stars (number only)	1934		£1.00	£100.00
KP48	Film Stars 4th Series	1935	HB-163	40p	£20.00
KP48	Film Stars 5th Series	1937	HB-163	£1.75	£85.00
KP48	Film Stars 6th Series (F before No.)	1938		£2.00	—
P48	Film Stars 7th Series	1939		£1.75	£85.00
KP48	Film Stars 8th Series	1940	HB-164	60p	£30.00
KP48	Radio Stars 1st Series	1935		£1.50	£75.00
KP48	Radio Stars 2nd Series	1936	HB-165	40p	£20.00

BRIMSTONE PRODUCTIONS

10	Hollywood Beauties (of the 40s & 50s)	2009		—	£5.00

J.M. BRINDLEY

30	The Artist Impression Series Opera Stars	c1993		—	£15.00
30	Australian Cricketers	1986		—	£12.00
30	Bentley Cars	1993		—	£12.00
M20	Birds of Britain 1st Series Nos 1-20	1991		—	£10.00
M20	Birds of Britain 2nd Series Nos 21-40	1992		—	£10.00
M20	Birds of Britain 3rd Series Nos 41-60	1993		—	£10.00
M20	Birds of Britain 4th Series Nos 61-80	1993		—	£10.00
M20	Birds of Britain 5th Series Nos 81-100	1993		—	£10.00
M12	British Birds of Prey	1995		—	£8.00
20	Car Badges and Emblems	1987		—	£6.00
30	Cricketers 1st Series	1984		—	£20.00
30	Cricketers 2nd Series	1985		—	£20.00
L16	Cricketers 3rd Series	1985		—	£12.00
30	Cricketers 4th Series	1985		33p	£10.00
L20	Cricket (cartoons) 5th Series	1985		—	£10.00
12	Cricket Caricatures 1st Series Nos 1-12	1992		50p	£6.00
18	Cricket Caricatures 2nd Series Nos 13-30	1993		—	£9.00

J.M. BRINDLEY (continued)

Size & quantity		Date	Handbook reference	Price per card	Complete set
30	Cricket — The Old School	1987		—	£10.00
20	Cricket Old Timers	1993		—	£7.50
30	Cricket — Surrey v Yorkshire	1988		—	£9.00
20	Cricketers of the 1880s	1992		40p	£8.00
25	Cricketing Greats	1987		30p	£7.50
EL1	Cricketing Greats — W.G. Grace	1987		—	50p
18	Famous Operatic Roles	1992		—	£9.00
18	Fish	1989		—	£7.00
EL3	Fish	1989		50p	£1.50
EL35	Full Dress Uniforms of the British Army c1914 1st Series	1990		—	£12.00
EL35	Full Dress Uniforms of the British Army c1914 2nd Series	1990		—	£12.00
EL35	Full Dress Uniforms of the British Army c1914 3rd Series	1990		—	£12.00
EL35	Full Dress Uniforms of the British Army c1914 4th Series	1990		—	£12.00
EL35	Full Dress Uniforms of the British Army c1914 5th Series	1990		—	£12.00
20	Golf	1987		—	£10.00
38	Hampshire County Cricket Club	1991		40p	£16.00
24	Hampshire Cricket Sunday League Era	1987		—	£6.00
20	Horse Racing	1987		—	£6.00
20	Loco's	1987		40p	£8.00
30	London, Brighton and South Coast Railway	1986		—	£9.00
20	Military	1987		—	£6.00
EL1	Motor Car The Bentley	1993		—	50p
25	Old Golfing Greats	1987		60p	£15.00
EL1	Old Golfing Greats — H. Vardon	1987		—	50p
12	Old Motor Cycles	1993		50p	£6.00
30	Opera Stars	1988		—	£12.00
16	Players of the Past — 1930s Football	1992		—	£10.00
8	Pop Stars (Series of 15, but only 8 cards issued)	c1993		50p	£4.00
EL6	Regimental Drum Majors	1992		—	£3.00
EL7	The Royal Hussars Bandsmen 1979-1989	1989		50p	£3.50
20	S.E.C.R. Locos	1995		40p	£8.00
16	Sea Fish	1992		—	£8.00
20	South African Test Cricket 1888-1988	1989		50p	£10.00
20	Trains — London & S.W. Railways	1992		—	£7.00
	Victorian and Edwardian Soldiers in Full Dress:				
30	A Back in black	1988		50p	—
30	B Back in olive/green	1988		—	£12.00
30	C Back in white	1988		—	£12.00
M6	World Boxers 1st Series Nos 1-6	1992		—	£4.50
M6	World Boxers 2nd Series Nos 7-12	1993		—	£4.50

BRISTOL–MYERS CO. LTD

Size & quantity		Date	Handbook reference	Price per card	Complete set
25	Speed 1st Series	1966	HX-153	£5.00	—
25	Speed 2nd Series	1966	HX-153	£5.00	—

THE BRITISH AUTOMATIC CO. LTD (Weight Cards)

Size & quantity		Date	Handbook reference	Price per card	Complete set
K24	British Aircraft	1950		£1.80	£45.00
K24	British Birds	1950		£2.25	—
K24	British Locomotives	1948		£1.00	£25.00
K36	British Motor Cars	1950		£3.50	—
K44	Coronation Information	1953		£1.30	—

THE BRITISH AUTOMATIC CO. LTD (Weight Cards) (continued)

			Date	Handbook reference	Price per card	Complete set
K32	Dogs 1st Series:					
	A	Front with 'Weigh Daily' across picture	1953		75p	£24.00
	B	Front without 'Weigh Daily' across picture	1953		£1.50	—
K32	Dogs 2nd Series		1953		£1.10	£35.00
K24	Famous Trains of the World 1st Series		1952		£1.50	—
K24	Famous Trains of the World 2nd Series		1952		£1.25	£30.00
K37	Fortunes, Horoscopes, Quotations numbered		1953		£1.00	—
	Fortunes, Horoscopes, Quotations unnumbered:					
K37	A	With frame lines, no Serifs, horizontal	c1953	HB-166.1	£3.00	—
K33	B	Without frame line, no Serifs, horizontal	c1953	HB-166.2	£3.00	—
K32	C	Without frame line, or Serif, vertical	c1953	HB-166.3	£3.00	—
K33	D	Without frame line, with Serifs, horizontal	c1953	HB-166.4	£3.00	—
K32	Fortunes 2nd Series		1953		70p	—
K24	Fresh Water Fish		1950		£1.75	—
K24	History of Transport		1948		50p	£12.00
K44	Jokes		1951		60p	—
K24	Olympic Games		1952		£5.00	—
K24	Racing and Sports Cars		1957		£3.00	—
K24	Space Travel		1955		£2.00	—
K24	Speed		1949		50p	£12.00
K24	Sportsman		1955		£3.00	—
K20	Twenty Questions		1952		£2.50	—
K24	Warships of the World		1952		£1.00	£24.00

BRITISH EDUCATIONAL SERIES

		Date	Handbook reference	Price per card	Complete set
50	Modern Aircraft	1953	HX-35	20p	£10.00

BRITISH TOURIST AUTHORITY

		Date			Complete set
25	Industrial Heritage Year	1993		—	£15.00

C. BRITTON

		Date		Price per card	Complete set
L24	Golf Courses of the British Isles	1993		30p	£7.50

BROOK MOTORS LTD (Motor Engineers)

		Date		Price per card	Complete set
EL12	Motor Cars 1910-1931	1961		£2.50	£30.00
EL12	Railway Engines (size 120 × 83mm)	1962		£3.00	£36.00
EL12	Railway Engines (size 125 × 105mm)	c1970		£1.00	£12.00
EL12	Traction Engines	1968		£2.00	£24.00

BROOKE BOND & CO. LTD

(104-page illustrated reference book 'Brooke Bond Tea Cards', published 2007 — £12.50)

		Date		Price per card	Complete set
50	Adventurers and Explorers	1973		20p	£4.00
	Album			—	£4.00
50	African Wild Life:				
	A	Blue back	1961	25p	£12.50
	Album (original matt cover with price). Small print on front black		—	£40.00
	Album (original matt cover with price). Small print on front bluish grey		—	£30.00
	B	Black back	1973	20p	£4.00
	Album (re-issue glossy cover with price)		—	£20.00
	Album (re-issue glossy cover without price)		—	£15.00
50	Asian Wild Life	1962		20p	£10.00
	Album (price sixpence)			—	£35.00

BROOKE BOND & CO. LTD (continued)

Size & quantity			Date	Handbook reference	Price per card	Complete set
50	Bird Portraits:					
	A	With address	1957		£1.20	£60.00
	B	Without address	1957		£2.50	—
		Album (solid border to card space)			—	£90.00
		Album (dotted border to card space)			—	£75.00
50	British Butterflies:					
	A	Blue back	1963		70p	£35.00
		Album (original matt cover)			—	£30.00
	B	Black back	1973		20p	£6.00
		Album (re-issue glossy cover with price)			—	£20.00
		Album (re-issue glossy cover without price)			—	£15.00
50	British Costume:					
	A	Blue back	1967		20p	£5.00
		Error and Corrected Cards of Nos 3, 4, 23, 24			—	£30.00
		Album (original with price and printer's credit) ...			—	£25.00
	B	Black back	1973		20p	£4.00
		Album (re-issue with price, without printer's credit)			—	£5.00
		Album (re-issue without price, with printer's credit)			—	£18.00
50	British Wild Life:			HX-66		
	A	Brooke Bond (Great Britain) Ltd	1958		£1.80	—
	B	Brooke Bond Tea Ltd	1958		90p	£45.00
	C	Brooke Bond & Co. Ltd	1958		£1.80	—
		Album			—	£60.00
50	Butterflies of the World	1964	HX.67	20p	£7.50
		Album (price sixpence)			—	£30.00
	Creatures of Legend:					
M24	A	Standard set	1994		30p	£7.50
EL12	B	Two pictures per card	1994		80p	£10.00
		Album			—	£7.00
		Wallchart	1994		—	£5.00
	The Dinosaur Trail:					
20	A	Standard set:				
		i Postcode BB1 1PG	1993		80p	£16.00
		ii Postcode BB11 1PG	1993		20p	£3.50
L10	B	Two pictures per card:				
		i Postcode BB1 1PG	1993		£1.80	—
		ii Postcode BB11 1PG	1993		60p	£6.00
		Album (with © Marshall on back cover)			—	£30.00
		Album (without © Marshall on back cover)			—	£4.00
	Discovering Our Coast:					
50	A	Standard set Blue back	1989		20p	£4.00
50	B	Standard set Black back	1992		20p	£5.00
L25	C	Two pictures per card	1989		40p	£10.00
		Album			—	£4.00
		Wallchart	1989		—	£5.00
50	Famous People:					
	A	Blue back	1969		20p	£4.00
		Album (original with printer's credit and price) ..			—	£15.00
	B	Black back	1973		20p	£4.00
		Album (re-issue with price, without printer's credit)			—	£20.00
		Album (re-issue without price, with printer's credit)			—	£20.00
		Album (re-issue without price and printer's credit)			—	£5.00

BROOKE BOND & CO. LTD (continued)

Size & quantity			Date	Handbook reference	Price per card	Complete set
	Features of the World:					
50	A	Standard set	1984		20p	£5.00
L25	B	Two pictures per card	1984		£1.00	£25.00
		Album			—	£4.00
50	Flags and Emblems of the World:					
	A	Blue back	1967		20p	£5.00
		Album (original, matt cover with printer's credit)			—	£7.00
	B	Black back	1973		40p	£10.00
		Album (re-issue, glossy cover without printer's credit)			—	£4.00
48	40 Years of Cards:					
	A	Dark Blue back	1994		20p	£7.00
	B	Light Blue back	1994		20p	£6.00
	C	Black back	1994		20p	£6.00
LT40	40 Years of the Chimps Television Advertising	1995		25p	£10.00
		Album with '17 Roadworks' printed in red			—	£20.00
		Album without '17 Roadworks' printed in red			—	£5.00
20	Frances Pitt — British Birds:			HX-64		
	A	Cream Card	1954		£4.00	£80.00
	B	White Card...	1954		£3.00	£60.00
		Album (price 3d)			—	£150.00
50	Freshwater Fish:					
	A	Blue back	1960		£1.00	£50.00
		Album (original matt cover with price)			—	£35.00
	B	Black back	1973		50p	£25.00
		Album (re-issue glossy cover with price)			—	£20.00
		Album (re-issue glossy cover without price)			—	£18.00
	Going Wild — Wildlife Survival:					
M40	A	Standard set	1994		20p	£6.00
EL20	B	Two pictures per card	1994		50p	£10.00
		Album			—	£5.00
50	History of Aviation	1972		20p	£5.00
		Album (original matt inside cover)			—	£6.00
		Album (re-issue glossy inside cover)			—	£6.00
50	History of the Motor Car:					
	A	Blue back	1968		25p	£12.50
		Album (original with price, inside cover cream)			—	£8.00
	B	Black back	1974		25p	£12.50
		Album (re-issue without price, inside cover white)			—	£18.00
		Album (re-issue with price, inside cover white) ...			—	£20.00
	Incredible Creatures:					
40	A	Standard set:				
		i 'Sheen Lane' address	1985		30p	£12.00
		ii 'Walton' address with Dept. I.C.	1986		20p	£4.00
		iii 'Walton' address without Dept. I.C.	1986		50p	£20.00
L20	B	Two pictures per card:				
		i 'Sheen Lane' address	1985		£2.50	—
		ii 'Walton' address with Dept. I.C.	1986		£1.50	£30.00
		iii 'Walton' address without Dept. I.C.	1986		£3.00	—
	Set of 4 Wallcharts			—	£6.00
LT20	International Soccer Stars	1998		50p	£10.00
		Album			—	£5.00
50	Inventors and Inventions	1975		20p	£5.00
		Album			—	£15.00
	A Journey Downstream:					
25	A	Standard set	1990		20p	£3.50
L25	B	Two pictures per card	1990		50p	£12.50
		Album			—	£4.00

BROOKE BOND & CO. LTD (continued)

Size & quantity		Title	Date	Handbook reference	Price per card	Complete set
12		The Language of Tea (flags)	1988		20p	£2.50
		Wallchart			—	£15.00
LT45		The Magical, Mystical World of Pyramids:				
	A	Red & black back	1996		40p	£18.00
	B	Black back	1998		30p	£14.00
		Album			—	£4.00
		The Magical World of Disney:				
25	A	Standard set	1989		20p	£5.00
	B	Two pictures per card:				
L13		i Two pictures per card all 25 pictures			80p	£10.00
L25		ii Two pictures per card all varieties			—	£20.00
		Album			—	£4.00
		Natural Neighbours:				
40	A	Standard set	1992		25p	£10.00
L20	B	Two pictures per card	1992		50p	£10.00
		Album			—	£4.00
		Olympic Challenge 1992:				
40	A	Standard set	1992		25p	£10.00
L20	B	Two pictures per card	1992		60p	£12.00
		Album			—	£4.00
40		Olympic Greats:				
	A	Green back	1979		30p	£12.00
	B	Black back	1988		£1.25	—
		Album			—	£4.00
50		Out Into Space:				
	A	'Issued with Brooke Bond ...'	1956		£10.00	—
		Album (back cover without 'P.G. Tips')	1956		—	£25.00
	B	'Issued in packets ...'	1958		£1.20	£60.00
		Album (back cover with 'P.G. Tips')	1958		—	£45.00
40		Play Better Soccer	1976		20p	£4.00
		Album (original, inside pages cream)			—	£4.00
		Album (re-issue, inside pages white)			—	£12.00
40		Police File	1977		20p	£4.00
		Album			—	£4.00
EL10		Polyfilla Modelling Cards	1974		£9.00	—
50		Prehistoric Animals	1972		20p	£7.00
		Album			—	£20.00
		Queen Elizabeth I - Queen Elizabeth II:				
50	A	Blue/purple back	1983		20p	£6.00
50	B	Black back	1988		20p	£6.00
L25	C	Two pictures per card	1983		£1.40	£35.00
		Album			—	£4.00
50		The Race Into Space:				
	A	Blue back	1971		20p	£6.00
		Album (original, printer's credit 45mm)			—	£25.00
	B	Black back	1974		20p	£5.00
		Album (re-issue, printer's credit 39mm)			—	£30.00
50		Saga of Ships:				
	A	Blue back	1970		20p	£4.00
		Album (original, cover light blue sky)			—	£20.00
	B	Black back	1973		20p	£5.00
		Album (re-issue, cover dark blue sky)...			—	£4.00
50		The Sea — Our Other World	1974		20p	£4.00
		Album (original, with printer's credit)			—	£10.00
		Album (re-issue, without printer's credit)			—	£4.00
LT50		The Secret Diary of Kevin Tipps	1995		20p	£10.00
		Album			—	£4.00

BROOKE BOND & CO. LTD (continued)

Size & quantity		Date	Handbook reference	Price per card	Complete set
40	Small Wonders:				
	A Blue back	1981		20p	£5.00
	B Black back	1988		20p	£4.00
	Album			—	£4.00
LT19	Tea Leaf Oracle	1999		£4.00	—
	Teenage Mutant Hero Turtles:				
12	A Standard set	1991		21p	£2.50
L6	B Two pictures per card	1991		80p	£5.00
	Album			—	£4.00
12	30 Years of The Chimps:				
	A Thin Card plain back	1986		£6.00	—
	B Thick Card plain back	1986		85p	£10.00
	C Thin Card Tak Tik back	1986		£5.00	—
	Album			—	£20.00
50	Transport Through the Ages:		HX-158		
	A Blue back	1966		20p	£5.00
	Album			—	£25.00
	B Black back	1973		£1.00	—
50	Trees in Britain:				
	A Blue back	1966		20p	£4.00
	Album (original matt cover with letter 'T')			—	£8.00
	Album (original matt cover without letter 'T')			—	£35.00
	B Black back	1973		20p	£4.00
	Album (re-issue glossy cover with price and printer's credit)			—	£20.00
	Album (re-issue glossy cover with price, without printer's credit)			—	£5.00
	Album (re-issue glossy cover without price)			—	£15.00
50	Tropical Birds:				
	A Blue back	1961		35p	£17.50
	Album (original matt cover with price)			—	£25.00
	B Black back	1974		20p	£4.00
	Album (re-issue glossy cover with price)			—	£20.00
	Album (re-issue glossy cover without price or printer's credit)			—	£5.00
	Album (re-issue glossy cover without price with printer's credit)			—	£18.00
	Unexplained Mysteries of the World:				
40	A Standard set	1987		20p	£4.00
L20	B Two pictures per card	1987		50p	£10.00
	Album			—	£4.00
40	Vanishing Wildlife:				
	A Brown back	1978		20p	£4.00
	Album (original matt inside cover)			—	£6.00
	B Black back	1988		20p	£5.00
	Album (re-issue glossy inside cover)			—	£5.00
50	Wild Birds in Britain:				
	A Blue back	1965		20p	£4.00
	Album (original matt cover with price)			—	£20.00
	B Black back	1973		20p	£6.00
	Album (re-issue glossy cover with price)			—	£18.00
	Album (re-issue glossy cover without price)			—	£18.00
50	Wild Flowers, Series 1:				
	A Thick Card	1955		£3.00	£150.00
	B Paper Thin Card	1955		£9.00	—
	Album (cover with price)			—	£40.00
	Album (cover without price)			—	£80.00

BROOKE BOND & CO. LTD (continued)

Size & quantity		Date	Handbook reference	Price per card	Complete set
50	Wild Flowers, Series 2:				
	A Blue back with 'issued by …'	1959		25p	£12.50
	B Blue back without 'issued by …'	1959		£2.50	—
	Album (original matt cover with price)			—	£30.00
	C Black back	1973		20p	£5.00
	Album (re-issue glossy cover with price)			—	£20.00
	Album (re-issue glossy cover without price)			—	£5.00
50	Wild Flowers, Series 3	1964		20p	£6.00
	Album			—	£25.00
50	Wild Life in Danger:				
	A Blue back	1963		20p	£4.00
	Album (original matt cover with price sixpence)			—	£15.00
	B Black back	1973		20p	£4.00
	Album (re-issue glossy cover with price)			—	£20.00
	Album (re-issue glossy cover without price)			—	£20.00
LT30	The Wonderful World of Kevin Tipps	1997		40p	£12.00
	Album			—	£4.00
50	Wonders of Wildlife	1976		20p	£4.00
	Error and corrected card of No. 37			—	£18.00
	Album			—	£4.00
40	Woodland Wildlife:				
	A Green back	1980		20p	£7.00
	B Black back	1988		20p	£7.00
	Album			—	£4.00
L50	Zena Skinner International Cookery Cards	1974		£20.00	—

BROOKE BOND OVERSEAS ISSUES

IRELAND

40	Incredible Creatures	1986		£2.00	£80.00

CANADA

CU1 48	Songbirds of North America:				
	A Back 'Red Rose Tea & Coffee' Album clause reading:				
	i 'Mount Your Collection, Send 25c'	1959		£6.00	—
	ii 'Album available at your grocer's or from us 25c'	1959		£3.50	
	B Back 'Red Rose and Blue Ribbon Tea and Coffee'	1959		£1.80	£90.00
	Album (back cover 'Red Rose' only)			—	£70.00
	Album (back cover 'Red Rose & Blue Ribbon')			—	£60.00
CU2 48	Animals of North America:				
	A 'Rolland' back	1960		£3.00	—
	B 'Roland' back:				
	i Text between lines 47mm	1960		£2.50	£125.00
	ii Text between lines 49mm	1960		£14.00	—
	Album			—	£40.00
CU3 48	Wild Flowers of North America	1961		£1.00	£50.00
	Album			—	£40.00
CU4 48	Birds of North America	1962		£1.00	£50.00
	Album			—	£40.00
CU5 48	Dinosaurs	1963		£3.00	£150.00
	Album			—	£90.00
CU6 48	Tropical Birds:				
	A Top line in red	1964		£9.00	—
	B Top line in black	1964		90p	£45.00
	Album			—	£20.00

Size & quantity	TRADE CARD ISSUES	Date	Handbook reference	Price per card	Complete set

BROOKE BOND & CO. LTD (Overseas Issues, Canada continued)

Size & quantity		Date	Price per card	Complete set
CU7 48	African Animals	1964	20p	£6.00
	Album		—	£20.00
CU8 48	Butterflies of North America	1965	80p	£40.00
	Album		—	£30.00
CU9 48	Canadian/American Songbirds	1966	£2.50	£125.00
	Album		—	£20.00
CU10 48	Transportation Through the Ages:			
	A Top line in red	1967	£9.00	—
	B Top line in black	1967	35p	£17.50
	Album		—	£25.00
CU11 48	Trees of North America	1968	40p	£20.00
	Album (pages 3, 8, 9 etc. green)		—	£30.00
	Album (pages 3, 6, 7 etc. green)		—	£25.00
CU12 48	The Space Age	1969	30p	£15.00
	Album		—	£15.00
CU13 48	North American Wildlife in Danger	1970	20p	£9.00
	Album		—	£15.00
CU14 48	Exploring the Ocean	1971	20p	£6.00
	Album		—	£5.00
CU15 48	Animals and Their Young:			
	A Text ends 'Products'	1972	40p	£20.00
	B Text ends 'Tea/Coffee'	1972	£9.00	—
	Note: Without Brooke Bond name — see Liptons Tea			
	Album		—	£15.00
CU16 48	The Arctic	1973	20p	£10.00
	Album		—	£4.00
CU17 48	Indians of Canada	1974	£1.00	£50.00
	Album		—	£4.00

USA

		Date	Price per card	Complete set
CU2 48	Animals of North America:			
	A Blue text on back	1960	£9.00	—
	B Black text on back	1960	£12.00	—
CU3 48	Wild Flowers of North America:			
	A Dark Blue back	1961	£5.00	—
	B Light Blue back	1961	£20.00	—
CU4 48	Birds of North America	1962	£7.00	—
CU5 48	Dinosaurs	1963	£9.00	—
CU6 48	Tropical Birds	1964	£5.00	—
CU8 48	Butterflies of North America	1965	£5.00	—
CU9 48	Canadian/American Songbirds	1966	£3.00	—

SOUTHERN RHODESIA AND EAST AFRICA

		Date	Price per card	Complete set
SR2 50	African Wild Life	1961	£6.00	—
	Album (no price with red line under C.F. Tunnicliffe)		—	£150.00
SR3 50	Tropical Birds	1962	£6.00	—
	Album (no price with red line under C.F. Tunnicliffe)		—	£150.00
SR4 50	Asian Wild Life	1963	£6.00	—
	Album (East Africa issue price 50 cents)		—	£150.00
	Album (Rhodesia issue price 6c)		—	£150.00
SR5 50	Wild Life in Danger	1964	£6.00	—
	Album (East Africa issue price 50 cents)		—	£150.00
	Album (Rhodesia issue price nine pence)		—	£150.00
SR6 50	African Birds	1965	£5.00	—
	Album		—	£100.00
SR7 50	Butterflies of the World	1966	£5.00	£250.00
	Album (price 9d)		—	£125.00

BROOKE BOND & CO. LTD (Overseas Issues continued)

SOUTH AFRICA

SA1 50	Wild van Africa (alternate cards English and Afrikaans)	1965		£13.00	—
SA2 50	Wild van Africa (bilingual)	1965		£5.00	£250.00
	Album			—	£50.00
SA3 50	Out Into Space	1966		£5.00	£250.00
	Album			—	£50.00
SA4 50	Our Pets:				
	A Printing A	1967		£5.00	£250.00
	B Printing B (revised numbering)	1967		£16.00	—
	Album			—	£50.00

MUSGRAVE-BROOKE BOND (Eire)

MBB1 20	British Birds...	1964	HX-64	£10.00	—
	Album (price 6d)			—	£200.00
MBB2 50	British Wild Life	1964	HX-66	£10.00	—
	Album (Musgrave Brothers on back)			—	£200.00
MBB3 50	Butterflies of the World	1965	HX-67	£10.00	—
	Album (Musgrave Brooke Bond address)			—	£200.00
MBB4 50	Transport Through the Ages	1966	HX-158	£5.00	£250.00
	Album (Musgrave Brooke Bond on front cover)			—	£150.00

BROOKE BOND-LIEBIG (Italy)

EL6	F.1845 The Nativity	1971		—	£25.00
EL6	F.1850 Self-Portraits of Famous Artists	1972		—	£6.00
EL6	F.1851 Journey to the Moon (II)	1972		—	£10.00
EL6	F.1852 Historical Fights...	1972		—	£7.00
EL6	F.1853 The Resurrection	1972		—	£18.00
EL6	F.1854 History of the Typewriter	1972		—	£12.00
EL6	F.1855 How Animals See (I)	1973		—	£6.00
EL6	F.1856 Ludwig van Beethoven	1973		—	£8.00
EL6	F.1857 The Fight Against Microbes (I)	1973		—	£6.00
EL6	F.1858 How Animals See (II)	1973		—	£5.00
EL6	F.1859 The Story of the Circus	1973		—	£14.00
EL6	F.1860 The Fight Against Microbes (II)	1973		—	£15.00
EL6	F.1861 The Circus	1974		—	£15.00
EL6	F.1862 War at Sea	1974		—	£40.00
EL6	F.1863 Animals	1974		—	£15.00
EL6	F.1867 Journey to the Moon (I)	1975		—	£13.00
EL6	F.1868 Protected Birds	1975		—	£11.00
EL6	F.1869 Old Military Dress (I)	1975		—	£11.00
EL6	F.1871 Old Military Dress (II)	1975		—	£40.00

BROOKE BOND NOVELTY INSERTS
ADVERTISEMENT CARD INSERTS (Great Britain)

1	Why is Crown Cup 'Medium Roasted'?	1963		—	£5.00
1	3 Crown Cups and Saucers	1963		—	£12.00
2	Danish Designed Tableware	1964		£12.00	—
2	Radio London	1965		£12.00	—
2	Six-Piece Cutlery Set	1966		£12.00	—
1	Free Opal Glass Jar:				
	A Original card plain back	1967		—	£45.00
	B Reprint card printed back	2004		—	£3.00
	Place The Face Bingo:		HB-177		
15	A Single Face with PG Tips	1972		£35.00	—
15	B Single Face without PG Tips...	1972		£35.00	—
15	C Three Faces	1972		£35.00	—
K15	D Flap of Packet	1972		£40.00	—

BROOKE BOND & CO. LTD (Novelty Inserts continued)

1	Play Better Soccer set and album offer	1976		—	£5.00
1	Play Better Soccer 'Great New Series!'	1976		—	£12.00
1	Police File 'New picture Card Series'	1977		—	£45.00
LT1	P.G. Tips Tipps Family 1997 Calendar	1996		—	£10.00
LT3	Farewell to Picture Cards	1999		£1.50	£4.50
LT1	P.G. Tips Need Your Help	1999		—	£1.50
LT1	Thank You	1999		—	£1.50
LT1	PG Tips Bean Chimp:				
	A With Multi Coloured Circle	2001		—	£4.00
	B With Dark Brown Circle	2001		—	£8.00
EL1	World Cup 1966 Souvenir (booklet)	1966		—	£70.00

ADVERTISEMENT CARDS (Eire)

Match-Maker Cards:

	A Blue & black printing:				
39	a 'Musgrave Brooke Bond' on front	1967		£40.00	—
39	b 'PG Tips' on front	1967		£40.00	—
9	B Red & black printing	1967		£40.00	—

CARD GAMES

L36	British Costume	1974		—	£25.00
L36	Flags and Emblems	1974		—	£25.00
L36	Motor History	1974		—	£25.00
L55	P.G. Tips Card Game — Get Out	1995		—	£5.00
L54	P.G. Tips Card Game — Playing Cards	1995		—	£4.00
L36	P.G. Tips Card Game — Snap	1995		—	£4.00
L54	P.G. Tips Card Game — Trick Cards	1995		—	£4.00

BROOKFIELD SWEETS (Ireland)

50	Animals of the World	c1956	HX-93	£4.00	—
25	Aquarium Fish 1st Series	c1959	HX-87	£4.00	—
25	Aquarium Fish 2nd Series	c1959	HX-87	£4.00	—
25	Conquest of Space	c1956	HX-73	£4.00	—
25	Motor Cars	c1954	HX-15	£4.00	—

BROOKS DYE WORKS LTD

EL4	Interesting Shots of Old Bristol	c1950		£1.50	£6.00

BROWN & POLSON

L25	Brown & Polson Picture Cards (Recipe)	1925		£4.00	—

DAVID BROWN (Tractors)

EL3	Is Your Slip Showing?	1954		£3.00	£9.00

BROWNE BROS. LTD (Tea)

25	Birds	1963	HX-71	£1.60	—
25	British Cavalry Uniforms of the 19th Century	1964	HX-73	80p	—
25	Garden Flowers	1965	HX-46	£2.00	—
25	History of the Railway 1st Series	1964	HX-88	40p	£10.00
25	History of the Railway 2nd Series	1964	HX-88	36p	£9.00
24	The Island of Ceylon	1961	HX-47	£5.00	—
25	Passenger Liners	1966	HX-82	£2.00	—
25	People and Places	1967	HX-26	20p	£3.00
25	Tropical Birds	1966	HX-13.2	20p	£3.00
25	Wonders of the Deep	1965	HX-89	20p	£3.00
25	Wonders of the World	1967	HX-49	20p	£5.00

BRYANT & MAY

| L12 | The Thirties.. | 1992 | | — | £12.00 |

BUBBLES INC. (Chewing Gum)

| L55 | Mars Attacks .... | 1964 | | £25.00 | — |
| L50 | Outer Limits .... | 1966 | | £5.50 | — |

BUCHANAN'S (Jam)

| 24 | Birds and Their Eggs .... | 1923 | HX-164 | £10.00 | — |

JOHNNY BUNNY

| 25 | Football Clubs and Badges .... | c1960 | HX-137 | £3.00 | — |

BUNSEN CONFECTIONERY CO.

| 200 | Famous Figures Series........................ | c1925 | HB-186 | £18.00 | — |

BURDALL & BURDALL

| 30 | Wild Animals .... | c1920 | | £7.50 | — |

BURLINGTON SLATE

| L20 | Processing and Use of Slate .... | 1992 | | — | £15.00 |

BURTONS (Wagon Wheels)

25	Indian Chiefs	1972		70p	£17.50
EL8	NFL Heroes (American Football)	1987		—	£24.00
L7	Pictures of the Wild West	1983		£7.00	—
25	The West	1972		20p	£5.00
25	Wild West Action	1972		20p	£5.00

BUTTAPAT DAIRIES

| 25 | People of the World .... | 1915 | HB-188 | £20.00 | — |

BUTTERCUP BREAD (Australia)

M24	Allan Border Tribute	1994		—	£18.00
M24	Border's Ashes Heroes	1993		—	£18.00
M24	1993-94 World Series All Stars	1993		—	£18.00

BYRNES ENT. (USA)

| LT22 | Firemen in Action .... | 1981 | | — | £9.50 |
| LT22 | Firemen in Action .... | 1982 | | — | £12.00 |

C.B.S. LTD

| 30 | Glamorgan Cricketers .... | 1984 | | — | £20.00 |

CCC LTD

L15	Arsenal FC Cup Winners 1992/1993	1993		—	£7.50
L20	Doctor Who (TV Series)	1993		—	£15.00
L6	Wild Cats by Joel Kirk	1994		—	£3.50

C & G CONFECTIONERY CO.

| 25 | Box of Tricks 1st Series .... | 1963 | | £5.00 | — |
| 25 | Box of Tricks 2nd Series .... | 1963 | | £5.00 | — |

C.H. PUBLICATIONS

L6	MG World 1st Series Nos 1-6 (Cars)	1999		—	£3.00
L6	MG World 2nd Series Nos 7-12 (Cars)	1999		—	£3.00
L6	Triumph World 1st Series Nos 1-6 (Cars)	1999		—	£3.00
L6	Triumph World 3rd Series Nos 13-18 (Cars)	2000		—	£3.00

CMA (UK)

LT82	Hammer Horror Series 2	1996		—	£15.00
LT74	Hammer Horror Entombed	2000		—	£20.00

C.N.G. (New Zealand)

M10	Trees of New Zealand	1992		—	£8.00

C.S. LTD (Cadet Sweets)

50	Footballers and Club Colours	1963		£1.50	—
25	Record Holders of the World 1st Series	1962		50p	£12.50
25	Ships Through the Ages 1st Series	1963	HX-94	£1.20	—
25	Ships Through the Ages 2nd Series	1963	HX-94	£1.20	—

CADBURY BROS. LTD

EL12	Antarctic Series	c1915	HC-11	£30.00	—
EL6	Bay City Rollers	1975		£2.00	£12.00
L12	Birds in Springtime	1983		—	£3.50
6	Bourneville Series B	c1905		£20.00	—
6	Bourneville Village Series	c1905		£20.00	—
EL25	British Birds (Reward Cards)	c1910	HC-12	£9.00	—
12	British Birds and Eggs	c1910	HC-13	£12.00	—
EL12	British Birds and Their Eggs (Reward Cards)	c1910	HC-14	£11.00	—
EL32	British Butterflies and Moths (Reward Cards)	c1910	HC-15	£6.50	—
6	British Colonies, Maps and Industries	c1910		£20.00	—
120	British Marvels Vol. I	1936		£2.00	—
120	British Marvels Vol. II	1936		£2.00	—
12	British Trees Series	1911		£7.00	—
80	Cadbury's Picture Making	c1935		£2.00	—
	Cathedral Series:				
12	A Standard size (size 65 x 37mm)	1913		£8.00	—
EL6	B Strip of two (size 165 x 37mm)	1913		£20.00	—
EL6	C Strip of two (size 150 x 37mm)	1913		£20.00	—
6	Colonial Premiers Series	c1910		£20.00	—
	Constellations Series:				
12	A Standard size (size 65 × 37mm)	1912		£8.50	—
EL6	B Strip of two (size 152 × 36mm)	1912		£16.00	—
24	Copyright (Inventors) Series	c1915		£14.00	—
	Coronation:				
1	A Size 73 × 34mm	1911		—	£30.00
EL1	B Size 149 × 38mm	1911		—	£40.00
48	Dangerous Animals	1970		45p	£22.50
6	Dogs Series	c1910		£38.00	—
EL12	English Industries	c1910	HC-19	£32.00	—
25	Fairy Tales	1924		£4.00	—
27	Famous Steamships	1923		£3.50	—
12	Fish	c1910	HC-20	£12.00	—
EL6	Fish and Bait Series	c1910		£36.00	—
	Flag Series (horizontal):				
12	A Standard size (size 65 × 36mm)	1912		£4.00	—
EL6	B Strips of Two (size 150 × 36mm)	1912		£8.00	—

Size &   **TRADE CARD ISSUES**   *Date*   *Handbook*   *Price*   *Complete*

quantity   *reference*   *per card*   *set*

CADBURY BROS. LTD (continued)

Size & quantity		Date	Handbook reference	Price per card	Complete set
	Flag Series (vertical):				
EL12	A Size 107 × 35mm	1912		£26.00	—
EL12	B Size 146 × 50mm	1912		£26.00	—
EL12	Flight, The World's Most Spectacular Birds	1983		—	£6.00
1	Largest Steamers in the World	c1905		—	£80.00
6	Locomotive Series	c1910		£32.00	—
12	Match Puzzles	c1905		£35.00	—
6	Old Ballad Series	c1905		£22.00	—
EL6	Panama Series	c1910		£30.00	—
EL5	Pop Stars	1975		£1.50	—
EL8	Prehistoric Monsters	1975		£1.25	—
EL6	Rivers of the British Isles	c1910	HC-26	£16.00	—
24	Shadow Series	c1915		£16.00	—
6	Shipping Series:				
	A Size 84 × 40mm	c1910		£12.00	—
	B Size 134 × 58mm	c1910		£12.00	—
	C Size 153 × 39mm	c1910		£12.00	—
	D Size 164 × 81mm	c1910		£12.00	—
EL6	Sports Series	c1905		£50.00	—
24	Strange But True	1969		20p	£3.00
	Album			—	£20.00
25	Transport	1925		50p	£12.50

CADBURY-SCHWEPPES FOODS LTD

12	The Age of the Dinosaur	1971		50p	£6.00
	Folder/Album			—	£10.00

CADET (Sweets)

48	Adventures of Rin Tin Tin:				
	A Size 60 × 32mm	1960		£1.20	—
	B Size 65 × 37mm:				
	i 'Cadet Sweets' in two lines	1960		50p	£25.00
	ii 'Cadet Sweets' in one line	1960		£1.50	—
25	Arms and Armour	1960		20p	£2.50
50	Buccaneers:		HC-29A		
	A Size 58 × 30mm	1959		£1.00	—
	B Size 63 × 33mm	1959		40p	£20.00
50	Buccaneers (different Series) (size 65 × 35mm)	1959	HC-29B	60p	£30.00
50	Conquest of Space:		HX-73		
	A Size 64 × 35mm	1957		60p	—
	B Size 69 × 37mm	1957		30p	£15.00
25	Daktari	1968		40p	£10.00
50	Doctor Who and The Daleks	1965		£3.50	£175.00
25	Dogs 1st Series:				
	A Size 60 × 32mm	1958		50p	£12.50
	B Size 65 × 35mm	1958		£2.70	—
25	Dogs 2nd Series:				
	A Size 60 × 32mm	1958		50p	£12.50
	B Size 65 × 35mm	1958		£2.70	—
25	Evolution of the Royal Navy	1960	HX-90	20p	£4.00
22	Famous Explorers (Package Issue)	c1960		£8.00	—
50	Footballers Size 66 x 35mm	1957		60p	£30.00
50	Footballers Size 61 x 31mm. Title 28mm, large text print inverted backs	1958		35p	£17.50
50	Footballers Size 61 x 31mm. Title 19mm, small text print	1959		35p	£17.50

CADET (Sweets) (continued)

50	Footballers Size 61 x 31mm. Title 28mm, small text				
	print, standard backs… … … … … … … … … … …	c1960		£5.00	—
25	How? … … … … … … … … … … … … … … … …	1968		36p	£9.00
25	Prehistoric Animals … … … … … … … … … … …	1961	HX-92	£1.00	—
50	Railways of the World … … … … … … … … … …	1955		20p	£8.00
50	Record Holders of the World … … … … … … … …	1956		20p	£10.00
50	Stingray … … … … … … … … … … … … … … …	1965		70p	£35.00
25	Treasure Hunt … … … … … … … … … … … … …	1964		20p	£3.00
50	UNCLE (TV Series):				
	A Photos	1966		£1.30	£65.00
	B Drawings … … … … … … … … … …	1966		£2.50	—
25	What Do You Know? … … … … … … … … … …	1965	HX-67	60p	£15.00

A.J. CALEY & SON

K24	Film Stars … … … … … … … … … … … … … …	c1930	HC-34	£10.00	—
48	Mickey Mouse Wisequacks … … … … … … … …	1939		£11.00	—
L50	Tricks & Puzzles … … … … … … … … … … … …	c1930		£6.00	—

CALFUN INC (Canada)

LT100	Fantazy Cards (Pin Up Girls) … … … … … … … …	1992		—	£15.00

CALICO GRAPHICS (USA)

LT54	League of Nations 2nd Series … … … … … … …	1990		—	£9.50
EL1	League of Nations 2nd Series advert card … … … …	1990		—	£1.00

CALRAB (USA)

LT24	The California Raisins World Tour … … … … … … …	1988		—	£5.00

CALTEX OIL (Australia)

EL6	Stargazer (Haley's Comet) … … … … … … … … …	1986		—	£3.00

F.C. CALVERT & CO. LTD (Tooth Powder)

K25	Dan Dare … … … … … … … … … … … … … … …	1954		£4.00	£100.00
	Album … … … … … … … … … … … … … … … …			—	£50.00

CANDY GUM

M50	Auto Sprint 1st Series … … … … … … … … … … …	1975		30p	—
M30	Auto Sprint 2nd Series … … … … … … … … … … …	1975		20p	£6.00

CANDY NOVELTY CO.

25	Animals of the Countryside … … … … … … … … …	1960	HX-9	£5.00	—
50	Animals of the World … … … … … … … … … … …	c1960	HX-93	£4.00	—
M50	Dog Series A.1:				
	A Complete set … … … … … … … … … … … …	c1955		£1.50	—
	B 25 different… … … … … … … … … … … …	c1955		20p	£4.00
	Album … … … … … … … … … … … … … … …			—	£25.00
32	Motor Car Series:				
	A Blue green … … … … … … … … … … … …	c1953		£6.00	—
	B Orange … … … … … … … … … … … …	c1953		£6.00	—
25	Ships through the Ages 2nd Series… … … … … … …	c1960	HX-94	£5.00	—
32	Western Series:				
	A Black on blue green … … … … … … … …	c1953		£6.00	—
	B Green on blue green … … … … … … … …	c1953		£6.00	—

Size &
quantity
TRADE CARD ISSUES
Date
*Handbook
reference*
*Price
per card*
*Complete
set*

CANNING'S

25	Types of British Soldiers … … … … … … … …	c1914	HX-144	£16.00	—

CANNON PRESS

10	Screen Gems David Niven … … … … … … …	2010		—	£5.00
20	Screen Gems Lana Turner … … … … … … …	2009		—	£9.00
20	Screen Gems Natalie Wood… … … … … … … …	2009		—	£9.00
10	Screen Gems Rock Hudson … … … … … … …	2010		—	£5.00
10	Screen Gems Will Hay … … … … … … … … …	2009		—	£5.00
10	Treasure Island … … … … … … … … … … …	2009		—	£5.00

CAPERN (Bird Food)

7	Cage Birds (blue backgrounds) … … … … … … …	c1920	HC-43B	£12.00	—
7	Cage Birds (white backgrounds)… … … … … … …	c1920	HC-43A	£12.00	—
	Cage Birds:		HC-44		
EL51	A Plain back … … … … … … … … … … …	c1925		£4.50	—
EL8	B Postcard back … … … … … … … …	c1925		£5.00	—
EL1	C Text back … … … … … … … … … …	c1925		£8.00	—
24	Capern Picture Aviary … … … … … … … … …	1964		£1.00	—
	Album … … … … … … … … … … … … …			—	£20.00
1	Capern Picture Aviary Introductory Card … … … … …	1964		—	25p

CAR AND DRIVER (USA)

EL100	Cadillac Collection … … … … … … … … … …	1993		—	£15.00

CARAMAC

M42	Railway Locomotives … … … … … … … … …	1976		36p	£15.00

CARD CRAZY (New Zealand)

LT90	High Velocity New Zealand Cricketers… … … … … …	1996		20p	£12.00
LT90	New Zealand Rugby League Superstars … … … … …	1995		20p	£12.00
LT110	New Zealand Rugby Union Superstars … … … … …	1995		20p	£12.00
LT55	Shortland Street (TV Series) … … … … … … … …	1995		—	£6.00

CARD CREATIONS (USA)

LT100	Popeye … … … … … … … … … … … … … …	1994		—	£12.00

CARD INSERT LTD

1	Famous Footballers (only No.12 issued) … … … … …	c1955		—	£8.00

CARDLYNX

EL6	Bookmarks High Grade Series … … … … … … …	2008		—	£4.50
L6	Butterflies … … … … … … … … … … … …	2007		—	£3.00
L6	Eagles … … … … … … … … … … … … …	2007		—	£3.00
L6	Gangsters … … … … … … … … … … … …	2005		—	£3.00
L6	Golfers … … … … … … … … … … … … …	2006		—	£3.00
L6	Horses … … … … … … … … … … … … …	2007		—	£3.00
L6	Jazz Greats… … … … … … … … … … … …	2005		—	£3.00
L6	Lighthouses… … … … … … … … … … … …	2008		—	£3.00
L6	Owls … … … … … … … … … … … … … …	2004		—	£3.00
L6	Parrots … … … … … … … … … … … … …	2004		—	£3.00
L6	Poultry … … … … … … … … … … … … …	2005		—	£3.00
L6	Poultry Breeds… … … … … … … … … … …	2007		—	£3.00
L6	Sea Shells … … … … … … … … … … … …	2008		—	£3.00
L6	Space Firsts … … … … … … … … … … …	2004		—	£3.00
EL6	UFOs & Aliens From Space… … … … … … … … ..	2010		—	£4.50

CARDLYNX (continued)

L6	Victorian Poultry	2007		—	£3.00
EL6	Wild West Outlaws	2013		—	£4.50
EL6	Wizards Past, Present & Future/ World's Most				
	Valuable Baseball Cards	2010		—	£4.50

CARDS INC

LT72	Beyblade	2000		—	£8.00
LT72	Captain Scarlet	2002		20p	£9.50
LT72	Harry Potter and The Prisoner of Azkaban	2004		20p	£9.50
LT17	Harry Potter and The Prisoner of Azkaban				
	Foil Series	2004		25p	£4.00
LT72	The Prisoner Volume 1 (1960/70s TV Series)	2002		—	£12.00
LT30	Scarface The Film	2003		—	£8.00
LT72	Shrek 2 The Film:				
	A Standard Series	2004		20p	£12.00
	B Foil Parallel Series	2004		40p	£30.00
LT72	Thunderbirds	2001		20p	£9.50
LT72	Thunderbirds The Movie	2004		—	£11.00
LT100	U.F.O. (TV Series)	2004		—	£12.00
LT100	The Very Best of The Saint	2003		—	£12.00

CARDTOON CREATIONS

24	Championship Champions 2005-2006 (Reading F.C.)	2006		—	£7.50

CARDTOONS (USA)

LT95	Baseball Parodies	1993		—	£8.00
LT9	Baseball Parodies Field of Greed Puzzle...............	1993		—	£3.00
LT11	Baseball Parodies Politics in Baseball............	1993		—	£3.00

CARDZ (USA)

LT100	Hitchhiker's Guide to the Galaxy (Cartoon)	1994		—	£12.00
LT50	Lee MacLeod — Fantasy Art	1994		—	£6.00
LT10	Lee MacLeod Tekchrome Nos T1 to T10 — Fantasy				
	Art	1994		—	£8.00
LT100	The Mask — The Film	1994		—	£9.50
LT60	Maverick — The Movie	1994		—	£9.50
LT60	The Muppets	1993		—	£9.00
LT80	Muppets Take The Ice	1994		—	£8.00
LT60	Return of The Flintstones	1994		—	£9.00
LT110	San Diego Zoo	1993		—	£12.00
LT60	Tiny Toons Adventures	1994		—	£9.00
LT60	Tom & Jerry...	1993		—	£9.00
LT100	WCW Main Event (Wrestling)	1995		—	£9.50
LT100	William Shatner's Tek World	1993		—	£9.50
LT100	World War II	1994		—	£9.50
LT10	World War II Tekchrome Nos T1-T10	1994		—	£3.00

CARNATION (Tinned Milk)

EL12	Recipe Service	1971		33p	4.00

CARR'S BISCUITS

EL20	Cricketers	1968	£7.00		—
EL48	Sporting Champions..	1966	£7.00		—
EL20	Sports — Soccer Card Series	c1967	£10.00		—

CARSON'S CHOCOLATE

72	Celebrities		1901	HC-48	£17.00	—

CARTER'S LITTLE LIVER PILLS

28	Dominoes		c1910		£2.00	—

F.C. CARTLEDGE

L96	Epigrams (Rheuma Salts)		1939		21p	£20.00
L48	Epigrams (Knock-out Razor Blades)		1939	HC-52	20p	£10.00
L12	Epigrams (without maker's name)		1939	HC-53	—	£10.00
L64	Epigrams (without product)		1939	HC-54	20p	£12.00
50	Famous Prize Fighters:					
	A Complete set (matt)...		1938		—	£125.00
	B 49/50 (—No. 23) (matt)		1938		£2.00	£100.00
	C 2 variety cards (matt) (Nos 13 & 19)		1938		—	£8.00
	D Complete set (glossy)		1938		£3.00	—

CASEY CARDS

10	The Casey (Football Stars of the 1960s)		2010		—	£5.00

CASH & CO.

20	War Pictures		c1910	HX-122	£16.00	—

CASSELL'S

M6	British Engines		c1925		£11.00	—
M12	Butterflies and Moths Series		c1925		£7.50	—

CASTROL OIL

L18	Famous Riders (motorcyclists)		1956	HC-59	£5.00	£90.00
L24	Racing Cars		1955		£4.00	—

CAVE, AUSTIN & CO. LTD

20	Inventors Series		1928	HX-213	£12.00	—

C.E.D.E. LTD

25	Coins of the World		1956	HX-6	20p	£4.00

CENTRAL ELECTRICITY AUTHORITY

M10	Careers in the Central Electricity Board		1957	HC-61	30p	£3.00

CEREBOS

100	Sea Shells:					
	A Brown back		1925		£2.50	—
	B Grey back		1925		£4.50	—

CEYLON TEA CENTRE

24	Island of Ceylon		1955	HX-47	20p	£2.50
	Album				—	£15.00

CHAMPS (USA)

LT100	American Vintage Cycles Series 1		1992		—	£9.50
LT100	American Vintage Cycles Series 2		1993		—	£9.50

CHANNEL 4/CHEERLEADER

L20	All Time Great Quarterbacks		1989		£1.25	£25.00

H. CHAPPEL & CO.

?10	British Celebrities	1905	HC-65	£35.00	—
? 8	Characters from Nursery Rhymes	1905	HB-17	£45.00	—

CHARTER TEA & COFFEE CO LTD

25	Prehistoric Animals 1st Series	c1965	HX-151	£1.20	—
25	Prehistoric Animals 2nd Series	c1965	HX-151	£1.20	—
25	Strange but True 1st Series	1961	HX-96	80p	£20.00
25	Strange but True 2nd Series	1961	HX-96	60p	£15.00
25	Transport Through the Ages 1st Series	c1965	HX-97	80p	£20.00
25	Transport Through the Ages 2nd Series	c1965	HX-97	60p	£15.00
	Album for 1st and 2nd Series combined			—	£20.00

CHEF & BREWER

L20	Historic Pub Signs	1984		£1.00	—

CHESDALE (New Zealand)

M6	Action Sports	1983		60p	£3.50

CHIVERS & SONS LTD

M10	Firm Favourites 1st Series...	c1930		£4.00	—
M10	Firm Favourites 2nd Series	c1930		£4.00	—
M10	Firm Favourites 3rd Series	c1930		£4.00	—
M95	Firm Favourites (Nos 31 to 125)...	c1930		£3.00	—
EL6	Studies of English Fruits (Series 1)...	c1930		£6.00	—
EL6	Studies of English Fruits (Series 2)...	c1930		£6.00	—
24	Wild Wisdom	c1960		£3.20	—
48	Wild Wisdom in Africa	c1960		£3.20	—
48	Wild Wisdom, River and Marsh	c1960		£3.20	—
	Package Issues:				
L15	Children of Other Lands	c1955		£1.25	—
L15	Chivers British Birds	c1955		£1.50	—
L20	On Chivers Farms	c1955		£1.25	—

CHIX CONFECTIONERY CO. LTD

M12	Batman P.C. inset (Package issue)...	1989		—	£6.00
M48	Facts & Feats (Waxed Paper issue)	c1960		£4.50	—
	Famous Footballers No.1 Series:				
L24	A Inscribed 'Set of 48' (Nos 1-24 only issued) ...	1955		£4.50	—
L24	B Inscribed 'Numbers 1 to 24'	1955		£4.50	—
L24	C Inscribed 'Numbers 25 to 48'	1955		£4.50	—
L48	D Inscribed 'Numbers 1 to 48'	1955		£4.50	—
L48	Famous Footballers 2nd Series	1957		£5.50	—
L48	Famous Footballers 3rd Series	1958		£6.50	—
L50	Famous Footballers	1961		£7.00	—
L50	Famous Last Words	1969		£1.50	—
L48	Footballers (double picture):				
	A 'Ask for Chix' back	1960		£2.00	—
	B Anonymous back	1960		80p	£40.00
L50	Funny Old Folk	1970		50p	£25.00
L50	Happy Howlers	1969		£1.20	—
L6	Joker P.C. inset (Double Package issue)...	1990		—	£9.00
L50	Krazy Kreatures from Outer Space...	1968		£2.00	£100.00
L50	Military Uniforms	1969		70p	—
L50	Moon Shot	1966		£2.50	—
L50	Popeye	1959		£3.50	—
L24	Scottish Footballers (SFBL 1 back)...	c1960		£9.00	—

CHIX CONFECTIONERY CO. LTD (continued)

L50	Ships of the Seven Seas	1964		£2.00	—
L50	Soldiers of the World	1960		£1.50	—
L50	Sports Through the Ages	1963		£3.50	—
96	TV and Radio Stars	1955		£4.00	£400.00
L50	Wild Animals	c1960		£2.00	—

CHOCOLAT DE VILLARS

24	British Birds and Their Eggs	1926	HX-164	£4.60	£115.00

CHUMS

MP23	'Chums' Cricketers	1923		£5.50	—
MP20	'Chums' Football Teams	1922		£4.50	—
P8	'Chums' Football Teams, New Series	c1925		£4.50	—
LP10	'Chums' Real Colour Photos	c1925		£8.00	—

CHURCH & DWIGHT (USA)

M60	Beautiful Flowers, New Series	c1888		£4.00	—
EL10	Birds of Prey	1975		—	£25.00
M30	Fish Series	1900		£4.00	—
M30	New Series of Birds	1908		£3.50	—
M30	Useful Birds of America (no series number)	1915		£3.50	—
M30	Useful Birds of America 1st Series	1915		£3.00	—
M30	Useful Birds of America 2nd Series	1918		£3.00	—
M30	Useful Birds of America 3rd Series	1922		£3.00	—
M30	Useful Birds of America 4th Series	1924		£3.00	—
M15	Useful Birds of America 5th Series	1928		£3.00	—
M15	Useful Birds of America 6th Series	1931		£3.00	—
M15	Useful Birds of America 7th Series	1933		£3.00	—
M15	Useful Birds of America 8th Series	1936		£3.00	—
M15	Useful Birds of America 9th Series	1938		£1.00	£15.00
M15	Useful Birds of America 10th Series	1938		£1.00	£15.00

THE CITY BAKERIES LTD

8	The European War Series	1916	HX-129	£45.00	—
4	Shadow Series	1916		£40.00	—

CLARNICO

30	Colonial Troops	c1910	HX-100	£30.00	—
25	Great War Leaders	c1915	HC-101	£22.00	—
29	Wolf Cubs	c1910		£40.00	—

CLASSIC COLLECTIONS

50	Newcastle United FC (Football)	1993		—	£20.00

CLASSIC GAMES INC. (USA)

LT100	Deathwatch 2000	1993		—	£9.50
LT50	McDonalds History	1996		—	£8.00
LT150	WWF The History of Wrestle Mania Series 2	1990		—	£15.00
LT150	World Wrestling Federation Superstars	1991		—	£15.00

CLEVEDON CONFECTIONERY LTD

K50	British Aircraft:				
	A Title in one line	1956		£3.20	—
	B Title in two lines	1956		£3.20	—

CLEVEDON CONFECTIONERY LTD (continued)

Size & quantity		Date	Handbook reference	Price per card	Complete set
K25	British Orders of Chivalry and Valour:				
	A Black back ...	1960		£5.40	—
	B Blue back	1960		£5.40	—
K50	British Ships	1956		£3.50	—
M50	British Trains and Engines...	1958		£8.00	—
K25	Dan Dare	1960		£8.00	—
K40	Did You Know?	1957		£5.50	—
K40	Famous Cricketers	c1960		£12.00	—
K25	Famous Cricketers	c1960		£12.00	—
K50	Famous Football Clubs...	1961		£5.00	—
K50	Famous Footballers	1961		£7.00	—
K50	Famous International Aircraft...	1963	HX-98	£2.00	—
M50	Famous Screen Stars, Series A.1	1959		£4.50	—
K40	Film Stars	1958		£4.50	—
K50	Football Club Managers	1959		£15.00	—
K50	Hints on Association Football:				
	A Black back & front	1957		£4.00	—
	B Blue back, coloured front...	1957		£4.00	—
	C Blue back & front	1957		£9.00	—
K50	Hints on Road Safety	1958		£3.00	—
K50	International Sporting Stars	1960		£4.50	—
M50	Regimental Badges	1956		£3.80	—
EL25	Sporting Memories	1960		£12.00	—
K50	The Story of the Olympics...	1960		£3.00	—
K50	Trains of the World	1962		£2.80	—

CLEVELAND PETROL

EL20	Golden Goals (numbered 1-41)	1972		£1.00	—
	Album			—	£15.00

CLIFFORD

50	Footballers	c1950		£25.00	—

CLOVER DAIRIES LTD

25	Animals and Reptiles	1965	HX-99	20p	£3.00
25	British Rail	1973	HX-107	20p	£3.00
25	People and Places	1970	HX-26	20p	£3.00
25	Prehistoric Animals	1966	HX-92	30p	£7.50
25	Science in the 20th Century	1965	HX-18	20p	£4.00
25	Ships and Their Workings...	1966	HX-85	20p	£3.50
25	The Story of Milk...	1964	HX-3	30p	£7.50
25	Transport Through the Ages	1967	HX-101	20p	£3.00

COACH HOUSE STUDIOS

50	Railway Locomotives	1987		40p	—

COCA-COLA (UK)

LT10	Football Match World Cup USA (scratch cards)	1994		—	£4.00
LT49	Football World Cup (yellow back)	2002		—	£15.00

COCA-COLA (South Africa)

M100	Our Flower Paradise...	1964		55p	£55.00

COCA-COLA (USA)

The World of Nature:

EL12	Series I — Earth and Air and Sky	c1960	£1.00	—
EL12	Series II — Man's Closest Friends and Most Inveterate Enemies	c1960	£1.00	—
EL12	Series III — Trees and Other Plants Useful to Man	c1960	£1.00	—
EL12	Series IV — Some Common Wild Flowers	c1960	£1.00	—
EL12	Series V — Among Our Feathered Friends	c1960	£1.00	—
EL12	Series VI — Native Wild Animals	c1960	£1.00	—
EL12	Series VII — Life In and Around the Water	c1960	£1.00	—
EL12	Series VIII — Insects, Helpful and Harmful	c1960	£1.00	—

COFTON COLLECTIONS

L7	Alice in Wonderland	2002	—	£3.00
15	Birmingham City F.C. Stars of The 1970s	2007	—	£5.50
25	Dogs 1st Series	1988	24p	£6.00
25	Dogs 2nd Series	1988	24p	£6.00
25	Dogs 3rd Series	1988	24p	£6.00
L25	Nursery Rhymes	1992	—	£7.50
15	West Brom. Heroes & Legends (Footballers)	2012	—	£5.50
L20	Worcestershire County Cricketers	1989	—	£7.50

CECIL COLEMAN LTD

24	Film Stars	c1935	£8.00	—

COLGATE-PALMOLIVE

EL4	Coronation Souvenir	1953	£2.50	£10.00
M24	Famous Sporting Trophies	1979	25p	£6.00
	Album		—	£6.00

COLINVILLE LTD

L28	Fantasy of Space 1st Series	1956	£9.00	—
L28	Fantasy of Space 2nd Series	1956	£9.00	—
L25	Prairie Pioneers	1960	£5.00	—

COLLECT-A-CARD (USA)

LT50	Adventures of Ronald McDonald — McDonald Land 500	1996	—	£6.00
LT100	American Bandstand (T.V. Music Show)	1993	—	£8.00
LT72	The Campbell's (Soup) Collection	1995	—	£8.00
LT120	Centennial Olympic Games	1996	—	£9.50
LT100	The Coca Cola Collection 2nd Series	1994	—	£15.00
K8	The Coca Cola Collection 2nd Series Coke Caps	1994	—	£3.00
LT100	The Coca Cola Collection 3rd Series	1994	—	£12.50
LT100	The Coca Cola Collection 4th Series	1995	—	£12.50
LT50	The Coca Cola Polar Bears South Pole Vacation	1996	—	£8.00
LT100	Country (Music) Classics	1992	—	£9.50
LT72	Dinotopia — Fantasy Art Dinosaurs	1995	—	£9.50
LT100	Harley Davidson Series 2	1992	—	£9.50
LT100	Harley Davidson Series 3	1993	—	£9.50
LT100	King Pins (Ten Pin Bowling)	1990	—	£10.00
LT50	Norfin Trolls	1992	—	£5.00
LT72	Power Rangers 1st Series	1994	—	£9.50
LT72	Power Rangers 2nd Series	1994	—	£9.50
LT72	Power Rangers New Season	1994	—	£9.50
LT100	Stargate Plus Set LT12 Puzzle	1994	—	£9.50

COLLECT-A-CARD (USA) (continued)

LT100	Vette Set (Corvette Cars)	1991	—	£9.50
LT10	Vette Set (Corvette Cars) Bonus Series	1991	—	£4.00

COLLECTABLE PICTURES

L13	England Win The Ashes 2005 (Cricket)	2005	—	£8.50
L20	Liverpool F.C. European Champions 2005	2005	—	£12.00
L7	Views of Bath	2005	—	£5.00

COLLECTABLES OF SPALDING

25	British Cavalry Uniforms	1987	—	£7.50
25	Military Maids	1987	—	£7.50
25	Warriors Through the Ages	1987	30p	£7.50

THE COLLECTOR AND DEALER MAGAZINE

6	Animal Series	1953	£3.00	—

THE COLLECTOR & HOBBYIST

25	Fascinating Hobbies	1950	HX-74	20p	£2.50

COLLECTORS' CORNER

L20	Halifax As It Was	1989	—	£4.50

COLLECTORS FARE

16	Reading Football Club Simod Cup Winners	1990	—	£7.50
EL16	Reading Football Club Simod Cup Winners	1990	—	£5.00

COLLECTORS SHOP

25	Bandsmen of the British Army	1960	HX-62	70p	£17.50

COLONIAL BREAD (USA)

LT33	Star Trek The Motion Picture	1979	—	£9.50

COMET (Sweets)

25	Armand & Michaela Denis on Safari 1st Series	1961		40p	£10.00
25	Armand & Michaela Denis on Safari 2nd Series	1961		40p	£10.00
25	Modern Wonders:		HX-130		
	A Black back	1961		20p	£3.00
	B Blue back	1961		80p	—
25	Olympic Achievements 1st Series	1959		60p	£15.00
25	Olympic Achievements 2nd Series	1959		60p	£15.00

COMIC ENTERPRISES

L15	Superman Action Comics	2005	—	£6.50

COMIC IMAGES (USA)

LT70	The Art of Coca Cola	1999	—	£9.50
LT90	The Beast Within — Ken Barr Fantasy Art	1994	—	£9.50
LT72	The Beatles — Yellow Submarine	1999	—	£13.00
LT90	Beyond Bizarre — Jim Warren Surrealism Fantasy Art	1993	—	£9.50
LT90	Bill Ward (Saucy Cartoons)	1994	—	£12.00
LT90	Blueprints of The Future — Vincent Di Fate Fantasy Art	1994	—	£9.50
LT90	Bone	1994	—	£9.50

COMIC IMAGES (USA) (continued)

Size & quantity		Date	Handbook reference	Price per card	Complete set
LT90	The Brothers Hildebrandt — Fantasy Art	1994		—	£8.00
LT72	The Cat In The Hat — The Film	2003		—	£8.00
LT72	Coca Cola — The Art of Haddon Sundblom	2001		—	£12.00
LT90	Colossal Conflicts (Marvel Heroes & Villains) Series 2	1987		—	£9.50
LT72	Comic Greats 98	1998		—	£9.50
LT90	Conan The Marvel Years	1996		—	£12.00
LT72	Crimson Embrace — Adult Fantasy Art	1998		—	£9.50
LT72	Dark Horse Presents Ghost	1997		—	£9.50
LT72	Elvira Mistress of Omnichrome	1997		—	£9.50
LT72	Final Fantasy — The Spirits Within...	2001		—	£8.50
LT90	Frazetta II The Legend Continues — Fantasy Art	1993		—	£8.00
LT90	Greg Hildebrandt II — 30 Years of Magic...	1993		—	£8.00
LT90	Harlem Globetrotters	1992		—	£9.50
LT90	Jack Kirby The Unpublished Archives — Fantasy Art	1994		—	£8.00
LT72	Judgment Day (cartoon)	1997		—	£8.00
LT72	Julie Strain Queen of the 'B' Movies	1996		—	£9.50
LT72	Madagascar The Film	2005		—	£9.50
LT90	Magnificent Myths — Boris 4 Fantasy Art	1994		—	£9.50
LT90	Maxfield Parrish Portrait of America — Fantasy Art ...	1994		—	£8.00
LT61	Meanie Babies...	1998		—	£8.00
LT90	Moebius — Fantasy Art...	1993		—	£9.50
LT90	More Than Battlefield Earth — Ron Hubbard Fantasy Art	1994		—	£9.50
LT72	The New American Pin Up (Pin Up Girls)	1997		—	£12.00
LT72	Olivia 98 (Adult Fantasy Art)	1998		—	£9.50
LT72	Olivia Obsessions in Omnichrome (Adult Fantasy Art)	1997		—	£9.50
LT90	Other Worlds — Michael Whelan Fantasy Art	1995		—	£9.50
LT90	Other Worlds — Michael Whelan II Fantasy Art	1995		—	£9.50
LT72	The Painted Cow	1997		—	£9.50
LT90	The Phantom	1995		—	£9.50
LT90	Prince Valiant	1995		—	£8.00
LT90	Richard Corben Fantasy Art	1993		—	£9.50
LT72	The Rock's Greatest Matches — WWF	2000		—	£15.00
LT90	Ron Miller's Firebrands Heroines of Science Fiction & Fantasy	1994		—	£9.50
LT90	Sachs & Violens	1993		—	£8.00
LT90	The Savage Dragon	1992		—	£8.00
LT90	Shadow Hawk (Comic Book Art by Jim Valentino)... ...	1992		—	£8.00
LT90	Shi Visions of The Golden Empire	1996		—	£9.50
LT72	Shrek 2 The Film	2004		—	£9.50
LT70	South Park	1998		—	£9.50
LT90	Species — The Movie	1995		—	£9.50
LT90	Spiderman The McFarlane Era	1992		—	£9.50
LT90	Spiderman II 30th Anniversary	1992		—	£9.50
LT90	Strangers in Paradise	1996		—	£8.00
LT90	Supreme — Adult Fantasy Art	1996		—	£9.50
LT72	Terminator 3 Rise of The Machines — The Movie... ...	2003		—	£9.50
LT90	30th Salute G.I. Joe	1994		—	£9.50
LT90	24 — TV Series	2003		—	£12.00
LT90	Ujena Swimwear Illustrated	1993		—	£9.50
LT90	Ujena Swimwear Illustrated	1994		—	£9.50
LT90 ·	Unity Time Is Not Absolute	1992		—	£9.50
LT72	Van Helsing — The Film	2004		—	£9.50
LT90	William Stout 2 (Fantasy Art etc)	1994		—	£9.50
LT90	Wolverine From Then Till Now II...	1992		—	£9.50
LT81	World Wrestling Federation No Mercy	2000		—	£12.00
LT90	Young Blood (Super Heroes)	1992		—	£8.00

COMIC LIFE

MP4	Sports Champions	1922		£6.50	—

COMMODEX (Gum)

M88	Operation Moon	1969		£2.20	—
L120	Super Cars	1970		£2.20	—

COMMONWEALTH SHOE & LEATHER CO. (USA)

M12	Makes of Planes	c1930		£4.00	—

COMO CONFECTIONERY PRODUCTS LTD

K25	Adventures of Fireball XL5	c1970		£16.00	—
M25	History of the Wild West 1st Series...	1960		£5.00	—
M25	History of the Wild West 2nd Series	1963		£1.00	£25.00
50	Lenny's Adventures	1960		£1.00	£50.00
50	Noddy and His Playmates	1962		£2.20	—
	Noddy's Adventures 1st Series:				
M25	A Size 63 × 63mm	1961		£3.40	—
K25	B Size 46 × 46mm	c1970		£6.50	—
M25	Noddy's Adventures 2nd Series	1961		£3.40	—
25	Noddy's Budgie and Feathered Friends 1st Series ...	1959		£2.80	—
25	Noddy's Budgie and Feathered Friends 2nd Series ...	1959		£2.80	—
	Noddy's Friends Abroad:				
M50	A Size 62 × 62mm	1959		£3.00	—
K25	B Size 46 × 46mm	c1970		£6.50	—
	Noddy's Nursery Rhyme Friends:				
M50	A Size 63 × 60mm	1959		£2.50	—
K25	B Size 46 × 46mm	c1970		£6.50	—
M50	Sooty's Adventures	1961		£2.00	—
25	Sooty's Latest Adventures 3rd Series, No.1-25				
	A Black back	c1960		£2.00	—
	B Blue back	c1960		£2.00	—
	C Navy blue back	c1960		£2.00	—
	D Red back	c1960		£2.00	—
25	Sooty's Latest Adventures 3rd Series, No. 26-50				
	A Black back	c1960		£2.00	—
	B Blue back	c1960		£2.00	—
	C Navy blue back	c1960		£2.00	—
	D Red back	c1960		£2.00	—
M50	Sooty's New Adventures 2nd Series	1961		£2.00	—
25	Speed 1st Series	1962	HX-153	£1.60	£40.00
25	Speed 2nd Series	1962	HX-153	70p	£17.50
	Album for 1st and 2nd Series combined			—	£15.00
25	Supercar 1st Series	1962		£7.00	—
25	Supercar 2nd Series...	1962		£5.00	—
25	Top Secret 1st Series	1965		£2.60	—
25	Top Secret 2nd Series	1965		£2.60	—
M26	XL5 1st Series...	1965		£22.00	—
M26	XL5 2nd Series	1966		£22.00	—

COMPTONS

22	Footballers Series A (coloured)	1925		£27.00	—
22	Footballers Series A (black and white)...	1925		£27.00	—
22	Footballers Series B (coloured)	1925		£27.00	—
22	Footballers Series B (black and white)	1925		£27.00	—
22	Footballers Series C (coloured)	1925		£27.00	—
22	Footballers Series D (coloured)	1925		£27.00	—

CONNOISSEUR POLICIES

| M25 | The Dorking Collection (Antiques) ... ... | 2004 | | — | £7.50 |

CONTINENTAL CANDY CO. (U.K.)

| LT81 | Snoots Nosy Bodies... ... ... | 1989 | | — | £9.00 |

COOPER & CO. STORES LTD

50	Do You Know?...	1962	HX-166.1	20p	£5.00
25	Inventions and Discoveries 1st Series...	1962	HX-131	£1.60	—
25	Inventions and Discoveries 2nd Series	1962	HX-131	£1.60	—
25	Island of Ceylon	1958	HX-47	£4.00	—
25	Mysteries & Wonders of the World 1st Series	1960		60p	£15.00
25	Mysteries & Wonders of the World 2nd Series	1960		40p	£10.00
25	Prehistoric Animals 1st Series	1962	HX-151	£1.40	£35.00
25	Prehistoric Animals 2nd Series	1962	HX-151	£1.40	£35.00
25	Strange but True 1st Series	1960	HX-96	20p	£3.50
25	Strange but True 2nd Series	1960	HX-96	20p	£4.00
25	Transport Through the Ages 1st Series	1961	HX-97	32p	£8.00
25	Transport Through the Ages 2nd Series	1961	HX-97	40p	£10.00
	Album for 1st and 2nd Series combined			—	£15.00

COORS BREWING CO. (USA)

| LT100 | Coors ... ... | 1995 | | — | £9.50 |

CORNERSTONE (USA)

LT72	Austin Powers The Spy Who Shagged Me — The Movie	1999		—	£9.50
LT90	The Avengers in Colour Series 2	1993		—	£15.00
LT81	The Avengers Return Series 3	1995		—	£15.00
LT110	Doctor Who 1st Series (TV Series)...	1994		—	£25.00
LT110	Doctor Who 2nd Series (TV Series)	1995		—	£17.50
LT110	Doctor Who 3rd Series (TV Series)...	1996		—	£15.00
LT90	Doctor Who 4th Series (TV Series)...	1996		—	£15.00
LT90	Kiss Series 2, silver foil fronts (Pop Group)	1998		—	£12.00
LT81	Robot Carnival Masters of Japanese Animation	1994		—	£9.50

COUNTY PRINT SERVICES

M25	Australian Test Cricketers	1993		—	£15.00
25	Australiian Test Cricketers 1876-1896	c1992		—	£40.00
EL48	County Cricket Teams 1900-1914	1992		—	£10.00
50	County Cricketers 1990...	1990		—	£25.00
M25	Cricket Caricatures	1991		—	£40.00
20	Cricket Pavilions	1991		—	£15.00
EL24	Cricket Teams 1884-1900	1990		—	£7.00
M25	Cricket's Golden Age	1991		—	£10.00
EL12	Cricket's Pace Partners...	1996		—	£8.00
EL12	Cricket's Spin Twins	1996		—	£8.00
50	Cricketers 1890	1989		—	£8.00
50	Cricketers 1896	1989		—	£8.00
50	Cricketers 1900	1990		—	£8.00
50	Cricketers 1906	1992		—	£12.50
EL5	Cricketing Knights	1994		—	£15.00
L25	Derbyshire Test Cricketers...	1994		—	£12.50
14	England Cricket Team 1901-02	1991		—	£12.00
14	England Cricket Team 1903-04	1991		—	£4.00
15	England Cricket Team 1907-08	1992		—	£15.00
17	England Cricket Team 1932-33	1995		—	£6.00

COUNTY PRINT SERVICES (continued)

16	England Cricket Team 1990-91	1990	—	£6.00
L25	Essex Test Cricketers	1993	—	£15.00
M27	Famous Cricket Crests	1992	—	£12.50
M25	Famous Cricket Ties...	1992	—	£12.00
EL12	First Knock Cricket's Opening Pairs	1994	—	£9.00
L25	Glamorgan Test Cricketers	1993	—	£12.50
L25	Gloucestershire Test Cricketers	1994	—	£12.50
L25	Hampshire Test Cricketers...	1995	—	£12.50
L25	Kent Test Cricketers	1993	—	£12.50
L25	Lancashire Test Cricketers	1993	—	£12.50
L25	Leicestershire Test Cricketers	1995	—	£12.50
L25	Middlesex Test Cricketers	1994	—	£12.50
50	1912 Triangular Tournament Cricket	1992	—	£9.00
M24	1920s Test Cricketers 1st Series	1994	—	£10.00
M24	1920s Test Cricketers 2nd Series	1996	—	£10.00
25	1950s England Cricket Characters	1995	—	£20.00
50	1950s Test Cricketers	1992	—	£20.00
M50	1960s Test Cricketers	1992	—	£25.00
25	1995 England Cricket Characters	1996	—	£10.00
L25	Northamptonshire Test Cricketers	1993	—	£12.50
L25	Nottinghamshire Test Cricketers...	1994	—	£12.50
25	Prominent Cricketers of 1894...	c1991	—	£40.00
50	Somerset County Championship Cricket Series 1	1990	—	£10.00
50	Somerset County Championship Cricket Series 2	1990	—	£10.00
L25	Somerset Test Cricketers	1994	—	£12.50
16	The South African Cricket Team 1894	1990	—	£8.00
M15	The South African Cricket Team 1965	1994	—	£6.00
L25	Surrey Test Cricketers	1994	—	£12.50
L25	Sussex Test Cricketers	1994	—	£12.50
L25	Warwickshire Test Cricketers	1994	—	£12.50
L25	Worcestershire Test Cricketers	1995	—	£12.50
M30	World Stars of Cricket & Showbusiness	1992	—	£6.00
L25	Yorkshire Test Cricketers	1993	—	£20.00

CECIL COURT

L20	Christopher Columbus	1992	—	£7.00
L12	Class of 66 (England World Cup Team)	2002	—	£9.00
L20	Famous Film Directors	1992	—	£7.00

COW & GATE

L12	Advertisement Series 1st Series...	1928	HC-137.1	£2.50	£30.00
L12	Advertisement Series 2nd Series	1928	HC-137.2	£2.00	£24.00
L48	Happy Families	1928	HC-138	£1.25	—

COWAN CO. LTD (Canada)

EL24	Animal Cards	1923	£8.00	—
EL24	Birds Series	c1925	£8.00	—
EL24	Canadian Birds	1922	£8.00	—
EL24	Canadian Fish	c1924	£8.00	—
EL24	Chicken Cards...	c1924	£8.00	—
M24	Dog Pictures	c1925	£8.00	—
M24	Learn To Swim...	1929	£8.00	—
24	Noted Cats	c1927	£8.00	—
EL12	Scenic Canada	c1925	£12.00	—
EL24	Wild Flowers of Canada	c1925	£8.00	—

CRAIG & HALES (Australia)

30	Footballers			c1930		£25.00	—

CRAWLEY CAKE & BISCUIT CO.

| 24 | World's Most Beautiful Birds ... ... | | | c1925 | HX-22 | £10.00 | — |

CREATURE FEATURES

| 10 | Spooky TV (The Addams Family) ... ... | | | 2011 | | — | £5.00 |

CRESCENT CONFECTIONERY CO. LTD

| 85 | Footballers ... ... | | | c1925 | HC-139 | £40.00 | — |
| 97 | Sportsmen ... ... | | | c1925 | | £40.00 | — |

CRICKET MEMORABILIA SOCIETY

| L50 | Memorabilia Through the Ages (Cricket) ... ... | | | 2000 | | — | £10.00 |

CROMWELL STORES

1	Advertisement Card — Girl Bugler			c1963		—	£5.00
25	Do You Know?...			1963	HX-166.2	40p	£10.00
25	Racing Colours			1963		70p	£17.50

CROSBIE

| K54 | Miniature Playing Cards ... ... | | | c1930 | | £1.20 | — |

J. CROSFIELD

| 36 | Film Stars ... ... | | | 1924 | | £10.00 | — |

CROWN SPORTS CARDS (USA)

| LT10 | Landforce Series 2 (Military) ... ... | | | 1991 | | — | £5.00 |
| LT9 | Seaforce Series 3 (Naval) ... ... | | | 1991 | | — | £5.00 |

CROXLEY CARD CO.

L20	British Lions Series 1 (Rugby Union)			1999		—	£10.00
LT20	Leicester Tigers Series 3 (Rugby Union)			2001		—	£10.00
LT21	Leicester Tigers Series 5 (Rugby Union)			2001		—	£10.00
LT20	Saracens Series 2 (Rugby Union)			2000		—	£10.00
LT21	Saracens Series 4 (Rugby Union)			2001		—	£10.00

CRYPTOZOIC

LT95	Arrow Season 1			2015		—	£10.00
LT68	The Big Bang Theory Seasons 3 & 4			2012		—	£9.50
LT68	The Big Bang Theory Season 5			2013		—	£9.50
LT72	Castle Seasons 1 & 2			2012		—	£9.50
LT72	Castle Seasons 3 and 4			2014		—	£9.50
LT69	Ender's Game The Movie			2014		—	£10.00
LT72	Fringe — Imagine The Impossibilities Seasons 1 & 2			2012		—	£8.00
LT73	Fringe — Imagine The Impossibilities Seasons 3 & 4			2013		—	£8.50
LT101	The Hobbit An Unexpected Journey			2014		—	£10.00
LT63	The Vampire Diaries Season 1			2011		—	£9.50
LT69	The Vampire Diaries Season 2			2012		—	£9.50
LT72	The Vampire Diaries Season 3			2014		—	£9.50
LT72	The Walking Dead Season 3 Part 1			2014		—	£9.50
LT72	The Walking Dead Season 3 Part 2			2014		—	£9.50

CRYSELCO

EL25	Beautiful Waterways...............................	1939		£1.20	£30.00
EL25	Buildings of Beauty	1938		£1.40	£35.00
EL12	Interesting Events of 60 Years Ago...............	1955		£2.50	£30.00

CRYSTAL CAT CARDS

LT6	Attitude Cats by Louis Wain Series LW5	2005	—	£3.00
LT6	Cats in Black by Louis Wain Series LW6	2005	—	£3.00
LT6	Cats Prize Winners by Louis Wain Series LW1.........	2005	—	£3.00
LT6	Cats Sports & Leisure by Louis Wain Series LW2......	2005	—	£3.00
LT6	Diabolo Cats by Louis Wain Series LW7	2005	—	£3.00
EL6	First World War Cats by Louis Wain Series LW12......	2009	—	£3.00
LT6	Happy Days Cats by Louis Wain Series LW4	2005	—	£3.00
EL6	Mascots Cats by Louis Wain Series LW10.............	2009	—	£3.00
EL6	Mikado Cats by Louis Wain Series LW13	2010	—	£3.00
EL6	Out In All Weathers Cats by Louis Wain Series LW8 ...	2009	—	£3.00
EL6	Persians 1st Series Cats by Louis Wain Series LW9 ...	2009	—	£3.00
EL6	Persians 2nd Series Cats by Louis Wain Series LW11	2009	—	£3.00
LT6	Purr-Fect Reaction Cats by Louis Wain Series LW3 ...	2005	—	£3.00

CULT-STUFF

LT27	Adventures of Sherlock Holmes	2013	—	£10.00
LT27	The Art of Burlesque 'Kiss' Limited Edition	2013	—	£15.00
LT18	Beyond Stoker's Dracula	2013	—	£12.00
LT27	Bram Stoker's Dracula	2012	—	£10.00
LT36	Civil War Chronicles Volume 1	2013	—	£12.00
LT36	Civil War Chronicles Volume 2	2015	—	£12.00
LT18	Civil War Chronicles Portraits (Chase Sets Volume 1 & 2 combined)	2015	—	£9.00
LT18	Dixon's Vixens 1st Series (Numbered 1 to 18 LCC issue)	2015	—	£10.00
LT18	Dixon's Vixens 2nd Series (Numbered 19 to 36)	2015	—	£10.00
1	Largest Steamers in the World (Olympic & Titanic) (reprint)	2013	—	£1.50
LT27	Memoirs of Sherlock Holmes 2nd Series	2014	—	£15.00
LT6	1914 Preview (World War I)	2014	—	£3.00
LT36	Propaganda and Poster Series 1 (World War 1 & 2) ...	2013	—	£12.00
LT27	RMS Titanic	2012	—	£10.00
LT18	Sherlock Holmes and Victorian Crime	2013	—	£9.00
LT36	Vintage Erotica (postcard back)	2013	—	£13.00
LT6	Vintage Erotica Sectional Chase Set	2013	—	£6.00
LT21	The War Illustrated (World War I)	2015	—	£10.00
LT27	War of the Worlds – H.G. Wells	2013	—	£10.00
LT28	War of the Worlds Earth Under the Martians	2014	—	£12.00

D. CUMMINGS & SON

64	Famous Fighters (Boxers)...........................	1948	£4.00	—

THE CUNNING ARTIFICER

6	Advertising Cards Discworld Emporium	2009	—	£3.00
20	Bernard Pearson's Clare Craft Pottery	2009	—	£6.00
	Album......................................		—	£5.00
20	Discworld Advertisements and Labels	2009	—	£6.00
	Album......................................		—	£5.00
25	Discworld Scout Insignia Collection (Terry Pratchett's Scouting For Trolls)	2009	—	£10.00
	Album......................................		—	£5.00

THE CUNNING ARTIFICER (Continued)

M25	The Discworld Stamp Collection (based on Terry Pratchett's Discworld Books)	2009		—	£10.00
	Album			—	£5.00
M10	Discworld Toy Shop Collection (Props from The Hogfather film)	2009		—	£5.00
	Album			—	£5.00
22	Famous Footballers of Ankh-Morpork (Terry Pratchett's Discworld)	2010		—	£10.00
	Album			—	£6.00

D.S.I. (USA)

LT50	Desert Storm	1991		—	£9.00

DAILY HERALD

32	Cricketers	1954		£4.25	—
32	Footballers	1954	HD-7	£4.25	—
32	Turf Personalities	1955		£1.10	£35.00

DAILY ICE CREAM CO.

24	Modern British Locomotives	1954		£1.50	£36.00

DAILY MIRROR

M100	Star Soccer Sides	1971		75p	—
EL60	Star Soccer Sides 'My Club' Premium Issue	1971	HD-15	£8.00	—

DAILY SKETCH

40	World Cup Souvenir	1970		£3.00	—
	Album			—	£25.00

DAILY TELEGRAPH

26	England Rugby World Cup	1995		—	£7.50
26	Ireland Rugby World Cup	1995		—	£7.50
26	Scotland Rugby World Cup	1995		—	£7.50
26	Wales Rugby World Cup	1995		—	£7.50

DAINTY NOVELS

10	World's Famous Liners	1915	HD-20	£12.00	—

DANDY GUM

M200	Animal Fables:				
	A Black back	1971		40p	—
	B Red back	1971		40p	—
M160	Cars and Bikes:				
	A Black back with 'Dandy'	1977		80p	—
	B Blue back, anonymous...	1977		80p	—
M116	Flag Parade	1965		30p	£35.00
M160	Flag Parade	1978		30p	—
M210	Football Clubs and Colours of the World	c1970		50p	—
M54	Football — European Cup (without firm's name)	1988		50p	—
M55	Football World Cup (with firm's name)...	1986		50p	—
M80	Hippy Happy Tattoos (black and white)	c1965		80p	—
M72	Motor Cars	c1960		£1.25	—
M53	Our Modern Army...	1956		£1.00	—
M53	Pin-up Girls (Original Set)	1955		£2.00	—

DANDY GUM (continued)

Size & quantity		Date	Handbook reference	Price per card	Complete set
M53	Pin-up Girls (with 'Substitute' cards)	1955	HD-30	£2.00	–
M54	Pin-up Girls	1977		60p	–
M80	Pirate Tattoos (coloured)	c1965		80p	–
M70	Pop Stars Series P	1977		£1.00	–
M56	Rock 'N' Bubble Pop Stars	1987		35p	£20.00
M100	Soldier Parade	1969		70p	–
	Album			–	£12.00
M200	Struggle for the Universe (black back)	1970		30p	–
M72	Veteran and Vintage Cars:				
	A Numbers 1 to 48 British Issue	1966		£1.50	–
	B Numbers 49 to 72 Overseas Issue	1966		£1.50	–
M100	Wild Animals:				
	A Danish/English text	1969		30p	£30.00
	B Arabic/English text	1978		35p	£35.00
M200	Wonderful World	c1975		30p	–

DART FLIPCARDS (USA)

Size & quantity		Date		Price per card	Complete set
LT72	Battlestar Galactica	1996		–	£9.50
LT72	Betty Boop	2001		–	£20.00
LT100	Fern Gully The Last Rainforest	1992		–	£9.50
LT72	The Frighteners — The Film	1996		–	£12.00
LT72	I Love Lucy 50th Anniversary	2001		–	£9.50
LT72	The Lone Ranger	1997		–	£15.00
LT72	Mr Bean (Rowan Atkinson)	1998		–	£9.50
LT72	The Munsters All New Series	1998		–	£12.00
LT100	100 Years of Hersheys	1995		–	£9.50
LT100	Pepsi Cola 1st Series	1994		–	£13.00
LT100	Pepsi Cola 2nd Series	1995		–	£9.50
LT72	Sabrina The Teenage Witch	1999		–	£9.50
LT72	Sailor Moon	1997		–	£9.50
LT72	Shrek The Film	2001		–	£8.00
LT72	Titanic (The Liner)	1998		–	£20.00
LT100	Vietnam Series 2	1991		–	£9.50

DE BEUKELAER BISCUITS

Size & quantity		Date	Handbook reference	Price per card	Complete set
KP100	All Sports	1932		70p	£70.00
M125	Dumbo	c1940		£1.50	–
KP100	Film Stars 1st Series (Nd 1-100)	c1930	HB-199	–	–
KP100	Film Stars 2nd Series (Nd 101-200)	c1930		£1.20	–
KP100	Film Stars 3rd Series (Nd 201-300)	c1930		£1.20	–
KP100	Film Stars 4th Series (Nd 301-400)	1932		£1.20	£120.00
KP100	Film Stars 5th Series (Nd 401-500)	c1935	HB-97	£1.20	–
KP100	Film Stars 6th Series (Nd 501-600)	c1935		£1.20	–
KP100	Film Stars 7th Series (Nd 601-700)	c1935		£1.20	–
KP100	Film Stars 8th Series (Nd 701-800)	c1935		£1.20	–
KP100	Film Stars 9th Series (Nd 801-900)	c1935		£1.20	–
KP100	Film Stars 10th Series (Nd 901-1,000)	c1935		£1.20	–
KP100	Film Stars 11th Series (Nd 1,001-1,100)	1940		£1.20	–
KP100	Film Stars (A) (B1-B100) small figure	c1935		£1.20	–
KP100	Film Stars (B) (B1-B100) large figure	c1935		£1.20	–
K160	Film Stars (gold background)	1938		£1.60	–
132	Film Stars (gold background)	1939	HB-98	£1.60	£210.00
M125	Gulliver's Travels	c1940		£1.25	–
	Album			–	£25.00
M125	Pinocchio Series	c1940		£1.50	–

DE BEUKELAER BISCUITS (continued)

M60	Sixty Glorious Years	c1940		£2.00	—
	Album			—	£40.00
M100	Snow White Series	c1940		£1.50	—

DERBY EVENING TELEGRAPH

EL8	150 Years of British Railways (Derby)	1980		—	£5.00

DESIGN AT LONDON COLOUR LTD

10	Bizarre Imagination	2013		—	£4.00
10	More Bizarre Imagination Series	2013		—	£4.00
10	The Story of Barratt's Sweets Factory — The Early Years	2013		—	£5.50

DESIGNS ON SPORT

25	Test Cricketers	1992		—	£7.50

LIAM DEVLIN & SONS LTD

M36	Coaching Gaelic Football	c1960		£11.00	—
48	Corgi Toys	1971		£2.50	—
50	Do You Know?	1964	HX-166.2	20p	£6.00
M50	Famous Footballers New Series	1952	HX-102	£16.00	—
M50	Famous Footballers, Series A1	1953	HX-57	£16.00	—
M50	Famous Footballers, Series A2	1954	HX-58	£16.00	—
50	Famous Footballers, Series A3	1955	HX-59	£16.00	—
M45	Famous Speedway Stars	c1960	HD-38	£16.00	—
M45	Fastest on Earth	c1953	HX-60	£5.00	—
36	Flags of All Nations	1958		£5.00	—
48	Gaelic Sportstars	c1960		£11.00	—
48	Irish Fishing	1962		70p	£35.00
50	Modern Transport	1966	HX-125	20p	£10.00
48	Our Dogs	c1960		£10.00	—
48	Right or Wrong	c1960		£6.00	—
M35	Walt Disney Characters	c1955	HX-65	£7.00	—
M50	Wild Animals by George Cansdale	1954	HX-68	£6.00	—
48	Wild Wisdom	c1965		£3.20	—
50	Wonders of the World	1968	HX-49	20p	£7.50
100	World Flag Series	c1965	HD-40	£6.00	—

DIAMOND COLLECTION (UK)

L20	Rock 'n' Roll	1998		—	£7.50

DICKSON, ORDE & CO. LTD

50	Footballers	1960		40p	£20.00
25	Ships Through the Ages	1960	HX-94	£3.40	—
25	Sports of the Countries	1962		£1.20	£30.00

DIGIT CARDS

LT40	Happy Puppy Your Best Friends (Game Cards)	c1995		—	£6.00

DIGITAL IMPACT

L20	Caricatures From The Movies	2002		—	£8.00
30	Victorian & Edwardian Soldiers in Full Dress	2001		—	£12.00

DINERS CLUB

EL8	Reminders	1976		40p	£3.00

DINKIE PRODUCTS LTD (Hair Grips)

M24	Stars and Starlets	1947		£3.00	—
M20	Stars and Starlets 2nd Series	1947		£3.00	—
M20	MGM Films 3rd Series	1948		£3.00	—
M24	Warner Bros. Artists 4th Series	1948		£5.00	—
M20	Gone With the Wind 5th Series	1948		£6.00	—
M24	Warner Bros. Films 6th Series	1949		£4.00	—
M24	MGM Stars 7th Series	1949		£4.00	—
M24	Paramount Pictures 8th Series	1950		£4.00	—
M24	M.G.M. Films 9th Series	1950		£6.50	
M24	M.G.M. Films 10th Series	1951		£8.00	—
M24	United Artists Releases 11th Series	1951		£8.00	—

(N.B. these prices are for complete cards with space for grips.
If cards have grip holder cut off these will be 80% of prices shown.)

DINOCARDZ (USA)

| LT80 | Dinosaurs Series 1 | 1992 | | — | £9.50 |

DIRECT ACCESS

| L8 | Atlanticard (British Sports Stars) | 1992 | | £1.25 | £10.00 |

DIRECT TEA SUPPLY CO.

| 25 | British Uniforms of the 19th Century | c1960 | HX-78 | £1.00 | £25.00 |

J. ARTHUR DIXON

Collectacard Series:

EL15	Vintage Steam (GWR), Set 6	1978		—	£3.50
EL15	Vintage Steam (SR), Set 7	1978		—	£3.50
EL15	Vintage Steam (LMS), Set 8	1978		—	£3.50
EL15	Vintage Steam (LNER), Set 9	1978		—	£3.50
EL15	Vintage Steam (Scottish), Set 10	1978		—	£3.50

F. & M. DOBSON (SOUTHERN) LTD

L72	Flags of the World, Nos 1-72	1978		—	£10.00
L72	Flags of the World, Nos 73-144	1978		—	£10.00
100	Newcastle and Sunderland's Greatest Footballers	1981		—	£20.00

A. & J. DONALDSON LTD

| 534 | Sports Favourites | c1950 | HD-48 | £9.00 | — |
| 64 | Sports Favourites Golden Series (Footballers) | c1950 | | £25.00 | — |

DONRUSS (USA)

LT56	Dallas	1981		—	£15.00
LT78	The Dark Crystal — The Film	1982		—	£10.00
LT66	Elvis	1978		—	£40.00
LT55	Knight Rider	1982		—	£20.00
LT66	Magnum P.I.	1983		—	£15.00
EL60	Major League All-Stars Baseball	1986		—	£12.00
LT66	Sgt Pepper's Lonely Hearts Club Band	1978		—	£15.00
LT66	Tron (including set 8 stickers)	1981		—	£15.00
LT92	Twister The Film	1996		—	£9.50

DORMY COLLECTION

| 25 | Golf — The Modern Era | 1994 | | 60p | £15.00 |

DOUBLE Z ENTERPRISE (USA)

LT66	Zig & Zag	1994		—	£8.00

DRIFTER

M24	Pop Stars	1983		£1.00	—

DRYFOOD LTD

50	Animals of the World	1956	HX-93	20p	£4.00
K50	Zoo Animals	1955		20p	£4.00

DUCHESS OF DEVONSHIRE DAIRY CO. LTD

L25	Devon Beauty Spots...	1936		£4.40	£110.00

DUNHILLS

25	Ships and Their Workings	1962	HX-85	50p	£12.50

DUNKIN (Malta)

L88	Martial Arts	c1975		£1.00	—
M50	Motor Cycles of the World	1976		£2.20	—

DUNN'S LONDON

60	Animals	1924	HX-140	£9.00	—
48	Birds	1924	HX-141	£9.00	—

J.A. DUNN & CO.

26	Actresses 'FROGA A'	1902	HX-155	£45.00	—

DUO (USA)

LT72	Abbott & Costello...	1996		20p	£12.00
EL72	The Beatles — Yellow Submarine (152 × 102mm) ...	1999		—	£15.00
LT90	Gone with the Wind — The Film...	1996		—	£9.50
LT72	Happy Days (1970s TV Series)	1998		—	£9.50
LT72	It's A Wonderful Life (The 1946 Film)	1996		—	£9.50
LT72	Lionel Greatest Trains	1998		—	£20.00
LT72	Lionel Legendary Trains	1997		—	£12.00
LT72	Lionel Legendary Trains 1900-2000 Centennial	2000		—	£20.00
LT81	The Outer Limits	1997		—	£9.50
LT72	The Wizard of Oz...	1996		—	£15.00
LT72	WWF Smack Down (Wrestling)	1999		—	£12.00
LT72	Zorro — The Film...	1998		—	£9.50

MICKEY DURLING (Sunday Empire)

(Cards issued with staple holes.)

48	Footballers of Today c1950			£5.00	—

DUTTON'S BEERS

12	Team of Sporting Heroes	1980		25p	£3.00
	Folder/Album			—	£8.00

DYNAMIC (Australia)

LT100	Disney's Aladdin	1995		20p	£9.50
LT60	Escape of the Dinosaurs	1997		—	£9.50
LT55	New Zealand All Blacks	1995		20p	£8.00

DYNAMIC FORCES (USA)

LT72	Lexx Premiere Series (TV, Sci-Fi Series)...	2002		—	£9.50

THE EAGLE

16	Soccer Stars	1965		£4.00	—

EAST KENT NATIONAL BUS CO.

L8	British Airways Holidays	1984		—	£4.00

EBRO

EL69	Pop Singers	c1963	HE-4	£5.00	—

ECLIPSE ENTERPRISES (USA)

LT110	The Beverly Hillbillies	1993		—	£9.50
LT110	National Lampoon Loaded Weapon I	1993		—	£9.50

EDGE ENTERTAINMENT (USA)

LT82	Judge Dredd — Movie & Comic	1995		—	£9.50

J. EDMONDSON & CO. LTD

26	Actresses 'FROGA'	c1901	HE-6	£60.00	—
4	Aeroplane Models	1939	HE-7	£20.00	—
?72	Art Pictures	c1914	HE-8	£14.00	—
14	Birds and Eggs	c1925	HE-9	£12.00	—
?22	Boy Scout Proficiency Badges	c1925	HE-10	£35.00	—
25	British Army Series	c1915	HX-144	£25.00	—
20	British Ships	1925		£3.50	—
20	Dogs	c1930	HE-11	£9.00	—
20	Famous Castles	1925		£7.50	—
30	Flags & Flags With Soldiers (Flags only)	c1905		£22.00	—
42	Flags of All Nations (3 printings)	c1930	HE-12	£10.00	—
24	Pictures from the Fairy Stories	c1930	HE-15	£6.00	—
24	Popular Sports	c1925	HE-17	£12.00	—
25	Sports and Pastimes	c1910	HX-225	£16.00	—
12	Throwing Shadows on the Wall:				
	A Light blue background	1937		£5.00	—
	B Dark blue background	1937		£5.00	—
25	War Series	c1916	HX-290	£15.00	—
12	Woodbine Village	c1930	HE-18	£5.00	—
26	Zoo Alphabet	c1930		£8.00	—

EDWARDS & SONS (Confectionery)

27	Popular Dogs	1954		£4.50	—
12	Products of the World	1957		20p	£2.50
25	Transport — Present and Future:				
	A Descriptive back	1955		20p	£3.00
	B Album offer back	1955		30p	£7.50
25	Wonders of the Universe:		HX-14		
	A With title	1956		20p	£3.50
	B Without title	1956		£1.00	£25.00

THE 'ELITE' PICTURE HOUSE

50	War Portraits	1916	HX-86	£100.00	—

ELKES BISCUITS LTD

25	Do You Know? (Mechanical)	1964	HX-166.1	20p	£3.00

ELY BREWERY CO. LTD

M24	Royal Portraits	1953	HX-10	£2.50	£60.00

EMERALD COLLECTABLES

M72	Birds & their Eggs	1996		—	£15.00

EMPIRE MARKETING BOARD

12	Empire Shopping	c1925		£3.50	£42.00

H.E. EMPSON & SON LTD

25	Birds	1962	HX-71	80p	—
25	British Cavalry Uniforms of the 19th Century	1963	HX-43	70p	£17.50
25	Garden Flowers	1966	HX-46	£1.00	£25.00
25	History of the Railways 1st Series	1966	HX-88	£1.60	—
25	History of the Railways 2nd Series	1966	HX-88	£1.60	—
24	The Island of Ceylon	1962	HX-47	£4.00	—
25	Passenger Liners	1964	HX-82	£1.60	—
25	Tropical Birds	1966	HX-13	50p	£12.50
25	Wonders of the Deep	1965	HX-89	20p	£3.50

ENESCO (USA)

LT16	Precious Moments	1993		—	£8.00

ENGLAND'S GLORY

15	England '66 (Football World Cup)	2004		—	£5.50

ENGLISH AND SCOTTISH CWS

?23	British Sports Series	c1910	HE-24	£40.00	—
25	Humorous Peeps into History (Nd 1-25)	1927		£3.40	£85.00
25	Humorous Peeps into History (Nd 26-50)	1928		£5.00	—
25	In Victoria's Days	1930		£3.40	£85.00
L12	The Rose of the Orient, Film Series	1925	HE-29.1	50p	£6.00
L12	The Rose of the Orient 2nd Film Series	1925	HE-29.2	50p	£6.00
L12	The Story of Tea (brown back)	1925	HE-31	£1.00	£12.00
L12	The Story of Tea (blue back)	1925		£1.50	£18.00

ENSIGN FISHING TACKLE

L6	Advertising Blotters	2002		—	£3.00
L6	Advertising Cards	2002		—	£3.00
L6	The Art of Angling 1st Series	1997		—	£3.00
L6	The Art of Angling 2nd Series	1997		—	£3.00
L6	The Art of Angling 3rd Series	2002		—	£3.00
L6	Birds of Prey	1997		—	£3.00
L6	Fisherman's Lore	2002		—	£3.00
L6	Fishing Tackle Advertisements	1995		—	£3.00
L20	Freshwater Fish	1995		—	£7.50
L6	Game Birds (By Graham Payne)	1996		—	£3.00
L6	Garden Birds	1997		—	£3.00
L6	It's A Dog's Life	2002		—	£3.00
L6	Lifeboats	2002		—	£3.00
L6	Lighthouses	2002		—	£3.00
L6	Norman Neasom's Rural Studies Series 1	2002		—	£3.00
L6	Norman Neasom's Rural Studies Series 2	2002		—	£3.00
L6	Owls	1997		—	£3.00
L25	Salmon Flies	1995		—	£7.50
L6	Sea Fish	2002		—	£3.00
L6	Sharks	2002		—	£3.00
L6	Water Loving Birds	2002		—	£3.00

EPOL (South Africa)

M30	Dogs	1974		70p	£20.00

JOHN E. ESSLEMONT LTD (Tea)

25	Before Our Time	1966	HX-103	40p	£10.00
25	Into Space	1966	HX-147	80p	£20.00
24	The Island of Ceylon	c1960	HX-47	£6.00	—

ESSO

EL20	Olympics (Nd 1-40)	1972		£2.00	—
M16	Squelchers Booklets (Football)	1970		£2.00	—

ESSO (Australia)

L18	Australia's Great Mineral Discoveries	1971		£1.00	£18.00

EUROSTAR

LT125	Tour de France (Cycling)	1997		20p	—

EVERSHED AND SON LTD

25	Sports and Pastimes	c1910	HX-225	£18.00	—

EVERY GIRLS PAPER

MP17	Film Stars	c1924	HE-42	£5.00	—

EWBANKS LTD

25	Animals of the Farmyard	1960		30p	£7.50
25	British Uniforms	1957	HX-108	20p	£4.00
25	Miniature Cars and Scooters	1959		24p	£6.00
50	Ports and Resorts of the World	1958	HX-38	20p	£9.00
25	Ships Around Britain...	1961		20p	£3.00
25	Sports and Games	1958	HX-154	40p	£10.00
25	Transport Through the Ages:		HX-101		
	A Black back	1957		20p	£3.00
	B Blue back	1957		50p	£12.50

EXPRESS WEEKLY

The Wild West:

25	A No overprint	1958	HX-55.3	30p	£7.50
25	B Red overprint	1958		20p	£4.00
L25	C 2 Pictures per card	1958		80p	—

EXTRAS

24	Prehistoric Monsters and the Present	1979		£3.00	—

F1 SPORTS CARD MARKETING INC. (Canada)

LT200	Grid Formula 1 Racing	1992		—	£20.00

F.P.G. (USA)

LT90	Barclay Shaw — Fantasy Art	1995		—	£9.50
LT90	Bernie Wrightson More Macabre Series 2 — Fantasy				
	Art	1994		—	£9.50
LT90	Bob Eggleton — Fantasy Art	1995		—	£9.50
LT90	Chris Foss — Fantasy Art	1995		—	£9.50
LT90	Christos Achilleos — Fantasy Art	1992		—	£9.50
LT90	Darrell Sweet — Fantasy Art	1994		—	£9.50

F.P.G. (USA) (continued)

Size & quantity		Date	Handbook reference	Price per card	Complete set
LT90	David Cherry — Fantasy Art	1995		—	£9.50
LT90	David Mattingly — Fantasy Art	1995		—	£9.50
LT90	Everway Vision Cards — Fantasy Art	1995		—	£12.00
LT90	James Warhola — Fantasy Art	1995		—	£9.50
LT60	Janny Wurts — Fantasy Art	1996		—	£8.00
LT90	Jeffrey Jones Series 1 — Fantasy Art	1993		—	£9.50
LT90	Jeffrey Jones Series 2 — Fantasy Art	1995		—	£9.50
LT90	Joe Devito — Fantasy Art	1995		—	£9.50
LT60	Joe Jusko's Edgar Rice-Burroughs Collection 1 (Tarzan)	1994		—	£12.00
LT60	Joe Jusko's Edgar Rice-Burroughs Collection 2	1995		—	£15.00
LT90	John Berkey Series 2 — Fantasy Art	1996		—	£9.50
LT90	Michael Kaluta 1st Series — Fantasy Art...	1994		—	£9.50
LT90	Michael Kaluta 2nd Series — Fantasy Art	1995		—	£9.50
LT90	Mike Ploog — Fantasy Art...	1994		—	£9.50
LT90	Paul Chadwick — Fantasy Art	1995		—	£9.50
LT90	Robh Ruppel — Fantasy Art	1996		—	£9.50
LT90	Thomas Canty — Fantasy Art	1996		—	£9.50

FACCHINO

	Cinema Stars:				
K50	A Inscribed Series of 50	1936		£7.00	—
K100	B Inscribed Series of 100	1936		65p	£65.00
K50	How or Why	1937		60p	£30.00
K50	People of All Lands	c1935		£2.00	—
K50	Pioneers	c1935		£2.00	—

FACTORY ENTERTAINMENT

LT50	The Prisoner Volume 2	2010		—	£8.00

FAIRLEY'S RESTAURANT

20	The European War Series	1916	HX-129	£25.00	—

FAITH PRESS

10	Boy Scouts	1928		£8.00	—
10	Girl Guides	1928		£8.00	—

FAMILY STAR

EL8	Good Luck Song Cards...	c1930		£3.50	—
K52	Miniature Playing Cards	c1955		80p	—
M4	Film Stars	c1955	HF-3	£5.00	—

FANTASY (USA)

LT50	Rocketship X-M	1979		—	£10.00

FANTASY TRADE CARD CO. (USA)

LT60	Alien Nation	1990		—	£18.00

FARM-TO-DOOR SUPPLIES

25	Castles of Great Britain...	1965	HX-161	£4.00	—
25	Cathedrals of Great Britain	1965	HX-162	£4.00	—

FARROW'S

50	Animals in the Zoo	1925		£8.00	—

FAULDERS CHOCOLATE

10	Ancient v Modern Sports	1924		£10.00	—
10	Birds and Nests	1924		£7.00	—
10	Fruits	1924		£7.00	—
10	Game...	1924		£8.00	—
10	Zoology	1924		£8.00	—

FAX PAX

L40	The American West (19th Century).....................	1992		—	—
L40	Birds of the British Isles	1991		—	—
L40	Britain's Royal Heritage..............................	1991		—	£5.00
LT50	Butterflies of the British Isles	1996		—	£5.00
L40	Castles	1990		—	—
L40	Cathedrals and Minsters	1989		—	£5.00
L39	Dinosaurs	1993		—	£5.00
L36	Equestrianism	1987		—	—
LT40	Famous Golfers	1993		—	£6.00
L42	First Ladies of the United States	1997		—	£5.00
L36	Football Greats	1989		—	—
L36	Football Stars	1989		—	£6.00
L40	Forty Great Britons	1992		—	—
L36	Golf	1987		—	£15.00
L40	Historic Houses	1990		—	£5.00
L40	Kings and Queens	1988		—	£5.00
L40	The Lake District	1993		—	£5.00
L40	London	1992		—	£5.00
	Presidents of the United States 1993:				
L41	A Complete set	1993		—	—
L40	B Different (minus George Bush 1989-93)	1993		—	£5.00
L40	Scotland's Heritage	1990		—	£5.00
L38	Tennis	1987		—	£8.00
LT50	Wild Flowers of the British Isles	1996		—	£5.00
L40	Wildlife of the British Isles	1991		—	£5.00
LT40	World of Sport	1993		—	£6.00

FEATHERED WORLD

EL?	Poultry, Pigeons, Cage Birds, etc. postcards	c1910	HF-6.8	£2.50	—

ALEX FERGUSON

20	The European War Series	1917	HX-129	£25.00	—
41	VC Heroes	1917	HX-220	£20.00	—

FESTIVAL OF 1000 BIKES

L24	The Vintage Motor Cycle Club	1993		—	£6.00

FIELD GALLERIES

L7	Racehorses & Jockeys 1st Series	1997		—	£3.00
L7	Racehorses & Jockeys 2nd Series	1997		—	£3.00

FIFE POLICE

L36	British Stamps	1987		20p	£6.00
EL20	Intercity British Rail	1990		40p	£8.00

FILM PICTORIAL

EL2	Film Stars (paper-backed silks)	c1930		£35.00	—

FILSHILL

24	Birds and Their Eggs	c1920	HX-164	£9.00	—
25	Footballers	1922	HF-18	£22.00	—
25	Types of British Soldiers	c1920	HX-144	£26.00	—

FINDUS (Frozen Foods)

20	All About Pirates	1967		30p	£6.00

FINE FARE TEA

25	Inventions and Discoveries 1st Series	1962	HX-131	70p	£17.50
25	Inventions and Discoveries 2nd Series	1962	HX-131	70p	£17.50
	Album for 1st and 2nd Series combined			—	£20.00
12	Your Fortune in a Teacup	1965		30p	£3.50

FISH MARKETING BOARD

18	Eat More Fish	c1930		£3.75	—

FIZZY FRUIT

25	Buses and Trams	c1960	HX-109	£1.00	£25.00

FLEER

LT84	Believe It or Not	c1970		40p	—
LT192	Mad	1985		40p	—

FLEER (USA)

LT90	Aaahh! Real Monsters	1995		—	£8.00
LT10	Aaahh! Real Monsters Colouring Cards	1995		—	£3.00
LT120	Batman Forever:				
	A Fleer 1995 on front	1995		—	£9.50
	B Fleer 95 Ultra on front	1995		—	£9.50
LT100	Batman Forever Metal	1995		—	£12.00
LT119	Casper — The Movie (Nos 13 & 77 unissued, 2 different Nos 12 & 69)	1995		—	£9.50
LT42	Christmas Series	1995		—	£12.00
LT66	Grossville High	1986		—	£8.00
LT72	Here's Bo Derek	1981		20p	£10.00
LT146	MTV Animation	1995		—	£12.00
LT42	Nursery Rhymes	1995		—	£10.00
LT150	Power Rangers The Movie	1995		—	£12.00
LT24	Power Rangers The Movie Power Pop Up	1995		—	£5.00
LT150	Reboot (TV Series)	1995		—	£12.00
LT100	Skeleton Warriors	1995		—	£8.00
LT50	Spiderman '97 with Fleer on front	1997		—	£9.50
LT50	Spiderman '97 without Fleer on front	1997		—	—
LT80	World Wrestling Federation Clash	2001		—	£10.00
LT100	WWF Wrestlemania	2001		—	£10.00

FLEETWAY PUBLICATIONS LTD

L72	Adventures of Sexton Blake	1968		£4.00	—
EL1	The Bobby Moore Book of The F.A. Cup (booklet)	1968		—	£15.00
EL28	Football Teams 1958-59 (issued with 'Lion/Tiger')	1958	HF-27	£4.00	—
EL28	Football Teams 1959-60 (issued with 'Lion/Tiger')	1959	HF-27	£4.00	—
EL2	Pop Stars (Roxy)	1961		£1.50	£3.00
50	Star Footballers of 1963 (issued with 'Tiger')	1963		£1.80	—

FLORENCE CARDS

24	Luton Corporation Tramways … … … … … … … … …	1983		—	£3.00
M20	Tramway Scenes … … … … … … … … … … … … …	1984		—	£4.00

FOOTBALL ASSOCIATION OF WALES

LT17	The Dragons Dream Team (Welsh International Footballers) … … … … … … … … … … …	2000		—	£6.00

FOOTBALL CARD COLLECTOR

10	Association Footballers (of the 1960s) 1st Series … …	2012		—	£5.00
10	Association Footballers (of the 1960s) 2nd Series …	2012		—	£5.00
10	Association Footballers (of the 1950/60s) 3rd Series…	2012		—	£5.00
10	Footballers 1960s 1st Series … … … … … … … … …	2011		—	£4.50
10	Footballers 1960s 2nd Series … … … … … … …	2011		—	£4.50
10	Footballers 1960s 3rd Series … … … … … … … …	2011		—	£4.50
10	Footballers 1960s 4th Series … … … … … … … …	2011		—	£4.50
10	Soccer Heroes (1945-66) 1st Series … … … … …	2014		—	£5.00
10	Soccer Heroes (1950-60s) 2nd Series… … … … … …	2014		—	£5.00

FOOTBALL COLLECTOR CARDS

20	Football (1950s Footballers) blue fronts 1st Series …	2011		—	£7.50
20	Football (1950s Footballers) yellow fronts 2nd Series	2011		—	£7.50
20	Football (1950s Footballers) green fronts 3rd Series …	2011		—	£7.50

FOOTBALL FANFARE

20	Football Fanfare (1950s Footballers) 1st Series … …	2010		—	£7.50
20	Football Fanfare (1950s Footballers) 2nd Series … …	2010		—	£7.50
20	Football Fanfare (1950/60s Footballers) 3rd Series …	2010		—	£7.50
20	Football Fanfare (1950/60s Footballers) 4th Series …	2010		—	£7.50

FOOTBALL STAR COLLECTOR CARDS

20	Football Star … … … … … … … … … … … … …	2010		—	£7.50

FOOTBALL TRADER

16	Legends of The Orient (Leyton Orient F.C.) … … … …	2011		—	£5.00

FOOTBALLER MAGAZINE

24	Hall of Fame (Footballers)… … … … … … … … …	1994		50p	£12.00
	Album … … … … … … … … … … … … … … …			—	£12.00

FORD MOTOR CO. LTD

L50	Major Farming … … … … … … … … … … … … …	c1955		£9.00	—

FOSTER CLARK (Malta)

50	The Sea Our Other World … … … … … … … … …	1974		50p	£25.00

FOTO BUBBLE GUM

25	Wonders of the Universe … … … … … … … … …	1957	HX-14	20p	£3.00

FRAME SET & MATCH

25	Wembley Magpies (Newcastle Utd Footballers) … …	1995		24p	£6.00

FRAMEABILITY

L17	British Steam Locomotives … … … … … … … …	2002		—	£6.00
L16	Fire Engines 1st Series… … … … … … … … … …	1996		—	£5.00
L16	Fire Engines 2nd Series … … … … … … … … …	1998		—	£6.00

FRAMEABILITY (continued)

L10	Highwaymen	2003			—	£4.00
L17	Police — British Police Vehicles	2002			—	£6.00
L6	Traction Engines	1999			—	£3.00
L10	World Cup Winners 1966 England	2002			—	£5.00

FRAMES OF MIND

L11	World Cup Winners 1966 (Football)	1997			—	£11.00

A.C.W. FRANCIS (West Indies)

25	British Uniforms of the 19th Century	c1965			£1.00	—
25	Castles of Britain	c1965			£1.00	—
25	The Circus	1966			£1.00	—
25	Football Clubs and Badges	c1965			£1.00	—
25	Pond Life	1967			36p	£9.00
25	Sports of the Countries:					
	A Black back	1967			£1.20	—
	B Blue back	1967			£1.20	—

FRANK'S SWEETS

32	Felix Pictures	c1922	HX-56		£50.00	—

FREEDOM PRESS (USA)

LT40	The JFK Assassination	1991			—	£8.00
LT16	Official Currier and Ives Civil War	1994			—	£5.00

LES FRERES

25	Aircraft of World War II:		HX-7			
	A Black back	1966			£2.00	£50.00
	B Blue black	1966			£1.20	£30.00

FRESHMAID LTD (Jubbly)

50	Adventurous Lives	1966			20p	£4.50

J.S. FRY & SONS LTD (Chocolate)

4	Advertisement Cards:					
	A G.H. Elliott (size 63 × 38mm), dark brown	c1910			—	£30.00
	B G.H. Elliott (size 66 × 38mm), light brown	c1910			—	£30.00
	C Hello Daddy (size 66 × 38mm)	c1910			—	£30.00
	D Vinello (size 80 × 62mm)	c1920			—	£40.00
50	Ancient Sundials:					
	A With series title, text back...	1924			£3.20	—
	B Without series title, plain back	1924			£7.50	—
50	Birds and Poultry	1912			£3.20	£160.00
24	Birds and Their Eggs	1912			£4.50	£110.00
15	China and Porcelain	1907			£14.00	—
25	Days of Nelson	1906			£12.00	—
25	Days of Wellington	1906			£12.00	—
25	Empire Industries	1924			£8.00	—
	Exercises for Men and Women:					
13	A Exercises for Men	1926			£6.00	—
12	B Exercises for Men and Boys	1926			£6.00	—
13	C Exercises for Women	1926			£6.00	—
12	D Exercises for Women and Girls...	1926			£6.00	—
K48	Film Stars	1934			£3.50	—
50	Fowls, Pigeons and Dogs	1908			£4.50	£225.00

J.S. FRY & SONS LTD (Chocolate) (continued)

EL12	Fun Cards	1972		20p	£2.50
25	Match Tricks	c1921		£34.00	—
15	National Flags	1908		£8.00	—
50	Nursery Rhymes	1917		£4.00	£200.00
50	Phil May Sketches	1905		£5.00	—
25	Red Indians...	1927		£8.00	—
25	Rule Britannia	1915		£6.00	—
50	Scout Series	1912		£8.00	—
48	Screen Stars	1928		£3.50	—
120	This Wonderful World	1935		£3.00	—
50	Time and Money in Different Countries	1908		£3.50	£175.00
50	Tricks and Puzzles (blue back)	1918		£4.00	£200.00
50	Tricks and Puzzles (black back)	1924		£4.00	£200.00
6	War Leaders — Package Issue	1915	HF-58	£30.00	—
25	With Captain Scott at the South Pole	1912		£13.00	£325.00

J.S. FRY & SONS LTD (Canada)

50	Children's Pictures	c1915	£14.00	—
25	Hunting Series...	c1915	£20.00	—
25	Radio Series	c1930	£12.00	—
50	Scout Series 2nd Series	c1930	£13.00	—
50	Treasure Island Map...	c1915	£10.00	—

FUTERA (Australia)

LT60	Cricket Elite...	1996	—	£15.00
LT110	Cricketers	1994	—	£16.00

FUTERA
(SEE ALSO TRADE CARDS (EUROPE) LTD)

LT18	Aston Villa F.C.	2000	—	£12.00
LT18	Derby County F.C.	2000	—	£12.00
LT18	Manchester City F.C.	2000	—	£15.00
LT18	Middlesbrough F.C.	2000	—	£12.00
LT64	Red Dwarf (TV Series)	2002	—	£15.00
LT18	West Ham United F.C.	2000	—	£15.00
LT50	World Stars Platinum Series (Footballers)	2001	—	£16.00
M24	World Stars 3D Footballers	2002	—	£8.00

G.B. & T.W.

L20	Golfing Greats ...	1989	—	£10.00

G. D. S. CARDS

L25	American Civil War Battles	2006	—	£12.50
L25	Birds by C.R. Bree	2007	—	£9.50
L25	Birds by Cassell 1860	2007	—	£9.50
L20	Birds of North America by John Cassin	2007	—	£8.50
L20	Birds of The United States...	2007	—	£8.50
L20	British Birds of Prey Series 1	2006	—	£8.50
L20	British Birds of Prey Series 2	2008	—	£8.50
L20	British Butterflies (1841) Series 1	2008	—	£8.50
L20	British Butterflies (1841) Series 2	2008	—	£8.50
L20	British Fresh-Water Fish	2006	—	£8.50
EL4	Cattle Breeds	2007	—	£4.50
L20	Champion Hurdle — Winners 1976-1995...	1997	—	£12.00
L20	Cheltenham Gold Cup — Winners 1976-1995	1997	—	£12.00

G. D. S. CARDS (continued)

Size & quantity	Title	Date	Handbook reference	Price per card	Complete set
L20	Clippers and Yachts	2007		—	£8.50
L16	Derby Winners 1953-1968	1994		—	£10.00
L20	Dogs	2006		—	£8.50
L20	Earl of Derby Collection of Racehorse Paintings	2004		—	£13.00
L20	European Birds	2007		—	£9.50
L20	Famous Jockeys	2001		—	£9.50
L20	Famous Jockeys of Yesterday, Series 1	2003		—	£12.00
L20	Famous Titled Owners and Their Racing Colours, Series 1	2003		—	£12.00
L20	Famous Trainers (Horse Racing)	2001		—	£9.50
L20	Finches by Butler and Frohawk (1899)	2010		—	£7.00
EL4	Fusiliers by Richard Simkin (1890-1905)	2008		—	£4.50
L20	Grand National — Winners 1976-1995	1997		—	£12.00
L20	Great Racehorses	2003		—	£12.00
L16	Great Racehorses of Our Time	1994		—	£14.00
L25	Hawks and Owls of The America	2007		—	£9.50
L20	Heads of Famous Winners (Racehorses)	2001		—	£9.50
L20	Horses	2008		—	£8.50
L20	Hummingbirds by M.E. Mulsant & J.B.E. Verreaux (1876-77)	2010		—	£7.00
L25	Indian Chiefs of North America Series 1	2006		—	£9.50
L25	Indian Chiefs of North America Series 2	2007		—	£9.50
L20	Indian Tribes of North America	2007		—	£8.50
L16	Lester Piggott's Classic Winners	1994		—	£10.00
L25	Light Infantries and Regiments by Richard Simkin (1890-1905)	2008		—	£9.50
EL4	Military (1890-1905) by Richard Simkin	2008		—	£4.50
L25	Monkeys by J.G. Keulemans	2007		—	£9.50
L25	1950's Racehorse Winners	2008		—	£10.50
L20	1960's Racehorse Winners	2007		—	£10.50
L25	1970's Racehorse Winners	2007		—	£10.50
L20	One Thousand Guineas Winners 1981-2000	2005		—	£10.50
L20	Orchids by Robert Warner & Thomas Moore (1882)	2010		—	£7.00
L20	Parakeets and Parrots (1903) by David Seth-Smith	2008		—	£8.50
L25	Parrots	2007		—	£9.50
L25	Pigeons	2006		—	£9.50
L20	Poultry	2006		—	£8.50
L25	Poultry by Harrison Weir 1904	2008		—	£9.50
L20	St Leger 1776-1815 Winning Owners Colours	2005		—	£10.50
EL6	Soldiers and Cavalry by Richard Simkin (1890-1905)	2008		—	£7.00
L20	Tropical Birds	2007		—	£8.50
L20	Trotters (American Style Horse Racing)	2006		—	£8.50
L20	Two Thousand Guineas Winners 1981-2000	2005		—	£10.50
L25	World's Birds of Prey (1876) Series 1	2008		—	£9.50
L25	World's Birds of Prey (1876) Series 2	2008		—	£9.50

GALBRAITH'S STORES

25	Animals in the Service of Man	c1964	HX-51	£5.00	—
50	Strange Creatures	c1963	HX-120	£5.00	—

GALLERY OF LEGENDS

72	The British Open Golf Collection	1999		—	£15.00

GAMEPLAN LTD

L25	Open Champions (Golf)	1993		—	£9.00
L25	Vauxhall Motor Sport	1993		—	£10.00

GANONG BROS. LTD (Canada)

50	Big Chief...	c1925		£8.00	—

GARDEN RAILWAYS MAGAZINE (USA)

20	Daventry Garden Railway	1991		—	£6.00
20	Garden Railway Structures Set E	1991		—	£6.00
20	Trains in the Garden: USA Set C	1991		—	£6.00
20	Trains in the Garden: Britain Set D	1991		—	£6.00

GAUMONT CHOCOLATE

K50	Film Stars	1936		£4.00	—

GAYCON PRODUCTS LTD (Confectionery)

25	Adventures of Pinky and Perky 1st Series:				
	A Blue back	1961		£4.00	—
	B Black back	1961		£4.00	—
25	Adventures of Pinky and Perky 2nd Series:				
	A Blue back	1961		£4.00	—
	B Black back	1961		£4.00	—
50	British Birds and Their Eggs	1961	HX-105	30p	£15.00
25	British Butterflies 1st Series	1963		80p	£20.00
25	Do You Know? 1st Series	1962	HX-166.3	£1.60	£40.00
25	Do You Know? 2nd Series...	1962	HX-166.3	£1.60	£40.00
50	Flags of All Nations	1963	HX-112	£2.50	—
25	History of the Blue Lamp 1st Series	1961		80p	£20.00
25	History of the Blue Lamp 2nd Series	1961		80p	£20.00
30	Kings and Queens	1961	HX-116	20p	£3.00
25	Modern Motor Cars	1959	HX-39	£5.00	—
25	Modern Motor Cars of the World 1st Series	1962		£5.00	—
25	Modern Motor Cars of the World 2nd Series	1962		£5.00	—
25	Red Indians 1st Series	1960	HX-118	80p	£20.00
25	Red Indians 2nd Series...	1960	HX-118	80p	£20.00
25	Top Secret 1st Series	1967	HX-156	£3.40	—
25	Top Secret 2nd Series	1967	HX-156	£3.40	—

GEE'S FOOD PRODUCTS

30	Kings and Queens	1961	HX-116	60p	£18.00
16	See Britain by Coach	1955	HX-84	22p	£3.50

THE GEM LIBRARY

MP15	Footballers Special Action Photo	1922		£5.00	—
MP6	Footballers Autographed Real Action Photo Series ...	1922		£5.00	—
MP4	Footballers Autographed Action Series	1923		£5.50	—
L16	Marvels of the Future	1929		£3.25	—

GENERAL FOODS (South Africa)

L50	Animals and Birds	1973		20p	£9.00
	Album			—	£15.00

GENERAL MILLS (Canada)

LT6	Baseball Players (10 players per card)	1989		—	£5.00

THE GIRLS FRIEND

M6	Actresses (Silk)	1912	HG-12	£10.00	—

GIRLS MIRROR

MP10	Actors and Actresses		c1922	HG-14	£4.50	—

GIRLS WEEKLY

12	Flower Fortune Cards		1912		£15.00	—

GLENGETTIE TEA

25	Animals of the World		1964	HX-61	20p	£3.00
25	Birds and Their Eggs		1970	HX-1.3	24p	£6.00
25	The British Army, 1815:					
	A Black back		1976		30p	£7.50
	B Blue back		1976		30p	£7.50
25	British Locomotives		1959	HX-157	20p	£3.50
25	Do You Know?		1970	HX-166.4	20p	£3.00
25	Historical Scenes		1968	HX-143	20p	£3.50
25	History of the Railway 1st Series		1974		20p	£4.00
25	History of the Railway 2nd Series		1974		20p	£4.00
25	International Air Liners		1963	HX-125.1	60p	—
25	Medals of the World:			HX-110		
	A Black back		1961		20p	£3.00
	B Blue back		1961		60p	£15.00
25	Modern Transport:			HX-125.1		
	A Black back		1963		70p	£17.50
	B Blue back		1963		70p	£17.50
25	Naval Battles		1971	HX-21	20p	£3.00
25	Rare British Birds		1967		20p	£5.00
25	Sovereigns, Consorts and Rulers of Great Britain,					
	1st Series		1970	HX-201	£1.00	—
25	Sovereigns, Consorts and Rulers of Great Britain,					
	2nd Series		1970	HX-201	£1.00	£25.00
25	Trains of the World		1966	HX-121.2	20p	£5.00
25	Veteran and Vintage Cars		1966	HX-159	80p	£20.00
25	Wild Flowers		1961	HX-124	40p	£10.00

GLENTONS LTD

24	World's Most Beautiful Butterflies		c1920	HX-23	£9.00	—

GLOUCESTERSHIRE C.C.C.

M12	Gloucestershire Cricketers of 1990		1990		30p	£3.50

J. GODDARD & SONS LTD

	Back 'Eighty'					
M3	Four Generations		c1925	HG-24	£2.00	£6.00
M12	London Views		c1925	HG-25	£2.00	£24.00
M12	Old Silver		c1925	HG-26	£1.50	£18.00
M2	Use and Cleaning of Silverware I		c1925		£1.25	£2.50
	Back 'Eighty-five'					
M4	Cleaning a Silver Teapot		c1930	HG-23	£4.00	£16.00
M12	Ports of the World		c1930	HG-28	£2.50	—
M4	Silverware and Flowers I		c1930	HG-29	£2.50	£10.00
M12	Views of Old Leicester		c1930		£5.00	—
	Back 'Ninety'					
M9	Old Silver at the Victoria and Albert Museum		c1935	HG-27	£2.00	£18.00
M8	Silverware and Flowers II		c1935	HG-30	£3.50	—
M8	Views of Leicester		c1935		£5.00	—
	Back '95'					

J. GODDARD & SONS LTD (continued)

M12	Present Day Silverware...	c1940		£2.00	£24.00
M6	Use and Cleaning of Silverware II	c1940	HG-31	£4.00	—

GOLDEN CHICK

24	World's Most Beautiful Birds	c1920	HX-22	£10.00	—

GOLDEN ERA

L7	A.J.S. Motor Cycles	1995		—	£3.00
L25	Aircraft of the First World War	1994		—	£7.50
L7	Alfa Romeo (Cars)	1998		—	£3.00
LT10	American Automobiles of the 1950s	2003		—	£4.50
LT7	Anglia, Prefect, Popular Small Fords 1953-1967	2005		—	£3.75
L7	Antique Dolls	1996		—	£3.00
L7	Ariel Motor Cycles	1995		—	£3.00
L7	Aston Martin (Cars)	1993		—	£3.00
L7	Aston Martin Post-War Competition Cars...	2001		—	£3.00
L10	Austin Cars	1996		—	£3.75
L7	Austin Healey Motor Cars	1995		—	£3.00
L9	BMW (Cars)	1999		—	£3.75
L7	BSA 1st Series (Motor Cycles)	1993		—	£3.00
L7	BSA 2nd Series (Motor Cycles)	1999		—	£3.00
L10	British Buses of the 1950s...	1999		—	£3.75
L10	British Buses of the 1960s...	1999		—	£3.75
L10	British Lorries of the 1950s	2000		—	£3.75
EL4	British Lorries of the 1950s (numbered 081-084)	1999		—	£2.25
L10	British Lorries of the 1950s & 1960s	1999		—	£3.75
L10	British Lorries of the 1960s	2000		—	£3.75
L10	British Military Vehicles of WWII...	2000		—	£3.75
L25	British Motor Cycles of the Fifties	1993		—	£7.50
L7	British Tanks of WWII	2000		—	£3.00
L10	British Trucks (1950s and 1960s)	2010		—	£3.75
L7	British Vans of The 1950s	2002		—	£3.00
L7	British Vans of The 1960s	2002		—	£3.00
LT10	Buses in Britain 1950s	2005		—	£4.50
LT10	Buses in Britain 1960s	2005		—	£4.50
L10	Bygone Buses (1950s and 1960s)...	2010		—	£3.75
L7	Capri Mk1 1969-74	2007		—	£3.00
L7	Capri Mk3 1978-86	2007		—	£3.00
LT7	Capri Mk I Performance Models (1969-74)	2004		—	£3.75
LT7	Capri Mk II Performance Models (1974-78)	2004		—	£3.75
LT7	Capri Mk III Performance Models (1978-86)...	2004		—	£3.75
L25	Cats (Full Length)	1994		—	£7.50
L26	Cats (Heads)	1995		—	£7.50
LT7	Chevrolet Camaro 1967-69	2004		—	£3.75
L7	Citroen (Cars)	2001		—	£3.00
L10	Classic American Motor Cycles	1998		—	£3.75
L7	Classic Bentley (Cars)	1997		—	£3.00
L26	Classic British Motor Cars	1992		—	£7.50
L25	Classic British Motor Cycles of the '50s & '60s	1993		—	£7.50
L7	Classic Citroen 2CV	2001		—	£3.00
LT10	Classic Corvette (Cars)	1994		—	£4.50
L7	Classic Ferrari (Cars)	1993		—	£7.00
L7	Classic Ferrari F1 1961-2000...	2002		—	£3.00
L7	Classic Fiat	2002		—	£3.00
L7	Classic Honda (Motor Cycles)	1999		—	£3.00
EL4	Classic Jaguar Series 1 (numbered 153-156)	2010		—	£2.25

GOLDEN ERA (continued)

Size & quantity		Date	Handbook reference	Price per card	Complete set
L10	Classic Jeep	2002		—	£3.75
L7	Classic Kawasaki (Motor Cycles)	1999		—	£3.00
EL6	Classic Lambretta — The Golden Era of Scootering	2008		—	£3.00
L10	Classic Lorries (1950s and 1960s)	2010		—	£3.75
L7	Classic Lotus (Cars) 1st Series	1995		—	£3.00
L7	Classic Lotus (Cars) 2nd Series	1997		—	£3.00
L7	Classic MG (Cars) 1st Series	1992		—	£3.00
L7	Classic MG (Cars) 2nd Series	1994		—	£3.00
L7	Classic MG Sports Cars	1996		—	£3.00
L10	Classic Mercedes	2000		—	£3.75
LT10	Classic Mini	2005		—	£4.50
L7	Classic Morgan Sports Cars	1997		—	£3.00
LT10	Classic Mustang (Cars)	1994		—	£6.00
L13	Classic Porsche Cars	1996		—	£4.50
L7	Classic Rally Cars of the 1970s	2001		—	£3.00
L7	Classic Rally Cars of the 1980s	2001		—	£3.00
EL6	Classic Riley	2008		—	£3.00
L7	Classic Rolls-Royce (Cars)	1997		—	£3.00
L7	Classic Rover (Cars)	1995		—	£3.00
L10	Classic Scooters	2000		—	£3.75
L7	Classic Suzuki	1999		—	£3.00
L10	Classic Tractors	1998		—	£3.75
L7	Classic T.V.R. (Cars)	1997		—	£3.00
L7	Classic Vauxhalls of the 1950s & 1960s	2002		—	£3.00
L7	Classic Volkswagen Karmann Ghia 1955-74	2002		—	£3.00
L7	Classic Volkswagen Transporter 1950-79	1999		—	£3.00
L7	Classic Volkswagen VW Beetle 1949-66	1999		—	£3.00
L7	Classic Volkswagen VW Beetle 1967-80	1999		—	£3.00
L7	Classic Volkswagen VW Golf GTI 1975-92	2002		—	£3.00
L7	Classic Volvo (Cars)	2003		—	£3.00
L13	Classic VW (Cars)	1993		—	£4.50
EL6	Classic VW Transporter	2008		—	£3.00
EL6	Classic Wolseley	2008		—	£3.00
L7	Classic Yamaha	1999		—	£3.00
L7	Cobra The Sports Car 1962-1969	1996		—	£3.00
LT7	Consul, Zephyr, Zodiac Big Fords 1951-1971	2005		—	£3.75
L7	Cortina Mk1 1962-1966	2007		—	£3.00
L7	Daimler Classics	2004		—	£3.00
L7	Dolls	1996		—	£3.00
L7	Ducati (Motor Cycles)	1999		—	£3.00
L7	E-Type Jaguar (Cars)	1993		—	£3.00
L10	Eight Wheelers Classic British Lorries	2007		—	£3.75
L7	Escort Mk1 R S Models	2007		—	£3.00
L7	Escort Mk2 1975-80	2007		—	£3.00
L7	Escort Twin-cam, RS & Mexico 1969-80	1999		—	£3.00
L7	Escort Works Rally Mk I, MK II	1999		—	£3.00
LT7	Escort Mk I The Performers	2004		—	£3.75
LT7	Escort Mk II The Performers	2004		—	£3.75
LT10	Famous Bombers (Aircraft)	1997		—	£4.50
LT10	Famous Fighters (Aircraft)	1997		—	£4.50
M20	Famous Footballers by Stubbs — Arsenal	2001		—	£5.00
M20	Famous Footballers by Stubbs — Aston Villa	2002		—	£5.00
M20	Famous Footballers by Stubbs — Chelsea	2001		—	£5.00
M20	Famous Footballers by Stubbs — Leeds	2001		—	£5.00
M20	Famous Footballers by Stubbs — Liverpool	2001		—	£5.00
M20	Famous Footballers by Stubbs — Manchester United	2001		—	£5.00

GOLDEN ERA (continued)

M20	Famous Footballers by Stubbs — Newcastle United ...	2002	—	£5.00
M20	Famous Footballers by Stubbs — Spurs	2001	—	£5.00
M20	Famous Footballers by Stubbs — West Ham United ...	2002	—	£5.00
L7	Famous Fords — Capri Mk2 1974-78	2008	—	£3.00
L7	Famous Fords — Cortina Mk2 1966-70	2008	—	£3.00
L10	Famous T.T. Riders (Motorcyclists)	1998	—	£3.75
L7	Ferrari 1950s & 1960s	2003	—	£3.00
L7	Ferrari 1970s & 1980s	2003	—	£3.00
L7	Ford and Fordson Tractors 1945-1970	2010	—	£3.00
L10	The Ford Capri (Cars)	1995	—	£3.75
L7	Ford Cortina Story 1962-82	2002	—	£3.00
L7	Ford Executive (Cars)	1994	—	£3.00
L10	Ford in the Sixties (Cars)	1996	—	£3.75
L7	Ford RS Models 1983-92	2001	—	£3.00
LT7	Ford Sierra — The Performers	2005	—	£3.75
L7	Ford XR Performance Models 1980-89	2001	—	£3.00
L10	Formula 1 (Grand Prix)	1996	—	£3.75
L10	F1 Champions 1991-2000	2001	—	£3.75
L7	German Military Vehicles of WWII	2001	—	£3.00
L7	Graham & Damon Hill (Grand Prix Drivers)	2000	—	£3.00
LT7	Granada-Consul and Granada MkI and MkII	2005	—	£3.75
L10	Grand Prix Greats	1996	—	£3.75
L26	Grand Prix The Early Years (Cars)	1992	—	£7.50
L10	Heavy Haulage (Lorries etc)	2000	—	£3.75
EL4	Jaguar At Le Mans (numbered 029-032)	1995		£2.25
L7	Jaguar Classic (Cars) 1st Series	1992	—	£3.00
L7	Jaguar Classic (Cars) 2nd Series	1993	—	£3.00
L7	Jaguar Classic (Cars) 3rd Series	1997	—	£3.00
L7	Jaguar Classics (Cars) 4th Series	2003	—	£3.00
EL4	Jaguar E-Type (numbered 149-152)	2010	—	£2.25
L7	Jaguar Modern Classics (Cars) 5th Series	2003	—	£3.00
L7	Jim Clark (Grand Prix Driver)	2000	—	£3.00
L7	Lambretta (Motor Cycles)	2000	—	£3.00
EL6	Lambretta Innocetti — The Golden Era of Scootering	2008	—	£3.00
L10	Lambretta The World's Finest Scooter...	2007	—	£3.75
EL6	Lambrettability — The Golden Era of Scootering	2008	—	£3.00
L7	Lancia (Cars)	1998	—	£3.00
L7	Land Rover 1st Series	1996	—	£3.00
EL4	Land Rover 1st Series (numbered 049-052)...	1997	—	£4.00
L7	Land Rover 2nd Series	1996	—	£3.00
EL4	Land Rover 2nd Series (numbered 053-056)	1997	—	£4.00
L7	Land Rover 3rd Series	1996	—	£3.00
EL4	Land Rover 3rd Series (numbered 057-060)	1997	—	£4.00
L7	Land Rover Discovery	2001	—	£3.00
L7	Land Rover Legends Series 1	2000	—	£3.00
EL4	Land Rover Legends Series 1 (numbered 093-096) ...	2000	—	£2.25
L7	Land Rover Legends Series 2	2000	—	£3.00
EL4	Land Rover Legends Series 2 (numbered 097-100) ...	2000	—	£2.25
L7	Land Rover Legends Series 3	2000	—	£3.00
EL4	Land Rover Legends Series 3 (numbered 101-104) ...	2000	—	£2.25
L7	Land Rover, Ninety, One Ten & Defender	2000	—	£3.00
EL4	Land Rover Ninety, One Ten & Defender (numbered 105-108)	2000	—	£2.25
L7	The Legend Lives On, Ayrton Senna (Grand Prix ... ... Driver)...	2000	—	£3.00
L10	London Buses of the Post-War Years	1997	—	£3.75
EL4	London Buses Post-War (numbered 069-072)	1999	—	£2.25

GOLDEN ERA (continued)

Size & quantity		Date	Price per card	Complete set
L10	London Buses of the Pre-War Years	1997	—	£3.75
EL4	London Buses Pre-War (numbered 065-068)	1999	—	£2.25
L7	The London Taxi	2001	—	£3.00
L10	London's Country Buses	2000	—	£3.75
EL4	London's Country Buses (numbered 061-064)	2000	—	£2.25
L7	Mansell (by Wayne Vickery)	1994	—	£3.00
L7	Matchless Motor Cycles	1995	—	£3.00
L7	Mercedes SL (Cars)	1994	—	£3.00
EL4	M.G. Greats (Cars) (numbered 033-036)	1995	—	£2.25
EL4	M.G.B. (Cars) (numbered 037-040)	1995	—	£2.25
L10	Micro & Bubble Cars	2000	—	£3.75
EL4	Midland Red Buses (numbered 117-120)	2000	—	£2.25
L7	Mini Cooper (Cars)	1994	—	£3.00
EL4	Mini Cooper (Cars) (numbered 001-004)	1994	—	£2.25
EL4	Mini Cooper (numbered 161-164)	2010	—	£2.25
L10	Mini Cooper The 1960's	2007	—	£3.75
L10	The Mini Legend (Cars)	1995	—	£3.75
L7	Mini Moke 1961-89	2007	—	£3.00
L10	Mini (Cars) — Special Edition	1999	—	£3.75
EL4	Mini Vans (numbered 025-028)	1995	—	£2.25
EL4	Monte Carlo Minis (Cars) (numbered 009-012)	1994	—	£2.25
L9	Morris Minor (Cars)	1993	—	£3.75
EL4	Morris Minor (Cars) (numbered 045-048)	1995	—	£2.25
L9	Morris Minor — Fifty Years (Cars)	1998	—	£3.75
EL4	Morris Minor (Vans) (numbered 005-008)	1994	—	£2.25
L10	Motorcycling Greats	1997	—	£3.75
L10	Municipal Buses of The 1950s and 1960s	2007	—	£3.75
L7	Norton (Motor Cycles) 1st Series	1993	—	£3.00
L7	Norton (Motor Cycles) 2nd Series	1998	—	£3.00
L7	Old Teddy Bears	1995	—	£3.00
L10	On The Move Classic British Lorries	2004	—	£3.75
EL6	Original Vespa — The Golden Age of Scootering	2009	—	£3.00
EL4	Police Vehicles (numbered 013-016)	1994	—	£2.25
LT7	Pontiac GTO 1964-74	2004	—	£3.75
L7	Porsche 356 (1950-65)	2003	—	£3.00
L7	Porsche 911 (1963-77)	2003	—	£3.00
L7	Porsche 911 (1978-98)	2003	—	£3.00
L7	Racing & Rallying Mini Coopers of the 60's	2000	—	£3.00
LT7	Racing Legends (Formula 1 Drivers)	2004	—	£3.75
L7	Range Rover (Cars)	1996	—	£3.00
L7	The Ringmaster — Michael Schumacher	2002	—	£3.00
L10	Road Haulage Classic British Lorries	2004	—	£3.75
LT10	Rootes Sixties Classics (Cars)	2005	—	£4.50
EL4	Southdown Buses (numbered 121-124)	2000	—	£2.25
L7	Spitfire (Cars)	1994	—	£3.00
L7	Sporting Ford (Cars)	1992	—	£3.00
EL4	Sporting Mini Cooper (numbered 157-160)	2010	—	£2.25
L7	Spridget — Austin Healey Sprite & MG Midget 1958-79	2002	—	£3.00
L13	Superbikes of the 70s	2000	—	£4.50
L7	Tanks of WWII	2000	—	£3.00
L7	Teddies	1997	—	£3.00
L7	Teddy Bears	1994	—	£3.00
EL4	Teddy Bears (numbered 021-024)	1995	—	£2.25
EL4	Teddy Bear Families (numbered 017-020)	1995	—	£2.25
L10	35 Years of the Mini 1959-1994	1994	—	£3.75
LT7	Thunderbird American Classics 1955-63 (Cars)	2003	—	£4.00
L10	Traction Engines	1999	—	£3.75

GOLDEN ERA (continued)

Size & quantity		Date	Handbook reference	Price per card	Complete set
EL4	Traction Engines (numbered 109-112)...	2000		—	£2.25
EL4	Tractors 1st Series (numbered 073-076)	1999		—	£4.00
EL4	Tractors 2nd Series (numbered 077-080)	1999		—	£4.00
L7	Tractors of the Fifties	1999		—	£3.00
L7	Tractors of the Sixties	1999		—	£3.00
L7	TR Collection (Triumph Cars)...	1992		—	£3.00
L7	Triumph (Motor Cycles) 1st Series	1993		—	£3.00
L7	Triumph (Motor Cycles) 2nd Series...	1998		—	£3.00
L10	Triumph Herald 1959-71	2007		—	£3.75
L7	Triumph Saloon Cars 1960s & 1970s	2002		—	£3.00
L7	Triumph Spitfire 1962-80	2007		—	£3.00
L7	Triumph Stag Motor Cars	1995		—	£3.00
L7	Triumph TR2 and TR3 1953-61	2007		—	£3.00
L7	Triumph TR4, TR5 and TR6 1961-76	2007		—	£3.00
L7	Triumph Vitesse 1962-71	2007		—	£3.00
L7	U.S. Military Vehicles of WWII	2001		—	£3.00
L7	Velocette (Motor Cycles)	1993		—	£3.00
L7	Vespa (Motor Cycles)	2000		—	£3.00
L7	Vincent Motor Cycles	1995		—	£3.00
L7	Vintage Vespa 1958-1966...	2005		—	£3.00
EL4	Volkswagen Beetle (numbered 085-088)	1999		—	£4.00
EL4	Volkswagen Transporter (numbered 089-092)	1999		—	£4.00
L7	VW Transporter 1956-1961	2005		—	£3.00
EL6	VW Transporter Bus 1950-67...	2008		—	£3.00
L7	VW Transporter 1968-80 Bay Window Models	2007		—	£3.00
EL6	VW Transporter Type 2...	2008		—	£3.00
LT7	World Champions (Formula 1 Drivers)	2004		—	£3.75

GOLDEN FLEECE (Australia)

L36	Dogs ...	1967		55p	£20.00

GOLDEN GRAIN TEA

25	Birds ...	1963	HX-71	£1.20	—
25	British Cavalry Uniforms of the 19th Century	1965	HX-43	60p	£15.00
25	Garden Flowers	1965	HX-46	20p	£3.50
25	Passenger Liners...	1966	HX-82	36p	£9.00

GOLDEN WONDER

24	Soccer All Stars	1978		50p	£12.00
	Album...			—	£6.00
14	Space Cards (yellow background)	1978		22p	£3.00
14	Space Cards (coloured)	1979		22p	£3.00
24	Sporting All Stars...	1979		20p	£4.00
	Album...			—	£6.00
24	TV All Stars...	1979		20p	£3.00
	Album ...			—	£15.00
36	World Cup Soccer All Stars	1978		50p	£18.00
	Album...			—	£6.00

GOLF GIFTS LTD

M24	Ryder Cup 1989	1991		—	£15.00

GOOD TIMES CREATIONS

21	Blades Legends (Sheffield United F.C. from 1889 to 2014	2014		—	£12.00

GOOD TIMES CREATIONS (continued)

Size & quantity		Date		Price per card	Complete set
34	Colours of Brazil (2014 Football World Cup)	2014		—	£12.00
13	Golf Legends	2012		—	£8.50
23	Great Britons (Olympic Athletes Post War Gold Medalists)	2012		—	£12.00
13	Ladies of Rock...	2013		—	£8.50
13	Legends of Rock	2012		—	£8.50
20	Lendas Brasileiras (Brazilian Football Legends)	2013		—	£12.00
25	24 Lions in Brazil (English World Cup Footballers) ...	2014		—	£12.00
13	Silkmen Legends (Macclesfield Town F.C.)	2012		—	£8.50
13	Twelve Days of Christmas...	2012		—	£8.50

GOODIES LTD

50	Doctor Who and the Daleks	1969		£10.00	—
25	Flags and Emblems	1961		20p	£3.50
25	Indian Tribes	1969		£5.40	—
25	Mini Monsters	1970		£2.00	£50.00
25	The Monkees 1st Series	1967		£1.20	£30.00
25	The Monkees 2nd Series	1968		£5.00	—
24	Olympics...	1972		£3.00	—
25	Pirates	1970		£3.20	—
25	Prehistoric Animals	1969		£3.00	—
25	Robbers and Thieves	1971		£2.40	—
25	Vanishing Animals	1971		£2.00	—
25	Weapons Through the Ages	1970		£2.00	—
25	Wicked Monarchs	1973		£1.60	£40.00
25	Wide World/People of Other Lands...	1968		£1.40	£35.00
25	Wild Life	1969		£2.00	—
25	World Cup	1974		£3.20	—

D.W. GOODWIN & CO.

36	Careers for Boys and Girls	c1930		£8.00	—
24	Extra Rhymes 2nd Series	c1930		£14.00	—
	Flags of All Nations (12 different backs):				
36	Series A Home Nursing...	c1930		£6.00	—
36	Series B Common Ailments and Their Cures	c1930		£6.00	—
36	Series C Tenants' Rights	c1930		£6.00	—
36	Series D Gardening Hints	c1930		£6.00	—
36	Series E Household Hints	c1930		£6.00	—
36	Series F Poultry Keeping	c1930		£6.00	—
36	Series G Beauty Aids	c1930		£6.00	—
36	Series H The World's Great Women	c1930		£6.00	—
36	Series I First Aid	c1930		£6.00	—
36	Series J Cookery Recipes...	c1930		£6.00	—
36	Series K Cookery Recipes...	c1930		£6.00	—
36	Series L General Knowledge	c1930		£6.00	—
36	Jokes Series (multi-backed)	c1930	HG-34	£11.00	—
36	Optical Illusions (multi-backed)	c1930	HG-35	£12.00	—
36	Ships Series (multi-backed)	c1930	HG-37	£11.00	—
24	Wireless Series	c1930		£14.00	—
36	World Interest Series (multi-backed)	c1930	HG-38	£7.00	—
24	World's Most Beautiful Birds	c1930	HX-22	£10.00	—
24	World's Most Beautiful Fishes	c1930	HX-24	£10.00	—

W. GOSSAGE & SONS LTD

48	British Birds and their Eggs	1924	HX-141	£3.00	—
48	Butterflies and Moths	1925		£2.00	—

GOWERS & BURGONS

25	British Birds and Their Nests	1967	HX-104	30p	£7.50
25	The Circus	1966	HX-79	£2.40	—
25	Family Pets	1967	HX-136	20p	£3.50
25	People and Places	1966	HX-26	20p	£3.00
25	Prehistoric Animals	1967	HX-92	£1.20	£30.00
25	Sailing Ships Through the Ages	1963	HX-119	£1.20	£30.00
25	Veteran and Vintage Cars	1965	HX-159	£1.20	£30.00
25	Veteran Racing Cars	1963	HX-19	£1.20	£30.00

GRAFFITI INC. (USA)

LT90	Goldeneye, James Bond 007	1997	—		£9.50

GRAIN PRODUCTS (New Zealand)

M20	Adventuring in New Zealand	1982	—		£10.00
M20	American Holiday	1986	—		£10.00
M20	Amusement Parks	1987	—		£10.00
M20	Cats	1983	—		£15.00
M20	European Holiday	1980	—		£10.00
M20	Farming in N.Z.	1986	—		£12.00
M20	Fire Engines	1988	—		£15.00
M20	Fish of the New Zealand Seas	1981	—		£15.00
M20	Hong Kong Highlights	1991	—		£12.00
M20	Horse and Pony World	1978	—		£12.00
EL9	How to Cartoon	1989	—		£9.00
M20	Kennel Companions	1976	—		£20.00
M25	National Costumes of the Old World	1977	—		£25.00
M20	New Zealand Police	1984	—		£15.00
M20	Our Heritage on Parade	1980	—		£12.00
M20	Our Mighty Forests	1979	—		£15.00
M20	Passport Los Angeles	1990	—		£12.00
M20	Space Exploration	1986	—		£15.00
M20	Television in New Zealand	1983	—		£10.00
EL10	Vintage and Veteran Cars	1985	—		£10.00
M20	World of Bridges	1981	—		£15.00

GRAMPUS PHOTOS

M20	Film Favourites (of 1920s)	1993	—		£10.00
M20	Modern Beauties (topless pin-up girls)	1992	—		£15.00

GRANDSTAND

LT100	Scottish Footballers Nos 1-100	1993		20p	£10.00
LT102	Scottish Footballers Nos 101-202	1993		20p	£10.00

GRANGER'S

12	Dr. Mabuse	c1920		£12.00	—

GRANOSE FOODS LTD

M48	Adventures of Billy the Buck	1952		20p	£4.00
M16	Air Transport	1957	HG-40.1	40p	£6.00
M16	Animal Life	1957	HG-40.2	25p	£4.00
25	Animals in the Service of Man	c1965		£3.00	—
M16	Aquatic and Reptile Life	1957	HG-40.3	40p	£6.00
M48	King of the Air	1956		60p	—
M48	Life Story of Blower the Whale	1956		60p	—
M48	Lone Leo the Cougar	1955		60p	—
M20	150 Years of British Locomotives	1980		75p	£15.00

GRANOSE FOODS LTD (continued)

M16	Our Winged Friends	1957	HG-40.4	75p	—
M16	Plant Life	1957	HG-40.5	75p	—
M48	Silver Mane, The Timber Wolf	1955		30p	£15.00
M16	Space Travel	1957	HG-40.6	60p	£10.00
M48	Tippytail the Grizzly Bear	1956		20p	£7.50
M16	Water Transport	1957	HG-40.7	25p	£4.00
M16	World Wide Visits	1957	HG-40.8	25p	£4.00

W. GRANT & SONS LTD

25	Clan Tartans	1992		—	£15.00

GREATER MANCHESTER POLICE

L24	British Lions (Rugby League)	1992		—	£7.50
EL15	British Stamps	1986		30p	£4.50
L24	Riversiders Wigan R.L.F.C.	1990		30p	£7.50
L12	Rugby 13 Hall of Fame	1992		—	£6.00
L24	Wigan R.L.F.C. Simply the Best	1996		—	£12.00
L24	Wigan Rugby League F.C. (As Safe As ...)	2001		—	£6.00

D. GREEN

15	Alexandra The Greats (Crewe Alexandra F.C. Footballers)	2006		—	£4.50

GREGG (New Zealand)

M48	Aquatic Birds	1965		40p	£20.00
	Album			—	£15.00
M40	Birds (Land Birds)	1963		60p	—
	Album			—	£20.00
M40	Introduced Birds	1967		60p	£24.00
	Album			—	£20.00
M40	Native Birds of New Zealand	1971		30p	£12.00
	Album			—	£20.00
M35	Rare and Endangered Birds	1977		60p	—
	Album			—	£25.00
M40	Remarkable Birds	1969		60p	£24.00
	Album			—	£20.00
M35	Unusual Birds of the World	1981		60p	—
	Album			—	£25.00

GUINNESS

EL6	Famous Guinness Alice Posters	1951		£15.00	£90.00
EL6	Famous Guinness for Strength Posters	1951		£15.00	£90.00
EL6	Guinness Advertisements, Set A	1932		£20.00	—
EL6	Guinness Advertisements, Set B	1932		£20.00	—
EL6	Guinness Advertisements, Set C	1932		£20.00	—

H.M.A.F. TOYS

EL9	H.M. Armed Forces	2009		—	£9.00

HADDEN'S

24	World's Most Beautiful Butterflies	c1920	HX-23	£10.00	—

NICHOLAS HALL

25	War Series	1915	HX-290	£20.00	—

B. HALLS

Size & quantity		Date	Handbook reference	Price per card	Complete set
M35	Cricket Sudocards	2006		—	£5.00
M25	Rowing Sudocards	2006		—	£4.00

HALPIN'S WILLOW TEA

	Aircraft of the World:				
25	A Standard Set	1958	HX-180	20p	£3.00
M20	B Two Pictures per Card, 25 Subjects	1958		£1.00	£20.00
25	Nature Studies...	1957	HX-9	20p	£5.00

T. P. K. HANNAH (Confectionery)

25	Top Flight Stars (Sport)...	1960		£3.60	—

THE HAPPY HOME

M8	Child Studies (silks) (multi-backed)...	c1915	HH-5	£16.00	—
M9	Flags (silks)...	c1915	HH-6	£8.00	—
K14	The Happy Home Silk Button (silks)	c1915		£8.00	—
M9	Our Lucky Flowers (silks) (multi-backed)	c1915	HH-8	£14.00	—
M12	Women on War Work (silks)	c1915	HH-9	£10.00	—

HARBOUR DIGITAL

M12	Birds in Flight	1997		—	£6.00
30	Cars At the Turn of the Century	1996		—	£9.00
M18	Cricket Teams of the 1890s	1997		—	£9.00
12	England & South Africa Cricketers	1996		—	£8.00
12	European Locomotives	1996		—	£6.00
L38	Famous Cricketers 1895	2000		—	£10.00
24	Golden Oldies Extracts from Famous Cricketer 1890	1996		—	£10.00
M20	Harry Vardon's Golf Clinic	1997		—	£6.00
24	Historic Hampshire	1996		—	£6.00
24	Jaguar Cars	1996		—	£9.00
20	More Golden Oldies — Cricketers	1995		60p	£12.00
30	The Old Fruit Garden	1995		40p	£12.00
20	The Operatic Stage	1996		—	£7.00
L18	The Romance of India	2000		—	£6.00
M10	The Sea Mens Dress	1997		—	£8.00
18	Ships That Battle the Seas	1996		—	£9.00
M12	World Boxers 3rd Series	1996		—	£6.00

HARDEN BROTHERS & LINDSAY LTD

50	Animals of the World	1959	HX-93	40p	£20.00
	Album (titled Wild Animals of the World)			—	£6.00
50	British Birds and Their Eggs	1960	HX-105	£1.00	—
	Album			—	£40.00
50	National Pets	1961	HX-145	20p	£4.00
	Album...			—	£6.00

HAROLD HARE

L16	Animals and Pets plus album...	1960		—	£10.00

HARRISON

25	Beauties	c1910	HH-10	£26.00	—
25	Types of British Soldiers	c1910	HX-144	£40.00	—

HAT-TRICK CARDS

15	Burnley (Footballers of the 1960s) … … … … … … …	2011		—	£5.50
10	Everton Heroes (Footballers of the 1960s) … … … …	2011		—	£5.00
10	Hat-Trick Football Cards 1960/70s (black and white)…	2011		—	£4.50
10	Hat-Trick Football Cards 1st Series (1970s footballers) coloured … … … … … … … … … … … … … … …	2011		—	£5.00
10	Hat-Trick Football Cards 2nd Series (1970s footballers) coloured … … … … … … … … … … … … … …	2011		—	£5.00
10	Hat-Trick Football Cards 3rd Series (1970s footballers) coloured … … … … … … … … … … … … … …	2011		—	£5.00
10	Hat-Trick Football Cards 4th Series (1970s footballers) coloured … … … … … … … … … … … … … …	2011		—	£5.00
10	Hat-Trick Football Cards 5th Series (1970s footballers) coloured … … … … … … … … … … … … … …	2011		—	£5.00
10	Hat-Trick Football Cards 6th Series (1970s footballers) coloured … … … … … … … … … … … … … …	2011		—	£5.00
10	Hat-Trick Football Cards 7th Series (1970s footballers) coloured … … … … … … … … … … … … … …	2011		—	£5.00
10	Hat-Trick Football Cards 8th Series (1970s footballers) coloured … … … … … … … … … … … … … …	2013		—	£5.00
10	Hat-Trick Football Cards 9th Series (1970s footballers) coloured … … … … … … … … … … … … … …	2013		—	£5.00
10	Kick Off 1st Series (Footballers of the 1960/70s) … …	2012		—	£5.00
10	Kick Off 2nd Series (Footballers of the 1960/70s) … …	2012		—	£5.00

J. HAWKINS & SONS LTD

M30	The Story of Cotton … … … … … … … … … … …	c1920		£6.00	—

HAYMAN

24	World's Most Beautiful Butterflies … … … … … …	c1920	HX-23	£10.00	—

HEDNESFORD TOWN FOOTBALL CLUB

24	Hednesford Town Football Stars (including Information Sheets) … … … … … … … … … …	1986		25p	£6.00

HEINZ

EL1	Australian Cricket Team England … … … … … …	1964		—	£15.00

HERALD ALARMS

10	Feudal Lords … … … … … … … … … … … … …	1986		—	£20.00
EL10	Feudal Lords … … … … … … … … … … … … …	1986		£1.20	£12.00

HERTFORDSHIRE POLICE

L12	Stamp Out Crime … … … … … … … … … … …	1983		—	£6.00

HITCHMAN'S DAIRIES LTD

25	Aircraft of World War II:		HX-7		
	A Black back … … … … … … … … … … … …	1966		36p	£9.00
	B Blue back … … … … … … … … … … … …	1966		£1.00	£25.00
25	Animals of the World … … … … … … … … … …	1965	HX-61	70p	£17.50
25	British Birds and their Nests … … … … … … …	1966	HX-104	£1.00	—
25	British Railways … … … … … … … … … … …	1964	HX-107	20p	£3.50
25	Buses & Trams:		HX-109		
	A White card … … … … … … … … … … …	1966		20p	£5.00
	B Cream card … … … … … … … … … …	1966		20p	£5.00
25	Merchant Ships of the World … … … … … … …	1962	HX-63	70p	£17.50

HITCHMAN'S DAIRIES LTD (continued)

25	Modern Wonders	1965	HX-130	40p	£10.00
25	Naval Battles	1971	HX-21	20p	£5.00
25	People and Places	1971	HX-26	24p	£6.00
25	Regimental Uniforms of the Past	1973		20p	£3.00
25	Science in the 20th Century	1966	HX-18	30p	£7.50
25	The Story of Milk	1965	HX-3	70p	£17.50
25	Trains of the World	1970	HX-121	£1.00	—

F. HOADLEY LTD

24	World's Most Beautiful Birds	c1920	HX-22	£12.00	—

HOADLEY'S CHOCOLATES LTD (Australia)

50	The Birth of a Nation	c1940		£2.25	—
50	British Empire Kings and Queens	c1940		£1.80	—
?33	Cricketers (black and white)	1928		£18.00	—
36	Cricketers (brown)	1933		£12.00	—
50	Early Australian Series	c1940		£2.00	—
50	Empire Games and Test Teams	1934		£10.00	—
32	Gulliver's Travels	1939		£6.00	—
50	National Safety Council...	c1937		£3.50	—
40	Test Cricketers...	1936		£15.00	—
M36	Test Cricketers...	1938		£15.00	—
50	Victorian Footballers 1st Series nd 1-50	c1940		£8.00	—
50	Victorian Footballers 2nd Series nd 51-100	c1940		£8.00	—
50	Victorian Footballers (action studies)	c1940		£8.00	—
50	Wild West Series	c1940		£2.50	—

HOBBYPRESS GUIDES

20	Preserved Railway Locomotives...	1983		—	£3.00
20	Preserved Steam Railways 1st Series...	1983		—	£3.00
20	Preserved Steam Railways 2nd Series	1984		—	£4.00
20	The Worlds Great Cricketers	1984		—	£6.00

THOMAS HOLLOWAY LTD

EL60	Natural History Series — Animals (full length)	c1900		£10.00	—
EL39	Natural History Series — Animals' Heads	c1900		£8.00	—
EL39	Natural History Series — Birds	c1900		£8.00	—
EL50	Pictorial History of the Sports and Pastimes of All Nations	c1900		£12.00	—

HOME AND COLONIAL STORES LTD

26	Advertising Alphabet (boxed letters)	1913	HH-27.1	£8.00	—
26	Advertising Alphabet different series (unboxed letters)	1913	HH-27.2	£15.00	—
M100	Flag Pictures	1915	HH-28	£4.50	—
100	War Pictures	1915		£4.25	—
M40	War Pictures (Personalities)	c1915	HH-29.1	£7.50	—
M40	War Pictures (Scenes)	c1915	HH-29.2	£7.50	—

HOME COUNTIES DAIRIES TEA

25	Country Life	1964	HX-11	20p	£5.00
25	International Air Liners	1968	HX-125	20p	£3.00
25	The Story of Milk	1965	HX-3	20p	£4.50

THE HOME MIRROR

M4	Cinema Star Pictures (silks)	1919	HH-31	£15.00	—

HOME PUBLICITY LTD

?98	Merry Miniatures	c1950	HH-32	£13.00	—

HOME WEEKLY

12	Little Charlie Cards	c1915	£18.00	—

HORNIMAN TEA

EL10	Boating Ways	c1910	HH-38	£22.00	—
EL12	British Birds and Eggs	c1910	HH-37	£22.00	—
48	Dogs	1961		20p	£5.00
	Album			—	£25.00
EL10	Naval Heroes	c1910	HH-39	£22.00	—
48	Pets	1960		20p	£5.00
	Album...			—	£10.00
48	Wild Animals	1958		20p	£5.00
	Album (titled 'On Safari')			—	£25.00

HORSLEY'S STORES

25	British Uniforms of the 19th Century	1968	HX-79	40p	£10.00
25	Castles of Britain	1968	HX-134	£1.80	—
25	Family Pets...	1968	HX-136	50p	£12.50

HUDDERSFIELD TOWN F.C.

M37	Huddersfield Town Players and Officials Season 1935-36	1936	£16.00	—

HULL CITY FOOTBALL CLUB

L20	Footballers	1950	£12.00	—

HULL DAILY MAIL

EL8	100 Years of Hull Public Transport	1980	—	£5.00

HUMBERSIDE POLICE

EL36	East Yorkshire Scenes of Natural Beauty	1987	30p	£10.00

HUNT, CROP AND SONS

15	Characters from Dickens	1912	£12.00	—

D.J. HUNTER

Infantry Regimental Colours:

L7	The Argyll & Sutherland Highlanders 1st Series:			
	A Error Set with light yellow border	2008	—	£3.00
	B Corrected Set with orange border	2008	—	£3.00
L7	The Argyll & Sutherland Highlanders 2nd Series ...	2011	—	£3.00
L7	The Bedfordshire & Herefordshire Regiment...	2009	—	£3.00
L7	The Black Watch 1st Series	2006	—	£3.00
L7	The Black Watch 2nd Series	2011	—	£3.00
L7	The Border Regiment	2005	—	£3.00
L7	The Buffs (Royal East Kent Regiment)	2005	—	£3.00
L7	The Cameronians (Scottish Rifles)	2009	—	£3.00
L7	The Cheshire Regiment...	2006	—	£3.00
L7	The Coldstream Guards 1st Series	2009	—	£3.00
L7	The Coldstream Guards 2nd Series	2009	—	£3.00
L7	The Coldstream Guards 3rd Series	2009	—	£3.00
L7	The Connaught Rangers	2010	—	£3.00
L7	The Devonshire Regiment 1st Series	2006	—	£3.00

D. J. HUNTER (continued)

Infantry Regimental Colours (continued):

		Date	Handbook reference	Price per card	Complete set
L7	The Devonshire Regiment 2nd Series	2012		—	£3.00
L7	The Dorset Regiment 1st Series	2010		—	£3.00
L7	The Dorset Regiment 2nd Series	2012		—	£3.00
L7	The Duke of Cornwall's Light Infantry	2007		—	£3.00
L7	The Duke of Wellington's Regiment 1st Series	2006		—	£3.00
L7	The Duke of Wellington's Regiment 2nd Series... ...	2011		—	£3.00
L7	The Durham Light Infantry 1st Series	2009		—	£3.00
L7	The Durham Light Infantry 2nd Series	2012		—	£3.00
L7	The East Lancashire Regiment 1st Series	2007		—	£3.00
L7	The East Lancashire Regiment 2nd Series	2012		—	£3.00
L7	The East Surrey Regiment...	2004		—	£3.00
L7	The East Yorkshire Regiment 1st Series	2010		—	£3.00
L7	The East Yorkshire Regiment 2nd Series	2011		—	£3.00
L7	The Essex Regiment	2007		—	£3.00
L7	The Gloucestershire Regiment 1st Series	2006		—	£3.00
L7	The Gloucestershire Regiment 2nd Series	2013		—	£3.00
L7	The Gordon Highlanders 1st Series...	2004		—	£3.00
L7	The Gordon Highlanders 2nd Series	2013		—	£3.00
L7	The Green Howards	2010		—	£3.00
L7	The Grenadier Guards 1st Series	2009		—	£3.00
L7	The Grenadier Guards 2nd Series	2009		—	£3.00
L7	The Grenadier Guards 3rd Series	2009		—	£3.00
L7	The Highland Light Infantry	2007		—	£3.00
L7	The Irish Guards 1st Series	2009		—	£3.00
L7	The Irish Guards 2nd Series	2009		—	£3.00
L7	The King's Own Royal Regiment (Lancaster) 1st Series	2005		—	£3.00
L7	The King's Own Royal Regiment (Lancaster) 2nd Series	2012		—	£3.00
L7	The King's Own Scottish Borderers 1st Series	2004		—	£3.00
L7	The King's Own Scottish Borderers 2nd Series (includes errors and two number 3s but no number 4)	2013		—	£3.00
L7	The King's Own Yorkshire Light Infantry	2009		—	£3.00
L7	The King's Regiment (Liverpool)	2005		—	£3.00
L7	The King's Shropshire Light Infantry 1st Series... ...	2004		—	£3.00
L7	The King's Shropshire Light Infantry 2nd Series ...	2008		—	£3.00
L7	The Lancashire Fusiliers 1st Series:				
	A Error Set with 'Royal' in title	2005		—	£3.00
	B Corrected Set without 'Royal' in title	2006		—	£3.00
L7	The Lancashire Fusiliers 2nd Series	2011		—	£3.00
L7	The London Regiment 1st Series	2008		—	£3.00
L7	The London Regiment 2nd Series	2008		—	£3.00
L7	The Loyal Regiment (North Lancashire)	2009		—	£3.00
L7	The Manchester Regiment 1st Series	2005		—	£3.00
L7	The Manchester Regiment 2nd Series...	2012		—	£3.00
L7	The Middlesex Regiment (Duke of Cambridge Own)	2007		—	£3.00
L9	Miscellaneous Colours	2013		—	£3.00
L7	The North Staffordshire Regiment 1st Series	2004		—	£3.00
L7	The North Staffordshire Regiment 2nd Series	2008		—	£3.00
L7	The Northamptonshire Regiment 1st Series	2007		—	£3.00
L7	The Northamptonshire Regiment 2nd Series	2013		—	£3.00
L7	The Oxfordshire & Buckinghamshire Light Infantry 1st Series	2007		—	£3.00
L7	The Oxfordshire & Buckinghamshire Light Infantry 2nd Series	2011		—	£3.00

D. J. HUNTER (continued)

Infantry Regimental Colours (continued):

		Date		Price per card	Complete set
L7	The Prince of Wales's Leinster Regiment	2010		—	£3.00
L7	The Queen's Own Cameron Highlanders 1st Series .	2006		—	£3.00
L7	The Queen's Own Cameron Highlanders 2nd Series	2012		—	£3.00
L7	The Queen's Own Royal West Kent Regiment	2005		—	£3.00
L7	The Queen's Royal Regiment (West Surrey) 1st Series	2004		—	£3.00
L7	The Queen's Royal Regiment (West Surrey) 2nd Series	2012		—	£3.00
L7	The Royal Berkshire Regiment	2010		—	£3.00
L7	The Royal Dublin Fusiliers	2010		—	£3.00
L7	The Royal Fusiliers (City of London Regiment)	2005		—	£3.00
L7	The Royal Hampshire Regiment	2008		—	£3.00
L7	The Royal Inniskilling Fusiliers 1st Series...	2005		—	£3.00
L7	The Royal Inniskilling Fusiliers 2nd Series	2011		—	£3.00
L7	The Royal Irish Fusiliers	2008		—	£3.00
L7	The Royal Irish Regiment (18th Foot) 1st Series ...	2006		—	£3.00
L7	The Royal Irish Regiment (18th Foot) 2nd Series ...	2012		—	£3.00
L7	The Royal Irish Rifles	2010		—	£3.00
L7	The Royal Leicestershire Regiment 1st Series	2006		—	£3.00
L7	The Royal Leicestershire Regiment 2nd Series... ...	2013		—	£3.00
L7	The Royal Lincolnshire Regiment	2006		—	£3.00
L7	The Royal Marines 1st Series...	2008		—	£3.00
L7	The Royal Marines 2nd Series	2008		—	£3.00
L7	The Royal Munster Fusiliers	2010		—	£3.00
L7	The Royal Norfolk Regiment	2004		—	£3.00
L7	The Royal Northumberland Fusiliers	2005		—	£3.00
L7	The Royal Scots 1st Series	2004		—	£3.00
L7	The Royal Scots 2nd Series	2007		—	£3.00
L7	The Royal Scots Fusiliers 1st Series	2006		—	£3.00
L7	The Royal Scots Fusiliers 2nd Series	2012		—	£3.00
L7	The Royal Sussex Regiment	2007		—	£3.00
L7	The Royal Warwickshire Fusiliers	2005		—	£3.00
L7	The Royal Welch Fusiliers 1st Series	2008		—	£3.00
L7	The Royal Welch Fusiliers 2nd Series	2011		—	£3.00
L7	The Scots Guards 1st Series	2009		—	£3.00
L7	The Scots Guards 2nd Series...	2009		—	£3.00
L7	The Scots Guards 3rd Series	2009		—	£3.00
L7	The Seaforth Highlanders 1st Series	2006		—	£3.00
L7	The Seaforth Highlanders 2nd Series	2012		—	£3.00
L7	The Seaforth Highlanders 3rd Series	2012		—	£3.00
L7	The Sherwood Foresters 1st Series	2004		—	£3.00
L7	The Sherwood Foresters 2nd Series	2007		—	£3.00
L7	The Somerset Light Infantry 1st Series	2010		—	£3.00
L7	The Somerset Light Infantry 2nd Series	2011		—	£3.00
L7	The South Lancashire Regiment...	2007		—	£3.00
L7	The South Staffordshire Regiment 1st Series	2004		—	£3.00
L7	The South Staffordshire Regiment 2nd Series	2008		—	£3.00
L7	The South Wales Borderers 1st Series	2006		—	£3.00
L7	The South Wales Borderers 2nd Series	2011		—	£3.00
L7	The Suffolk Regiment 1st Series...	2004		—	£3.00
L7	The Suffolk Regiment 2nd Series:				
	A Error Set with light yellow border	2008		—	£3.00
	B Corrected Set with orange border	2008		—	£3.00
L7	The Welch Regiment...	2005		—	£3.00
L7	The Welsh Guards	2009		—	£3.00
L7	The West Yorkshire Regiment	2010		—	£3.00

D. J. HUNTER (continued)

Infantry Regimental Colours (continued):

		Date	Handbook reference	Price per card	Complete set
L7	The Wiltshire Regiment 1st Series	2010		—	£3.00
L7	The Wiltshire Regiment 2nd Series	2011		—	£3.00
L7	The Worcestershire Regiment 1st Series	2004		—	£3.00
L7	The Worcestershire Regiment 2nd Series				
	(Error on No. 6 marked 1st Series)	2007		—	£3.00
L7	The York and Lancaster Regiment 1st Series	2009		—	£3.00
L7	The York and Lancaster Regiment 2nd Series	2011		—	£3.00

HUNTLEY & PALMERS

		Date	Handbook reference	Price per card	Complete set
EL12	Animals and Birds	c1900	HH-95	£10.00	—
EL12	Aviation	c1908		£50.00	—
EL12	Biscuits in Various Countries	c1900	HH-96	£10.00	—
EL6	Biscuits with Travellers	c1900	HH-97	£10.00	—
EL12	Children of Nations (Gold Border)	c1900	HH-98	£10.00	—
EL12	Children of Nations (White Border)	c1900	HH-99	£10.00	—
EL12	Children at Leisure and Play (No Captions)	c1900	HH-100	£10.00	—
EL12	Harvests of the World	c1900	HH-101	£20.00	—
EL12	Hunting	c1900	HH-102	£12.50	—
EL8	Inventors	c1900	HH-103	£25.00	—
EL11	Rhondes Enfantines (Children's Rhymes)	c1900	HH-104	£25.00	—
EL12	Scenes with Biscuits	c1900	HH-105	£10.00	—
EL12	The Seasons	c1900		£15.00	—
EL8	Shakespearian Subjects	c1900	HH-106	£12.50	—
EL12	Soldiers of Various Countries	c1900	HH-107	£15.00	—
EL12	Sports (With Semi-Circular Effect)	c1900	HH-108	£20.00	—
EL12	Sports (Without Semi-Circular Effect)	c1900	HH-108	£20.00	—
EL12	Travelling During the 19th Century	1900	HH-109	£25.00	—
EL12	Views of Italy and the French Riviera	c1900	HH-110	£12.50	—
EL12	Warships	c1900	HH-111	£15.00	—
EL8	Watteau	c1900	HH-112	£10.00	—
EL8	Wonders of the World	c1900	HH-113	£25.00	—

R. HYDE & CO. LTD

		Date	Handbook reference	Price per card	Complete set
80	British Birds	1929		£2.40	—
80	Cage Birds	1930		£1.60	—
80	Canary Culture	1930		£1.30	—
?M63	Hyde's Cartoons (multi-backed)	1908	HH-114	£14.00	—

IDEAL ALBUMS

		Date		Price per card	Complete set
L25	Boxing Greats	1991		—	£12.50

IKON (Australia)

		Date		Price per card	Complete set
LT81	Buffy The Story Continues	2003		—	£16.00
LT81	Buffy The Story So Far	2000		—	£16.00
LT81	Cricketer Australia 2003	2003		—	£15.00

IMPEL (USA)

		Date		Price per card	Complete set
LT150	An American Tail — Fievel Goes West	1991		—	£12.00
LT80	Laffs	1991		—	£8.00
LT160	Minnie 'N' Me	1991		—	£12.00
LT120	Star Trek The Next Generation	1992		—	£14.00
LT5	Star Trek The Next Generation Bonus Foreign				
	Language	1992		—	£5.00
LT160	Star Trek 25th Anniversary 1st Series	1991		—	£12.00
LT150	Star Trek 25th Anniversary 2nd Series	1991		—	£12.00

IMPEL (USA) (continued)

LT140	Terminator 2 — The Film		1991		—	£9.50
LT36	Trading Card Treats (Cartoon Characters)		1991		—	£8.00
LT90	U.S. Olympic Hall of Fame		1991		20p	£9.50
LT162	WCW Wrestling		1991		—	£12.00

IMPERIAL PUBLISHING

L20	American Golfers		1990		—	£8.50
L24	Birds of Britain		2000		—	£8.50
L6	Breeds of Cats		2000		—	£3.00
L6	Dogs — Airedale Terriers		1999		—	£3.00
L6	Dogs — Border Collies		1999		—	£3.00
L6	Dogs — Boxers		1999		—	£3.00
L6	Dogs — Bulldogs		1999		—	£3.00
L6	Dogs — Cocker Spaniels		1999		—	£3.00
L6	Dogs — Dachshunds		1999		—	£3.00
L6	Dogs — Dalmatians		1999		—	£3.00
L6	Dogs — Dobermann		1999		—	£3.00
L6	Dogs — German Shepherds		1999		—	£3.00
L6	Dogs — Golden Retrievers		1999		—	£3.00
L6	Dogs — Greyhounds		2000		—	£3.00
L6	Dogs — Jack Russell Terriers		1999		—	£3.00
L6	Dogs — Labrador Retrievers		1999		—	£3.00
L6	Dogs — Pekingese		1999		—	£3.00
L6	Dogs — Poodles		1999		—	£3.00
L6	Dogs — Scottish Terriers		1999		—	£3.00
L6	Dogs — Staffordshire Bull Terriers		2000		—	£3.00
L6	Dogs — West Highland White Terriers		2000		—	£3.00
L6	Dogs — Yorkshire Terriers		1999		—	£6.00
L24	The History of The Olympic Games		1996		—	£12.00
L20	Native North Americans		1995		—	£8.50
L48	Olympic Champions		1996		—	£15.00
L18	Snooker Celebrities		1993		—	£12.00

IN LINE (USA)

LT56	Motor Cycles		1993		—	£9.50

INDIA & CEYLON TEA CO LTD

24	The Island of Ceylon		c1955	HX-47	£6.00	—

INDIAN MOTOCYCLE CO (USA)

LT10	Indian Motorcycles		1993		—	£10.00

INKWORKS (USA)

LT90	The Adventures of Pinocchio		1996		—	£9.50
LT81	Alias Season 1		2002		—	£11.00
LT81	Alias Season 2		2003		—	£10.00
LT81	Alias Season 3		2004		—	£9.50
LT81	Alias Season 4		2006		—	£9.50
LT90	Alien Legacy (The Four Films)		1998		—	£9.50
LT90	Alien vs Predator — The Film		2004		—	£12.00
LT81	Aliens vs Predator Requiem		2007		—	£8.50
LT45	American Pride		2000		—	£5.00
LT90	Andromeda Season 1		2001		—	£9.50
LT90	Andromeda Reign of The Commonwealth		2004		—	£8.00
LT90	Angel Season 1		2000		—	£9.50
LT90	Angel Season 2		2001		—	£9.50

INKWORKS (USA) (continued)

Size & quantity		Date	Handbook reference	Price per card	Complete set
LT90	Angel Season 3	2002		—	£9.50
LT90	Angel Season 4	2003		—	£9.50
LT90	Angel Season 5	2004		—	£9.50
LT90	Buffy The Vampire Slayer Season 3	1999		—	£15.00
LT90	Buffy The Vampire Slayer Season 4	2000		—	£12.00
LT90	Buffy The Vampire Slayer Season 5	2001		—	£12.00
LT90	Buffy The Vampire Slayer Season 6	2002		—	£12.00
LT90	Buffy The Vampire Slayer Season 7	2003		—	£9.50
LT72	Buffy The Vampire Slayer Big Bads	2004		—	£12.00
LT72	Buffy The Vampire Slayer Connections	2003		—	£18.00
LT50	Buffy The Vampire Slayer Evolution	2002		—	£15.00
LT90	Buffy The Vampire Slayer Memories	2006		—	£8.50
LT81	Buffy The Vampire Slayer Men of Sunnydale	2005		—	£8.00
LT72	Buffy The Vampire Slayer Reflections	2000		—	£15.00
LT90	Buffy The Vampire Slayer 10th Anniversary	2007		—	£8.50
LT90	Buffy The Vampire Slayer Women of Sunnydale	2004		—	£9.50
LT72	Catwoman — The Movie	2004		—	£12.00
LT72	Charmed Season 1	2000		—	£9.50
LT72	Charmed Connections	2004		—	£11.00
LT72	Charmed Conversations	2005		—	£8.00
LT72	Charmed Destiny	2006		—	£8.00
LT72	Charmed Forever	2007		—	£8.00
LT72	Charmed The Power of Three	2003		—	£12.00
LT72	Family Guy Season 1	2005		—	£7.50
LT72	Family Guy Season 2	2006		—	£7.50
LT72	Firefly The Complete Collection	2006		—	£9.50
LT72	The 4400 Season 1	2006		—	£8.00
LT81	The 4400 Season 2	2007		—	£8.50
EL72	Godzilla — The Film	1998		—	£9.50
LT72	The Golden Compass — The Film	2007		—	£9.50
LT72	Hell Boy — The Film	2004		—	£12.00
LT72	Hellboy Animated Sword of Storms	2006		—	£7.50
LT90	James Bond 007 3rd Series	1997		—	£20.00
LT72	Jericho Season 1	2007		—	£8.50
LT72	Jurassic Park III — The Movie	2001		—	£8.50
LT72	Looney Tunes Back in Action	2003		—	£9.50
LT90	Lost Season 1	2005		—	£8.50
LT90	Lost Season 2	2006		—	£8.50
LT90	Lost Season 3	2007		—	£8.50
LT81	Lost Revelations	2006		—	£8.00
LT90	Lost in Space — The Film	1998		—	£9.50
LT72	Lost in Space Archives	1997		—	£8.00
LT9	Lost in Space Archives Movie Preview	1997		—	£4.00
LT90	Men in Black — The Film	1997		—	£9.50
LT81	Men In Black II — The Film	2002		—	£12.00
LT81	Mummy Returns — The Movie	2001		—	£9.50
LT72	The Osbournes	2002		—	£8.00
LT90	The Phantom — The Movie	1996		—	£9.50
LT90	Robots — The Movie	2005		—	£9.50
LT90	Roswell Season 1	2000		—	£9.50
LT72	Scooby Doo — The Movie	2002		—	£9.50
LT72	Scooby Doo 2 Monsters Unleashed	2004		—	£11.00
LT72	The Scorpion King — The Movie	2002		—	£12.00
LT72	Serenity — The Film	2005		—	£8.00
LT81	The Simpsons Anniversary Celebration	2000		—	£16.00
LT72	Simpsons Mania	2001		—	£12.00
LT90	Sleepy Hollow — The Movie	1999		—	£9.50

INKWORKS (USA) (continued)

LT72	Sliders (TV Sci-Fi Series)	1997		—	£9.50
LT90	Small Soldiers — The Film	1998		—	£9.50
LT90	Smallville Season 1	2002		—	£9.50
LT90	Smallville Season 2	2003		—	£14.00
LT90	Smallville Season 3	2004		—	£12.00
LT90	Smallville Season 4	2005		—	£9.50
LT90	Smallville Season 5	2007		—	£9.50
LT90	Smallville Season 6	2008		—	£9.50
LT72	The Sopranos Season 1	2005		—	£9.50
LT81	Spawn The Movie	1997		—	£9.50
LT90	Spawn The Toy Files	1999		—	£9.50
LT72	Spike The Complete Story (Buffy & Angel)	2005		—	£11.00
LT72	The Spirit — The Film	2008		—	£8.00
LT81	Starship Troopers — The Movie	1997		—	£9.50
LT90	Supernatural Season 1	2006		—	£9.50
LT90	Supernatural Season 2	2007		—	£8.50
LT81	Supernatural Season 3	2008		—	£9.50
LT72	Supernatural Connections	2008		—	£8.00
LT90	Titan A.E.	2000		—	£9.50
LT90	Tomb Raider — The Movie	2001		—	£9.50
LT81	Tomb Raider 2 — The Cradle of Life	2003		—	£9.50
LT90	Tomorrow Never Dies — James Bond 007	1997		—	£12.00
LT90	TV's Coolest Classics Volume One	1998		—	£9.50
LT72	Veronica Mars Season 1	2006		—	£9.50
LT81	Veronica Mars Season 2	2007		—	£9.50
LT81	Witchblade	2002		—	£9.50
LT90	The World Is Not Enough James Bond 007 the Movie	1999		20p	£12.00
LT90	The X Files Season 4 & 5	2001		20p	£9.50
LT90	The X Files Season 6 & 7	2001		—	£12.00
LT90	The X Files Season 8	2002		20p	£12.00
LT90	The X Files Season 9	2003		20p	£12.00
LT72	The X Files Connections	2005		—	£9.50
LT72	The X Files I Want to Believe — The Film	2008		—	£8.00

INTERNATIONAL HERITAGE

L20	Squadrons and Aircraft of the RAF	1993		—	£12.00

INTREPID (Australia)

LT100	Tennis — A.T.P. Tour	1996		—	£15.00
LT90	X-Files	1996		—	£9.50

IPC MAGAZINES LTD

M25	Lindy's Cards of Fortune	1975		20p	£5.00
	My Favourite Soccer Stars (blue back):				
M32	Issued with 'Buster' including album	1970		£1.25	—
M32	Issued with 'Lion' including album	1970		£1.25	—
M32	Issued with 'Scorcher' including album	1970		£1.25	—
M32	Issued with 'Smash' including album	1970		£1.25	—
M32	Issued with 'Tiger' including album	1970		£1.25	—
	My Favourite Soccer Stars — (red back):				
M32	Issued with 'Buster and Jet' including album	1971		—	£28.00
M32	Issued with 'Lion and Thunder' including album	1971		—	£28.00
M32	Issued with 'Scorcher and Score' including album	1971		—	£28.00
M32	Issued with 'Tiger' including album	1971		—	£28.00
M32	Issued with 'Valiant and TV21' including album	1971		—	£28.00

283

JOHN IRWIN & SON

		Date	Handbook reference	Price per card	Complete set
12	Characters from Dickens' Works	1912	HX-172	£17.00	—
6	Characters from Shakespeare	c1910	HI-6	£17.00	—

J. F. SPORTING COLLECTIBLES

		Date			
LT24	Abbeys, Monasteries & Priorys in The 20th Century ...	2011		—	£16.00
LT24	Academy Award Winners 1st Series (Film Stars)	2010		—	£16.00
LT24	Academy Award Winners 2nd Series (Film Stars)	2013		—	£16.00
LT24	Ali — His Fights, His Opponents	2004		—	£16.00
LT24	The Armies of India	2010		—	£16.00
LT36	Association Footballers 1920/30s 1st Series	2013		—	£27.00
LT36	Association Footballers 1920/30s 2nd Series	2014		—	£27.00
LT24	Association Footballers 1950s 1st Series..............	2013		—	£16.00
LT24	Association Footballers in Action 1920/30s 1st Series	2014		—	£16.00
LT15	Australian Cricketers 1930...........................	1999		—	£10.00
LT28	Australian Rugby League Tourists 1948	2002		—	£21.00
LT36	Battle of The Roses Pre War Personalities (Cricketers)	2003		—	£27.00
LT24	Belle Vue Speedway Aces............................	2001		—	£16.00
LT24	Birds in Britain and Their Eggs 1st Series	2013		—	£16.00
LT24	Boer War Officers...................................	2008		—	£16.00
LT25	Boxers World Champions	2000		—	£16.00
L24	British Yeomanry Uniforms	2004		—	£16.00
LT24	Bygone Railway Stations and Architecture	2012		—	£16.00
LT24	Castles in Britain in the 20th Century 1st Series	2009		—	£16.00
LT24	Castles in Britain in the 20th Century 2nd Series	2010		—	£16.00
LT25	Centenarians Cricket's 100 100s Club................	2008		—	£18.00
LT24	Classic Movies of the 1930s 1st Series	2013		—	£16.00
LT24	Classic Movies of the 1930s 2nd Series	2015		—	£16.00
LT24	Classic Steam Locos 1st Series.....................	2007		—	£16.00
LT24	Classic Steam Locos 2nd Series	2008		—	£16.00
LT24	Country Seats in the 19th Century in Great Britain & Ireland	2013		—	£16.00
LT24	County Cricketers 1940/50s 1st Series	2014		—	£16.00
LT24	Cowboy Film & TV Stars	2011		—	£16.00
LT24	Cricket England One Cap Winners	2011		—	£16.00
LT24	Cricket Parade 1940/50s	2001		—	£24.00
LT24	Cricket Personalities 1940/50s 1st Series	2000		—	£16.00
LT24	Cricket Personalities 1940/50s 2nd Series	2003		—	£16.00
LT24	Cricket Personalities 1940/50s 3rd Series	2004		—	£16.00
LT24	Cricket Personalities 1940/50s 4th Series	2005		—	£16.00
LT24	Cricket Personalities 1940/50s 5th Series	2006		—	£16.00
LT24	Cricket Personalities 1940/50s 6th Series	2007		—	£16.00
LT24	Cricket Personalities 1940/50s 7th Series	2009		—	£16.00
LT24	Cricket Personalities 1940/50s 8th Series	2013		—	£16.00
LT24	Cricket Personalities 1940/50s 9th Series	2014		—	£16.00
LT24	Cricket Personalities 1940/50s 10th Series	2015		—	£16.00
LT24	Cricket Personalities 1960s 1st Series	2007		—	£16.00
LT24	Cricket Personalities 1960s 2nd Series	2007		—	£16.00
LT24	Cricket Personalities 1960s 3rd Series	2008		—	£16.00
LT24	Cricket Personalities 1960s 4th Series	2010		—	£16.00
LT24	Cricket Personalities 1970s 1st Series	2014		—	£16.00
LT24	Cricket Personalities 1970s 2nd Series	2014		—	£16.00
LT24	Cricketers From Overseas 1919-1939 1st Series	2009		—	£16.00
LT36	Cricketers From Overseas 1940/50s 1st Series	2005		—	£27.00
LT36	Cricketers From Overseas 1960s	2007		—	£27.00
LT24	Cricketers in Action 1940/50s 1st Series	2004		—	£16.00
LT24	Cricketers in Action 1940/50s 2nd Series...	2005		—	£16.00

J. F. SPORTING COLLECTIBLES (continued)

Size & quantity		Date	Handbook reference	Price per card	Complete set
LT24	Cricketers In Action 1940/50s 3rd Series	2005		—	£16.00
LT24	Cricketers In Action 1940/50s 4th Series	2006		—	£16.00
LT24	Cricketers in Action 1960s 1st Series	2007		—	£16.00
LT24	Cricketers in Action 1960s 2nd Series	2007		—	£16.00
LT24	Cricketers in Action 1960s 3rd Series	2008		—	£16.00
LT24	Cricketers The Golden Age Pre Great War 1st Series	2009		—	£16.00
LT24	Cricketers The Golden Age Pre Great War 2nd Series	2010		—	£16.00
LT24	Cricketers The Golden Age Pre Great War 3rd Series	2010		—	£16.00
LT24	Cricketers The Golden Age Pre Great War 4th Series	2011		—	£16.00
LT24	Cricketers The Golden Age Pre Great War 5th Series	2011		—	£16.00
LT24	Cricketers The Golden Age Pre Great War 6th Series	2012		—	£16.00
LT24	Cricketers The Golden Age Pre Great War 7th Series	2014		—	£16.00
LT24	Cricketers 1919-1939 1st Series	2008		—	£16.00
LT24	Cricketers 1919-1939 2nd Series	2008		—	£16.00
LT24	Cricketers 1919-1939 3rd Series	2008		—	£16.00
LT24	Cricketers 1919-1939 4th Series	2009		—	£16.00
LT24	Cricketers 1919-1939 5th Series	2009		—	£16.00
LT24	Cricketers 1919-1939 6th Series	2010		—	£16.00
LT24	Cricketers 1919-1939 7th Series	2011		—	£16.00
LT24	Cricketers 1919-1939 8th Series	2013		—	£16.00
LT24	Cricketers 1919-1939 9th Series	2013		—	£16.00
LT24	Cricketers 1919-1939 10th Series	2015		—	£16.00
LT24	The Empire's Air Power World War II	2007		—	£16.00
LT36	England Footballers One Cap Winners 1st Series	2013		—	£27.00
LT36	England Footballers One Cap Winners 2nd Series ...	2013		—	£27.00
LT24	Families in First Class Cricket	2011		—	£16.00
LT24	Famous British Film & Stage Stars 1920-40s				
	1st Series	2009		—	£16.00
LT24	Famous Film Stars 1940/50s 1st Series	2008		—	£16.00
LT24	Famous Film Stars 1940/50s 2nd Series	2009		—	£16.00
LT24	Famous Film Stars 1940/50s 3rd Series	2009		—	£16.00
LT36	Famous Footballers Pre-Great War 1st Series	2003		—	£27.00
LT36	Famous Footballers Pre-Great War 2nd Series	2005		—	£27.00
LT20	Famous Heavyweight Fights	2007		—	£12.50
LT24	50s Glamour Girls	2015		—	£16.00
LT24	Film Stars of The World 1930s 1st Series	2009		—	£16.00
LT24	Film Stars of The World 1930s 2nd Series	2013		—	£16.00
LT24	Films and Their Stars 1940/50s 1st Series	2012		—	£16.00
LT24	Films and Their Stars 1940/50s 2nd Series	2013		—	£16.00
LT36	Football Club Managers 1940/50s 1st Series	2001		—	£27.00
LT24	Football Fallen Heroes of WWI	2014		—	£16.00
LT24	Football Forgotten Caps of WWII (World War 2)	2014		—	£16.00
LT24	Football Personalities Pre-Great War 1st Series	2015		—	£16.00
LT24	Football Personalities Pre-Great War 2nd Series	2015		—	£16.00
LT36	Football Personalities 1940/50s 1st Series	2007		—	£27.00
LT36	Football Stars of the Seventies 1st Series	2000		—	£27.00
LT36	Football Stars of the Seventies 2nd Series	2002		—	£27.00
LT36	Football Wartime Guests 1st Series	2011		—	£27.00
LT36	Football Wartime Guests 2nd Series	2011		—	£27.00
LT36	Football Wartime Guests 3rd Series	2012		—	£27.00
LT36	Football Wartime Guests 4th Series	2013		—	£27.00
LT36	Footballers 1980s 1st Series	2010		—	£27.00
LT36	Footballers 1980s 2nd Series	2011		—	£27.00
LT36	Footballers in Action 1919-1939 1st Series	2010		—	£27.00
LT36	Footballers in Action 1919-1939 2nd Series	2010		—	£27.00
LT24	Footballers In Action 1940/50s 1st Series	1999		—	£16.00

J. F. SPORTING COLLECTIBLES (continued)

LT24	Footballers in Action 1940/50s 2nd Series	1999	—	£16.00
LT24	Footballers in Action 1940/50s 3rd Series	2000	—	£16.00
LT24	Footballers in Action 1940/50s 4th Series	2003	—	£16.00
LT36	Footballers in Action 1950s 1st Series	2008	—	£27.00
LT36	Footballers in Action 1950s 2nd Series	2009	—	£27.00
LT36	Footballers in Action 1960s 1st Series	2002	—	£27.00
LT36	Footballers in Action 1960s 2nd Series	2004	—	£27.00
LT36	Footballers in Action 1970s 1st Series	2007	—	£27.00
LT36	Footballers in Action 1970s 2nd Series	.2009	—	£27.00
LT36	Footballers of the 1920/30s 1st Series	2013	—	£27.00
LT36	Footballers of the 1920/30s 2nd Series	2013	—	£27.00
LT36	Footballers of the 50s 1st Series	2012	—	£27.00
LT36	Footballers of the 50s 2nd Series	2012	—	£27.00
LT36	Footballers of the 50s 3rd Series	2012	—	£27.00
LT36	Forties Favourites in Action (Footballers) 1st Series ...	2004	—	£27.00
LT36	Forties Favourites in Action (Footballers) 2nd Series...	2005	—	£27.00
LT36	Forties Favourites in Action (Footballers) 3rd Series ...	2005	—	£27.00
LT36	Forties Favourites in Action (Footballers) 4th Series ...	2006	—	£27.00
LT36	Forties Favourites in Action (Footballers) 5th Series ...	2007	—	£27.00
LT24	Gentlemen v Players Pre-War Personalities (Cricketers) 1st Series	2003	—	£16.00
LT24	Gentlemen v Players Pre-War Personalities (Cricketers) 2nd Series	2004	—	£16.00
LT24	Gentlemen v Players Pre-War Personalities (Cricketers) 3rd Series	2007	—	£16.00
LT24	George Formby Tribute	2011	—	£16.00
LT24	Golf Personalities 1940/50s	2005	—	£16.00
LT24	Great Goalies 1920-30s 1st Series	2015	—	£16.00
LT24	Great Goalscorers 1920-30s 1st Series	2015	—	£16.00
LT24	Music Hall Artistes	2013	—	£16.00
LT24	Ocean Steamers Through The Ages	2010	—	£16.00
LT24	Personalities on the TV and Radio 1950/60s 1st Series	2015	—	£16.00
LT24	Popular Footballers 1919-1939 1st Series	2002	—	£16.00
LT24	Popular Footballers 1919-1939 2nd Series	2002	—	£16.00
LT24	Popular Footballers 1919-1939 3rd Series	2002	—	£16.00
LT36	Popular Footballers 1919-1939 4th Series	2002	—	£27.00
LT36	Popular Footballers 1919-1939 5th Series	2003	—	£27.00
LT36	Popular Footballers 1919-1939 6th Series	2006	—	£27.00
LT36	Popular Footballers 1919-1939 7th Series	2007	—	£27.00
LT36	Popular Footballers 1919-1939 8th Series	2007	—	£27.00
LT36	Popular Footballers 1919-1939 9th Series	2008	—	£27.00
LT36	Popular Footballers 1919-1939 10th Series	2009	—	£27.00
LT36	Popular Footballers 1919-1939 11th Series	2012	—	£27.00
LT36	Popular Footballers 1950s 1st Series	1998	—	£27.00
LT36	Popular Footballers 1950s 2nd Series	1999	—	£27.00
LT36	Popular Footballers 1950s 3rd Series	1999	—	£27.00
LT36	Popular Footballers 1960s 1st Series	1999	—	£27.00
LT36	Popular Footballers 1960s 2nd Series	2000	—	£27.00
LT36	Popular Footballers 1960s 3rd Series	2000	—	£27.00
LT36	Popular Footballers 1960s 4th Series	2000	—	£27.00
LT36	Popular Footballers 1960s 5th Series	2000	—	£27.00
LT36	Popular Footballers 1960s 6th Series	2005	—	£27.00
LT36	Popular Footballers 1970s 1st Series	2001	—	£27.00
LT36	Popular Footballers 1970s 2nd Series	2001	—	£27.00
LT36	Popular Footballers 1970s 3rd Series	2002	—	£27.00
LT36	Popular Footballers 1970s 4th Series	2004	—	£27.00

J. F. SPORTING COLLECTIBLES (continued)

Size & quantity		Date	Handbook reference	Price per card	Complete set
LT36	Popular Footballers 1970s 5th Series … … … … …	2004		–	£27.00
LT36	Popular Footballers 1970s 6th Series … … … … …	2005		–	£27.00
LT36	Popular Footballers 1970s 7th Series … … … … …	2006		–	£27.00
LT36	Popular Footballers 1970s 8th Series … … … … …	2007		–	£27.00
LT36	Popular Footballers 1970s 9th Series … … … … …	2008		–	£27.00
LT36	Popular Footballers in Action 1970s 1st Series … … … …	2006		–	£27.00
LT36	Popular Footballers in Action 1970s 2nd Series … …	2006		–	£27.00
LT36	Popular Footballers in Action 1970s 3rd Series … …	2007		–	£27.00
LT36	Popular Footballers in Action 1970s 4th Series … …	2008		–	£27.00
LT36	Popular Footballers in Action 1970s 5th Series … …	2008		–	£27.00
LT36	Popular Footballers in Action 1970s 6th Series… … …	2010		–	£27.00
LT24	Rugby League Stars 1940/50s 1st Series … … … … …	2002		–	£16.00
LT24	Rugby League Stars In Action 1940/50s … … … … …	2007		–	£16.00
	Scottish Clan Tartans 1st Series:				
L24	A Titled Scottish Clan Tartans … … … … … … … …	2002		–	–
LT24	B Titled Scottish Tartans … … … … … … … … … …	2012		–	£16.00
L24	Scottish Clan Tartans 2nd Series … … … … … … …	2003		–	£16.00
LT24	Seaside Piers in England and Wales in The 20th Century 1st Series … … … … … … … … … … … .	2009		–	£16.00
LT24	Seaside Piers in England and Wales in The 20th Century 2nd Series … … … … … … … … … …	2010		–	£16.00
LT24	Sheffield Tigers Speedway Post-War Legends … … …	2001		–	£16.00
LT24	Sherlock Holmes Film Stars … … … … … … … … … …	2011		–	£16.00
LT24	Silent Movie Stars 1st Series … … … … … … … … …	2009		–	£16.00
LT24	Silver Screen Actors 1930s … … … … … … … … …	2012		–	£16.00
LT24	Silver Screen Actresses 1930s … … … … … … … … …	2009		–	£16.00
L24	Soldiers of Queen Victoria's Army 1837-1901 1st Series … … … … … … … … … … … … …	2004		–	£16.00
L24	Soldiers of Queen Victoria's Army 1837-1901 2nd Series … … … … … … … … … … … …	2007		–	£16.00
LT24	Soldiers of Queen Victoria's Army 1837-1901 3rd Series	2015		–	£16.00
LT24	Speedway All-Time Greats 1st Series … … … … … …	1999		–	£16.00
LT24	Speedway All-Time Greats 2nd Series … … … … … …	1999		–	£16.00
LT24	Speedway All-Time Greats 3rd Series … … … … … …	2000		–	£16.00
LT24	Speedway Personalities In Action 1st Series … … … …	2000		–	£16.00
LT24	Speedway Personalities In Action 2nd Series … … … …	2000		–	£16.00
LT24	Speedway Riders From Overseas 1st Series … … … …	2006		–	£16.00
LT24	Stars of Bradford Speedway … … … … … … … … …	2004		–	£16.00
LT30	Stars of Football 1940s … … … … … … … … … … … …	2002		–	£21.00
LT24	Stars of London Speedway … … … … … … … … … …	2002		–	£16.00
LT24	Stars of Midland Speedway 1st Series … … … … … …	2006		–	£16.00
LT36	Stars of Scottish Football Pre-Great War 1st Series …	2004		–	£27.00
LT25	Stars of Scottish Speedway … … … … … … … … …	2002		–	£17.50
LT24	Stars of the Radio Shows 1940/50s 1st Series … … …	2013		–	£16.00
LT20	Tennis Stars 1950/60s … … … … … … … … … … …	2007		–	£13.00
LT24	Test Cricketers 1950s/60s 1st Series … … … … … …	2013		–	£16.00
L24	Uniforms of The Royal Regiment of Artillery … … … … …	2003		–	£16.00
LT28	Victorian Cricket Personalities … … … … … … … … …	2000		–	£20.00
LT24	Victorian Cricketers … … … … … … … … … … … …	2012		–	£16.00
LT24	Victorian Railway Stations … … … … … … … … … …	2011		–	£16.00
LT15	Wembley Speedway Stars 1st Series … … … … … … …	1999		–	£10.00
LT21	Wembley Speedway Stars 2nd Series… … … … … … …	2000		–	£16.00
LT24	Western Films and Their Stars … … … … … … … …	2013		–	£16.00
L24	World Heavyweight Boxing Champions … … … … … …	1999		–	£16.00
LT20	World Heavyweight Championship Contenders … … …	2000		–	£12.00
LT24	World War II Films and Their Stars … … … … … … … …	2013		–	£16.00

JACOB & CO.

Qty	Title	Date	Handbook reference	Price per card	Complete set
EL24	Banknotes that Made History	1975		20p	£3.00
	Album			—	£3.50
EL6	Build Your Own Prize	1972		£3.00	£18.00
EL16	Circus	c1970		£3.00	—
EL8	Doodles	1970		£3.00	—
32	Famous Picture Cards from History	1978		20p	£3.00
EL18	Happy Families	1967	HJ-2	£3.00	—
EL6	Nursery Rhymes	1969		£3.00	—
M30	School of Dinosaurs	1994		30p	£9.00
	Album			—	£15.00
EL10	Through the Looking Glass	1971		£3.00	—
25	Vehicles of All Ages	1924	HX-111	£2.80	£70.00
25	Zoo Series:		HX-186		
	A (brown back)	1924		£2.00	£50.00
	B (green back)	1924		£1.60	£40.00

M.V. JASINSKI (USA)

Qty	Title	Date	Handbook reference	Price per card	Complete set
LT36	Flash Gordon 1st Series	1990		—	£15.00
LT36	Flash Gordon's Trip to Mars 2nd Series	1991		—	£15.00
LT36	Flash Gordon Conquers the Universe 3rd Series	1992		—	£15.00

JENSEN PRINT

Qty	Title	Date	Handbook reference	Price per card	Complete set
10	Soccer Stars (1960s Footballers) 1st Series	1998		—	£4.50
10	Soccer Stars (1960s Footballers) 2nd Series	1998		—	£4.50

JERMYN'S

Qty	Title	Date	Handbook reference	Price per card	Complete set
25	National Heroes	c1975		£2.60	—

JESK CONFECTIONERY

Qty	Title	Date	Handbook reference	Price per card	Complete set
25	Buses and Trams	1959	HX-109	£1.20	£30.00

JIFFI

Qty	Title	Date	Handbook reference	Price per card	Complete set
M64	Kama Sutra	1989		80p	£50.00

JONDER (UK)

Qty	Title	Date	Handbook reference	Price per card	Complete set
L53	Doctor Who — Playing Cards	1996		—	£20.00

R.L. JONES & CO. LTD

Qty	Title	Date	Handbook reference	Price per card	Complete set
24	Jet Aircraft of the World	1957		20p	£4.00

JUNIOR EXPRESS WEEKLY

Qty	Title	Date	Handbook reference	Price per card	Complete set
25	Jeff Hawke & Space Gen.	1956		£3.20	—

JUNIOR PASTIMES

(Cards issued with staple holes)

Qty	Title	Date	Handbook reference	Price per card	Complete set
52	Popular English Players:				
	A 51 different (minus No. 21)	c1960		£3.80	—
	B Number 21	c1960		£25.00	—
52	Popular Players (Footballers)	c1960		£8.00	—
52	Popular Railway Engines:				
	A 51 different (minus No. 38)	c1960		£3.00	—
	B Number 38	c1960		£25.00	—
M80	Star Pix	c1960	HX-187	£2.00	—

JUST SEVENTEEN (Periodical)

M17	Advertisement Stickers		1985		—	£3.00

K.P. FOODS

K30	Flintstones, Wackey Races, Tom & Jerry		1996		—	£15.00
20	Wonderful World of Nature		1983		75p	£15.00

KADLE KARDS

10	Who (Doctor Who)		2007		—	£4.50

KANE PRODUCTS LTD

50	British Birds and Their Eggs		1960	HX-105	60p	£30.00
25	Cricket Clubs & Badges		1957		20p	£3.00
L50	Disc Stars		1959		£1.80	£90.00
M50	Disc Stars		1960		£3.20	—
50	Dogs		1955	HX-205	£3.00	—
L72	Film Stars		1955	HX-30-2	£2.00	—
50	Flags of All Nations		1959	HX-112	30p	£15.00
25	Football Clubs and Colours		1957		20p	£3.50
50	Historical Characters		1957		25p	£12.50
25	International Football Stars		1958		£1.20	£30.00
30	Kings and Queens		1959	HX-116	60p	£18.00
L30	Kings and Queens		1959	HX-116	70p	£20.00
25	Modern Motor Cars		1959	HX-39	70p	£17.50
50	Modern Racing Cars...		1954		60p	£30.00
25	National Pets Club 1st Series		1958	HX-145	24p	£6.00
25	National Pets Club 2nd Series		1958	HX-145	£2.40	—
25	1956 Cricketers 1st Series		1956		80p	£20.00
25	1956 Cricketers 2nd Series		1956		80p	£20.00
25	Red Indians 1st Series		1957	HX-118	£1.00	£25.00
25	Red Indians 2nd Series...		1958	HX-118	£1.00	£25.00
25	Roy Rogers Colour Series...		1958		£2.40	£60.00
25	Roy Rogers Series		1957		£4.00	—
50	Space Adventure		1955		70p	£35.00
50	20th Century Events...		1959		£1.50	—
K50	Wild Animals		1954		20p	£4.00

KARDOMAH

K50	Wild Animals		c1920	HX-216	£5.00	—
K50	Wonders of the Deep		c1920	HK-4.2	£5.00	—

M. & S. KEECH

15	Australian Cricket Team 1905		1986		—	£4.00
15	English Cricketers 1902		1987		—	£6.00

KEEPSAKE (USA)

LT72	The Blue and the Gray — Civil War Art by Kunstler ...		1997		—	£17.50
LT72	Wild West by Mort Kunstler		1996		—	£12.00

JAMES KEILLER & SON LTD

ELP18	Film Favourites		c1925		£10.00	—
25	Scottish Heritage		c1970		50p	£12.50

KELLOGG COMPANY OF GREAT BRITAIN LTD

K16	Animals — 3D		c1968	HK-17	£3.50	—
M56	Crunchy Nut Corn Flakes Playing Cards		1986		—	£4.00

KELLOGG COMPANY OF GREAT BRITAIN LTD (continued)

Size & quantity		Date	Handbook reference	Price per card	Complete set
12	Famous Firsts	1963		25p	£3.00
M20	Gardens to Visit	1987		30p	£6.00
	Album			—	£15.00
16	History of British Military Aircraft	1963		£1.50	£24.00
12	International Soccer Stars	1961		£1.00	£12.00
	Album			—	£30.00
M8	International Soccer Tips	c1978		£5.00	—
40	Motor Cars:				
	A Black and white	1949		£3.75	—
	B Coloured	1949		£6.50	—
M20	Olympic Champions	1991		£1.50	—
K8	Prehistoric Monsters and the Present	1985		£1.50	£12.00
16	Ships of the British Navy	1962		£1.50	£24.00
12	The Story of the Bicycle	1960		£3.50	—
	Story of the Locomotive 1st Series:		HK-25		
16	A Inscribed 'A Series of 16'	1962		£1.50	£24.00
12	B Inscribed 'A Series of 12'	1962		£4.00	—
16	The Story of the Locomotive 2nd Series:				
	A Inscribed 'Series 2'	1965		£1.50	£24.00
	B Without 'Series 2'	1965		£3.50	—
K8	Tony Racing Stickers	1988		40p	£3.00
16	Veteran Motor Cars	1962		£1.00	£16.00

KELLOGG (Canada)

Size & quantity		Date	Price per card	Complete set
M32	Dinosaur Stickers	1992	—	£6.00
	General Interest Set 1:			
M15	Aeroplanes	c1937	£2.00	—
M15	Campcraft	c1937	£2.00	—
M15	Firearms	c1937	£2.00	—
M15	People of the World	c1937	£2.00	—
M15	Ships of War	c1937	£2.00	—
M15	Sports Records	c1937	£2.00	—
M30	Sports Tips	c1937	£2.00	—
M15	Strange Animals	c1937	£2.00	—
M15	Vehicles of War	c1937	£2.00	—
	General Interest Set 2:			
M15	Aeroplanes	c1938	£2.00	—
M15	Denizens of the Deep	c1938	£2.00	—
M15	Dogs	c1938	£2.00	—
M15	Great Deeds in Canada	c1938	£2.00	—
M15	Histories of Flight	c1938	£2.00	—
M30	Sports Tips	c1938	£2.00	—
M15	Things to Make	c1938	£2.00	—
M15	Tricks	c1938	£2.00	—
M15	Uniforms	c1938	£2.00	—
	General Interest Set 3:			
M15	Aeroplanes	c1939	£2.00	—
M15	Boats	c1939	£2.00	—
M15	First Aid Tips	c1939	£2.00	—
M15	Historic Automobiles	c1939	£2.00	—
M15	Picture Puzzles	c1939	£2.00	—
M15	Sports History	c1939	£2.00	—
M30	Sports Tips	c1939	£2.00	—
M15	Strange Birds	c1939	£2.00	—
M15	Things to Make	c1939	£2.00	—

KENT COUNTY CONSTABULARY

L24	England World Cup Squad	1982	£3.00	—
L30	England World Cup Squad	1986	£2.50	—
L30	Olympic Athletes	1988	£1.50	£45.00

KENT COUNTY CRICKET CLUB

50	Cricketers of Kent	1985	—	£9.00

KENTUCKY FRIED CHICKEN

M20	Star Wars Episode 1...	1999	38p	£7.50

KICK OFF CARDS

10	Kick Off (Footballers of the 1970s)	2011	—	£5.00

KIDDY'S FAVOURITES LTD
(Cards issued with staple holes)

52	New Popular Film Stars	c1950	£4.00	—
50	Popular Boxers:			
	A 49 different (minus No. 46)	c1950	£3.00	—
	B Number 46	c1950	£25.00	—
52	Popular Cricketers:	HX149		
	A 51 different (minus No. 48)	1948	£4.00	—
	B Number 48	1948	£30.00	—
65	Popular Film Stars	c1950	£5.00	—
52	Popular Footballers:			
	A 51 different (minus No. 52)	c1950	£4.00	—
	B Number 52	c1950	£25.00	—
52	Popular Olympics...	c1950	£3.00	—
	'Popular' Players (Footballers):			
75	A Five red hearts at top of front	c1950	£7.00	—
52	B Three red shamrocks at top of front:			
	i 51 different (minus No. 44)	1949	£4.00	—
	ii Number 44	1949	£25.00	—
52	'Popular' Speedway Riders	c1950	£3.50	—

KILPATRICKS BREAD (USA)

LT33	Star Trek The Motion Picture	1979	—	£12.00

KIMBALL (USA)

LT12	The Space Shuttle	1992	—	£6.00

KINGS, YORK (Laundry)

K25	Flags of all Nations (silks)	1954	£3.00	—
30	Kings and Queens of England	1954	HX-116	20p	£5.00

KING'S LAUNDRIES LTD (Walthamstow)

25	Famous Railway Engines	c1955	£5.00	—
25	Modern British Warplanes	1953	£4.00	—
25	Modern Motor Cycles	c1955	£4.00	—
25	Radio and Television Stars	c1955	£4.00	—

KING'S SPECIALITIES

26	Alphabet Rhymes...	c1915	£12.00	—
24	'Don'ts' or Lessons in Etiquette	c1915	£11.00	—
25	Great War Celebrities & Warships	c1915	HK-37	£12.00	—
25	Heroes of Famous Books	1914	£11.00	—

KING'S SPECIALITIES (continued)

Size & quantity		Date	Handbook reference	Price per card	Complete set
25	King's Discoveries	c1915	HK-38	£11.00	—
25	King's Servants	c1915	HK-39	£11.00	—
24	Proverbs...	c1915		£11.00	—
37	Unrecorded History	c1915		£11.00	—
100	War Pictures	c1915	HX-200	£12.00	—
25	Where King's Supplies Grow	1913	HK-40	£11.00	—

KITCHEN SINK (USA)

LT90	The Crow — City of Angels — The Film	1996		—	£9.50
LT90	Universal Monsters of the Silver Screen	1996		—	£12.00

KLENE (GUM)

L50	Footballers (Val Footer Gum)...	1936		£35.00	—
L80	Shirley Temple and Film Stars (Nos 1 to 80)	1935		£6.00	—
L70	Shirley Temple (black and white) (Nos 81 to 100 & 161 to 210)	1935		£7.00	—
L80	Shirley Temple (coloured) title in blue (Nos 81 to 160)	1935		£7.00	—
L60	Shirley Temple (coloured) title in black (Nos 101 to 160)	1935		£7.00	—

J. KNIGHT (Hustler Soap)

20	Animals of the World (cut outs):				
	A Corner officially cut	1925		£1.25	£25.00
	B Uncut card	1925		£1.50	£30.00
20	Animals of the World 2nd Series (cut outs):				
	A Corner officially cut	1925		£1.25	£25.00
	B Uncut card	1925		£1.50	£30.00
20	Animals of the World 3rd Series (cut outs):				
	A Corner officially cut	1925		£1.25	£25.00
	B Uncut card	1925		£1.50	£30.00
30	Regimental Nicknames:				
	A Corner officially cut	1925		£2.25	—
	B Uncut card	1925		£2.75	—

KNOCKOUT

20	Super Planes of Today	c1960		30p	£6.00

KNORR

L6	Great Trains of Europe	1983		£5.00	—

KRAFT CHEESE

12	Historic Military Uniforms	1971		20p	£2.50
	Album...			—	£4.00

KROME (USA)

LT50	Betty Boop 1st Series	1996		—	£20.00
LT45	Betty Boop 2nd Series	1997		—	£20.00
LT100	Bloom County Outland Chromium	1995		—	£12.00
LT50	Creed Chromium From Lightning Comics	1996		—	£12.00

LACEY'S CHEWING GUM

50	Footballers	c1925		£32.00	—
40	Uniforms...	c1925	HL-1	£25.00	—

F. LAMBERT & SONS LTD (Tea)

Qty	Title	Date	Handbook reference	Price per card	Complete set
25	Before our Time	1961	HX-103	20p	£2.50
25	Birds & Their Eggs	1960	HX-1.1	£1.00	£25.00
25	Butterflies & Moths	1966	HX-2	30p	£7.50
25	Cacti	1962	HX-133	20p	£2.50
25	Car Registration Numbers 1st Series	1959		40p	£10.00
25	Car Registration Numbers 2nd Series	1960		£1.20	—
25	Football Clubs and Badges	1958	HX-137	20p	£4.00
25	Game Birds and Wild Fowl	1964		60p	£15.00
25	Historic East Anglia	1963		20p	£2.50
25	Interesting Hobbies	1965		60p	£15.00
25	Passenger Liners	1965	HX-82	60p	£15.00
25	Past and Present	1964		20p	£3.00
25	People and Places	1966	HX-26	20p	£5.00
25	Pond Life	1964	HX-81	50p	£12.50
25	Sports and Games	1964	HX-154	20p	£5.00

LAMPORT AND HOLT

Qty	Title	Date	Price per card	Complete set
L1	TSS Vandyck and TSS Voltaire:			
	A Criss Cross border	1925	—	£12.00
	B Chain border with circles at corners	1925	—	£25.00

LANCASHIRE CONSTABULARY

Qty	Title	Date	Price per card	Complete set
L12	Austin Rover Motor Cars	1987	50p	£6.00
11	History of the Police	1989	30p	£3.00
24	Lancashire Police File	1986	50p	£12.00

LANCASHIRE COUNTY CRICKET CLUB

Qty	Title	Date	Price per card	Complete set
M150	Lancashire Greats (Cricketers)	2014	—	£15.00

LANG'S BREAD CO LTD

Qty	Title	Date	Price per card	Complete set
25	Holsum Series (Recipe Cards)	c1920	£12.00	—

LATARCHE

Qty	Title	Date	Price per card	Complete set
L25	Skiing Through the Ages	1994	—	£8.50

LEAF GUM CO. (USA)

Qty	Title	Date	Price per card	Complete set
L72	Star Trek	1967	—	—

LEAF SALES CONFECTIONERY LTD

Qty	Title	Date	Handbook reference	Price per card	Complete set
L50	Cliff Richard	1961		£4.00	—
EL50	Do You Know?	1961		60p	£30.00
EL90	Famous Artists	1963		£2.20	—
EL50	Famous Discoveries and Adventures	1961		£2.60	—
EL40	The Flag Game	1960		70p	£28.00
EL50	Footballers (Portraits and Caricatures)	1961	HL-7	£2.80	—
EL50	Totem Pole Talking Signs	1960		£1.00	£50.00

LEEDS POLICE

Qty	Title	Date	Price per card	Complete set
L20	Leeds Rugby League F.C.	1992	—	£8.00
L20	Leeds Rugby League F.C.	1993	—	£6.00
L20	Leeds Rugby League F.C.	1994	—	£6.00
L20	Leeds Rugby League F.C.	1995	—	£6.00

LEESLEY (USA)

Qty	Title	Date	Price per card	Complete set
LT100	Big Foot (Trucks)	1988	—	£9.50

LEGENDS

L20	British Rock Legends	1993		—	£9.00

LEICESTER MERCURY

LT40	Leicester City Footballers	2003		—	£30.00

LEVER BROS

20	British Birds and Their Nests ('Sunlight Soap')	1961	HX-104	20p	£4.00
152	Celebrities, white borders large and small	1905	HL-15	£4.00	—
M39	Celebrities, black border	1905	HL-16	£7.00	—

LIFEGUARD PRODUCTS (Soap etc.)

25	British Butterflies	1955		20p	£5.00

LIME ROCK (USA)

LT40	Dallas Cowboys Cheerleaders	1992		—	£6.00
LT110	Dream Machines Nos 1-110 (Motoring)	1991		—	£15.00
LT55	Dream Machines Nos 111-165 (Motoring & Powerboats)	1992		—	£9.50
LT110	Heroes of the Persian Gulf	1991		—	£9.50
LT49	Los Angeles Raiderettes Cheerleaders	1992		—	£6.00
LT31	Miami Dolphins Cheerleaders	1992		—	£6.00
LT36	New Orleans Saintsations Cheerleaders	1992		—	£6.00
LT44	Pro Cheerleaders (basketball)	1991		—	£6.00
LT55	Space Art	1993		—	£9.50

JOSEPH LINGFORD & SON LTD (Baking Powder)

36	British War Leaders	1950		£1.65	£60.00

LIPTON LTD (Tea)

50	Conquest of Space	1962	HX-73	90p	—
60	Flags of the World	1966		20p	£12.00
	Album			—	£6.00

LIPTON TEA (Canada)

48	Animals and Their Young	1991		60p	£30.00

LIPTON TEA (Overseas)

EL30	Birds of Prey (Arabic text)	c1970		—	£25.00

J. LIVINGSTONE

11	Flags, Arms and Types of Nations	c1905	HL-45	£25.00	—

LOBO (Portugal)

L12	David Bowie 1993 Calendar Back	1992		—	£5.00
L12	Iron Maiden (Pop Group) 1990 Calendar Back	1989		—	£5.00
L16	Iron Maiden (Pop Group) 1992 Calendar Back	1991		—	£5.00
L12	Michael Jackson 1992 Calendar Back	1991		—	£5.00
L12	Mick Jagger (Rolling Stones) 1992 Calendar Back	1991		—	£5.00

LOCAL AUTHORITIES CATERERS ASSOCIATION

5	British Sporting Personalities	1997		—	£3.00

LODGE PLUGS LTD

M20	Vintage Cars	c1950	HL-47	£12.00	—

LONGLEAT HOUSE

25	Longleat House	...	1966		20p	£3.00

LOS ANGELES POLICE (USA)

EL30	Dodgers Baseball Players ...		1988		—	£10.00

LOT-O-FUN

MP4	Sports Champions ...		1922		£6.00	—

G.F. LOVELL & CO. LTD

?31	British Royalty Series ...		1911		£35.00	—
36	Football Series ...		1910		£65.00	—
25	Photos of Football Stars ...		1928	HX-188	£25.00	—

B. LUND

6	Rugby Union Six Nations 2000 ...		2000		—	£1.50
6	Rugby Union Six Nations 2001 ...		2001		—	£1.50
8	Rugby Union World Cup 1999 ...		1999		—	£1.50

LYCHGATE PRESS

10	Amazing World ...		2004		—	£3.50
10	The Beatles...		2002		—	£4.00
12	The Beatles 1963...		2005		—	£4.75
10	Crystal Palace Legends 1st Series ...		2014		—	£5.00
10	Crystal Palace Legends 2nd Series ...		2015		—	£5.00
10	Eloise (Adult Fantasy Art) ...		2001		—	£4.00
10	Flags of Micronations ...		2014		—	£5.00
10	Hendrix (Jimi) ...		2010		—	£5.00
10	Images of the Great War 1st Series ...		2013		—	£5.00
10	Images of the Great War 2nd Series ...		2013		—	£5.00
10	Images of the Great War 3rd Series ...		2013		—	£5.00
10	Images of the Great War 4th Series ...		2013		—	£5.00
10	Kings of Comedy ...		2005		—	£4.00
10	Punk Icons 1st Series ...		2014		—	£5.00
10	Punk Icons 2nd Series ...		2015		—	£5.00
10	Rock Icons 1st Series ...		2015		—	£5.00
10	Rock'N'Roll Greats ...		2005		—	£4.50
10	60's Soccer Stars...		2006		—	£4.50
L25	Soccer Gallery (Footballers of the 1960s) ...		2000		—	£10.00
10	Soccer Parade (Footballers of the 1960/70s) 1st Series		2015		—	£5.00
10	Soccer Parade (Footballers of the 1960/70s) 2nd Series (not marked 2nd Series) ...		2015		—	£5.00
18	Tottenham (Footballers) ...		2000		—	£6.50
10	The Wonderful World of Inventions...		2004		—	£4.00

J. LYONS

48	Australia...		1959		20p	£8.00
	Album ...				—	£25.00
L16	Catweazle Magic Cards ...		1971	HL-80	40p	£6.00
32	HM Ships 1902-1962:			HL-81		
	A Descriptive Back...		1962		25p	£8.00
	B Advertisement Back ...		1962		40p	£12.00
	Album ...				—	£25.00
	Illustrated Map of the British Isles:					
M35	A Set of 35 ...		1959		£1.00	—
M1	B Key card ...		1959		—	£2.00
EL6	150th Anniversary of the Postage Stamp...		1990		50p	£3.00

J. LYONS (continued)

Size & quantity		Date	Handbook reference	Price per card	Complete set
K100	Tricks and Puzzles ...	1926		£3.50	—
48	What Do You Know? ...	1957		20p	£4.00
	Album ...			—	£25.00
24	Wings Across the World:		HL-83		
	A Descriptive Back ...	1961		25p	£6.00
	B Advertisement Back ...	1961		40p	£10.00
	Album ...			—	£20.00
24	Wings of Speed:		HL-84		
	A Descriptive Back ...	1960		20p	£5.00
	B Advertisement Back ...	1960		32p	£8.00
	Album ...			—	£20.00

LYONS MAID (Ice Cream)

Size & quantity		Date	Handbook reference	Price per card	Complete set
40	All Systems Go ...	1967		£2.00	—
M20	Banknotes ...	1974		50p	£10.00
M12	Beautiful Butterflies ...	1974		50p	£6.00
25	Birds and Their Eggs ...	1963		£1.20	—
40	British Wildlife ...	1970		£1.25	£50.00
M20	County Badge Collection ...	1974		25p	£5.00
EL12	Did You Know? ...	1975		50p	£6.00
40	European Adventure ...	1969		£1.65	—
40	Famous Aircraft ...	1965		50p	£20.00
	Album ...			—	£6.00
40	Famous Cars ...	1966		£2.00	—
	Album. ...			—	£20.00
40	Famous Locomotives ...	1964		£2.50	—
48	Famous People:		HX-53		
	A Panel at top 29mm ...	1962		£1.50	£75.00
	B Panel at top 32mm ...	1962		£1.00	£50.00
M12	Farmyard Stencils ...	1977		75p	£8.00
M14	Flowers ...	c1976		—	£28.00
EL12	Horses in the Service of Man ...	1984		32p	£4.00
40	International Footballers ...	1971		£5.00	—
40	Into the Unknown ...	1968		£1.50	£60.00
15	Jubilee Kings and Queens of England ...	1977		£2.00	—
EL10	Junior Champs ...	1983		35p	£3.50
50	100 Years of Motoring ...	1961	HX-117	£1.40	—
40	On Safari ...	1969		£1.40	—
40	Pop Scene ...	1970		£2.50	—
40	Pop Stars ...	1969		£2.50	—
M10	Pop Stars (shaped) ...	1975		50p	£5.00
40	Soccer Stars ...	1970		£4.50	—
40	Space Age Britain ...	1968		£1.70	—
40	Space Exploration ...	1963		£2.00	—
25	Space 1999 ...	1976		£6.00	—
25	Star Trek ...	1980		£6.00	—
50	Train Spotters ...	1962	HX-157	70p	£35.00
40	Views of London ...	1967		90p	£36.00

M.P. CARDS

Size & quantity		Date		Price per card	Complete set
L12	The Geisha Collection ...	1997		—	£10.00
L14	Nishikigo — Koi Carp ...	1997		—	£15.00
L6	The Staffordshire Bull Terrier ...	1996		—	£6.00

MAC FISHERIES

Size & quantity		Date		Price per card	Complete set
L12	Gallery Pictures ...	1924		£1.50	£18.00
L14	Japanese Colour Prints ...	1924		£1.50	—

MAC FISHERIES (continued)

L12	Poster Pointers … … … … … … … … … … … …	1925		£1.25	£16.00
L12	Sporting Prints… … … … … … … … … … … …	1923		£4.50	—

Wm. McEWAN & CO. LTD

25	Old Glasgow … … … … … … … … … … … …	1929		£13.00	—

McVITIE & PRICE

8	The European War Series … … … … … … … …	1915	HX-129	£18.00	—

MADISON CONFECTIONERY PRODUCTS LTD

L48	Disc Jockey 1st Series … … … … … … … …	1957		£2.50	—
L48	Disc Jockey 2nd Series… … … … … … … …	1958		£1.80	£90.00
L50	Recording Stars … … … … … … … … … …	c1960		£2.00	—

THE MAGNET LIBRARY

MP6	Football Teams (11.11.22 to 16.12.22)… … … …	1922	HM-13.1	£5.00	—
MP4	Football Teams (2.2.23 to 24.2.23) … … … …	1923	HM-13.2	£5.00	—
MP15	Footballers … … … … … … … … … … …	1922		£4.50	—

MAINSTREAM PUBLISHING

13	The Story of Newcastle United's No. 9 Heroes … … …	2004		—	£6.00

MANCHESTER EVENING NEWS

L30	Manchester City & United Footballers … … … … …	1976		£3.00	—

MANOR BREAD (USA)

LT33	Star Trek The Motion Picture … … … … … …	1979		—	£15.00

R. MARCANTONIO LTD

50	Interesting Animals (black and white) … … … …	1953	HX-115	20p	£4.00

MARKET-SCENE LTD (New Zealand)

M21	Super Stars of Wrestling 1st Series … … … …	1989		£1.00	—
M21	Super Stars of Wrestling 2nd Series … … … …	1989		£1.00	—
M21	Super Stars of Wrestling 3rd Series … … … …	1990		£1.00	—

A.T. MARKS

14	Australian Cricketers 1893… … … … … … … …	1993		—	£3.00
8	Buses in Luton… … … … … … … … … …	1991		—	£2.50
M35	Cricket (1900 Period) unnumbered … … … … …	1994		—	£5.00
M16	Cricket (1900 Period) 1st Series nos 1-16 … …	1994		—	£3.00
M16	Cricket (1900 Period) 2nd Series nos 17-32… … …	1995		—	£3.00
M16	Cricket (1900 Period) 3rd Series nos 33-48 … … …	1995		—	£3.00
M8	Cricket (1900 Period) 4th Series nos 49-56 … …	1995		—	£2.50
12	Derbyshire Cricketers 1895 … … … … … …	1993		—	£3.00
13	Essex Cricketers 1895 … … … … … … …	1993		—	£3.00
11	Gloucestershire Cricketers 1892… … … … …	1990		—	£2.50
13	Gloucestershire Cricketers 1894… … … … …	1993		—	£3.00
13	Hampshire Cricketers 1895 … … … … …	1993		—	£3.00
11	Kent Cricketers 1892 … … … … … …	1991		—	£3.00
14	Kent Cricketers 1897 … … … … … …	1993		—	£3.00
13	Kent Cricketers 1909 … … … … … …	1991		—	£3.00
12	Lancashire Cricketers 1892 … … … … …	1992		—	£3.00
14	Lancashire Cricketers 1895 … … … … …	1993		—	£3.00
13	Leicestershire Cricketers 1895 … … … …	1993		—	£3.00

A.T. MARKS (continued)

		Date	Handbook reference	Price per card	Complete set
11	Middlesex Cricketers 1892	1990		—	£2.50
12	Middlesex Cricketers 1895	1993		—	£3.00
12	Middlesex Cricketers 1903	1990		—	£2.50
11	Northamptonshire Cricketers 1912	1990		—	£3.00
13	Nottinghamshire Cricketers 1895	1992		—	£3.00
12	Somerset Cricketers 1894	1992		—	£3.00
11	Surrey Cricketers 1892	1990		—	£3.00
13	Surrey Cricketers 1896	1993		—	£3.00
11	Sussex Cricketers 1892	1990		—	£3.00
15	Sussex Cricketers 1895	1993		—	£3.00
12	Warwickshire Cricketers 1895	1992		—	£3.00
12	Yorkshire Cricketers 1892	1991		—	£3.00
17	Yorkshire Cricketers 1898	1993		—	£3.00
12	Yorkshire Cricketers 1903	1990		—	£2.50

MARLOW CIVIL ENGINEERING

		Date	Handbook reference	Price per card	Complete set
25	Famous Clowns	1990		—	£30.00

MARS CONFECTIONS LTD

		Date	Handbook reference	Price per card	Complete set
25	Ceremonies of the Coronation:				
	A Caption on front in black, back in black	1937		£2.00	—
	B Caption on front in blue, back in black	1937		£1.40	£35.00
	C Caption on front in blue, back in blue	1937		£5.00	—
50	Famous Aeroplanes, Pilots and Airports	1938		£1.80	£90.00
50	Famous Escapes	1937		£1.50	£75.00
50	Famous Film Stars	1939		£1.80	£90.00
25	Wonders of the 'Queen Mary'	1936		£1.80	£45.00

JAMES MARSHALL (GLASGOW) LTD

		Date	Handbook reference	Price per card	Complete set
30	Colonial Troops	1900	HX-100	£37.00	—
10	Recipes/House Hints	c1930		£5.00	—
10	Recipes (coloured)	c1930		£5.00	—

THE MASTER VENDING CO. LTD (Chewing Gum)

		Date	Handbook reference	Price per card	Complete set
L25	A Bombshell for the Sheriff	1959		£1.00	£25.00
L16	Cricketer Series, New Zealand	1958		£1.25	£20.00
L50	Did You Know? (Football Cards)	1959		£1.50	—
L50	Football Tips (2 printings)	1958	HM-28	£1.80	—
L100	Jet Aircraft of the World:		HM-29		
	A Send 3/6 for 20 page album	1958		£2.00	—
	B Send for details of the Album	1958		£2.00	—
	C German Text	1958		£2.50	—
L25	Taxing the Sheriff	1959		£1.00	£25.00
L36	Tommy Steele	1960		£3.50	—

MASTERS

		Date	Handbook reference	Price per card	Complete set
L12	Food From Britain	1986		25p	£3.00

MATCH WEEKLY

		Date	Handbook reference	Price per card	Complete set
M36	Euro Football	1988		—	£2.50
L31	FA Cup Facts File	1986		25p	£7.50

MATCHBOX INT. LTD

		Date	Handbook reference	Price per card	Complete set
75	Matchbox Models	1985		70p	£50.00
	Album			—	£25.00

MATCHDAY CARDS

EL18	Stockport County F.C. 2010-11	2010		—	£6.00
EL16	Stockport County F.C. 2011-12	2011		—	£6.00

MAXILIN MARKETING CO. LTD

25	Motor Cars	1951		20p	£5.00

MAXX (UK)

LT76	British Athletics nos 1-76	1992		20p	£10.00
LT74	British Athletics nos 77-150	1992		20p	£10.00

MAYNARDS LTD

12	Billy Bunter Series	c1920	HM-31	£22.00	—
8	European War Series	c1915	HX-129	£17.00	—
17	Football Clubs	1932	HM-32	£35.00	—
18	Girl Guides	c1920	HM-33	£17.00	—
50	Girls of All Nations	1924	HM-34	£5.00	—
12	Strange Insects	c1920		£5.00	—
12	Wonders of the Deep	c1920		£6.00	—
	World's Wonder Series:				
12	A Numbered	c1920		£5.00	—
10	B Unnumbered	c1920	HM-35	£6.00	—

MAYPOLE

25	War Series	1915		£11.00	—

MAZAWATTEE (Tea)

L39	Kings and Queens	c1905	HM-37	£5.00	—

MEADOW DAIRY CO.

50	War Series	1914	HX-290	£10.00	—

MELOX

L50	Famous Breeds of Dogs	1937		£7.00	—
M32	Happy Families (Dogs)	1937		£8.00	—

MERCURY HOUSE CONSUMER PUBLICATIONS LTD

L4	PM Car Starter ('Popular Motoring')	1972		75p	£3.00

MERLIN

LT120	Football Premier League	1994		—	£10.00
LT88	Football Premier League	1996		—	£18.00
LT161	Football Premier League Gold	1997		—	£25.00
LT150	Football Premier League Gold	1998		—	£20.00
LT150	Football Premier League Gold	1999		—	£20.00
LT20	Football Premier League Gold Club Badges Nos A1 to A20	1999		—	£15.00
LT10	Football Premier League Gold World Cup Superstars etc. Nos B1 to B10	1999		—	£15.00
LT105	Football Premier League Gold	2000		—	£15.00
LT20	Football Premier League Gold — Top Scorers	2000		—	£12.00
LT20	Football Premier League Gold — Key Players	2000		—	£12.00
LT80	Rugby League Footballers Nos 1-80	1991		20p	£9.00
LT80	Rugby League Footballers Nos 81-160	1991		20p	£9.00
LT100	Shooting Stars (Footballers) Nos 1-100	1991		20p	£10.00
LT100	Shooting Stars (Footballers) Nos 101-200	1991		20p	£10.00

MERLIN (continued)

LT100	Shooting Stars (Footballers) Nos 201-300	1991		20p	£10.00
LT96	Shooting Stars (Footballers) Nos 301-396	1991		20p	£10.00
LT125	Star Wars Trilogy	1997		20p	£15.00
LT96	World Wrestling Federation Gold Series Part 1	1992		20p	—
LT96	World Wrestling Federation Gold Series Part 2	1992		20p	—
LT75	World Wrestling Federation Stars Nos 1-75	1991		20p	—
LT75	World Wrestling Federation Stars Nos 76-150	1991		20p	—

MERRYSWEETS LTD

L48	Telegum TV Stars	1958		£1.60	—
L48	World Racing Cars	1959		£3.00	—

GEOFFREY MICHAEL PUBLISHERS LTD

40	Modern Motor Cars (booklets)	1953		£1.50	—

MIDLAND CARTOPHILIC BRANCH

L24	Silhouettes of Veteran & Vintage Cars	1991		—	£6.00

MIDLAND COUNTIES

M20	Banknotes	1974		—	£12.50
M12	Farmyard Stencils	1977		—	£4.00
M24	Kings of the Road	1977		—	£8.00
EL10	Steam Power	1978		50p	£5.00

MIDLAND COUNTIES & CADBURY

12	Action Soldiers	1976		35p	£4.00

MILK MARKETING BOARD

25	Prehistoric Animals	1964		24p	£6.00
	Album			—	£15.00

MILLERS (Tea)

25	Animals and Reptiles	1962	HX-99	20p	£3.50

MINUTE MAID/UPPER DECK (USA)

LT25	World Cup All Stars (Football)	1994		—	£10.00

ROBERT R. MIRANDA LTD

50	150 Years of Locomotives:		HX-178		
	A White lettering on black panel	1957		20p	£6.00
	B Black lettering on white background	1958		20p	£5.00
50	100 Years of Motoring	1955	HX-117	20p	£5.00
25	Ships Through the Ages	1958	HX-94	40p	£10.00
50	Strange Creatures	1960	HX-120	20p	£7.50

MIS-SPENT YOUTH

L55	Toon Traders (Newcastle Utd. Footballers)	1996		—	£12.00

MISTER SOFTEE LTD (Ice Cream)

M12	Beautiful Butterflies	1977		60p	£7.00
M20	County Badge Collection	1976		25p	£5.00
L12	Did You Know?	1976		35p	£4.00
25	Do You Know?	1961	HX-166.1	£3.50	—

MISTER SOFTEE LTD (Ice Cream) (continued)

Size & quantity		Date	Handbook reference	Price per card	Complete set
L20	Famous Sports Trophies (shaped) … … … … … …	1975		—	£12.00
M12	Farmyard Stencils … … … … … … … … …	1977		40p	£5.00
M24	1st Division Football League Club Badges … … … …	1972		—	£8.00
L12	Horses in the Service of Man… … … … … … …	1977		£1.25	£15.00
M24	Kings of the Road (car radiator badges) … … … … …	1977		30p	£7.50
20	Mister Softee's TOP 20 … … … … … … … …	1963		70p	£14.00
EL12	Mister Softee TOP 10 ('Record Mirror' blue printed back — no address) … … … … … … …	1964	HM-61	50p	£6.00
EL12	First 12 Subjects: Mister Softee's Top Ten (black printing on back 'Win a Big Prize') … … … … … … … …	1965		£1.50	£18.00
EL12	Second 12 Subjects:				
	A Mister Softee's Top Ten — address '350 King Street' … … … … … … … … … …	1966		£5.00	—
	B Lord Neilson's Star Cards, address '350 King Street' … … … … … … … … …	1966		£2.00	—
EL12	Third 12 Subjects: Lord Neilson's Star Cards — no address … … … …	1967		£1.50	£18.00
EL24	Lord Neilson's Star Cards ('Disc and Music Echo') unnumbered … … … … … … … … …	1968	HM-62	£1.50	£36.00
EL24	Mister Softee's Pop Parade ('Disc and Music Echo') numbered … … … … … … … …	1969		£1.25	£30.00
EL24	Lord Neilson's Star Cards ('Disc and Music Echo') numbered … … … … … … … … …	1969		£1.75	—
M24	Mister Softee Pop Discs (circular card) … … …	1973	HM-63B	£1.25	£30.00
L24	Lord Neilson Star Discs (circular card) … … … …	1970	HM-63A	£1.50	£36.00
15	Moon Mission … … … … … … … … … …	1962		£2.50	—
M10	Pop Stars (star shaped) … … … … … … …	1975		—	£10.00
M20	Stamp in a Million … … … … … … …	1976		—	£10.00
L10	Steam Power … … … … … … … … …	1978		30p	£3.00
M4	Super Human Heroes … … … … … … …	1979		—	£3.00
25	TV Personalities … … … … … … … … …	1962		£3.00	—
EL12	Your World … … … … … … … … … …	1963		20p	£3.00

MISTER SOFTEE & CADBURY

12	Action Soldiers … … … … … … … … …	1976		40p	£5.00

MITCHAM FOODS LTD

25	Aircraft of Today … … … … … … … … …	1960		20p	£5.00
25	Aquarium Fish 1st Series … … … … … … …	1957	HX-87	£2.00	£50.00
25	Aquarium Fish 2nd Series … … … … … … …	1957	HX-87	20p	£3.00
50	Butterflies and Moths (issued in pairs)… … … … …	1959		£1.20	—
25	Footballers … … … … … … … … …	1956	HX-54	£3.00	—
50	Mars Adventure … … … … … … … …	c1960	HX-138	£6.00	—
25	Motor Racing … … … … … … … … …	1957		£2.00	£50.00

MOBIL OIL CO. LTD

M30	Football Club Badges (Canvas) … … … … … …	1977		£2.50	—
EL36	The Story of Grand Prix Motor Racing… … … … …	1970		55p	£20.00
25	Veteran and Vintage Cars … … … … … … …	1963	HX-159	£2.40	£60.00
24	Vintage Cars … … … … … … … … …	1966		20p	£5.00
	Album … … … … … … … … … …			—	£15.00

MODERN BOY

16	Fighting Planes of the World … … … … … …	1936		£4.50	—
32	Mechanical Wonders of 1935… … … … … … …	1935		£2.50	—

MOFFAT BROS

L100	Cinema Artistes	1914		£13.00	—

MOFFAT (B. & G. LTD)

EL102	Money That Made History	1971		20p	£9.00

MOLASSINE (Vims)

50	Dogs (full length):		HX-135		
	A Title boxed	1963		£1.50	—
	B Title unboxed	1963		£1.50	—
50	Dogs (head and shoulder)	1964		£2.00	—
25	Dogs at Work	1971		20p	£4.00
12	Dogs of All Countries	1925		£10.00	—
50	Puppies	1966		£2.00	—

MONTAGU MOTOR MUSEUM

M24	Veteran & Vintage Cars 1st Series	1961		£3.50	—
	Album			—	£30.00
M24	Veteran & Vintage Cars 2nd Series	1961		£5.00	—

MONTY GUM

M54	Bay City Rollers (Playing Card inset)	1978		60p	£32.00
L72	Daily Fables	1969		33p	£25.00
M94	Dallas...	1981		—	£12.00
LT50	Elvis	1978		—	£80.00
M98	Flags + 2 varieties (nos. 59 and 92 not issued)	c1980		—	£8.00
L56	Footballers (Playing Card inset)	1961	HM-73	£3.00	—
M54	Hitmakers (Playing Card inset)	1978		50p	—
M72	Kojak	1975		—	£36.00
M54	Kojak (Playing Card inset) black back	1976		50p	£27.00
M56	Kojak (Playing Card inset) red back	1976		70p	—
L55	Motor Cars (Playing Card inset) Symbols 36-38mm apart	1960		£1.75	—
L56	Motor Cars (Playing Card inset) Symbols 33-34mm apart	1960		£1.50	—
M64	Space Alpha 1999	1978		50p	£32.00
L56	Vintage Cars	1962		£1.40	—
L52	World Aircraft (Playing Card inset)	c1960		£3.00	—

MORLEY LTD

10	The Morley Circus	c1960		£3.00	—

MORNING FOODS LTD

1	Advertisement Card	c1955		—	£5.00
P25	British Planes:		HM-78		
	A Unnumbered	1953		60p	£15.00
	B Numbered	1953		£7.00	—
P50	British Trains	1952		£7.00	—
25	British Uniforms	1954	HX-108	24p	£6.00
12	The Cunard Line:				
	A Black back	1957		25p	£3.00
	B Blue back	1957		35p	£4.00
50	Modern Cars	1954		40p	£20.00
50	Our England	1955		20p	£6.00
25	Test Cricketers...	1953		£2.40	—

MORNING FOODS LTD (continued)

25	World Locomotives:		HX-70		
	A Black back ...	1956		20p	£3.00
	B Blue back ...	1956		£1.00	£25.00

E.D.L. MOSELEY

M25	Historical Buildings ...	1956		20p	£3.00

MOTOR ART (USA)

LT110	Iditarod (Sled Dog Race Across Alaska) ...	1992		—	£9.50

MOTOR CYCLE NEWS

M24	Best of British Motor Cycling (including poster)...	1988		—	£3.00
L6	Motorcycle Classics ...	1995		—	£3.00

MOTOR MAGAZINE

24	The Great British Sports Car (including album)...	1988		25p	£6.00

MOTOR SPORT CHARITY MEMORABILIA

50	Formula 1 World Championship ...	1999		—	£10.00

MURCO PETROLEUM

50	Airlines of the World ...	1978		—	£4.00

R.S. MURRAY & CO.

9	Alphabet Cards ...	c1930		£27.00	—

MUSEUM OF BRITISH MILITARY UNIFORMS

25	British Cavalry Uniforms ...	1987		—	£7.50
25	Military Maids ...	1987		—	£7.50
25	Warriors Through the Ages ...	1987		—	£7.50

MUSGRAVE BROTHERS LTD

25	Birds ...	1961	HX-71	£1.20	£30.00
25	Into Space ...	1961	HX-147	30p	£7.50
25	Modern Motor Cars ...	1963	HX-39	80p	£20.00
25	Pond Life ...	1963	HX-81	60p	£15.00
25	Products of the World ...	1961	HX-152	20p	£5.00
25	Tropical Birds ...	1965	HX-13	30p	£7.50
25	Wild Flowers ...	1961	HX-124	60p	£15.00

MUSICAL COLLECTABLES

25	Gilbert & Sullivan 1st Series ...	1995		—	£6.00
25	Gilbert & Sullivan 2nd Series ...	1995		—	£6.00

MY WEEKLY

M9	Battle Series (silk) ...	1916	HM-87	£8.00	—
M12	Floral Beauties (silk) ...	c1915	HM-82	£8.00	—
M15	Language of Flowers (silk) ...	c1915	HM-84	£8.00	—
M54	Lucky Emblems (silk) ...	c1915	HM-85	£9.00	—
M6	Lucky Flowers (silk) ...	c1915	HM-86	£12.00	—
M12	Our Soldier Boys (silk) ...	c1915	HM-88	£8.00	—
M14	Soldiers of the King (silk) ...	c1915	HM-91	£8.00	—
M6	Sweet Kiss Series (silk) ...	c1915	HM-94	£8.00	—
M6	War Heroes (silk) ...	c1915	HM-95	£8.00	—

MYERS & METREVELI

K48	Film Stars 1st Series (Numbered 1 to 48, Wow Gum				
	issue)	c1955		£4.00	—
K48	Film Stars 2nd Series (Numbered 49 to 96 Anonymous				
	issue)	c1955		£4.00	—
	Film Stars and Biographies:		HM-97		
L59	A Back Stupendous News	c1953		£7.00	—
L1	B Back Wow News...	c1953		£10.00	—
L60	Hollywood Peep Show	c1953		£5.00	—
L50	Spot the Planes (Strato Gum issue)	c1954		£7.00	—

NABISCO FOODS LTD

K5	Aces in Action	1980		£4.00	—
M24	Action Shots of Olympic Sports	1980		£2.00	—
L4	Adventure Books	1970		£6.00	—
EL20	Champions of Sport	1961		£3.50	—
EL6	Eagle Eye	1979		—	£3.00
12	ET — The Extra-Terrestrial	1982		40p	£5.00
M24	Footballers	1970		£3.25	—
EL8	Football Tactics (England Soccer Stars)	1977		—	£12.00
EL12	Freshwater Fishes of Britain	1974		—	£15.00
M10	History of Aviation	1970		£2.50	£25.00
K4	Johan Cruyff Demonstrates	1980	HN-3	£5.00	—
EL10	Kevin Keegan's Keep Fit with the Stars	1977		—	£12.00
EL6	Kevin Keegan's Play 'N' Score	1977		—	£7.00
EL10	Motor Show...	1960		£3.00	—
L6	World Super Stars and Sporting Trophies	1980		£4.00	—

NAC (USA)

| LT100 | Branson on Stage (TV Music Show) ... ... | 1992 | | — | £8.00 |

NASSAR (Gold Coast)

| 25 | Transport — Present and Future ... ... | 1955 | | 24p | £6.00 |

NATIONAL GALLERY

| EL24 | Masterpieces ... ... | 1978 | | — | £6.00 |

NATIONAL SPASTICS SOCIETY

| 24 | Famous County Cricketers (booklet) ... ... | 1958 | | £2.00 | £50.00 |
| 24 | Famous Footballers ... ... | 1958 | | 80p | £20.00 |

NECA

| LT24 | Beetlejuice The Movie ... ... | 2001 | | — | £6.00 |

NEEDLERS

| 13 | Military Series ... ... | 1916 | HX-128 | £27.00 | — |

PHILIP NEILL

15	Arsenal Double Legends of 1970/71	2002		—	£5.50
15	Arsenal 79 (A Tribute To The Classic FA Cup Winners				
	of 1979)	2009		—	£5.50
15	Aston Villa F.C. European Champions 81/82	2013		—	£6.00
10	Bizarre Club Shirts (Football)	2001		—	£4.00
15	Blackburn Rovers Heroes & Legends	2009		—	£5.50
15	Blades Heroes & Legends (Sheffield United F.C)	2014		—	£6.00

PHILIP NEILL (continued)

Size & quantity		Date	Handbook reference	Price per card	Complete set
12	Brazil '70 (Football)	2005	—		£4.75
10	Brazilliant — The Story of Pele (Footballer)	2001	—		£4.00
20	British Internationals 1950-2 (Football)	1999	—		£7.00
15	The Busby Babes 1st Series (Manchester United F.C.)	2002	—		£5.50
15	The Busby Babes 2nd Series (Manchester United F.C.)	2005	—		£5.50
L8	Celtic '67 The Lisbon Lions (Footballers)	2003	—		£4.25
15	Chelsea F.C. 1970 (F.A. Cup Winners)	2008	—		£5.50
10	Chelsea's Top Ten Goalscorers	2013	—		£5.00
15	Claret Heroes of The 1970s (Burnley F.C.)	2008	—		£5.50
15	Classic F.A. Cup Winners Tottenham Hotspur 1981	2013	—		£6.00
10	Classic Kits (Football Team Colours)	2001	—		£4.00
15	Classic Soccer Strips	2006	—		£5.50
10	Crystal Palace Heroes and Legends (Footballers)	2012	—		£5.00
15	Derby County Champions of 1971/72	2007	—		£5.50
18	Derby County Champions of 1974/75 40th Anniversary Edition	2015	—		£7.50
L10	Elvis in Pictures	2003	—		£5.75
15	England World Cup Winners 1966	2006	—		£5.50
10	England's Top Goal Scorers	2002	—		£4.00
10	Everton Heroes and Legends	2012	—		£5.00
20	Favourite Footballers Pre 1st & 2nd World War 1st Series	2009	—		£7.00
20	Favourite Footballers Pre 1st & 2nd World War 2nd Series	2009	—		£7.00
20	Favourite Footballers Pre 1st & 2nd World War 3rd Series	2009	—		£7.00
20	Favourite Footballers Pre 1st & 2nd World War 4th Series	2009	—		£7.00
25	Fergie's Heroes 2003/04 — Manchester United Footballers	2003	—		£7.50
10	Football Favourites (Prominent Players of the 1960s)	2015	—		£5.00
10	Football Heroes (Stars of the 1960s)	2001	—		£4.00
10	Football Icons 1st Series	2014	—		£5.00
10	Football Icons 2nd Series	2015	—		£5.00
10	Football in the Fifties	2001	—		£4.00
10	Football League Stars	2005	—		£3.75
25	Football Stars of the '20s and '30s	2004	—		£5.25
15	Football Stars of The Seventies 1st Series	2002	—		£5.50
15	Football Stars of The Seventies 2nd Series	2003	—		£5.50
15	Footballer of the Year (1948-1965)	1999	—		£5.50
10	Footy Star (Soccer Stars of the 1950s)	2008	—		£4.00
12	Forest Kings of Europe 1979 (Nottingham Forest F.C.)	2005	—		£4.50
10	George Formby 50th Anniversary Issue	2011	—		£5.50
10	Greavsie — A Tribute to Jimmy Greaves (Footballer)	2001	—		£4.00
10	Hotshot Football (Soccer Stars of the 1960s)	2008	—		£4.00
10	International Stars of Yesteryear 1st Series (Footballers)	2000	—		£4.00
10	International Stars of Yesteryear 2nd Series (Football)	2001	—		£4.00
15	Ipswich Town F.C. (UEFA Cup Winners 1981)	2008	—		£5.50
15	Kings of Europe (Manchester United F.C.)	1999	—		£5.50
15	Leeds United The Revie Era	2002	—		£5.50
12	The Lisbon Lions (Celtic European Cup Winning Legends)	1999	—		£4.50
15	Liverpool F.C. Champions League 2005	2005	—		£5.50
15	Liverpool F.C. Kings of Europe 1977	2005	—		£5.50
15	Liverpool Legends (Footballers)	2000	—		£5.50
15	Maine Road Heroes (Manchester City Footballers)	2003	—		£5.50

PHILIP NEILL (continued)

Size & quantity		Date	Handbook reference	Price per card	Complete set
15	Manchester City's Euro Kings of '70	2006		—	£5.50
15	Manchester United Classic Kits	2004		—	£5.50
10	Masters of Horror	2015		—	£5.00
15	Moscow Magic (Manchester United Champions League Winners)	2008		—	£5.50
15	Newcastle Heroes — Post War Toon Legends	2004		—	£5.50
10	Nicole Kidman	1999		—	£4.00
15	Premiership Burnley Tribute To The Turf Moor Play-off Heroes	2009		—	£6.00
15	Rangers Euro Kings of '72	2006		—	£5.50
20	Red Legends (Manchester United Footballers)	1998		—	£5.50
10	Scottish Footballers of the 1930s	2000		—	£4.00
10	Scottish Internationals (1960s Footballers)	2002		—	£4.00
15	70's Soccer Stars	2003		—	£5.50
10	Soccer in the 60s 1st Series	1999		—	£4.00
10	Soccer in the 60s 2nd Series	2000		—	£4.00
15	Soccer Portraits of the 1950s Series 1	2008		—	£5.00
15	Soccer Portraits of the 1960s Series 1	2008		—	£5.00
15	Soccer Portraits of the 1970s Series 1	2008		—	£5.00
10	Soccer Selection (Footballing Greats)	2004		—	£4.00
10	Soccer 70 (1970s Footballers)	2002		—	£4.00
10	Soccer Sketch (Footballers of 50s and 60s)	2010		—	£4.50
10	Soccer Stars of The 50s	2001		—	£4.00
10	Soccer Stars of The 60s	2001		—	£4.00
15	Stamford Bridge Superstars — Chelsea F.C.	2006		—	£5.50
10	Striker Soccer Cards (of the '70s) 1st Series	2009		—	£5.00
10	Striker Soccer Cards (of the '70s) 2nd Series	2009		—	£5.00
15	Sunderland FA Cup Winners of 1973	2008		—	£5.50
L18	Super Reds (Manchester United Footballers)	1998		—	£7.50
10	Ten of the Best — George Best (Footballer)	2000		—	£4.00
10	10 Select Manchester United Footballers	2011		—	£5.50
10	Third Lanark Favourites (Footballers)	2009		—	£5.00
15	Tottenham Double Winners 1960-61	2004		—	£5.50
10	Tottenham Heroes & Legends	2012		—	£5.00
25	United Legends (Manchester United Footballers)	2000		—	£7.50
15	United '68 (Manchester United F.C.)	2006		—	£5.50
12	Villa Cup Winners 1957 (Aston Villa F.C.)	2005		—	£4.50
10	Vintage Footballers of the 1900s	2005		—	£4.00
15	Vintage Soccer Heroes	2005		—	£5.00
L7	Visions of Marilyn Munroe	2003		—	£4.25
15	West Ham United Cup Winning Sides of 1964 and 1965	2007		—	£5.50
15	Wolves Heroes and Legends (Wolverhampton Wanderers F.C.)	2011		—	£6.00
10	World Cup Heroes and Legends 1st Series (Football)	2009		—	£5.00
10	World Cup Heroes and Legends 2nd Series (Football)	2010		—	£5.00
10	World Soccer Heroes 1st Series	2009		—	£5.00
10	World Soccer Heroes 2nd Series	2009		—	£5.00
10	World Soccer Stars (1960s to 1980s)	2013		—	£5.00

NEILSON'S

50	Interesting Animals	1954	HX-115	20p	£4.00

THE NELSON LEE LIBRARY

MP15	Footballers	1922		£5.00	—
MP6	Modern British Locomotives	1922		£7.00	—

NESTLE (Chocolate)

EL12	Animal Bar (wrappers)	1970	HN-23	—	£3.00
49	Happy Families	1935	HN-31	£1.20	—
100	Stars of the Silver Screen, Vol I	1936		£1.80	—
50	Stars of the Silver Screen, Vol II...	1937		£2.20	—
136	This England	1936		£1.20	—
156	Wonders of the World, Vol I	1932		£1.20	—
144	Wonders of the World, Vol II	1933		£1.20	—
288	Wonders of the World, Vol III	1934		£1.20	—

NEW ENGLAND CONFECTIONERY (USA)

M12	Real Airplane Pictures	c1930		£3.00	£36.00

NEW SOUTH WALES CRICKET ASSOCIATION (Australia)

L20	The Blues — N.S.W. Cricketers 1998-99 (inscribed 'Toyota')	1998		—	£6.00
L20	The Blues — N.S.W. Cricketers 1999-2000 (without 'Toyota')	1999		—	£6.00

NEW SOUTH WALES FIRE SERVICE (Australia)

L10	Fire Appliances and Equipment 1st Series	1980		75p	—
L10	Fire Appliances and Equipment 2nd Series	1981		75p	—
L10	Fire Appliances and Equipment 3rd Series	1982		75p	—
L10	Fire Appliances and Equipment 4th Series	1983		75p	—
L10	Fire Appliances and Equipment 5th Series	1984		75p	—
L10	Fire Appliances and Equipment 7th Series	1986		75p	—
L10	Fire Appliances and Equipment 8th Series	1987		75p	£7.50
L10	Fire Appliances and Equipment 9th Series	1988		75p	£7.50
L10	Fire Appliances and Equipment 10th Series	1989		75p	£7.50
L10	Fire Appliances and Equipment 11th Series	1990		75p	£7.50

NEWMARKET HARDWARE

L24	Some of Britain's Finest (Motor) Bikes	1993		—	£6.00

NEWS CHRONICLE

L12	Cricketers — England v S Africa 1955...	1955	HN-37.1	£15.00	—
	Football Players:				
L13	Barrow RFC...	1955	HN-39.1	£2.00	—
L14	Blackburn Rovers FC	1955	HN-37.5A	£2.00	—
L12	Bradford City FC	1955	HN-37.7A	£2.00	—
L11	Chesterfield FC	1955	HN-37.13	£2.00	—
L12	Everton FC (no stars at base)	1955	HN-37.18A	£2.00	—
L10	Everton FC (two stars at base)	1955	HN-37.18B	£2.00	—
L15	Manchester City FC	1955	HN-37.27	£2.00	—
L12	Newcastle United FC	1955	HN-37.29	£3.00	—
L14	Rochdale Hornets RFC	1955	HN-39.7	£2.00	—
L13	Salford RFC...	1955	HN-39.9	£2.00	—
L17	Stockport County FC...	1955	HN-37.47	£2.00	—
L13	Sunderland FC...	1955	HN-37.49	£2.50	—
L13	Swinton RFC	1955	HN-39.10	£2.00	—
L11	Workington AFC	1955	HN-37.56	£2.00	—
L11	York City FC	1955	HN-37.57	£2.00	—
L12	The Story of Stirling Moss	1955	HN-40	£10.00	—

NEWTON, CHAMBERS & CO.

EL18	Izal Nursery Rhymes 1st Series	c1930		£4.00	—
EL18	Izal Nursery Rhymes 2nd Series	c1930		£4.00	—

NEW ZEALAND MEAT PRODUCERS BOARD

EL6	New Zealand Pastoral Scenes	c1930		50p	£3.00
M25	Scenes of New Zealand Lamb	c1930		£4.00	—

NINETY MINUTES

20	Ninety Minutes Footballers of the 1950s 1st Series	2009		—	£9.00
20	Ninety Minutes Footballers of the 1950s 2nd Series	2009		—	£9.00
20	Ninety Minutes Footballers of the 1950s 3rd Series	2010		—	£7.50
20	Ninety Minutes Footballers of the 1950s 4th Series	2010		—	£7.50
20	Ninety Minutes Footballers of the 1950s 5th Series	2010		—	£7.50

NORTHAMPTONSHIRE COUNTY CRICKET CLUB

30	Northamptonshire County Cricket 1905-1985	1985		50p	£15.00

NORTHERN CONFECTIONS LTD

48	Aeroplanes	c1955		£5.00	—

NORTHERN CO-OPERATIVE SOCIETY LTD

25	Birds	1963	HX-71	£1.20	—
25	History of the Railways 1st Series	1964	HX-88	50p	£12.50
25	History of the Railways 2nd Series	1964	HX-88	70p	£17.50
25	Passenger Liners	1963	HX-82	20p	£3.00
25	Then and Now	1963	HX-27	40p	£10.00
25	Tropical Birds	1967	HX-13	50p	£12.50
25	Weapons of World War II	1962		80p	£20.00
25	Wonders of the Deep	1966	HX-89	20p	£4.00

NORTH'S BREAD (New Zealand)

LT16	Canterbury Crusaders (Rugby Union)	1997		—	£5.00
	Album			—	£5.00

NORTHUMBRIA POLICE

EL21	Sunderland AFC (Footballers)	1991		—	£12.00

NORTON'S

25	Evolution of The Royal Navy	c1965	HX-90	£1.60	—

NUGGET POLISH CO.

EL30	Allied Series	c1910		£15.00	—
50	Flags of all Nations	c1925	HN-47	£5.00	—
EL40	Mail Carriers and Stamps	c1910	HN-48	£15.00	—

NUMBER ONE MAGAZINE

EL5	Get Fit And Have Fun	1991		—	£3.00

NUNBETTA

25	Motor Cars	1955	HN-49	£10.00	—

NUNEATON F C

L30	Nuneaton Borough Footballers	1995		—	£10.00
L30	Nuneaton Football Greats	1992		—	£15.00

O'CARROLL KENT LTD

50	Railway Engines	c1955		£4.50	—

OCTUS SPORTS (USA)

LT44	Rams NFL Cheerleaders	1994		—	£6.00

ODLING & WILLSON

25	Bygone Locomotives	1999		—	£10.00

N. OLDHAM

12	Blackpool Legends (Footballers)	2015		—	£7.50
13	Golf Legends	2005		—	£6.00

OLDHAM EDUCATIONAL COMMITTEE

M40	Reward Cards	c1915	HO-8	£7.00	—

TONY L. OLIVER

1	Advert Card for German Orders & Decorations...	1963		—	£3.00
25	Aircraft of World War II	c1970	HX-7	£5.00	—
50	German Orders and Decorations	1963		£2.50	—
50	German Uniforms...	1971		25p	£12.50
M25	Vehicles of the German Wehrmacht	c1970		£1.20	£30.00

ORBIS LTD

EL90	Dinosaurs	1992		20p	£10.00

ORBIT ADVERTISING

15	Engines of the London & North Eastern Railway	1986		—	£4.00
20	Famous Douglas Aeroplanes	1986		—	£10.00
28	Great Rugby Sides New Zealand Tourists 1905	1986		20p	£4.00
16	New Zealand Cricketers of 1958	1988		—	£7.00

OVALTINE

25	Do You Know?...	1968	HX-166.2	32p	£8.00

O.V.S. TEA CO.

K25	Modern Engineering	1955		30p	£7.50

OXO LTD

K?	Advertisement Cards	c1925	HL-96/9	£8.00	—
K20	British Cattle	1924		£4.50	£90.00
15	Bull Series	1927		£3.00	£45.00
K24	Feats of Endurance	1926		£3.00	£75.00
K20	Furs and their Story	1924		£3.00	£60.00
K36	Lifeboats and their History...	1925		£3.25	—
K30	Mystery Painting Pictures	1928		£3.00	£90.00
EL6	Oxo Cattle Studies	c1920		£35.00	—
25	Oxo Recipes	1936		£3.00	—

P.C.G.C. (Gum)

LT88	War Bulletin...	1966		£2.00	—

P.M.R. ASSOCIATES LTD

25	England The World Cup Spain '82	1982		20p	£3.00

P.Y.Q.C.C. (USA)

LT100	Great Guns	1993		—	£15.00

PACIFIC TRADING (USA)

LT110	American Soccer Players 1987-88	1987	—	£10.00
LT110	American Soccer Players 1988-89	1989	—	£10.00
LT110	American Soccer Players 1989-90	1990	—	£10.00
LT220	American Soccer Players 1990-91	1990	—	£15.00
LT110	American Soccer Players NPSL 1992/93...	1993	20p	£15.00
LT110	Bingo — The Film	1991	—	£8.00
LT110	The College Years Saved By the Bell (TV Show)	1994	—	£7.50
LT110	Eight Men Out — The Film	1998	—	£9.50
LT110	Gunsmoke (1950-60s TV Show)	1993	—	£9.50
LT110	I Love Lucy (TV Series)	1991	—	£12.00
LT110	Operation Desert Shield (Gulf War)	1991	—	£9.50
LT110	Total Recall — The Movie	1990	—	£9.50
LT110	Where Are They	1992	—	£9.50
LT110	The Wizard of Oz...	1991	—	£15.00
LT110	World War II	1992	—	£9.50

H.J. PACKER LTD

K30	Footballers	c1930	£50.00	—
50	Humorous Drawings...	1936	£4.00	—

PAGE WOODCOCK

20	Humorous Sketches (multi-backed)	c1905	HP-4	£25.00	—

PALMER MANN & CO. LTD

Sifta Sam Salt Package Issues

24	Famous Cricketers	c1953	£20.00	—
24	Famous Footballers	c1954	£20.00	—
12	Famous Jets	c1955	£12.00	—
12	Famous Lighthouses	c1956	£12.00	—

PALS

M8	Famous Footballers Fineart Supplements	1922	HP-8	£10.00	—
MP12	Football Series	1922		£5.00	—

PANINI (UK)

Cards:

LT150	Disney's Aladdin	1994	20p	£15.00
LT45	England Football Stars Gold Collection	1996	—	£15.00
LT100	Footballers 92 Nos 1-100	1991	20p	—
LT100	Footballers 92 Nos 101-200	1991	20p	—
LT100	Footballers 92 Nos 201-300	1991	20p	—
LT122	Footballers 92 Nos 301-422	1991	20p	—

Sticker sets complete with albums:

M180	The Adventures of the Animals of Farthing Wood	1995	—	£22.00
M255	Care Bears News...	1987	—	£22.00
M120	ET — The Extra Terrestrial	1982	—	£22.00

PANINI (USA and Canada)

Cards:

LT100	Antique Cars 1st Series	c1995	—	£9.50
EL72	Austin Powers	1998	—	£12.00
LT198	Barbie and Friends	1992	—	£12.00
LT100	Dream Cars 1st Series	1991	—	£9.50
LT100	Dream Cars 2nd Series	1992	—	£9.50
LT90	The Lion King — Walt Disney Film	1995	—	£9.50
EL108	NSYNC (Pop Group) (Nos 34 & 100 blurred as issued)	1999	—	£12.00

PANINI (USA and Canada) (continued)

Size & quantity		Date	Handbook reference	Price per card	Complete set
LT100	Wildlife in Danger...	c1993		—	£9.50
LT100	Wings Of Fire (Military Aircraft etc)	1992		—	£9.50
	Sticker Sets complete with albums:				
M240	Star Trek — The Next Generation (Factory Set)	1993		—	£12.00

PARAMINT CARDS

10	Arthur Askey — Comedy Heroes	2012		—	£5.00
10	Classic Football Stars 1st Series	2015		—	£5.00
10	Classic Football Stars 2nd Series	2015		—	£5.00
20	Football Favourites (1960s/70s Footballers)				
	1st Series	2014		—	£8.00
20	Football Favourites (1960s/70s Footballers)				
	2nd Series	2014		—	£8.00
10	Football Stars (of the 1970s) 1st Series	2012		—	£5.00
10	Football Stars (of the 1970s) 2nd Series	2012		—	£5.00
10	Football Stars (of the 1970s) 3rd Series	2012		—	£5.00
10	Football Stars (of the 1970s) 4th Series	2012		—	£5.00
10	Football Stars (of the 1970s) 5th Series	2012		—	£5.00
10	Gracie Fields From Rochdale to Capri	2012		—	£5.00
10	Margaret Rutherford	2012		—	£5.00
10	Norman Wisdom — Comedy Heroes	2012		—	£5.00
10	Scottish Football Stars (1970s footballers)	2011		—	£5.00

PARAMOUNT LABORATORIES LTD

50	Fifty Years of Flying	1954		90p	£45.00
50	Motor Cars	1954		£1.75	—
50	Railways of the World:				
	A 'Paramount Sweets':				
	(i) Correct numbering	1955		50p	£25.00
	(ii) Incorrect numbering	1955		£1.00	—
	B 'Paramount Laboratories Ltd'	1955		80p	£40.00

PARRS

L20	Famous Aircraft	1953		£7.00	—

JAMES PASCALL LTD

48	Boy Scouts Series (multi-backed)	c1910	HP-14	£12.00	—
24	British Birds...	1925		£3.50	—
30	Devon Ferns	1927		£2.00	—
30	Devon Flowers:				
	A Without Red Overprint	1927		£2.00	—
	B With Red Overprint	1927		£4.00	—
24	Devon Worthies	1927		£2.50	—
18	Dogs	1924		£4.50	—
12	Felix the Film Cat...	c1920	HP-15	£35.00	—
15	Flags and Flags with Soldiers (with bow, cord)				
	(multi-backed)	c1910	HX-41	£15.00	—
15	Flags and Flags with Soldiers (without bow, cord)				
	(multi-backed)	c1910	HX-41	£15.00	—
30	Glorious Devon	1929		£2.20	—
36	Glorious Devon 2nd Series:				
	A Marked 2nd Series	1929		£2.20	—
	B Marked Aids for Mothers	1929		£7.50	—
36	Glorious Devon (Ambrosia black back)	c1930		£2.20	—
2	King George V and Queen Mary (multi-backed)	c1915	HP-16	£30.00	—
44	Military Series (multi-backed)...	c1910	HP-17	£20.00	—

JAMES PASCALL LTD (continued)

20	Pascall's Specialities (multi-backed)	c1920	HP-18	£20.00	—
12	Royal Navy Cadet Series (multi-backed)	c1915	HP-19	£20.00	—
8	Rulers of the World	c1910	HP-20	£30.00	—
68	Town and Other Arms (multi-backed)	c1910	HP-21	£12.00	—
50	Tricks and Puzzles	c1920		£11.00	—
13	War Portraits	c1915		£25.00	—

J. PATERSON & SON LTD

M48	Balloons	1964		90p	£45.00

PATRICK GARAGES

The Patrick Collection (Motor Cars):

M24	A Without Coupon	1986		60p	£15.00
EL24	B With Coupon	1986		£1.00	£25.00

GEORGE PAYNE (Tea)

25	American Indian Tribes:		HX-28		
	A Cream Card	1962		£1.00	£25.00
	B White Card	1962		£1.00	£25.00
25	British Railways	1962	HX-107	30p	£7.50
	Characters from Dickens' Works:		HX-172		
12	A Numbered	c1912		£15.00	—
6	B Unnumbered	c1912		£15.00	—
25	Dogs' Heads	1963	HX-16	50p	£12.50
25	Mickey Mouse Pleasure Cruise	c1920		£32.00	—
25	Science in the 20th Century	1963	HX-18	20p	£3.00

PENGUIN BISCUITS

EL10	Home Hints	c1974		£2.50	—
EL10	Making the Most of Your Countryside	1975		£2.50	—
EL10	Pastimes	c1972		£2.50	—
EL12	Penguin Farm Animal Series	c1968		£2.50	—
EL10	Penguin Zoo Animal Series	c1968		£2.50	—
EL10	Playday	c1974		£2.50	—
EL12	Wildlife	1973		£2.50	—

PENNY MAGAZINE

M12	Film Stars	c1930		£4.00	—

PEPSI (UK)

L7	Star Wars Episode 1 The Phantom Menace	1999		—	£5.00

PEPSI (Thailand)

LT8	Britney Spears	2002		—	£8.00
LT32	World Football Stars	2002		—	£8.00

PEPSICO FOODS (Saudi Arabia)

M22	World Soccer	1998		30p	£7.00

PERENNIAL MUSIC

M45	Forever Gold Entertainment Legends	2000		—	£12.00

PERFETTI GUM

40	Famous Trains	1983		£3.50	—

PERIKIM

L7	Dogs — The Boxer	2001		—	£3.00
L7	Dogs — The Bull Terrier	2005		—	£3.00
L7	Dogs — The Bulldog	2005		—	£3.00
L7	Dogs — The Cocker Spaniel	2001		—	£3.00
L7	Dogs — The Dalmatian	2005		—	£3.00
L7	Dogs — The Dobermann	2001		—	£3.00
L7	Dogs — The English Springer Spaniel	2001		—	£3.00
L7	Dogs — The German Shepherd	2001		—	£3.00
L7	Dogs — The Golden Retriever	2001		—	£3.00
L7	Dogs — The Irish Setter	2005		—	£3.00
L7	Dogs — The Jack Russell	2001		—	£3.00
L7	Dogs — The King Charles Cavalier	2005		—	£3.00
L7	Dogs — The Rottweiler	2005		—	£3.00
L7	Dogs — The Rough Collie	2005		—	£3.00
L7	Dogs — The Staffordshire Bull Terrier	2005		—	£3.00
L7	Dogs — The West Highland	2005		—	£3.00
L7	Dogs — The Yorkshire Terrier	2005		—	£3.00
L13	Nursery Rhymes	1996		—	£5.00

PETER MAX (USA)

LT6	Peter Max Posters	1994		—	£3.00

PETERKIN

M8	English Sporting Dogs (multi-backed)	c1930	HP-43	£14.00	—

PETPRO LTD

35	Grand Prix Racing Cars (64 × 29mm)	1966		30p	£10.00

THE PHILATELIC POSTCARD PUBLISHING CO. LTD

EL10	Philatelic Anniversary Series	1983		—	£5.00

PHILLIPS TEA

25	Army Badges, Past and Present	1964		20p	£3.50
25	British Birds and Their Nests	1971	HX-104	£1.60	—
25	British Rail	1965	HX-107	30p	£7.50

PHILOSOPHY FOOTBALL

L20	Philosopher Footballers	1998		—	£12.00

PHOTAL

EL2	Duncan Edwards (Footballer)	2001		—	£5.00
EL4	Manchester United F.C. 1967 Series 1	2001		—	£8.00
EL10	Manchester United F.C. 1968 Series 2 Nos 1-10	2001		—	£15.00
EL10	Manchester United F.C. 1968 Series 2 Nos 11-20	2001		—	£15.00
EL6	Northern Footballing Knights	2001		—	£12.00
EL10	Sir Tom Finney (Footballer)	2001		—	£16.00

PHOTO ANSWERS MAGAZINE

EL12	Holiday Fax	1990		—	£3.00

PHOTO PRECISION

EL20	Fighting Aircraft of World War II	1978		—	£5.00
EL10	Flowers	1979		—	£2.50
EL10	Old English Series	1979		—	£2.50
EL10	Traction Engines	1979		—	£2.50

PHOTO PRECISION (continued)

EL12	Vintage Cars	1975		—	£2.50
EL10	Wild Birds	1979		—	£2.50
EL10	Wild Life	1979		—	£2.50

PILOT

32	Aeroplanes and Carriers	1937		£3.50	—
32	Football Fame Series	1935	HP-52	£4.00	—

GEO. M. PITT

25	Types of British Soldiers	1914	HX-144	£27.00	—

PIZZA HUT

EL12	Football Skill Cards	c1995		—	£6.00

PLANET LTD

L50	Racing Cars of the World	1959		£3.00	—

PLANTERS NUT AND CHOCOLATE CO. (USA)

M25	Hunted Animals	1933		£3.00	£75.00

PLAY HOUR

M24	Zoo plus album	c1960		—	£10.00

PLAYER PARADE

20	Player Parade (Footballers of the 50s) 1st Series	2010		—	£7.50
20	Player Parade (Footballers of the 50s) 2nd Series	2011		—	£7.50

PLAYERS INTERNATIONAL

LT40	Boxing Personalities — Ringlords	1991		—	£5.00

PLUCK

MP27	Famous Football Teams	1922	HP-56	£4.00	—

PLYMOUTH COUNTY COUNCIL

EL20	Endangered Species	1985		—	£5.00

POLAR PRODUCTS LTD (BARBADOS)

25	International Air Liners	c1970		60p	£15.00
25	Modern Motor Cars	c1970		80p	£20.00
25	Tropical Birds	c1970		60p	£15.00
25	Wonders of the Deep	c1970		50p	£12.50

POLYDOR

16	Polydor Guitar	1975		50p	£8.00

PONY MAGAZINE

EL26	Horse & Pony Breeds (Trumps Cards)	2008		—	£6.00

H. POPPLETON & SONS

50	Cricketers Series	1926		£27.00	—
16	Film Stars	1928	HP-58	£8.00	—
15	War Series	c1915	HP-59	£27.00	—
12	Wembley Empire Exhibition Series	c1920	HP-60	£27.00	—

POPULAR GARDENING

| EL6 | Colour Schemes With Garden Flowers ... ... | 1939 | HP-61 | £2.00 | — |

PORTFOLIO INTERNATIONAL (USA)

LT50	Endless Summer (Pin Up Girls)	1993	—	£9.50
LT50	Portfolio (Pin Up Girls)	1992	—	£9.50
LT50	Portfolio (Pin Up Girls)	1993	—	£9.50
LT36	Portfolio's Secret (Pin Up Girls) (No. 12 unissued, 2 different No. 15s)	1994	—	£9.50

PoSTA

| 25 | Modern Transport... ... ... | 1957 | 20p | £5.00 |

PRESCOTT CONFECTIONERY

| L36 | Speed Kings ... ... | 1966 | 75p | £27.00 |

PRESCOTT — PICKUP

EL60	Action Portraits of Famous Footballers	1979	—	£15.00
	Album		—	£15.00
EL60	Interregnum (Military)	1978	—	£20.00
	Album		—	£15.00
EL64	Our Iron Roads (Railways)	1980	—	£12.00
	Album		—	£15.00
EL60	Queen and People	1977	—	£12.00
	Album		—	£15.00
EL60	Railway Locomotives:			
	A Post Card back	1976	—	£12.00
	B Textback	1978	—	£12.00
	Album		—	£15.00
50	Railway Locomotives	1978	25p	£12.50
	Album		—	£12.00
EL12	The Royal Wedding	1981	—	£9.00
EL60	Sovereign Series No. 1 Royal Wedding	1981	—	£20.00
	Album		—	£15.00
EL60	Sovereign Series No. 2 30 Years of Elizabeth II	1982	—	£15.00
	Album		—	£15.00
EL30	Sovereign Series No. 3 — Charles & Diana in the Antipodes	1983	—	£8.00
EL15	Sovereign Series No. 3 — Charles & Diana in Canada	1983	—	£4.00
EL70	Sovereign Series No. 4 — Royal Family	1982	—	£15.00
	Album		—	£15.00
EL63	Sovereign Series No. 6 — Papal Visit	1982	—	£10.00
	Album		—	£15.00
EL63	Sovereign Series No. 7 — Falklands Task Force	1982	—	£25.00
	Album		—	£15.00
EL63	Sovereign Series No. 8 — War in the South Atlantic ...	1983	—	£20.00
	Album		—	£15.00
EL60	Tramcars & Tramways	1977	—	£15.00
	Album		—	£15.00
EL60	Tramcyclopaedia	1979	—	£18.00
	Album		—	£15.00

PRESS PASS (USA)

| LT100 | Elvis Is (Elvis Presley) ... ... | 2008 | — | £20.00 |
| LT110 | Royal Family ... ... | 1993 | 20p | £9.50 |

PRESTON DAIRIES

25	Country Life	………………………………………	1966	HX-11	20p	£3.00

PRICE'S PATENT CANDLE CO. LTD

EL12	Famous Battles	……………………………………	c1910	HP-68	£12.00	—

W.R. PRIDDY

80	Famous Boxers	………………………………	1992		—	£15.00

PRIMROSE CONFECTIONERY CO. LTD

24	Action Man ………………………………………	1976		£3.40	—
50	Amos Burke, Secret Agent:				
	A With 'printed in England' …………………………	1970		£1.00	£50.00
	B Without 'printed in England' …………………	1966		£1.20	
50	Andy Pandy ………………………………………	1960		40p	£20.00
50	Bugs Bunny ………………………………………	1964		£1.20	£60.00
50	Burke's Law ………………………………………	1966		£5.00	—
25	Captain Kid ………………………………………	1975		£5.50	—
50	Chitty Chitty Bang Bang:				
	A Thick card ……………………………………	1969		£1.00	£50.00
	B Paper thin card …………………………………	1969		40p	£20.00
50	Cowboy ……………………………………………	1961		25p	£12.50
25	Cup Tie Quiz ……………………………………	1973		20p	£3.00
25	Dad's Army ………………………………………	1973		80p	£20.00
50	Famous Footballers (F.B.S.1) back………………	1961		40p	£20.00
50	Flintstones ………………………………………	1963		£1.00	—
25	Football Funnies …………………………………	1974		30p	£7.50
25	Happy Howlers ……………………………………	1975		20p	£4.00
50	Joe 90:				
	A Thick card ……………………………………	1969		£2.00	—
	B Paper thin card ………………………………	1970		£1.70	—
50	Krazy Kreatures from Outer Space:				
	A Thick card ……………………………………	1970		60p	£30.00
	B Thin card ……………………………………	1972		20p	£6.00
	C Paper thin card ……………………………	1972		20p	£5.00
50	Laramie …………………………………………	1964		£1.60	£80.00
50	Laurel & Hardy:				
	A Thick card ……………………………………	1968		£3.00	—
	B Thin card ……………………………………	1972		£1.60	£80.00
	C Paper thin card ……………………………	1972		£1.20	£60.00
22	Mounties (Package Issue)…………………………	1960		£7.00	—
50	Popeye 1st Series ………………………………	1960		£6.00	—
50	Popeye 2nd Series ………………………………	1960		£5.50	£275.00
50	Popeye 3rd Series ………………………………	1961		25p	£12.50
50	Popeye 4th Series:				
	A Back headed '4th Series Popeye No. …' Address 'Argyle Avenue', Album clause 'send only 9d …' ………………………………………	1963		25p	£12.50
	B Back headed 'Popeye … 4th Series' Address 'Farnham Road'				
	i Thick card ………………………………	1970		30p	£15.00
	ii Thin card ……………………………………	1970		25p	£12.50
50	Queen Elizabeth 2 (The Cunard Liner):				
	A Cream card …………………………………	1969		£1.00	£50.00
	B White card …………………………………	1969		90p	£45.00
50	Quick Draw McGraw, Series Q.1 ………………	1965		£1.50	£75.00

PRIMROSE CONFECTIONERY CO. LTD (continued)

Size & quantity		Date	Price per card	Complete set
50	Space Patrol:			
	A Thick card	1968	30p	£15.00
	B Thin card	1968	20p	£10.00
50	Space Race	1969	20p	£6.00
12	Star Trek..	1971	65p	£7.50
50	Superman:			
	A Thick card	1968	80p	—
	B Paper thin card	1972	50p	£25.00
50	Yellow Submarine	1968	£5.00	—
50	Z Cars Album. Text on back 'send only 9d'	1964	25p	£12.50
50	Z Cars Album. Text on back 'send only 1/-' (different Series)	1968	50p	£25.00

A.S. PRIOR (Fish and Chips)

		Date	Handbook reference	Price per card	Complete set
25	Evolution of the Royal Navy c1965		HX-90	£1.40	—

S. PRIOR (Bookshop)

		Date	Handbook reference	Price per card	Complete set
25	British Uniforms of the 19th Century c1965		HX-78	£1.40	—
25	Do You Know? c1965		HX-166.2	£1.20	—

PRIORY TEA & COFFEE CO. LTD

Size & quantity		Date	Price per card	Complete set
1	Advert Card Set Completion Offer	1966	—	£10.00
50	Aircraft	1961	£1.20	—
	Album..		—	£6.00
50	Birds	1963	£1.00	—
	Album		—	£25.00
24	Bridges	1959	20p	£3.00
50	Cars	1964	60p	£30.00
	Album		—	£6.00
24	Cars	1958	£4.00	—
50	Cycles and Motorcycles	1960	£2.00	—
	Album		—	£20.00
24	Dogs	1957	20p	£3.50
24	Flowering Trees	1959	20p	£3.00
24	Men at Work	1959	20p	£3.00
24	Out and About...	1957	40p	£10.00
24	People in Uniform	1957	£2.00	—
24	Pets	1957	20p	£3.00
50	Wild Flowers	1961	80p	£40.00
	Album		—	£20.00
	Album for Bridges and Men at Work combined		—	£20.00
	Album for Cars (24) and Flowering Trees combined		—	£15.00
	Album for Dogs and People in Uniform combined ...		—	£20.00
	Album for Out and About and Pets combined		—	£20.00

PRISM LEISURE

		Date	Price per card	Complete set
L30	George Formby	1993	—	£15.00
L12	Patsy Cline (Country Singer)	1993	—	£10.00

PRO SET (UK)

		Date	Price per card	Complete set
LT100	Bill & Ted's Excellent Adventure	1992	20p	£9.00
LT100	Football Fixtures/Footballers	1991	20p	£10.00
LT110	Footballers 1990-91 Nos 1-110	1990	20p	£9.00
LT110	Footballers 1990-91 Nos 111-220	1990	20p	£9.00
LT108	Footballers 1990-91 Nos 221-328	1990	20p	£9.00
LT115	Footballers 1991-92 Nos 1-115	1991	20p	£9.00

PRO SET (UK) (continued)

LT115	Footballers 1991-92 Nos 116-230	1991		20p	£9.00
LT125	Footballers 1991-92 Nos 231-355	1992		20p	£9.00
LT124	Footballers 1991-92 Nos 356-479	1992		20p	£9.00
LT100	Footballers — Scottish 1991-92	1991		20p	£8.00
LT100	Guinness Book of Records	1992		20p	£7.50
LT75	Super Stars Musicards (Pop Stars) Nos 1-75	1991		20p	£7.50
LT75	Super Stars Musicards (Pop Stars) Nos 76-150	1991		20p	£7.50
LT100	Thunderbirds	1992		20p	£8.00

PRO SET (USA)

LT150	American Football World League	1991		—	£12.00
LT95	Beauty and The Beast	1992		—	£8.00
LT90	The Little Mermaid (Disney Film) + 37 Bonus Cards ...	1991		—	£12.00
LT160	NFL Super Bowl XXV	1991		—	£15.00
LT100	PGA Golf	1990		—	£12.00
LT285	PGA Golf Tour	1991		—	£25.00
LT100	PGA Golf nos E1-E20, 1-80	1992		20p	£10.00
LT100	PGA Golf nos 81-180	1992		20p	£10.00
LT100	PGA Golf nos 181-280	1992		20p	£10.00
LT50	Petty Family Racing (Motor Racing)	1991		—	£7.00
LT100	Yo MTV Raps Musicards Nos 1-100	1991		—	£8.00
LT50	Yo MTV Raps Musicards Nos 101-150	1991		—	£6.00
LT95	The Young Indiana Jones Chronicles	1992		20p	£8.00
LT8	The Young Indiana Jones Chronicles Hidden				
	Treasures	1992		30p	£2.50
LT11	The Young Indiana Jones Chronicles 3-D	1992		20p	£2.50

PRO TRAC'S (USA)

LT100	Formula One Racing Series 1 Nos 1-100	1991		—	£15.00
LT100	Formula One Racing Series 1 Nos 101-200.............	1991		—	£15.00

PROMATCH

LT200	Premier League Footballers 1st Series	1996		—	£25.00
LT110	Premier League Footballers 2nd Series (10 numbers				
	unissued)	1997		—	£25.00
LT200	Premier League Footballers 3rd Series	1998		—	£18.00
LT198	Premier League Footballers 4th Series (number 163				
	not issued, 2 different number 162s)	1999		—	£18.00

PROPERT SHOE POLISH

25	British Uniforms	1955	HX-108	24p	£6.00

PUB PUBLICITY

M45	Inns of East Sussex	1975		20p	£9.00

PUBLICATIONS INT (USA)

M100	Micro Machines 1st Series (Cars, etc)...................	1989		—	£10.00
M100	Micro Machines 2nd Series (Cars, etc)	1989		—	£10.00

PUKKA TEA CO. LTD

50	Aquarium Fish	1960	HX-87	£1.00	£50.00

PURITY PRETZEL CO. (USA)

M56	US Air Force Planes, US Navy Planes, Ships of the				
	US Navy	c1930		£1.50	—

PYREX

EL16	The Pyrex Guide to Simple Cooking		1975		20p	£3.00

QUADRIGA

M126	Snooker Kings		1985		—	£20.00
	Album				—	£6.00

QUAKER OATS

EL12	Armour Through the Ages		1963		£1.25	£15.00
M4	Famous Puffers		1978		£5.00	—
M54	Historic Arms of Merry England		c1938		£1.50	—
EL8	Historic Ships		1965		£4.00	—
15	Honey Monster Crazy Games		1982		£1.50	—
M16	Jeremy's Animal Kingdom		1970		£1.50	—
L8	Legends of Batman		1995		£1.50	—
12	Monsters of the Deep		1984		£2.00	—
M6	Nature Trek		1976		50p	£3.00
EL12	Prehistoric Animals		1964		£5.00	—
EL12	Space Cards		1963	HQ-6	£5.00	—
EL12	Vintage Engines		1964		£5.00	—
	Package Issues:					
	Quaker Cards blue border issues:					
L36	British Landmarks		1961		£1.25	—
L36	Great Moments of Sport		1961		£3.00	—
L36	Household Hints		1961		£1.25	—
L36	Phiz Quiz		1961		£1.50	—
L36	Railways of the World		1961		£3.00	—
L36	The Story of Fashion		1961		£2.00	—
	Quaker Quiz Cards yellow border issues:					
M12	British Customs		1961		£1.50	—
M12	Famous Explorers		1961		£1.50	—
M12	Famous Inventors		1961		£2.00	—
M12	Famous Ships		1961		£2.00	—
M12	Famous Women		1961		£1.50	—
M12	Fascinating Costumes		1961		£1.25	—
M12	Great Feats of Building		1961		£1.25	—
M12	History of Flight		1961		£2.00	—
M12	Homes and Houses		1961		£1.25	—
M12	On the Seashore		1961		£1.50	—
M12	The Wild West		1961		£2.00	—
M12	Weapons & Armour		1961		£2.00	—
	Sugar Puffs Series (text back):					
12	Exploration & Adventure		1974		£1.50	—
12	National Maritime Museum		1974		£1.50	—
12	National Motor Museum		1974		£1.50	—
12	Royal Air Force Museum		1974		£1.50	—
12	Science & Invention		1974		£1.50	—

QUEENS

30	Kings and Queens of England		1955	HX-116	£1.20	£36.00

QUORN SPECIALITIES LTD

25	Fish and Game		1963		£6.00	—

RADIO FUN

20	British Sports Stars		1956		25p	£5.00

RADIO REVIEW

L36	Broadcasting Series		1935		£5.00	—
EL20	Broadcasting Stars		c1935	HR-3	£5.00	—

RAIL ENTHUSIAST

EL48	British Diesel and Electric Railway Engines		1984		—	£6.00

RAILWAY TAVERN

L12	Preserved British Locomotives		2000		—	£7.50
12	Steam Locomotives		1999		—	£10.00

RAINBO BREAD (USA)

LT33	Star Trek The Motion Picture		1979		—	£9.50

RAINBOW PRESS

L26	Grand Prix The Early Years (Cars)		1992		—	£12.50

RALEIGH BICYCLES

M48	Raleigh, The All Steel Bicycle		1957		£1.50	£75.00

RED AND GREEN

20	Football Heroes (1950s Footballers) 1st Series		2009		—	£9.00
20	Football Heroes (1950s Footballers) 2nd Series		2010		—	£7.50
20	Football Heroes (1950s Footballers) 3rd Series		2010		—	£7.50

RED HEART

EL6	Cats		1954	HR-7	—	£40.00
EL6	Dogs 1st Series		1955	HR-8.1	—	£40.00
EL6	Dogs 2nd Series		1955	HR-8.2	—	£40.00
EL6	Dogs 3rd Series		1956		—	£40.00

RED LETTER, RED STAR WEEKLY

L104	Fortune Cards		c1930	HR-11	£3.50	—
EL8	Good Luck Song Cards...		c1930		£3.00	—
	Midget Message Cards (Gravures):					
L6	A Green – Fragments From France (cartoons) ...		1915		£4.00	—
L26	B Brown – Rhymes letters of the alphabet...		c1930		£3.00	—
L6	C Brown – Pictures of woman, short verse beneath		1915		£3.00	—
L12	D Green – Dark green borders with small picture inset...		1915		£3.00	—
L12	E Green – White frameline inside fancy green border		1915		£3.00	—
L12	F Green – White borders		1915		£3.00	—
L12	G Light brown Set 1		1915	HR-13	£3.00	—
L12	H Light brown Set 2		1915	HR-13	£3.00	—
L12	Red Letter Message Cards		c1920		£3.20	—

RED ROSE RADIO

EL6	Disc Jockeys from Gold AM		1992		—	£4.00
EL5	Disc Jockeys from Rock FM		1992		—	£3.00

RED, WHITE & BLUE PRINT

15	Aston Villa European Champions 81/82		2010		—	£6.50

REDDINGS TEA COMPANY

25	Castles of Great Britain...	1965	HX-161	£2.20	£55.00
	Album			—	£25.00
25	Cathedrals of Great Britain	1965	HX-162	£2.20	£55.00
25	Heraldry of Famous Places	1966		£2.20	£55.00
48	Ships of the World	1963		20p	£7.50
25	Strange Customs of the World:				
	A Text back	1969		20p	£3.00
	B Advertisement back...	1969		£5.00	—
	Album			—	£25.00
24	Warriors of the World 1st Series...	1962		£2.00	£50.00
24	Warriors of the World 2nd Series	1962		£2.00	£50.00
	Album for 1st and 2nd Series combined			—	£20.00
24	Warriors of the World with Ships of the World fronts ...	1963		£7.00	—

REDDISH MAID CONFECTIONERY

K50	Famous International Aircraft	1963	HX-98	£3.00	—
K25	Famous International Athletes	1965		£8.00	—
25	International Footballers of Today	1966		£8.00	—

REDSKY

10	Audrey Hepburn	2011		—	£5.00
10	Ava Gardner	2012		—	£5.00
10	Brigitte Bardot	2011		—	£5.00
10	Claudia Cardinale	2011		—	£5.00
10	Doris Day	2011		—	£5.00
10	Elizabeth Taylor	2011		—	£5.00
10	Gene Tierney	2014		—	£5.00
10	Grace Kelly	2012		—	£5.00
10	Hedy Lamarr	2014		—	£5.00
10	Ingrid Bergman	2011		—	£5.00
10	Jane Russell	2012		—	£5.00
10	Jayne Mansfield	2011		—	£5.00
10	Joan Fontaine	2014		—	£5.00
10	Lauren Bacall	2011		—	£5.00
10	Leslie Caron	2014		—	£5.00
10	Olivia De Havilland	2014		—	£5.00
10	Rita Hayworth	2011		—	£5.00
10	Sophia Loren	2011		—	£5.00
10	Susan Hayward	2011		—	£5.00

REDSTONE (USA)

LT50	Dinosaurs	1993		20p	£8.00

REEVES LTD

25	Cricketers	1912		£32.00	—

REFLECTIONS

12	Nottingham Heritage/Poster	1996	—	£2.25
12	Nottingham Trams	2004/07	—	£2.25
4	Nottingham Trams	2008/10	—	£1.50
6	Nottinghamshire Towns 1st Series	1999	—	£1.50
4	Nottinghamshire Towns 2nd Series	2009	—	£1.50
6	Railways Around Nottingham	1996	—	£1.50
4	Rugby Union World Cup 2003	2003	—	£1.50
6	Sporting Occasions	2002	—	£1.50
6	St Pancras International (Railway Station)	2008	—	£1.50

REFLECTIONS (continued)

6	Steam Around Britain 1st Series Nos 1-6 (Railways) ...	1999		—	£1.50
6	Steam Around Britain 2nd Series Nos 7-12 (Railways)	2001		—	£1.50
6	Steam Around Britain 3rd Series Nos 13-18 (Railways)	2003		—	£1.50
6	Steam Around Britain 4th Series Nos 19-24 (Railways)	2005		—	£1.50
6	Steam Around Britain 5th Series Nos 25-30 (Railways)	2008		—	£1.50
6	Steam Around Britain 6th Series Nos 31-36 (Railways)..	2009		—	£1.50
6	Steam Around Britain 7th Series Nos. 37-42 (Railways)	2012		—	£1.50

REGENT OIL

L25	Do You Know?...	1964		20p	£3.00

REMLAP WORKS

50	Keep Fit Games and Exercise Ball Games 1st Series	c1930		£15.00	—
50	Keep Fit Games and Exercise Ball Games 2nd Series	c1930		£12.00	—

RICHARDS COLLECTION

25	Soccer Stars of Yesteryear 1st Series...	1995		—	£8.75
25	Soccer Stars of Yesteryear 2nd Series	1997		—	£8.75
25	Soccer Stars of Yesteryear 3rd Series...	1997		—	£8.75
25	Soccer Stars of Yesteryear 4th Series...	1998		—	£5.00
5	Soccer Stars of Yesteryear 5th Series...	2002		—	£2.50
20	Sporting Stars by Jos Walker (Cricketers)	1997		—	£5.00
21	Stars of the Past (Football)	1994		—	£8.75

RINGSIDE TRADING (USA)

LT80	Ringside Boxing	1996		—	£15.00

RINGTONS LTD (Tea)

25	Aircraft of World War II	1962	HX-7	£2.40	—
25	British Cavalry Uniforms of the 19th Century	1971	HX-43	£1.20	£30.00
25	Do You Know?...	1964	HX-166.4	20p	£3.00
25	Fruit of Trees and Shrubs	1963	HX-45	20p	£2.50
25	Head Dresses of the World	1973	HX-197	20p	£3.00
25	Historical Scenes	1964	HX-143	20p	£4.00
25	Old England	1964		20p	£3.00
25	People and Places	1964	HX-26	20p	£2.50
25	Regimental Uniforms of the Past	1966		24p	£6.00
25	Sailing Ships Through the Ages	1964	HX-119	24p	£6.00
25	Ships of the Royal Navy	1963		40p	£10.00
25	Sovereigns, Consorts and Rulers of Great Britain, 1st Series	1961	HX-201	32p	£8.00
25	Sovereigns, Consorts and Rulers of Great Britain, 2nd Series	1961	HX-201	32p	£8.00
25	Then and Now...	1970	HX-27	£1.20	—
25	Trains of the World	1970	HX-121	20p	£3.50
25	The West	1968	HX-42	20p	£5.00

RISCA TRAVEL AGENCY

25	Holiday Resorts	1966	HX-38	£1.00	£25.00

RITTENHOUSE ARCHIVES (USA)

LT72	Agents of S.H.I.E.L.D Season 1	2015		—	£9.50
LT81	Art and Images of Star Trek The Original Series	2005		—	£9.50
LT120	Babylon 5 The Complete Series...	2002		—	£16.00
LT72	Battlestar Galactica	2005		—	£9.50

RITTENHOUSE ARCHIVES (USA) (continued)

Size & quantity	Title	Date	Handbook reference	Price per card	Complete set
LT72	Battlestar Galactica Colonial Warriors	2005		−	£8.00
LT72	Battlestar Galactica The Complete Series	2004		−	£11.00
LT81	Battlestar Galactica Season 1	2006		−	£8.00
LT72	Battlestar Galactica Season 2	2007		−	£8.00
LT63	Battlestar Galactica Season 3	2008		−	£8.00
LT63	Battlestar Galactica Season 4	2009		−	£8.00
LT72	The Chronicles of Riddick	2004		−	£9.50
LT81	The Complete Avengers 1963-Present	2007		−	£12.00
LT72	Conan Art of The Hyborian Age	2004		−	£11.00
LT69	Continuum Seasons 1 & 2	2014		−	£8.00
LT50	D C Legacy	2007		−	£9.00
LT100	The Dead Zone	2004		−	£12.00
LT90	Die Another Day James Bond 007	2002		−	£15.00
LT100	The Fantasy Worlds of Irwin Allen	2003		−	£9.50
LT72	Farscape Season 1	2001		−	£9.50
LT72	Farscape Season 2	2001		−	£8.00
LT72	Farscape Season 3	2002		−	£9.50
LT72	Farscape Season 4	2003		−	£8.00
LT72	Farscape Through The Wormhole	2004		−	£8.00
LT72	Game of Thrones Season I	2012		−	£8.00
LT88	Game of Thrones Season 2	2013		−	£8.50
LT98	Game of Thrones Season 3	2014		−	£9.50
LT100	Game of Thrones Season 4	2015		−	£9.50
LT72	Hercules and Xena The Animated Adventures	2005		−	£9.50
LT120	Hercules The Legendary Journeys	2001		−	£9.50
LT72	Heroes Archives	2010		−	£8.00
LT126	Highlander The Complete Series	2003		20p	£18.00
LT72	The Hobbit The Desolation of Smaug	2015		−	£9.50
LT70	Iron Man The Film	2008		−	£8.00
LT66	James Bond 007 Archives	2009		−	£8.50
LT99	James Bond 007 Casino Royale	2014		−	£9.50
LT189	James Bond 007 The Complete Series	2007		−	£18.00
LT110	James Bond 007 Dangerous Liaisons	2006		−	£9.50
LT60	James Bond 007 40th Anniversary	2002		−	£18.00
LT19	James Bond 007 40th Anniversary − Bond Extras	2002		−	£10.00
LT19	James Bond 007 40th Anniversary − Bond Villains	2002		−	£12.00
LT99	James Bond 50th Anniversary Series 1 (only odd numbers issued)	2012		−	£9.50
LT99	James Bond 50th Anniversary Series 2 (only even numbers issued)	2012		−	£9.50
LT81	James Bond 007 Heroes and Villains	2010		−	£8.00
LT63	James Bond 007 In Motion (3-D)	2008		−	£9.50
LT66	James Bond 007 Mission Logs	2011		−	£8.00
LT90	James Bond 007 Quantum of Solace	2015		−	£9.50
LT100	James Bond 007 Quotable Series	2004		−	£9.50
LT110	James Bond 007 Skyfall	2013		−	£9.50
LT72	Lost Archives	2010		−	£8.00
LT108	Lost Seasons 1 Thru 5	2009		−	£9.50
LT90	Lost In Space (The Complete Series)	2005		−	£9.50
LT81	The Outer Limits Sex, Cyborgs & Science Fiction	2003		−	£8.00
LT81	Six Feet Under	2004		20p	£8.50
LT72	Six Million Dollar Man	2004		−	£9.50
LT72	Spiderman Archives	2009		−	£8.00
LT79	Spiderman III − The Film	2007		−	£8.00
LT100	Star Trek Aliens	2014		−	£9.50
LT90	Star Trek Celebrating 40 Years	2006		−	£9.50
LT189	Star Trek Deep Space Nine The Complete Series	2003		−	£18.00

RITTENHOUSE ARCHIVES (USA) (continued)

Size & quantity		Date	Handbook reference	Price per card	Complete set
LT108	Star Trek Deep Space Nine Quotable Series	2007		—	£9.50
LT81	Star Trek Enterprise Season I	2002		—	£12.00
LT81	Star Trek Enterprise Season 2	2003		—	£12.00
LT72	Star Trek Enterprise Season 3	2004		—	£9.50
LT72	Star Trek Enterprise Season 4	2005		—	£9.50
LT110	Star Trek Into Darkness	2014		—	£9.50
LT81	Star Trek Movie	2009		—	£8.00
LT60	Star Trek Movies In Motion (3-D)	2008		—	£15.00
LT90	Star Trek Movies The Complete Series	2007		—	£9.50
LT90	Star Trek Movies Quotable Series	2010		—	£8.00
LT72	Star Trek Nemesis	2002		20p	£9.50
LT90	Star Trek The Next Generation Complete Series 1 (1987-1991) (Nos 1 to 88, 177 & 178)	2011		—	£8.00
LT90	Star Trek The Next Generation Complete Series 2 (1991-1994) (Nos 89 to 176, 179 & 180)	2012		—	£9.50
LT100	Star Trek The Next Generation Heroes and Villains ...	2013		—	£9.50
LT110	Star Trek The Next Generation Quotable Series	2005		—	£9.50
LT110	Star Trek The Original Series Archives	2009		—	£9.50
LT80	Star Trek The Original Series Artwork by Juan Ortiz ...	2014		—	£8.50
LT110	Star Trek The Original Series 40th Anniversary 1st Series	2006		—	£9.50
LT110	Star Trek The Original Series 40th Anniversary 2nd Series	2008		—	£9.50
LT100	Star Trek The Original Series Heroes and Villains... ...	2013		—	£9.50
EL24	Star Trek The Original Series in Motion (3D)	1999		—	£20.00
LT110	Star Trek The Original Series Quotable	2004		—	£12.00
LT81	Star Trek The Remastered Original Series	2010		—	£8.00
LT183	Star Trek Voyager The Complete Series	2002		—	£18.00
LT72	Star Trek Voyager Quotable Series...	2012		—	£8.00
LT63	Stargate Atlantis Season 1	2005		—	£8.00
LT72	Stargate Atlantis Season 2	2006		—	£7.50
LT81	Stargate Atlantis Seasons 3 and 4	2008		—	£8.00
LT72	Stargate SG1 Season 1 to 3	2001		—	£9.50
LT72	Stargate SG1 Season 4	2002		—	£8.00
LT72	Stargate SG1 Season 5	2002		20p	£9.50
LT72	Stargate SG1 Season 6	2004		—	£9.50
LT3	Stargate SG1 Season 6 Checklist Corrected Cards ...	2004		—	£2.00
LT72	Stargate SG1 Season 7	2005		—	£8.00
LT81	Stargate SG1 Season 8	2006		—	£7.50
LT72	Stargate SG1 Season 9	2007		—	£7.50
LT72	Stargate SG1 Season 10	2008		—	£8.00
LT90	Stargate SG1 Heroes	2009		—	£8.50
LT72	Stargate Universe SG-U Season 1	2010		—	£8.00
LT98	Trueblood Seasons 1 to 4	2012		—	£9.50
LT72	Trueblood Archives Season 5 (Nos. 99 to 122 plus Character Profiles Nos. 1 to 48)	2013		—	£8.50
LT72	Twilight Zone 1st Series	1999		—	£9.50
LT72	Twilight Zone 2nd Series	2000		—	£9.50
LT8/9	Twilight Zone 2nd Series Challenge Game (Minus 'S')	2000		—	£2.50
LT72	Twilight Zone 3rd Series	2002		—	£9.50
LT72	Twilight Zone 4th Series	2005		—	£9.50
LT79	Twilight Zone 50th Anniversary...	2009		—	£8.50
LT81	Under the Dome Season 1	2014		—	£8.50
LT72	Warehouse 13	2010		—	£8.00
LT63	Women of James Bond in Motion (3-D)	2003		—	£20.00
LT81	The Women of Star Trek	2010		—	£8.00
EL32	Women of Star Trek in Motion (3-D)	1999		—	£25.00

Size & quantity		Date	Handbook reference	Price per card	Complete set

RITTENHOUSE ARCHIVES (USA) (continued)

LT70	Women of Star Trek Voyager Holofex Series	2001		—	£16.00
LT72	X-Men Origins Wolverine	2009		—	£9.50
LT72	X-Men The Last Stand	2006		—	£8.00
LT72	Xena Warrior Princess Season 4 and 5	2001		—	£9.50
LT72	Xena Warrior Princess Season 6	2001		—	£9.50
LT63	Xena Warrior Princess Art & Images	2004		—	£9.50
LT72	Xena Warrior Princess Beauty & Brawn (No 70 not issued)	2002		20p	£9.50
LT72	Xena Warrior Princess Dangerous Liaisons	2007		—	£9.50
LT135	Xena Warrior Princess Quotable Series	2003		—	£15.00
LT9	Xena Warrior Princess Quotable Series Words from the Bard	2003		—	£4.00

RIVER GROUP (USA)

LT150	Dark Dominion	1993		—	£12.00
LT150	Plasm O	1993		—	£12.00
LT31	Splatter Bowl	1993		—	£6.00

RIVER WYE PRODUCTIONS

LT81	D-Day Commemorative Series	2005		—	£25.00
LT72	Hammer Horror Behind The Screams	2004		—	£20.00
LT9	Laurel and Hardy Babes At War (Limited Edition)	2006		—	£12.00
LT90	Laurel & Hardy 70th Anniversary	1997		—	£20.00
LT72	Laurel & Hardy Millennium 2000 Celebration	2000		—	£18.00
LT72	Sherlock Holmes	2002		—	£25.00

THE 'RK' CONFECTIONERY CO. LTD

32	Felix	1922	HX-56	£40.00	—

ROB ROY

L20	Manchester United Footballers	1995		—	£15.00

ROBERTSON LTD (Jam)

1	Advertisement Gollies:				
	A Shaped figure	c1960		—	£4.00
	B Medium card 60 × 47mm	c1960		—	£4.00
10	Musical Gollies:		HR-26.2		
	A Shaped figure	c1960		£4.00	—
	B Medium card 60 × 47mm	c1960		£4.00	—
10	Sporting Gollies:		HR-26.3		
	A Shaped figure	c1960		£4.00	—
	B Medium card 60 × 47mm	c1960		£4.00	—

ROBERTSON & WOODCOCK LTD

50	British Aircraft Series	1930		£3.00	—

C. ROBINSON ARTWORKSHOP

L16	Plymouth Argyle FA Cup Squad 1983-84	1984		—	£8.00

ROBINSON'S BARLEY WATER

EL30	Sporting Records	1983		20p	£5.00

ROBINSON BROS. & MASTERS

25	Tea from the Garden to the House	c1930		£12.00	—

ROCHE & CO. LTD

K50	Famous Footballers	1927		—	£750.00
	49/50 (— No. 21)	1927		£12.00	—

THE ROCKET

MP11	Famous Knock-Outs	1923		£9.00	—

ROCKWELL

	Airship The Story of the R101:				
10	A Standard size	2003		—	£4.50
L10	B Large size	2003		—	£7.00
	Arsenal Goalscorers The Modern Era:				
10	A Standard size	2010		—	£4.50
L10	B Large size	2010		—	£7.00
	Bodyline — The Fight For The Ashes 1932-33:				
10	A Standard size	2005		—	£4.50
L10	B Large size	2005		—	£7.00
	Britain's Lost Railway Stations:				
10	A Standard size	2005		—	£4.50
L10	B Large size	2005		—	£7.00
	British Armoured Vehicles of World War II:				
10	A Standard size	2001		—	£4.50
L10	B Large size	2001		—	£7.00
	British Fighting Jets:				
10	A Standard size	2003		—	£4.50
L10	B Large size	2003		—	£7.00
	British Warplanes of the Second World War:				
10	A Standard size	2000		—	£4.50
L10	B Large size	2000		—	£7.00
10	Bygone Chingford	1998		—	£4.50
10	Bygone Highams Park	1998		—	£4.50
	Children's Book Illustrators of The Golden Age:				
10	A Standard size	2005		—	£4.50
L10	B Large size	2005		—	£7.00
L7	Classic Chelsea F.C.	2005		—	£5.00
L7	Classic Everton F.C.	2005		—	£5.00
	Classic Football Teams Before The First World War:				
10	A Standard size	2000		—	£4.50
L10	B Large size	2000		—	£7.00
	Classic Football Teams of the 1960s:				
10	A Standard size	1999		—	£4.50
L10	B Large size	1999		—	£7.00
	Classic Gunners (Arsenal F.C.):				
7	A Standard size	2010		—	£4.50
L7	B Large size	2001		—	£5.00
L7	Classic Hammers (West Ham United F.C.)	2003		—	£5.00
L7	Classic Liverpool F.C.	2005		—	£5.00
L7	Classic Reds (Manchester United F.C.)	2003		—	£5.00
	Classic Sci-Fi 'B' Movies:				
10	A Standard size	2007		—	£4.50
L10	B Large size	2007		—	£7.00
	Classic Spurs (Tottenham Hotspur F.C.):				
7	A Standard size	2010		—	£4.50
L7	B Large size	2002		—	£5.00
	Cunard In The 1950s:				
10	A Standard size	2003		—	£4.50
L10	B Large size	2003		—	£7.00

ROCKWELL (continued)

Early Allied Warplanes:

				Date	Price per card	Complete set
10	A	Standard size		2000	–	£4.50
L10	B	Large size (79 × 62mm)		2000	–	£7.00
LT10	C	Large size (89 × 64mm)		2000	–	£7.50

Early Balloon Flight:

| 10 | A | Standard size ... ... | 2001 | – | £4.50 |
| L10 | B | Large size ... ... | 2001 | – | £7.00 |

Early Locomotives Series One:

| 10 | A | Standard size ... ... | 2005 | – | £4.50 |
| L10 | B | Large size ... ... | 2005 | – | £7.00 |

Early Locomotives Series Two:

| 10 | A | Standard size ... ... | 2005 | – | £4.50 |
| L10 | B | Large size ... ... | 2005 | – | £7.00 |

Family Cars of the 1950s:

10	A	Standard size	2000	–	£4.50
L10	B	Large size (79 × 62mm)	2000	–	£7.00
LT10	C	Large size (89 × 64mm)	2000	–	£7.50

Flying So High – West Ham United F.C. 1964-66:

| 10 | A | Standard size ... ... | 2005 | – | £4.50 |
| L10 | B | Large size ... ... | 2005 | – | £7.00 |

German Armoured Vehicles of World War II:

10	A	Standard size	2001	–	£4.50
L10	B	Large size (79 × 62mm)	2001	–	£7.00
LT10	C	Large size (89 × 64mm)	2001	–	£7.50

German Warplanes of the Second World War:

10	A	Standard size	2000	–	£4.50
L10	B	Large size (79 × 62mm)	2000	–	£7.00
LT10	C	Large size (89 × 64mm)	2000	–	£7.50

The Great Heavyweights (Boxers):

| 10 | A | Standard size ... ... | 2002 | – | £4.50 |
| L10 | B | Large size ... ... | 2002 | – | £7.00 |

The Great Middleweights (Boxers):

| 10 | A | Standard size ... ... | 2002 | – | £4.50 |
| L10 | B | Large size ... ... | 2002 | – | £7.00 |

Heath Robinson At The Seaside:

| 10 | A | Standard size ... ... | 2010 | – | £4.50 |
| L10 | B | Large size ... ... | 2010 | – | £7.00 |

Heath Robinson Sporting Eccentricities:

| 10 | A | Standard size ... ... | 2010 | – | £4.50 |
| L10 | B | Large size ... ... | 2005 | – | £7.00 |

Heath Robinson Urban Life:

| 10 | A | Standard size ... ... | 2010 | – | £4.50 |
| L10 | B | Large size ... ... | 2005 | – | £7.00 |

The Hornby Book of Trains:

| 10 | A | Standard size ... ... | 2005 | – | £4.50 |
| L10 | B | Large size ... ... | 2005 | – | £7.00 |

Hurricane Flying Colours:

| 10 | A | Standard size ... ... | 2002 | – | £4.50 |
| L10 | B | Large size ... ... | 2002 | – | £7.00 |

Images of World War One:

10	A	Standard size	1999	–	£4.50
L10	B	Large size (79 × 62mm)	1999	–	£7.00
LT10	C	Large size (89 × 64mm)	1999	–	£7.50

Lost Warships of WWII:

| 10 | A | Standard size ... ... | 2002 | – | £4.50 |
| L10 | B | Large size ... ... | 2002 | – | £7.00 |

ROCKWELL (continued)

			Date	Price per card	Complete set
	Meccano The Aviation Covers:				
10	A	Standard size	2006	—	£4.50
L10	B	Large size	2006	—	£7.00
	Meccano The Railway Covers:				
10	A	Standard size	2006	—	£4.50
L10	B	Large size	2006	—	£7.00
	Mighty Atoms The All Time Greats (Boxers):				
10	A	Standard size	2004	—	£4.50
L10	B	Large size	2004	—	£7.00
	Modern Family Cars:				
15	A	Standard size	2001	—	£7.00
L15	B	Large size (79 × 62mm)	2001	—	£10.00
LT15	C	Large size (89 × 64mm)	2001	—	£11.00
	The 1948 Australians (Cricketers):				
10	A	Standard size	2006	—	£4.50
L10	B	Large size...	2006	—	£7.00
	Olympic, Titanic, Britannic (Liners):				
25	A	Standard size	2001	—	£9.50
L25	B	Large size	2001	—	£11.00
	Post War Wimbledon Ladies Champions 1st Series:				
10	A	Standard size	2004	—	£4.50
L10	B	Large size	2004	—	£7.00
	Post-War Wimbledon Ladies Champions 2nd Series:				
10	A	Standard size	2005	—	£4.50
L10	B	Large size	2005	—	£7.00
	Post War Wimbledon Men's Champions 1st Series:				
10	A	Standard size	2004	—	£4.50
L10	B	Large size	2004	—	£7.00
	Post-War Wimbledon Men's Champions 2nd Series:				
10	A	Standard size	2005	—	£4.50
L10	B	Large size	2005	—	£7.00
	Relegated to History England's Lost Football Grounds:				
10	A	Standard size	2004	—	£4.50
L10	B	Large size	2004	—	£7.00
	Solar System:				
10	A	Standard size	2001	—	£4.50
L10	B	Large size	2001	—	£7.00
	Spitfire Flying Colours:				
10	A	Standard size	1999	—	£4.50
L10	B	Large size (79 × 62mm)	1999	—	£7.00
LT10	C	Large size (89 × 64mm)	1999	—	£7.50
	Spurs Great Post-War Goalscorers Series 1 (Tottenham Hotspur F.C.):				
10	A	Standard size	2007	—	£4.50
L10	B	Large size	2007	—	£7.00
	Spurs Great Post-War Goalscorers Series 2 (Tottenham Hotspur F.C.):				
10	A	Standard size	2007	—	£4.50
L10	B	Large size	2007	—	£7.00
	Spurs 1960-1963 — The Glory Years (Tottenham Hotspur F.C.):				
10	A	Standard size	2005	—	£4.50
LT10	B	Large size	2005	—	£7.50
	Suffragettes:				
10	A	Standard size	2005	—	£4.50
L10	B	Large size	2005	—	£7.00

ROCKWELL (continued)

The Titanic Series:

			Date	Price per card	Complete set
25	A	Standard size	1999	—	£9.50
L25	B	Large size (79 × 62mm)	1999	—	£11.00
LT25	C	Large size (89 × 64mm)	1999	—	£15.00

Twopenny Tube Edwardian Sketches of The Central Railway:

10	A	Standard size	2010	—	£4.50
L10	B	Large size	2010	—	£7.00
L7		World Cup 1966	2005	—	£5.00

World War I Posters:

10	A	Standard size	2001	—	£4.50
L10	B	Large size	2001	—	£7.00

World War II Posters — The Home Front:

10	A	Standard size	2001	—	£4.50
L10	B	Large size	2001	—	£7.00

World War II Posters — Industry:

10	A	Standard size	2005	—	£4.50
L10	B	Large size	2007	—	£7.00

World War II Posters — Morale:

10	A	Standard size	2005	—	£4.50
L10	B	Large size	2007	—	£7.00

World War II Posters — The Services:

10	A	Standard size	2001	—	£4.50
L10	B	Large size	2001	—	£7.00

ROGERSTOCK

LT13	American Cars of the 1950s		2007	—	£6.50
LT13	American Cars of the 1960s		2007	—	£6.50
LT13	Ferrari — Classic Ferrari Models 1958-92		2007	—	£6.50
LT13	Jaguar — Classic Jaguar Models 1950-96		2007	—	£6.50

ROLLS-ROYCE MOTORS

			Date	Price per card	Complete set
L25	Bentley Motor Cars 1st Series:				
	A	Original Issue Thin frameline back	1985	£2.40	£60.00
	B	Inscribed 'Second Edition' thin frameline back	1987	£2.00	£50.00
L25	Bentley Motor Cars 2nd Series thick frameline to two sides		1987	£2.00	£50.00
L25	Rolls Royce Motor Cars 1st Series:				
	A	Original Issue Thin frameline back	1985	—	£60.00
	B	Inscribed 'Second Edition' thin frameline back	1987	£2.00	£50.00
L25	Rolls Royce Motor Cars 2nd Series thick frameline to two sides		1987	—	£50.00

ROSSI'S ICES

			Price per card	Complete set
M48	Flags of the Nations	1975	20p	£6.00
	Album		—	£15.00
25	History of Flight 1st Series	1966	60p	£15.00
25	History of Flight 2nd Series	1966	60p	£15.00
	Album for 1st and 2nd Series combined		—	£30.00
25	World's Fastest Aircraft	1966	60p	£15.00
	Album		—	£30.00

ROUND HOUSE

10	Sound of the Psychedelic 60s 1st Series	2014	—	£5.00
10	Sound of the 60s 1st Series (Pop Stars)	2013	—	£5.00

ROUND HOUSE (continued)

10	Sound of the 60s 2nd Series (Pop Stars)	2013		—	£5.00
10	Sound of the 60s 3rd Series (Pop Stars)	2014		—	£5.00
10	Sound of the 60s 4th Series (Pop Stars)	2014		—	£5.00
10	Sound of the 60s 5th Series (Pop Stars)	2014		—	£5.00
10	Sound of the 60s 6th Series (Pop Stars)	2014		—	£5.00
10	Sound of the 60s 7th Series (Pop Stars)	2014		—	£5.00
10	Sound of the 70s 1st Series (Pop Stars)	2014		—	£5.00
10	Sound of the 70s 2nd Series (Pop Stars)	2014		—	£5.00

D. ROWLAND

L20	Arsenal F.C. 2002-03	2004		—	£15.00
25	Association Footballers Series 1	1999		—	£12.50
25	Association Footballers Series 2	1999		50p	£12.50
25	Association Footballers Series 3	1999		—	£7.50
25	Association Footballers Series 4	1999		—	£7.50
25	Association Footballers Series 5	1999		30p	£7.50
20	Boxers Series 1	1999		—	£7.50
20	Boxing Legends Series 1	1999		—	£7.50
L20	Chelsea F.C. 2002-03	2004		—	£12.00
25	Cricketers Series 1	1999		30p	£7.50
25	Cricketers Series 2	1999		—	£7.50
20	Famous Footballers Series 1	1999		—	£6.00
20	Famous Footballers Series 2	1999		30p	£6.00
20	Famous Footballers Series 3	1999		50p	£10.00
20	Famous Footballers Series 4 (Managers)	1999		30p	£6.00
20	Famous Footballers Series 5	1999		—	£10.00
L10	Famous Footballers Series 6 (Teams)	2000		—	£5.00
L10	Famous Footballers Series 7 (Teams)	2000		—	£5.00
L20	Liverpool F.C. 2002-03	2004		—	£12.00
L20	Manchester City F.C. 2002-03	2004		—	£12.00
L20	Manchester United F.C. 2002-03	2004		—	£12.00
L20	Wolverhampton Wanderers F.C. 2002-03	2004		—	£12.00

ROWNTREE & CO.

25	Celebrities of 1900 Period	1900	HR-35	£30.00	—
M20	Merry Monarchs	1977		20p	£4.00
	The Old and the New:		HR-40		
25	A i Rowntree's Elect Chocolate (with coupon)	1912		£10.00	—
25	A ii Rowntree's Elect Chocolate (without coupon)	1912		£6.00	—
48	B i Rowntree's Elect Chocolate Delicious (with coupon)	1912		£10.00	—
48	B ii Rowntree's Elect Chocolate Delicious (without coupon)	1912		£6.00	—
M18	Prehistoric Animals	1978		30p	£5.00
M10	Texan Tall Tales of The West	1977		—	£20.00
120	Treasure Trove Pictures	c1930		£2.20	—
24	York Views:		HR-41		
	A Unicoloured	c1920		£15.00	—
	B Coloured	c1920		£15.00	—

ROYAL ARMY MEDICAL CORPS HISTORICAL MUSEUM

M16	Centenary Year Royal Army Medical Corps Victoria Crosses 1898-1998	1998		—	£6.00

ROYAL LEAMINGTON SPA

25	Royal Leamington Spa	1971		20p	£2.50
	Album			—	£4.00

ROYAL NATIONAL LIFEBOAT INSTITUTION

| M16 | Lifeboats... ... ... | 1979 | | 30p | £5.00 |

ROYAL NAVY SUBMARINE MUSEUM

| M25 | History of R.N. Submarines (including album) ... ... | 1996 | | — | £10.00 |

ROYAL SOCIETY FOR THE PREVENTION OF ACCIDENTS (RoSPA)

24	Modern British Cars	1953		£2.00	£50.00
22	Modern British Motor Cycles	1953		£3.60	—
25	New Traffic Signs...	1966		24p	£6.00
	Album			—	£18.00
24	Veteran Cars 1st Series	1955		£1.50	£36.00
24	Veteran Cars 2nd Series	1957		£2.00	£50.00
	Album			—	£20.00

ROY ROGERS BUBBLE GUM

| M24 | Roy Rogers — In Old Amarillo (plain back) ... ... | 1955 | | 25p | £6.00 |
| M24 | Roy Rogers — South of Caliente (plain back) ... ... | 1955 | | 25p | £6.00 |

RUBY

| L10 | Famous Beauties of the Day ... ... | 1923 | | £10.00 | — |
| L6 | Famous Film Stars ... ... | 1923 | | £10.00 | — |

RUBY CARDS

| 10 | A Tribute to Dad's Army ... ... | 2009 | | — | £5.00 |

RUGBY FOOTBALL UNION

| 50 | English Internationals 1980-1991 ... ... | 1991 | | — | £15.00 |

RUGLYS

L12	England Rugby Stars (Series Ref 1003)	2000		—	£6.00
L8	England Soccer Stars (Series Ref 1006)	2000		—	£4.00
L20	Manchester United Soccer Stars (Series Ref 1004) ...	2000		—	£10.00
L4	Shearer (Alan) Soccer Star (Series Ref 1005)	2000		—	£2.50
L8	Snooker Stars (Series Ref 1007)	2000		—	£4.00
L12	Wales Rugby Classics (Series Ref 1002)...	2000		—	£6.00
L20	Wales Rugby Stars (Series Ref 1001)...	2000		—	£10.00

S. & B. PRODUCTS

| ?69 | Torry Gillicks's Internationals ... ... | c1950 | | £10.00 | — |

S.C.M.C.C.

| 15 | Stoke's Finest Hour (1972 Football Cup Final) ... ... | 2002 | | — | £5.50 |

S.P.C.K.

L12	Bible Promises Illustrated, Series VIII	c1940		£2.00	—
L12	Cathedrals of Northern England, Series VII	c1940		£2.00	—
L12	Palestine, Series II	c1940		£2.00	—
L12	Scenes from English Church History, Series V	c1940		60p	£7.50
L12	Scenes from Genesis, Series XI...	c1940		£2.00	—
L12	Scenes from Lives of the Saints, Series VI	c1940		£1.00	£12.00
L12	Southern Cathedrals, Series XVI	c1940		£2.00	—
L12	Stories of Joseph and David, Series I	c1940		£2.00	—

SSPC (USA)

| LT45 | 200 Years of Freedom 1776-1976 ... ... | 1976 | | — | £7.50 |

SAINSBURY LTD

M12	British Birds............	1924		£8.00	—
M12	Foreign Birds	1924		£8.00	

SANDERS BROTHERS

25	Birds, Poultry, etc...	1924		£7.00	—
20	Dogs	1924		£4.00	£80.00
25	Recipes	1924		£4.40	—

SANDERSON

24	World's Most Beautiful Birds	c1925	HX-22	£10.00	—

SANITARIUM HEALTH FOOD CO. LTD (New Zealand)

EL12	Airliners of the 90's	1991		—	£6.00
EL12	Alpine Flora of New Zealand	1975		40p	£5.00
EL12	Alpine Sports	1986		35p	£4.00
EL12	Amazing Animals of the World	1985		60p	—
LT8	Amazing Facts...	1998		—	£4.00
M30	Another Look at New Zealand	1971		20p	£4.50
M30	Antarctic Adventure	1972		30p	—
M20	The Aviation Card Series	1995		—	£3.50
LT16	Babe & Friends — The Film	1999		—	£4.00
EL12	Ball Sports	1989		50p	£6.00
M4	Bee — 3D Motion Cards	1998		—	£2.50
EL12	Big Cats	1992		—	£4.50
M20	Big Rigs	1983		20p	£3.50
M20	Big Rigs at Work	1986		20p	£3.50
M20	Big Rigs 3	1992		—	£3.00
EL12	Big Sea Creatures	1994		35p	£4.00
L12	Boarding Pass (Landmarks Around the World)	1998		—	£5.00
EL12	Bush Birds of New Zealand	1981		50p	—
M20	Cars of the Seventies	1976		30p	£6.00
LT20	Centenaryville	1999		—	£4.00
EL12	Clocks Through the Ages	1990		40p	£5.00
M20	Conservation Caring for Our Land	1974		25p	£5.00
EL12	Curious Conveyances	1984		40p	£5.00
EL12	Did You Know	1994		35p	£4.00
M4	Discount Destination Passport	1991		—	£4.00
M20	Discover Indonesia	1977		20p	£3.00
M20	Discover Science With the DSIR	1989		20p	£3.00
EL12	Discovering New Zealand Reptile World	1983		35p	£4.00
M20	Exotic Cars	1987		25p	£5.00
M20	Exploring Our Solar System	1982		25p	—
M24	Famous New Zealanders	1971		25p	£6.00
M20	Farewell to Steam	1981		30p	£6.00
M30	Fascinating Orient	1966		20p	£4.00
EL12	Focus on New Zealand 1st Series	1982		35p	£4.00
EL12	Focus on New Zealand 2nd Series...	1982		35p	£4.00
LT12	Have You Had Your Weet-Bix (Sports)	1997		—	£4.00
EL12	High Action Sports	1994		35p	£4.00
EL12	Historic Buildings 1st Series	1982		50p	£6.00
EL12	Historic Buildings 2nd Series	1984		35p	£4.00
M30	The History of New Zealand Railways...	1968		50p	—
M20	History of Road Transport in New Zealand	1979		25p	£5.00
EL12	Horse Breeds	1990		40p	£5.00
LT15	Hunchback of Notre Dame (Disney)	1996		—	£5.00
EL10	Hunchback of Notre Dame (Disney)	1996		—	£4.50

SANITARIUM HEALTH FOOD CO. LTD (New Zealand) (continued)

Size & quantity	Title	Date	Price per card	Complete set
LT8	It's Showtime (Disney)	1997	—	£4.00
EL12	Jet Aircraft	1974	60p	—
M20	Kiwi Heroes	1994	20p	£3.00
LT9	Kiwi Kids Tryathlon	1999	—	£4.00
M20	Kiwis Going for Gold	1992	—	£3.00
EL12	The Lion King (Disney)	1995	—	£4.00
M20	Living in Space	1992	—	£3.00
M20	Looking at Canada	1978	20p	£3.00
M20	Mammals of the Seas	1985	20p	£3.00
EL12	Man Made Wonders of the World	1987	35p	£4.00
M20	The Many Stranded Web of Nature	1983	25p	£6.00
M30	Marineland Wonders	1967	50p	£15.00
M20	Motor Bike Card Series	1995	—	£5.00
EL12	Mountaineering	1987	35p	£4.00
LT10	Mr Men	1997	40p	£4.00
M25	National Costumes of the Old World	1968	50p	£12.50
M20	New Zealand's Booming Industries	1975	20p	£3.00
EL12	New Zealand Custom Vans	1994	—	£4.00
EL12	New Zealand Disasters	1991	35p	£4.00
M20	N.Z. Energy Resources	1976	20p	£3.50
EL12	New Zealand Inventions and Discoveries	1991	35p	£4.00
EL12	New Zealand Lakes 1st Series	1977	60p	—
EL12	New Zealand Lakes 2nd Series	1978	35p	£4.00
M30	New Zealand National Parks	1973	33p	£10.00
M20	New Zealand Reef Fish	1984	20p	£3.00
M20	New Zealand Rod & Custom Cars	1979	25p	£5.00
M20	New Zealand Summer Sports	1984	20p	£3.50
M30	New Zealand Today	1966	25p	£7.50
EL12	New Zealand Waterfalls	1981	50p	—
M20	New Zealanders in Antarctica	1987	25p	£5.00
M20	New Zealanders on Top of the World	1991	20p	£3.00
EL12	N.Z.R. Steam Engines	1976	—	£12.00
M20	The 1990 Commonwealth Games	1989	20p	£4.00
M20	1990 Look How We've Grown	1990	20p	£3.00
EL12	Ocean Racers	1986	35p	£4.00
M20	100 Years of New Zealand National Parks	1987	20p	£3.00
EL12	Our Fascinating Fungi	1980	50p	—
M20	Our Golden Fleece	1981	20p	£3.00
M20	Our South Pacific Island Neighbours	1974	25p	£5.00
M20	Our Weather	1980	20p	£3.00
EL12	Party Tricks	1993	—	£4.00
M20	Peanuts (Cartoon Characters)	1993	50p	—
M20	The Phonecard Collection	1994	—	£3.00
EL12	Power Boats in New Zealand	1990	35p	£4.00
EL12	Robin Hood (Disney)	1996	—	£4.00
M20	Saving the World's Endangered Wildlife	1991	20p	£3.00
EL12	Shipping in Our Coastal Waters	1988	50p	£6.00
EL12	Silly Dinosaurs	1997	—	£4.00
M8	Snow White & the Seven Dwarfs (3-D)	1997	—	£4.00
EL12	Spanning New Zealand	1992	—	£4.00
M20	Spectacular Sports	1974	25p	£5.00
LT12	Speed	1998	—	£4.00
M20	The Story of New Zealand Aviation	1977	25p	£5.00
M20	The Story of New Zealand in Stamps	1977	25p	£5.00
M20	Super Cars	1972	50p	£10.00
EL12	Surf Life Saving	1986	35p	£4.00
LT12	Then & Now	1998	—	£4.00

SANITARIUM HEALTH FOOD CO. LTD (New Zealand) (continued)

M20	Timeless Japan	1975		25p	£5.00
M20	Treasury of Maori Life	1980		20p	£3.00
EL12	Veteran Cars	1971		50p	—
M20	Vintage Cars	1973		40p	£8.00
M20	Weet-bix Stamp Album (Stamp Collecting)	1994		30p	£6.00
M30	What Makes New Zealand Different	1967		60p	£18.00
EL12	Wild Flowers of New Zealand	1979		50p	£6.00
EL12	Wildlife Wonders — Endangered Animals of NZ	1993		—	£4.00
M20	The Wild South	1986		20p	£3.00
EL12	Windsports	1989		35p	£4.00
M20	Wonderful Ways of Nature	1978		20p	£3.00
EL12	Wonderful Wool	1988		50p	—
M20	The Wonderful World of Disney	1993		30p	£6.00
LT17	World Ball (Basketball)	1997		—	£4.00
M20	World's Greatest Fun Parks	1990		20p	£4.00
M20	Your Journey Through Disneyland	1988		35p	£7.00

SAVOY PRODUCTS

M56	Aerial Navigation	c1925		£2.50	—
M56	Aerial Navigation Series B	c1925		£2.25	—
M56	Aerial Navigation, Series C	c1925		£2.25	—
M56	Famous British Boats	1928		£2.00	—

SCANLEN (Australia)

M208	Cricket Series No. 3	1984		—	£30.00
L84	Cricketers 1989/90	1989		—	£20.00
L84	Cricketers 1990/91	1990		—	£20.00
L90	World Series Cricket	1981		—	£20.00

SCHOOL & SPORT

M4	British Railway Engines	1922	HS-135.1	£7.00	—
M4	British Regiments	1922	HS-135.2	£7.00	—
M4	County Cricket Captains	1922	HS-135.3	£15.00	—
M4	Wild Animals	1922	HS-135.4	£7.00	—

THE SCHOOL FRIEND

LP6	Famous Film Stars	1927	HS-8	£10.00	—
EL10	Popular Girls of Cliff House School	1922		£10.00	—
L6	Popular Pictures	1923	HS-9	£4.00	—

THE SCHOOL GIRL

M12	Zoological Studies	1923	HS-21	£3.00	—
M4	Zoological Studies (anonymous)	1923	HS-21	£3.00	—

THE SCHOOLGIRLS OWN PAPER

L3	Royal Family Portraits (anonymous)	c1925		£4.00	—

THE SCHOOLGIRLS' WEEKLY

L1	HRH The Duke of York	1922		—	£6.00
L4	Popular Pictures	1922	HS-17	£4.00	—

SCORE (USA)

LT704	Baseball	1990		—	£30.00
LT47	Dallas Cowboys Cheerleaders	1993		—	£12.00
LT110	1991 NHL Rookie and Traded (Ice Hockey)	1991		—	£6.00

SCORE CARD COLLECTABLES

10	Score (Footballers of the 1970s) 1st Series	2011		—	£5.00
10	Score (Footballers of the 1970s) 2nd Series	2011		—	£5.00

SCOTTISH DAILY EXPRESS

EL24	Scotcard — Scottish Footballers	1973		£7.00	—

SCOTTISH TOURIST BOARD

L40	Places of Interest	1992		20p	£4.00

THE SCOUT

M9	Birds Eggs	1925		£7.00	—
M12	Railway Engines	1924		£7.00	—

SCRAPBOOK MINICARDS

27	Pendon Museum (model railway and village)	1978		20p	£3.00

SCREEN ICONS

10	Cary Grant	2013		—	£5.00
10	Frankie Howerd	2013		—	£5.00
10	Gregory Peck	2013		—	£5.00
10	Paul Newman	2013		—	£5.00
10	Robert Redford	2013		—	£5.00
10	Steve McQueen	2013		—	£5.00

SEAGRAM

25	Grand National Winners	1995		—	£20.00

SECRETS

K52	Film Stars Miniature Playing Cards	c1930	HS-26	£1.70	—

SELF SERVICE LAUNDERETTES

50	150 Years of Locomotives	1955	HX-178	£5.00	—

SELLOTAPE PRODUCTS LTD

35	Great Homes and Castles	1974		50p	£17.50

SEMIC

LT275	Equestrianism	1997		—	£18.00

SEW & SEW

25	Bandsmen of the British Army	1960	HX-62	£2.20	—

A.J. SEWARD & CO. LTD

40	Stars of the Screen	1935		£11.00	—

SEYMOUR MEAD & CO. LTD (Tea)

24	The Island of Ceylon	1961	HX-47	20p	£2.50

SHARMAN NEWSPAPERS

L24	Golden Age of Flying	1979		40p	£10.00
	Album			—	£3.00
L24	Golden Age of Motoring	1979		40p	£10.00
	Album			—	£3.00

SHARMAN NEWSPAPERS (continued)

L24	Golden Age of Steam	1979		40p	£10.00
	Album			—	£3.00

EDWARD SHARP & SONS

20	Captain Scarlet	c1970		£8.00	—
25	Hey Presto!...	1968		20p	£2.50
100	Prize Dogs	c1925		£6.00	—

T. SHELDON COLLECTIBLES

L18	Central Lancashire Cricket League Clubs and Pavilions	1997		—	£7.00
20	The Don (Reproductions of Don Bradman Cricket Cards) 2nd Series...	2010		—	£10.00
10	Famous Old Standians	2002		40p	£4.00
20	Fryer's Roses	1999		—	£10.00
20	Kenyan Cricket I.C.C. World Cup	1999		40p	£8.00
L6	Mailey Master of His Art (Cricketers)	2003		—	£4.00
L10	Match of The Day Aldershot Town v Accrington Stanley (10.8.03)	2004		—	£4.00
L10	Match of The Day Cwmbran Town v Maccabi Haifa (14.8.03)	2004		—	£4.00
L10	Match of The Day Rochdale v Yeovil Town (9.8.03) ...	2003		—	£4.00
20	Olden Goldies (Cricketers)	1998		—	£10.00
L18	Out of the Blue into the Red (Labour Politicians)	1997		40p	£7.00
18	Prominent Cricketers 1924 (reprint, G. Goode, Australia)...	1999		—	£9.50
20	Stalybridge Celtic Football Club	1996		—	£4.50
L18	We're Back Halifax Town A.F.C. 1998/99	1999		—	£7.00

SHELL (Oil)

14	Bateman Series	1930		£8.00	—
EL20	Great Britons	1972	HS-34	£1.50	£30.00
	Album			—	£20.00
16	History of Flight (metal coins)...	1970	HS-35	£1.50	—
M12	Olympic Greats including album	1992		—	£7.00
M16	3-D Animals	1971	HS-37	£1.50	—
M16	Wonders of the World	c1975		£1.50	—

SHELL (Oil) (Australia)

M60	Beetle Series (Nd 301-360)	1962		60p	£36.00
M60	Birds (Nd 121-180)	1960		60p	—
M60	Butterflies & Moths (Nd 181-240)	1960		70p	—
M60	Citizenship (Nd 1-60)	1964		40p	£24.00
M60	Discover Australia with Shell (Nd 1-60)	1959		60p	—
M60	Meteorology (Nd 361-420)...	1963		40p	£24.00
M60	Pets (Nd 481-540)	1965		50p	£30.00
M60	Shells, Fish and Coral (Nd 61-120)...	1959		50p	—
M60	Transportation (Nd 241-300)	1961		40p	£24.00

SHELL (Oil) (New Zealand)

M48	Aircraft of the World	1963		—	£20.00
M60	Cars of the World...	1964		50p	£30.00
M40	Cars of the World...	1992		—	£7.00
M20	The Flintstones (Film)	1994		40p	£8.00
M48	Racing Cars of the World	1964		—	£30.00

SHELL (Oil) (New Zealand) (continued)

M37	Rugby Greats (The All Blacks)	1992		—	£12.00
M40	World of Cricket	1992		30p	£12.00

SHELLEY'S ICE CREAM

25	Essex — County Champions (cricket)	1984		—	£9.00

SHEPHERDS DAIRIES

100	Shepherds War Series	1915	HX-200	£10.00	—

SHERIDAN COLLECTIBLES

LT12	Bobby Jones at St Andrews (Golf)	1995		—	£6.50
LT12	The Bobby Jones Story (Golfer)	1993		—	£6.50
L6	Golf Adventures of Par Bear	1994		—	£3.00
LT25	Players of the Ryder Cup '93 (Golf)	1994		—	£10.00
L7	Railway Posters — Golf	1996		—	£2.50
LT12	The Tom Morris Story (Golfer)	1994		—	£6.50
L7	Underground Art — Football & Wembley	1996		—	£2.50
L7	Underground Art — Rugby	1996		—	£2.50
L7	Underground Art — Wimbledon (Tennis)	1996		—	£2.50
L7	Underground Art — Windsor	1996		—	£2.50
L12	Winners of the Ryder Cup 95	1996		—	£6.50

SHERMAN'S POOLS LTD

EL8	Famous Film Stars	1940	HS-39	75p	£6.00
EL38	Searchlight on Famous Players	1937	HS-40	£5.50	—
EL37	Searchlight on Famous Teams (Football):		HS-41		
	A 35 different	1938		£5.00	—
	B Aston Villa and Blackpool	1938		75p	£1.50

W. SHIPTON LTD

Trojan Gen-Cards Series 1:

5	Group 1 Famous Buildings	1959		£1.00	—
5	Group 2 Characters of Fiction	1959		£1.00	—
5	Group 3 Stars of Entertainment	1959		£1.00	—
5	Group 4 Fight Against Crime	1959		£1.00	—
5	Group 5 Prehistoric Monsters	1959		£1.00	—
5	Group 6 Railways	1959		£1.00	—
5	Group 7 Racing Cars	1959		£1.00	—
5	Group 8 Insect World	1959		£1.00	—
5	Group 9 Stars of Sport	1959		£1.00	—
5	Group 10 Animal World	1959		£1.00	—
5	Group 11 Nursing	1959		£1.00	—
5	Group 12 Under the Sea	1959		£1.00	—
5	Group 13 Ballet	1959		£1.00	—
5	Group 14 Wild West	1959		£1.00	—
5	Group 15 Motor Cars	1959		£1.00	—

SIDELINES

M23	19th Century Cricket Teams	1987		20p	£4.00

SILVER KING & CO

1	Advertisement Card	1905		—	£15.00

SILVER SHRED

6	British Medals	c1920	HR-25	£20.00	—

SKETCHLEY CLEANERS

25	Communications	1960		30p	£7.50
25	Nature Series	1960	HX-148	36p	£9.00
25	Tropical Birds	1960	HX-13.2	60p	£15.00

SKYBOX (USA)

LT90	The Adventures of Batman & Robin (Cartoon)	1995	—	£9.50
LT60	Babylon 5	1996	—	£10.00
EL10	Babylon 5 Posters	1996	—	£6.00
LT100	Babylon 5 Profiles	1999	—	£9.50
LT81	Babylon 5 Season Four	1998	—	£9.50
LT81	Babylon 5 Season Five	1998	—	£9.50
LT72	Babylon 5 Special Edition	1997	—	£9.50
EL72	Batman & Robin the Film	1997	—	£12.00
EL24	Batman & Robin Storyboards	1997	—	£12.00
LT90	Batman Master Series (Cartoon)	1995	—	£9.50
LT100	Batman Saga of The Dark Knight	1994	—	£12.00
LT94	Bill Nye The Science Guy	1995	—	£8.50
LT90	Blue Chips (Basketball Film)	1994	—	£8.00
LT90	Cinderella — Walt Disney Film	1996	—	£9.50
LT45	D.C. Comics Stars	1994	—	£7.50
EL90	D.C. Comics Vertigo	1994	—	£9.50
LT100	D.C. Milestone (Comic Book Story)	1993	—	£8,00
LT100	Demolition Man — The Film	1993	—	£9.50
LT90	Disney's Aladdin	1993	—	£9.50
LT90	Free Willy 2 — The Film	1995	—	£8.00
LT75	Gargoyles Series 2	1996	—	£9.50
LT90	Harley Davidson Motor Cycles	1994	—	£9.50
LT101	Hunchback of Notre Dame — Disney Film	1996	—	£9.50
LT90	Jumanji — The Film	1995	—	£9.50
LT90	The Lion King 1st Series — Walt Disney Film	1995	—	£9.50
LT80	The Lion King 2nd Series — Walt Disney Film	1995	—	£9.50
LT90	Lois & Clark — New Adventures of Superman	1995	—	£9.50
LT100	The Making of Star Trek The Next Generation	1994	—	£12.00
LT90	Mortal Kombat The Film	1995	—	£9.50
LT101	101 Dalmations — The Movie	1996	—	£9.50
LT90	The Pagemaster (Film)	1994	—	£12.50
LT102	Pocahontas (Disney film)	1997	—	£9.50
LT100	The Return of Superman	1993	—	£8.50
LT100	Sea Quest DSV	1993	—	£12.00
LT90	Snow White and the Seven Dwarfs	1994	—	£12.50
LT100	Star Trek Cinema 2000	2000	—	£12.00
LT48	Star Trek Deep Space Nine	1993	—	£9.50
LT100	Star Trek Deep Space Nine	1993	—	£15.00
LT100	Star Trek Deep Space Nine Memories From the Future	1999	—	£9.50
LT82	Star Trek Deep Space Nine Profiles	1997	—	£9.50
EL60	Star Trek — First Contact	1996	—	£10.00
EL72	Star Trek — Generations	1994	—	£15.00
EL72	Star Trek — Insurrection	1998	—	£13.00
LT90	Star Trek Master Series 1st Series	1993	—	£13.50
LT100	Star Trek Master Series 2nd Series	1994	—	£12.00
LT39	Star Trek The Next Generation Behind the Scenes	1993	—	£9.50
LT82	Star Trek The Next Generation Profiles	2000	—	£12.00
LT96	Star Trek The Next Generation Season Two	1995	—	£9.50
LT108	Star Trek The Next Generation Season Three	1995	—	£9.50
LT108	Star Trek The Next Generation Season Four	1996	—	£9.50
LT108	Star Trek The Next Generation Season Five	1996	—	£9.50

SKYBOX (USA) (continued)

Size & quantity		Date	Handbook reference	Price per card	Complete set
LT6	Star Trek The Next Generation Season Five foil embossed	1996		—	£24.00
LT108	Star Trek The Next Generation Season Six	1997		—	£9.50
LT103	Star Trek The Next Generation Season Seven	1999		—	£12.00
LT90	Star Trek The Original Series, Series One	1997		—	£9.50
LT81	Star Trek The Original Series, Series Two	1998		—	£9.50
LT75	Star Trek The Original Series, Series Three	1999		—	£15.00
LT12/13	Star Trek The Original Series, Series Three Challenge Game (minus Letter C)	1999		—	£5.00
LT58	Star Trek The Original Series Character Log, 1st Series	1997		—	£9.50
LT52	Star Trek The Original Series Character Log, 2nd Series	1998		—	£9.50
LT48	Star Trek The Original Series Character Log, 3rd Series	1999		—	£12.00
LT100	Star Trek 30 Years Phase One	1995		—	£12.00
LT100	Star Trek 30 Years Phase Two	1996		—	£15.00
LT100	Star Trek 30 Years Phase Three	1996		—	£12.00
LT100	Star Trek Voyager — Closer to Home	1999		—	£13.00
LT90	Star Trek Voyager Profiles	1998		—	£14.00
LT98	Star Trek Voyager Season One, Series 1	1995		—	£9.50
LT90	Star Trek Voyager Season One, Series 2	1995		—	£9.50
LT100	Star Trek Voyager Season Two	1996		—	£9.50
LT3	Star Trek Voyager Season Two Xenobio	1997		—	£9.00
EL90	Superman Platinum Series	1994		—	£12.00
LT90	The Three Musketeers — The Movie	1997		—	£9.50
LT98	Toy Story — The Film	1996		—	£9.50
LT74	Toy Story 2 — The Film	1996		—	£9.50
LT100	Ultraverse	1993		—	£9.50
LT81	Wild Wild West — The Movie	1999		—	£9.50

SKYFOTOS LTD

48	Merchant Ships	c1965	HS-53	£2.50	—

SLADE & BULLOCK LTD

25	Cricket Series	c1925		£60.00	—
25	Football Terms	c1925		£30.00	—
	Modern Inventions:				
25	A Front light and dark blue	c1925		£12.00	—
25	B Front yellow and purple	c1925		£15.00	—
20	Now and Then Series	c1925		£15.00	—
25	Nursery Rhymes	c1925		£15.00	—
25	Science and Skill Series	c1925		£15.00	—
25	Simple Toys and How to Make Them	c1925		£15.00	—
24	World's Most Beautiful Butterflies	c1925	HX-23	£10.00	—

SLOAN & GRAHAM

L20	Magnificent Magpies 92/93 squad (Newcastle FC)	1993		—	£6.00
L5	Magnificent Magpies 92-93 2nd Series (Newcastle F.C.)	1993		—	£4.00
25	Newcastle All Time Greats (Football)	1993		—	£6.00
L2	Newcastle Footballers (Keegan/Beardsley) Plain back	1993		—	£2.00
L12	Sunderland All Time Greats (Football)	1993		—	£6.00
L14	Sunderland Legends of '73 (Football)	1993		—	£6.00

P. SLUIS

EL30	Tropical Birds	1962	HS-54	£1.00	£30.00

SMART NOVELS

MP12	Stage Artistes and Entertainers	c1925	HS-58	£5.00	—

SNAP CARDS PRODUCTS LTD

L50	ATV Stars 1st Series	1958		£3.00	—
L48	ATV Stars 2nd Series	1960		£2.20	£110.00
L50	Associated Rediffusion Stars	1960		£3.00	£150.00
L25	Dotto (Celebrities) (photo)	1959		£2.00	—
L25	Dotto (Celebrities) (sketches)...	1959		£2.00	—

H.A. SNOW

12	Hunting Big Game in Africa	c1920	HU-5	£7.00	—

SOCCER BUBBLE GUM

L48	Soccer Teams, No. 1 Series	1957		£2.50	—
L48	Soccer Teams, No. 2 Series	1958		£3.50	—

SOCCER STAR CARDS

20	Soccer Star 1st Series	2010		—	£7.50
20	Soccer Star 2nd Series	2010		—	£7.50
20	Soccer Star 3rd Series...	2010		—	£7.50
20	Soccer Star 4th Series...	2010		—	£7.50

SODASTREAM

25	Historical Buildings	1957	HX-72	20p	£5.00

SOLDIER MAGAZINE

M24	The British Army	1993		—	£5.00

SOMPORTEX LTD

L50	The Exciting World of James Bond 007	1965		£7.50	—
L60	Famous TV Wrestlers	1964		£4.00	—
L60	Film Scene Series James Bond 007	1964		£7.00	—
L72	John Drake — Danger Man	1966		£6.50	—
L72	The Saint	1967		£7.00	—
L26	Sean Connery as James Bond (You Only Live Twice) (real colour film, issued in strips of 3)	1967		£11.00	—
L72	Thunderball James Bond 007:		HS-65		
	A Complete set	1966		—	£330.00
	B 71 different (minus No. 24)	1966		£4.00	£280.00
L73	Thunderbirds (coloured)	1966		£7.50	—
L72	Thunderbirds (black and white):				
	A Size 90 × 64mm	1966		£3.50	—
	B Size 77 × 57mm	1966		£6.00	—
L36	Weirdies	1968	HS-66	£1.50	—

SONNY BOY

50	Railway Engines:				
	A White back...	c1960		20p	£8.00
	B Cream back	c1960		20p	£8.00

SOUTH WALES CONSTABULARY

EL36	British Stamps	1983		—	£12.00
EL36	Castles and Historic Places in Wales	1988		33p	£12.00
EL36	City of Cardiff	1989		60p	—
EL35	The '82 Squad (rugby union)	1982		£1.25	—
EL36	Merthyr Tydfil Borough Council	1987		—	£12.00
EL37	Payphones Past and Present	1987		70p	£25.00
EL36	Rhymney Valley District Council	1986		—	£12.00
EL20	South Wales Constabulary	1990		—	£10.00
M32	Sport-a-Card	1991		—	£16.00

SOUTH WALES ECHO

L36	Cardiff City Legends (Footballers)	2003		—	£7.50
50	Great Welsh Rugby Players	1992		—	£7.50

SPACE VENTURES (USA)

LT37	Moon Mars Space Shots (embossed)	1991		—	£10.00
LT110	Space Shots 1st Series	1990		—	£16.00
LT110	Space Shots 2nd Series	1991		—	£9.50
LT110	Space Shots 3rd Series	1992		—	£12.00

SPAR GROCERS

EL30	Walt Disney	1972	HS-67	£2.00	£60.00

SPILLERS NEPHEWS

25	Conundrum Series	c1910		£22.00	—
40	Views of South Wales and District	c1910		£22.00	—

SPOOKTASTIC CARDS

10	Karloff (Boris Karloff Tribute to the Horror Legend)	2010		—	£5.00

SPORT AND ADVENTURE

M46	Famous Footballers	1922		£4.50	—

SPORT IN PRINT

M64	Nottinghamshire Cricketers	1989		—	£35.00

SPORT IN VIEW

25	Pro's and Poetry 1920s Football and Cricket	2012		—	£7.00
	The Sporting Art of Amos Ramsbottom from 1900s:				
L16	Set 1 Football and Rugby	2012		—	£6.00
EL10	Set 2 Football	2012		—	£6.00
EL10	Set 3 Cricket	2012		—	£6.00
EL6	Set 4 Lancashire League Cricket	2012		—	£5.00
EL7	Set 5 Rugby Union	2012		—	£5.00
EL6	Set 6 Rugby League	2012		—	£5.00
EL5	Set 7 General Sport	2012		—	£4.50

P. J. SPORTING

L10	International Cricketers	2001		—	£8.00

SPORTING PROFILES

L8	Arsenal F.C. F.A. Cup Winners 1930 Programme Covers	2006		—	£5.00
L9	Arsenal F.C. F.A. Cup Winners 1971 Programme Covers	2006		—	£5.00

SPORTING PROFILES (continued)

		Date	Handbook reference	Price per card	Complete set
L13	Ashes Set Match Action — Cricketers...............	2005		—	£6.50
L5	Ashes Set Match Action — Cricket Bonus Set				
	Programme Covers..	2005		—	£3.50
L10	Aston Villa F.C. European Cup Winners 1982				
	Programme Covers	2006		—	£6.00
L15	Ayrton Senna 1960-1994	2005		—	£6.50
L12	The Beatles Magazine Covers	2006		—	£6.00
L20	Bob Dylan Concert Posters	2009		—	£7.50
L15	Bon Jovi Concert Posters	2014		—	£6.50
15	Boxing Greats	2003		—	£5.00
L15	Bruce Lee Film Posters	2005		—	£6.50
L15	Bruce Springsteen Concert Posters	2009		—	£6.50
L20	Cardiff City F.C. European Adventure 1964-70				
	Programme Covers	2005		—	£7.50
L20	Carry On Up The Card Set (Carry On Film Stars).........	2005		—	£9.00
L16	Cassius Clay The Early Years	2002		—	£9.00
L10	Celtic F.C. 1967 European Cup Winners Programme				
	Covers	2004		—	£6.50
L20	Charles Buchan's Football Monthly Magazine Covers	2004		—	£9.50
L10	Chelsea F.C. European Cup Winners 1971				
	Programme Covers..	2006		—	£6.00
L10	Chelsea F.C. F.A Cup Winners 1970 Programme				
	Covers	2006		—	£5.00
L8	Circus Posters From Around 1900	2005		—	£5.00
L15	Classic Le Mans Posters	2007		—	£6.50
L15	Classic Monaco Posters (Grand Prix)	2007		—	£6.50
EL8	Classic Teams Arsenal F.C.	2006		—	£4.00
EL8	Classic Teams Chelsea F.C.	2006		—	£4.00
EL8	Classic Teams Liverpool F.C.	2006		—	£4.00
EL8	Classic Teams Manchester United F.C.	2006		—	£4.00
EL8	Classic Teams Tottenham Hotspur F.C.	2006		—	£4.00
EL8	Classic Teams West Ham United F.C................	2006		—	£4.00
L15	The Cliff Richard Collection	2004		—	£7.50
L10	Dads Army	2006		—	£5.00
L15	David Bowie Concert Posters	2010		—	£6.50
L12	Depeche Mode (Concert Posters etc.).............	2015		—	£6.00
L12	England Players World Cup 1966	2007		—	£6.00
L6	England World Cup 1966 (Programme Covers,				
	Posters & Ticket)	2006		—	£4.50
L9	Everton F.C. F.A. Cup Winners 1966 Programme				
	Covers	2007		—	£5.00
L17	F.A. Cup Final Programme Covers 1923-1939	2001		—	£8.00
L20	F.A. Cup Final Programme Covers 1946-1965	2003		—	£8.00
L20	F.A. Cup Final Programme Covers 1966-1982	2004		—	£8.00
L21	F.A. Cup Final Programme Covers 1983-2000	2006		—	£8.00
L12	Fawlty Towers	2005		—	£6.50
L20	Frank Bruno Programme Covers	2005		—	£7.50
L9	The Golden Age of Middleweights 1980-1989	2006		—	£5.00
L15	Great British Cars of the 1950s	2004		—	£7.50
L12	The Greatest Cassius Clay Bonus Card Set				
	Programme Covers 1958-1962	2010		—	£6.00
L50	The Greatest Muhammad Ali (Boxer)	1993		—	£12.00
L4	Heavyweight Champions of the Naughty 1890s				
	(Boxing)	2000		—	£2.50
L40	Henry Cooper (Boxer)	1997		—	£10.50
L20	Heroes of the Prize Ring	1994		—	£6.00
L14	Houdini Show Posters	2007		—	£6.50

SPORTING PROFILES (continued)

Size & quantity		Date	Handbook reference	Price per card	Complete set
L8	Ipswich Town F.C. F.A. Cup Winners 1978 Programme Covers	2007	—		£5.00
L15	Iron Maiden Concert Posters	2010	—		£6.50
L30	'Iron' Mike Tyson (Boxer)	2004	—		£10.00
L5	'Iron' Mike Tyson (Boxer) Bonus Series	2004	—		£2.50
L20	Jack Nicklaus — Sports Illustrated	2005	—		£7.50
L25	Joe Louis A Career History (Boxer)...	2000	—		£12.50
L1	Joe Louis A Career History Wild Card (Joe Louis v Billy Conn 1941)	2000	—		£1.00
L20	Johnny Cash Concert Posters	2009	—		£7.50
L20	The Krays	2009	—		£7.50
L36	Larry Holmes (Boxer) Programme Covers	2006	—		£10.00
L10	Led Zeppelin Album Covers	2006	—		£5.00
L8	Leeds United F.C. F.A. Cup Winners 1972 Programme Covers	2007	—		£5.00
L30	Lennox Lewis Programme Covers	2006	—		£10.00
L15	Liverpool F.C. Champions League Winners 2005 Programme Covers	2005	—		£6.50
L6	Liverpool F.C. European Cup Finals 1977-2005 Programme Covers	2006	—		£4.00
L9	Liverpool F.C. F.A. Cup Winners 1974 Programme Covers	2008	—		£5.00
L10	Madonna (Concert Posters)	2015	—		£6.00
L7	Manchester City F.C. F.A. Cup Winners 1969 Programme Covers	2007	—		£5.00
L10	Manchester United 1968 European Cup Winners	2004	—		£6.50
L15	Marilyn Monroe	2006	—		£6.50
L20	Marvin Hagler (Boxer) Programme Covers	2006	—		£8.00
L30	Movie Idols — Alfred Hitchcock	2005	—		£10.00
L12	Movie Idols — Audrey Hepburn	2015	—		£6.00
L15	Movie Idols — Basil Rathbone is Sherlock Holmes ...	2004	—		£7.50
L30	Movie Idols — Errol Flynn	2004	—		£10.00
L10	Movie Idols — Fred Astaire & Ginger Rogers	2005	—		£5.50
L10	Movie Idols — Greta Garbo	2007	—		£5.00
L30	Movie Idols — Humphrey Bogart Film Posters	2003	—		£10.00
L15	Movie Idols — James Cagney	2008	—		£6.50
L20	Movie Idols — John Wayne Series 1 (Cowboy Films)	2007	—		£7.50
L30	Movie Idols — John Wayne Series 2 (Cowboy Films) ..	2006	—		£10.00
L15	Movie Idols — John Wayne Series 3 (War Films)	2010	—		£6.50
L30	Movie Idols — Marlon Brando	2004	—		£10.00
L12	Movie Idols — The Marx Brothers	2006	—		£6.00
L15	Movie Idols — Modern Gangster Classics	2008	—		£6.50
L15	Movie Idols — Paul Newman Classics	2010	—		£6.50
L15	Movie Idols — Steve McQueen Film Posters	2006	—		£6.50
L30	Muhammad Ali — Sports Illustrated	2002	—		£12.00
L10	The Muhammad Ali Story	2010	—		£6.00
L12	Newcastle United 1968/69 Fairs Cup Winners Programme Covers	2005	—		£7.00
L10	Nottingham Forest European Cup Winners 1980 Programme Covers	2006	—		£6.00
L25	Olympic Posters — Summer Games	2003	—		£8.50
L20	Olympic Posters — Winter Games	2003	—		£8.00
L15	Only Fools & Horses (Caricatures)	2002	—		£9.00
L15	Only Fools & Horses Volume 1 (Scenes)	2003	—		£9.00
L20	Only Fools & Horses Volume II (Scenes)	2005	—		£7.50
L4	Only Fools & Horses Bonus Set A	2003	—		£2.50
L15	Pele (Footballer)	2005	—		£6.50

SPORTING PROFILES (continued)

Size & quantity	Title	Date	Handbook reference	Price per card	Complete set
L12	Pink Floyd — Album Covers and Concert Posters	2008		—	£6.00
L20	Princess Diana Magazine Covers	2006		—	£7.50
L15	Queen Concert Posters	2010		—	£6.50
L8	Rocky Marciano (Boxer)	2001		—	£5.00
L20	Rod Stewart Concert Posters	2013		—	£7.50
L13	The Rolling Stones Concert Posters	2006		—	£6.00
L20	Smokin' Joe Frazier — A Career History	2005		—	£9.00
L20	Steptoe & Son	2003		—	£9.00
L12	Stoke City F.C. 1972 League Cup Winners Programme Covers	2005		—	£6.00
LT11	John L. Sullivan (Boxer) Cradle to Grave	1997		—	£6.00
L9	Sunderland F.C. F.A. Cup Winners 1973 Programme Covers	2007		—	£5.00
L20	Team GB 19 Golds Beijing 2008 Olympics	2008		—	£7.50
L9	Tony Hancock	2002		—	£6.50
L8	Tottenham Hotspur F.A. Cup Winners 1961 Programme Covers	2008		—	£5.00
L9	Tottenham Hotspur F.A. Cup Winners 1967 Programme Covers	2008		—	£5.00
L9	Tottenham Hotspur F.A. Cup Winners 1981 Programme Covers	2008		—	£5.00
L6	Tottenham Hotspur League Cup Winners 2008 Programme Covers	2008		—	£4.50
L10	West Bromwich Albion F.A. Cup Winners 1968 Programme Covers	2007		—	£6.00
L7	West Ham United F.A. Cup Winners 1964 Programme Covers	2005		—	£5.00
L8	West Ham United F.A. Cup Winners 1975 Programme Covers	2007		—	£5.00
L8	West Ham United F.A. Cup Winners 1980 Programme Covers	2005		—	£5.00
L20	When Ali Met Pele	2007		—	£7.50
L20	The Who Concert Posters	2009		—	£7.50
L7	Wolverhampton Wanderers F.A. Cup Winners 1960 Programme Covers	2007		—	£5.00
L15	World Cup 1966 England	2002		—	£9.00
L17	World Cup Posters 1930-2002 (Football)	2002		—	£8.00
L4	The Young Ones (TV Comedy Show)	2006		—	£3.00
L20	Zulu The Movie	2014		—	£7.50

SPORTS TIME (USA)

Size & quantity	Title	Date	Handbook reference	Price per card	Complete set
LT100	The Beatles	1996		—	£16.00
LT100	Marilyn Monroe 1st Series	1993		20p	£16.00
LT100	Marilyn Monroe 2nd Series	1995		—	£16.00

SPRATTS PATENT LTD

Size & quantity	Title	Date	Handbook reference	Price per card	Complete set
K100	British Birds (numbered)	c1925	HS-77.1	£6.50	—
K50	British Birds (unnumbered)	c1925	HS-77.2	£4.50	—
42	British Birds	c1925	HS-78	£6.50	—
25	Bonzo Series	1924	HS-76	£6.00	—
36	Champion Dogs	c1930	HS-79	£14.00	—
K20	Fish	c1925	HS-21	£14.00	—
K100	Poultry	c1925	HS-82	£14.00	—
12	Prize Dogs (multi-backed)	c1910	HS-83	£45.00	—
12	Prize Poultry (multi-backed)	c1910	HS-84	£45.00	—

THE STAMP CORNER

25	American Indian Tribes		1962	HX-28	£3.00	—

STAMP KING

L7	Robin Hood...		2002		—	£3.00

STAMP PUBLICITY

M40	1990 Cricket Tours		1990		—	£10.00
	Album...				—	£8.00

STAR CARDS

LT99	Riders of the World (Equestrian)		1995		20p	£9.50

STAR DISC ENTERPRISE (Canada)

K58	Star Trek The Next Generation (circular)		1994		—	£9.50

STAR INTERNATIONAL (USA)

LT100	Venus Swimwear International Model Search		1994		20p	£9.50

STAR JUNIOR CLUB

10	Do You Know About Animals		1960		£1.50	—
10	Do You Know About Sports and Games		1960		£2.50	—
5	Do You Know About Sports and Games		1960		£2.50	—

STAR PICS (USA)

LT80	Alien 3 — The Movie		1992		—	£9.50
LT72	All My Children		1991		—	£8.00
LT6	All My Children Insert Set		1991		—	£3.00
LT80	Dinamation (Dinosaurs)		1992		—	£8.50
LT72	Playboy (Magazine)		1992		—	£12.00
LT150	Saturday Night Live		1992		—	£12.00
LT76	Twin Peaks (TV Series)		1991		—	£8.00

STARLINE (USA)

LT250	Americana (USA History)		1992		—	£18.00
LT125	Hollywood Walk of Fame Nos 1-125		1991		—	£9.50
LT125	Hollywood Walk of Fame Nos 126-250		1991		—	£9.50

STATE OF THE ARTS

L6	Sex, Drugs & Rock 'n Roll...		1994		—	£7.50

STAVELEY'S LUDGATE HILL

24	World's Most Beautiful Birds		c1920	HX-22	£10.00	—
24	World's Most Beautiful Butterflies		c1920	HX-23	£10.00	—

STERLING CARDS (USA)

LT100	Country Gold (Country & Western Singers)		1992		—	£9.50
LT150	Country Gold (Country & Western Singers)		1993		—	£12.00

STOKES & DALTON LTD

M20	Dick Dalton in The Mystery of the Crimson Cobra... ...		1950		£3.25	—
28	Dominoes (without the dot)		1939		20p	£5.00

STOLL

25	The Mystery of Dr. Fu-Manchu	c1930		£12.00	—
25	Stars of Today	c1930		£8.00	—

STOLLWERCK

L216	Animal World	c1910		£1.50	—
?93	Views of the World (multi-backed)	c1910	HS-93	£6.00	—

STRICTLY INK

LT100	The Avengers Series 1	2003		20p	£10.00
LT100	The Avengers Series 2 Season 4 and 5 1965-1967 ...	2005		—	£15.00
LT54	The Avengers 3rd Series Additions The Archive Collection	2010		—	£7.50
LT100	CSI — Crime Scene Investigation Series 1	2003		—	£9.50
LT100	CSI — Crime Scene Investigation Series 2	2004		—	£9.50
LT72	CSI — Crime Scene Investigation Series 3	2006		—	£8.50
LT100	CSI Miami Series 1	2004		—	£9.50
LT72	CSI Miami Series 2	2007		—	£8.00
LT72	CSI NY Series 1	2008		—	£8.50
LT10	Doctor Who Promotional Series	2000		—	£10.00
LT120	Doctor Who 1st Series	2000		20p	£12.00
LT120	Doctor Who 2nd Series...	2001		20p	£12.00
LT120	Doctor Who 3rd Series	2002		20p	£12.00
LT200	Doctor Who	2006		—	£20.00
LT100	Doctor Who Big Screen	2003		20p	£12.00
	Doctor Who Big Screen Additions Collection:				
LT72	A Coloured	2008		—	£9.50
LT72	B Black and white	2008		—	£9.50
LT100	Doctor Who 40th Anniversary	2003		20p	£12.00
LT54	Hammer Horror Series 2	2010		—	£8.00
LT72	The New Avengers Season 1...	2006		—	£15.00

SUMMER COUNTY SOFT MARGARINE

Countryside Cards: HB-95

5	Birds	c1975		£2.00	—
5	Birds of Prey	c1975		£2.00	—
5	Butterflies	c1975		£2.00	—
5	Corn Crops	c1975		£2.00	—
5	Herbs & Berries	c1975		£2.00	—
5	The Hedgerow	c1975		£2.00	—
5	Horses & Ponies	c1975		£2.00	—
5	Mills	c1975		£2.00	—
5	Nocturnal Animals...	c1975		£2.00	—
5	Trees	c1975		£2.00	—
5	Water Fowl	c1975		£2.00	—
5	Water Life	c1975		£2.00	—
5	Wild Animals	c1975		£2.00	—
5	Wild Flowers	c1975		£2.00	—

SUMMER'S PRODUCTIONS

EL3	War Effort Cartoons	1943		£10.00	—

THE SUN

M134	Football	1970		60p	£80.00
M52	Gallery of Football Action	1972	HS-106.2	£3.00	—
	6 different numbers			—	£6.00
M6	How To Play Football	1972	HS-106.3	£4.00	—

THE SUN (continued)

M54	Page 3 Playing Cards (Pin-Up Girls)	1979		—	£8.00
50	Soccercards — Nos 1 to 50	1979		25p	£12.50
50	Soccercards — Nos 51 to 100	1979		25p	£12.50
50	Soccercards — Nos 101 to 150	1979		25p	£12.50
50	Soccercards — Nos 151 to 200	1979		25p	£12.50
50	Soccercards — Nos 201 to 250	1979		25p	£12.50
50	Soccercards — Nos 251 to 300	1979		25p	£12.50
50	Soccercards — Nos 301 to 350	1979		25p	£12.50
50	Soccercards — Nos 351 to 400	1979		25p	£12.50
50	Soccercards — Nos 401 to 450	1979		25p	£12.50
50	Soccercards — Nos 451 to 500	1979		25p	£12.50
50	Soccercards — Nos 501 to 550	1979		25p	£12.50
50	Soccercards — Nos 551 to 600	1979		25p	£12.50
50	Soccercards — Nos 601 to 650	1979		25p	£12.50
50	Soccercards — Nos 651 to 700	1979		25p	£12.50
50	Soccercards — Nos 701 to 750	1979		25p	£12.50
50	Soccercards — Nos 751 to 800	1979		25p	£12.50
50	Soccercards — Nos 801 to 850	1979		25p	£12.50
50	Soccercards — Nos 851 to 900	1979		25p	£12.50
50	Soccercards — Nos 901 to 950	1979		25p	£12.50
50	Soccercards — Nos 951 to 1000	1979		25p	£12.50
EL50	3-D Gallery of Football Stars	1972	HS-106.1	£5.00	—

SUNBLEST TEA

25	Inventions and Discoveries 1st Series	1962	HX-131	50p	£12.50
25	Inventions and Discoveries 2nd Series	1962	HX-131	60p	£15.00
	Album for 1st and 2nd Series combined			—	£20.00
25	Prehistoric Animals 1st Series	1966	HX-151	30p	£7.50
25	Prehistoric Animals 2nd Series	1966	HX-151	30p	£7.50
	Album for 1st and 2nd Series combined			—	£20.00

SUNBLEST (Australia)

M25	Great Explorers	c1975		50p	£12.50
M24	Sports Action Card Series	c1975		—	£12.00

SUNDAY STORIES

M6	Flags (silk)	1915	HS-113	£15.00	—
M6	The King and His Soldiers (silk)	1916	HS-114	£15.00	—

SUNNY BOY

50	British Naval Series	c1960	HX-76	£2.00	—

SWEETACRES (Australia)

48	Aircraft of the World	c1930		£5.00	—
36	Cricketers (back in red & green)	1926		£18.00	—
32	Cricketers – Test Match Record Nos. 1 to 32	1932		£6.00	—
32	Cricketers – Prominent Cricketers 2nd Series Nos. 33 to 64	1932		£6.00	—
24	Cricketers (Caricatures)	1938		£30.00	—
48	My Favourite Dogs	c1930		£6.00	—
36	Footballers	c1930		£8.00	—
48	Sports Champions	c1930		£7.00	—
48	Steamships of the World	c1930		£5.00	—
48	This World is Ours	c1930		£6.00	—

SWEETULE PRODUCTS LTD

Size & quantity	Title	Date	Handbook reference	Price per card	Complete set
25	Animals of the Countryside	1959	HX-9	20p	£3.00
25	Archie Andrews' Illustrated Jokes	1957		£9.00	—
25	Birds and Their Eggs ('Junior Service')	1955		20p	£3.00
25	Birds and Their Eggs:		HX-102		
	A Black back	1959		20p	£5.00
	B Blue back	1959		20p	£5.00
25	Birds and Their Haunts	1958		£5.00	—
25	Birds of the British Commonwealth (Canada):				
	A Black back	1958		20p	£5.00
	B Blue back	1958		20p	£5.00
25	Do You Know?	1963	HX-166.2	20p	£5.00
25	Family Crests	1961		20p	£3.00
25	Famous Sports Records:				
	A Blue back	1956		70p	£17.50
	B Black back	1956		£1.20	—
25	Football Club Nicknames	1959		40p	£10.00
K18	Historical Cars and Cycles	1957		50p	£9.00
25	Junior Service Quiz	1958		20p	£3.00
50	Modern Aircraft	1954	HX-35	20p	£6.00
25	Modern Transport	1955	HX-125.2	30p	£7.50
50	Motor Cycles Old and New	1963		£1.60	—
30	National Flags and Costumes	1957		70p	£20.00
52	Natural History Playing Card inset	1961		40p	£20.00
25	Nature Series	1959	HX-148	20p	£3.00
25	Naval Battles	1959	HX-21	20p	£3.00
25	Products of the World	1960	HX-152	20p	£3.00
25	Sports Quiz	1958		24p	£6.00
25	Stamp Cards	1960		24p	£6.00
EL30	Trains of the World	1960	HX-121.1	£1.65	—
25	Treasure Island	1958		30p	£7.50
25	Tropical Birds	1954	HX-13.1	20p	£3.00
25	Vintage Cars	1964	HX-33	50p	£12.50
25	Weapons of Defence	1959		20p	£3.00
25	Wild Animals	1958	HX-160	20p	£3.00
25	Wild Flowers	1960		20p	£3.00
25	The Wild West:		HX-55		
	A Black back	1960		60p	£15.00
	B Blue back	1960		20p	£4.00
25	Wonders of the World	1956	HX-142	20p	£3.50

Package Issues:

18	Aircraft	1954		£6.00	—
M12	Coronation Series	1953		£7.00	—
M18	Home Pets	1955		£7.00	—
25	International Footballers	1959		£9.00	—
18	Landmarks of Flying	1958		£7.00	—
25	Racing Cars of the World	1960		£10.00	—
M18	Railway Engines	1956		£7.00	—
M18	Railway Engines Past & Present	1957		£7.00	—
24	The World of Ships	c1960		£9.00	—

SWETTENHAM TEA

25	Aircraft of the World	1959	HX-180	60p	£15.00
25	Animals of the Countryside	1958	HX-9	20p	£3.00
25	Birds and Their Eggs	1958	HX-1.2	20p	£2.50
25	Butterflies and Moths	1960	HX-2	20p	£2.50
25	Evolution of the Royal Navy	1957	HX-90	20p	£3.50

SWETTENHAM TEA (continued)

25	Into Space	1959	HX-147	24p	£6.00
25	Wild Animals	1958	HX-160	30p	£7.50

W. SWORD & CO.

25	British Empire at Work	c1930	HX-113	£15.00	—
20	Dogs	c1930	HX-211	£17.00	—
20	Inventors and Their Inventions	c1930	HX-213	£17.00	—
25	Safety First	c1930	HX-199	£13.00	—
25	Sports and Pastimes Series	c1930	HX-225	£17.00	—
25	Vehicles of All Ages	c1930	HX-111	£15.00	—
25	Zoo Series (brown gravures)	c1930		£10.00	£250.00
25	Zoo Series (coloured)	c1930	HX-186	£12.00	—

SYMONDS CIDER (Scrumpy Jacks)

M100	Sporting Greats (early 1900s) 10 pictures with 10 varieties on each	1994		75p	—
	76 Different including varieties			—	£57.00
	10 Pictures only without varieties			—	£7.50

T C M ASSOCIATES (USA)

LT100	Earthmovers 2nd Series (Tractors etc)	1994		—	£12.00
LT72	Santa Around the World (Premier Edition)	1994		—	£9.50
LT72	Santa Around The World 2nd Series (with snowflake border)	1994		—	£9.50
LT100	Winnebago (Mobile Homes etc.)	1994		—	£9.50

T & M ENTERPRISES (USA)

LT45	The Bikini Open	1992		—	£8.00

TAMWORTH POLICE

L18	Keepers of the Peace	1990		25p	£4.50
	Album			—	£5.00

DES TAYLOR

L20	My Favourite Fish	2000		—	£7.50

TEA TIME ASSORTED BISCUITS (NABISCO)

12	British Soldiers Through the Ages	1974		25p	£3.00
	Album			—	£4.00

TEACHERS WHISKY

L12	Scottish Clans:		HT-2		
	A Back circular advert Teacher's Highland Cream:				
	i Thick card	1955		£6.00	—
	ii Thin card	1955		£6.00	—
	B Back circular advert Teacher's Highland Cream Scotch Whisky	1955		£7.00	—
	C Back rectangular advert	1971		£3.50	£42.00

TEASDALE & CO.

25	Great War Series	c1920		£25.00	—

TELLY CLASSICS

10	Telly Classics Nearest & Dearest 1960/70s Comedy with Jimmy Jewell & Hilda Baker	2009		—	£5.00

TENNYSON ENTERPRISES (USA)

LT100	Super Country Music	1992		—	£9.50

TESCO

EL6	Nature Trail	1988		—	£3.00

TETLEY TEA

48	British Birds...	c1975		£5.00	—

TEXACO (Petrol)

12	Cricket	1984		40p	£5.00
	Folder/Album			—	£12.00
K24	England Squad 2006 (Football)	2006		—	£7.50
K5	England Squad 2006 Additions (Carson, Downing,				
	Hargreaves, Lennon, Walcott) (Football)	2006		—	£5.00
K24	F.A. Cup Winners Hall of Fame	2007		—	£10.00
	Album and DVD	2007		—	£7.00

D.C. THOMSON

	Adventure Pictures:				
L10	Set 1 White borders, glazed	1922	HT-12.1	£3.50	—
L10	Set 2 White borders, matt	1922	HT-12.2	£3.50	—
L10	Set 3 Brown borders, glazed	1922	HT-12.3	£3.50	—
M16	Badges of the Fighting Fliers	1937	HT-14	£4.50	—
	Battles for the Flag:				
EL13	Inscribed 'Rover'	c1935	HT-15.1	£5.50	—
EL13	Inscribed 'Wizard' (different)	c1935	HT-15.2	£5.50	—
K80	Boys of All Nations	1936	HT-17	£1.30	—
LP11	British Team of Footballers	1922	HT-19	£3.25	—
L20	Canvas Masterpieces (silk)	1925		£10.00	—
16	Catch-My-Pal Cards	1938	HT-20	£2.25	—
M12	Coloured Photos of Star Footballers	c1930	HT-21	£8.00	—
16	County Cricketers (Adventure)	1957		£2.50	—
16	County Cricketers (Hotspur)	1957		£2.50	—
16	County Cricketers (Rover)	1957		£2.50	—
16	County Cricketers (Wizard)	1957		£2.50	—
	Cricketers:				
EL12	Inscribed 'Rover'	1924		£8.00	—
EL12	Inscribed 'Vanguard'	1924		£8.00	—
KP8	Cricketers	1923	HT-22	£3.50	—
EL16	Cup Tie Stars of All Nations (Victor)	1962	HT-24	£4.50	—
K28	Dominoes — School Caricatures	c1935		£2.50	—
MP35	Famous British Footballers:		HT-26		
	A 18 Different English Players	c1925		£3.25	—
	B 17 Different Scottish Players...	c1925		£9.00	—
K80	Famous Feats	1937	HT-27	£1.40	—
24	Famous Fights...	c1935		£3.00	—
24	Famous Footballers (Wizard)	1955		£2.40	—
25	Famous Footballers (Wizard)	c1955		£2.40	—
L32	Famous Ships	1931	HT-29	£4.50	—
EL12	Famous Teams in Football History	1961	HT-30	£5.00	—
EL16	Famous Teams in Football History 2nd Series				
	(New Hotspur)	1962	HT-31	£5.00	—
K80	Flags of the Sea	1937	HT-33	£1.40	—
P40	Football Photos	c1925		£6.50	—
48	Football Stars (Adventure and Hotspur)	1957		£2.50	—
44	Football Stars of 1959 (Wizard)	1959		£3.00	—

D.C. THOMSON (continued)

Size & quantity		Date	Handbook reference	Price per card	Complete set
K64	Football Team Cards:				
	A 63 Different (Minus No. 43)	1933		£1.50	—
	B Number 43	1933		£15.00	—
64	Football Tips and Tricks	1959		£1.00	—
L32	Football Towns and Their Crests	1931	HT-35	£6.50	—
KP137	Footballers	c1925	HT-37	£1.50	—
L8	Footballers	c1930	HT-38	£7.50	—
MP18	Footballers	1922	HT-36	£3.20	—
K52	Footballers — Hunt the Cup Cards	c1935	HT-41	£3.00	—
24	Footballers — Motor Cars (Double Sided)	c1930		£8.00	—
MP35	Footballers — Signed Real Photos:		HT-43		
	A 22 Different English Players	c1930		£2.50	—
	B 13 Different Scottish Players	c1930		£9.00	—
L12	Great Captains (Wizard)	c1970		£6.00	—
12	Guns in Action	1940		£2.25	—
M8	Hidden Treasure Clue Cards	1926		£13.00	—
EL16	International Cup Teams (Hornet)	1963	HT-51	£5.00	—
6	Ju-Jitsu Cards	1929		£6.00	—
24	Motor Bike Cards	1929		£6.50	—
K100	Motor Cars	1934	HT-53	£1.50	—
11	Mystic Menagerie	c1930	HT-56	£6.00	—
36	1930 Speedway Stars	1930		£8.00	—
K80	Punishment Cards	1936	HT-59	£1.40	—
	Puzzle Prize Cards:				
12	Dandy Dogs	1928		£5.00	—
12	Queer Animals	1928		£3.50	—
12	Speedsters of the Wilds	1928		£3.50	—
	Q Prize Cards:				
16	Cricket Crests	1929		£9.00	—
16	Flags of All Nations	1929		£3.00	—
16	Queer Birds	1929		£3.00	—
K80	Secrets of Cricket	1936	HT-62	£2.50	—
36	Spadger's Monster Collection of Spoofs	c1935		£3.50	—
48	Speed	1932		£1.20	—
EL22	Star Teams of 1961	1961		£4.00	—
24	Stars of Sport and Entertainment (Hotspur)	1958		£2.20	—
24	Stars of Sport and Entertainment (Rover)	1958		£2.20	—
L24	Superstars of '72 (Footballers) (Victor) (16 size 65 x 47mm, 8 size 95 x 65mm)	1972		£2.50	—
24	This Year's Top Form Footballers	1924		£3.60	—
EL12	Top Cup Teams	1964	HT-71	£6.00	—
10	Vanguard Photos Gallery	1923		£14.00	—
32	V.P. Flips (Adventure)	1932		£1.75	—
32	V.P. Flips (Rover)	1932		£1.75	—
32	V.P. Flips (Skipper)	1932		£1.75	—
24	Warrior Cards	1929		£2.75	—
K28	Warrior Cards (back with Dominoes)	1935		£2.20	—
K80	Warrior Cards	1937	HT-74	£1.40	—
K28	Wild West Dominoes	c1935		£2.20	—
	Wizard Series:				
20	British Birds and Eggs	1923	HT-18	£3.25	—
20	Easy Scientific Experiments	1923	HT-25	£3.00	—
20	Famous Liners	1923	HT-28	£4.00	—
20	Motor Cycles	1923	HT-54	£7.00	—
20	Why?	1923	HT-75	£3.00	—
20	The Wireless Telephone	1923	HT-76	£3.00	—
20	Wonders of the Rail	1923	HT-77	£5.00	—
20	Wonders of the World	1923	HT-78	£2.75	—

D.C. THOMSON (continued)

16	World Cup Footballers (Adventure)	1958	£3.00	—
16	World Cup Footballers (Hotspur)	1958	£3.00	—
16	World Cup Footballers (Rover)	1958	£3.00	—
16	World Cup Footballers (Wizard)	1958	£3.00	—
M72	World Cup Stars (Hornet/Hotspur)	1970	£3.00	—
32	The World's Best Cricketers (back in very dark green)	1932	£3.00	—
	The World's Best Cricketers:			
12	Inscribed 'Adventure' (back in mauve)	1930	£6.00	—
12	Inscribed 'Rover' (back in mauve)	1930	£6.00	—
12	Inscribed 'Wizard' (back in mauve)	1930	£6.00	—
18	The World's Best Cricketers (Adventure)	1956	£3.25	—
18	The World's Best Cricketers (Hotspur)	1956	£3.25	—
18	The World's Best Cricketers (Rover)	1956	£3.25	—
18	The World's Best Cricketers (Wizard)	1956	£3.25	—

HY. THORNE & CO.

25	Royalty	c1905	HT-82	£32.00	—

THUNDER PRODUCTIONS (USA)

LT100	Custom Motorcycles	1993	—	£9.50

TIMARU MILLING CO. (New Zealand)

M36	Focus on Fame	1948	75p	£27.00
M37	Peace and Progress	1947	75p	£28.00
M36	Victory Album Cards	1946	£1.00	—

TIMES CONFECTIONERY CO. LTD

M24	Roy Rogers — In Old Amarillo	1955	50p	£12.00
M24	Roy Rogers — South of Caliente	1955	50p	£12.00

TITBITS

K54	Pin-Up Girls (playing cards)	1976		24p	£12.50
M20	Star Cover Girls	1953	HT-84	£5.50	—

CHOCOLAT TOBLER LTD

12	Famaza Pedagogi (Famous People) Series 17	c1960	—	£3.00
50	Famous Footballers with 'Tobler' on front	c1937	£13.00	—
50	Famous Footballers without 'Tobler' on front	c1939	£13.00	—
12	Infanto En Arto (Children in Art) Series 21	c1960	—	£3.00
12	Planets and Fixed Stars, Series 45	c1960	—	£7.50
12	Infanto — Ludi (Children's Games) Series 52	c1960	—	£3.50
12	Tobler Posters 2nd Series, Series 58	c1960	—	£3.00
12	Different Ways of Travelling, Series 62	c1960	—	£5.00
L192	General Interest Series (30 sets of 6, 2 sets of 12)	c1900	£2.50	—

TOBY

24	Dogs 1st Series	c1920	£4.50	—
24	Dogs 2nd Series	c1920	£4.50	—
24	Sights of London	c1920	£4.00	—
24	Toby's Bird Series	c1920	£4.00	—
24	Toby's Ship Series	c1920	£4.00	—
24	Toby's Travel Series	c1920	£4.00	—

TODAY NEWSPAPER

LT14	Around Britain	1991	—	£3.00

TOM THUMB (New Zealand)

M24	Supercars (issued in strips of 3)	1980		£1.50	£12.00

TOMMY GUN

50	Medals	1971		20p	£4.00

TONIBELL (Ice Cream)

M20	Banknotes of the World...	1974		25p	£5.00
M12	Beautiful Butterflies	1977		35p	£4.00
M20	County Badge Collection	1976		20p	£4.00
L12	Did You Know	1976		£1.50	—
25	Did You Know?	1963	HX-166.2	20p	£3.00
EL12	England's Soccer Stars...	1970	HT-86	£4.00	£50.00
L19	Famous Sports Trophies	c1970	HT-87	50p	£10.00
M12	Farmyard Stencils	1977		40p	£5.00
M24	1st Division Football League Club Badges	1972		£2.50	—
EL12	Horses in the Service of Man...	1977		£1.00	£12.00
25	Inventions that Changed the World...	1963	HX-18	20p	£3.00
EL10	Junior Champs	1979		60p	£6.00
M24	Kings of the Road (car radiator badges)	1977		£1.00	—
M24	Pop Star Cameos (circular cards)	c1970		40p	£10.00
M10	Pop Stars (Star Shaped)	c1975		—	£15.00
K36	Team of All Time (English footballers)	1971		£2.25	£80.00
25	This Changing World:				
	A Black line under Tonibell	1963		36p	£9.00
	B Without black line under Tonibell	1963		40p	£10.00
25	Wonders of the Heavens	1963	HX-48	60p	£15.00
25	World's Passenger Liners	1963	HX-82	20p	£3.00

TONIBELL & CADBURY

12	Action Soldiers	1976		30p	£4.00

TOP SELLERS LTD

M54	Crazy Stickers	1975		—	£6.00

TOP TRUMPS

L30	Football South Africa 2010 World Cup Goalscorers ...	2010		—	£4.00
L30	Football South Africa 2010 World Cup Keepers &				
	Defenders	2010		—	£4.00
L30	Football South Africa 2010 World Cup Legends	2010		—	£4.00
L30	Football South Africa 2010 World Cup Managers	2010		—	£4.00
L30	Football South Africa 2010 World Cup Moments	2010		—	£4.00
L30	Football South Africa 2010 World Cup Stadiums	2010		—	£4.00
L35	Prehistoric Monsters...	1979		—	£4.00
L33	Rockets	1980		—	£4.00

TOPICAL TIMES

EL8	Cricketers in Action	1937		£20.00	—
M24	Footballers — English (Head and Shoulders)	1939	HT-98.1	£3.50	£85.00
M24	Footballers — Scottish (Head and Shoulders)	1939	HT-98.2	£12.00	—
L48	Footballers — English (size 125 × 46mm):		HT-97		
	A First 24 Subjects...	1937		£3.50	£85.00
	B Second — 24 Subjects	1938		£3.50	£85.00
L48	Footballers — Scottish (size 125 × 46mm):				
	A First 24 Subjects	1937	HT-97.2	£12.00	—
	B Second 24 Subjects	1938	HT-97.4	£12.00	—

TOPICAL TIMES (continued)

Size & quantity		Date	Handbook reference	Price per card	Complete set
EL120	Footballers (size 250 × 95mm), black and white	c1935	HT-99	£4.50	—
EL16	Footballers (size 250 × 95mm), coloured	1936	HT-95.1	£6.00	—
MP10	Footballers (2 players per card)	c1930	HT-92	£5.00	—
EL8	Footballers (3 players per card)	1937	HT-96.1	£7.00	—
EL8	Footballers (size 253 × 190mm), coloured	1936	HT-94.1	£7.00	—
MP6	Football Teams (card)	c1930	HT-91	£6.00	—
M6	Football Teams (metal)	c1925	HT-90	£15.00	—

TOPPS (Australia)

LT63	Australian Cricket...	2000		—	£25.00

TOPPS (Germany)

LT99	Jurassic Park (including Sticker Set)	1993		—	£10.00

TOPPS (UK)

Size & quantity		Date		Price per card	Complete set
M80	Alf His Life and Times	1988		20p	£12.00
M88	American Baseball	1988		20p	£18.00
M88	American Baseball	1989		20p	£18.00
M88	American NFL Football	1987		22p	£20.00
LT99	Autos of 1977	1977		£1.75	—
M132	Batman (size 77 x 55mm)	1989		20p	£7.50
M22	Batman stickers	1989		20p	£2.50
LT88	Batman Returns	1992		20p	£8.50
M10	Batman Returns stickers	1992		25p	£2.50
LT66	Battlestar Galactica (Nos 1-66) (white card)	1979		20p	£12.00
LT66	Battlestar Galactica (Nos 67-132) (white card)	1979		20p	£12.00
LT66	Bay City Rollers	1976		40p	—
LT132	Beavis and Butt-Head (No 6934 unissued, 7769 not on check list)	1994		20p	£11.00
LT88	Beverly Hills 90210	1991		20p	£9.50
M11	Beverly Hills 90210 stickers	1991		25p	£2.50
LT88	The Black Hole	1980		25p	£22.00
LT49	Comic Book Heroes	1977		£2.20	—
LT88	Desert Storm	1991		20p	£16.00
M22	Desert Storm Stickers	1991		20p	£2.50
LT60	England 2002 (Football)	2002		—	£14.00
LT10	England 2002 (Football) Electric Foil Series Nd. E1 to E10	2002		—	£7.00
EL30	English League Football Internationals	1980		70p	£21.00
LT88	The Flintstones (The Movie)	1994		20p	£5.00
M11	The Flintstones (The Movie) stickers	1994		25p	£2.50
LT124	Football Premier Gold	2001		—	£20.00
LT125	Football Premier Gold	2002		—	£20.00
LT125	Football Premier Gold	2003		—	£20.00
LT125	Football Premier Gold	2004		—	£20.00
	Football Saint and Greavsie:				
M175	A Complete set	1988		20p	£25.00
M264	B Complete set plus varieties	1988		—	£30.00
LT132	Footballers, Nd 1-132 (red back)	1975		£1.75	—
LT88	Footballers, Nd 133-220 (red back)...	1975		£1.75	—
LT88	Footballers, Scottish (blue back)	1975		£2.50	—
LT110	Footballers, Nd 1-110 (blue back)	1976		£1.20	—
LT110	Footballers, Nd 111-220 (blue back)	1976		£1.20	—
LT110	Footballers, Nd 221-330 (blue back)	1976		£1.20	—
LT132	Footballers, Scottish (red back)	1976		£2.20	—
LT110	Footballers, Nd 1-110 (red back)	1977		£1.25	—

TOPPS (UK) (continued)

Size & quantity		Date	Handbook reference	Price per card	Complete set
LT110	Footballers, Nd 111-220 (red back)	1977		£1.25	—
LT110	Footballers, Nd 221-330 (red back)	1977		£1.25	—
LT132	Footballers, Scottish (yellow back)	1977		£1.50	—
LT132	Footballers, Nd 1-132 (orange back)	1978		35p	£45.00
LT132	Footballers, Nd 133-264 (orange back)	1978		35p	£45.00
LT132	Footballers, Nd 265-396 (orange back)	1978		35p	£45.00
LT132	Footballers, Scottish (green back)	1978		£1.50	—
LT132	Footballers, Nos 1-132 (light blue back)	1979		£1.50	—
LT132	Footballers, Nos 133-264 (light blue back)	1979		£1.50	—
LT132	Footballers, Nos 265-396 (light blue back)	1979		£1.50	—
LT132	Footballers, Scottish (red back)	1979		£1.75	—
LT66	Footballers (pink back) (3 numbers per card)	1980		£1.25	£90.00
EL18	Footballers Posters	1980		80p	£14.00
LT65	Footballers (blue back) (3 numbers per card)	1981		£1.00	£65.00
	Album			—	£8.00
LT100	Footballers Stadium Club nos 1-100	1992		20p	£16.00
LT100	Footballers Stadium Club nos 101-200	1992		20p	£16.00
LT10/14	Footballers Stadium Club Promotional Series	1992		25p	£2.50
LT21	Funny Puzzles	1978		£1.50	—
M39	The Garbage Gang nd 1a-39a	1990		40p	—
M39	The Garbage Gang nd 1b-39b (except for subjects 15b & 39b, incorrectly numbered 15a & 39a)	1990		40p	£16.00
M42	The Garbage Gang Nos 418A-459A	1991		40p	—
M41	The Garbage Gang Nos 460A-500A	1991		40p	—
M41	Garbage Pail Kids 1st Series A	1986		40p	—
M41	Garbage Pail Kids 1st Series B	1986		40p	—
M42	Garbage Pail Kids 2nd Series A	1986		40p	—
M42	Garbage Pail Kids 2nd Series B	1986		40p	—
M44	Garbage Pail Kids 3rd Series A	1987		40p	—
M37	Garbage Pail Kids 3rd Series B	1987		40p	—
M42	Garbage Pail Kids 4th Series A	1987		40p	—
M42	Garbage Pail Kids 4th Series B	1987		40p	—
M39	Garbage Pail Kids 5th Series A	1987		40p	—
M39	Garbage Pail Kids 5th Series B	1987		40p	—
M44	Garbage Pail Kids 6th Series A	1988		40p	—
M44	Garbage Pail Kids 6th Series B	1988		40p	£17.50
M86	The Goonies	1986		30p	—
M15	The Goonies stickers	1986		30p	—
LT88	Gremlins 2 The Movie (white card)	1990		20p	£9.00
LT66	Home Alone 2 The Movie	1993		20p	£4.50
M11	Home Alone 2 The Movie stickers	1993		25p	£2.50
LT44	Home & Away	1990		20p	£5.00
LT99	Hook — The Film	1992		20p	£8.50
M11	Hook — The Film stickers	1992		25p	£2.50
LT88	Jurassic Park	1993		20p	£9.50
M11	Jurassic Park stickers	1993		25p	£2.50
LT66	Kings of Rap (including stickers)	1991		20p	£8.00
M111	Mad Cap Alphabet (including All Varieties)	1994		20p	£12.00
LT49	Marvel Super Heroes	1980		£1.70	£85.00
LT83	Match Attax Extra 2007/08 (red backs)	2007		—	£9.50
LT20	Match Attax Extra 2007/08 Club Captains (foil fronts)	2007		—	£6.00
LT92	Match Attax Extra 2008/09 (blue backs)	2008		—	£9.50
LT20	Match Attax Extra 2008/09 Club Captains	2008		—	£5.00
LT20	Match Attax Extra 2008/09 Fans Favourite (foil fronts)	2008		—	£6.00
LT112	Match Attax Extra 2009/10 (orange backs)	2010		—	£9.50
LT20	Match Attax Extra 2009/10 I-Card Chromium	2010		—	£10.00
LT20	Match Attax Extra 2009/10 Man of The Match	2010		—	£18.00

TOPPS (UK) (continued)

Size & quantity		Date	Handbook reference	Price per card	Complete set
LT224	Match Attax World Cup 2010 (red backs)...	2010	—		£12.00
LT32	Match Attax World Cup 2010 International Legends ...	2010	—		£5.00
LT8	Match Attax World Cup 2010 International Masters (foil fronts)	2010	—		£4.00
LT28	Match Attax World Cup 2010 Man of the Match (foil fronts)...	2010	—		£14.00
LT16	Match Attax World Cup 2010 Managers	2010	—		£5.00
LT4	Match Attax World Cup 2010 100 Club (foil fronts) ...	2010	—		£12.00
LT6	Match Attax World Cup 2010 Star Legends (foil fronts)	2010	—		£5.00
LT25	Match Attax World Cup 2010 Star Players (foil fronts)	2010	—		£5.00
LT66	Michael Jackson	1984		50p	—
LT49	Monster in My Pocket	1991		20p	£5.00
LT66	Neighbours 1st Series	1988		20p	£5.00
LT66	Neighbours 2nd Series	1988		20p	£5.00
LT88	New Kids on the Block	1990		20p	£6.00
M11	New Kids on the Block stickers, red borders	1990		25p	£2.50
M11	New Kids on the Block stickers, yellow borders	1990		25p	£2.50
LT66	Planet of the Apes (TV Series)	1974		£1.50	£100.00
LT90	Pokemon (TV animation series) 1st Series	2000		25p	£16.00
LT72	Pokemon (TV animation series) 2nd Series	2000		25p	£16.00
LT72	Pokemon (TV animation series) 3rd Series	2000		—	£16.00
LT72	Pokemon The Movie...	2000		25p	£16.00
LT72	Pokemon 2000 The Movie...	2000		—	£16.00
M75	Pro-Cycling	1988		20p	£10.00
M66	Put On Stickers (including varieties)	1992		20p	£8.00
LT50	Shocking Laffs (No.17 not issued, but two Nos 47):				
	A Grey card	1977		£2.40	—
	B White card	1977		£2.60	—
LT88	The Simpsons	1991		20p	£18.00
M22	The Simpsons Stickers	1991		40p	—
LT66	Spitting Image	1990		20p	£10.00
LT88	Star Trek, The Motion Picture	1980		£1.50	£130.00
LT66	Star Wars, Nd 1-66	1978		£1.75	£115.00
LT66	Star Wars, Nd 1A-66A	1978		£3.00	—
LT80	Star Wars Attack of The Clones (white Star Wars on front)	2002		—	£15.00
LT10	Star Wars Attack of The Clones — Characters	2002		—	£10.00
LT5	Star Wars Attack of The Clones — Planets	2002		—	£5.00
LT10	Star Wars Attack of The Clones — Vehicles...	2002		—	£10.00
LT66	Stingray — Thunderbirds — Captain Scarlet	1993		20p	£8.00
M44	Stupid Smiles	1990		30p	—
M64	Super Mario Bros — Nintendo	1992		20p	£7.00
LT66	Superman The Movie 1st Series	1979		27p	£18.00
LT66	Superman The Movie 2nd Series	1979		24p	£16.00
LT66	Take That (Pop Group)	1994		20p	£5.00
M11	Take That (Pop Group) stickers	1994		25p	£2.50
LT66	Teenage Mutant Hero Turtles...	1990		20p	£5.00
M11	Teenage Mutant Hero Turtles Stickers...	1990		25p	£2.50
LT132	Teenage Mutant Ninja Turtles Movie	1990		20p	£6.50
M11	Teenage Mutant Ninja Turtles Movie Stickers	1990		25p	£2.50
M44	Terminator 2 (size 77 × 55mm)	1991		20p	£5.00
LT77	Toxic Crusaders	1993		20p	£9.50
M11	Toxic Crusaders stickers	1993		25p	£2.50
M54	Toxic High School	1991		30p	—
M23	Toxic High School Senior stickers	1991		20p	£4.00
M44	Trash Can Trolls nos 1A-44A	1993		40p	£17.50
M44	Trash Can Trolls nos 1B-44B	1993		50p	—

TOPPS (UK) (continued)

LT66	Trolls (glossy backs)..........................	1992		20p	£7.50
M11	Trolls stickers	1992		25p	£2.50
LT38	Wacky Packages 1st Series	c1978		£1.50	–
LT38	Wacky Packages 2nd Series	c1978		£1.50	–
M30	Wacky Packages	1982		70p	–
LT42	Wanted Posters	1978		80p	–
LT66	World Championship Wrestling	1992		20p	£7.00
EL18	World Cup Supersquad England (Football)	1990		60p	£11.00
EL18	World Cup Supersquad Scotland (Football)	1990		70p	£12.00

TOPPS (USA)

LT66	The 'A' Team	1984		–	£8.00
LT84	Alien – The Movie	1979		–	£15.00
LT66	Baby	1985		–	£8.00
LT88	Back to the Future Part II – The Film......	1989		–	£8.00
LT72	Barb Wire (Pamela Anderson Film).........	1996		–	£9.50
LT12	Barb Wire Embossed Series (Pamela Anderson Film)	1996		–	£5.00
LT132	Batman (size 89 x 64mm)	1989		20p	£7.50
LT90	Batman Begins – The Film	2005		–	£12.00
LT100	Batman Returns (Stadium Club).............	1992		–	£9.50
LT72	The Blair Witch Project – The Movie	1999		–	£9.50
LT88	Buck Rogers in the 25th Century	1979		–	£18.00
LT66	Charlie's Angels 3rd Series	1977		–	£25.00
LT66	Close Encounters of The Third Kind – The Movie ...	1978		–	£12.00
LT72	Daredevil – The Movie	2003		20p	£12.00
LT72	Dark Angel 1st Series	2002		–	£9.50
LT88	Desert Storm 2nd Series	1991		–	£9.50
LT88	Desert Storm 3rd Series	1991		–	£8.00
LT88	Dick Tracy – The Movie	1990		–	£8.00
LT55	Dinosaurs Attack (including Set LT11 Stickers).........	1988		–	£9.50
EL72	Dragon Heart The Film – Widevision	1996		–	£9.50
LT87	ET – The Extra Terrestrial	1982		–	£9.00
LT54	Goosebumps	1996		–	£8.00
LT99	Greatest Olympians	1983		–	£12.00
LT88	Gremlins 2 – The Movie (grey card)	1990		–	£9.00
LT66	Growing Pains (TV Series)	1988		–	£9.50
LT77	Harry and The Hendersons	1987		–	£9.50
LT90	Heroes Series 1	2008		–	£9.50
LT90	Heroes Volume 2	2008		–	£8.50
LT77	Howard The Duck	1986		–	£8.00
LT88	In Living Colour – Fox TV Series	1992		–	£9.50
LT72	The Incredible Hulk	2003		–	£9.50
EL72	Independence Day – The Film Widevision	1996		–	£9.50
LT90	Indiana Jones and The Kingdom of The Crystal Skull	2008		–	£8.00
LT90	Indiana Jones Masterpieces	2008		–	£8.00
LT59	Jaws 2	1978		–	£15.00
LT44	Jaws 3-D The Film	1983		–	£8.00
LT80	Kong The 8th Wonder of The World	2005		–	£9.50
LT88	Last Action Hero – The Film	1993		–	£9.50
LT44	Little Shop of Horrors	1986		–	£7.50
LT72	Lord of The Rings Evolution	2006		–	£9.50
LT90	Lord of The Rings Fellowship of the Ring Series 1 ...	2001		–	£30.00
LT72	Lord of The Rings Fellowship of the Ring Series 2 ...	2002		–	£12.00
LT90	Lord of The Rings Masterpieces Series 1	2006		–	£9.50
LT72	Lord of The Rings Masterpieces Series 2	2008		–	£8.50
LT90	Lord of The Rings The Return of the King Series 1 ...	2003		–	£9.50

TOPPS (USA) (continued)

Size & quantity		Date	Handbook reference	Price per card	Complete set
LT72	Lord of The Rings The Return of the King Series 2 ...	2004		—	£12.00
LT90	Lord of The Rings The Two Towers Series 1	2002		—	£12.00
LT72	Lord of The Rings The Two Towers Series 2	2003		—	£12.00
LT72	The Lost World of Jurassic Park + Set L11 Stickers ...	1997		—	£9.50
LT56	Mars Attacks	1962		—	—
EL72	Mars Attacks — Widevision	1996		—	£9.50
LT66	Menudo (Pop Group)	1983		—	£9.50
LT33	Michael Jackson 1st Series	1984		—	£10.00
LT33	Michael Jackson 2nd Series	1984		—	£10.00
LT99	Moonraker James Bond 007	1979		—	£20.00
LT99	Mork and Mindy	1978		—	£18.00
LT88	Nicktoons	1993		—	£9.50
LT50	NSYNC (Pop Group)	2000		—	£9.50
LT50	Outer Limits	1964		—	—
LT33	Pee Wee's Playhouse	1989		—	£7.50
LT55	Perlorian Cats ...	1982		—	£7.50
LT90	Planet of the Apes — The Movie	2001		—	£9.50
LT44	Return to Oz	1985		—	£12.00
LT55	Robin Hood Prince of Thieves — The Film	1991		—	£8.00
LT88	Robocop 2 — The Film	1990		—	£8.00
LT99	The Rocketeer — The Film	1991		—	£8.00
LT99	Rocky II	1979		—	£10.00
LT90	The Shadow — The Movie	1994		—	£8.00
LT100	Star Wars Attack of The Clones (silver Star Wars on front)	2002		—	£16.00
EL80	Star Wars Attack of The Clones — Widevision ...	2002		—	£18.00
LT90	Star Wars Clone Wars	2004		—	£12.00
LT90	Star Wars The Clone Wars — The Film	2008		—	£9.50
EL80	Star Wars The Clone Wars (Widevision)	2009		—	£9.50
LT90	Star Wars Clone Wars Rise of The Bounty Hunters ...	2010		—	£8.00
LT132	Star Wars The Empire Strikes Back 1st Series	1980		—	£20.00
LT132	Star Wars The Empire Strikes Back 2nd Series	1980		—	£20.00
EL48	Star Wars The Empire Strikes Back 30th Anniversary (3-D) Widevision	2010		—	£15.00
EL80	Star Wars Episode 1 Series 1 — Widevision (red) ...	1999		—	£15.00
EL80	Star Wars Episode 1 Series 2 — Widevision (blue) ...	1999		—	£15.00
LT93	Star Wars Evolution ...	2001		—	£15.00
LT120	Star Wars Galaxy Series 4	2009		—	£9.50
LT120	Star Wars Galaxy Series 5	2010		—	£9.50
LT120	Star Wars Galaxy Series 6	2011		—	£9.50
LT110	Star Wars Galaxy Series 7	2012		—	£9.50
LT12	Star Wars Galaxy Lucas Art	1995		—	£15.00
LT120	Star Wars Heritage	2004		—	£12.00
LT90	Star Wars Jedi Legacy ...	2013		—	£9.50
LT132	Star Wars Return of The Jedi 1st Series ...	1983		—	£20.00
LT88	Star Wars Return of The Jedi 2nd Series...	1983		—	£20.00
LT90	Star Wars Revenge of The Sith	2005		—	£9.50
EL80	Star Wars Revenge of The Sith — Widevision ...	2005		—	£14.00
LT120	Star Wars The 30th Anniversary ...	2007		—	£9.50
EL72	Star Wars Trilogy — Widevision ...	1997		—	£16.00
LT72	Star Wars Vehicles	1997		—	£15.00
LT44	Supergirl — The Film	1994		—	£6.00
LT88	Superman II — The Film	1980		—	£9.50
LT99	Superman III — The Film	1983		—	£9.50
LT90	Superman Returns — The Film ...	2007		—	£9.50
LT44	T.2 — Terminator 2 — The Movie (size 89 × 64mm) ...	1991		—	£5.00
LT90	Terminator Salvation Movie	2009		—	£8.50

TOPPS (USA) (continued)

LT16	Three's Company (Puzzle Picture)	1978	—	£5.00
LT72	WCW Nitro (Wrestling)	1999	—	£8.00
LT132	Who Framed Roger Rabbit — The Movie	1987	—	£9.50
LT100	Wild C.A.T.S Covert Action Teams by Jim Lee (2 different No. 66, No.68 not issued)	1983	—	£8.00
LT72	World Championship Wrestling Embossed	1999	—	£10.00
LT72	The X Files Fight for the Future	1998	—	£12.00
LT72	The X Files Season 1	1996	—	£9.50
LT72	The X Files Season 2	1996	—	£9.50
LT72	The X Files Season 3	1997	—	£9.50
EL72	The X Files Showcase — Widevision	1997	—	£12.00
LT72	X-Men — The Movie	2000	—	£9.50
LT72	X-Men 2 United — The Movie	2003	—	£8.00
LT72	Xena Warrior Princess Season 1	1998	—	£9.50
LT72	Xena Warrior Princess Season 2	2000	—	£12.00

JOHN TORDOFF & SON

K25	The Growth and Manufacture of Tea	c1930		£12.00	—
25	Safety First	c1930	HX-199	£12.00	—

TOTAL UK

L25	Return to Oz	1985		20p	£4.00
	Album			—	£5.00

TOURISM RESOURCES

L24	Historic Irish Houses	1993	—	£15.00

TOURIST BOARD

L40	Places to Visit Cumbria	1992	—	£4.00
L40	Places to Visit Cumbria	1993	—	£4.00
L40	Places to Visit Cumbria	1995	—	£4.00
L40	Places to Visit North West	1991	—	£5.00
L40	Places to Visit North West	1992	—	£5.00
L40	Places to Visit North West	1993	—	£4.00
L40	Places to Visit North West	1994	—	£4.00
L40	Places to Visit North West	1995	—	£4.00
L40	Places to Visit North West	1996	—	£4.00
L40	Places to Visit North West	1999	—	£4.00
L40	Places to Visit Stockport	1992	—	£4.00
L40	Places to Visit Stockport	1993	—	£4.00
L40	Places to Visit Stockport	1994	—	£4.00
L40	Places to Visit Trafford	1990	—	£4.00
L40	Places to Visit Trafford	1991	—	£4.00
L40	Places to Visit Wigan & District	1991	—	£4.00
L40	Places to Visit Wigan & District	1992	—	£4.00

TOWER TEA

24	Illustrated Sayings	c1910	HT-100	£27.00	—

TRADE CARDS (EUROPE) LTD
(SEE ALSO FUTERA)

LT90	Arsenal F.C. — Fans Selection	1998	—	£16.00
LT18	Arsenal F.C. — Fans Selection (embossed)	1998	—	£5.00
LT99	Arsenal F.C. plus Set LT9 embossed	1999	20p	£15.00
LT9	Arsenal F.C. Hot Shots (foil fronts)	1999	£2.00	£18.00

TRADE CARDS (EUROPE) LTD (continued)

		Date	Handbook reference	Price per card	Complete set
LT9	Arsenal F.C. Vortex (foil fronts)	1999		£2.00	£18.00
LT50	Arsenal F.C. Greatest	1999		—	£25.00
LT50	Arsenal F.C. — Main Series	2000		20p	£7.50
LT6	Arsenal F.C. — Electric Series	2000		£3.00	£18.00
LT90	Aston Villa F.C. — Fans Selection	1998		—	£17.50
LT18	Aston Villa F.C. — Fans Selection (embossed)	1998		—	£5.00
LT99	Aston Villa F.C. plus Set LT9 embossed	1999		20p	£15.00
LT9	Aston Villa F.C. Hot Shots (foil fronts)	1999		£2.00	£18.00
LT9	Aston Villa F.C. Vortex (foil fronts)	1999		£2.00	£18.00
LT90	Celtic F.C. — Fans Selection	1998		—	£17.50
LT18	Celtic F.C. — Fans Selection (embossed)	1998		—	£5.50
LT99	Celtic F.C. plus Set LT9 embossed	1999		20p	£15.00
LT9	Celtic F.C. Hot Shots (foil fronts)	1999		£2.00	£18.00
LT9	Celtic F.C. Vortex (foil fronts)	1999		£2.00	£18.00
LT50	Celtic F.C. — Main Series	2000		20p	£7.50
LT4	Celtic F.C. — Electric Series	2000		£3.00	£12.00
LT90	Chelsea F.C. — Fans Selection	1998		—	£17.50
LT18	Chelsea F.C. — Fans Selection (embossed)	1998		—	£6.00
LT99	Chelsea F.C. plus Set LT9 embossed	1999		20p	£15.00
LT9	Chelsea F.C. Hot Shots (foil fronts)	1999		£2.00	£18.00
LT9	Chelsea F.C. Vortex (foil fronts)	1999		£2.00	£18.00
LT50	Chelsea F.C. Greatest	1999		—	£25.00
LT90	Leeds United F.C. — Fans Selection	1998		—	£17.50
LT18	Leeds United F.C. — Fans Selection (embossed)	1998		—	£6.00
LT99	Leeds United F.C. plus Set LT9 embossed	1999		20p	£15.00
LT9	Leeds United F.C. Hot Shots (foil fronts)	1999		£2.00	£18.00
LT9	Leeds United F.C. Vortex (foil fronts)	1999		£2.00	£18.00
LT50	Leeds United F.C. Greatest	1999		—	£25.00
LT50	Leeds United F.C. — Main Series	2000		20p	£7.50
LT4	Leeds United F.C. — Electric Series	2000		£3.00	£12.00
LT99	Liverpool F.C. — Main Series	1998		—	£16.00
LT99	Liverpool F.C. plus Set LT9 embossed	1999		20p	£15.00
LT9	Liverpool F.C. Hot Shots (foil fronts)	1999		£2.00	£18.00
LT9	Liverpool F.C. Vortex (foil fronts)	1999		£2.00	£18.00
LT50	Liverpool F.C. — Main Series	2000		20p	£7.50
LT6	Liverpool F.C. — Electric Series	2000		£3.00	£18.00
LT100	Manchester United F.C.	1997		—	£17.50
LT90	Manchester United F.C. — Fans Selection	1998		—	£16.00
LT18	Manchester United F.C. — Fans Selection (embossed)	1998		—	£5.00
LT99	Manchester United F.C. — Main Series	1998		—	£17.50
LT99	Manchester United F.C. plus Set LT9 embossed	1999		20p	£15.00
LT9	Manchester United F.C. Hot Shots (foil fronts)	1999		£2.00	£18.00
LT9	Manchester United F.C. Vortex (foil fronts)	1999		£2.00	£18.00
LT99	Manchester United F.C. — Main Series	2000		20p	£15.00
LT9	Manchester United F.C. — Electric Series	2000		£3.00	—
LT99	Newcastle United F.C. plus Set LT9 embossed	1999		20p	£15.00
LT9	Newcastle United F.C. Hot Shots (foil fronts)	1999		£2.00	£18.00
LT9	Newcastle United F.C. Vortex (foil fronts)	1999		£2.00	£18.00
LT50	Newcastle United F.C. Greatest	1999		—	£25.00

TRADING CARDS INTERNATIONAL (USA)

LT50	Princess Diana 1961-1997	1997		—	£9.50

TREASURE

L18	Zoo Time plus album	1966		—	£9.00

TREBOR LTD

M42	Space Series (Waxed Paper issue):				
	A Top 'Victory Bubble Gum'	1964		£5.00	—
	B Top 'Trebor Zip Bubble Gum'	1964		£5.00	—
M48	V.C. Heroes (Waxed Paper issue):		HX-215		
	A Inscribed 'Zip'	1967		£5.00	—
	B Inscribed 'Zoom Bubble Gum'	1967		£5.00	—

TREBOR BASSETT LTD (SEE GEO. BASSETT)

TREBOR/SHARP

24	Famous Pets	1972		20p	£3.00
	Album			—	£5.00

TRIBUTE COLLECTABLES

10	Abbott and Costello	2010		—	£5.00
10	Astaire Legend of Dance (Fred Astaire)	2010		—	£5.50
10	Carole Lombard	2015		—	£5.00
10	Charlie Parker	2014		—	£5.00
10	Cyd Charisse	2010		—	£5.50
10	Debbie Reynolds	2014		—	£5.00
10	Dizzy Gillespie	2014		—	£5.00
10	Ella Fitzgerald	2010		—	£5.50
15	Gina Lollobrigida	2014		—	£6.50
10	Ginger Rogers	2010		—	£5.50
10	Humphrey Bogart	2010		—	£5.50
10	John Wayne A Tribute To The Duke	2010		—	£5.00
10	Josephine Baker (Dancer & Actress)	2010		—	£5.50
10	Marty (Marty Feldman Commemorating the British Comedy Star)	2010		—	£5.00
20	Paulette Goddard	2015		—	£9.50
10	Sammy Davis Jr.	2015		—	£5.00
15	Satchmo	2014		—	£6.50
10	Screen Sirens — Veronica Lake	2015		—	£5.00
10	A Tribute to Danny Kaye	2010		—	£5.50
10	A Tribute to Dean Martin	2010		—	£5.00
10	A Tribute to Diana Dors	2010		—	£5.00
20	A Tribute to Gene Kelly	2010		—	£9.00
10	A Tribute to Judy Garland	2010		—	£5.50
15	A Tribute to On The Buses (1970s TV Show)	2014		—	£6.50
10	Victor Mature	2010		—	£5.50

TRUCARDS

M30	Animals	1970		20p	£3.00
M30	Battle of Britain	1970		20p	£4.00
M30	Flowers	1970		20p	£3.00
M30	History of Aircraft	1970		20p	£3.00
M30	Sport	1970		20p	£3.00
M30	Veteran and Vintage Cars	1970		20p	£3.00
M30	World War I	1970		20p	£3.00
M30	World War II	1970		20p	£3.00

TUCKETTS

25	Cricketers	1926		£35.00	—
50	Film Stars	1935	HT-105	£6.00	—
25	Football Stars	1928	HX-188	£25.00	—

TUCKFIELD (Australia)

M32	Australiana Animals	c1970		£1.60	—
M48	Australiana Birds Nos 1-48	c1970		70p	—
M48	Australiana Birds Nos 49-96	c1970		70p	—
M48	Australiana Birds Nos 97-144	c1970		70p	—
M48	Australiana Birds Nos 145-192	c1970		70p	—
M48	Australiana Birds Nos 193-240	c1970		70p	—
M48	Australiana Birds Nos 241-288	c1970		70p	—
M48	Australiana Birds Nos 289-336	c1970		70p	—
M48	Australiana Birds Nos 337-384	c1970		70p	—

TUFF STUFF (USA)

LT33	Peanuts by Schulz	1992		—	£6.00
LT50	Remember Pearl Harbor	1991		—	£15.00
LT15	World War II Propaganda Diamond Edition	1991		—	£6.50

W.E. TURNER

20	War Pictures	1915	HX-122	£18.00	—

21st CENTURY ARCHIVES (USA)

LT50	The Comic Art Tribute To Joe Simon and Jack Kirby	1994		—	£8.00
LT100	National Lampoon	1993		—	£9.50

TWININGS TEA

30	Rare Stamps 1st Series	1958		80p	£24.00
30	Rare Stamps 2nd Series				
	A No overprint	1960		20p	£5.00
	B Red overprint	1960		20p	£3.00

TYPHOO TEA
(36 page Illustrated Reference Book — £4.50)

25	Aesop's Fables	1924	HT-117	£3.20	£80.00
M12	The Amazing World of Doctor Who................	1976		£2.25	£27.00
25	Ancient and Annual Customs....................	1924		£2.60	£65.00
L25	Animal Friends of Man	1927	HT-118	£5.00	—
L25	Animal Offence and Defence	1928		£1.60	£40.00
24	British Birds and Their Eggs	1914	HX-164	£13.00	—
L25	British Birds and Their Eggs	1936		£1.80	£45.00
	British Empire at Work:				
30	1 Normal set with pictures	1925		£1.70	£50.00
30	2 Wording only 'This is a Continuation Card'	1925		£7.00	—
1	3 The Last Chance Card....................	c1925		—	£10.00
25	Calendar 1934 (Dogs)	1933		£30.00	—
25	Calendar...	1936	HT-120	£16.00	—
L1	Calendar..	1937		—	£9.00
L25	Characters from Shakespeare	1937		£1.40	£35.00
25	Common Objects Highly Magnified (multi-backed) ...	1925		£1.60	£40.00
25	Conundrums	1915		£20.00	—
24	Do You Know?.....................................	1962		20p	£3.50
	Album			—	£12.00
L25	Famous Voyages (multi-backed)	1933	HT-123	£1.80	£45.00
M20	Flags and Arms of Countries	1916	HT-124	£16.00	—
24	Great Achievements	1967		£1.40	£35.00
	Album			—	£20.00
L25	Historical Buildings	1939		£2.00	£50.00
L25	Homes of Famous Men (multi-backed)	1934		£1.40	£35.00
L25	Horses	1934		£1.80	£45.00

TYPHOO TEA (continued)

Size & quantity		Date	Handbook reference	Price per card	Complete set
L25	Important Industries of the British Empire (multi-backed)	1938	HT-127	50p	£12.50
L25	Interesting Events in British History (multi-backed) ...	1938	HT-127	50p	£12.50
10	Nursery Rhymes ...	c1910	HT-130	£25.00	—
24	Our Empire's Defenders	c1915		£32.00	—
48	Puzzle Pictures	c1915		£32.00	—
L30	Robin Hood and His Merry Men:				
	A Back with Oval Imprint...	1926		£8.00	—
	B Back without Oval Imprint...	1926		£8.00	—
L25	Scenes from John Halifax, Gentleman	1931		£2.40	£60.00
L25	Scenes from Lorna Doone:		HT-132		
	A Lemon borders to picture side (multi-backed) ...	1930		£3.60	—
	B Orange borders to picture side (multi-backed) ...	1930		£3.60	—
L25	Scenes from a Tale of Two Cities by Charles Dickens:				
	A Back inscribed '897.1/31' ...	1931		£3.60	£90.00
	B Back inscribed '897.10/31'	1931		£4.50	—
L30	The Story of David Copperfield:				
	A Coupon inscribed 'until 30th September' ...	1930		£3.00	£90.00
	B Coupon inscribed 'until end of October' ...	1930		£6.00	—
	C With coupon cut off...	1930		£2.50	£75.00
L25	The Swiss Family Robinson (multi-backed) ...	1935	HT-133	£2.00	£50.00
24	Travel Through the Ages	1961		20p	£3.50
	Album ...			—	£12.00
L25	Trees of the Countryside (multi-backed) ...	1937	HT-127	80p	£20.00
L25	Whilst We Sleep Series:				
	A Back with inscription '79610/10/28'	1928		£3.40	—
	B Back without inscription '79610/10/28' ...	1928		£3.00	£75.00
24	Wild Flowers	1963		24p	£6.00
	Album ...			—	£12.00
L25	Wild Flowers in Their Families 1st Series	1935		£1.20	£30.00
L25	Wild Flowers in Their Families 2nd Series	1936		£1.20	£30.00
L25	Wonder Cities of the World (multi-backed)	1933	HT-134	£1.80	£45.00
M24	Wonderful World of Disney	1975		£3.60	—
L25	Work on the Farm (No. 1 multi-backed)	1932	HT-135	£4.00	£100.00
25	Zoo Series ...	1932	HX-186	£1.40	£35.00
	Package issues:				
	Children's series of:				
L20	By Pond and Stream...	1960		50p	£10.00
L20	Common British Birds	1954		50p	£10.00
L20	Costumes of the World	1961		70p	—
L20	Famous Bridges	1958		50p	—
L20	Famous Buildings...	1953		50p	£10.00
L20	Pets	1959		50p	—
L20	Some Countryside Animals	1957		50p	—
L20	Some Popular Breeds of Dogs	1955		80p	£16.00
L20	Some World Wonders	1959		50p	£10.00
L20	Types of Ships ...	1956		50p	£10.00
L20	Wild Animals	1952		50p	£10.00
L24	Do You Know?...	1962		50p	£12.00
L24	Famous Football Clubs...	1964		£2.00	—
	Famous Football Clubs 2nd Series:				
L24	A With 'Second Series' in red above picture ...	1965		£2.50	—
L24	B Without 'Second Series' in red above picture ...	1965		£2.50	—
L26	Football Club Plaques	1973	HT-125	£7.00	—
L24	Football Stars, New Series	1973		£2.80	—
L24	Great Voyages of Discovery	1966		50p	£12.00

TYPHOO TEA (continued)

L24	International Football Stars		1967		£2.80	—
L24	International Football Stars 2nd Series		1969		£2.80	—
L24	100 Years of Great British Achievements		1972		75p	—
	Album				—	£25.00
L24	Travel Through the Ages		1961		50p	—
L24	Wild Flowers		1963		60p	£15.00
	Premium issues:					
EL24	Famous Football Clubs 1st Series		1964	HT-121	£12.00	—
EL24	Famous Football Clubs 2nd Series		1965	HT-122	£10.00	—
EL24	Football Stars		1973	HT-126	£9.00	—
EL24	International Football Stars 1st Series		1967	HT-128	£9.00	—
EL24	International Football Stars 2nd Series		1969	HT-129	£9.00	—
EL24	100 Years of Great British Achievements:					
	A Plain back		1972		£1.25	£30.00
	B Printed back		1972		£5.00	£125.00

TYSON & CO. LTD

28	Semaphore Signals		c1912		£18.00	—

'UNION JACK'

MP6	Monarchs of the Ring		1923		£10.00	—
M8	Police of All Nations		1922		£7.50	—

UNITED AUTOMOBILE SERVICES

Kodak Views Series:

25	Castles, Series No. 1		1925		£7.00	—
25	Churches, Series No. 2		1925		£7.00	—
25	United, Series No. 3		1925		£7.00	—
25	Places of Interest, Series No. 4		1925		£7.00	—

THE UNITED CONFECTIONERY CO. LTD

50	Wild Animals of the World		1905	HX-216	£12.00	—

UNITED DAIRIES (Tea)

25	Aquarium Fish		1964	HX-87	28p	£7.00
25	Birds and Their Eggs		1961	HX-1.3	70p	£17.50
25	British Uniforms of the 19th Century		1962	HX-78	70p	£17.50
25	The Story of Milk		1966	HX-3	30p	£7.50
25	The West		1963	HX-42	80p	£20.00

UNIVERSAL AUTOMATICS LTD

L30	Trains of the World		1958	HX-121	£1.35	—

UNIVERSAL CCC

15	Australia Cricket Team 1905		1986		—	£3.00
15	English Cricketers 1902		1987		—	£3.00

UNSTOPABLE CARDS

LT72	The Avengers 50 (TV Series of the 1960s)		2012		—	£8.00
LT54	Blake's 7 1st Series (1970/80s TV Series)		2013		—	£7.50
LT54	Blake's 7 2nd Series (1970s/80s TV Series)		2014		—	£7.50
LT54	Doctor Who and the Daleks (Movies)		2015		—	£7.50
LT54	The Man Who Fell to Earth		2014		—	£8.50
LT54	The Wicker Man		2014		—	£7.50
LT54	The Women of The Avengers		2014		—	£7.50

UPPER DECK (Germany)

LT45	Werder Bremen F.C...............................	1997	—	£6.00

UPPER DECK (Italy)

LT45	Italian Footballers World Cup.............................	1998	—	£6.00
LT90	Juventus F.C. 1994/95	1994	—	£7.50
LT45	Juventus F.C. Centenary 1897-1997	1997	—	£7.50

UPPER DECK (Spain)

LT45	Spanish Footballers World Cup	1998	—	£6.00

UPPER DECK (Sweden)

LT224/225	Swedish Hockey League (minus No. 36) 1997/98	1997	20p	£15.00
LT30	Swedish Hockey League Crash Cards 1997/98	1997	—	£10.00
LT15	Swedish Hockey League Stickers 1997/98	1997	—	£5.00
LT15	Swedish Hockey League Update Series 1997/98	1997	—	£10.00

UPPER DECK (UK)

LT34	Digimon Digital Monsters	2000	—	£7.00
LT45	England's Qualifying Campaign (Football World Cup) 1st Series Nos 1 to 45	1997	—	£10.00
LT37	England's Qualifying Campaign (Football World Cup) 2nd Series Nos 46 to 82	1998	—	£10.00
LT135	Manchester United F.C. 2001............................	2001	20p	£17.50
LT14	Manchester United F.C. 2001 Legends of Old Trafford	2001	—	£14.00
LT7	Manchester United F.C. 2001 Magnificent 7's	2001	—	£7.00
LT7	Manchester United F.C. 2001 Strike Force	2001	—	£7.00
LT14	Manchester United F.C. 2001 We Are United	2001	—	£14.00
LT90	Manchester United F.C...................................	2002	—	£17.50
LT100	Manchester United F.C. Play Makers	2003	—	£17.50
LT100	Manchester United F.C. Strike Force	2003	—	£17.50
LT90	Manchester United Legends	2002	—	£17.50
LT45	Manchester United World Premiere	2001	—	£20.00
LT45	The Mini (Car) Collection	1996	—	£15.00
LT250	World Cup Football	1994	—	£25.00
LT17	World Cup Football nos 251-267 Unissued	1994	—	£10.00
LT30	World Cup Football All Stars	1994	—	£5.00

UPPER DECK (USA)

LT90	Adventures in Toon World	1993	—	£9.50
LT99	Anastasia — The Movie	1998	—	£8.50
LT90	Battlefield Earth — The Film	2000	—	£8.00
LT198	Beauty and the Beast	1992	—	£12.00
LT90	Congo The Film	1995	—	£9.50
LT89	Disney Treasures 1st Series	2003	—	£15.00
LT45	Disney Treasures 1st Series — Mickey Mouse	2003	—	£18.00
LT10	Disney Treasures 1st Series — Walt Disney Retrospective	2003	—	£3.50
LT90	Disney Treasures 2nd Series...........................	2003	—	£12.00
LT45	Disney Treasures 2nd Series — Donald Duck	2003	—	£15.00
LT10	Disney Treasures 2nd Series The Lion King Special Edition	2003	—	£3.50
LT89	Disney Treasures 3rd Series	2004	—	£12.00
LT10	Disney Treasures 3rd Series Aladdin Special Edition...	2004	—	£3.50
LT45	Disney Treasures 3rd Series — Winnie The Pooh	2004	—	£18.00
LT75	Disney Treasures Celebrate Mickey 75 Years of Fun...	2004	—	£12.00

UPPER DECK (USA) (continued)

		Date		Price	Complete set
LT75	Iron Man 2 — The Film	2010	—	—	£8.00
LT55	Looney Tunes Olympics 1996	1996	—	—	£8.00
LT210	N.H.L. Hockey Players 1st Series 1997/98	1997	—	20p	£15.00
LT55	Princess Gwenevere and The Jewell Riders	1996	—	—	£8.00
LT60	Space Jam — The Film	1996	—	—	£7.50
LT120	The Valiant Era	1993	—	—	£12.00
LT120	World Cup Toons	1994	—	—	£9.50

UPPER DECK/HOOLA HOOPS (UK)

L40	Basketball Players (NBA) (No. HH1 to HH40)	1997	—	—	£8.00

VAN DEN BERGHS LTD

EL8	Birds	1974	—	45p	£3.50
LT24	Pirates	1968	—	£3.00	—
LT24	This Modern World	1968	—	£2.25	£60.00

VAUXHALL MOTORS

L25	Vauxhall's 90th Anniversary Series	1993	—	—	£10.00

VENORLANDUS LTD

M48	Our Heroes, World of Sport	1979	—	50p	£24.00
	Album		—		£5.00

VERKADE (Holland)

L120	Cactussen (Cacti)	1931	—	25p	—
L140	De Bloemen en Haar Vrienden (Flowers and Their Friends)	1933	—	20p	£20.00
L140	De Boerderil (The Farm)	c1930	—	30p	—
L138	Hans de Torenkraai (Hans the Crow)	c1930	—	20p	£20.00
L132	Kamerplanten (House Plants)	1928	—	25p	—
L126	Mijn Aquarium (My Aquarium)	1925	—	30p	—
L132	Texel District	1927	—	30p	—
L126	Vetplanten (Succulents)	1932	—	20p	£25.00

VICTORIA GALLERY

L6	A Gathering of Spirits (Red Indians)	1994	—	—	£3.00
L20	American Civil War Leaders	1992	—	—	£7.00
L25	Ashes Winning Captains (cricket)	1993	—	—	£8.50
L20	Boxing Champions 1st Series	1991	—	—	£10.00
L21	Boxing Champions 2nd Series	1992	—	—	£7.00
L6	British Birds of Prey by D. Digby	1994	—	—	£3.00
L6	British Birds of Prey 2nd Series	1996	—	—	£3.00
L20	Caricatures of the British Army 1st Series	1994	—	—	£7.00
L20	Caricatures of the British Army 2nd Series	1994	—	30p	£7.00
L6	Classic Motor Cycles (Harley Davidson)	1993	—	—	£3.00
50	Deep Sea Diving	1997	—	20p	£10.50
L20	Embassy Snooker Celebrities	1988	—	—	£7.00
L20	Endangered Wild Animals	1992	—	—	£7.00
L10	Formula One 91 (Cars)	1991	—	—	£8.00
L25	Hollywood Moviemen	1993	—	—	£8.50
L20	Legends of Hollywood	1991	—	—	£7.00
L25	Olympic Greats	1992	—	—	£8.50
L20	Partners (Film Stars)	1992	—	—	£7.00
L15	The Ryder Cup (Golf)	1987	—	—	£15.00
L25	The Ryder Cup 1991 (Golf)	1991	—	—	£15.00

VICTORIA GALLERY (continued)

L12	Samurai Warriors	1996		—	£10.00
L10	Spirit of a Nation (Red Indians)	1991		—	£5.00
L12	Twelve Days of Christmas	1992		—	£6.00
L20	Uniforms of the American Civil War	1992		—	£7.00
L24	Uniforms of the American War of Independence	1993		—	£8.50
L12	Wild West — Frontiersmen	1993		—	£4.00
L12	Wild West — Indians	1993		—	£4.00
L12	Wild West — Lawmen	1993		—	£4.00
L12	Wild West — Outlaws	1993		—	£4.00

VICTORIAN CRICKET ASSOCIATION (Australia)

L20	Bushrangers Cricketers	1998		—	£6.00
L20	Bushrangers Cricketers	1999		—	£6.00

VINCENT GRAPHICS

M48	The Life and Times of Nelson	1991		—	£20.00

VISION (USA)

LT150	Generation Extreme (Extreme Sports)	1994		—	£15.00

VOMO AUTOMATICS

LT50	Flags of the World	c1960		£1.10	—

WAKEFORD

30	Army Pictures, Cartoons, etc	1916	HX-12	£100.00	—

JONATHAN WALES LTD

25	The History of Flight 1st Series	1963		£7.00	—
25	The History of Flight 2nd Series	1963		£7.00	—

WALES ON SUNDAY

L40	British Lions on Tour Australia (Rugby Union)	2001		20p	£8.00
L36	World Cup Heroes (Rugby Union Players)	1995		33p	£12.00
L24	World Cup Rugby Greats (including album)	1999		—	£10.00

WALES ON SUNDAY/WESTERN MAIL

EL13	Welsh Rugby Union — Graham Henry's Wales	2001		—	£4.00

WALKER HARRISON AND GARTHWAITE LTD

M15	Dogs	1902	HW-1	£25.00	—

WALKERS SNACK FOODS

K50	Looney Tunes — Tazos Nos 1-50 (circular)	1996		20p	£10.00
K10	Monster Munch Tazos (circular)	1996		—	£3.00
K35	Pokemon Tazos (circular)	2001		40p	—
K50	Star Wars Trilogy — Tazos (circular)	1997		25p	£12.50
K20	World Tazos Nos 51-70 (circular)	1996		25p	£5.00

T. WALL & SONS

24	Do You Know?	1965		20p	£4.00
	Album			—	£20.00
36	Dr. Who Adventure	1967		£3.00	£110.00
20	Incredible Hulk	1979		£1.00	£20.00
M6	Magicards — Prehistoric Animals	1971	HW-4	50p	£3.00
48	Moon Fleet	1966		25p	£12.50

T. WALL & SONS (continued)

EL6	Sea Creatures		1971		50p	£3.00
20	Skateboard Surfer		1978		25p	£5.00
20	Time Travel with Starship 4		1984		£3.50	—

WALLIS CHOCOLATES

24	British Birds...		c1920		£12.00	—

WALTERS' 'PALM' TOFFEE

50	Some Cap Badges of Territorial Regiments		1938		50p	£25.00

WAND CONFECTIONERY LTD

EL10	Chubby Checker — How To Do the Twist		1964	HW-7	£8.00	—
25	Commemoration Stamp Series		1962		£3.00	£75.00
EL35	Pop DJs		1967		£4.00	—
25	They Gave Their Names		1963	HX-52	50p	£12.50

F. WARNE & CO LTD

Observer's Picture Cards (issued with Presentation Box)

L32	Series	I	British Birds	c1955	£1.25	—
L32	Series	II	Wild Flowers	c1955	£1.25	—
L32	Series	III	British Wild Flowers	c1955	£1.25	—
L32	Series	IV	Dogs	c1955	£1.25	—
L32	Series	V	Domestic Animals	c1955	£1.25	—
L32	Series	VI	Trees	c1955	£1.25	—
L32	Series	VII	Flags	c1955	£1.25	—
L32	Series	VIII	Ships	c1955	£1.25	—
L32	Series	IX	Insects	c1955	£1.25	—

WARUS (UK)

10	The Beatles — Abbey Road	1998		—	£5.00
10	The Beatles — Beatles for Sale	1998		—	£5.00
10	The Beatles — Beatles for Sale No. 2 EP Series...	2005		—	£5.00
10	The Beatles — Beatles Second Album	2005		—	£5.00
10	The Beatles — Beatles 65...	2005		—	£5.00
10	The Beatles — EP Series...	2005		—	£5.00
10	The Beatles — Hard Day's Night	1998		—	£5.00
10	The Beatles — Help	1998		—	£5.00
10	The Beatles — Hits EP Series	2005		—	£5.00
10	The Beatles — Let It Be	1998		—	£5.00
10	The Beatles — Long Tall Sally EP Series	2005		—	£5.00
10	The Beatles — Magical Mystery Tour	1998		—	£5.00
10	The Beatles — Meet The Beatles	2005		—	£5.00
10	The Beatles — Million Sellers EP Series	2005		—	£5.00
10	The Beatles — Nowhere Man EP Series	2005		—	£5.00
10	The Beatles — Please Please Me	1998		—	£5.00
10	The Beatles — Revolver	1998		—	£5.00
10	The Beatles — Rubber Soul	1998		—	£5.00
10	The Beatles — Sgt. Pepper	1998		—	£5.00
10	The Beatles — Something New	2005		—	£5.00
10	The Beatles — Twist and Shout EP Series	2005		—	£5.00
10	The Beatles — White Album	1998		—	£5.00
10	The Beatles — With the Beatles...	1998		—	£5.00
10	The Beatles — Yellow Submarine	1998		—	£5.00
10	The Beatles — Yesterday and Today	2005		—	£5.00
10	The Beatles — Yesterday EP Series	2005		—	£5.00
10	The Rolling Stones Urban Jungle Tour	1998		—	£5.00

WARWICK DISTRICT COUNCIL

30	England's Historic Heartland		1980		20p	£3.50

WATFORD BISCUITS

KP48	Cinema Stars 1st Series		1955		£3.00	—
KP48	Cinema Stars 2nd Series		1956		£5.00	—

JOHN WATSON

M56	Norfolk Churches		2012		—	£9.50
M52	Taverns of East Anglia Series 1		2004		—	£9.50
M56	Taverns of Norfolk Series 2		2008		—	£9.50

WEBCOSA & CO. LTD

L20	Trail Town		1964	HW-15.1	£2.50	£50.00
M48	Victoria Cross Heroes (waxed paper issue)		c1963		£4.00	—

WEEKLY WELCOME

12	'Lest We Forget' cards		1916		£10.00	—

WEETABIX LTD

L25	Animal Cards		1960		70p	£17.50
L28	Asterix — His Friends and Foes...		1976		£2.50	—
L18	Batman and Wonderwoman		1979		£3.00	—
L25	British Birds...		1962		£2.40	—
L25	British Cars		1963		£3.60	—
L25	Conquest of Space, Series A		1958		£2.60	£65.00
	Album				—	£20.00
L25	Conquest of Space, Series B...		1959		£2.60	£65.00
	Album				—	£20.00
L24	Dr. Who — Coloured background		1977		£6.00	—
L24	Dr. Who — White background		1975		£6.00	—
L18	Flash Gordon		1981		£2.50	—
L18	Huckleberry Hound		1977		£2.50	—
L25	Our Pets...		1961		80p	£20.00
L18	Robin Hood Characters from Walt Disney		1974		£3.00	—
L18	Star Trek...		1979		£4.00	£70.00
L18	Superman		1978		£2.50	—
L25	Thrill Cards		1961		£2.40	—
L18	Walt Disney Cartoon Characters		1978		£3.00	—
L25	The Western Story		1959		£1.80	£45.00
L25	Working Dogs		1960		30p	£7.50
L18	World of Sport		1986		£4.00	—

WELSH RUGBY UNION

50	Great Welsh Rugby Players		1980		20p	£7.50

WEST BROMWICH ALBION FOOTBALL CLUB

M25	West Bromwich Albion Footballers		1993		—	£15.00
L12	West Bromwich Albion Footballers Plus Folder (VE/VJ Day Issue)		1995		—	£6.00

J. WEST FOODS LTD

M8	Famous Sea Adventurers (inscribed series of 14, only 8 cards issued)...		1972		40p	£3.00

WEST LONDON HOSPITAL

EL1	Calendar 1947 (size 125 × 75mm)	1947		—	£1.50

WEST LONDON SYNAGOGUE

25	Hebrew Texts Illustrated	1960		£2.00	—

WEST MIDLANDS COLLECTORS

24	Busby Babes (Football)	1990		—	£12.00
12	Busby Babes Nos 25-36 (Football)	1991		—	£3.00
36	Busby Babes (revised combined 1990/91 issues)	1994		—	£15.00
2	Busby Babes Additional Cards Nos 24 & 25 Error Marked Series of 25	1991		—	£1.50
30	England Captains (Football)	1997		—	£6.00
24	Golden Wolves (Football)	1989		25p	£6.00
24	Vintage Spurs (Football)	1993		—	£15.00

WEST MIDLANDS POLICE

EL24	The Old Bill Collection	1990		20p	£5.00
	Album			—	£5.00
EL36	Pictorial History of Walsall and District	1986		50p	£18.00
EL8	Play Safe — Stay Safe (including Album)	1992		—	£5.00

WEST RIDING COUNTY COUNCIL

20	Health Cards	c1920		£6.50	—

WEST YORKSHIRE FIRE SERVICE

M29	Huddersfield Giants R.L.F.C.	1999		—	£10.00

WEST YORKSHIRE POLICE

EL20	Great Britain Rugby League Stars	2003		—	£6.00

WESTERN MAIL

L24	Wales Soccer Stars	2003		—	£6.00
L36	Welsh Grand Slam (Rugby Union)	2005		—	£6.00

WESTON BISCUITS CO. LTD (Australia)

50	Dogs	c1965		£3.00	—
M24	Veteran and Vintage Cars 1st Series	1961		£2.00	£50.00
	Album			—	£5.00
M24	Veteran and Vintage Cars 2nd Series	1962		30p	£7.50

WHAT CAMERA

EL12	Photocards	1988		—	£3.00

R. WHEATLEY

36	Animal Pictures	c1920		£6.50	—

WHITBREAD & CO. LTD

M1	The Britannia Inn Sign:				
	A Printed Back	1958		—	£60.00
	B Plain Back	1958		—	£40.00
M1	Duke Without a Head Inn Sign	1958		—	£10.00

WHITBREAD & CO. LTD (continued)

Size & quantity		Date	Handbook reference	Price per card	Complete set
M50	Inn Signs 1st Series (metal)	1951		£3.80	£190.00
M50	Inn Signs 2nd Series (metal)	1951		£3.80	£190.00
M50	Inn Signs 3rd Series:				
	A Metal	1951		£4.50	£225.00
	B Card	1952		£3.80	£190.00
M50	Inn Signs 4th Series (card)	1952		£3.80	£190.00
M50	Inn Signs 5th Series (card)	1953		£3.80	£190.00
M4	Inn Signs (special issue)	1951		£7.00	—
M25	Inn Signs, Bournemouth	1973		£7.50	—
M25	Inn Signs, Devon and Somerset	1973		£2.00	£50.00
M25	Inn Signs, Isle of Wight	1974		£7.50	—
M25	Inn Signs, Kent	1973		£7.50	—
M15	Inn Signs, London:				
	A Complete set	1973		—	£100.00
	B 12 different (minus Nos 3, 10 & 13)	1973		£3.25	£40.00
M10	Inn Signs, London	1974		£5.00	—
	Album			—	£8.00
M25	Inn Signs, Maritime	1974		30p	£7.50
	Album			—	£12.00
M25	Inn Signs, Marlow	1973		£7.50	—
M25	Inn Signs, Portsmouth	1973		£9.00	—
M25	Inn Signs, Stratford-upon-Avon	1974		£6.00	—
M25	Inn Signs, West Pennine	1973		£7.50	—
M1	The Railway Inn Sign	1958		—	£13.00
M1	The Startled Saint Inn Sign:				
	A With Printed in Great Britain	1958		—	£65.00
	B Without Printed in Great Britain	1958		—	£45.00

THE WHITE FISH AUTHORITY

25	Fish We Eat	1954		20p	£3.00

WHITEHAVEN MUSEUM

M6	The Port of Whitehaven	1978		85p	£5.00

WHITEHEAD (NOTTINGHAM) LTD

L25	Kings and Queens	1980		20p	£3.50

WIKO (Germany)

50	Soldaten Der Welt	1969		30p	£15.00

WILCOCKS & WILCOCKS LTD

25	Birds	1965	HX-71	£2.40	—
25	British Cavalry Uniforms of the 19th Century	1964	HX-43	60p	£15.00
25	Garden Flowers	1964	HX-46	20p	£5.00
24	The Island of Ceylon	1964	HX-47	£5.00	—
25	Passenger Liners	1967	HX-82	80p	£20.00
25	People and Places	1967	HX-26	20p	£4.00
25	Tropical Birds	1965	HX-13	50p	£12.50
25	Wonders of the Deep	1965	HX-89	20p	£3.50
25	Wonders of the World (1st 25 cards only issued)	1971	HX-49	20p	£5.00

A.S. WILKIN LTD

25	Into Space	1960	HX-147	30p	£7.50

W.R. WILKINSON & CO. LTD

M25	Popular Footballers	c1955		£45.00	—

WILKINSON SWORD LTD

K4	Garden Tools (Firm's name in black on white background)...	1961	HW-30	£2.50	£10.00
K2/4	Garden Tools (Firm's name in white on black background)...	1961	HW-30	—	£2.00
K16	Regimental Swords	1995		£4.00	—
	Album			—	£20.00

WILLARDS CHOCOLATE LTD (Canada)

50	Indian Series c1925			£8.00	—

R.J. WILSON

L5	B.R. Preserved Diesel-Electric Locomotives...	2005		—	£5.00
LT6	British Birds...	2005		—	£3.00
L10	British Steam Locomotives	2000		—	£5.50
L6	Eggs of British Birds...	2004		—	£4.00
L6	Glamour Girls (Pin Up Girls)	2004		—	£4.00
L10	Hunting With the South Wold...	2000		—	£6.25
LT6	Lincolnshire Village Churches 1st Series	2006		—	£5.00
LT6	Lincolnshire Village Churches 2nd Series	2007		—	£5.00
LT6	Nests and Eggs of British Birds 1st Series	2005		—	£4.00
LT6	Nests and Eggs of British Birds 2nd Series...	2005		—	£4.00
LT6	Nests and Eggs of British Birds 3rd Series...	2006		—	£4.00
LT6	Nests and Eggs of British Birds 4th Series	2007		—	£4.00
L6	Railway Engines	2004		—	£3.00
10	Railway Locomotives	2000		—	£5.00
L4	The South Wold (Lincolnshire) Foxhounds	2004		—	£2.50
L10	Traditional Lincolnshire Country Life	2001		—	£6.25
L6	Vintage Agricultural Traction	2003		—	£6.50
L6	Vintage Motive Power	2004		—	£5.00
L10	Vintage Tractors	2002		—	£4.50
LT6	Wilford Bowls Club	2007		—	£4.00
LT6	Young of British Birds	2007		—	£4.00

WILTSHIRE LIBRARY

EL13	Wiltshire Railcards 1st Series	1978		—	£3.50
EL8	Wiltshire Railcards 2nd Series	1979		—	£3.00

WIMPY

M20	Super Heroes Super Villains	1979		£1.50	£30.00

WINGATE CARDS

10	Team Line—Ups (1950/60s Football Teams)	2014		—	£4.50

WINGS

M5	Back to the Egg — Paul McCartney	c1980		£3.00	—

WINTERLAND (USA)

LT10	Backstreet Boys Awards	2000		—	£4.00
LT4	Backstreet Boys Black & Blue	2000		—	£3.00
LT15	Backstreet Boys Hot Shots	2000		—	£4.00
LT25	Backstreet Boys Millennium	2000		—	£5.00

WIZARDS

EL81	Harry Potter & The Sorcerer's Stone		2001		—	£20.00
	A Nos 1 to 40				30p	—
	B Nos 41 to 81				20p	£8.00
EL40	Harry Potter & The Sorcerer's Stone Parallel Series ...		2001		£2.00	—

WOMAN'S OWN

8	Film Stars		c1955	HW-45	£6.50	—

WONDERBREAD (USA)

LT24	Close Encounters of The Third Kind		1977		—	£12.00

WONDERBREAD/TOPPS (USA)

LT24	American Football Stars		1976		—	£6.00

E. WOODHEAD & SONS

25	Types of British Soldiers		1914	HX-144	£30.00	—

WOOLWORTHS

M24	Guinness Book of Records		1989		—	£6.00

WOOLWORTHS-TOPPS (USA)

LT33	Baseball Highlights		1988		—	£8.00

WORLD CRICKET INC (New Zealand)

LT18	New Zealand Cricketers 2007		2007		75p	—
LT27	New Zealand Cricketers 2008		2008		—	£9.50
LT25	New Zealand Cricketers 2009		2009		50p	—

WORTHINGTON (BEST BITTER)

36	Sportsmen from 1920 to 1940 (Reprints from various cigarette card issues)		1992		£1.25	—

WRIGHTS BISCUITS LTD

24	Marvels of the World		1968		20p	£3.00
24	Mischief Goes to Mars:					
	A 'Join the Mischief Club' at base...		1954		20p	£5.00
	B 'Issued by Wright's Biscuits Ltd' at base		1954		40p	£10.00
	C Name at side, but not at base		1954		20p	£3.50

YORKSHIRE FRAMING CO

25	England World Cup 2006 (Football)		2006		—	£6.00
14	The 36th Ryder Cup		2006		—	£4.50

YOUNG BRITAIN

MP15	Favourite Cricketers Series (2 pictures per card)		1922		£7.00	—

YOUR CLASSIC MAGAZINE

50	Cars		c1980		£4.00	—

ZELLERS (Canada)

L24	Batman Returns		1992		—	£10.00

ANONYMOUS

Size & quantity		Date	Handbook reference	Price per card	Complete set
50	Animals of the World	1954	HX-93	20p	£5.00
4	Birds, Nests and Eggs	c1960		75p	£3.00
25	Bridges of the World	1958	HX-132	20p	£3.00
25	British Coins and Costumes	1958	HX-191	20p	£3.00
25	British Uniforms of the 19th Century:		HX-78		
	A Black back	c1965		32p	£8.00
	B Blue back	c1965		20p	£3.50
20	Budgerigars (officially indented by issuer)	1957		60p	£12.00
25	Cacti	c1965	HX-133	20p	£3.00
25	Castles of Britain	c1960	HX-134	50p	—
25	Children of All Nations	1958		20p	£3.00
25	The Circus	1964	HX-79	50p	—
25	Family Pets	1964	HX-136	30p	£7.50
? K300	Film & Entertainment Stars	c1960		40p	—
	A 10 Different Male Stars (size 44 x 28mm)				
	(our selection)	c1960		—	£3.00
	B 10 Different Female Stars (size 50 x 25mm)				
	(our selection)	c1960		—	£3.00
25	Flags and Emblems	c1965	HX-17	24p	£6.00
25	Flowers	c1970		20p	£3.00
25	Football Clubs and Badges	c1960	HX-137	20p	£4.00
110	General Interest Series	c1970		—	£12.00
40	Greats from the States (Golf)	1994		—	£20.00
50	Jewish Life in Many Lands	c1960		£1.20	£60.00
	Jewish Symbols & Ceremonies:				
50	A Complete set	1961		£2.00	£50.00
25	B Numbers 1 to 25 only	1961		20p	£3.00
25	Modern Aircraft	1958	HX-219	20p	£5.00
L12	Motor Cycles 1907-1950	1987		20p	£3.00
25	Musical Instruments	1967		20p	£3.00
25	Pigeons	1971		20p	£5.00
25	Pond Life	c1970	HX-81	20p	£3.00
1	Soldier — Bugler	c1970		—	£2.50
25	Sports of the Countries	c1970		80p	—
25	Tropical Birds	c1960	HX-13.1	20p	£4.00
1	Venice in London	c1970		—	£1.00

FILM AND ENTERTAINMENT
* * * STARS * * *

CLIFF RICHARD

These miniature glossy photographs
were issued anonymously around
1960 and we can supply the
following at 40p each

SUSAN HAYWARD
M.G.M.

Size approx 44 x 28mm

Pier Angelli	Robert Horton	Kenneth More
Brigitte Bardot	* Jeffrey Hunter	George Nader
* Warren Beatty	Glynis Johns	Sheree North
Ann Blyth	Shirley Jones	Kim Novak
Dirk Bogarde	Kay Kendall	Debra Paget
Marlon Brando	Deborah Kerr	Laya Raki
Rossano Brazzi	Frankie Laine	Johnnie Ray
Max Bygraves	Mario Lanza (light suit)	Debbie Reynolds (swimsuit)
* Eddie Byrnes	Piper Laurie	Debbie Reynolds (head)
Rory Calhoun	June Laverick	* Cliff Richard
Rosemary Clooney	Belinda Lee	Jane Russell
Perry Como	Janet Leigh	Janette Scott
Doris Day	Liberace	Jean Simmons
Yvonne De Carlo	Gina Lollobrigida	* Roger Smith
Diana Dors	Sophia Loren	* Tommy Steele
* Duanne Eddy	Dennis Lotis	Maureen Swanson
Anita Ekberg	Virginia McKenna	Elizabeth Taylor
Vera-Ellen	Gordon Macrae	Dickie Valentine
Ava Gardner	Jayne Mansfield	Mamie Van Doren
* James Garner	Dean Martin	* Frankie Vaughan (h&s)
Mitzi Gaynor	Victor Mature	Frankie Vaughan (singing)
Richard Greene	Virginia Mayo	Esther Williams
Susan Hayward	* Sal Mineo	Shelley Winters
Audrey Hepburn	Guy Mitchell	Natalie Wood
	Terry Moore	

Size approx 50 x 25mm

Lucille Ball	Yvonne De Carlo	* Hedy Lamarr
* Cyd Charisse	* Dale Evans (sitting)	Ann Miller
Jeanne Crain	* Dale Evans (standing)	* Gale Robbins
* Linda Darnell (black top)	Ava Gardner (black top)	* Jane Russell
Linda Darnell (swimsuit)	* Ava Gardner (skirt)	* Beryl Wallace
Doris Day	* Gloria Grahame	Esther Williams
	Susan Hayward	

SPECIAL OFFER:
The 10 male stars marked with an asterisk * for £3.00
The 10 female stars marked with an asterisk * for £3.00

375

TOP TRUMPS

We have available the following
Top Trumps sets that were
issued between 1978
and 1980.
These sets of colour
photos can also
be used as a
card game.

TOP TRUMPS (UK) (CARD GAMES)

L33	Dragsters (Series 7)	1978	£4.00
L33	Flowers (Quartets)	1978	£4.00
L35	Prehistoric Monsters	1979	£4.00
L33	Rockets	1980	£4.00

MINI TRUMPS SERIES 1

K25	Dragsters	1978	£3.00

MINI TRUMPS SERIES 2

* K25	Grand Prix Cars	1978	£3.00
* K25	Hot Rods	1978	£3.00
* K25	Jumbos and Jets	1978	£3.00
K25	Rally Cars	1978	£3.00
K25	Super Trains	1978	£3.00

SUPER MINI TRUMPS SERIES 1

* M25	Dragster Bikes	1978	£3.00
* M25	Formula Cars	1978	£3.00
M25	Helicopters	1978	£3.00
* M25	Stock Cars	1978	£3.00

SUPER MINI TRUMPS SERIES 2

M25	Dragsters	1978	£3.00
* M25	H P Giants (Lorries etc)	1978	£3.00
* M25	Super Cars	1978	£3.00
* M25	Super Dragsters	1978	£3.00

SPECIAL OFFER:
The 9 sets marked with an asterisk * for £19.00 (saving £8.00)

SECTION 5

LIEBIG CARD ISSUES .

In 1847, Justus von Liebig, an eminent German chemist at the Royal Pharmacy in Munich, published a treatise titled *Extractum Carnis* in which he described how a concentrated essence could be made from fresh meat. However, the cost of production was prohibitive until the vast herds of cattle on the grasslands of South America could be exploited

In 1863 an engineer, George Giebert, established a factory at Frey Bentos in Uruguay and began shipping low-cost extract to Liebig in Europe. After testing at a depot in Antwerp, the extract was sold in stone jars each with a distinctive label bearing the signature of Baron von Liebig who had been honoured for his contribution to science. The business expanded rapidly and in 1865 the Liebig's Extract of Meat Company Limited, with a capital of half a million pounds, was set up in London.

Trade cards had been circulating on the Continent since the 1850s, and the Liebig Company soon latched on to the fact that colourful cards were an excellent form of advertisement. In 1872, only a short time before the Baron died, the first cards or 'chromos' were published to show the production of Liebig extract. During the following 100 years, no fewer than 1863 different series were to be issued, ending in 1973, a few years after Liebig merged with Brooke Bond and became part of Brooke Bond Oxo.

Except for the earliest series issued before 1883, almost all the sets comprise six cards, although a few later issues were of 12 or 18. In a large format, approximately 100 x 70 mm, the cards were distributed in many countries and were printed in a number of languages, the most common of which were Italian, German and French, plus Bohemian, Danish, Dutch, Flemish, Hungarian, Russian, Spanish and Swedish. A few were in English, but these are rarely seen.

The cards were given away as complete sets in exchange for coupons. On the backs of many of the earlier cards was printed the signature 'J. v Liebig' in large blue script, a reflection of the number of imitation products which were marketed, some ending in protracted lawsuits. On one of the English language issues appears the words 'Caution. – A sort called 'Baron Liebig's Extract' with photo of Baron Liebig has no connection whatever with the Baron. Insist on having Liebig Company's Extract – avoid all imitation extracts.'

There is no doubt as to the authenticity of the cards, however. Printed on coated cardboard by the hand lithographic method using up to twelve colours, they are fine examples of the printer's art. The subjects cover almost every field of knowledge and human activity; the arts, places and scenes from many countries, historical events, the customs of different peoples, their fashions and occupations, ancient and colourful festivals, weapons of war and military uniforms, natural history in its many forms, bird, animal, insect and marine life, science, social and industrial life of past ages, various forms of transport old and new, sports and pastimes, etc. The Liebig 'chromos' provide very wide scope and a most fertile field for the specialist.

In the ensuing pages, we list all but the earliest three hundred series showing the number in the set, the internationally recognised 'Fada reference number', a translation of the subject description, an approximate date of issue, and the price per set. Only the 'Chromos' are covered, and collectors are referred to Section 4 Trade Card Issues for details of pre-war Oxo cards and the many post-war issues of Brooke Bond.

Incidentally, readers may be interested to know that the fascinating story of the Liebig Oxo Company and its card issues was published in numbers 484 to 486 of *Card Collectors News*, copies of which are still available @ £6.75 for the 3 copies plus £2.00 handling fee.

How to Use this Section

The series are listed in the same order as shown in the Italian-language Fada Liebig Catalogue, officially recognised by the Liebig Company. These are the 'F' reference numbers shown in the left-hand column. The second column shows the 'S' numbers which refer to the Sanguinetti Liebig listings which some collectors use for their numbering reference. The third column is the number of cards in the set, followed by an English language translation of the series title. The right-hand columns show the approximate date of issue and the price per set, in good average condition. Please see front of the catalogue for how to order cards etc

F No.	S No.	Qty	Title (English Translation)	Date	Set Price
301	293	6	Popular Songs	1891	£180.00
302	294	6	Playing Cards	1891	£140.00
303	295	6	Horses in the Circus	1891	£90.00
304	296	6	Child Clowns	1891	£140.00
305	297	6	Shells	1891	£90.00
306	299	6	Little Chefs III	1891	£250.00
307	298	6	Little Chefs IV	1891	—
308	300	6	National Dances II	1891	£80.00
309	303	6	Famous Explorers	1891	£110.00
310	304	6	Liebig in Africa	1891	£40.00
311	301	6	Where Liebig is Used	1891	£60.00
312	306	6	Adventures on the Railway	1891	—
313	307	6	Scattered Flowers	1891	£220.00
314	317	6	The Thieving Magpie (Opera by Rossini)	1891	£110.00
315	308	6	Nymphs with Sashes	1891	£80.00
316	309	6	Puzzle Pictures IX	1891	—
317	310	6	Puzzle Pictures X	1891	£100.00
318	320	6	Inventions of the 19th Century	1891	£75.00
319	311	6	Italian Plays	1891	£40.00
320	312	6	The Beautiful Melusina	1891	£45.00
321	313	6	Caricatures of Negroes	1891	£125.00
322	314	6	Marriage Costumes of different countries	1891	£100.00
323	318	6	Pierrot's Illness	1891	—
324	319	6	Food and Meals - menus	1891	£90.00
325	321	6	Proverbs II	1891	£90.00
326	322	6	The Illness of Pierrot	1891	£50.00
327	325	6	Symbols (Bird and People)	1891	£50.00
328	326	6	Coats of Arms	1891	—
329	327	6	Tea	1891	£50.00
330	329	12	Alphabet Girls	1892	£175.00
331	330	6	The Argonauts	1892	£70.00
332	355	6	Planets	1892	£140.00
333	332	6	The Bull	1892	£40.00
334	333	6	Songs IX	1892	—
335	334	6	The Coalman and The Englishman	1892	£450.00
336	335	6	Venetian Carnivals	1892	£50.00
337	336	6	Playing Cards IV	1892	—
338	337	6	The Ant and the Grasshopper	1892	£70.00
339	338	6	Father, Son and Donkey	1892	£55.00
340	339	6	Christopher Columbus II	1892	£60.00
341	340	6	National Dances III	1892	£100.00
342	341	6	National Dances IV	1892	£85.00
343	331	6	National Beauties II	1892	£75.00
344	342	6	Flower Girls IV	1892	£175.00
345	353	6	Faust (opera)	1892	£65.00
346	343	6	Gargantua (Giant)	1892	£85.00
347	344	6	Children's Games	1892	£75.00
348	345	6	Gnomes	1892	£90.00
349	365	6	The Trojan War	1892	£60.00
350	348	6	Puzzle Pictures XI	1892	£60.00
351	347	6	Puzzle Pictures XII	1892	£90.00
352	346	6	Puzzle Pictures XIII	1892	£70.00
353	349	6	Language of Flowers III	1892	£90.00
354	350	6	Natural Resources II	1892	£60.00
355	351	6	Christmas in Different Countries	1892	—
356	386	6	Christmas Customs in different countries	1892	£50.00
357	354	6	Geological Periods	1892	£50.00
358	356	6	Sleeping Beauty	1892	£50.00

F No.	S No.	Qty	LIEBIG CARD ISSUES Title (English Translation)	Date	Set Price
359	357	6	Problems II	1892	£70.00
360	358	6	Proverbs III	1892	£65.00
361	360	6	When you are alone and in Company	1892	£85.00
362	363	6	Puzzle Pictures VIII	1892	£110.00
363	362	6	Puzzle Pictures IX	1892	£110.00
364	361	6	Puzzle Pictures X	1892	£110.00
365	359	6	Grannie's Present, Mr. Punch	1892	£175.00
366	364	6	History of Writing I	1892	£50.00
367	366	6	Birds and Flowers	1892	£80.00
368	367	6	The Emperor William's Voyage	1892	£175.00
369	368	6	The Liebig Tree	1893	£50.00
370	369	12	Alphabet of Male Operatic Characters	1893	£110.00
371	375	6	Commerce, Industry and Culture	1893	£45.00
372	371	6	Calendar for 1893 January to June	1893	—
373	372	6	Charlemagne	1893	£45.00
374	373	6	Celebrated Castles	1893	£40.00
375	374	6	Famous Composers I	1893	£80.00
376	376	6	An Unfortunate Mistake	1893	—
377	377	6	Falstaff (Opera)	1893	£55.00
378	379	6	Symbolic Flowers	1893	£40.00
379	380	6	Flowers, Birds and Butterflies	1893	£50.00
380	370	6	Boats II	1893	£130.00
381	381	6	Puzzle Pictures XIV	1893	£70.00
382	382	6	Puzzle Pictures XV	1893	£60.00
383	383	6	Puzzle Pictures XVI	1893	£175.00
384	384	6	Puzzle Pictures XVII	1893	£110.00
385	388	6	Lohengrin Opera by Wagner	1893	£70.00
386	385	6	Italian Masquerade VIII	1893	£40.00
387	352	6	Shadowgraphs I	1893	£45.00
388	387	6	Shadowgraphs II	1893	£60.00
389	392	6	Precious Stones	1893	£50.00
390	393	6	Problems III	1893	£70.00
391	421	6	Proverbs IV	1893	£250.00
392	394	6	Picture Puzzle XI	1893	—
393	395	6	Picture Puzzle XII	1893	£175.00
394	391	6	Opera Scenes III	1893	£40.00
395	389	6	A Midsummer's Night Dream	1893	£35.00
396	396	6	States of America	1893	£110.00
397	397	6	Styles of Architecture	1893	£40.00
398	398	6	Story of France	1893	£45.00
399	399	6	The Magic Table	1893	£80.00
400	400	6	The Telephone	1893	—
401	401	6	The Trumpeter from Sakkingen	1893	£100.00
402	402	6	The Voyage of Mr. Durand	1893	£70.00
403	403	6	Travel Around the World	1893	£40.00
404	390	6	The Walkyries (Opera)	1893	£90.00
405	434	6	The Weather	1894	—
406	435	6	Adventure in the Congo	1894	—
407	405	6	Popular Songs X	1894	£60.00
408	436	6	Seaside Towns	1894	£90.00
409	406	6	Famous Composers II	1894	£60.00
410	407	6	The Legend of Frithjof	1894	£40.00
411	408	6	In Japan	1894	£55.00
412	409	6	Magic	1894	£90.00
413	410	6	Months of the Year	1894	£70.00
414	411	6	Children's Occupations	1894	£70.00
415	412	6	Scandinavian Mythology	1894	£70.00
416	413	6	The World of Children	1894	£60.00

F No.	S No.	Qty	Title (English Translation)	Date	Set Price
417	414	6	Monograms	1894	£45.00
418	415	6	The Dwarf Nose (Fairy Tale)	1894	£40.00
419	416	6	Christmas Scenes I	1894	£60.00
420	417	6	Marriage	1894	—
421	419	6	Theft IV (Pierrott)	1894	£90.00
422	420	6	Problems IV	1894	£40.00
423	422	6	Proverbs V	1894	£70.00
424	423	6	Puzzle Pictures XIII	1894	—
425	424	6	Puzzle Pictures XIV	1894	£130.00
426	404	6	Masked Ball	1894	—
427	425	6	Carnival Scenes	1894	£110.00
428	418	6	Opera Scenes IV (Caricatures)	1894	£50.00
429	431	6	Views of Venice	1894	£50.00
430	428	6	Leisure Sports	1894	£50.00
431	427	6	Theatre Scenes	1894	£60.00
432	426	6	The Story of Writing II	1894	£40.00
433	429	6	Story of France II	1894	—
434	430	6	History of Transport	1894	—
435	432	6	Around the Mediterranean	1894	£40.00
436	433	6	Arts and Crafts	1895	£45.00
437	438	6	Hunting	1895	£45.00
438	439	6	The Wild Hunter (poem by Wolff)	1895	£65.00
439	454	6	Carmen (Opera)	1895	£80.00
440	441	6	Circus Scenes with children	1895	£250.00
441	449	6	Letters of Liebig with Flowers	1895	£40.00
442	447	6	Times of the Day	1895	£50.00
443	444	6	Children's Faces with Flowers	1895	£55.00
444	445	6	Flower Girls' Bodies	1895	£50.00
445	459	6	On and Off Stage	1895	£65.00
446	446	6	Winged People	1895	£55.00
447	448	6	Puzzle Pictures XVIII	1895	£80.00
448	450	6	Madame Sans-Gene by Sardov	1895	£130.00
449	451	6	The Seven Wonders of the World	1895	£60.00
450	437	6	Barometer Children	1895	£225.00
451	452	6	Christmas II	1895	£80.00
452	453	6	Shipping Through the Ages	1895	£60.00
453	455	6	The Oyster and the Pilgrims	1895	£55.00
454	442	6	Children with Kitchen Utensils	1895	£80.00
455	456	6	Children Growing Up	1895	£80.00
456	457	6	Provinces of France III	1895	£70.00
457	458	6	Romeo and Juliet	1895	£45.00
458	443	6	Scenes in the Moonlight	1895	£75.00
459	460	6	Snow White and the Seven Dwarfs	1895	£100.00
460	461	6	Sport I (English)	1895	—
461	462	6	Sport II	1895	£100.00
462	494	6	Sports III	1895	£90.00
463	495	6	Winter Sports I	1895	£75.00
464	463	6	Till the Buffoon	1895	£60.00
465	464	6	Wine	1895	£50.00
466	485	6	The African (Opera)	1896	£55.00
467	465	6	The Arts II	1896	£45.00
468	467	6	The Hunt	1896	£300.00
469	468	6	Views of Cities	1896	£40.00
470	500	6	The Course of Life I	1896	£90.00
471	469	6	Ancient Gods	1896	£60.00
472	471	6	Women and Children in Different Countries	1896	£50.00
473	472	6	Mythological Scenes	1896	£50.00
474	473	6	Fables of La Fontaine II	1896	—

F No.	S No.	Qty	Title (English Translation)	Date	Set Price
475	474	6	Alpine Flowers	1896	£55.00
476	475	6	Flowers with Cupids	1896	£50.00
477	476	6	The Two Smokers	1896	–
478	477	6	Gargantua II (Giant)	1896	–
479	478	6	The Policemen and the Apple Thieves	1896	£60.00
480	488	6	People Young and Old	1896	£50.00
481	479	6	Hansel and Gretel	1896	£70.00
482	480	6	Puzzle Pictures XIX	1896	£45.00
483	481	6	Musical Instruments	1896	£65.00
484	482	6	The Kaethchen Von Hielbronn (Play)	1896	£50.00
485	490	6	Mountain People	1896	£50.00
486	484	6	Christmas III	1896	£50.00
487	487	6	German Town Halls	1896	£35.00
488	489	6	Celebrated Painters	1896	£35.00
489	491	6	Famous Queens	1896	£35.00
490	470	6	Old German Proverbs	1896	£50.00
491	492	6	French Provinces IV	1896	£40.00
492	493	6	The Valiant Tailor	1896	£80.00
493	466	6	Comic Animal Scenes II	1896	£70.00
494	483	6	Army on Manoeuvres	1896	£45.00
495	496	6	Bible Stories V	1896	£45.00
496	497	6	Wandering Musicians	1896	£75.00
497	486	6	Tannhauser (Opera)	1896	£50.00
498	498	6	Theatre of Berlin I	1896	£45.00
499	499	6	Theatre of Berlin II	1896	£55.00
500	501	6	Trees of Different Latitudes	1897	£30.00
501	502	6	Types of Warships	1897	£35.00
502	507	6	German Dramatists	1897	£45.00
503	504	6	Variety Acts	1897	£30.00
504	505	6	Popular Songs XI	1897	£60.00
505	506	6	The Carnival in Rome	1897	£25.00
506	508	6	Shells II	1897	£40.00
507	509	6	Cooper's Adventures with the Red Indians	1897	£40.00
508	510	6	Special Army Corps	1897	£25.00
509	511	6	Biggest Natural Phenomena	1897	£30.00
510	512	6	Crusades I	1897	£30.00
511	513	6	Crusades II	1897	£30.00
512	514	6	Famous Women in History	1897	£22.00
513	515	6	Natural Tricks of Light	1897	£30.00
514	516	6	Scenes from the time of the Caliphs	1897	£30.00
515	517	6	Journey into the Alps	1897	£23.00
516	518	6	Butterflies of Central Europe IV	1897	£35.00
517	519	6	Butterflies and Moths V	1897	£35.00
518	520	6	Flowers and Lovers	1897	£30.00
519	526	6	The Letters of Liebig with Flowers	1897	£50.00
520	521	6	Postage Stamps I	1897	£30.00
521	522	6	Fungi	1897	£32.00
522	523	6	In Japan II	1897	£25.00
523	524	6	The Discovery of the Route to the Indies	1897	£20.00
524	525	6	Puzzle Pictures XX	1897	£30.00
525	527	6	The Conquest of Mexico	1897	£25.00
526	529	6	Orders of Chivalry I	1897	£25.00
527	530	6	Pastimes for Winter and Summer	1897	£30.00
528	528	6	The Prophet (Opera)	1897	£20.00
529	533	6	Provinces of France V	1897	£25.00
530	539	6	The Pied Piper	1897	£55.00
531	503	6	Cattle Breeds	1897	£20.00
532	531	6	Types of Poultry	1897	£40.00

F No.	S No.	Qty	Title (English Translation)	Date	Set Price
533	532	6	The First Pipe Tobacco or sweets	1897	£40.00
534	541	6	The Snow Ball	1897	£50.00
535	534	6	Famous Sculptors	1897	£30.00
536	535	6	The Five Senses II	1897	£25.00
537	536	6	History of France III	1897	£30.00
538	537	6	History of the Telegraph	1897	£30.00
539	538	6	Horse-drawn Carriages	1897	£45.00
540	540	6	Exotic Flowers and Birds VII	1897	£40.00
541	542	6	Signs of the Zodiac	1897	£70.00
542	543	12	The Alphabet (Male National Costumes)	1898	£50.00
543	545	6	Fishing for Whales	1898	£30.00
544	546	6	Hunting Scenes XII	1898	£25.00
545	547	6	Cantons of Switzerland	1898	£30.00
546	570	6	Children's Nursery Rhymes III	1898	£300.00
547	548	6	Popular Folksongs XIII	1898	£35.00
548	549	6	Carnival Serenades	1898	£22.00
549	550	6	Royal Castles of Bavaria	1898	£25.00
550	551	6	Children with Kitchen Utensils	1898	£35.00
551	552	6	Don Quixote	1898	£25.00
552	556	6	Flower Girls V	1898	£32.00
553	578	6	Uses of Liebig IV	1898	—
554	554	6	Flower Children	1898	£30.00
555	555	6	Moths of the Night of Central Europe	1898	£28.00
556	557	6	Rivers of Europe	1898	£25.00
557	558	6	Happy Children	1898	£30.00
558	559	6	Puzzle Pictures XXI	1898	£25.00
559	560	6	Puzzle Pictures XXII	1898	£25.00
560	561	6	National Musical Instruments II	1898	£25.00
561	562	6	The Book	1898	£25.00
562	563	6	Language of Flowers IV	1898	£25.00
563	564	6	Monuments of Ancient Rome	1898	£25.00
564	565	6	Children and Balloons	1898	£35.00
565	566	6	The Cultivation of Plants in Warm Countries	1898	£20.00
566	567	6	Celebrated Poets	1898	£20.00
567	568	6	Provinces of Spain	1898	£30.00
568	569	6	Provinces of Italy	1898	£22.00
569	572	6	Robezahl (Fable)	1898	£50.00
570	571	6	Nursery Rhymes IV	1898	£90.00
571	553	6	Elephant Tales	1898	£35.00
572	544	6	Snow White and Rose Red	1898	£55.00
573	574	6	Sport (Grand Ballet of L. Manzotti)	1898	£25.00
574	575	6	Styles of Architecture II	1898	£22.00
575	573	6	Scenes of Old France IV	1898	£25.00
576	576	6	Children's Natural History	1898	£30.00
577	577	6	Variety Actions	1898	£30.00
578	579	6	Modes of Travel	1898	£25.00
579	609	12	Alphabet (Female National Costumes) IV	1899	£80.00
580	602	6	Beasts of Burden	1899	£20.00
581	580	6	National Drinks	1899	£22.00
582	581	6	Bismark	1899	£25.00
583	582	6	The Naughty Dog	1899	£50.00
584	583	6	Famous Waterfall	1899	£20.00
585	596	6	Musical Celebrities	1899	£25.00
586	584	6	Views of European Cities	1899	£20.00
587	586	6	The Danube	1899	£22.00
588	585	6	Cuba	1899	£20.00
589	587	6	The Making of Iron	1899	£20.00
590	588	6	Popular Festivals Masked	1899	£18.00

F No.	S No.	Qty	Title (English Translation)	Date	Set Price
591	589	6	Postage Stamps II	1899	£35.00
592	590	6	Gnomes	1899	£40.00
593	591	6	The Development of Artificial Illuminations	1899	£20.00
594	592	6	Puzzle Pictures XXIII	1899	£25.00
595	593	6	National Anthems II (with music)	1899	£70.00
596	594	6	Inventors I	1899	£22.00
597	595	6	Marine Fauna	1899	£18.00
598	597	6	Orders of Chivalry II	1899	£22.00
599	598	6	The Tit Family	1899	£20.00
600	599	6	Fish and Fishing II	1899	£28.00
601	600	6	Famous Bridges	1899	£18.00
602	601	6	Art Forms	1899	£22.00
603	603	6	Richard III by Shakespeare	1899	£20.00
604	604	6	Sea Rescues	1899	£20.00
605	605	6	Comic Situations	1899	£20.00
606	606	6	In Transvaal	1899	£20.00
607	608	6	European Military Uniforms	1899	£20.00
608	607	6	Birds - Fowl	1899	£25.00
609	638	6	Hamlet (Opera)	1900	£18.00
610	610	6	Balloons	1900	£40.00
611	611	6	Children's Army	1900	£60.00
612	612	6	Doll Making	1900	£35.00
613	613	6	Country Children	1900	£25.00
614	629	6	Little Brother and Sister	1900	£40.00
615	614	6	At the Races	1900	£25.00
616	615	6	Breeds of Dogs I	1900	£50.00
617	616	6	Popular Songs	1900	£65.00
618	617	6	German Colonies	1900	£40.00
619	618	6	Colours II	1900	£32.00
620	619	6	Military Uniforms in Different Ages	1900	£25.00
621	620	6	National Dances V	1900	£20.00
622	651	6	In the World of the Birds	1900	£35.00
623	621	6	Famous Words of Schiller & Goethe	1900	£50.00
624	622	6	Asiatic Women	1900	£40.00
625	623	6	Duelling	1900	£20.00
626	624	12	World Exhibition 1900 Paris	1900	£75.00
627	625	6	Fable of La Fontaine III	1900	£35.00
628	626	6	Neapolitan Festivals	1900	£18.00
629	627	6	From Field and Forest	1900	£22.00
630	628	6	Postage Stamps III	1900	£30.00
631	630	6	Fruits and Women in Costume	1900	£20.00
632	631	6	Edible Fungi II	1900	£30.00
633	632	6	Gnomes and Elves	1900	£40.00
634	633	6	Grottos and Caves	1900	£25.00
635	634	6	William Tell	1900	£18.00
636	635	6	Inventors	1900	£65.00
637	636	6	The Philippine Islands	1900	£20.00
638	637	6	Monuments of Naval Heroes	1900	£20.00
639	639	6	Gold	1900	£18.00
640	640	6	The Poor Fisherman from 1001 Nights	1900	£35.00
641	641	6	Famous Regiments	1900	£25.00
642	642	6	Salt	1900	£18.00
643	648	6	Opera Scenes	1900	£25.00
644	643	6	The Swan Princess	1900	£40.00
645	644	6	Sinbad the Sailor	1900	£28.00
646	647	6	Bible Story VI	1900	£20.00
647	645	6	Dreams	1900	£25.00
648	646	6	Story of France V	1900	£18.00

F No.	S No.	Qty	Title (English Translation)	Date	Set Price
649	649	6	The World and its Inhabitants	1900	£18.00
650	650	6	Treasures of the Earth	1900	£16.00
651	652	6	The Glass Industry I	1900	£20.00
652	653	6	Volcanoes	1900	£18.00
653	654	6	The Manufacture of Sugar	1900	£20.00
654	667	6	Adventures of a Kite	1901	£60.00
655	657	6	Weapons of War through the Ages	1901	£18.00
656	658	6	Bicycle Games	1901	£40.00
657	664	6	What the Children Find in the Forest	1901	£50.00
658	659	6	Scenes of China I	1901	£18.00
659	660	6	Scenes of China II	1901	£20.00
660	661	6	Cyrano de Bergerac (Play)	1901	£15.00
661	662	6	Colours of the Rainbow	1901	£28.00
662	663	6	French Theatre	1901	—
663	689	6	The Course of Life	1901	£25.00
664	665	6	Easter Customs	1901	£15.00
665	666	6	Marriage Costumes	1901	£15.00
666	655	6	The Restaurant	1901	£18.00
667	668	6	Pheasants	1901	£25.00
668	669	6	Festivals of Ancient Times	1901	£16.00
669	675	6	Fidelio (Opera)	1901	£35.00
670	676	6	Der Freischutz (Opera)	1901	£16.00
671	685	6	The Two Envious Sisters from 1001 Nights	1901	£40.00
672	670	6	Seaside Children's Games	1901	—
673	671	6	The Island of Caroline	1901	£15.00
674	672	6	Famous Lakes	1901	£15.00
675	673	6	The Three Musketeers	1901	£18.00
676	656	6	The Christmas Tree	1901	£25.00
677	677	6	The Sparrow with Split Tongue (Japanese Fable)	1901	£15.00
678	678	6	Mountain Passes	1901	£14.00
679	679	6	Prince Achmed & Fairy Paribanu from 1001 Nights	1901	£45.00
680	680	6	The Rhine from Bingen to Coblenz	1901	£125.00
681	681	6	Course of the Rhine	1901	£15.00
682	682	6	The Rhine in History	1901	£14.00
683	683	6	Medieval War Scenes	1901	£15.00
684	674	6	Dutch Scenes	1901	£20.00
685	684	6	Composers	1901	£40.00
686	686	6	Famous Street Scenes from around the World	1901	£20.00
687	687	6	Johann Strauss and His Operas	1901	£15.00
688	688	6	Types and People of Hindustan	1901	£20.00
689	690	6	Unusual Trees	1902	£16.00
690	691	6	Special Armies	1902	£16.00
691	692	6	Architectural Art	1902	£15.00
692	694	6	Spa Towns	1902	£14.00
693	695	6	Famous City Ruins	1902	£40.00
694	715	6	Cultivation of Tobacco in Sumatra	1902	£14.00
695	696	6	Commerce	1902	£14.00
696	697	6	The Count of Monte Cristo	1902	£15.00
697	726	6	The Seven Ravens and the True Sister (Story)	1902	£35.00
698	728	6	Ancient Customs of the Provinces of France	1902	—
699	698	6	Whitsun Customs	1902	£14.00
700	699	6	Entertainments and Festivals in the Middle Ages	1902	£15.00
701	700	6	Spices	1902	£15.00
702	701	6	The Elephant	1902	£22.00
703	702	6	France in Olden Times	1902	£15.00
704	703	6	Game Bird Shooting	1902	£20.00
705	693	6	Famous Leaders	1902	£20.00
706	704	6	The Island of Samoa	1902	£15.00

F No.	S No.	Qty	Title (English Translation)	Date	Set Price
707	709	6	King Drosselbart	1902	£28.00
708	705	6	Naval Manoeuvres	1902	£22.00
709	706	6	Bread	1902	£15.00
710	707	6	Useful Plants	1902	£14.00
711	708	6	Homing Pigeon	1902	£20.00
712	710	6	Famous Rocks	1902	£12.00
713	711	6	Scenes from the History of Civilisation	1902	£14.00
714	712	6	Schools	1902	£14.00
715	713	6	Symbolic Flowers	1902	£40.00
716	714	6	History of France in the 16th Century VI	1902	£15.00
717	716	6	Treasures of the Sea	1902	£18.00
718	717	6	The Life of Verdi	1902	£17.00
719	752	6	The Life of a Director	1902	—
720	718	6	Culinary Art Through the Ages	1903	£15.00
721	719	6	The Art of Medicine	1903	£16.00
722	720	6	Feasts Through the Ages	1903	£14.00
723	722	6	Canals I	1903	£15.00
724	723	6	Canons Through the Ages	1903	£15.00
725	724	6	Horsemen I	1903	£15.00
726	761	6	Chasing the Butterfly	1903	£45.00
727	727	6	Constellations	1903	£25.00
728	729	6	The Heroines from Wagner's Operas	1903	£30.00
729	730	6	Various Scenes of the Uses of Liebig	1903	£28.00
730	731	6	Flower Festivals	1903	£15.00
731	732	6	Japanese Fable – The Mouse's Daughter	1903	£18.00
732	733	6	Rivers in France	1903	£15.00
733	734	6	Ice	1903	£14.00
734	735	6	Gulfs and Bays	1903	£14.00
735	725	6	Famous Conquerors 1st Series	1903	£15.00
736	765	6	Famous Conquerors 2nd Series	1903	£15.00
737	721	6	Types of Boats	1903	£18.00
738	736	6	Useful Insects	1903	£15.00
739	738	6	Alpine Troop Manoeuvres	1903	£12.00
740	739	6	Scenes with Gnomes	1903	£28.00
741	740	6	Flora and Fauna of the Alps	1903	£14.00
742	741	6	Monuments of Famous Captains	1903	£14.00
743	742	6	Monuments of Famous Scientists	1903	£14.00
744	743	6	La Muta dei Portici (Opera)	1903	£15.00
745	744	6	Sea Fishing	1903	£20.00
746	745	6	Use of Stone	1903	£14.00
747	746	6	Nomadic People	1903	£14.00
748	747	6	Clowns	1903	£25.00
749	737	6	Scenes from the Life of Liebig	1903	£12.00
750	748	6	Poisonous Snakes	1903	£18.00
751	750	6	Biblical Scenes VII	1903	£18.00
752	749	6	Sport	1903	£35.00
753	751	6	Drinking Vessels	1903	£14.00
754	754	6	The History of Needlework	1904	£12.00
755	755	6	Inns	1904	£14.00
756	758	6	Animals in Art	1904	£15.00
757	757	6	Famous Animals from History I	1904	£14.00
758	756	6	Famous Animals from History II	1904	£15.00
759	759	6	The Plough	1904	£14.00
760	784	6	The Elements II	1904	£25.00
761	760	6	Butter	1904	£14.00
762	762	6	Uncle Tom's Cabin	1904	£20.00
763	763	6	Cavaliers of Ancient Times II	1904	£18.00
764	764	6	Different Foods	1904	£35.00

F No.	S No.	Qty	Title (English Translation)	Date	Set Price
765	766	6	In Korea	1904	£10.00
766	767	6	Processions and Fetes	1904	£15.00
767	768	6	Ancient German Customs	1904	£15.00
768	769	6	Wedding Costumes	1904	£12.00
769	770	6	Dances Through The Ages	1904	£12.00
770	802	6	The Path of Life	1904	£25.00
771	772	6	The Seasons	1904	£20.00
772	774	6	In the Land of the Pharaohs	1904	£15.00
773	775	6	Trans-Siberian Railway	1904	£16.00
774	776	6	Popular Fetes	1904	£14.00
775	800	6	Harvest Ceremonies	1904	£40.00
776	777	6	Children Experimenting	1904	£28.00
777	778	6	Norwegian Fjords	1904	£15.00
778	782	6	The Glove	1904	£45.00
779	783	6	The Goose Girl	1904	£50.00
780	779	6	Water Creatures	1904	£14.00
781	780	6	Life in Japan	1904	£18.00
782	781	6	Cereals	1904	£12.00
783	753	6	Dwellings	1904	£55.00
784	785	6	The Italian Lakes II	1904	£14.00
785	786	6	The Letter	1904	£13.00
786	851	6	The Story of Mother Holle	1904	£50.00
787	787	6	Grandmothers	1904	£25.00
788	798	6	Birds and Their Nests	1904	£55.00
789	788	6	Parsifal (Opera)	1904	£100.00
790	790	6	Parliament Buildings	1904	£13.00
791	791	6	Plants in Decorative Art	1904	£14.00
792	792	6	Poisonous Plants	1904	£14.00
793	793	6	Precious Stones II	1904	£14.00
794	771	6	Scenes in the Lives of Famous Painters	1904	£14.00
795	794	6	Italian Renaissance Art	1904	£14.00
796	789	6	Operas IV	1904	£20.00
797	796	6	Scenes in Spain I	1904	£10.00
798	840	6	Scenes in Spain II	1904	£14.00
799	773	6	Children's Scenes	1904	£65.00
800	795	6	In Servia	1904	£12.00
801	797	6	Modes of Transport	1904	£60.00
802	799	6	Useful Birds	1904	£16.00
803	801	6	One Hundred Years of Travelling	1904	£45.00
804	803	6	Ducks	1905	£15.00
805	804	6	Antwerp in the Middle Ages	1905	£13.00
806	805	6	Dogs – (Head Silhouettes)	1905	£90.00
807	806	6	Views of Capital Cities	1905	£14.00
808	807	6	Rural Dwelling Places in Europe	1905	£13.00
809	808	6	Historic Castles	1905	£15.00
810	809	6	Life in Feudal Castles	1905	£12.00
811	810	6	Popular Customs of India	1905	£13.00
812	811	6	The Crusades	1905	£15.00
813	812	6	Emotions	1905	£25.00
814	813	6	Episodes in the History of Belgium 1st Series	1905	£13.00
815	814	6	Episodes in the History of Belgium 2nd Series	1905	£13.00
816	815	6	Factories of the Hanseatic Towns	1905	£45.00
817	816	6	The Fire in Artistic Industries	1905	£12.00
818	817	6	In Japan III	1905	£13.00
819	823	6	Types of Transport in Japan	1905	£12.00
820	839	6	Days of the Week	1905	£25.00
821	818	6	The War of the Roses	1905	£15.00
822	819	6	House Interiors	1905	£45.00

F No.	S No.	Qty	Title	Date	Set Price
823	820	6	Useful Trees	1905	£13.00
824	821	6	Places of Worship	1905	£11.00
825	822	6	Ancient War Machines	1905	–
826	824	6	Migration of People	1905	£12.00
827	825	6	Feminine Dress	1905	£25.00
828	826	6	Windmills	1905	£14.00
829	827	6	Wedding Procession	1905	£18.00
830	828	6	The Marriage of Figaro (Opera)	1905	£25.00
831	829	6	Oberon (Opera)	1905	£20.00
832	831	6	Medals Given to Females	1905	£15.00
833	832	6	Time Pieces	1905	£15.00
834	833	6	In Panama	1905	£15.00
835	834	6	The Fisherman and His Wife	1905	£40.00
836	836	6	Raphael	1905	£14.00
837	837	6	In Rumania	1905	£15.00
838	835	6	Opera Scenes – Leading Ladies	1905	£18.00
839	838	6	Famous Sculptors	1905	£18.00
840	841	6	History of France VII	1905	–
841	842	6	The Theatre - Old and New	1905	£14.00
842	830	6	Le Trouvere (Opera)	1905	£30.00
843	843	6	In Abyssinia	1906	£12.00
844	844	6	Dutch Head-Dress	1906	£14.00
845	846	6	Astronomers	1906	£17.00
846	847	6	Celebrated Colosseums	1906	£14.00
847	848	6	Popular Russian Costume	1906	£15.00
848	849	6	Heroes of Wagner's Operas	1906	£30.00
849	850	6	The Production of a Liebig Card	1906	£30.00
850	852	6	Gardens	1906	£13.00
851	853	6	In India	1906	£16.00
852	854	6	Views of Morocco	1906	£14.00
853	855	6	Materials for Artistic Industries III	1906	£12.00
854	856	6	Life of Mozart	1906	£20.00
855	857	6	Old Holland	1906	£13.00
856	859	6	Famous Italian Town Halls	1906	£12.00
857	860	6	Children in National Dress	1906	£25.00
858	861	6	Pompeii - Then and Now	1906	£14.00
859	862	6	Wells and Fountains	1906	£12.00
860	863	6	The Life of Rembrandt	1906	£13.00
861	864	6	History of Rome	1906	£12.00
862	858	6	Samson and Delilah (Opera)	1906	£18.00
863	845	6	Scenes of Africa	1906	£16.00
864	865	6	The Life of Shakespeare	1906	£16.00
865	866	6	Nymphs	1906	£15.00
866	867	6	Straits of Europe	1906	£15.00
867	868	6	Straits Outside Europe	1906	£16.00
868	869	6	In Sweden	1906	£13.00
869	870	6	The Simplon Tunnel	1906	£13.00
870	871	6	Famous Tragedies	1906	£15.00
871	872	6	Birds of Prey	1906	£15.00
872	873	6	Ensigns and Standards	1906	£15.00
873	874	6	Voyage in the Mediterranean	1906	£13.00
874	875	6	Ancient Dwellings	1907	£13.00
875	876	6	Sources of Water	1907	£13.00
876	877	6	In East Africa	1907	£13.00
877	878	6	Fruit Trees	1907	£13.00
878	879	6	Art in the Metal Industry	1907	£13.00
879	880	6	The Art of Different Races	1907	£13.00
880	881	6	Automobiles	1907	£30.00

F No.	S No.	Qty	LIEBIG CARD ISSUES Title (English Translation)	Date	Set Price
881	882	6	Cacti	1907	£13.00
882	883	6	The Carnival in Different Ages	1907	£13.00
883	884	6	Flourishing Towns in the Middle Ages	1907	£13.00
884	885	6	Guilds of Middle Ages	1907	£13.00
885	886	6	History of Female Dress	1907	£13.00
886	887	6	History of Male Costume	1907	£13.00
887	888	6	Berceaux Dynastiques	1907	£13.00
888	903	6	Don Juan (Opera)	1907	£25.00
889	889	6	Electricity	1907	£15.00
890	890	6	History of Belgium	1907	£10.00
891	891	6	Lighthouses	1907	£22.00
892	892	6	The Puppets Story	1907	£22.00
893	893	6	Popular Japanese Fetes	1907	£13.00
894	894	6	Markets and Fairs in Different Countries	1907	£13.00
895	895	6	In Finland	1907	£13.00
896	896	6	Flowers and Dragonflies	1907	£14.00
897	897	6	Roman Emperors	1907	£13.00
898	898	6	Inventions of the 19th Century	1907	—
899	899	6	Malta	1907	£20.00
900	900	6	Materials Used for Clothing	1907	£13.00
901	901	6	Famous Merchants	1907	£13.00
902	902	6	Parasols and Umbrellas	1907	£15.00
903	904	6	In Indo-China	1907	£13.00
904	905	6	In Persia	1907	£13.00
905	906	6	Medical Plants	1907	£13.00
906	907	6	In Spring	1907	£45.00
907	908	6	Queens	1907	£40.00
908	909	6	The Legend of Roland	1907	£50.00
909	910	6	In Scandinavia	1907	£13.00
910	911	6	Italian Scenes	1907	£13.00
911	912	6	The Story of Silk	1907	£13.00
912	913	6	On the Beach	1907	£22.00
913	914	6	In Turkistan	1907	£13.00
914	915	6	Views and Costumes in the Alp	1907	£14.00
915	916	6	In Venezuela	1907	£13.00
916	917	6	Afghanistan	1908	£12.00
917	918	6	The Hunter of Furs	1908	£20.00
918	919	6	In the Caucasus	1908	£15.00
919	920	6	In Chile	1908	£18.00
920	921	6	Money of Different Periods	1908	£15.00
921	922	6	Flowers of the Desert	1908	£15.00
922	923	6	Ancient Roman Buildings	1908	£15.00
923	924	6	The Manufacture of Perfume from Roses	1908	£17.00
924	925	6	In the Far West (Cowboys and Indians)	1908	£30.00
925	926	6	Aquatic Plant Life	1908	£17.00
926	927	6	Festival of Flowers II	1908	£15.00
927	928	6	Fetes in Olden Days	1908	£12.00
928	929	6	Flowers of the Night	1908	£15.00
929	930	6	The Flora in the Upper Mountain	1908	£13.00
930	931	6	Fruits and their Enemies in the Animal Kingdom	1908	£15.00
931	932	6	The Making of a Fire	1908	£14.00
932	933	6	Military Uniforms of Different Countries	1908	£15.00
933	934	6	Islands of the Mediterranean	1908	£15.00
934	935	6	The Feminine Arts	1908	£15.00
935	936	6	The Story of Steam Machines	1908	£20.00
936	937	6	Madagascar	1908	£15.00
937	939	6	The Merchant of Venice	1908	£15.00
938	940	6	In Mexico	1908	£15.00

F No.	S No.	Qty	LIEBIG CARD ISSUES Title (English Translation)	Date	Set Price
939	942	6	Mignon (Opera)	1908	£17.00
940	941	6	The Story of Nala and Damavanti	1908	£15.00
941	943	6	Historic Gateways to Cities	1908	£13.00
942	944	6	Harvesting in Different Countries	1908	£13.00
943	938	6	In the Domain of the Medusas (Jellyfish, etc)	1908	£14.00
944	945	6	The Sources Of Important Rivers	1908	£15.00
945	946	6	Birds Who Cannot Fly	1908	£15.00
946	947	6	Journey of Suen-Hedin to Tibet	1908	£20.00
947	948	6	Feminine Head-dress	1909	£20.00
948	949	6	In Burma	1909	£18.00
949	950	6	Famous Cloisters	1909	£13.00
950	951	6	French Colonies	1909	£15.00
951	952	6	The Culture of Cotton	1909	£14.00
952	953	6	The Coast of France	1909	£14.00
953	954	6	Curious and Ancient Writings	1909	£12.00
954	955	6	Episodes from Russian History	1909	£13.00
955	956	6	Children's Occupations	1909	£35.00
955A	956A	6	Children's Occupations	1909	£90.00
956	957	6	Episodes in the History of Famous Towns	1909	£13.00
957	958	6	Alpine Animals	1909	£20.00
958	959	6	Different Railway Systems	1909	£14.00
959	960	6	The Magic Flute (Opera)	1909	£30.00
960	961	6	Living in the Extreme North	1909	£13.00
961	962	6	Light and Illumination	1909	£14.00
962	963	6	Islands of New Guinea	1909	£14.00
963	966	6	Law Courts in Different Countries	1909	£17.00
964	967	6	Road Surfaces	1909	£13.00
965	968	6	Hobbies	1909	£14.00
966	969	6	Medicinal Plants	1909	£13.00
967	970	6	Useful Exotic Plants	1909	£14.00
968	971	6	Coastal Ports	1909	£15.00
969	973	6	In the Republic of Argentina	1909	£16.00
970	964	6	Robert the Devil (Opera)	1909	£15.00
971	974	6	Frederic de Schiller	1909	£16.00
972	975	6	Servicing at the Table in Ancient Times	1909	£12.00
973	976	6	Solanum (Plants)	1909	£13.00
974	977	6	Monarchs Among Their People	1909	£13.00
975	978	6	Styles of Furniture	1909	£13.00
976	979	6	The History of Weaving	1909	£13.00
977	965	6	La Traviata (Opera)	1909	£20.00
978	972	6	Picturesque Corners in Venice	1909	£14.00
979	981	6	Coaches and Carriages of the Ages	1909	£13.00
980	980	6	Old Costumes of France	1909	£100.00
981	982	6	Life in Siam	1909	£17.00
982	983	6	Armies of the Balkan States	1910	£14.00
983	984	6	In Australia	1910	£18.00
984	985	6	In Bulgaria	1910	£12.00
985	986	6	Carnival Scenes	1910	£14.00
986	987	6	Rubber Cultivation	1910	£14.00
987	988	6	The Story of the Round Table	1910	£14.00
988	989	6	Colonies of European Origin	1910	£14.00
989	990	6	The Flight of the Dragon	1910	£12.00
990	991	6	Summer Pastimes	1910	£14.00
991	992	6	The Story of Nibelungen	1910	£20.00
992	993	6	Evolution of Commerce and Industry	1910	£13.00
993	994	6	Wedding Feasts in Different Countries	1910	£13.00
994	995	6	Garibaldi and His Expedition 1860	1910	£14.00
995	996	6	Episodes of the Thirty Years War	1910	£15.00

F No.	S No.	Qty	Title (English Translation)	Date	Set Price
996	997	6	The Delivery of Jerusalem	1910	£10.00
997	998	6	Winter in Sunny Countries	1910	£12.00
998	999	6	Pastimes at the Sea Side	1910	£20.00
999	1002	6	The Master Singers of Nuremberg (Opera)	1910	£22.00
1000	1000	6	Monuments of the Renaissance	1910	£14.00
1001	1001	6	The Nine Muses	1910	£20.00
1002	1003	6	History of Porcelain	1910	£14.00
1003	1004	6	In Portugal	1910	£14.00
1004	1005	6	Scenes of Egypt	1910	£18.00
1005	1006	6	Performing Monkeys	1910	£14.00
1006	1007	6	History of France VIII (Louis XIV 1643-1715)	1910	£12.00
1007	1008	6	Evolution of Musical Instruments	1910	£14.00
1008	1009	6	The Good Old Times	1910	£13.00
1009	1010	6	In Turkey	1910	£17.00
1010	1011	6	Famous Old Churches	1910	£15.00
1011	1012	6	Picturesque Algeria	1911	£14.00
1012	1013	6	Exotic Dolls and Games	1911	£12.00
1013	1014	6	Uses of Bells	1911	£14.00
1014	1015	6	Famous Castles of Italy (Laziali)	1911	£20.00
1015	1016	6	Famous Castles of Italy (Piemontesi)	1911	£22.00
1016	1017	6	Celebrated Italian Military Leaders	1911	£12.00
1017	1026	6	Le Cid (Opera)	1911	£17.00
1018	1027	6	The Damnation of Faust (Opera)	1911	£14.00
1019	1018	6	Dances of Different Countries VI	1911	£14.00
1020	1019	6	Scented Flowers	1911	£13.00
1021	1020	6	In the Kingdom of Flowers	1911	£20.00
1022	1021	6	Ancient Roman Leaders	1911	£13.00
1023	1022	6	Iceland	1911	£12.00
1024	1023	6	Mountain People	1911	£14.00
1025	1024	6	Famous Dwarfs	1911	£40.00
1026	1025	6	Aerial Navigation	1911	£26.00
1027	1029	6	The Age of Pericles	1911	£10.00
1028	1028	6	Sacred Plants	1911	£15.00
1029	1060	6	The French Riviera	1911	£85.00
1030	1030	6	The Dardanelles	1911	£10.00
1031	1031	6	The Truffle	1911	£13.00
1032	1032	6	Towers	1911	£10.00
1033	1033	6	In Hungary	1911	£15.00
1034	1034	6	The History of Glass	1911	£12.00
1035	1035	6	Curious Animals	1912	£13.00
1036	1036	6	Sacred Animals	1912	£13.00
1037	1040	6	Ancient Norwegian Costumes	1912	£12.00
1038	1037	6	The Art of Cooking in Different Ages	1912	£12.00
1039	1038	6	In Brittany	1912	£13.00
1040	1039	6	Corsica	1912	£14.00
1041	1057	6	Curious Natural Bridges	1912	£12.00
1042	1041	6	Gods of the Hindus	1912	£18.00
1043	1043	6	Buildings in Rome	1912	£10.00
1044	1044	6	Italian Celebrities in their Childhood	1912	£20.00
1045	1045	6	Military Manoeuvres in Italy	1912	£12.00
1046	1046	6	Italian-Turkish War	1912	£17.00
1047	1047	6	The Library Through the Ages	1912	£11.00
1048	1048	6	Macbeth	1912	£15.00
1049	1049	6	The Masque	1912	£11.00
1050	1050	6	History of Lace	1912	£15.00
1051	1051	6	Gothic Monuments	1912	£12.00
1052	1052	6	Buildings in Italy	1912	£12.00
1053	1054	6	Equatorial Countries	1912	£12.00

F No.	S No.	Qty	LIEBIG CARD ISSUES Title (English Translation)	Date	Set Price
1054	1055	6	Imperial Palaces in China	1912	£9.00
1055	1056	6	Historic French Town Halls	1912	£12.00
1056	1042	6	Places in Paris	1912	£14.00
1057	1058	6	Ports of France	1912	£14.00
1058	1053	6	The Queen of Sheba (Opera - Goldmark)	1912	£14.00
1059	1059	6	The Republic of Andorra	1912	£12.00
1060	1061	6	St. Louis King of France	1912	£13.00
1061	1062	6	The Champagne Industry	1912	£15.00
1062	1063	6	Sleighs in Different Countries	1912	£14.00
1063	1064	6	Ancient and Modern Villas	1912	£12.00
1064	1065	6	Camouflage with Insects	1913	£12.00
1065	1066	6	Courage and Discipline of Italian Army	1913	£22.00
1066	1067	6	History of Beer	1913	£20.00
1067	1068	6	The History of Paper	1913	£20.00
1068	1069	6	Chateaux and Forts of Italy	1913	£13.00
1069	1070	6	How Films are Made	1913	£22.00
1070	1071	6	Crowns and Coronations	1913	£14.00
1071	1072	6	The Cat Family	1913	£22.00
1072	1073	6	Memorable Journeys Across the Alps	1913	£15.00
1073	1074	6	Monuments in the Baroque Style	1913	£18.00
1074	1075	6	Monuments of Vittorio Emanuel II in Rome	1913	£13.00
1075	1076	6	Countries where Romany is Spoken	1913	£15.00
1076	1077	6	Vanished Civilisations	1913	£13.00
1077	1078	6	Robinson Crusoe	1913	£14.00
1078	1079	6	Scenes of Dutch Life	1913	£22.00
1079	1080	6	Historic Sicily	1913	£12.00
1080	1081	6	Fans of Different Countries	1913	£20.00
1081	1082	6	Verdi and His Works	1913	£22.00
1082	1083	6	Richard Wagner	1913	£20.00
1083	1084	6	The Provisioning of Armies on Campaign	1914-15	£14.00
1084	1085	6	Art Among Primitive People	1914-15	£15.00
1085	1088	6	Costumes of Servia	1914-15	£125.00
1086	1089	6	Costumes and Views of Austria	1914-15	£140.00
1087	1114	6	Gluck the Composer	1914-15	£350.00
1088	1094	6	Famous Navigators	1914-15	—
1089	1098	6	In Palestine	1914-15	£150.00
1090	1105	6	In Tunisia	1914-15	£375.00
1091	1106	6	Remains of the Roman Empire in Africa	1914-15	£12.00
1092	1086	6	The Panama Canal	1919-20	£25.00
1093	1113	6	Canals II	1919-20	£95.00
1094	1087	6	Cavaliers	1919-20	£20.00
1095	1090	6	Dante (Poet) I	1919-20	£30.00
1096	1116	6	Dante (Poet) II	1919-20	£15.00
1097	1091	6	The History of Iron	1919-20	£15.00
1098	1092	6	Mountain Railways	1919-20	£20.00
1099	1117	6	Foundries	1919-20	£40.00
1100	1093	6	Symbolic Stamps	1919-20	£30.00
1101	1095	6	Toothless Mammals	1919-20	£45.00
1102	1096	6	Gold Mines of Mont-Rose	1919-20	£12.00
1103	1097	6	Forges Throughout the Ages	1919-20	£14.00
1104	1099	6	Weights and Measures	1919-20	£50.00
1105	1100	6	Useful Plants and Their Promoters	1919-20	£40.00
1106	1101	6	The Winter's Tale (Shakespeare)	1919-20	£22.00
1107	1102	6	The Republic of San Marino	1919-20	£22.00
1108	1103	6	Scenes from Ural Mountains	1919-20	£25.00
1109	1104	6	Tramways Old and New	1919-20	£40.00
1110	1107	6	Travelling in Corsica	1919-20	£40.00
1111	1108	6	The Six Altitudinal Zones	1919-20	£24.00

F No.	S No.	Qty	Title (English Translation)	Date	Set Price
1112	1109	6	Ancient Commercial Centres	1921	£18.00
1113	1110	6	Famous Astronomers	1921	£45.00
1114	1111	6	Amateur Dramatics	1921	£20.00
1115	1112	6	In Canada I	1921	£45.00
1116	1115	6	Curious Experiments in Physics	1921	£35.00
1117	1118	6	The Story of Gas	1921	£35.00
1118	1119	6	Giants	1921	£125.00
1119	1120	6	The Pass of St. Gothard	1921	£30.00
1120	1121	6	Leonardo da Vinci	1921	£50.00
1121	1122	6	The Migration of Birds	1921	£22.00
1122	1123	6	The Pre-Historic Animal World	1921	£900.00
1123	1124	6	Animals in Human Situations	1921	£65.00
1124	1126	6	The Discoveries of Famous Scientists	1921	£55.00
1125	1127	6	Items of Yesterday and Today	1921	£45.00
1126	1128	6	Animals and Their Furs	1921	£30.00
1127	1125	6	Sapho (Opera)	1921	£30.00
1128	1129	6	Ruins in Sicily	1921	£40.00
1129	1130	6	Winter Sports	1921	£65.00
1130	1131	6	Zone Language in Italy	1921	£22.00
1131	1132	6	In East Africa II	1922-23	£22.00
1132	1133	6	Deep Sea Animals and Plants	1922-23	£20.00
1133	1134	6	Sacred Animals	1922-23	£22.00
1134	1135	6	Bees and Bee Keepers	922-23	£22.00
1135	1136	6	Roman Construction	1922-23	£22.00
1136	1137	6	Famous Women	1922-23	£22.00
1137	1138	6	Episodes in the History of the Middle Eastern Empire	1922-23	£22.00
1138	1139	6	The Founders of Large Empires	1922-23	£22.00
1139	1140	6	Uses of Fire	1922-23	£20.00
1140	1141	6	Episodes from the Lives of Famous Historians	1922-23	£20.00
1141	1142	6	The Glove as a Symbol	1922-23	£22.00
1142	1143	6	Lakes in Mountains	1922-23	£22.00
1143	1144	6	Flour Mills II	1922-23	£22.00
1144	1145	6	Military Music	1922-23	£28.00
1145	1146	6	The Origin of Different Colonies	1922-23	£22.00
1146	1147	6	Plants and Their Uses	1922-23	£22.00
1147	1148	6	Scenes from the Lives of Famous Painters	1922-23	£22.00
1148	1149	6	Birds in the Life of Man	1922-23	£20.00
1149	1150	6	People of Asia Minor	1922-23	£22.00
1150	1151	6	Tasso	1922-23	£18.00
1151	1152	6	Remains of Bygone Civilisations	1922-23	£20.00
1152	1153	6	Famous Roman Villas	1922-23	£14.00
1153	1154	6	Water and the Ancient Romans and Egyptians	1924	£10.00
1154	1155	6	History of Culinary Art	1924	£9.00
1155	1156	6	Natural Catastrophes	1924	£8.00
1156	1157	12	Milan Cathedral	1924	£30.00
1157	1158	6	The Miller, His Son and the Ass	1924	£12.00
1158	1159	6	The Little Marat (Opera)	1924	£15.00
1159	1160	6	Robert the Bruce	1924	£8.00
1160	1161	6	Holy Shrines	1924	£20.00
1161	1162	6	Historic Military Expeditions	1924	£15.00
1162	1163	6	Famous Opera Houses	1924	£20.00
1163	1164	6	Holy Year 1925	1925	£8.00
1164	1165	6	Famous Italian Towers	1925	£8.00
1165	1166	6	Different Sleeping Places	1925	£11.00
1166	1167	6	Swiss Guard at the Vatican	1925	£10.00
1167	1175	6	Liebig Transported by Elephant (Humorous)	1925	£15.00
1168	1168	6	Natural Light Phenomena	1925	£15.00
1169	1169	6	Nero – Opera	1925	£15.00

F No.	S No.	Qty	Title (English Translation)	Date	Set Price
1170	1170	6	Famous Belgian Town Halls	1925	£10.00
1171	1171	6	Unusual Plant Life	1925	£10.00
1172	1172	6	Famous Italian Squares	1925	£10.00
1173	1173	6	Death and Burial of Tutankhamen	1925	£22.00
1174	1174	6	Picturesque Views of Spain	1925	£10.00
1175	1176	6	Rearing of Useful Creatures	1926	£10.00
1176	1177	6	Famous Diplomats and Ambassadors	1926	£11.00
1177	1178	6	Popular Fables	1926	£20.00
1178	1179	6	War in the Alps	1926	£11.00
1179	1180	6	Art in Japan	1926	£10.00
1180	1181	6	The Promised Bride by Manzoli	1926	£12.00
1181	1182	6	Greetings of Primitive Peoples	1926	£8.00
1182	1183	6	The Life of St. Francis of Assisi	1926	£14.00
1183	1184	6	Architectural Treasures of Latium	1926	£7.00
1184	1185	6	Leaning Towers	1926	£12.00
1185	1186	6	Historical Vehicles	1926	£12.00
1186	1187	6	Pictures of Olden Times	1926	£11.00
1187	1188	6	'L'Aiglon' - Drama by Rostand	1927	£10.00
1188	1203	6	Beethoven	1927	£14.00
1189	1189	6	'Boris Goudonov' by Mussorgsky	1927	£15.00
1190	1190	6	British Castles	1927	£12.00
1191	1191	6	'Cyrano de Bergerac' by Rostand	1927	£10.00
1192	1192	6	Sun Worshippers	1927	£9.00
1193	1193	6	Glaciers and Alpine Flowers	1927	£8.00
1194	1194	6	Gulliver's Travels in Lilliput	1927	£14.00
1195	1195	6	Gulliver's Travels in Brobdingnag	1927	£14.00
1196	1196	6	The Iliad - Roman Mythology	1927	£12.00
1197	1197	6	The Odyssey	1927	£10.00
1198	1198	6	The Story of Bread	1927	£10.00
1199	1199	6	Perseus	1927	£8.00
1200	1200	6	Rain	1927	£10.00
1201	1201	6	Famous Scenes from the Napoleonic Era	1927	£10.00
1202	1202	6	Sailing Ships Through the Ages	1927	£12.00
1203	1205	6	Diogenes	1928	£9.00
1204	1206	6	The Twelve Labours of Hercules I	1928	£9.00
1205	1207	6	The Twelve Labours of Hercules II	1928	£9.00
1206	1208	6	Historic Invasions of Italy	1928	£8.00
1207	1209	6	The Working of Copper and Bronze	1928	£8.00
1208	1210	6	The Legend of St. Nicholas	1928	£15.00
1209	1211	6	Women and Children of the World	1928	£9.00
1210	1212	6	Mohammed	1928	£7.00
1211	1213	6	Dangerous Occupations	1928	£7.00
1212	1215	6	Uses of Feathers	1928	£7.00
1213	1216	6	Sensitive Plants	1928	£6.00
1214	1204	6	Conquest of the North Pole	1928	£20.00
1215	1217	6	Unusual Outdoor Occupations	1928	£8.00
1216	1218	6	Arctic Russia	1928	£8.00
1217	1219	6	Schubert	1928	£12.00
1218	1232	6	Humorous Sports	1928	£12.00
1219	1220	6	Theseus	1928	£8.00
1220	1214	6	New Zealand Views	1928	£7.00
1221	1221	6	The Inhabitants of Tierra del Fuego	1929	£6.00
1222	1222	6	Scenes of Canada	1929	£10.00
1223	1224	6	Chocolate	1929	£10.00
1224	1225	6	Dante - Divine Comedy I The Inferno	1929	£8.00
1225	1226	6	Dante - Divine Comedy II Purgatory	1929	£10.00
1226	1227	6	Dante - Divine Comedy III Paradise	1929	£8.00
1227	1228	6	Cheese Industry in Different Lands	1929	£8.00

F No.	S No.	Qty	LIEBIG CARD ISSUES Title (English Translation)	Date	Set Price
1228	1229	6	Combat Formations	1929	£12.00
1229	1230	6	The Apple as an Historical Symbol	1929	£7.00
1230	1231	6	The Mediterranean Coast	1929	£7.00
1231	1233	6	Evolution of the Earth	1929	£11.00
1232	1234	6	The Life of Buddha	1930	£12.00
1233	1223	6	Famous Chemists	1930	£7.00
1234	1235	6	Belgian Churches	1930	£5.00
1235	1236	6	Confucius	1930	£7.00
1236	1237	6	Electing a Doge of Venice	1930	£8.00
1237	1238	6	Legend of Aeneid I	1930	£6.00
1238	1239	6	Legend of Aeneid II	1930	£6.00
1239	1240	6	Classical Italian Gardens	1930	£5.00
1240	1241	6	Gems of Sicilian Architecture	1930	£6.00
1241	1242	6	Historic Buildings and Gateways of Milan	1930	£25.00
1242	1243	6	Hindu Monuments	1930	£6.00
1243	1244	6	Microscopic Water Life	1931	£6.00
1244	1245	6	Great Greek Tragedies	1931	£6.00
1245	1246	6	Pictorial History of Switzerland	1931	£6.00
1246	1247	6	Mahabharata - Ancient Legend of India	1931	£8.00
1247	1248	6	Ancient Egyptian Monuments	1931	£10.00
1248	1249	6	Prehistoric Monuments	1931	£8.00
1249	1250	6	Famous Mosques	1931	£6.00
1250	1252	6	Ramayana - Ancient Legend of India	1931	£6.00
1251	1253	6	Bizarre Rocks	1931	£5.00
1252	1254	6	Scenes from Venetian History	1931	£6.00
1253	1255	6	The Story of Medieval Switzerland	1931	£6.00
1254	1256	6	Loading and Unloading Ships	1932	£6.00
1255	1257	6	Paper Making	1932	£7.00
1256	1258	6	Methods of Fixing a Position at Sea	1932	£7.00
1257	1259	6	Building a Liner	1932	£7.00
1258	1260	6	Faust I	1932	£7.00
1259	1261	6	Faust II	1932	£7.00
1260	1262	6	Aesop's Fables	1932	£8.00
1261	1263	6	Ants	1932	£8.00
1262	1264	6	Jupiter	1932	£6.00
1263	1251	6	Orpheus	1932	£5.00
1264	1265	6	Parasitic Plants	1932	£7.00
1265	1266	6	Transmission of News Among Primitive People	1932	£8.00
1266	1267	6	Bees	1933	£6.00
1267	1271	6	Hydroelectricity	1933	£5.00
1268	1270	6	Coal-Mining	1933	£6.00
1269	1272	6	Chateaux of the Loire	1933	£9.00
1270	1273	6	Castles of the Rhine	1933	£6.00
1271	1275	6	Story of China I	1933	£8.00
1272	1276	6	Story of China II	1933	£9.00
1273	1277	6	Climate and Vegetation	1933	£6.00
1274	1278	6	The Comedy of Aristophanes	1933	£10.00
1275	1281	6	Cloud Formations	1933	£6.00
1276	1280	6	Isis and Osiris - Ancient Egyptians	1933	£12.00
1277	1283	6	Symbiosis	1933	£6.00
1278	1284	6	Japanese Theatre	1933	£10.00
1279	1285	6	Living in the Alps	1933	£7.00
1280	1268	6	Apollo	1934	£8.00
1281	1286	6	Pre-Colombian Architecture in South America	1934	£12.00
1282	1269	6	Ancient Athens	1934	£35.00
1283	1287	6	The Isle of Capri	1934	£6.00
1284	1289	12	Medieval German Cathedrals	1934	£30.00
1285	1274	6	Swiss Chalets	1934	£7.00

F No.	S No.	Qty	LIEBIG CARD ISSUES Title (English Translation)	Date	Set Price
1286	1288	12	Chateaux of Belgium	1934	£35.00
1287	1290	6	How and Why Flowers Attract Insects	1934	£6.00
1288	1301	6	German Youth Movement	1934	£95.00
1289	1300	6	German Girls	1934	£125.00
1290	1291	6	Edda - Mythological Saga	1934	£9.00
1291	1292	6	Head Adornment in Primitive People	1934	£6.00
1292	1279	6	European Alpine Fauna	1934	£15.00
1293	1293	6	Match Making	1934	£10.00
1294	1295	6	Iceland	1934	£5.00
1295	1296	6	Geological Times	1934	£5.00
1296	1297	6	Fishing in the North Sea	1934	£8.00
1297	1298	6	Production of Petroleum	1934	£6.00
1298	1282	6	Carnivorous Plants	1934	£9.00
1299	1294	6	Preparation of an Illustrated Journal	1934	£5.00
1300	1299	6	Legend of Prometheus	1934	£5.00
1301	1302	6	Samarkand - (City of Tamerlane)	1934	£8.00
1302	1303	12	The Legend of Till Uilenspeigel	1934	£100.00
1303	1304	12	The Life of the People of the Congo	1934	£27.00
1304	1306	6	Strange Trees of the World	1935	£5.00
1305	1307	6	Arabian Scenes	1935	£5.00
1306	1308	6	Construction of Spiders' Webs	1935	£5.00
1307	1321	6	Types of Jellyfish	1935	£11.00
1308	1310	6	The Vatican City	1935	£6.00
1309	1311	6	Historical Aspects of Modern Cities	1935	£8.00
1310	1312	6	Travel in our Grandfather's Time	1935	£6.00
1311	1313	6	Conquering the Air I	1935	£20.00
1312	1314	6	Conquering the Air II	1935	£20.00
1313	1309	6	Evolution of Cacti	1935	£5.00
1314	1315	6	Tropical Butterflies and Beetles	1935	£11.00
1315	1318	6	Irish Scenes	1935	£16.00
1316	1305	6	Unusual German Youth Hostels	1935	£50.00
1317	1319	6	Great Engineering Feats of Modern Europe	1935	£5.00
1318	1320	6	Lhasa, Holy City of the Himalayas	1935	£10.00
1319	1322	6	Luxurious Ships of Bygone Days	1935	£6.00
1320	1324	6	Views of Tierra Del Fuego	1935	£5.00
1321	1325	6	Famous Abbeys of Belgium	1936	£8.00
1322	1327	6	Hamlet (Shakespeare)	1936	£15.00
1323	1330	6	Belfries of Belgium	1936	£9.00
1324	1329	6	Blooms of Aquatic Flowers	1936	£9.00
1325	1323	6	De Rozenkavalier (Opera)	1936	£18.00
1326	1337	6	'El Cid' Tragedy by Corneille	1936	£5.00
1327	1332	6	Hummimg Birds	1936	£10.00
1328	1333	6	Folk Dances of the World	1936	£6.00
1329	1334	6	Don Quixote II	1936	£7.00
1330	1316	6	The Coast of Europe	1936	£5.00
1331	1336	6	Landscaped Gardens	1936	£18.00
1332	1317	6	Great American Sky-Scrapers	1936	£16.00
1333	1338	6	Legend of Roland	1936	£6.00
1334	1339	6	Exotic Aquarium Fish	1936	£7.00
1335	1341	6	Processions and Pilgrimages in Belgium	1936	£7.00
1336	1342	12	King Albert of Belgium	1936	£23.00
1337	1346	12	The Life of Queen Astrid of Belgium	1936	£25.00
1338	1343	6	River and Maritime Signals	1936	£7.00
1339	1344	6	Distribution of Seeds by the Wind	1936	£8.00
1340	1345	6	Views of Submarine Life	1936	£7.00
1341	1347	6	Legend of Zarathustra	1936	£6.00
1342	1348	6	Unusual Dwellings	1937	£6.00
1343	1326	6	Climbing in the Alps	1937	£10.00

F No.	S No.	Qty	Title (English Translation)	Date	Set Price
1344	1349	12	Wild Animals of the Congo	1937	£45.00
1345	1328	6	The Antarctic	1937	£12.00
1346	1350	12	Chinese Art	1937	£40.00
1347	1351	6	Moroccan Art	1937	£17.00
1348	1331	6	Wooden Churches	1937	£7.00
1349	1335	6	Alpine Flowers	1937	£7.00
1350	1353	6	Life of a River	1937	£6.00
1351	1354	6	Flora of the Riviera	1937	£6.00
1352A	1356	6	The Italian Empire (Nos 1-6)	1937	£12.00
1352B	1356	6	The Italian Empire (Nos 7-12)	1937	£12.00
1352C	1356	6	The Italian Empire (Nos 13-18)	1937	£12.00
1353	1355	6	Joan of Arc II	1937	£9.00
1354	1359	6	Strange Mammals	1937	£7.00
1355	1361	6	Marvellous Grottoes of Belgium	1937	£8.00
1356	1362	6	Orchids	1937	£12.00
1357	1363	6	The Reign of Albert and Isabella	1937	£8.00
1358	1364	6	Lifestyle of Termites	1937	£6.00
1359	1365	6	Birds	1937	£10.00
1360	1368	6	Glass Industry II	1937	£9.00
1361	1366	6	Customs of Belgium	1937	£6.00
1362	1367	6	Old Houses	1937	£10.00
1363	1372	6	Belgium	1938	£6.00
1364	1385	6	German Town Halls	1938	£350.00
1365	1374	6	The Gods of Egypt	1938	£10.00
1366	1352	6	Animals and the Plants They Eat	1938	£5.00
1367	1376	6	The Fountains of Rome	1938	£6.00
1368A	1377	6	History of Japan (Nos 1-6)	1938	£6.00
1368B	1377	6	History of Japan (Nos 7-12)	1938	£6.00
1369	1378	6	Caesar	1938	£7.00
1370	1380	6	Famous Historical People of Latin America	1938	£6.00
1371	1381	6	The Grottoes of Postumia	1938	£11.00
1372	1386	6	William Tell (Opera)	1938	£15.00
1373	1358	6	Development of Insects from Water to Air	1938	£8.00
1374	1357	6	Water Insects	1938	£8.00
1375	1383	6	Justus Von Liebig	1938	£35.00
1376	1382	6	G. Marconi	1938	£22.00
1377	1360	6	Submarine Life at 500 Fathoms	1938	£12.00
1378	1384	6	Marriage Through the Ages	1938	£9.00
1379	1387	6	The Master Singers (Opera)	1938	£400.00
1380	1340	6	Women's Hair Styles	1938	£6.00
1381	1371	6	School of Horse Riding	1938	£15.00
1382	1388	6	Industries of Italy	1938	£20.00
1383	1375	6	History of the U.S.A.	1938	£9.00
1384	1390	6	Characteristic Houses of the Pacific Islands	1939	£5.00
1385	1369	6	Inside an Iron Foundry	1939	£5.00
1386	1391	6	Emperor Augustus	1939	£5.00
1387	1370	6	Farming Silk Worms	1939	£10.00
1388	1392	6	Benvenuto Cellini	1939	£5.00
1389	1394	6	Riders of the World	1939	£6.00
1390	1395	6	Famous Italian Knights	1939	£11.00
1391	1411	6	Coral	1939	£5.00
1392	1373	6	Crustacea	1939	£5.00
1393	1393	6	German Provincial Halls	1939	£125.00
1394	1397	6	Italian Festivals	1939	£6.00
1395	1389	6	The Life of a Glacier	1939	£5.00
1396	1403	6	Amber	1939	£160.00
1397	1379	6	Modern Drilling, Excavating and Dredging Plant	1939	£5.00
1398A	1400	6	History of India (Nos 1-6)	1939	£6.00

F No.	S No.	Qty	Title (English Translation)	Date	Set Price
1398B	1400	6	History of India (Nos 7-12)	1939	£6.00
1399	1399	6	Popular Games	1939	£6.00
1400	1401	6	Flax Industry in Belgium	1939	£6.00
1401	1404	6	Fishing III	1939	£6.00
1402	1398	6	Rivers of the Ardennes	1939	£6.00
1403	1406	6	Scipio and Hannibal	1939	£6.00
1404	1405	6	Skiing	1939	£25.00
1405	1402	6	Turandot (Opera)	1939	£15.00
1406	1409	6	Museums in Houses	1939	£7.00
1407	1396	6	Folk Costumes of Germany	1939	£140.00
1408	1412	6	Ancient Dwellings	1940	£6.00
1409	1413	6	Castles of Tuscany	1940	£6.00
1410	1414	6	Flora and Fauna of Ethiopia	1940	£8.00
1411	1415	6	Primitive Production and Uses of Fire	1940	£7.00
1412	1416	6	Giants	1940	£5.00
1413	1419	6	The History of the Post	1940	£10.00
1414	1417	6	Gastropods (Snails, etc.)	1940	£9.00
1415	1418	6	The Albert National Park, Africa	1940	£6.00
1416	1420	6	Rhine and Lake Boats	1940	£140.00
1417	1421	6	The Life of Rubens	1940	£4.00
1418	1422	6	Skiing II	1940	£60.00
1419	1407	6	Tobacco	1940	£10.00
1420	1408	6	Bearded Birds	1940	£8.00
1421	1424	6	Death Valley	1940	£4.00
1422	1425	6	Traditional Belgian Farmhouses	1940	£6.00
1423	1410	6	Life in an Ancient Village	1940	£5.00
1424	1423	6	Winter Sport	1940	£160.00
1425	1426	6	Animals Used for Fur	1941	£8.00
1426	1427	6	Bamboo	1941	£6.00
1427	1428	6	Exotic Wedding Costumes	1941	£5.00
1428	1429	6	Majesty of the Alps	1941	£12.00
1429	1430	6	Sea Mammals	1941	£8.00
1430	1431	6	Marco Polo	1941	£5.00
1431	1432	6	Molluscs and Oysters	1941	£6.00
1432	1433	6	Unusual Fish	1941	£7.00
1433	1434	6	Useful Plants of the Congo	1941	£5.00
1434	1436	6	Water Sports	1941	£9.00
1435	1435	6	Old Belgian Bridges I	1941	£8.00
1436	1437	6	Artistic Craftsman of the Congo	1942	£7.00
1437	1438	6	Famous Waterfalls	1942	£10.00
1438	1439	6	Dances of Ancient Greece	1942	£6.00
1439	1441	6	Belgian Windmills	1942	£5.00
1440	1447	6	Mosquitoes	1942	£5.00
1441	1442	6	Birds Nests	1942	£10.00
1442	1443	6	The Origin and History of Writing	1942	£6.00
1443	1444	6	Italian Bridges	1942	£8.00
1444	1440	6	Popular Festivals	1942	£5.00
1445	1445	6	The Discovery of America	1942	£5.00
1446	1446	6	Indian Temples	1942	£7.00
1447	1448	6	Legendary Beings	1943	£6.00
1448	1449	6	The Story of Gil Blas	1943	£5.00
1449	1455	6	Birds of Paradise	1943	£12.00
1450	1450	6	Sponge Fishing	1943	£5.00
1451	1451	6	Medicinal Plants II	1943	£5.00
1452	1452	6	The Four Sons of Aymon	1943	£5.00
1453	1453	6	The Sahara	1943	£5.00
1454	1454	6	Life in the Sahara Desert	1943	£8.00
1455	1456	6	Cephalopods (Shells)	1947	£22.00

|-------|-------|-----|---|------|-----------|
1456	1457	6	The Cheese Industry	1947	£18.00
1457	1462	6	History of Egypt	1947	£35.00
1458	1458	6	Insects of the Locust Family	1947	£20.00
1459	1459	6	The Kalevala	1947	£7.00
1460	1460	6	Water Mills	1947	£10.00
1461	1461	6	San Giovani Bosco	1947	£17.00
1462	1463	6	Italian Leaders and Events of 1848	1948	£12.00
1463	1464	6	Baudouin - Arms of Iron	1948	£8.00
1464	1465	6	Song of Hiawatha	1948	£8.00
1465	1466	6	Journey of a Rich Roman	1948	£8.00
1466	1467	6	Baby Mammals	1948	£16.00
1467	1468	6	Miguel of Cervantes	1948	£7.00
1468	1469	6	Applications of Science	1948	£6.00
1469	1471	6	The Life of Albert Durer	1948	£6.00
1470	1470	6	Old Arches	1948	£5.00
1471	1472	6	Picturesque Abruzzo	1949	£12.00
1472	1473	6	History of Christianity in Italy I	1949	£4.00
1473	1474	6	History of Christianity in Italy II	1949	£4.00
1474	1475	6	History of Christianity in Italy III	1949	£8.00
1475	1476	6	Beetles of Europe	1949	£6.00
1476	1477	6	Winter Plants	1949	£14.00
1477	1483	6	The Discovery of America	1949	£6.00
1478	1478	6	Famous Italian Navigators	1949	£10.00
1479	1479	6	Masks of the World	1949	£10.00
1480	1480	6	Street Tradesmen	1949	£8.00
1481	1481	6	The Life of Rembrandt	1949	£5.00
1482	1482	6	Reptiles	1949	£5.00
1483	1484	6	The Life of Socrates	1949	£5.00
1484	1485	6	Antonie van Dyck	1949	£4.00
1485	1487	6	Alexander, the Founder of the Empire	1950	£6.00
1486	1488	6	Cavalry	1950	£8.00
1487	1489	6	Sea Shells	1950	£8.00
1488	1490	6	Inhabitants of Mexico Before Colombo	1950	£8.00
1489	1491	6	Erasme	1950	£5.00
1490	1492	6	Edible Fungi II	1950	£15.00
1491	1493	6	Poisonous Fungi	1950	£12.00
1492	1494	6	Belgian Generals	1950	£6.00
1493	1496	6	The Gaules at War	1950	£5.00
1494	1507	6	The History of the Horse	1950	£5.00
1495	1501	6	Bread, Wine, Oil, made in Rome	1950	£5.00
1496	1497	6	Moths	1950	£5.00
1497	1498	6	Lusitanian's	1950	£6.00
1498	1499	6	The Life of Moliere	1950	£4.00
1499	1500	6	Palissy Bernard	1950	£4.00
1500	1502	6	Monuments	1950	£5.00
1501	1503	6	Plants in Ceremonies	1950	£6.00
1502	1504	6	Picturesque Portugal	1950	£5.00
1503	1495	6	The First Tour Around the World	1950	£4.00
1504	1505	6	The Retreat of the Ten Thousand	1950	£5.00
1505	1506	6	Robin Hood	1950	£12.00
1506	1508	6	History of Ceramics	1950	£12.00
1507	1510	6	Some Occupations of Belgians	1951	£4.00
1508	1509	6	Albanians and Volscions	1951	£5.00
1509	1511	6	Plant and Animal Life on the Heath	1951	£5.00
1510	1512	6	The Hunter and His Dog	1951	£8.00
1511	1514	6	'Cuore' E. De Amicis	1951	£7.00
1512	1516	6	Flowers of the Marsh	1951	£6.00
1513	1517	6	Gardens of Italy	1951	£7.00

F No.	S No.	Qty	LIEBIG CARD ISSUES Title (English Translation)	Date	Set Price
1514	1515	6	King Herod Antipas	1951	£5.00
1515	1522	6	The History of Anvers	1951	£5.00
1516	1523	6	The History of Flanders (West)	1951	£6.00
1517	1549	6	The History of Flanders (East)	1951	£5.00
1518	1524	6	The History of Hainault	1951	£4.00
1519	1548	6	The History of Brabant	1951	£5.00
1520	1525	6	History of Leige	1951	£5.00
1521	1526	6	The History of Limbourg	1951	£5.00
1522	1527	6	History of Luxembourg	1951	£5.00
1523	1550	6	The History of Namur	1951	£5.00
1524	1513	6	The Court of Bourgogne	1951	£4.00
1525	1530	6	The Life of Manzoni Alessanoro	1951	£5.00
1526	1521	6	The History of Pasta	1951	£18.00
1527	1518	6	Princesses Visiting Belgium	1951	£4.00
1528	1519	6	Occupations of Animals and Birds	1951	£5.00
1529	1520	6	Sports of the World	1951	£22.00
1530	1528	6	History of Italy I	1951	£7.00
1531	1529	6	Parasites and their Hosts	1951	£7.00
1532	1531	6	Admirals and Buccaneers of Belgium	1951	£5.00
1533	1532	6	Garden Shrubs	1952	£4.00
1534	1533	6	Italian Cars	1952	£8.00
1535	1541	6	The Masked Ball (Opera by Verdi)	1952	£12.00
1536	1535	6	Natural Catastrophes	1952	£6.00
1537	1534	6	Fishing and Hunting in the Belgian Congo	1952	£4.00
1538	1539	6	The Belgian Emperors in Constantinople	1952	£4.00
1539A	1554	6	Historical Battles (Nos 1-6)	1952	£7.00
1539B	1555	6	Historical Battles (Nos 7-12)	1952	£7.00
1540	1536	6	Large Flowers	1952	£6.00
1541	1537	6	Fruits	1952	£6.00
1542	1545	6	History of the Belgian Congo 1st Series	1952	£4.00
1543	1546	6	History of the Belgian Congo 2nd Series	1952	£4.00
1544	1547	6	History of the Belgian Congo 3rd Series	1952	£5.00
1545	1551	6	History of Luxembourg	1952	£5.00
1546	1538	6	Flowers	1952	£6.00
1547	1540	6	Mercator	1952	£4.00
1548	1542	6	Astronomy	1952	£8.00
1549	1543	6	Coastal Fishing	1952	£9.00
1550	1544	6	Flowers of the Meadow	1952	£5.00
1551	1552	6	History of Italy II	1952	£6.00
1552	1553	6	History of Italy III	1952	£7.00
1553	1556	6	The River Po Right Bank	1953	£6.00
1554	1557	6	Algae	1953	£4.00
1555	1558	6	Sites of Milan	1953	£6.00
1556	1559	6	The Antelope	1953	£4.00
1557	1560	6	Archimedes' Principles	1953	£4.00
1558	1561	6	Suez Canal	1953	£4.00
1559	1562	6	Mountain Songs	1953	£9.00
1560	1564	6	Carnivores	1953	£6.00
1561	1565	6	Sea Mammals	1953	£5.00
1562	1563	6	Charles-Joseph, Prince of Ligne	1953	£4.00
1563	1566	6	The Civilisation of Minoica	1953	£4.00
1564	1567	6	Mountain Costumes	1953	£6.00
1565	1568	6	Forest Flowers	1953	£4.00
1566	1569	6	William of Orange	1953	£4.00
1567	1577	6	Plant Life	1953	£5.00
1568	1570	6	The Production of Timber	1953	£7.00
1569	1571	6	Marsupials	1953	£5.00
1570	1580	6	Flightless Birds	1953	£6.00

F No.	S No.	Qty	LIEBIG CARD ISSUES Title (English Translation)	Date	Set Price
1571	1572	6	Wild Animals	1953	£5.00
1572	1575	6	Pierre Le Grand	1953	£4.00
1573	1574	6	House Plants	1953	£4.00
1574	1573	6	Freshwater Fish	1953	£7.00
1575	1576	6	Solomon the Great	1953	£4.00
1576	1578	12	Expanding the Colonies of Belgium	1953	£8.00
1577	1579	6	Trees and Their Blossom	1953	£4.00
1578	1581	6	Virgil the Poet	1953	£4.00
1579	1584	6	Ancient Boats	1954	£5.00
1580	1583	6	Fishing Craft of Belgium	1954	£5.00
1581	1586	6	Paddle Footed Carnivora	1954	£8.00
1582	1587	6	Catherine II of Russia	1954	£4.00
1583	1588	6	Nuptial Dances of Birds	1954	£9.00
1584	1589	6	The Fall of Constantinople in 1452/3	1954	£4.00
1585	1591	6	The Empire of the Incas	1954	£5.00
1586	1590	6	The Horse Family	1954	£8.00
1587	1585	6	Falconry	1954	£6.00
1588	1596	6	Oysters	1954	£4.00
1589	1593	6	Invasion of the Moors	1954	£4.00
1590	1594	6	The Use of Marble	1954	£6.00
1591	1595	6	Picturesque Lazio	1954	£5.00
1592	1610	6	Sea Birds	1954	£5.00
1593	1597	6	Fish and their Habitat	1954	£4.00
1594	1592	6	Insects and Molluscs of the Shore	1954	£4.00
1595	1598	6	Primates	1954	£6.00
1596	1599	6	Francois Rabaelais	1954	£4.00
1597	1600	6	Rodents	1954	£4.00
1598	1601	6	Rodents	1954	£5.00
1599	1602	6	Inventors of Belgium	1954	£4.00
1600	1603	6	Monkeys I	1954	£7.00
1601	1604	6	Monkeys II	1954	£4.00
1602	1605	6	The History of Italy IV	1954	£10.00
1603	1606	6	The History of Italy V	1954	£18.00
1604	1607	6	The History of Italy VI	1954	£5.00
1605	1608	6	The History of Italy VII	1954	£7.00
1606	1609	6	Tuscany	1954	£8.00
1607	1611	6	The Life of S. Ambrogioa	1954	£6.00
1608	1612	6	Australian Mammals	1955	£4.00
1609	1613	6	Architecture in Spain	1955	£4.00
1610	1582	6	Sailing Ships Through the Ages	1955	£4.00
1611	1616	6	Bats	1955	£9.00
1612	1617	6	New Varieties of Flowers	1955	£7.00
1613	1631	6	History of England	1955	£5.00
1614	1630	6	History of Germany	1955	£4.00
1615	1629	6	History of France	1955	£4.00
1616	1614	6	The Poems of Leopardi	1955	£5.00
1617	1628	6	The Storage and Use of Methane	1955	£4.00
1618	1619	6	Monster Sculptures of Bomarzo	1955	£5.00
1619	1634	6	Fish Eating Birds	1955	£5.00
1620	1620	6	Bears	1955	£5.00
1621	1621	6	Parrots	1955	£7.00
1622	1623	6	Fish and Fishing	1955	£4.00
1623A	1626	6	Natives of the Belgian Congo (Nos 1-6)	1955	£4.00
1623B	1626	6	Natives of the Belgian Congo (Nos 7-12)	1955	£4.00
1623C	1626	6	Natives of the Belgian Congo(Nos 13-18)	1955	£4.00
1624	1625	6	Desert Plants	1955	£4.00
1625	1624	6	Climbing Plants (White Boarders)	1955	£5.00
1625A	1624A	6	Climbing Plants (Inner Coloured boarders)	1955	£6.00

LIEBIG CARD ISSUES   *Date*   *Set Price*
Title (English Translation)

F No.	S No.	Qty	Title	Date	Set Price
1626	1622	6	Life in Sand-Dunes	1955	£4.00
1627	1627	6	Prosimiae - Tree Living Mammals	1955	£8.00
1628	1615	6	The Cultivation of Rice	1955	£4.00
1629	1618	6	Rice from Field to Table	1955	£6.00
1630	1632	6	Birds of the Congo	1955	£5.00
1631	1633	6	Social Birds	1955	£6.00
1632	1635	6	The River Po Left Bank	1956	£5.00
1633	1636	6	Dog, Friend of Man	1956	£6.00
1634	1648	6	Teaching Children to Walk	1956	£4.00
1635	1637	6	Harmful Insects of the Congo	1956	£4.00
1636	1638	6	Space Travel	1956	£6.00
1637	1639	6	Caterpillars	1956	£5.00
1638	1640	6	Cities of Switzerland	1956	£5.00
1639	1658	6	History of Spain	1956	£4.00
1640	1659	6	History of the U.S.A.	1956	£5.00
1641	1657	6	History of Holland	1956	£4.00
1642	1641	6	Indians of the North American Plains	1956	£5.00
1643	1642	6	North American Indians	1956	£5.00
1644	1644	6	Large Insects of the Belgian Congo	1956	£4.00
1645	1645	6	Insect Eaters	1956	£4.00
1646	1646	6	Ivan the Terrible	1956	£4.00
1647	1647	6	Pilgrimages	1956	£4.00
1648	1649	6	Features of the World I	1956	£6.00
1649	1650	6	Features of the World II	1956	£5.00
1650	1651	6	Places on Athos	1956	£4.00
1651	1652	6	The Career of Mozart	1956	£10.00
1652	1653	6	Jet Propulsion and Reaction	1956	£4.00
1653	1654	6	Holy Places	1956	£4.00
1654	1655	6	Rodents	1956	£4.00
1655	1656	6	Caving	1956	£4.00
1656	1660	6	History of Italy VIII	1956	£11.00
1657	1643	6	The Manufacture of Sulphur	1956	£5.00
1658	1670	6	Alaska	1957	£5.00
1659	1661	6	Types of Frog	1957	£4.00
1660	1665	6	Cradles of Different People	1957	£4.00
1661	1663	6	Armies from 1848	1957	£7.00
1662	1666	6	Cats	1957	£9.00
1663	1664	6	The Dolomites	1957	£6.00
1664	1681	6	History of Hungary	1957	£4.00
1665	1680	6	History of Portugal	1957	£4.00
1666	1667	6	Childhood of Jesus	1957	£4.00
1667	1668	6	Harmful Agricultural Insects of the Congo	1957	£4.00
1668	1669	6	Leopold I	1957	£4.00
1669	1673	6	Life in a Brook	1957	£4.00
1670	1671	6	Aromatic Plants	1957	£5.00
1671	1672	6	Scarce Plants	1957	£4.00
1672	1674	6	Plankton	1957	£4.00
1673	1662	6	Ancient Roman Buildings	1957	£4.00
1674	1675	6	Saladin	1957	£4.00
1675	1676	6	Siberia	1957	£4.00
1676	1677	6	History of Italy IX	1957	£7.00
1677	1678	6	History of Italy X	1957	£7.00
1678	1679	6	History of Italy XI	1957	£7.00
1679	1682	6	Jousting Tournament	1957	£4.00
1680	1683	6	Wind Flight	1957	£4.00
1681	1695	6	Spiders	1958	£4.00
1682	1684	6	Pirates	1958	£5.00
1683	1685	6	Doctors' Dress Through the Ages I	1958	£6.00

F No.	S No.	Qty	**LIEBIG CARD ISSUES** *Title (English Translation)*	*Date*	*Set Price*
1684	1686	6	Doctors' Dress Through the Ages II	1958	£5.00
1685	1687	6	Costumes of Sicily	1958	£5.00
1686	1688	6	Infantry	1958	£6.00
1687	1701	6	History of Italy	1958	£4.00
1688	1697	6	History of Denmark	1958	£4.00
1689	1702	6	History of Mexico	1958	£4.00
1690	1689	6	Parasites of Agriculture	1958	£4.00
1691	1690	6	The Legends of the Grottoes of Italy	1958	£6.00
1692	1691	6	Landscapes of Planets	1958	£8.00
1693	1692	6	National Parks	1958	£5.00
1694	1693	6	Living Prehistoric Plants	1958	£4.00
1695	1694	6	Creative Work by Well Known Belgians	1958	£4.00
1696	1696	6	Learned Men of Ancient Times	1958	£4.00
1697	1698	6	History of Italy XII	1958	£5.00
1698	1699	6	History of Italy XIII	1958	£4.00
1699	1700	6	History of Italy XIV	1958	£4.00
1700	1703	6	Tortoise	1958	£4.00
1701	1705	6	Living Prehistoric Animals	1959	£5.00
1702	1704	6	Luminous Animals	1959	£4.00
1703	1706	6	Artillery	1959	£6.00
1704	1707	6	The Grasshopper	1959	£5.00
1705	1708	6	How Children are Carried	1959	£4.00
1706	1709	6	Costumes of Sardinia	1959	£5.00
1707	1710	6	Dinosaurs	1959	£8.00
1708	1711	6	Letters and Numbers on Butterflies	1959	£8.00
1709	1712	6	Gaul Before Julius Caesar	1959	£4.00
1710	1713	6	Grenadiers of Sardinia	1959	£8.00
1711	1717	6	History of Argentina	1959	£4.00
1712	1723	6	History of Moscow	1959	£4.00
1713	1718	6	History of Poland	1959	£4.00
1714	1714	6	Leopold II	1959	£4.00
1715	1716	6	Aquarium Plants	1959	£4.00
1716	1715	6	Inedible Fish	1959	£4.00
1717	1719	6	History of Italy XV	1959	£5.00
1718	1720	6	History of Italy XVI	1959	£6.00
1719	1721	6	History of Italy XVII	1959	£6.00
1720	1722	6	History of Italy XVIII	1959	£7.00
1721	1724	6	Vincent van Gogh	1959	£4.00
1722	1725	6	Alchemy	1960	£4.00
1723	1749	6	The Alpine Brigade	1960	£12.00
1724	1726	6	Brillat-Savarin (18th century Personality)	1960	£4.00
1725	1727	6	The Story of Coffee	1960	£4.00
1726	1728	6	Famous Italian Benefactresses	1960	£4.00
1727	1758	6	Winged Gods and Heroes of Ancient Greece	1960	£4.00
1728	1733	6	Peer Gynt	1960	£4.00
1729	1743	6	History of Bulgaria	1960	£4.00
1730	1744	6	History of Ancient Greece	1960	£4.00
1731	1745	6	History of Roumania	1960	£4.00
1732	1746	6	History of Yugoslavia	1960	£4.00
1733	1730	6	Italian Lakes	1960	£10.00
1734	1731	6	Legends of Poland	1960	£4.00
1735	1736	6	Quentin Metsyr	1960	£4.00
1736	1732	6	Insect Nests	1960	£4.00
1737	1734	6	The Conquering Races of Asia	1960	£4.00
1738	1729	6	Parasites and their Hosts	1960	£4.00
1739	1735	6	National Prisons & Celebrated Historical Prisoners	1960	£4.00
1740	1737	6	San Carlo Borromeo	1960	£10.00
1741	1738	6	Artificial Satellites	1960	£8.00

403

F No.	S No.	Qty	LIEBIG CARD ISSUES Title (English Translation)	Date	Set Price
1742	1739	6	The Story of the Manger	1960	£12.00
1743	1740	6	History of Italy XIX	1960	£9.00
1744	1741	6	History of Italy XX	1960	£11.00
1745	1742	6	History of Italy XXI	1960	£17.00
1746	1769	6	History of Italy XXII	1960	£18.00
1747	1747	6	Songbirds of Europe I	1960	£12.00
1748	1770	6	Types of Italian Dwellings	1961	£6.00
1749	1748	6	Military Aircraft	1961	£11.00
1750	1751	6	Bilharzia - Lifecycle of a Parasite	1961	£4.00
1751	1753	6	Cavalry	1961	£14.00
1752	1752	6	Dogs	1961	£10.00
1753	1754	6	Cicero	1961	£4.00
1754	1755	6	Scottish Clans	1961	£4.00
1755	1756	6	The Conquest of Mountains by Climbers	1961	£9.00
1756	1757	6	Costumes of Doctors Through the Ages	1961	£8.00
1757	1762	6	The Daughters of Joric	1961	£8.00
1758	1760	6	Cable Cars	1961	£8.00
1759	1761	6	Owls	1961	£5.00
1760	1767	6	History of Finland	1961	£4.00
1761	1768	6	History of Czechoslovakia	1961	£4.00
1762	1776	6	Olden Day Children's Games	1961	£4.00
1763	1759	6	Butterflies	1961	£4.00
1764	1750	6	The Adventures of Pinnocchio	1961	£10.00
1765	1782	6	Regimental Paintings	1961	£11.00
1766	1763	6	Mountain Dwellings	1961	£6.00
1767	1764	6	Van Der Neyden (15th century Artist)	1961	£4.00
1768	1765	6	Mountain Chairlifts	1961	£5.00
1769	1766	6	Story of the Knights Templar	1961	£10.00
1770	1771	6	Songbirds of Europe II	1961	£9.00
1771	1772	6	Motorways of the World	1962	£4.00
1772	1777	6	Belgian Air Force Battles	1962	£4.00
1773	1773	6	Belgian Army Overseas	1962	£4.00
1774	1774	6	Great Dams	1962	£4.00
1775	1775	6	Textile Fabrics	1962	£4.00
1776	1778	6	Da Vinci's Inventions	1962	£4.00
1777	1779	6	The Dead Sea Scrolls	1962	£4.00
1778	1780	6	Aquarium Fish	1962	£6.00
1779	1781	6	Pierre Bruegel (16th century Artist)	1962	£4.00
1780	1783	6	Famous Bridges	1962	£6.00
1781	1784	6	Italian Ports	1962	£4.00
1782	1785	6	Predatory Submarine Life	1962	£6.00
1783	1786	6	History of the Gun	1962	£9.00
1784	1787	6	Story of the Army Engineers	1962	£8.00
1785	1788	6	Famous Italian Tunnels	1962	£5.00
1786	1789	6	Crossbows	1963	£4.00
1787	1790	6	Sea Creatures	1963	£9.00
1788	1791	6	Goldeni – Opera	1963	£9.00
1789	1792	6	Strange Insects	1963	£5.00
1790	1795	6	History of the Rifle	1963	£8.00
1791	1793	6	Riddles	1963	£7.00
1792	1794	6	History of String Instruments	1963	£9.00
1793	1796	6	Sea Birds	1963	£8.00
1794	1797	6	Tropical Birds	1963	£7.00
1795	1798	6	Lithographic Art	1964	£5.00
1796	1799	6	Beautiful Italian Islands	1964	£6.00
1797	1800	6	Famous Tall Buildings	1964	£6.00
1798	1801	6	Etruria (Ancient Italy)	1964	£6.00
1799	1802	6	Antique Guns	1964	£8.00

F No.	S No.	Qty	LIEBIG CARD ISSUES Title (English Translation)	Date	Set Price
1800	1803	6	The Story of Sail	1964	£8.00
1801	1804	6	Protected Birds (without Brooke Bond name)	1964	£8.00
1802	1806	6	The Life and Opera of Moliere	1964	£8.00
1803	1807	6	The Life and Opera of Vittorio Alfieri	1964	£7.00
1804	1808	6	Medieval Armour	1965	£8.00
1805	1811	6	The Inferno (Dante)	1965	£12.00
1806	1809	6	The Story of Jade	1965	£13.00
1807	1810	6	The Life of Dante	1965	£7.00
1808	1812	6	The Life of Galileo	1965	£7.00
1809	1813	6	The Life of Michelangelo	1965	£8.00
1810	1805	6	The Life and Work of Emilio Salgari	1965	£7.00
1811	1814	6	The World Cup (Football)	1966	£15.00
1812	1815	6	Religious Council	1966	£5.00
1813	1816	6	Antique Furniture	1966	£10.00
1814	1818	6	Paradise (Dante)	1966	£13.00
1815	1817	6	Purgatory (Dante)	1966	£7.00
1816	1819	6	History of the Motorcar	1966	£12.00
1817	1820	6	History of Photography	1966	£13.00
1818	1821	6	Cradles of the World	1967	£6.00
1819	1822	6	Famous Marriage Places	1967	£12.00
1820	1823	6	Massimo D'Azeglio	1967	£6.00
1821	1826	6	The Life and Work of Giotto	1967	£8.00
1822	1824	6	The Life of Pope Pius XII	1967	£8.00
1823	1825	6	The Life of Pope Giovanni XXIII	1967	£10.00
1824	1827	6	The First Aeroplanes	1968	£18.00
1825	1828	6	Italian Army	1968	£25.00
1826	1829	6	Philosophers and Scientists	1968	£10.00
1827	1830	6	Locomotives from 1815-1872	1968	£14.00
1828	1831	6	Old Military Dress I (without Brooke Bond name)	1968	£10.00
1829	1832	6	Old Military Dress II (without Brooke Bond name)	1968	£14.00
1830	1833	6	Old Military Dress III	1968	£16.00
1831	1834	6	Aircraft of the Future	1969	£10.00
1832	1835	6	Aircraft	1969	£10.00
1833	1836	6	Scenes Based on Chessmen	1969	£10.00
1834	1837	6	Locomotives	1969	£12.00
1835	1838	6	Principal Countries of the Middle East	1969	£16.00
1836	1839	6	The Life and Work of Rossini	1969	£15.00
1837	1840	6	Astronomy I	1970	£6.00
1838	1841	6	Astronomy II	1970	£10.00
1839	1842	6	Ancient Cavalry	1970	£8.00
1840	1843	6	Ancient Helmets	1970	£16.00
1841	1844	6	Giovanni Pascoli	1970	£8.00
1842	1845	6	Dangerous Occupations I	1970	£6.00
1843	1846	6	Dangerous Occupations II	1970	£8.00
1844	1847	6	Journey to the Moon I (without Brooke Bond name)	1971	£17.00
1845	1852	6	The Nativity	1971	£25.00
1846	1848	6	Crowns I	1971	£16.00
1847	1849	6	Crowns II	1971	£4.00
1848	1850	6	Bullfighting I	1971	£6.00
1849	1851	6	Bullfighting II	1971	£10.00
1850	1853	6	Self-Portraits of Famous Artists	1972	£6.00
1851	1854	6	Journey to the Moon II	1972	£10.00
1852	1855	6	Historical Fights	1972	£7.00
1853	1856	6	The Resurrection	1972	£18.00
1854	1857	6	History of the Typewriter	1972	£12.00
1855	1860	6	How Animals See I	1973	£6.00
1856	1862	6	Ludwig Van Beethoven	1973	£8.00
1857	1858	6	The Fight Against Microbes I	1973	£6.00

F No.	S No.	Qty	LIEBIG CARD ISSUES Title (English Translation)	Date	Set Price
1858	1861	6	How Animals See II	1973	£5.00
1859	1863	6	The Story of the Circus I	1973	£14.00
1860	1859	6	The Fight Against Microbes II	1973	£15.00
1861	1864	6	The Story of the Circus II	1974	£15.00
1862	1865	6	War at Sea	1974	£40.00
1863	1866	6	Animals	1974	£15.00
1867	1867	6	Journey to the Moon I (with Brooke Bond name)	1975	£13.00
1868	1868	6	Protected Birds (with Brooke Bond name)	1975	£11.00
1869	1869	6	Old Military Dress I (with Brooke Bond name)	1975	£11.00
1871	1871	6	Old Military Dress II (with Brooke Bond name)	1975	£40.00